Enduring Voices

Document Sets to Accompany

The Enduring Vision

A History of the American People

Fourth Edition

Volume Two: From 1865

by

Paul S. Boyer • Clifford E. Clark, Jr. • Joseph F. Kett
Neal Salisbury • Harvard Sitkoff • Nancy Woloch

James J. Lorence

University of Wisconsin
Marathon County

Houghton Mifflin Company
Boston   New York

Sponsoring Editor: Jeffrey Greene
Editorial Assistant: Shoma Aditya
Editorial Assistant: Heather Hubbard
Associate Production/Design Coordinator: Jodi O'Rourke
Senior Cover Design Coordinator: Deborah Azerrad Savona
Senior Manufacturing Coordinator: Marie Barnes
Senior Marketing Manager: Sandra McGuire
Cover Design: Sara Melhado Bishins
Cover Image: Cold drinks inside the Red Robin Cafe, Vale, Oregon. Photo by Russell Lee, July 4, 1941.
Reproduced from the collections of the Library of Congress.

Printed in the U.S.A.

ISBN: 0-395-96086X

56789-DHH-03 02

PREFACE

Enduring Voices: Document Sets to Accompany The Enduring Vision: A History of the American People, Fourth Edition, has been prepared with the objectives of exploiting students' latent interest in history, stimulating critical thinking, and immersing students in the historian's process—evaluating the kinds of evidence from which the historian builds interpretations of past events and developments. By plunging into documentary analysis, students not only become familiar with the tools of the historian's trade but experience firsthand the excitement and satisfaction of "doing history" and of unlocking the "secrets" of the past in a systematic way.

Yet using documents can be complicated, and the history instructor must instill in students a healthy skepticism. As students engage in the analytical process, they will discover on their own, often with some unease, that it is an oversimplification to "let the documents speak for themselves." They will realize that multiple readings of the evidence are frequently possible. An equally important goal in using *Enduring Voices,* then, becomes sensitizing students to interpretive complexity—making them comfortable with uncertainty.

For every chapter of *The Enduring Vision, Enduring Voices* presents several sets of documents, each built around a "problem" closely related to a major theme in the corresponding textbook chapter. In all, over four hundred individual pieces of historical evidence—comprising traditional forms such as letters, petitions, speech excerpts, and testimony, as well as nontraditional evidence like patent applications and product advertisements—are represented in the two-volume *Enduring Voices* anthology. Each Document Set is introduced by a brief essay establishing background and textual linkage and spotlighting a central analytical question, and by a series of questions for students' consideration. The instructor is free to photocopy any and all Document Sets for classroom use with *The Enduring Vision;* Houghton Mifflin has obtained all the necessary permissions.

Other relevant aspects of the format and objectives of *Enduring Voices* include the following.

- *Each Document Set focuses on a limited body of evidence.* Instructors will want to select the specific issues that will be emphasized in their own classroom discussions.

- *Each set also provides maximum opportunity for instructors to set students free to make their own sense of the evidence.* It is assumed that instructors will encourage students to think creatively—to exercise historical imagination by taking the final intuitive leap. By engaging in the historian's process, the student should develop the ability to frame and test hypotheses and to arrive at informed conclusions.

- *Part and parcel of this process is the matter of defining basic terms such as* primary source *and* document. By incorporating nontraditional evidence, *Enduring Voices* aims to stimulate students to consider the nature of documentation itself. A broadened definition of admissible evidence should result.

In the last analysis, the Document Sets are based on the belief that history can be a discipline second to none in its potential appeal to students. It is my hope that *Enduring Voices* will demonstrate how stimulating and rewarding is the pursuit of historical knowledge. By providing small windows into the past, these documents confirm our oneness with the people of generations long gone. As students use the historical record to understand their world, they will themselves become part of a new and distinguished group, the society of educated people. Exposure to the historian's craft can ease the way.

ACKNOWLEDGMENTS

A comprehensive project such as *Enduring Voices: Document Sets to Accompany The Enduring Vision, Fourth Edition,* must necessarily reflect the ideas and insights of teacher-scholars throughout the historical profession. The preparation of this collection has been especially influenced by the creative work of William Bruce Wheeler, Susan D. Becker, James West Davidson, Mark Hamilton Lytle, Robert Kelley, John and Selma Appel, Dimitri Lazo, John E. O'Connor, Stanley Mallach, Verna Posever Curtis, and the editors of *Restoring Women to History: Materials for US I, II* (1984). Moreover, these materials are the product of countless discussions of teaching techniques with my colleagues in the University of Wisconsin's Department of History. Particular acknowledgment is due Professor Donald Dennis of the University of Wisconsin Center—Fond du Lac for his work on the first drafts of several early chapters. In preparing the revisions, I have benefited from the advice of Paul S. Boyer, Clifford E. Clark, Jr., Joseph F. Kett, Neal Salisbury, Harvard Sitkoff, and Nancy Woloch, the authors of *The Enduring Vision;* and from Michael L. Krenn and John L. Rector. The editors at D. C. Heath have eased the task of manuscript preparation. I am especially grateful to Pat Wakeley, Sylvia Mallory, Shoma Aditya, and Jeffrey Greene for their criticism and encouragement. Andrew Mergendahl provided cheerful assistance with source checking and other matters of detail. Any errors in judgment and execution are mine.

James J. Lorence

CONTENTS

CHAPTER 18   *51*

CHAPTER 33   *407*

CHAPTER 16

DOCUMENT SET 1
Ensuring Suffrage: Equal Rights for Whom?

One important theme in Chapter 16 is the drive to expand suffrage as a consequence of the Civil War. Just as emancipation had altered the meaning of the war, southern recalcitrance transformed Reconstruction into a process that held potential for social revolution. Although revolution was not to be, dramatic political and constitutional changes were implemented before radicalism was contained.

The following documents explore the forces operating in the postwar era to encourage the extension of civil rights to the freedmen. Stressing the arguments that framed the debate, these materials place heavy emphasis on the voting franchise, regarded by most observers as the key to black political and social aspirations. As you review the evidence, pay careful attention to the justifications for and criticisms of a constitutional remedy.

African American initiative is evident in the interview granted by President Andrew Johnson to Frederick Douglass and George Downing. Compare their argument with the position taken by Missouri Senator Carl Schurz in his effort to persuade the president to endorse suffrage. Given the politically charged atmosphere that dominated postwar Washington, you should note the partisan backgrounds of the persons involved. The political context is clarified by your textbook's account of debate over the black codes, the civil rights bill, and the Freedmen's Bureau.

An important aspect of the struggle for equal rights was the close link between abolitionism and feminism. Insisting on "natural rights" for all adult citizens, proponents of women's rights moved in 1866 to establish the American Equal Rights Association, which blended the campaigns for both African American and female suffrage. As your text notes, however, Radical Republicans tried to play down the link between their goals for freedmen and feminist insistence on women's enfranchisement. As you compare Elizabeth Cady Stanton's bitter attack on feminism's abolitionist and Radical "friends" with Henry B. Blackwell's baldly practical argument for female suffrage, be conscious of the relationship between the two reform movements.

As partisan strife increased, Johnson became even more uncooperative. Review your textbook's description of his split with the Radical Congress as you examine his annual message of 1867. Consider the grounds on which Johnson based his argument, including the constitutional implications of his views. His annual message establishes the president's position on the hotly debated Fourteenth Amendment.

As you reflect on the documents, focus on a definition of civil liberties and political equality. In the context of the 1860s, which groups in American society could claim title to equal rights?

Questions for Analysis

1. What arguments were used by African Americans and Republicans to support the extension of suffrage to freedmen in 1865–1866? Were there underlying, yet unspoken, reasons for the endorsement of full political equality?

2. On what grounds did President Johnson base his position on suffrage? How would you account for his position on the Fourteenth Amendment? What is the relationship between the president's social/political background and his views on the voting franchise?

3. What was the relationship between abolitionism and the women's rights movement? What do the documents reveal about the obstacles to female suffrage in the 1860s? What were the ultimate consequences of the tension between abolitionism and feminism?

4. Elizabeth Cady Stanton and Henry B. Blackwell both supported female suffrage, yet they took different positions concerning reform priorities in the 1860s. Do the documents reveal anything of the priorities each established? As you examine their respective arguments for women's voting rights, what differences are evident?

5. What was the purpose of the Fourteenth Amendment? What did this constitutional amendment reflect about the Radicals' conception of federalism? In what ways was the constitutional balance in the American political system affected by the amendment?

1. Republican Carl Schurz Urges Black Suffrage, 1865

The Ballot Necessary for the Negro

The interference of the national authority in the home concerns of the southern States would be rendered less necessary, and the whole problem of political and social reconstruction be much simplified, if, while the masses lately arrayed against the government are permitted to vote, the large majority of those who were always loyal . . . were not excluded from all influence upon legislation. In all questions concerning the Union, the national debt, and the future social organization of the south, the feelings of the colored man are naturally in sympathy with the views and aims of the national government. While the southern whites fought against the Union, the negro did all he could to aid it; while the southern white sees in the national government his conqueror, the negro sees in it his protector; while the white owes to the national debt his defeat, the negro owes to it his deliverance; while the white considers himself robbed and ruined by the emancipation of the slaves, the negro finds in it the assurance of future prosperity and happiness. In all the important issues the negro would be led by natural impulse to forward the ends of the government, and by making his influence, as part of the voting body, tell upon the legislation of the States, render the interference of the national authority unnecessary.

As the most difficult of the pending questions are intimately connected with the status of the negro in southern society, it is obvious that a correct solution can be more easily obtained if he has a voice in the matter. In the right to vote we would find the best permanent protection against oppressive class-legislation, as well as against individual persecution. . . . It is a notorious fact that the rights of a man of some political power are far less exposed to violation than those of one who is, in matter of public interest, completely subject to the will of others. A voter is a man of influence; small as the influence may be in the single individual, it becomes larger when the individual belongs to a numerous class of voters. . . . Such an individual is an object of interest to the political parties that desire to have the benefit of his ballot. . . . The first trials ought certainly to be made while the national power is still there to prevent or repress disturbances; but the practice once successfully inaugurated under the protection of that power, it would probably be more apt than anything else to obliterate old antagonisms.

2. George Downing and Frederick Douglass Argue the Case for Enfranchisement, 1866

Our coming is a marked circumstance, noting determined hope that we are not satisfied with an amendment prohibiting slavery, but that we wish it enforced with appropriate legislation. This is our desire. We ask for it intelligently, with the knowledge and conviction that the fathers of the Revolution intended freedom for every American; that they should be protected in their rights as citizens, and be equal before the law. We are Americans, native born Americans. We are citizens; we are glad to have it known to the world that you bear no doubtful record on this point.

On this fact, and with confidence in the triumph of justice, we base our hope. We see no recognition of color or race in the organic law of the land. It knows no privileged class, and therefore we cherish the hope that we may be fully enfranchised, not only here in this District, but throughout the land. We respectfully submit that rendering anything less than this will be rendering to us less than our just due; that granting anything less than our full rights will be a disregard of our just rights and of due respect for our feelings. If the powers that be do so it will be used as a license, as it were, or an apology, for any community, or for individuals thus disposed, to outrage our rights and feelings. It has been shown in the present war that the Government may justly reach its strong arm into States, and demand for them, from those who owe it allegiance, their assistance and support. May it not reach out a like arm to secure and protect its subjects upon whom it has a claim?

Following upon Mr. Downing, Mr. Fred. Douglass advanced and addressed the President, saying:

Mr. President, we are not here to enlighten you, sir, as to your duties as the Chief Magistrate of this Republic, but to show our respect, and to present in brief the claims of our race to your favorable consid-eration. In the order of Divine Providence you are placed in a position where you have the power to save or destroy us, to bless or blast us—I mean our whole race. Your noble and humane predecessor placed in our hands the sword to assist in saving the nation, and we do hope that you, his able successor, will favorably regard the placing in our hands the ballot with which to save ourselves.

We shall submit no argument on that point. The fact that we are the subjects of Government, and subject to taxation, subject to volunteer in the service of the country, subject to being drafted, subject to bear the burdens of the State, makes it not improper that we should ask to share in the privileges of this condition.

3. Henry B. Blackwell Appeals to Racism in the Cause of Female Suffrage, 1867

To the Legislatures of the Southern States:—I write to you as the intellectual leaders of the Southern people—men who should be able and willing to transcend the prejudices of section—to suggest the only ground of settlement between North and South which, in my judgment, can be successfully adopted.

Let me state the political situation. The radical principles of the North are immovably fixed upon negro suffrage as a condition of Southern State reconstruction. The proposed Constitutional Amendment is not regarded as a finality. It satisfies nobody, not even its authors. In the minds of the Northern people the negroes are now associated with the idea of loyalty to the Union. They are considered citizens. They are respected as "our allies." It is believed in the North that a majority of the white people of the South are at heart the enemies of the Union. The advocates of negro suffrage daily grow stronger and more numerous. . . .

Now the radicalism of the North is actual, organic, and progressive. Recognize the fact. But if "governments derive their just powers from the consent of the governed"—if "taxation without representation is tyranny"—and "on these two commandments hang all the (Republican) law and the prophets"—then these propositions are as applicable to women as to negroes. . . .

The radicals demand suffrage for the black men on the ground named above. Very good. Say to them, as Mr. Cowan said to the advocates of negro male suffrage in the District, "Apply your principle! Give the suffrage to all men and women of mature age and sound mind, and we will accept it as the basis of State and National reconstruction."

Consider the result from the Southern standpoint. Your 4,000,000 of Southern white women will counterbalance your 4,000,000 of negro men and women, and thus the political supremacy of your white race will remain unchanged. . . .

But the propriety of your making the proposal lies deeper than any consideration of sectional expediency. If you must try the Republican experiment, try it fully and fairly. Since you are compelled to union with the North, remove every seed of future controversy. If you are to share the future government of your States with a race you deem naturally and hopelessly inferior, avert the social chaos, which seems to you so imminent, by utilizing the intelligence and patriotism of the wives and daughters of the South. Plant yourselves upon the logical Northern principle. Then no new demands can ever be made upon you. No future inroads of fanaticism can renew sectional discord.

The effect upon the North would be to revolutionize political parties. "Justice satisfies everybody." The negro, thus protected against oppression by possessing the ballot, would cease to be the prominent object of philanthropic interest. Northern distrust, disarmed by Southern magnanimity, would give place to the liveliest sentiments of confidence and regard. The great political desideratum would be attained. The negro question would be forever removed from the political arena. National parties would again crystallize upon legitimate questions of

National interest—questions of tariff, finance, and foreign relations. The disastrous conflict between Federal and State jurisdictions would cease. North and South, no longer hammer and anvil, would forget and forgive the past.

4. Elizabeth Cady Stanton Questions Abolitionist Support for Female Enfranchisement, 1868

Though many of the leading minds of this country have advocated woman's enfranchisement for the last twenty years, it has been more as an intellectual theory than a fact of life, hence none of our many friends were ready to help in the practical work of the last few months, neither in Kansas or the Constitutional Convention of New York. So far from giving us a helping hand, Republicans and Abolitionists, by their false philosophy—that the safety of the nation demands ignorance rather than education at the polls—have paralyzed the women themselves.

To what a depth of degradation must the women of this nation have fallen to be willing to stand aside, silent and indifferent spectators in the reconstruction of the nation, while all the lower stratas of manhood are to legislate in their interests, political, religious, educational, social and sanitary, moulding to their untutored will the institutions of a mighty continent. . . .

While leading Democrats have been thus favorably disposed, what have our best friends said when, for the first time since the agitation of the question [the enfranchisement of women], they have had an opportunity to frame their ideas into statutes to amend the constitutions of two States in the Union.

Charles Sumner, Horace Greeley, Gerrit Smith and Wendell Phillips, with one consent, bid the women of the nation stand aside and behold the salvation of the negro. Wendell Phillips says, "one idea for a generation," to come up in the order of their importance. First negro suffrage, then temperance, then the eight hour movement, then woman's suffrage. In 1958, three generations hence, thirty years to a generation, Phillips and Providence permitting, woman's suffrage will be in order. What an insult to the women who have labored thirty years for the emancipation of the slave, now when he is their political equal, to propose to lift him above their heads. Gerrit Smith, forgetting that our great American idea is "individual rights," in which abolitionists have ever based their strongest arguments for emancipation, says, this is the time to settle the rights of races; unless we do justice to the negro we shall bring down on ourselves another bloody revolution, another four years' war, but we have nothing to fear from woman, she will not revenge herself! . . .

Horace Greeley has advocated this cause for the last twenty years, but to-day it is too new, revolutionary for practical consideration. The enfranchisement of woman, revolutionizing, as it will, our political, religious, and social condition, is not a measure too radical and all-pervading to meet the moral necessities of this day and generation.

Why fear new things; all old things were once new. . . . We live to do new things! When Abraham Lincoln issued the proclamation of emancipation, it was a new thing. When the Republican party gave the ballot to the negro, it was a new thing, startling too, to the people of the South, very revolutionary to their institutions, but Mr. Greeley did not object to all this because it was new. . . .

And now, while men like these have used all their influence for the last four years, to paralyze every effort we have put forth to rouse the women of the nation, to demand their true position in the reconstruction, they triumphantly turn to us, and say the greatest barrier in the way of your demand is that "the women themselves do not wish to vote." What a libel on the intelligence of the women of the nineteenth century. What means the 12,000 petitions presented by John Stuart Mill in the British Parliament from the first women in England, demanding household suffrage? What means the late action in Kansas, 10,000 women petitioned there for the right of suffrage, and 9,000 votes at the last election was the answer. What means the agitation in every State in the Union? In the very hour when Horace Greeley brought in his adverse report in the Constitutional Convention of New York, at least twenty members rose in their places and presented petitions from every part of the State, demanding woman's suffrage. What means that eloquent speech of George W. Curtis in the Convention, but to show that the ablest minds in the State are ready for this onward step?

5. President Johnson Opposes Black Suffrage, 1867

It is manifestly and avowedly the object of these laws to confer upon negroes the privilege of voting and to disfranchise such a number of white citizens as will give the former a clear majority at all elections in the Southern States. This, to the minds of some persons, is so important that a violation of the Constitution is justified as a means of bringing it about. The morality is always false which excuses a wrong because it proposes to accomplish a desirable end. We are not permitted to do evil that good may come. But in this case the end itself is evil, as well as the means. The subjugation of the States to negro domination would be worse than the military despotism under which they are now suffering. It was believed beforehand that the people would endure any amount of military oppression for any length of time rather than degrade themselves by subjection to the negro race. Therefore they have been left without a choice. Negro suffrage was established by act of Congress, and the military officers were commanded to superintend the process of clothing the negro race with the political privileges torn from white men.

The blacks in the South are entitled to be well and humanely governed, and to have the protection of just laws for all their rights of person and property. If it were practicable at this time to give them a Government exclusively their own, under which they might manage their own affairs in their own way, it would become a grave question whether we ought to do so, or whether common humanity would not require us to save them from themselves. But under the circumstances this is only a speculative point. It is not proposed merely that they shall govern themselves, but that they shall rule the white race, make and administer State laws, elect Presidents and members of Congress, and shape to a greater or less extent the future destiny of the whole country. Would such a trust and power be safe in such hands?

The peculiar qualities which should characterize any people who are fit to decide upon the management of public affairs for a great state have seldom been combined. It is the glory of white men to know that they have had these qualities in sufficient measure to build upon this continent a great political fabric and to preserve its stability for more than ninety years, while in every other part of the world all similar experiments have failed. But if anything can be proved by known facts, if all reasoning upon evidence is not abandoned, it must be acknowledged that in the progress of nations negroes have shown less capacity for government than any other race of people. No independent government of any form has ever been successful in their hands. On the contrary, wherever they have been left to their own devices they have shown a constant tendency to relapse into barbarism. In the Southern States, however, Congress has undertaken to confer upon them the privilege of the ballot. Just released from slavery, it may be doubted whether as a class they know more than their ancestors how to organize and regulate civil society.

6. Text of the Fourteenth Amendment, 1868

Section 1. All persons born or naturalized in the United States, and subject to the jurisdiction thereof, are citizens of the United States and of the State wherein they reside. No State shall make or enforce any law which shall abridge the privileges or immunities of citizens of the United States; nor shall any State deprive any person of life, liberty, or property, without due process of law; nor deny to any person within its jurisdiction the equal protection of the laws.

Section 2. Representatives shall be apportioned among the several States according to their respective numbers, counting the whole number of persons in each State, excluding Indians not taxed. But when the right to vote at any election for the choice of electors for President and Vice-President of the United States, Representatives in Congress, the executive and judicial officers of a State, or the members of the legislature thereof, is denied to any of the male inhabitants of such State, being twenty-one years of age, and citizens of the United States, or in any way abridged, except for participation in rebellion, or other crime, the basis of representation therein shall be reduced in the proportion which the number of such male citizens shall bear to the whole number of male citizens twenty-one years of age in such State.

Section 3. No person shall be a Senator or Representative in Congress, or elector of President and Vice-President, or hold any office, civil or military, under the United States or under any State, who, having previously taken an oath as a member of Congress, or as an officer of the United States, or as a member of any State legislature, or as an executive or judicial officer of any State, to support the Constitution of the United States, shall have engaged in insurrection or rebellion against the same, or given aid or comfort to the enemies thereof. But Congress may, by a vote of two-thirds of each house, remove such disability.

Section 4. The validity of the public debt of the United States, authorized by law, including debts incurred for payment of pensions and bounties for services in suppressing insurrection or rebellion, shall not be questioned. But neither the United States nor any State shall assume or pay any debt or obligation incurred in aid of insurrection or rebellion against the United States, or any claim for the loss or emancipation of any slave; but all such debts, obligations, and claims shall be held illegal and void.

Section 5. The Congress shall have power to enforce, by appropriate legislation, the provisions of this article.

Chapter 16:
Document Set 1 References

1. Republican Carl Schurz Urges Black Suffrage, 1865
   Carl Schurz to Andrew Johnson, 1865, Senate Executive Document No. 2, 39th Cong., 1st Sess., p. 42.

2. George Downing and Frederick Douglass Argue the Case for Enfranchisement, 1866
   Interview with the President of the United States, Andrew Johnson, by a delegation of Negroes, headed by Frederick Douglass and George Downing, February 7, 1866.

3. Henry B. Blackwell Appeals to Racism in the Cause of Female Suffrage, 1867
   Henry B. Blackwell, "What the South Can Do: How the Southern States Can Make Themselves Masters of the Situation," 1867, from Elizabeth Cady Stanton *et al., History of Women's Suffrage* (New York: Fowler and Wells, 1887), Vol. II, pp. 929–931.

4. Elizabeth Cady Stanton Questions Abolitionist Support for Female Enfranchisement, 1868
   Elizabeth Cady Stanton, "Who Are Our Friends?" *The Revolution,* 15 (January 1868).

5. President Johnson Opposes Black Suffrage, 1867
   Andrew Johnson, "Third Annual Message," December 3, 1867, James D. Richardson, ed., *A Compilation of the Messages and Papers of the Presidents, 1789–1908* (Washington, D.C.: Bureau of National Literature and Art, 1909), Vol. VI, pp. 564–565.

6. Text of the Fourteenth Amendment, 1868
   James Morton Smith and Paul L. Murphy, *Liberty and Justice: A Record of American Constitutional Development* (New York: Alfred A. Knopf, 1963), p. 253.

CHAPTER 16

"Free at Last": The African American Response to Emancipation

As noted in Chapter 11, African American testimony from the Civil War and Reconstruction era presents special interpretive problems for the historian. Despite questions about the reliability of oral accounts, however, the words of freedmen provide a rich resource for the scholar willing to apply careful analytic rigor in their use. In this chapter, oral tradition is combined with contemporary records to provide insight on the black response to emancipation and the social/economic experience of the freedmen.

The central feature of these documents is their clear description of the freedmen's day-to-day social and economic life. Faced with the challenges and opportunities of freedom, blacks struggled to maintain dignity, initiative, and independence. As noted in your textbook, families were reunited, marriages legalized, education sought, and employment obtained as both black and white southerners worked at racial accommodation and economic adjustment. The following documents indicate that the transition was not easy.

As you analyze the evidence, pay special attention to the critical problem of the southern labor system. Using the textbook material as background, review the documents with an eye to the development of an eco-nomic system that would satisfy the conflicting goals of planters and freedmen. As you examine these materials, try to make a judgment on African American progress toward economic independence, as well as the implications of the new regime for planter interests.

Be alert to the immediate problems faced by African Americans following emancipation and the enactment of the Thirteenth Amendment. Try to identify the primary concerns of African Americans as they first experienced freedom. Note common responses to the social confusion resulting from the end of enslavement; in doing so, consider connections between white initiatives and the African American adjustment to the new social relationships.

Eventually, the extension of civil rights led to a white counterreaction in the form of vigilante-paramilitary activity after 1867. In interpreting the Ku Klux Klan, determine what the group's primary goals were.

As you reconstruct the African American response to liberation, be aware of the economic challenge and social uncertainty that pervaded the early Reconstruction years. What answers to the new questions surfaced after 1868? With what results?

Questions for Analysis

1. What do the documents suggest about the first reaction to liberation? How was the black family affected? Do you detect any pattern of response in the black and white accounts of the freedmen's initial actions? How would you explain the reaction that occurred?

2. What do the documents reveal about the economic impact of emancipation? How did African American goals and planter needs relate to one another? How would you account for conflicting objectives? What solution to the labor problem emerged? With what economic consequences?

3. What was the purpose of the black codes? What did they reveal about white perceptions of the outcome of the Civil War and emancipation?

4. In what ways do the documents clarify the origins and purposes of the Ku Klux Klan? How were its goals related to the African American response to freedom? What were the future implications of Klan activity? What did the Klan's efforts reveal about the constitutional guarantees discussed in Chapter 16, Document Set 1?

5. What impression do the documents leave with regard to the goals, functions, and results of Freedmen's Bureau activity? How does knowing the identity of the commentators help you understand the views expressed? Comparing the documentary evidence with your textbook's account of the bureau's efforts, how would you assess its work? What is the relationship between the social principle the bureau represented and the modern American social system?

1. The Louisiana Black Code, 1865

Sec. 1. *Be it ordained by the police jury of the parish of St. Landry,* That no negro shall be allowed to pass within the limits of said parish without special permit in writing from his employer. Whoever shall violate this provision shall pay a fine of two dollars and fifty cents, or in default thereof shall be forced to work four days on the public road, or suffer corporeal punishment as provided hereinafter. . . .

Sec. 3. . . . No negro shall be permitted to rent or keep a house within said parish. Any negro violating this provision shall be immediately ejected and compelled to find an employer; and any person who shall rent, or give the use of any house to any negro, in violation of this section, shall pay a fine of five dollars for each offence.

Sec. 4. . . . Every negro is required to be in the regular service of some white person, or former owner, who shall be held responsible for the conduct of said negro. But said employer or former owner may permit said negro to hire his own time by special permission in writing, which permission shall not extend over seven days at any one time. . . .

Sec. 5. . . . No public meeting or congregations of negroes shall be allowed within said parish after sunset; but such public meetings and congregations may be held between the hours of sunrise and sunset, by the special permission in writing of the captain of patrol, within whose beat such meetings shall take place. . . .

Sec. 6. . . . No negro shall be permitted to preach, exhort, or otherwise declaim to congregations of colored people, without a special permission in writing from the president of the police jury. . . .

Sec. 7. . . . No negro who is not in the military service shall be allowed to carry fire-arms, or any kind of weapons, within the parish, without the special written permission of his employers, approved and endorsed by the nearest and most convenient chief of patrol. . . .

Sec. 8. . . . No negro shall sell, barter, or exchange any articles of merchandise or traffic within said parish without the special written permission of his employer, specifying the article of sale, barter or traffic. . . .

Sec. 9. . . . Any negro found drunk within the said parish shall pay a fine of five dollars, or in default thereof work five days on the public road, or suffer corporeal punishment as hereinafter provided.

Sec. 11. . . . It shall be the duty of every citizen to act as a police officer for the detection of offences and the apprehension of offenders, who shall be immediately handed over to the proper captain or chief of patrol.

2. A Planter's Wife Recalls the African American Response to Emancipation, 1865

After Emancipation, Lewis remained with us many years. His home was only a short distance from our home. He cultivated a farm successfully, and soon had acquired not only the necessaries of life, but some luxuries. He had a pair of nice horses, a buggy and wagon, and other things, and lived well; but he had never known freedom entirely without Mars' Henry's supervision. One day he came to the conclusion that he would move away and enjoy freedom to its fullest extent. He came to see Mr. Clayton in the fall to say something about it. He seemed embarrassed when Mr. Clayton addressed him: "Lewis, what is it you want?" "Well, Mars' Henry, I want to move away and feel ontirely free and see whut I cen do by mysef. You has been kind to me and I has done well, but I want to go anyhow." Mr. Clayton said,

"Very well, Lewis, that is all right, move when you please; but when you leave, nail up the door of your house and leave it until you want to come back. No one shall go into it."

Lewis and his brother, Ned, rented a farm some miles beyond Clayton, moved, and we heard no more of them until the next fall, when Lewis made his appearance, very much dejected. Mr. Clayton said, "How are you, Lewis? How are you getting on?" "Bad, Mars' Henry. I have come to ask ef I cen go into my house again."

Lewis and Ned had hired hands, gotten a merchant to furnish them, and lost almost everything they had started out with. Lewis moved back, and has been loth to leave the Claytons since, and is now with us, an old man.

3. African American Testimony on the Aftermath of Enslavement, 1866

Question. Where do you live?

Answer. Hampton, Virginia. . . .

Question. How do the rebels down there, about Hampton, treat the colored people?

Answer. The returned rebels express a desire to get along in peace if they can. There have been a few outrages out upon the roadside there. One of the returned Union colored soldiers was met out there and beaten very much.

Question. By whom was he beaten?

Answer. It was said they were rebels; they had on Union overcoats, but they were not United States soldiers. Occasionally we hear of an outrage of that kind, but there are none in the little village where I live.

Question. What appears to be the feeling generally of the returned rebels towards the freedmen; is it kind or unkind?

Answer. Well, the feeling that they manifest as a general thing is kind, so far as I have heard.

Question. Are they willing to pay the freedmen fair wages for their work?

Answer. No, sir; they are not willing to pay the freedmen more than from five to eight dollars a month.

Question. Do you think that their labor is worth more than that generally?

Answer. I do, sir; because, just at this time, everything is very dear, and I do not see how people can live and support their families on those wages.

Question. State whether the black people down there are anxious to go to school?

Answer. Yes, sir; they are anxious to go to school; we have schools there every day that are very well filled; and we have night schools that are very well attended, both by children and aged people; they manifest a great desire for education. . . .

Question. How do you feel about leaving the State of Virginia and going off and residing as a community somewhere else?

Answer. They do not wish to leave and go anywhere else unless they are certain that the locality where they are going is healthy and that they can get along.

Question. Are they not willing to be sent back to Africa?

Answer. No, sir.

Question. Why not?

Answer. They say that they have lived here all their days, and there were stringent laws made to keep them here; and that if they could live here contented as slaves, they can live here when free.

Question. Do you not think that to be a very absurd notion?

Answer. No, sir; if we can get lands here and can work and support ourselves, I do not see why we should go to any place that we do not want to go to.

Question. If you should stay here, is there not danger that the whites and blacks would intermarry and amalgamate?

Answer. I do not think there is any more danger now than there was when slavery existed. At that time there was a good deal of amalgamation.

4. James D. B. DeBow Expresses Southern Skepticism of the Freedmen's Bureau, 1866

Question. What is your opinion of the necessity or utility of the Freedmen's Bureau, or of any agency of that kind?

Answer. I think if the whole regulation of the negroes, or freedmen, were left to the people of the communities in which they live, it will be administered for the best interest of the negroes as well as of the white men. I think there is a kindly feeling on the part of the planters towards the freedmen. They are not held at all responsible for anything that has happened. They are looked upon as the innocent cause. In talking with a number of planters, I remember some of them telling me they were succeeding very well with their freedmen, having got a preacher to preach to them and a teacher to teach them, believing it was for the interest of the planter to make the negro feel reconciled; for, to lose his services as a laborer for even a few months would be very disastrous. The sentiment prevailing is, that it is for the interest of the employer to teach the negro, to educate his children, to provide a preacher for him, and to attend to his physical wants. And I may say I have not seen any exception to that feeling in the south. Leave the people to themselves, and they will manage very well. The Freedmen's Bureau, or any agency to interfere between the freedman and his former master, is only productive of mischief. There are constant appeals from one to the other and continual annoyances. It has a tendency to create dissatisfaction and disaffection on the part of the laborer, and is in every respect in its result most unfavorable to the system of industry that is now being organized under the new order of things in the south. . . .

Question. What is your opinion as to the relative advantages . . . of the present system of free labor, as compared with that of slavery as it heretofore existed in this country?

Answer. If the negro would work, the present system is much cheaper. If we can get the same amount of labor from the same persons, there is no doubt of the result in respect to *economy*. Whether the same amount of labor can be obtained, it is too soon yet to decide. We must allow one summer to pass first. They are working now very well on the plantations. That is the general testimony. The negro women are not disposed to field work as they formerly were, and I think there will be less work from them in the future than there has been in the past. The men are rather inclined to get their wives into other employment, and I think that will be the constant tendency, just as it is with the whites. Therefore, the real number of agricultural laborers will be reduced. I have no idea the efficiency of those who work will be increased. If we can only keep up their efficiency to the standard before the war, it will be better for the south, without doubt, upon the mere money question, because it is cheaper to hire the negro than to own him. Now a plantation can be worked without any outlay of capital by hiring the negro and hiring the plantation. . . .

Question. What arrangements are generally made among the landholders and the black laborers in the south?

Answer. I think they generally get wages. A great many persons, however, think it better to give them an interest in the crops. That is getting to be very common.

5. African American Recollections of Freedom's Impact: Mingo White and Charles Davenport

Mingo White

Interviewed at Burleson, Alabama
Interviewed by Levi D. Shelby, Jr.
Age when interviewed: 85–90

De day dat we got news dat we was free, Mr. White called us niggers to the house. He said: "You are all free, just as free as I am. Now go and get yourself somewhere to stick your heads."

Just as soon as he say dat, my mammy hollered out: "Dat's 'nough for a yearlin'." She struck out across de field to Mr. Lee Osborn's to get a place for me and her to stay. He paid us seventy-five cents a day, fifty cents to her and two bits for me. He gave us our dinner along with de wages. After de crop was gathered for that year, me and my mammy cut and hauled wood for Mr. Osborn. Us left Mr. Osborn dat fall and went to Mr. John Rawlins. Us made a sharecrop with him. Us'd pick two rows of cotton and he'd pick two rows. Us'd pull two rows of corn and he'd pull two rows of corn. He furnished us with rations and a place to stay. Us'd sell our cotton and open corn and pay Mr. John Rawlins for feedin' us. Den we moved with Mr. Hugh Nelson and made a sharecrop with him. We kept movin' and makin' sharecrops till us saved up 'nough money to rent us a place and make a crop for ourselves.

Us did right well at dis until de Ku Klux got so bad, us had to move back with Mr. Nelson for protection. De mens that took us in was Union men. Dey lived here in the South but dey taken us part in de slave business. De Ku Klux threat to whip Mr. Nelson, 'cause he took up for de niggers. Heap of nights we would hear of de Ku Klux comin' and leave home. Sometimes us was scared not to go and scared to go away from home.

One day I borrowed a gun from Ed Davis to go squirrel huntin'. When I taken de gun back I didn't unload it like I always been doin'. Dat night de Ku Klux called on Ed to whip him. When dey told him to open de door, he heard one of 'em say, "Shoot him time he gets de door open." "Well," he says to 'em, "Wait till I can light de lamp." Den he got de gun what I had left loaded, got down on his knees and stuck it through a log and pulld de trigger. He hit Newt Dobbs in de stomach and kilt him.

He couldn't stay round Burleson any more, so he come to Mr. Nelson and got 'nough money to get to Pine Bluff, Arkansas. The Ku Klux got bad sure 'nough den and went to killin' niggers and white folks, too.

Charles Davenport

Interviewed at Natchez, Mississippi
Interviewed by Edith Wyatt Moore
Age at interview: About 100

Like all de fool niggers o' dat time I was right smart bit by de freedom bug for awhile. It sounded powerful nice to be told: "You don't have to chop cotton no more. You can throw dat hoe down and go fishin' whensoever de notion strikes you. And you can roam 'round at night and court gals just as late as you please. Ain't no marster gwine to say to you, "Charlie, you's got to be back when de clock strikes nine."

I was fool 'nough to believe all dat kind o' stuff. But to tell de honest truth, most o' us didn't know ourselfs no better off. Freedom meant us could leave where us'd been born and bred, but it meant, too, dat us had to scratch for us ownselfs. Dem what left de old plantation seemed so all fired glad to get back dat I made up my mind to stay put. I stayed right with my white folks as long as I could.

My white folks talked plain to me. Dey say real sadlike, "Charlie, you's been a dependence, but now you can go if you is so desirous. But if you wants to stay with us you can sharecrop. Dey's a house for you and wood to keep you warm and a mule to work. We ain't got much cash, but dey's de land and you can count on havin' plenty o' victuals. Do just as you please."

When I looked at my marster and knowed he needed me, I pleased to stay. My marster never forced me to do nary thing about it. . . .

Lord! Lord! I knows about de Kloo Kluxes. I knows a-plenty. Dey was sure 'nough devils a-walkin' de earth a-seekin' what dey could devour. Dey larruped de hide off de uppity niggers an' drove de white trash back where dey belonged.

Us niggers didn't have no secret meetin's. All us had was church meetin's in arbors out in de woods. De preachers would exhort us dat us was de chillen o' Israel in de wilderness an' de Lord done sent us to take dis land o' milk and honey. But how us gwine-a take land what's already been took?

I sure ain't never heard about no plantations bein' divided up, neither. I heard a lot o' yaller niggers spoutin' off how dey was gwine-a take over de white folks' land for back wages. Dem bucks just took all dey wages out in talk. 'Cause I ain't never seen no land divided up yet.

In dem days nobody but niggers and "shawl-strap" folks voted. Quality folks didn't have nothin' to do with such truck. If dey hada wanted to de Yankees wouldn'ta let 'em. My old marster didn't vote and if anybody knowed what was what he did. Sense didn't count in dem days. It was powerful ticklish times and I let votin' alone. . . . [O]ne night a bunch o' uppity niggers went to a entertainment in Memorial Hall. Dey dressed deyselfs fit to kill and walked down de aisle and took seats in de very front. But just about time dey got good set down, de curtain dropped and de white folks rose up without a-sayin' a word. Dey marched out de buildin' with dey chins up and left dem niggers a-sittin' in a empty hall.

Dat's de way it happen every time a nigger tried to get too uppity. Dat night after de breakin' up o' dat entertainment, de Kloo Kluxes rode through de land. I heard dey grabbed every nigger what walked down dat aisle, but I ain't heard yet what dey done with 'em.

6. A Freedman Recalls a Visit from the Ku Klux Klan, 1871

They came to my door and they said "Hey!" I was asleep. They called, "Hey, hey!" My wife says, "Lewis, listen." . . . "What are you doing there?" I says; and they said, "By Christ, come out; I will show you what I am doing." . . . and I got up and sat on the bed, with my legs hanging out, and peeped out. . . . They says, "Lewis, by Christ, arn't you going to get up and open the door?" . . . I spoke and said, "What do you want; do you want to whip me? I have done nothing to be whipped." . . . Says he, "How did you vote?" I says, "I voted the radical ticket." "You has, sir?" he says. I says, "Yes, sir." "Well, by Christ," says he, "Ain't you had no instruction?" I says, "I can't read, and I can't write, and I can't much more than spell." . . . I says, "How can a black man get along without there is some white gentleman or other with them? We go by instructions. We don't know nothing much." "O, by Christ," says he, "you radicals go side by side with one another, and by Christ us democrats go side and side with one another." I says, "I can't help that." . . . He says . . ."Get in the road and march," and in the road I went. They took me up the road pretty near to the edge of the woods. . . . Says he, "Off with your shirt." I says, "What do you all want to whip me for; what have I done?" "By Christ," he says, "Off with your shirt; if you don't

you shall go dead.["] . . . He says, "Now Lewis, by Christ, you get down on your knees." I says, "It is hard to get down on my knees and take a whipping for nothing." Then I dropped down. He says, "By Christ, don't you get up until we get done with you." They set to work on me and hit me ten or fifteen licks pretty keen, and I raised up. "Get down," he says; "if you ever raise up again you'll go dead before we quit you." Down I went again, and I staid down until they got done whipping me. Says he, "Now, by Christ, you must promise you will vote the democratic ticket?" I says, "I don't know how I will vote; it looks hard when a body thinks this way and that way to take a beating." . . . "You must promise to vote the democratic ticket, or you go dead before we leave you," he says. Then I studied and studied. They gathered right close up around me. "Come out with it—come, out with it, by Christ." Then I says, "Yes, sir, I reckon so."

Chapter 16:
Document Set 2 References

1. The Louisiana Black Code, 1865
   Senate Executive Document No. 2, 39th Cong., 1st Sess., p. 93.

2. A Planter's Wife Recalls the African American Response to Emancipation, 1865
   Mrs. Victoria V. Clayton, *White and Black Under the Old Regime* (Milwaukee: Young Churchman Company, 1899), pp. 172–174.

3. African American Testimony on the Aftermath of Enslavement, 1866
   Report of the Joint Committee on Reconstruction (Washington: Government Printing Office, 1866), Part II, pp. 55–56.

4. James D. B. DeBow Expresses Southern Skepticism of the Freedmen's Bureau, 1866
   Report of the Joint Committee, Part IV, pp. 132–135.

5. African American Recollections of Freedom's Impact: Mingo White and Charles Davenport
   Federal Writers' Project, Slave Narratives, "A Folk History of Slavery in the United States from Interviews with Former Slaves" (Washington, D.C.: Typewritten Records Prepared by the Federal Writers' Project, 1941).

6. A Freedman Recalls a Visit from the Ku Klux Klan, 1871
   Report to the Joint Select Committee to Inquire into the Condition of Affairs in the Late Insurrectionary States (Washington: Government Printing Office, 1872), Vol. I, p. 436.

DOCUMENT SET 3

Redemption and Salvation: The Reconstruction Experiment Abandoned

During President Grant's second term, the Republican hold on southern state governments weakened rapidly. Your textbook notes that the dramatic revival of the Democratic party coincided with an increase in violence, vigilante activity, and outright voter fraud in the South. Through a combination of economic pressure and voter intimidation, Democratic party leaders succeeded in sufficiently suppressing the African American vote to produce a revolution at the ballot box.

The term *Redemption* was commonly used by southern whites to denote the restoration of Democratic control of state governments in the South. As you examine the documents in this set, think about the emotional impact of Democratic rhetoric in these hotly contested political races. Consider the symbolic power of the concepts of redemption and salvation, especially as the foundation stones of southern folklore. As you review the documents, ask yourself what was saved and what was lost in the Reconstruction settlement. Who were the winners and who were the losers in the contest for social control in the South?

The focal point in these documents is the time-worn issue of ends and means. Concentrate on the devices resorted to by southern whites in the drive to reestablish Democratic party control. Evaluate the justifications offered for using extreme means to achieve the desired end. How did southern explanations affect future generations of historians as they interpreted the process of Redemption?

Beyond direct intimidation and vote fraud, deeper long-term social forces and institutional changes were occurring that sealed the fate of African-American citizens for nearly a century. While it seemed a short-run compromise, the crop-lien/sharecrop system was to shackle them to the land and condemn them to a position of long-term dependency. Probe the documents for indications of the economic system's impact on African American prospects for political participation and social equality.

As a complement to economic pressure, other methods of ensuring effective social control were evident in the post-Reconstruction South. Examine the words of the militant Ida B. Wells to gain a clearer understanding of the southern social system of the late nineteenth century. As you reflect upon the words of both Wells and Douglass, determine what the Redemption settlement meant for the future of a biracial society in America.

Questions for Analysis

1. Define the word *redemption*. What do the documents suggest concerning white southerners' reasons for using this term as they did in the 1870s?

2. What do the documents reveal about the formal and informal techniques used to reestablish white social control in the post-Reconstruction South?

3. How do the documents clarify the relationship between economic and political power in the South? In what ways do the documents provide evidence of a readjustment of the regional economy to normal conditions? What was the significance of the economic settlement for the political future of the African-American population?

4. What was the African-American response to Redemption and to the new political conditions and restraints under which they lived? What was the meaning of Ida B. Wells's reference to a "red record"? Why do you think Wells eventually chose to move out of her native South? What do her writings reveal about the unique aspects of the southern social system?

1. The Atlanta *News* Advocates Violence
to Redeem the South, 1874

Let there be White Leagues formed in every town, village and hamlet of the South, and let us organize for the great struggle which seems inevitable. If the October elections which are to be held at the North are favorable to the radicals, the time will have arrived for us to prepare for the very worst. The radicalism of the republican party must be met by the radicalism of white men. We have no war to make against the United States Government, but against the republican party our hate must be unquenchable, our war interminable and merciless. Fast fleeting away is the day of wordy protests and idle appeals to the magnanimity of the republican party. By brute force they are endeavoring to force us into acquiescence to their hideous programme. We have submitted long enough to indignities, and it is time to meet brute-force with brute-force. Every Southern State should swarm with White Leagues, and we should stand ready to act the moment Grant signs the civil-rights bill. It will not do to wait till radicalism has fettered us to the car of social equality before we make an effort to resist it. The signing of the bill will be a declaration of war against the southern whites. It is our duty to ourselves, it is our duty to our children, it is our duty to the white race whose prowess subdued the wilderness of this continent, whose civilization filled it with cities and towns and villages, whose mind gave it power and grandeur, and whose labor imparted to it prosperity, and whose love made peace and happiness dwell within its homes, to take the gage of battle the moment it is thrown down. If the white democrats of the North are men, they will not stand idly by and see us borne down by northern radicals and half-barbarous negroes. But no matter what they may do, it is time for us to organize. We have been temporizing long enough. Let northern radicals understand that military supervision of southern elections and the civil-rights bill mean war, that war means bloodshed, and that we are terribly in earnest, and even they, fanatical as they are, may retrace their steps before it is too late.

2. Senator Blanche K. Bruce Alleges Fraud
and Violence in Mississippi, 1876

MR. BRUCE: The conduct of the late election in Mississippi affected not merely the fortunes of partisans—as the same were necessarily involved in the defeat or success of the respective parties to the contest—but put in question and jeopardy the sacred rights of the citizen; and the investigation contemplated in the pending resolution has for its object not the determination of the question whether the offices shall be held and the public affairs of that State be administered by democrats or republicans, but the higher and more important end, the protection in all their purity and sig-nificance of the political rights of the people and the free institutions of the country. . . .

The truth of the allegations relative to fraud and violence is strongly suggested by the very success claimed by the democracy. In 1873 the republicans carried the State by 20,000 majority; in November last the opposition claimed to have carried it by 30,000; thus a democratic gain of more than 50,000. Now, by what miraculous or extraordinary interposition was this brought about? . . . [S]uch a change of front is unnatural. . . .

3. South Carolina Governor D. H. Chamberlain Attacks President Hayes's Betrayal of Southern Republicans, 1877

What is the President's Southern policy? In point of physical or external fact, it consists in withdrawing the military forces of the United States from the points in South Carolina and Louisiana where they had been previously stationed for the protection and support of the lawful Governments of those States.

In point of immediate, foreseen, and intended consequence, it consists in the overthrow and destruction of those State Governments, and the substitution in their stead of certain other organizations called State Governments.

In point of actual present results, it consists in the abandonment of Southern Republicans, and especially the colored race, to the control and rule not only of the Democratic party, but of that class at the South which regarded slavery as a Divine Institution, which waged four years of destructive war for its perpetuation, which steadily opposed citizenship and suffrage for the negro—in a word, a class whose traditions, principles, and history are opposed to every step and feature of what Republicans call our national progress since 1860.

In point of general political and moral significance it consists in the proclamation to the country and the world that the will of the majority of the voters of a State, lawfully and regularly expressed, is no longer the ruling power in our States, and that the constitutional guaranty to every State in this Union of a republican form of government and of protection against domestic violence, is henceforth ineffectual and worthless.

4. A Texas Shares Contract Creates the Structure for Economic Bondage, ca. 1860s

Said _____ of the first part furthermore agrees to furnish the said Freedmen of the second part with good and sufficient quarters, _____ wholesome food, fuel, and such medical treatment as can be rendered by the person superintending the place. Said *J C Mitchell* of the 1st part in consideration of the faithful discharge of the duties assumed by the parties of the second part, does hereby agree to furnish *the freedmen* the necessary tools and implements for the cultivation of the land, and allow said Freedmen *one third* interest in the crops raised on said *plantation* by their labor. It is also mutually agreed that ten hours shall constitute a day's work, and if any labor in excess of ten hours per day is rendered it shall be paid for as extra labor. Said parties of the second part do furthermore agree to do all necessary work on Sundays or at night when it is for the protection of plantation or crops against destruction by storms, floods, fire or frost, provided always that such service shall be paid for as extra labor; extra labor to be paid for at the rate of one day's labor and one-half rations extra for each six hours work. Provided that our employer failing to comply with any part of this agreement, this contract shall be annulled; also provided, that should any of the parties of the second part leave said *plantation* without proper authority, or engage elsewhere, or neglect or refuse to work as herein agreed, they or any part of them so offending shall be liable to be discharged and forfeit all wages due up to that time.

Also Provided, that this Contract shall constitute the first lien upon all crops raised by the labor of said parties of the Second part.

Said J C Mitchell shall have power to make such rules and regulations necessary to the management of the plantation as are not inconsistent with the term of this contract; all lost time to [be] deducted from the one third interest in crop to the freedmen.

5. Frederick Douglass Assesses the
Post-Reconstruction Economic Settlement, 1883

No more crafty and effective device for defrauding the southern laborers could be adopted than the one that substitutes orders upon shopkeepers for currency in payment of wages. It has the merit of a show of honesty, while it puts the laborer completely at the mercy of the land-owner and the shopkeeper. He is between the upper and the nether millstones, and is hence ground to dust. It gives the shopkeeper a customer who can trade with no other storekeeper, and thus leaves the latter no motive for fair dealing except his own moral sense, which is never too strong. While the laborer holding the orders is tempted by their worthlessness, as a circulating medium, to get rid of them at any sacrifice, and hence is led into extravagance and consequent destitution.

The merchant puts him off with his poorest commodities at highest prices, and can say to him take these or nothing. Worse still. By this means the laborer is brought into debt, and hence is kept always in the power of the land-owner. When this system is not pursued and land is rented to the freedman, he is charged more for the use of an acre of land for a single year than the land would bring in the market if offered for sale. On such a system of fraud and wrong one might well invoke a bolt from heaven—red with uncommon wrath.

It is said if the colored people do not like the conditions upon which their labor is demanded and secured, let them leave and go elsewhere. A more heartless suggestion never emanated from an oppressor. Having for years paid them in shop orders, utterly worthless outside the shop to which they are directed, without a dollar in their pockets, brought by this crafty process into bondage to the land-owners, who can and would arrest them if they should attempt to leave when they are told to go.

6. Ida B. Wells Denounces Southern
Social Control, 1895

Emancipation came and the vested interest of the white man in the Negro's body were lost. The white man had no right to scourge the emancipated Negro, still less has he a right to kill him. But the southern white people had been educated so long in that school of practice, in which might makes right, that they disdained to draw strict lines of action in dealing with the Negro. In slave times the Negro was kept subservient and submissive by the frequency and severity of the scourging, but, with freedom, a new system of intimidation came into vogue; the Negro was not only whipped and scourged; he was killed.

Not all nor nearly all of the murders done by white men, during the past thirty years in the South, have come to light, but the statistics as gathered and preserved by white men, and which have not been questioned, show that during these years more than ten thousand Negroes have been killed in cold blood, without the formality of judicial trial and legal execution. . . .

The first excuse given to the civilized world for the murder of unoffending Negroes was the necessity of the white man to repress and stamp out alleged "race riots." . . .

Then came the second excuse, which had its birth during the turbulent times of reconstruction. By an amendment to the Constitution the Negro was given the right of franchise, and, theoretically at least, his ballot became his invaluable emblem of citizenship. In a government "of the people, for the people, and by the people," the Negro's vote became an important factor in all matters of state and national politics. But this did not last long. The southern white man would not consider that the Negro had any right which a white man was bound to respect, and the idea of a republican form of government in the southern states grew into general contempt. It was maintained that "This is a white man's government," and regardless of numbers the white man should rule. "No Negro domination" became the new legend on the sanguinary banner of the sunny South, and under it rode the Ku Klux Klan, the Regulators, and the lawless mobs, which for any cause chose to murder one man or a dozen as suited their purpose best. . . .

But it was a bootless strife for colored people. The government which had made the Negro a citizen found itself unable to protect him. It gave him the right to vote, but denied him the protection which should have maintained that right. Scourged from his home; hunted through the swamps; hung by midnight raiders, and openly murdered in the light of day, the Negro clung to his right of franchise with a heroism which would have wrung admiration from the hearts of savages. He believed that in that small white ballot there was a subtle something which stood for manhood as well as citizenship, and thousands of brave black men went to their graves, exemplifying the one by dying for the other.

The white man's victory soon became complete by fraud, violence, intimidation and murder. The franchise vouchsafed to the Negro grew to be a "barren ideality," and regardless of numbers, the colored people found themselves voiceless in the councils of those whose duty it was to rule. With no longer the fear of "Negro Domination" before their eyes, the white man's second excuse became valueless. With the Southern governments all subverted and the Negro actually eliminated from all participation in state and national elections, there could be no longer an excuse for killing Negroes to prevent "Negro Domination."

Brutality still continued; Negroes were whipped, scourged, exiled, shot and hung whenever and wherever it pleased the white man so to treat them, and as the civilized world with increasing persistency held the white people of the South to account for its outlawry, the murderers invented the third excuse—that Negroes had to be killed to avenge their assaults upon women. There could be framed no possible excuse more harmful to the Negro and more unanswerable if true in its sufficiency for the white man. . . .

A word as to the charge itself. In considering the third reason assigned by the Southern white people for the butchery of blacks, the question must be asked, what the white man means when he charges the black man with rape. Does he mean the crime which the statutes of the civilized states describe as such? Not by any means. With the Southern white man, any mesalliance existing between a white woman and a colored man is a sufficient foundation for the charge of rape. The Southern white man says that it is impossible for a voluntary alliance to exist between a white woman and a colored man, and therefore, the fact of an alliance is a proof of force. In numerous instances where colored men have been lynched on the charge of rape, it was positively known at the time of lynching, and indisputably proven after the victim's death, that the relationship sustained between the man and woman was voluntary and clandestine, and that in no court of law could even the charge of assault have been successfully maintained. . . .

It is his regret, that, in his own defense, [the black] must disclose to the world that degree of dehumanizing brutality which fixes upon America the blot of a national crime. Whatever faults and failings other nations may have in their dealings with their own subjects or with other people, no other civilized nation stands condemned before the world with a series of crimes so peculiarly national. It becomes a painful duty of the Negro to reproduce a record which shows that a large portion of the American people avow anarchy, condone murder and defy the contempt of civilization.

7. The Economic Consequences of Redemption in Statistical Terms, 1880–1900

A. Percentage of Land in Farms Operated by Black Farmers, 1910

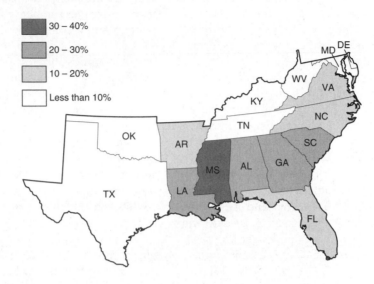

Source: U.S. Census Bureau, Bulletin 129, *Negroes in the U.S.* (Washington, D.C.: Government Printing Office, 1915).

B. Percentage of Farms Operated by Black Farmers, 1910

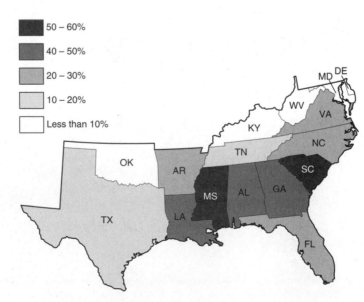

Source: U.S. Census Bureau, Bulletin 129.

C. Farms, by Color and Tenure of Operator: 1880 to 1900

Color and Tenure of Operator	Number of Farms		
	1900	*1890*	*1880*
South	**2,620,391**	**1,836,372**	**1,531,077**
Full Owner	1,237,114		
Part Owner	133,368	1,130,029	977,229
Manager	18,765		
Tenant	1,231,144	706,343	553,848
White	1,879,721		
Full Owner	1,078,635		
Part Owner	105,171		
Manager	17,172		
Tenant	678,743		
Nonwhite	740,670		
Full Owner	158,479		
Part Owner	28,197		
Manager	1,593		
Tenant	552,401		

Source: *Statistical History of the United States* (Stamford, CT: Fairfield Publishers, Inc., 1965), p. 278.

D. Value of Output per Worker and Value of Output per Family Member on Family Farms, by Type of Farm, Tenure, and Race of Farm Operator, Cotton South: 1880

Type of Farm	Value of Output Per Worker($)		Value of Output Per Family Member ($)	
	White	*Black*	*White*	*Black*
Small Family Farms	255.74	159.62	81.35	63.57
Owned	283.70	155.78	88.12	58.11
Tenanted	212.47	160.40	70.87	64.67
Rented	260.19	159.51	88.02	67.63
Sharecropped	200.69	160.81	66.64	63.30
Other Small Farms	262.78	153.79	143.73	127.94
Owned	262.29		149.18	
Tenanted	264.17	147.23	127.93	117.65

Source: Roger L. Ransom and Richard Sutch, *One Kind of Freedom: The Economic Consequences of Emancipation* (Cambridge University Press, 1977), p. 184.

E. **Number of Acres of Cropland per Worker on Family Farms, by Race and Tenure, Cotton South: 1880**

Form of Tenure	Acres of Crops per Worker	
	White	*Black*
Owner-Operated Farms	12.5	6.6
Rented Farms	14.5	7.3
Sharecropped Farms	11.7	8.0
All Farms	12.4	7.5

Source: Roger L. Ransom and Richard Sutch, *One Kind of Freedom: The Economic Consequences of Emancipation* (Cambridge University Press, 1977), p. 184.

F. **White and Black Proprietorships in Thirty-one Georgian Counties, 1873–1902**

Year	White		Black	
	Number	*Average Acreage*	*Number*	*Average Acreage*
1873	17,255	388.6	514	113.9
1880	20,725	339.5	1,865	93.8
1890	24,058	293.7	3,510	71.0
1902	26,957	264.8	5,221	64.3

Source: Enoch Banks, *The Economics of Land Tenure in Georgia* (New York: Columbia University Press, 1905), Appendix, Table B.

Chapter 16:
Document Set 3 References

1. The Atlanta *News* Advocates Violence to Redeem the South, 1874
   Atlanta *News*, September 10, 1874.

2. Senator Blanche K. Bruce Alleges Fraud and Violence in Mississippi, 1876
   Congressional Record, 44th Cong., 1st Sess., March 31, 1876, pp. 2100–2104.

3. South Carolina Governor D. H. Chamberlain Attacks President Hayes's Betrayal of Southern Republicans, 1877
   D. H. Chamberlain, Speech, July 4, 1877, W. A. Allen, *Governor Chamberlain's Administration in South Carolina,* p. 508, in Walter L. Fleming, ed., *Documentary History of Reconstruction,* Vol. 2 (New York: McGraw-Hill, 1966), pp. 387–388.

4. A Texas Shares Contract Creates the Structure for Economic Bondage, ca. 1860s
   "Records of the Assistant Commissioner for the State of Texas," Bureau of Refugees, Freedmen, and Abandoned Lands, Record Group 105, National Archives, Washington, D.C.

5. Frederick Douglass Assesses the Post-Reconstruction Economic Settlement, 1883
   Frederick Douglass, "Address to the People of the United States," delivered at Convention of Colored Men, Louisville, September 24, 1883.

6. Ida B. Wells Denounces Southern Social Control, 1895
   Ida B. Wells, *A Red Record* (Chicago: Privately Published, 1895), pp. 7–8, 9–10, 14–15.

7. The Economic Consequences of Redemption in Statistical Terms, 1880–1900
   A. Percentage of Land in Farms Operated by Black Farmers, 1910, U.S. Census Bureau, Bulletin 129, *Negroes in the U.S.* (Washington, D.C.: Government Printing Office, 1915).
   B. Percentage of Farms Operated by Black Farmers, 1910, U.S. Census Bureau, Bulletin 129.
   C. Farms, by Color and Tenure of Operator: 1880 to 1900, in *Statistical History of the United States* (Stamford, CT: Fairfield Publishers, Inc., 1965), p. 278.
   D. Value of Output per Worker and Value of Output per Family Member on Family Farms, by Type of Farm, Tenure, and Race of Farm Operator, Cotton South: 1880, Roger L. Ransom and Richard Sutch, *One Kind of Freedom: The Economic Consequences of Emancipation* (Cambridge: Cambridge University Press, 1977), p. 184.
   E. Number of Acres of Cropland per Worker on Family Farms, by Race and Tenure, Cotton South: 1880, in Ransom and Sutch, p. 184.
   F. White and Black Proprietorships in Thirty-one Georgian Counties, 1873–1902, in Enoch Banks, *The Economics of Land Tenure in Georgia* (New York: Columbia University Press, 1905), Appendix, Table B.

Chapter 16:
Document Set 3 Credits

CHAPTER 17

The Native American Presence: The Massacre at Sand Creek

Chapter 17 focuses on the exploitation of the trans-Mississippi West, the last major frontier region in the United States. Before the immense resources of the interior could be developed, however, an important residual problem had to be dealt with—the Native American presence. Even before the Civil War, the Indians' fate had been sealed as a result of the federal government's aggressive land-acquisition policy. This action dismissed the original inhabitants of scarce land as obstacles to the march of "civilization" (see Chapter 8).

The following documents describe an incident that tested American values. As the concentrated tribal reservations policy was implemented, the Plains Indians fought an unsuccessful rear-guard resistance, characterized by bitter hostilities and, as noted in your textbook, atrocities on both sides. One of the most brutal confrontations occurred in 1864 at Sand Creek, Colorado Territory, where the militia attacked a band of friendly Cheyennes and Arapahos in what became a vicious massacre. Within a few hours, nearly 500 were killed, many of them women and children. Public outrage ultimately led to a congressional investigation of the grisly event.

This incident provides the basis for a challenging exercise in historical analysis. Through an examination of the documents from the congressional investigation,

try to make an interpretive judgment of the evidence. Your responsibility is first to determine exactly what happened at Sand Creek and then to explain how and why those events transpired. Act as your own historian.

The documents included in this set are the report of the Congressional Committee (1865), the response by Colorado's Governor John Evans, Colonel J. M. Chivington's defense of his command, several eyewitness accounts (Lieutenant James D. Connor, Lieutenant Joseph A. Cramer, and Captain Presley Talbot), second-hand reports (Major E. W. Wynkoop), Black Kettle's peace pledge, and the account of reformer Helen Hunt Jackson. Your textbook provides background on the subjugation of the Plains Indians, government Indian policy, and reform efforts undertaken by "friends" of the Indian. Your task is to extract the "truth" from the evidence.

As you approach the documents, consider the reliability of the source. Try to decide whether a witness is credible or suspect. Determine what a given document reveals about its author. Does the document contribute to your interpretation of the Sand Creek incident? Develop a clear picture of the events in question and a hypothesis to explain them. Then determine how the incident fits into the history of the westward movement.

Questions for Analysis

1. What do the documents reveal about the Native Americans involved in the conflict at Sand Creek? How would you assess the military's understanding and perception of the Indians' intentions? To what extent were Chivington's and Evans's actions justified?

2. What do the events at Sand Creek tell us about the nature of Indian warfare on the Great Plains and the status of white relations with the Native American population in the nineteenth century? Do the documents speak to the matter of human weaknesses or strengths?

3. Why do you think Sand Creek became a political issue in 1864–1865? What do the documents suggest concerning the search for causes and the assignment of ultimate responsibility? Were the criticisms in the congressional report justified?

4. Why were Black Kettle, White Antelope, and their followers encamped at Sand Creek? What does their presence suggest about the Native American situation in 1864 and the white advance? Did the Cheyennes and Arapahos have a right to hold any land? What land? Why or why not? What realistic alternatives were there to Indian dependency on the white government?

5. Define *ethnocentrism* and explain how it was a factor in the Sand Creek incident. In what way do the documents demonstrate the inability of whites and Indians to move toward a successful cultural adjustment?

6. How can the views of Helen Hunt Jackson be best understood? How did the "friends of the Indian" propose to solve Native Americans' problems? What was the ultimate result of their efforts?

1. A Congressional Committee Decries the Violence at Sand Creek, 1865

The Joint Committee on the Conduct of the War submit the following report:

In the summer of 1864 Governor Evans, of Colorado Territory, as acting superintendent of Indian affairs, sent notice to the various bands and tribes of Indians within his jurisdiction that such as desired to be considered friendly to the whites should at once repair to the nearest military post in order to be protected from the soldiers who were to take the field against the hostile Indians. . . .

All the testimony goes to show that the Indians, under the immediate control of Black Kettle and White Antelope of the Cheyennes, and Left Hand of the Arapahoes, were and had been friendly to the whites, and had not been guilty of any acts of hostility or depredation. The Indian agents, the Indian interpreter and others examined by your committee, all testify to the good character of those Indians. Even Governor Evans and Major Anthony, though evidently willing to convey to your committee a false impression of the character of those Indians, were forced, in spite of their prevarication, to admit that they knew of nothing they had done which rendered them deserving of punishment. . . .

These Indians, at the suggestion of Governor Evans and Colonel Chivington, repaired to Fort Lyon and placed themselves under the protection of Major Wynkoop. They were led to believe that they were regarded in the light of friendly Indians, and would be treated as such as long as they conducted themselves quietly. . . .

Major Anthony having demanded their arms, which they surrendered to him, they conducted themselves quietly, and in every way manifested a disposition to remain at peace with the whites. . . . At the suggestion of Major Anthony (and from one in his position a suggestion was equivalent to a command) these Indians went to a place on Sand creek, about thirty-five miles from Fort Lyon, and there established their camp, their arms being restored to them. . . .

Upon observing the approach of the soldiers, Black Kettle, the head chief, ran up to the top of his lodge an American flag, which had been presented to him some years before by Commissioner Greenwood, with a small white flag under it, as he had been advised to do in case he met with any troops on the prairies. Mr. Smith, the interpreter, supposing they might be strange troops, unaware of the character of the Indians encamped there, advanced from his lodge to meet them, but was fired upon, and returned to his lodge.

And then the scene of murder and barbarity began—men, women, and children were indiscriminately slaughtered. In a few minutes all the Indians were flying over the plain in terror and confusion. A few who endeavored to hide themselves under the bank of the creek were surrounded and shot down in cold blood, offering but feeble resistance. From the sucking babe to the old warrior, all who were overtaken were deliberately murdered. Not content with killing women and children, who were incapable of offering any resistance, the soldiers indulged in acts of barbarity of the most revolting character; such, it is to be hoped, as never before disgraced the acts of men claiming to be civilized. No attempt was made by the officers to restrain the savage cruelty of the men under their command, but they stood by and witnessed these acts without one word of reproof, if they did not incite their commission. For more than two hours the work of murder and barbarity was continued, until more than one hundred dead bodies, three-fourths of them of women and children, lay on the plain as evidences of the fiendish malignity and cruelty of the officers who had so sedulously and carefully plotted the massacre, and of the soldiers who had so faithfully acted out the spirit of their officers.

It is difficult to believe that beings in the form of men, and disgracing the uniform of United States soldiers and officers, could commit or countenance the commission of such acts of cruelty and barbarity as are detailed in the testimony, but which your committee will not specify in their report. It is true that there seems to have existed among the people inhabiting that region of country a hostile feeling towards the Indians. Some of the Indians had committed acts of hostility towards the whites; but no effort seems to have been made by the authorities there to prevent these hostilities, other than by the commission of even worse acts. The hatred of the whites to the Indians would seem to have been inflamed and excited to the utmost; the bodies of persons killed at a great distance—whether by Indians or not, is not certain—were brought to the capital of the Territory and exposed to the public gaze for the purpose of inflaming still more the already excited feeling of the people. Their cupidity was appealed to, for the governor in a proclamation calls upon all, "either individually or in such parties as they may organize," "to kill and destroy as enemies of the country, wherever they may be found, all such hostile Indians," authorizing them to "hold to their own private use and benefit all the property of said hostile Indians that they may capture." . . .

As to Colonel Chivington, your committee can

hardly find fitting terms to describe his conduct. Wearing the uniform of the United States, which should be the emblem of justice and humanity; holding the important position of commander of a military district, and therefore having the honor of the government to that extent in his keeping, he deliberately planned and executed a foul and dastardly massacre which would have disgraced the veriest savage among those who were the victims of his cruelty. Having full knowledge of their friendly character, having himself been instrumental to some extent in placing them in their position of fancied security, he took advantage of their inapprehension and defenceless condition to gratify the worst passions that ever cursed the heart of man. . . .

[T]he truth is that he surprised and murdered, in cold blood, the unsuspecting men, women, and children on Sand creek, who had every reason to believe they were under the protection of the United States authorities, and then returned to Denver and boasted of the brave deeds he and the men under his command had performed.

2. Colonel J. M. Chivington Defends His Actions, 1865

Answer. My reason for making the attack on the Indian camp was, that I believed the Indians in the camp were hostile to the whites. That they were of the same tribes with those who had murdered many persons and destroyed much valuable property on the Platte and Arkansas rivers during the previous spring, summer and fall was beyond a doubt. When a tribe of Indians is at war with the whites it is impossible to determine what party or band of the tribe or the name of the Indian or Indians belonging to the tribe so at war are guilty of the acts of hostility. . . .

I had no reason to believe that Black Kettle and the Indians with him were in good faith at peace with the whites. The day before the attack Major Scott J. Anthony, 1st Colorado cavalry, then in command at Fort Lyon, told me that these Indians were hostile; that he had ordered his sentinels to fire on them if they attempted to come into the post, and that the sentinels had fired on them; that he was apprehensive

of an attack from these Indians, and had taken every precaution to prevent a surprise. . . .

I took every precaution to render the attack upon the Indians a surprise, for the reason that we had been chasing small parties of them all the summer and fall without being able to catch them, and it appeared to me that the only way to deal with them was to surprise them in their place of rendezvous. . . .

[W]hite men who had been trading with the Indians informed me that the Indians had determined to make war upon the whites as soon as the grass was green, and that they were making preparations for such an event by the large number of arrows they were making and the quantity of arms and ammunition they were collecting; that the settlers along the Platte and Arkansas rivers should be warned of the approaching danger; that the Indians had declared their intention to prosecute the war vigorously when they commenced. . . .

On my arrival at Fort Lyon, in all my conversations with Major Anthony, commanding the post, and Major Colley, Indian agent, I heard nothing of the recent statement that the Indians were under the protection of the government, &c.; but Major Anthony repeatedly stated to me that he had at different times fired upon these Indians, and that they were hostile, and, during my stay at Fort Lyon, urged the necessity of my immediately attacking the Indians before they could learn of the number of troops at Fort Lyon, and so desirous was Major Col-ley, Indian agent, that I should find and also attack the Arapahoes, that he sent a messenger after the fight at Sand creek, nearly forty miles, to inform me where I could find the Arapahoes and Kiowas; yet, strange to say, I have learned recently that these men, Anthony and Colley, are the most bitter in their denunciations of the attack upon the Indians at Sand creek. . . .

J. M. CHIVINGTON,
Lieu't Col. 1st Cavalry of Colorado, Com'd'g Dist. of Colorado.

3. Conflicting Testimony, 1865

[F]rom the time that Major Wynkoop left this post to go out to rescue the white prisoners until the arrival of Colonel Chivington here, which took place on the 28th of November last, no depredations of any kind had been committed by the Indians within two hundred miles of this post; that upon Colonel Chivington's arrival here with a large body of troops he was informed where these Indians were encamped, and was fully advised under what circumstances they had come into this post, and why they were then on Sand creek; that he was remonstrated with both by officers and civilians at this post against making war upon these Indians; that he was informed and fully advised that there was a large number of friendly Indians there, together with several white men, who were there at the request of himself (Colley) and by permission of Major Anthony; that notwithstanding his knowledge of the facts as above set forth, he is informed that Colonel Chivington did, on the morning of the 29th of November last, surprise and attack said camp of friendly Indians and massacre a large number of them, (mostly women and children,) and did allow the troops of his command to mangle and mutilate them in the most horrible manner.

S. G. COLLEY, *United States Indian Agent.*

Fort Lyon, Colorado Territory, *January* 16, 1865.

Personally appeared before me Lieutenant James D. Connor, first New Mexico volunteer infantry, who, after being duly sworn, says: That on the 28th day of November, 1864, I was ordered by Major Scott J. Anthony to accompany him on an expedition (Indian) as his battalion adjutant; the object of that expedition was to be a thorough campaign against hostile Indians, as I was led to understand. I referred to the fact of there being a friendly camp of Indians in the immediate neighborhood and remonstrated against simply attacking that camp, as I was aware that they were resting there in fancied security under promises held out to them of safety from Major E. W. Wynkoop, former commander of the post of Fort Lyon, as well as by Major S. J. Anthony, then in command. Our battalion was attached to the command of Colonel J. M. Chivington, and left Fort Lyon on the night of the 28th of November, 1864; about daybreak on the morning of the 29th of November we came in sight of the camp of the friendly Indians aforementioned, and were ordered by Colonel Chivington to attack the same, which was accordingly done. The command of Colonel Chivington was composed of about one thousand men; the village of the Indians consisted of from one hundred to one hundred and thirty lodges, and, as far as I am able to judge, of from five hundred to six hundred souls, the majority of which were women and children; in going over the battle-ground the next day I did not see a body of man, woman, or child but was scalped, and in many instances their bodies were mutilated in the most horrible manner—men, women, and children's privates cut out, &c; I heard one man say that he had cut out a woman's private parts and had them for exhibition on a stick; I heard another man say that he had cut the fingers off an Indian to get the rings on the hand; according to the best of my knowledge and belief these atrocities that were committed were with knowledge of J. M. Chivington, and I do not know of his taking any measures to prevent them; I heard of one instance of a child a few months old being thrown in a feed-box of a wagon, and after being carried some distance left on the ground to perish; I also heard of numerous instances in which men had cut out the private parts of females and stretched them over the saddle-bows, and wore them over their hats while riding in the ranks. All these matters were a subject of general conversation, and could not help being known by Colonel J. M. Chivington.

JAMES D. CONNOR,
First Lieutenant First Infantry
New Mexico Volunteers.

Fort Lyon, Colorado Territory.
Lieutenant Cramer sworn:

I am stationed at this post, 1st lieutenant company C, veteran battalion Colorado cavalry. I was at this post when Colonel Chivington arrived here, and accompanied him on his expedition. . . .Colonel Chivington moved his regiment to the front, the Indians retreating up the creek, and hiding under the banks. There seemed to be no organization among our troops; every one on his own hook, and shots flying between our own ranks. White Antelope ran towards our columns unarmed, and with both arms raised, but was killed. Several others of the warriors were killed in like manner. The women and children were huddled together, and most of our fire was concentrated on them. Sometimes during the engagement I was compelled to move my company to get out of the fire of our own men. Captain Soule did not order his men to fire when the order was given to commence the fight. During the fight, the battery on the opposite side of the creek kept firing at the bank while our men were in range. The Indian warriors, about one hundred in number, fought desperately; there were about five hundred all told. I estimated the loss of the Indians to be from one hundred and twenty-five to one hundred and seventy-five killed; no wounded fell into our hands, and all the dead were scalped. The Indian who was pointed out as White Antelope had his fingers cut off. Our force was so large that there was no necessity of firing on the Indians. They did not return the fire until after our troops had fired several rounds. We had the assur-

ance from Major Anthony that Black Kettle and his friends should be saved, and only those Indians who had committed depredations should be harmed. During the fight no officer took any measures to get out of the fire of our own men. Left Hand stood with his arms folded, saying he would not fight the white men, as they were his friends. I told Colonel Chivington of the position in which the officers stood from Major Wynkoop's pledges to the Indians, and also Major Anthony's, and that it would be murder, in every sense of the word, if he attacked those Indians. His reply was, bringing his fist down close to my face, "Damn any man who sympathizes with Indians." I told him what pledges were given the Indians. He replied, "That he had come to kill Indians, and believed it to be honorable to kill Indians under any and all circumstances"; all this at Fort Lyon. Lieutenant Dunn went to Colonel Chivington and wanted to know if he could kill his prisoner, young Smith. His reply was, "Don't ask me; you know my orders; I want no prisoners." Colonel Chivington was in position where he must have seen the scalping and mutilation going on. . . .

My name is Presley Talbot. I was in the third regiment Colorado cavalry, and held the position as captain of company M. I was at the battle of Sand creek; I was ordered to go into the fight by Colonel Chivington; ordered to cross Sand creek to the right side of the bank. There I received so very galling a fire from the Indians under the bank and from ditches dug out just above the bank that I ordered my company to advance, to prepare to dismount and fight on foot. . . . I furthermore state that the Indians were hostile, and acted with desperation and bravery; that Colonel John M. Chivington, commanding, acted with discretion and bravery. . . .

[I] had several consultations with Major Colley, Indian agent, and John Smith, Indian interpreter; stated that they had considerable sympathy for me, being wounded; would give me all the attention and assistance in their power, but they would do anything to damn Colonel John M. Chivington, or Major Downing; that they had lost at least six thousand dollars each by the Sand creek fight; that they had one hundred and five robes and two white ponies bought at the time of attack, independent of the goods which they had on the battle-ground, which they never had recovered, but would make the general government pay for the same, and damn old Chivington eventually.

4. Major E. W. Wynkoop Explains Indian Intent, 1864, 1865

Wynkoop's original report (September 28, 1864), before the massacre on November 29 of that year.

His excellency Governor Evans asked the Indians what they had to say.

Black Kettle then said: On sight of your circular of June 27, 1864, I took hold of the matter, and have now come to talk to you about it. . . . I want you to give all the chiefs of the soldiers here to understand that we are for peace, and that we have made peace, that we may not be mistaken by them for enemies. I have not come here with a little wolf's bark, but have come to talk plain with you. We must live near the buffalo or starve. When we came here we came free, without any apprehension, to see you, and when I go home and tell my people that I have taken your hand and the hands of all the chiefs here in Denver, they will feel well, and so will all the different tribes of Indians on the plains, after we have eaten and drunk with them.

Wynkoop's later report (1865), after the event.

In conclusion, allow me to say that from the time I held the consultation with the Indian chiefs on the headwaters of the Smoky Hill, up to the date of the massacre by Colonel Chivington, not one single depredation had been committed by the Cheyenne and Arapahoe Indians; the settlers of the Arkansas valley had returned to their ranches, from which they had fled, had taken in their crops, and had been resting in perfect security, under assurances from myself that they would be in no danger for the present—by that means saving the country from what must inevitably become almost a famine were they to lose their crops. The lines of communication to the State were opened, and travel across the plains rendered perfectly safe through the Cheyenne and Arapahoe country.

5. Governor John Evans Responds to the Congressional Report, 1865

Before leaving this subject, I desire to call attention to the following significant fact; the part of my proclamation from which the committee quote reads as follows:

"Now, therefore, I, John Evans, governor of Colorado Territory, do issue this, my proclamation, authorizing all citizens of Colorado, either individually or in such parties as they may organize, to go in pursuit of all hostile Indians on the plains, *scrupulously avoiding those who have responded to my call to rendezvous at the points indicated.* Also to kill and destroy, as enemies of the country, wherever they may be found, all such hostile Indians."

The language which I have italicized in the foregoing quotation shows that I forbade, in this proclamation, the disturbance of the friendly Indians and only authorized killing the hostile. . . .

I have thus noticed such portions of the report as refer to myself, and shown conclusively that the committee, in every mention they have made of me, have been, to say the least, mistaken.

First. The committee, for the evident purpose of maintaining their position that these Indians have not been engaged in the war, say the prisoners they held were purchased. The testimony is to the effect that they captured them.

Second. The committee say that these Indians were and always had been friendly, and had committed no acts of hostility or depredations. The public documents to which I refer show conclusively that they had been hostile, and had committed many acts of hostility and depredations.

Third. They say that I joined in sending these

Indians to Fort Lyon. The published report of the Commissioner of Indian Affairs, and of the Indian council, show that I left them entirely in the hands of the military authorities.

Fourth. They say nothing seems to have been done by the authorities to prevent hostilities. The public documents and files of the Indian bureau, and of my superintendency, show constant and unremitting diligence and effort on my part to prevent hostilities and protect the people.

Fifth. They say that I prevaricated for the purpose of avoiding the admission that these Indians "were and had been actuated by the most friendly feelings towards the whites." Public documents cited show conclusively that the admission they desired me to make was false, and that my statement, instead of being a prevarication, was true, although not in accordance with the preconceived and mistaken opinions of the committee.

6. Helen Hunt Jackson's Account of Sand Creek and the Aftermath, 1881

The Governor of Colorado called for military aid, and for authority to make a campaign against the Indians, which was given him. But as there was no doubt that many of the Indians were still peaceable and loyal, and he desired to avoid every possibility of their sharing in the punishment of the guilty, he issued a proclamation in June, requesting all who were friendly to come to places which he designated, where they were to be assured of safety and protection. This proclamation was sent to all the Indians of the plains. In consequence of it, several bands of friendly Arapahoes and Cheyennes came to Fort Lyon, and were there received by the officer in charge, rationed, and assured of safety. Here there occurred, on the 29th of November, one of the foulest massacres which the world has seen. . . .

In October of the next year some of the bands, having first had their safety assured by an old and true friend, I. H. Leavenworth, Indian Agent for the Upper Arkansas, gathered together to hold a council with United States Commissioners on the Little Arkansas. The commissioners were empowered by the President to restore to the survivors of the Sand Creek massacre full value for all the property then destroyed; "to make reparation," so far as possible. To each woman who had lost a husband there they gave one hundred and sixty acres of land; to each child who had lost a parent, the

same. Probably even an Indian woman would consider one hundred and sixty acres of land a poor equivalent for a murdered husband; but the offers were accepted in good part by the tribe, and there is nothing in all the history of this patient race more pathetic than the calm and reasonable language employed by some of these Cheyenne and Arapahoe chiefs at this council. Said Black Kettle, the chief over whose lodge the American flag, with a white flag tied below, was floating at the time of the massacre, "I once thought that I was the only man that persevered to be the friend of the white man; but since they have come and cleaned out our lodges, horses, and everything else, it is hard for me to believe white men any more. All my friends, the Indians that are holding back, they are afraid to come in; are afraid that they will be betrayed as I have been. I am not afraid of white men, but come and take you by the hand." Elsewhere, Black Kettle spoke of Colonel Chivington's troops as "that fool-band of soldiers that cleared out our lodges and killed our women and children. This is hard on us." With a magnanimity and common-sense which white men would have done well to imitate in their judgments of the Indians, he recognized that it would be absurd, as well as unjust, to hold all white men in distrust on account of the acts of that "fool-band of soldiers."

Chapter 17:
Document Set 1 References

1. A Congressional Committee Decries the Violence at Sand Creek, 1865
   Report, Joint Committee on the Conduct of the War, *Massacre of Cheyenne Indians,* 38th Cong., 2nd Sess., 1865, pp. 1–10.

2. Colonel J. M. Chivington Defends His Actions, 1865
   "Testimony of Colonel J. M. Chivington," April 26, 1865, *Massacre,* pp. 104, 106, 108.

3. Conflicting Testimony, 1865
   S. G. Colley, January 27, 1865; Lieutenant James D. Connor, January 16, 1865; Lieutenant Joseph A. Cramer, n.d., 1865; in *Massacre,* pp. 52–53, 73–74; Captain Presley Talbot, May 11, 1865. Report of the Secretary of War, 39th Cong., 2nd Sess., Senate Executive Document 26, 1867, pp. 207–208.

4. Major E. W. Wynkoop Explains Indian Intent, 1864, 1865
   Conference Record, September 28, 1864, Report of the Secretary of War, p. 213. Report, January 14, 1865, Report of the Secretary of War, p. 124.

5. Governor John Evans Responds to the Congressional Report, 1865
   John Evans, Statement, August 21, 1865, *Massacre,* pp. 85–86.

6. Helen Hunt Jackson's Account of Sand Creek and the Aftermath, 1881
   Helen Hunt Jackson, *A Century of Dishonor,* 1881 (New York: Harper Torchbooks, rep. 1965), pp. 87–88.

CHAPTER 17

DOCUMENT SET 2
The Farmer's Frontier: Life on the Great Plains

A significant portion of Chapter 17 is devoted to the farmer's frontier. While less dramatic than the exploitation of the miner's and cattleman's frontier, the settlement of the vast interior resulted in a stable and permanent presence in an area that would soon become the breadbasket of the United States. Complementing your textbook's description of pioneer life, the following documents concentrate on the everyday experience of the migrants who built a society in the trans-Mississippi West.

The first problem for promoters of western agricultural development was to publicize the economic opportunity. Your textbook notes that both the railroads and the government played a role in this process, whether through promotional activity or legislation such as the Homestead Act of 1862. Be aware of these enticements and compare them with the physical realities of life on the Great Plains frontier.

The most useful documents for purposes of comparison are the letters of homesteaders Howard Ruede and Mary Chaffee Abell, both immigrants to Kansas in the 1870s. These personal accounts provide evidence of the problems of daily life on the farmer's frontier. Together with writer Hamlin Garland's recollection of boyhood experiences in Iowa and the Dakota Territory, these letters paint a vivid picture of the work, pain, and hope encountered by agricultural pioneers.

For Ruede, the struggle ended in prosperity, but for Abell the result was death at the age of 29. Garland's musings reflect a deeper, thoughtful analysis of human existence on the Great Plains.

As you review the evidence, reflect on the similarities and differences between male and female experiences on the farmer's frontier. Until recently, the history of western society was written in terms of frontiers for men. In fact, western women functioned as domestic artisans, wage earners, and income-producers. These documents stress domestic production and nurturing roles, since home and farm tended to be women's workplace on the Great Plains. Be alert to the variety of female responsibilities on the farmer's frontier, as well as the impact of farm life on both men and women.

The heavy physical demands imposed on rural pioneers produced varied results. The last two documents suggest that economic success and personal gratification were not always possible. A descriptive article from the Emporia (Kansas) *Gazette* records the experience of a family broken by the plains environment, while the excerpt from a farm handbook unintentionally reveals the rigors of farm life. Try to determine what aspects of farming were responsible for the rising migration from farms to cities in the late nineteenth century.

Questions for Analysis

1. What do the documents reveal about the expectations of immigrants to the Great Plains frontier? How did they acquire these impressions of frontier life? What inducements drew them to the West? How did the realities of farm life as homesteaders compare with their expectations and aspirations?

2. How did the everyday life experiences of men, women, and children on the frontier differ? In what way did their lives contrast with those of farmers in more settled agricultural areas? How did women maintain contacts and values from their previous lives in more settled localities?

3. Why did a reverse migration pattern surface by 1900? Do the documents clarify the motives of farmers who returned to the East or of farm children attracted to urban communities?

4. Describe the sexual division of labor on the farmer's frontier. Do the documents reveal any gender-related differences in the physical or psychological impact of farm life on the rural pioneers? To what extent has the burden of responsibility and sex role definition changed over time?

1. Howard Ruede Homesteads a Claim, 1877–1878

Thursday, April 5, 1877
At Snyder's, Kill Creek, Kansas

This was another hot day, and we had heavy work too, laying up sod. Snyder broke a lot for us this A.M. and we began laying up the wall. It is 20 inches thick. These "Kansas brick" are from 2 to 4 inches thick, 12 wide and 20 long, and the joints between them we fill with ground. Just before sunset we got the ridgepole into position on the crotches, so that the room will be about 7 feet high. We expect to get the roof in and have the place in condition to live in by the end of the week. The sod is heavy and when you take 3 or 4 bricks on a litter or hand barrow, and carry it 50 to 150 feet, I tell you it is no easy work. . . .

Friday, April 6, 1877

Plenty of air stirring today, so it was not so hot. We finished off the gable ends of the dugout and got the boards on the rafters, ready for the straw. A lot more sod to carry tomorrow for the roof. Had jack rabbit for supper. . . .

Tuesday, December 8, 1877

At the well again. Sunk it to 25 feet and struck shale. Then we quit. We'll have to go to another place to dig now. We were not very badly disappointed, because we thought we'd find plenty shale. The chance was for water, but fortune did not smile upon us. There's 3¼ days' work for nothing. . . .

Monday, January 14, 1878

Directly after Breakfast Geo. and I went to boring where Hoot had said there was water. Down twelve feet and struck shale. Would have continued boring, to see how thick the shale is, but just then Geo. Lough came for the auger, and I could not tell him he couldn't have it. Went to Hoot's and borrowed a shovel; Bub and I went to the hole in the draw (not on my claim) where Pa bored and struck water. They had dug about three feet, and I dug about four more, and then had all the water we will need for the present, though I am not yet done digging wells. I intend to dig on my place till I get water. . . .

Sunday, February 24, 1878

. . . Priced all the wagons I could hear or think of, but could not get a satisfactory price. At last I came across C. G. Paris and asked him whether he knew of a wagon for sale. He replied that he had one. . . . I had not got out of town before he called me back, saying he'd take $30. So I tied the oxen, paid him and got a receipt. Then I again started for home. . . . Bud was down town yesterday and bought a curry comb, so now we can get the dirt out of the oxen's hides. I have something less than a dollar, and Pa has a whole dollar in cash, but we are happy anyhow. I'll have to trust to Providence to put work in my way to raise about $20 to buy a breaking plow, hoe, fork and rake, and timber for the new sod addition we intend to put to the ranch. . . .

Tuesday, June 18, 1878
Osborne, Kansas

Turned out about 5, and as soon as the wheat was dry enough went to cradling. Pa tied it awhile and between us we got ½ acre cut by noon. Then I started for town. It was awful hot, too. Took it easy and got to town about 6. . . .

The threshing was done Aug. 14th, Henry Hoot taking charge of the business. The wheat yielded 28½ bu. and the rye 33 bu., which was put into straw until the old house was vacated. During September I worked in the office, getting home very late. Pa and Geo. finished the new house and cut the corn fodder. On the 28th September we moved into the new house, after having occupied the dugout for 13 months.

2. Mary Chaffee Abell Confronts the Kansas Environment, 1871–1875

[Mary Abell to her sister Kate, June 29, 1871; this and the following letter are from Kansas.]

Robert has got a piece of land that suits him, and so near market that we can get every thing just as cheap as we could in Lawrence. It seems so fortunate. . . . There is a house to be built, fences to make—a well to be dug and a cow to be got beside a living—for the first year on a homestead brings in nothing—for the sod has to rot a year before a crop can be put in. I really cannot see how we are to get along—but in some way I hope. . . .

[Mary Abell to her sister Kate, Jan. 18, 1873]

Here we have been shut up all winter. Have not been anywhere since I was out to Miriams' last fall, do you wonder that I get nervous shut up so week after week with the children in a room 10 X 11 for that is every inch of room we have. Em talks about being crowded, but let her try keeping house in the further bedroom with four small children—a bedstead—bed on the floor—stove—table—big trunk, three chairs (stowed on the bed part of the time) and things that you can't get along without, and no sort of a storeroom and half a window to light it all and then what about being crowded, and yet we are just in that predicament. I have to cook and do everything right here. Get milk—make butter, eat, sleep etc. etc. . . .

[Mary Abell to her mother, Oct. 11, 1873]

I helped Rob in with the last of his hay Friday. Yesterday I cleaned all the lower part of the house excepting washing the doors and windows and mopping the other room floor. I was tired enough when night came. Nevertheless sat up till half past ten o'clock mending clean clothes for the little ones. They have all had the bowel complaint this fall, but are well and hearty again now. Baby has cut four double teeth at once. I felt motion soon after I wrote you last. Am over five months along, shall be sick the first part of Feb I expect—seems as if I have all I can tend to now. My head is much better, but I am bloated, and feel so uncomfortable most of the time. Have been at work all day even though it has been the Sabbath—washed the children all over, heads and all and put clean clothes on them—cut Rob's hair and whiskers etc. Everything has been neglected since I've been helping Robert. I have been his sole help in getting up and stacking at least 25 tons of hay and oats—some of the time I was deathly sick and faint while loading, but finally got through with it. My right limb is very bad. . . .

[Mary Abell to her family, Oct. 16, 1873]

I feel very little like writing, but you will be wanting to know the whys of course. One of those dreadful prairie fires, accompanied by a hurricane of wind swept through here Tuesday night, the 14th and took everything but our house and stock (horses and cattle). All our hay and oats that Rob and I had worked so hard to get up and stack, harness, saddle,

bridle, stable, 26 hens and chickens that I had had such work to raise—all the wooden part to the mower, hay rack posts planks all burned etc. At least a hundred dollars worth swept away in a few moments. The flames came rolling in, in huge billows—I rigged up in Robt's coat, boots and a flannel shirt with a wool comforter over my head and helped him fight fire—but no one could stand before this blinding smoke, heat and cinders. I burned the right side of my face raw. One of my eyes is half shut, it is so badly swollen. My back and hips are stiff enough. The fire came so suddenly that we had not much time to think or act. . . .

Rob is blue enough—and who wouldn't be? I don't feel much like writing.

[Mary Abell to her parents, Nov. 28, 1873]

Imagine yourselves for instance with nothing but land, house, and stock—for that's where we are. Not a tree, particle of water, grass, stable, fence or any thing else. Comfortable though right on the verge of winter—and the wherewith to get it with, about as vague. Eastern people may think us homesteaders are doing a fine thing to get 160 acres of land for nothing—all but the nothing. Oh, the suffering that the poor endure here, and privations you have not the remotest idea of, and poor means nearly all homesteaders.

[Mary Abell to her sister Kate, March 7, 1874]

I am beginning to look old—and no wonder I look yellow instead of pale after my latter confinements, and work and care soon tell on a body's looks—though I hope I shall be relieved after a while. Robert don't look any older—men don't you know. . . .

[Mary Abell to her father, Nov. 21, 1874]

We've been obliged to tell the children that Santa Claus will not come here this year, everybody is so poor, and need food and clothes so much it wont pay him to bring any playthings. I shall try and sell butter to get them some candy etc. . . . I have aches and pains somewhere all the time, and with all am cross and nervous. If I was only where I could run home once or twice a year and get a rest—but I am here and here I must stay, how long? . . .

[Mary Abell to her mother, Feb. 16, 1875]

Your two kind welcome letters have been received. I am sorry you worry about me so, but can't blame you. I am not as bad as I was in that coldest weather because I can sit up more, but I have no strength to do anything and the least little thing tires me all out. Baby has been quite sick for three days, and he is so heavy that the lifting and care of him has quite used me up. . . . The weather here is colder than with you, for with the cold is a fierce north wind which will freeze man or beast that happen to be out.

The children had to wear their hoods nights. My eyelids froze together so I picked off the ice, the tops of the sheets and quilts and all our beds were frozen stiff with the breath. The cold was so intense we could not breath the air without pain.

3. Hamlin Garland Recalls the Hardship of a Dakota Childhood, ca. 1880s

All that day I had studied the land, musing upon its distinctive qualities, and while I acknowledged the natural beauty of it, I revolted from the gracelessness of its human habitations. The lonely box-like farm-houses on the ridges suddenly appeared to me like the dens of wild animals. The lack of color, of charm in the lives of the people anguished me. I wondered why I had never before perceived the futility of woman's life on a farm. . . .

Looking at the sky above me, feeling the rush of the earth beneath my feet I saw how much I had dared and how little, how pitifully little I had won. Over me the ragged rainclouds swept, obscuring the stars and in their movement and in the feeling of the dawn lay something illimitable and prophetic. Such moments do not come to men often—but to me for an hour, life was painfully purposeless. "What does it all mean?" I asked myself. . . .

As I walked the street I met several neighbors from Dry Run as well as acquaintances from the Grove. Nearly all, even the young men, looked worn and weather-beaten and some appeared both silent and sad. Laughter was curiously infrequent and I wondered whether in my days on the farm they had all been as rude of dress, as misshapen of form and as wistful of voice as they now seemed to me to be.

"Have times changed? Has a spirit of unrest and complaining developed in the American farmer?"

I perceived the town from the triple viewpoint of a former resident, a man from the city, and a reformer, and every minutest detail of dress, tone and gesture revealed new meaning for me. Fancher and Gammons were feebler certainly, and a little more querulous with age, and their faded beards and rough hands gave pathetic evidence of the hard wear of wind and toil. At the moment nothing [glossed] the essential tragic futility of their existence. . . .

In those few days, I perceived life without its glamor. I no longer looked upon these toiling women with the thoughtless eyes of youth. I saw no humor in the bent forms and graying hair of the men. I began to understand that my own mother had trod a similar slavish round with never a full day of leisure, with scarcely an hour of escape from the tugging hands of children, and the need of mending and washing clothes. I recalled her as she passed from the churn to the stove, from the stove to the bedchamber, and from the bedchamber back to the kitchen, day after day, year after year, rising at daylight or before, and going to her bed only after the evening dishes were washed and the stockings and clothing mended for the night.

4. William Allen White Describes Some Kansas Refugees, 1895

There came through Emporia yesterday two old-fashioned "mover wagons," headed east. The stock in the caravan would invoice four horses, very poor and very tired; one mule, more disheartened than the horses; and one sad-eyed dog, that had probably been compelled to rustle his own precarious living for many a long and weary day.

A few farm implements of the simpler sort were in the wagon, but nothing that had wheels was moving except the two wagons. All the rest of the impedimenta had been left upon the battlefield, and these poor stragglers, defeated but not conquered, were fleeing to another field, to try the fight again.

These movers were from western Kansas—from

Gray County, a county which holds a charter from the state to officiate as the very worst, most desolate, God-forsaken, man-deserted spot on the sad old earth. They had come from the wilderness only after a ten years' hard, vicious fight, a fight which had left its scars on their faces, had beat their bodies, had taken the elasticity from their steps, and left them crippled to enter the battle anew.

For ten years they had been fighting the elements. They had seen it stop raining for months at a time. They had heard the fury of the winter wind as it came whining across the short burned grass, and their children huddling in the corner. They have strained their eyes watching through the long summer days for the rain that never came. They have seen that big cloud roll up from the southwest about one o'clock in the afternoon, hover over the land, and stumble away with a few thumps of thunder as the sun went down. They have tossed through hot nights wild with worry, and have arisen only to find their worst nightmares grazing in reality on the brown stubble in front of their sun-warped doors.

They had such high hopes when they went out there; they are so desolate now—no, not now, for now they are in the land of corn and honey. They have come out of the wilderness, back to the land of promise. They are now in God's own country down on the Neosho, with their wife's folks, and the taste of apple butter and good cornbread and fresh meat and pie—pie-plant [rhubarb] pie like mother used to make—gladdened their shrunken palates last night. And real cream, curdling on their coffee saucers last night for supper, was a sight so rich and strange that it lingered in their dreams, wherein they walked beside the still water, and lay down in green pastures.

5. John E. Read's Advice on Keeping Children on the Farm, 1881

How to keep the boys on the farm and induce them cheerfully to choose farming as their occupation for life is a question of deep interest to many parents. The stampede of young men from the country to cities and large towns is not an evil which finds its limit in the domestic circles which they leave, but is one which extends through society and makes its depressing influence felt everywhere. How to check this evil is a question of great importance and is well worthy of consideration.

In order to induce the boys to stay on the farm they must be informed of the true relation which exists between the city and the country. They must be shown that the expenses of living are so high that the city clerk, whom they envy because of his large salary, can hardly keep out of debt. And the fact that the man in the city is tied to his business a great deal more closely than the farmer is to his work should be set before them. . . .

Boys should be taught that farming is an *honorable occupation*. It is very true that the calling does not make the man, and that a man should not be respected because he follows one honest occupation or despised because he follows another. Character is what a man is, and cannot always be determined by reference to the kind of work which he performs. The farmer may be a gentleman or he can be a boor, he may build up a noble character or he may be a villain. He makes his own choice in these respects. Merely being a farmer will make him neither a good man nor a bad one. Still, farming is a business which does not open to its followers so many evil influences, and expose them to as many temptations, as some lines of business. It is the kind of labor which GOD directly marked out for man, and upon the cultivation of the soil the civilization and happiness of mankind must, in a great measure, depend. As far as occupation is concerned, the farmer has no occasion to "look up to" the merchant, manufacturer, or professional man. Clergymen and teachers are doing a work the value of which is beyond all price, and many boys will be called from the farm to fill the ranks of these professions. . . . But before a boy leaves the farm to become a merchant, or to go to a city as a laborer, or to engage in business of any kind, he should very carefully consider the question whether there is any good prospect that he can do better than the thousands of those who have preceded him, and who have soon been led to repent that they ever left the farm. . . .

The girls must be taught to respect farming as an occupation, and be required to help their mothers in the work of the house and the dairy. When farmers educate their girls in a manner which will fit them to become farmers' wives, and teach them that farming is one of the most honorable of all occupations, and that the girl who marries a farmer does fully as well as one who marries a merchant or a lawyer, they will thereby do a great deal towards keeping their boys on the farm. . . .

We are well aware that many farmers' wives have been terribly overworked, and we can sympathize with the mother who desires an easier lot for her child. But we know that this excessive labor is not an absolute necessity, and that with the aid of the labor-saving implements of the present day a farmer's wife can live as easily as the wives of men engaged in many other pursuits. . . . The wife of the farmer ought to be willing to work in order to help him, and if the man is what he should be he will see to it that she does not go beyond her strength.

Chapter 17:
Document Set 2 References

1. Howard Ruede Homesteads a Claim, 1877–1878
   Howard Ruede, *Sod-House Days. Letters from a Kansas Homesteader 1877–78,* John Ise, ed. (New York: Columbia University Press, 1937), pp. 39–40, 194, 203–204, 212–215, 233–234, 239.

2. Mary Chaffee Abell Confronts the Kansas Enviroment, 1871–1875
   "Hard Work Is the Watchword in Kansas: Mary Chaffee Abell," as reprinted in *Victorian Women: A Documentary Account of Women's Lives in Nineteenth-Century England, France, and the United States,* Erna Olafson Hellerstein *et al.,* eds. (Stanford: Stanford University Press, 1981).

3. Hamlin Garland Recalls the Hardship of a Dakota Childhood, ca. 1880s

Hamlin Garland, *A Son of the Middle Border,* 1917 (New York: Macmillan, rep. 1945), pp. 283–285.

4. William Allen White Describes Some Kansas Refugees, 1895
   William Allen White, Emporia (Kansas) *Gazette,* June 15, 1895.

5. John E. Read's Advice on Keeping Children on the Farm, 1881
   John E. Read, *Farming for Profit: A Handbook for the American Farmer* (Philadelphia: J. C. Moody and Co., 1881), pp. 848–850.

Chapter 17:
Document Set 2 Credits

CHAPTER 17

The Western Landscape: Nature's Gifts and Their Exploitation

The textbook describes the relationship between the findings of the explorers who went west to map the Rocky Mountain frontier and the origins of the conservation movement in the late nineteenth century. The observations of these early visitors emphasized the beauty, magnitude, and raw power of nature as they encountered it in the then-uncharted trans-Mississippi interior. Their accounts soon became important supporting evidence for those who sought to protect the nation's resources and scenic places from the encroachments of settlement and economic development.

The documents that follow attempt to capture the impressions created by western natural phenomena. As you examine these early descriptions of the American West, note especially the importance of scale in shaping the observers' responses to geographic features unfamiliar to easterners in the immediate post–Civil War era. Be aware of vast distances and bigger-than-life dimensions as common themes in the record left by those who charted the wilderness.

A useful complement to written accounts of the western landscape may be found in visual representations of nature and the physical environment. Through the photographic record, especially the work of William H. Jackson, it is possible to evaluate the sometimes subjective descriptions found in the printed sources.

Although the sheer mass and sweeping scale of the western landscape inspired a new respect for nature in many pioneer observers, alternative views of the environment were expressed by those interested in the economic development of the West. To the developers, the wilderness was composed of obstacles to be overcome through human ingenuity. As you review the evidence of early railroad development, consider the attitudes of the builders who were determined to make use of western resources. What opportunities did the western environment offer to the enterprising developer? What forms did frontier economic activity take?

The consequences of rapid economic development are evident in some of the documents in this set. As you compare the photographic and written records of resource use, think about the conflicting values expressed by those who assessed the costs and benefits of uncontrolled exploitation of the nation's resources. Relate their ideas to the textbook discussion of conservation as a seminal idea.

Questions for Analysis

1. What were the initial impressions of the early observers of the western landscape? What were their attitudes toward nature, and how were those attitudes shaped by the experiences of the early observers of the late-nineteenth-century West? Focusing your attention on the visual representation of the Rocky Mountains and High Plains, compare these impressions with then-prevailing conceptions of the East's natural environment. How would you account for the differences?

2. How did American entrepreneurs and developers regard the physical environment of the High Plains and Far West? In what ways did their ideas, proposals, and actions alter the landscape? How did the developers regard the potential consequences of their actions?

3. Analyze the human and environmental outcomes of frontier economic activity. How did observers regard the exploitation of nature in the late-nineteenth-century West? What solutions were advanced to deal with the use and misuse of resources? With what results?

4. To what extent was nature viewed as a receptive, resistant, or benign force by nineteenth-century observers? Using the documents as evidence, support one of these interpretations of the natural environment. How would you explain the ideas and impressions recorded by the authors or creators of the documents? What conditioned their views?

1. John Wesley Powell Describes the Grand Canyon, 1869

August 13—We are now ready to start on our way down the Great Unknown. Our boats, tied to a common stake, are chafing each other, as they are tossed by the fretful river. They ride high and buoyant, for their loads are lighter than we could desire. We have but a month's rations remaining. The flour has been resifted through the mosquito net sieve; the spoiled bacon has been dried, and the worst of it boiled; the few pounds of dried apples have been spread in the sun, and reshrunken to their normal bulk; the sugar has all melted, and gone on its way down the river; but we have a large sack of coffee. The lighting of the boats has this advantage: they will ride the waves better, and we shall have but little to carry when we make a portage.

We are three-quarters of a mile in the depths of the earth, and the great river shrinks into insignificance, as it dashes its angry waves against the walls and cliffs, that rise to the world above; they are but puny ripples, and we but pigmies, running up and down the sands, or lost among the boulders.

We have an unknown distance yet to run; and unknown river yet to explore. What falls there are, we know not; what rocks beset the channel, we know not; what walls rise over the river, we know not. Ah, well! we may conjecture many things. The men talk as cheerfully as ever; jests are bandied about freely this morning; but to me the cheer is somber and the jests are ghastly.

With some eagerness, and some anxiety, and some misgiving, we enter the cañon below, and are carried along by the swift water through walls which rise from its very edge. They have the same structure as we noticed yesterday—tiers of irregular shelves below, and, above these, steep slopes to the foot of marble cliffs. We run six miles in a little more than half an hour, and emerge into a more open portion of the cañon, where high hills and ledges of rock intervene between the river and the distant walls. . . .

August 14—At daybreak we walk down the bank of the river, on a little sandy beach, to take a view of a new feature in the cañon. Heretofore, hard rocks have given us bad river; soft rocks, smooth water; and a series of rocks harder than any we have experienced sets in. The river enters the granite!

We can see but a little way into the granite gorge, but it looks threatening.

After breakfast we enter on the waves. At the very introduction, it inspires awe. The cañon is narrower than we have ever before seen it; the water is swifter; there are but few broken rocks in the channel; but the walls are set, on either side, with pinnacles and crags; and sharp, angular buttresses, bristling with wind and wave polished spires, extend far out into the river. . . .

About eleven o'clock we hear a great roar ahead, and approach it very cautiously. The sound grows louder and louder as we run, and at last we find ourselves above a long, broken fall, with ledges and pinnacles of rock obstructing the river. There is a descent of, perhaps, seventy-five or eighty feet in a third of a mile, and the rushing waters break into great waves on the rocks, and lash themselves into a mad, white foam. We can land just above, but there is no foothold on either side by which we can make a portage. It is nearly a thousand feet to the top of the granite, so it will be impossible to carry our boats around, though we can climb to the summit up a side gulch, and, passing along a mile or two, can descend to the river. This we find on examination; but such a portage would be impracticable for us, and we must run the rapid, or abandon the river. There is no hesitation. We step into our boats, push off and away we go, first on smooth but swift water, then we strike a glassy wave, and ride to its top, down again into the trough, up again on a higher wave, and down and up on waves higher and still higher, until we strike one just as it curls back, and a breaker rolls over our little boat. Still, on we speed, shooting past projecting rocks, till the little boat is caught in a whirlpool, and spun around several times. At last we pull out again into the stream, and now the other boats have passed us. . . .

The walls, now, are more than a mile in height—a vertical distance difficult to appreciate. . . .

A thousand feet of this is up through granite crags, then steep slopes and perpendicular cliffs rise, one above another, to the summit. The gorge is black and narrow below, red and gray and flaring above, with crags and angular projections on the walls, which, cut in many places by side cañons, seem to be a vast wilderness of rocks. Down in these grand, gloomy depths we glide, ever listening, for the mad waters keep up their roar; ever watching, ever peering ahead, for the narrow cañon is winding, and the river is closed in so that we can see but a few hundred yards, and what there may be below we know not; but we listen for falls, and watch for rocks, or stop now and then, in the bay of a recess, to admire the gigantic scenery. . . .

August 18—The day is employed in making portages, and we advance but two miles on our journey. Still it rains.

While the men are at work making portages, I climb up the granite to its summit, and go away back over the rust colored sandstones and greenish yellow shales, to the foot of the marble wall. I climb so high that the men and boats are lost in the black depths below, and the dashing river is a rippling brook; and still there is more cañon above than below. All about me are interesting geological records. The book is open, and I can read as I run. All about me are grand views, for the clouds are playing again in the gorges. But somehow I think of the nine days' rations, and the bad river, and the lesson of the rocks, and the glory of the scene is but half seen. . . .

August 29—We start very early this morning. The river still continues swift, but we have no serious difficulty, and at twelve o'clock emerge from the Grand Cañon of the Colorado. We are in a valley now, and low mountains are seen in the distance, coming to the river below. We recognize this as the Grand Wash.

To-night we camp on the left bank, in a *mesquite* thicket.

The relief from danger, and the joy of success, are great. When he who has been chained by wounds to a hospital cot, until his canvas tent seems like a dungeon cell, until the groans of those who lie about, tortured with probe and knife, are piled up, a weight of horror on his ears that he cannot throw off, cannot forget, and until the stench of festering wounds and anaesthetic drugs has filled the air with its loathsome burthen, at last goes out into the open field, what a world he sees! How beautiful the sky; how bright the sunshine; what "floods of delirious music" pour from the throats of birds; how sweet the fragrance of earth, and tree, and blossom! The first hour of convalescent freedom seems rich recompense for all—pain, gloom, terror.

Something like this are the feelings we experience to-night. Ever before us has been an unknown danger, heavier than immediate peril. Every waking hour passed in the Grand Cañon has been one of toil. We have watched with deep solicitude the steady disappearance of our scant supply of rations, and from time to time have seen the river snatch a portion of the little left, while we were ahungered. And danger and toil were endured in those gloomy depths, where ofttimes the clouds hid the sky by day, and but a narrow zone of stars could be seen at night. Only during the few hours of deep sleep, consequent on hard labor, has the roar of the waters been hushed. Now the danger is over; now the toil has ceased; now the gloom has disappeared; now the firmament is bounded only by the horizon; and what a vast expanse of constellations can be seen!

2. Walt Whitman's View of the High Plains, 1879

The Spanish Peaks—Evening on the Plains

Between Pueblo and Bent's Fort, southward, in a clear afternoon sun-spell, I catch exceptionally good glimpses of the Spanish peaks. We are in southeastern Colorado—pass immense herds of cattle as our first-class locomotive rushes us along—two or three times crossing the Arkansas, which we follow many miles, and of which river I get fine views, sometimes for quite a distance, its stony, upright, not very high, palisade banks, and then its muddy flats. We pass Fort Lyon—lots of adobe houses, limitless pasturage, appropriately flecked with those herds of cattle—in due time the declining sun in the west, a sky of limpid pearl over all, and so evening on the Great Plains. A calm, pensive, boundless landscape; the perpendicular rocks of the North Arkansas, hued in twilight; a thin line of violet on the southwestern horizon; the palpable coolness and slight aroma; a belated cowboy with some unruly member of his herd; an emigrant wagon toiling yet a little further, the horses slow and tired; two men, apparently father and son, jogging along on foot—and around all the indescribable *chiaroscuro* and sentiment (profounder than anything at sea) athwart these endless wilds.

America's Characteristic Landscape

Speaking generally as to the capacity and sure future destiny of that plain and prairie area (larger than any European kingdom), it is the inexhaustible land of wheat, maize, wool, flax, coal, iron, beef and pork, butter and cheese, apples and grapes; land of ten million virgin farms, to the eye at present wild and unproductive—yet experts say that upon it, when irrigated, may easily be grown enough wheat to feed the world. Then, as to scenery (giving my own thought and feeling), while I know the standard claim is that Yosemite, Niagara Falls, the Upper Yellowstone, and the like afford the greatest natural shows, I am not so sure but the prairies and the Plains, while less stunning at first sight, last longer, fill the aesthetic sense fuller, precede all the rest, and make North America's characteristic landscape.

Indeed, through the whole of this journey, with all its shows and varieties, what most impressed me and will longest remain with me are these same prairies. Day after day, and night after night, to my eyes, to all my senses—the aesthetic one most of all—they silently and broadly unfolded. Even their simplest statistics are sublime.

3. Overcoming Natural Obstacles to Building the Union Pacific, 1869

"In 1853 Henry Farnam and T. C. Durant, the then contractors and builders of the Missouri River Railroad in Iowa, instructed Peter A. Dey to investigate the question of the proper point for the Mississippi and Missouri River road to strike the Missouri River to obtain a good connection with any road that might be built across the continent. I was assigned to the duty, and surveys were accordingly extended to and up the Platte Valley, to ascertain whether any road built on the central or then northern line would, from the formation of the country, follow the Platte and its tributaries over the plains, and thus overcome the Rocky Mountains. Subsequently, under the patronage of Mr. Farnam, I extended the examination westward to the eastern base of the Rocky Mountains and beyond, examining the practicable passes from the Sangre Christo to the South Pass; made maps of the country, and developed it as thoroughly as could be done without making purely instrumental surveys. The practicability of the route, the singular formation of the country between Long's Peak, the Medicine Bow Mountains, and Bridger Pass, on the south, and Laramie Peak and the Sweetwater and Wind River ranges on the north, demonstrated to me that through this region the road must eventually be built. I reported the facts to Mr. Farnam, and through his and his friends' efforts, the prospect for a Pacific railroad began to take shape. . . .

"The first grading was done in the autumn of 1864, and the first rail laid in July, 1865. When you look back to the beginning at the Missouri River, with no railway communication from the East, and 500 miles of the country in advance without timber, fuel, or any material whatever from which to build or maintain a road, except the sand for the bare roadbed itself, with everything to be transported, and that by teams or at best by steamboats, for hundreds and thousands of miles; everything to be created, with labor scarce and high, you can all look back upon the work with satisfaction and ask, Under such circumstances could we have done more or better? . . .

"Its future is fraught with great good. It will develop a waste, will bind together the two extremes of the nation as one, will stimulate intercourse and trade and bring harmony, prosperity, and wealth to the two coasts. A proper policy, systematically and persistently followed, will bring to the road the trade of the two oceans, and will give it all the business it can accommodate, while the local trade will increase gradually until the mining, grazing, and agricultural regions through which it passes will build up and create a business that will be a lasting and permanent support to the country."

4. John Muir on the Dominion of Nature, 1898

The tendency nowadays to wander in wildernesses is delightful to see. Thousands of tired nerve-shaken, over-civilized people are beginning to find out that going to the mountains is going home; that wildness is a necessity; and that mountain parks and reservations are useful not only as fountains of timber and irrigating rivers, but as fountains of life. Awakening from the stupefying effects of the vice of over-industry and the deadly apathy of luxury, they are trying as best they can to mix and enrich their own little ongoings with those of Nature, and to get rid of rust and disease. Briskly venturing and roaming, some are washing off sins and cobweb cares of the devil's spinning in all-day storms on mountains; sauntering in rosiny pinewoods or in gentian meadows, brushing through chaparral, bending down and parting sweet, flowery sprays; tracing rivers to their sources, getting in touch with the nerves of Mother Earth; jumping from rock to rock, feeling the life of them, learning the songs of them, panting in whole-souled exercise and rejoicing in deep, long-drawn breaths of pure wildness. This is fine and natural and full of promise. And so also is the growing interest in the care and preservation of forests and wild places in general, and in the half-wild parks and gardens of towns. Even the scenery habit in its most artificial forms, mixed with spectacles, silliness, and kodaks; its devotees arrayed more gorgeously than scarlet tanagers, frightening the wild game with red umbrellas,—even this is encouraging, and may well be regarded as a hopeful sign of the times. . . .

When, like a merchant taking a list of his goods, we take stock of our wildness, we are glad to see how much of even the most destructible kind is still unspoiled. Looking at our continent as scenery when it was all wild, lying between beautiful seas, the starry sky above it, the starry rocks beneath it, to compare its sides, the East and the West, would be like comparing the sides of a rainbow. But it is no longer equally beautiful. The rainbows of today are, I suppose, as bright as those that first spanned the sky; and some of our landscapes are growing more beautiful from year to year, notwithstanding the clearing, trampling work of civilization. New plants and animals are enriching woods and gardens, and many landscapes wholly new, with divine sculpture and architecture, are just now coming to the light of day as the mantling folds of creative glaciers are being withdrawn, and life in a thousand cheerful, beautiful forms is pushing into them, and new-born rivers are beginning to sing and shine in them. . . .

Man, too, is making many far-reaching changes. This most influential half animal, half angel is rapidly multiplying and spreading, covering the seas and lakes with ships, the land with huts, hotels, cathedrals, and clustered city shops and homes, so that soon, it would seem, we may have to go farther than Nansen to find a good sound solitude. None of Nature's landscapes are ugly so long as they are wild; and much, we can say comfortingly, must always be in great part wild, particularly the sea and the sky, the floods of light from the stars, and the warm, unspoilable heart of the earth, infinitely beautiful, though only dimly visible to the eye of imagination. The geysers, too, spouting from the hot underworld; the steady, long-lasting glaciers on the mountains, obedient only to the sun; Yosemite domes and the tremendous grandeur of rocky cañons and mountains in general,—these must always be wild, for man can change them and mar them hardly more than can the butterflies that hover above them.

5. The Early Photographic Record of the Western Wilderness, 1866–1888

A. Great Falls of the Yellowstone, 1871

B. Cathedral Rock, Yosemite, ca. 1866

C. The Grand Teton (Wyoming), 1872

6. The Eye of the Camera on the Altered Environment, 1866–1871

A. Gould and Curry Mill (Virginia City, Nevada), 1871

B. The Railroad Moves Westward: Newly Laid Ties, 1866

C. Urban Life on the Mining Frontier (Helena, Montana), ca. 1875

A. The Road to Agricultural Paradise, ca. 1880s

C. The Promise of the High Plains, ca. 1880s

B. The California Dream, ca. 1870s

Collection of The New York Historical Society.

Chapter 17:
Document Set 3 References

1. John Wesley Powell Describes the Grand Canyon, 1869
   John Wesley Powell, *Down the Colorado: Diary of the First Trip Through the Grand Canyon*, 1869, in Paul Schullery, ed., *The Early Grand Canyon: Early Impressions* (Niwot: Colorado Associated University Press, 1981), pp. 7–10, 16–17, 29–30.

2. Walt Whitman's View of the High Plains, 1879
   Walt Whitman, "Specimen Days and Collect," 1879, in Walt Whitman, *Complete Prose Works* (Boston, 1898), pp. 141–144.

3. Overcoming Natural Obstacles to Building the Union Pacific, 1869
   Grenville Dodge, Final Report to United States Government, February 1, 1869, in *How We Built the Union Pacific Railway and Other Railway Papers and Addresses* (Washington, D.C.: Government Printing Office, 1910), pp. 38–40.

4. John Muir on the Dominion of Nature, 1898
   John Muir, "The Wild Parks and Forest Reservations of the West," *Atlantic Monthly*, Vol. LXXXI, No. 483 (January 1898).

5. The Early Photographic Record of the Western Wilderness, 1866–1888
   A. Great Falls of the Yellowstone, 1871
      Photo by William Henry Jackson. In Clarence S. Jackson, *Picture Maker of the Old West: William H. Jackson* (New York: Charles Scribner's Sons, 1947), p. 153.
   B. Cathedral Rock, Yosemite, ca. 1866
      Photo by C. E. Watkins. Metropolitan Museum of Art, The Elisha Whittelsey Collection, The Elisha Whittelsey Fund, 1922 (1972.643.6). In Weston J. Naef *et al.*, *Era of Exploration: The Rise of Landscape Photography in the American West, 1860–1885* (New York: Albright-Knox Art Gallery and the Metropolitan Museum of Art, 1975).
   C. The Grand Teton (Wyoming), 1872
      Photo by William Henry Jackson. Explorers Club, New York City. In Jackson, p. 165.

6. The Eye of the Camera on the Altered Environment, 1866–1871
   A. Gould and Curry Mill (Virginia City, Nevada), 1871
      Photo by T. O'Sullivan. Library of Congress. In *Annals of America* (Chicago: Encyclopaedia Britannica, 1968), vol. 10, photo inset.
   B. The Railroad Moves Westward: Newly Laid Ties, 1866
      Photo by John Carbutt. Library of Congress. In Naef *et al.*, p. 43
   C. Urban Life on the Mining Frontier (Helena, Montana), ca. 1875
      Montana Historical Society.

7. Images of Nature's Bounty in Propaganda Aimed at New Settlers, 1870–1890
   A. The Road to Agricultural Paradise, ca. 1880s
      Editors of Time-Life Books, *The Railroaders* (New York: Time-Life Books, 1973), pp. 206–207. Photo courtesy Manuscript Division, Baker Library, Harvard University Graduate School of Business Administration.
   B. The California Dream, ca. 1870s
      The Railroaders, pp. 206–207. Courtesy of New York Historical Society.
   C. The Promise of the High Plains, ca. 1880s
      The Railroaders, pp. 206–207. Courtesy of Chicago Historical Society.

Chapter 17:
Document Set 3 Credits

5. A. Photograph by William Henry Jackson, from the collection of Mr. Horace M. Albright
   B. The Metropolitan Museum of Art. The Elisha Whittlesey Collection, The Elisha Whittelsey Fund, 1972. (1972.643.6)
   C. Photograph by William Henry Jackson/The Explorers Club, New York
6. A. Library of Congress
   B. Library of Congress
   C. Montana Historical Society
7. A. Photo Courtesy Manuscript Division, Baker Library, Harvard University Graduate School of Business Administration
   B. Collection of the New York Historical Society
   C. Chicago Historical Society

CHAPTER 18

DOCUMENT SET 1
The Impact of Industrial Change: The Work Process and the Work Force

The dominant feature of the American economy after the Civil War was the acceleration of industrialization, supported by sophisticated technology and more efficient business organization. Your textbook not only describes industrial change but also assesses its influence on a changing work force. The following documents stress the impact of industrialism on both the work process and the workers whose lives were affected by the new conditions of labor.

The first group of documents contains the reactions of a machinist and a shoe worker to the revolutionary changes in the work process caused by machine production. Although they worked at different trades, John Morrison and Horace M. Eaton shared an apprehensive response to the new manufacturing system. Try to relate their concerns to the textbook coverage of the transition from workshop to factory and of the changing nature of work. As you evaluate the testimony, be aware of the forum they chose in which to express their views.

The unsettling changes in work rhythms, skill levels, and worker self-image identified by Morrison and Eaton suggest a growing uneasiness over the altered work environment encountered in the factory system. One aspect of this atmosphere, as described in the congressional testimony of Robert D. Layton of the Knights of Labor, was that workers felt regimented. Try

to determine which aspects of the new industrial order Layton found most alarming. His testimony should also be linked with the problems of workers who were forced to accept scrip in payment for services (see illustration in the fourth document).

Since worker testimony may not be entirely objective, the observations of disinterested parties are especially useful in clarifying the impact of industrialism. Valuable insight is provided by French economist E. Levasseur's comparison of the work pace and pressures in the American and European industrial environments. Be particularly alert to his assessment of worker reaction to the new conditions.

The final two documents address the physical and moral impact of machinery and the factory system on employees. Compare the observations of Massachusetts physician Dr. John B. Whitaker and Carroll D. Wright, soon to become the first United States Labor Commissioner. As you review these analyses, account for their differences in perspective.

To assess the human impact of industrialization and modernization, observe how these system-wide changes translated into personal experience. By observing alterations in the worker's world and daily life, you should be able to understand the rising movement to reassert the dignity and status of labor.

Questions for Analysis

1. How did the work process itself change as a result of rapid industrialization? What do the documents reveal about the impact of those alterations on workers?

2. What was the meaning of the terms *craft* and *domestic system*? How were they affected by the acceleration of industrial change? What was the relationship between work responsibilities and worker self-image?

3. How did the relationship between capitalist/managers and labor/workers change as a result of industrialization? What was the position of labor in the economic structure by the end of the nineteenth century?

4. Dr. John B. Whitaker, Carroll D. Wright, and E. Levasseur were all observers of industrialism's impact on laborers. None of them was himself an industrial worker. In what ways did their assessments differ? How would you explain the conflicting interpretations? Which account is most credible? Why?

1. A Machinist Describes Specialization, 1883

Q. Is there any difference between the conditions under which machinery is made now and those which existed ten years ago?

A. A great deal of difference.

Q. State the differences as well as you can.

A. Well, the trade has been subdivided and those subdivisions have been again subdivided, so that a man never learns the machinist's trade now. Ten years ago he learned, not the whole of the trade, but a fair portion of it. Also, there is more machinery used in the business, which again makes machinery. In the case of making the sewing machine, for instance, you find that the trade is so subdivided that a man is not considered a machinist at all. Hence, it is merely laborers' work and it is laborers that work at that branch of our trade. The different branches of the trade are divided and subdivided so that one man may make just a particular part of a machine and may not know anything whatever about another part of the same machine. In that way machinery is produced a great deal cheaper than it used to be formerly, and in fact, through this system of work, 100 men are able to do now what it took 300 or 400 men to do fifteen years ago. By the use of machinery and the subdivision of the trade they so simplify the work that it is made a great deal easier and put together a great deal faster. There is no system of apprenticeship, I may say, in the business. You simply go in and learn whatever branch you are put at, and you stay at that unless you are changed to another. . . .

Q. Have you noticed the effect upon the intellect of this plan of keeping a man at one particular branch?

A. Yes. It has a very demoralizing effect upon the mind throughout. The man thinks of nothing else but that particular branch; he knows that he cannot leave that particular branch and go to any other; he has got no chance whatever to learn anything else because he is kept steadily and constantly at that particular thing, and of course his intellect must be narrowed by it.

Q. And does he not finally acquire so much skill in the manipulation of his particular part of the business that he does it without any mental effort?

A. Almost. In fact he becomes almost a part of the machinery. . . .

Q. What is the prospect for a man now working in one of these machine shops, a man who is temperate and economical and thrifty to become a boss or a manufacturer of machinery himself from his own savings? Could a man do it without getting aid from some relative who might die and leave him a fortune, or without drawing a lottery prize, or something of that sort?

A. Well, speaking generally, there is no chance. They have lost all desire to become bosses now.

Q. Why have they lost that desire?

A. Why, because the trade has become demoralized. First they earn so small wages; and, next, it takes so much capital to become a boss now that they cannot think of it, because it takes all they can earn to live. . . .

Q. I am requested to ask you this question: Dividing the public, as is commonly done, into the upper, middle, and lower classes, to which class would you assign the average workingman of your trade at the time when you entered it, and to which class would you assign him now?

A. I now assign them to the lower class. At the time I entered the trade I should assign them as merely hanging on to the middle class, ready to drop out at any time.

2. A Shoe Worker Comments on the Decline of Craft Consciousness, 1899

Q. What is the present condition of your trade now in reference to work and wages?

A. As to work, very good; as to wages, poor.

Q. How much less than they have been?

A. Well, that would be a difficult question to answer, more or less based upon opinion. I might go back in my own experience as a workman at the bench. Eleven years ago I used to be able to earn myself, lasting shoes, from $18 to $35 in a week, according to how hard I wanted to work; that is, in the city of Lynn. Today, on the same class of work, I would not be able, on any job in the city, to make over $15, and probably my wage would run nearer $12. That is based upon the experience of others that I know in the same kind of work. And another thing; where a man at that time would likely get eight or nine months' good work in a year, at the present time the season is shorter. Machinery is more largely used and of a more improved type. The manufacturers equip themselves to turn out their product in a shorter time, and the seasons of employment are shorter and more uncertain. . . . I would like to state one instance of the development of machinery. In respect to the operation of nailing the heel on to the boot or shoe, fastening the heel in with nails, about fifteen years ago I remember working at a factory where that operation was done by hand in the original way. A man stood up with a hammer and nailed those heels on, and 100 to 125 pairs of that grade of work was considered a good day's work. Five years later it is done by what they call the National nailing machine, where a man and a boy did five times as much. That man and the boy did the work that it would require five men to do. . . .

Q. Taking the material as it is prepared for the shoemaker, how many hands does a gentleman's finished shoe pass through in the process of manufacture?

A. To answer that question in another way, there are about one hundred subdivisions of labor in the manufacture of a shoe, varying more or less according to the factory and methods and the kind of shoe made. There are different combinations of these subdivisions.

Q. Now, let me ask, in connection with that, what effect has that specializing, if it might be so termed, upon the workman? Has it a beneficial effect or otherwise?

A. Oh, it has been detrimental to the workman.

Q. The workman only knows how to perform the labor of one department?

A. That is all, and he becomes a mere machine. You know we have the piece-work system almost entirely, and if we work for a week price, there is a stint that comes with it that makes it virtually a piece-work system, and it has come to be a race with a man. Now, take the proposition of a man operating a machine to nail on forty to sixty pairs cases of heels in a day. That is 2,400 pairs, 4,800 shoes, in a day. One not accustomed to it would wonder how a man could pick up and lay down 4,800 shoes in a day, to say nothing of putting them on a jack into a machine and having them nailed on. That is the driving method of the manufacture of shoes under these minute subdivisions.

Q. Under that system of special work, has the general worker of today the same opportunity to go out into the world and make a living as you think he had before this method was introduced?

A. No.

Q. Are there many workmen in the factory who can make a whole shoe?

A. No, the art of shoemaking, so far as the individual is concerned, has got to be a thing of the past. About all the actual shoemakers you can find today are located in small cobbling and custom shops—old-time workmen; and almost invariably you will find that they are old men.

3. A Union Leader Sees Worker Regimentation, 1883

Q. Can you give us some instances of the obnoxious rules of which you speak?

A. Yes; one instance was on the part of a large firm of carriage manufacturers at Rochester, N.Y.—James Cunningham, Sons & Co. Just a year ago this month their men rebelled against certain rules that they had established in their works—rules degrading to human nature. For instance, the faucets in the water sinks were locked up, and when an employee wanted a drink of water he had to go to the foreman of his department and ask for a drink; the foreman went and unlocked the faucet and gave him a cupful of water, and whether that was enough to satisfy his thirst or not, it was all he got. When the men entered in the morning they were numbered by checks. A man lost his identity as a man and took a number like a prisoner in a penitentiary. . . . Another obnoxious rule was that if a man was half or even a quarter of a minute late he was shut out. They had a gate and it would be shut down upon a man even when he was going in, sometimes so quickly that he would hardly have time to draw his foot back to keep it from being crushed by the gate, and that man would be kept out until nine o'clock, so that he would make only three-quarters of a day's work. The rule was that the men had to be *in* the works before the whistle blew.

4. Payment in Scrip, 1885

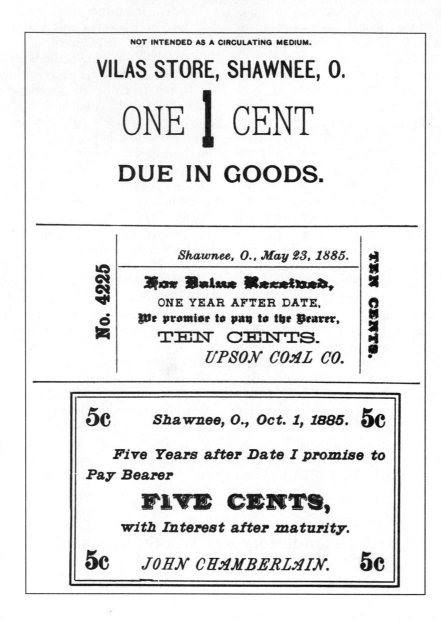

NOT INTENDED AS A CIRCULATING MEDIUM.

VILAS STORE, SHAWNEE, O.

ONE | CENT

DUE IN GOODS.

No. 4225

Shawnee, O., May 23, 1885.

For Value Received,

ONE YEAR AFTER DATE,

We promise to pay to the Bearer,

TEN CENTS.

UPSON COAL CO.

TEN CENTS.

5c *Shawnee, O., Oct. 1, 1885.* 5c

Five Years after Date I promise to Pay Bearer

FIVE CENTS,

with Interest after maturity.

5c *JOHN CHAMBERLAIN.* 5c

5. A French Economist Notes the Machine's Impact on American Workers, 1897

"The pay here is good, but the labor is hard," said an Alsatian blacksmith employed in a large [American] factory. I could verify nearly everywhere the truth of this remark, for I have seen such activity both in the small industry, where the tailors in the sweating-shops in New York worked with feverish rapidity, and in the great industry, where the butchers of the Armour packing house prepared 5800 hogs a day, where the cotton weavers tended as many as eight looms, or where the rolling-mill in Chicago turned out 1000 tons of rails in a day. Everywhere the machine goes very rapidly, and it commands; the workman has to follow. An English manufacturer, having read in one of Mr. [Jacob] Schoenhof's books that a silk spinner of New Jersey had renewed his machinery in order to obtain 7500 turns a minute, instead of 5000, told him that should he establish such machinery in his workshop all his workers would leave him. And, yet, in America, at the present time, the rapidity is from 10,000 to 13,000 turns. . . .

Several French laborers, delegates to the Exposition at Chicago, have brought back from their trip the notion that the laborer has to work hard and that he cannot loaf or chatter. "In the machine-shops," said one of them, "there is no movement, no going from place to place on the part of workmen, each one remains at his post without the discipline being more severe than in France." . . .

The laboring classes . . . reproach the machine with exhausting the physical powers of the laborer; but this can only apply to a very small number of cases to those where the workman is at the same time the motive power, as in certain sewing-machines. They reproach it with demanding such continued attention that it enervates, and of leaving no respite to the laborer, through the continuity of its movement. This second complaint may be applicable in a much larger number of cases, particularly in the spinning industries and in weaving, where the workman manages more than four looms. They reproach the machine with degrading man by transforming him into a machine, which knows how to make but one movement, and that always the same. They reproach it with diminishing the number of skilled laborers, permitting in many cases the substitution of unskilled workers and lowering the average level of wages. They reproach it with depriving, momentarily at least, every time that an invention modifies the work of the factory, a certain number of workmen of their means of subsistence, thus rendering the condition of all uncertain. They reproach it, finally, with reducing absolutely and permanently the number of persons employed for wages, and thus being indirectly injurious to all wage-earners who make among themselves a more disastrous competition, the more the opportunities for labor are restricted.

6. Dr. John B. Whitaker Explains the Impact of the Factory on Worker Health, 1871

1. Accidents and casualties are very numerous, partly owing to the exposed machinery and partly owing to carelessness. . . . It is really painful to go round among the operatives and find the hands and fingers mutilated, in consequence of accidents. 2. Unnatural or monotonous working positions . . . in some cases [make the worker] round-shouldered, in other cases producing curvature of the spine and bow-legs. 3. Exhaustion from overwork. In consequence of the long hours of labor, the great speed the machinery is run at, the large number of looms the weavers tend, and the general over-tasking, so much exhaustion is produced, in most cases, that immediately after taking supper, the tired operatives drop to sleep in their chairs. . . . 4. Work by artificial light. It is very injurious to the eyes. The affections consist principally in conjunctiviti, opacity of cornea, granulations of the lids, &c. 5. The inhalation of foreign articles. . . . I have been called to cases where I suspected this to be the cause of trouble in the stomach. After giving an emetic, they have in some cases vomited little balls of cotton. . . . 10. Predisposition to pelvic diseases . . . among the female factory operatives produces difficulty in parturition. The necessity for instrumental

delivery has very much increased within a few years, owing to the females working in the mills while they are pregnant and in consequence of deformed pelvis.... 11. ... Predisposition to sexual abuse. There is no doubt that this is very much increased, the passions being excited by contact and loose conversation....

They are, also, as a general thing, ignorant—at least to the extent that they do not know how to control their passions nor to realize the consequences.... 12. Predisposition to depression of spirits.... Factory life predisposes very much to depression of spirits.

7. Carroll D. Wright Assesses the Factory System's Influence, 1882

The usual mistake is to consider the factory system as the creator of evils, and not only evils, but of evil disposed persons. This can hardly be shown to be true, although it is [true] that the system may congregate evils or evil disposed persons, and thus give the appearance of creating that which already existed....

The spasmodic nature of work under the domestic system caused much disturbance, for handworking is always more or less discontinuous from the caprice of the operative, while much time must be lost in gathering and returning materials. For these and obvious reasons a hand weaver could very seldom turn off in a week much more than one-half what his loom could produce if kept continuously in action during the working hours of the day at the rate which the weaver in his working paroxysms impelled it.

The regular order maintained in the factory cures this evil of the old system and enables the operative to know with reasonable certainty the wages he is to receive at the next payday. His life and habits become more orderly, and he finds, too, that as he has left the closeness of his home shop for the usually clean and well-lighted factory, he imbibes more freely of the health giving tonic of the atmosphere....

The regularity required in mills is such as to render persons who are in the habit of getting intoxicated unfit to be employed there, and many manufacturers object to employing persons guilty of the vice; yet, notwithstanding all the efforts which have been made to stop the habit, the beer-drinking operatives of factory towns still constitute a most serious drawback to the success of industrial enterprises, but its effects are not so ruinous under the new as under the old system....

What is the truth as to wages? The vast influence of wages upon social life need not be considered here, but the question whether the factory system has increased them may be. I am constantly obliged, in my everyday labors, to refute the assertion that wages under the factory system are growing lower and lower. The reverse is the truth, which is easily demonstrated; the progress of improvement in machinery may have reduced the price paid for a single article, yard, or pound of product, or for the services of a skilled and intelligent operative, but the same improvement has enabled the workman to produce in a greater proportion and always with a less expenditure of muscular labor and in less time, and it has enabled a low grade of labor to increase its earnings. At the same time, a greater number have been benefited, either in consumption or production, by the improvement.

Experience has not only evolved but proven a law in this respect, which is, the more the factory system is perfected, the better will it reward those engaged in it, if not in increased wages to skill, certainly in higher wages to less skill.

Better morals, better sanitary conditions, better health, better wages, these are the practical results of the factory system, as compared with that which preceded it, and the results of all these have been a keener intelligence....

Industry and poverty are not handmaidens, and, as poverty is lessened, good morals thrive. If labor, employment of the mind, is an essential to good morals, then the highest kind of employment, that requiring the most application and the best intellectual effort, means the best morals. This condition, I take courage to assert, is superinduced eventually by the factory system, for by it the operative is usually employed in a higher grade of labor than that which occupied him in his previous condition. For this reason the present system of productive industry is constantly narrowing the limits of the class that occupies the bottom step of social order.

Chapter 18:
Document Set 1 References

1. A Machinist Describes Specialization, 1883
   Testimony, John Morrison, August 28, 1883, U.S. Congress, Senate, *Report of the Committee of the Senate upon the Relations between Labor and Capital* (Washington, D.C.: Government Printing Office, 1885), Vol. I, pp. 755–759.

2. A Shoe Worker Comments on the Decline of Craft Consciousness, 1899
   Testimony, Horace M. Eaton, September 21, 1899, U.S. Congress, House, *Report of the Industrial Commission on the Relations and Conditions of Capital and Labor Employed in Manufactures and General Business*, 56th Cong., 2nd Sess., House Doc. 495 (Washington, D.C.: Government Printing Office, 1901), Vol. 7, pp. 359, 361, 363.

3. A Union Leader Sees Worker Regimentation, 1883
   Testimony, Robert D. Layton, Grand Secretary, Knights of Labor, February 6, 1883, U.S. Congress, Senate, *Report of the Committee of the Senate upon the Relations Between Labor and Capital*, Vol. I, pp. 8–10.

4. Payment in Scrip, 1885
   Scrip, Shawnee, Ohio, 1885, in John A Garraty, ed., *The Transformation of American Society, 1870–1890* (New York: Harper and Row, 1968), p. 140.

5. A French Economist Notes the Machine's Impact on American Workers, 1897
   E. Levasseur, "The Concentration of Industry, and Machinery in the United Sates," *Annals of the American Academy of Political and Social Science*, Vol. 9, No. 2 (March 1897), pp. 12–14, 18–19, 21–24.

6. Dr. John B. Whitaker Explains the Impact of the Factory on Worker Health, 1871
   Dr. John B. Whitaker to the Gentlemen of the Massachusetts Bureau of Labor Statistics, Massachusetts Bureau of Labor Statistics, *Annual Report, 1870–1871*, pp. 504–506.

7. Carroll D. Wright Assesses the Factory System's Influence, 1882
   Carroll D. Wright, "The Factory System as an Element in Civilization," *Journal of Social Science*, Vol. 16 (December 1882).

Chapter 18:
Document Set 1 Credits

4. A. From John A. Garraty, editor, *The Transformation of American Society, 1870–1890*, New York: Harper and Row, 1968, page. 140.

CHAPTER 18

DOCUMENT SET 2
The Worker Response to Industrialism: Unionism and Labor Violence

Changes in work rhythms and work process did not take place without a challenge. One significant reaction was the outbreak of violence, often directed at workers and their supporters, in moments of sharp industrial conflict. The following documents explore some worker responses to the emergence of the modern industrial system. As you examine these materials, identify the strengths and weaknesses of nineteenth-century labor organizations, and account for the persistence of social tension and violence.

Your textbook cites the railroad strike of 1877 as an event that alarmed thoughtful social critics throughout the United States. By the time the violence receded, Americans had witnessed the country's first nationwide labor action, together with substantial bloodshed. As you review the reaction of journalist A. C. Buell, try to determine what aspect of the railroad strike most alarmed middle-class observers.

Another response to the pressures of the industrial system was the gradual growth of unionism following the Civil War. Particularly significant was the development of the Knights of Labor after 1869. Analyze the preamble to the Knights' Constitution, noting the organizing principles that separated the group from most other labor organizations of its time (the excerpt from grand master Terence V. Powderly's memoir will also be helpful).

The next group of documents focuses on the burgeoning eight-hour movement, which climaxed in Chicago with the Haymarket tragedy of 1886. The song lyrics shed light on worker endorsement of the shorter workday.

More significant in the long run was the outcome of the May demonstrations in Chicago and elsewhere. Police violence at Haymarket Square stunned observers, who drew back from the growing labor movement, its image now tarnished by charges of radicalism. Use your textbook material on strikes and violence as a resource in assessing the statement of convicted anarchist August Spies. As you evaluate Spies's remarks, be conscious of his background and the values of the Chicago officials whom he addressed. Compare his position to Samuel Gompers's plea for clemency. Use the Gompers argument as a guide in evaluating the convicted man's views, as well as an indicator of the political character of the American Federation of Labor. Consider the impact of these dramatic events on the development of American unionism.

Another issue addressed in the documents involves the role of women in the labor force and the union movement's view of their place in the organizational effort. The report of Knights' women's organizer Leonora M. Barry and the editorial from *American Federationist* provide evidence of organized labor's attitude toward female workers. As you compare the documents, develop an explanation for the positions of the two organizations.

When the furor over the "great upheaval" began to subside, it became clear that American workers had suffered a significant setback in the battle for public opinion. The confrontation of the 1880s revealed the widening gap between labor and capital that was the by-product of industrial expansion.

Questions for Analysis

1. What was the social significance of the railroad strike of 1877? What do the documents reveal about the public perception of the strikers' goals? What are the strike's wider implications?

2. As you review the assertions of workers and observers, what is your evaluation of labor's rationale for union organization? What evidence supports your position?

3. Given your reading of both the textbook and the documents, what distinctions can you make between the Knights of Labor and the American Federation of Labor? Do you observe similarities?

4. The Haymarket incident is one of the best-known and most widely analyzed labor disturbances in American history. Relying on the documents, evaluate the demonstrators' objectives and the role of the Chicago police in the events of May 3 and 4. What did this clash reveal about the character and history of the American labor movement?

5. How did the Knights of Labor and American Federation of Labor regard women? How do the documents contribute to an understanding of AFL attitudes? What were the underlying reasons for the union reaction to women?

6. Do the documents reveal any commitment to the concept of worker cooperatives? How did this idea influence the development of the American labor movement?

1. A. C. Buell Accounts for the Violence of the Railroad Strike, 1877

The most striking fact developed by this movement is the terrible antipathy which has grown up among the poor and laboring classes against those who possess great wealth.... John Jones and William Smith, laborers, regard William H. Vanderbilt, Jay Gould, and Tom Scott, capitalists, as their natural enemies, whose welfare means their loss and whose downfall would redound to their gain.... Today, Tom Scott could not get through Pittsburgh, or Vanderbilt through Buffalo, alive!... You may call it whatsoever name you please—Communism, Agrarianism, Socialism, or anything else— ... in the estimation of the vast majority of the American people the million-aire has come to be looked upon as a public enemy! ... We have just now had a foretaste of real Civil War; of that conflict of classes, which is the most terrible of all species of war.... The inadequacy of the present governmental system to combat servile insurrections has been forced home upon the capitalistic classes as a fact that can no longer be evaded.... The average citizen may forget the danger as soon as it is past, but not the man of millions. He has seen the ghost of the Commune, and it will stalk his dreams every night until he can feel with his prototype of the old world the security of mercenary bayonets enough to garrison every considerable town.

2. Terence V. Powderly Defines the Knights of Labor, 1878, 1889

The recent alarming development and aggression of aggregated wealth, which, unless checked, will invariably lead to the pauperization and hopeless degradation of the toiling masses, render it imperative, if we desire to enjoy the blessings of life, that a check should be placed upon its power and upon unjust accumulation, and a system adopted which will secure to the laborer the fruits of his toil; and as this much-desired object can only be accomplished by the thorough unification of labor, and the united efforts of those who obey the divine injunction that "in the sweat of thy brow shalt thou eat bread," we have formed the * * * * * with a view of securing the organization and direction, by co-operative effort, of the power of the industrial classes....

The belief was prevalent until a short time ago among workingmen, that only the man who was engaged in manual toil could be called a workingman. The man who labored at the bench or anvil; the man who held the throttle of the engine, or delved in the everlasting gloom of the coal mine, did not believe that the man who made the drawings from which he forged, turned, or dug could be classed as a worker. The draughtsman, the time-keeper, the clerk, the school teacher, the civil engineer, the editor, the reporter, or the worst paid, most abused and illy appreciated of all toilers—woman—could not be called a worker. It was essential that the mechanics of America should know who were workers. A more widespread knowledge of the true definition of the word labor must be arrived at, and the true relations existing between all men who labor must be more clearly defined. Narrow prejudice, born of the injustice and oppressions of the past, must be overcome, and all who interest themselves in producing for the world's good must be made to understand that their interests are identical.

3. "Eight Hour Day," ca. 1880s

We mean to make things over, we are tired of toil for
naught,
With but bare enough to live upon, and ne'er an hour
for thought;
We want to feel the sunshine, and we want to smell
the flowers,
We are sure that God has willed it, and we mean to
have eight hours.
We're summoning our forces from the shipyard,
shop, and mill.

Chorus:

Eight hours for work, eight hours for rest, eight
hours for what we will.

Eight hours for work, eight hours for rest, eight
hours for what we will.

The beasts that graze the hillside, and the birds that
wander free,
In the life that God has meted, have a better lot than we.
Oh hands and hearts are weary, and homes are heavy
with dole.
If our life's to be filled with drudgery, what need of a
human soul?
Shout, shout the lusty rally, from shipyard, shop,
and mill.

Ye deem they're feeble voices that are raised in
labor's cause?
But bethink ye of the torrent, and the wild tornado's
laws.
We say not toil's uprising in terror's shape will come,
Yet the world were wise to listen to the monetary hum.
Soon, soon the deep-toned rally shall all the nations
thrill.

From factories and workshops in long and weary lines,
From all the sweltering forges, and from out the sun-
less mines,
Wherever toil is wasting the force of life to live,
There the bent and battered armies come to claim
what God doth give,
And the blazon on the banner doth with hope the na-
tion fill.

Hurrah, hurrah for labor, for it shall arise in might;
It has filled the world with plenty, it shall fill the
world with light.
Hurrah, hurrah for labor, it is mustering all its powers
And shall march along to victory with the banner of
Eight Hours.
Shout, shout the echoing rally till all the welkin thrill.

4. August Spies Comments on the Haymarket Incident, 1886

No, I repeat, the prosecution has not established our legal guilt, notwithstanding the purchased and perjured testimony of some, and notwithstanding the originality of the proceedings of this trial. And as long as this has not been done, and you pronounce upon us the sentence of an appointed vigilance committee acting as a jury, I say, you, the alleged representatives and high priests of "law and order," are the real and only lawbreakers, and in this case to the extent of murder. It is well that the people know this. And when I speak of the people I don't mean the few coconspirators of Grinnell—the noble politicians who thrive upon the misery of the multitudes. These drones may constitute the state, they may control the state, they may have their Grinnells, their Bonfields, and other hirelings! No, when I speak of the people I speak of the great mass of human bees, the working people, who unfortunately are not yet conscious of the rascalities that are perpetrated in the "name of the people"—in their name.

The contemplated murder of eight men, whose only crime is that they have dared to speak the truth, may open the eyes of these suffering millions; may wake them up. Indeed, I have noticed that our conviction has worked miracles in this direction already. The class that clamors for our lives, the good, devout

Christians, have attempted in every way, through their newspapers and otherwise, to conceal the true and only issue in this case. By simply designating the defendants as anarchists and picturing them as a newly discovered tribe or species of cannibals, and by inventing shocking and horrifying stories of dark conspiracies said to be planned by them, these good Christians zealously sought to keep the naked fact from the working people and other righteous parties, namely: that on the evening of May 4, 200 armed men, under the command of a notorious ruffian, attacked a meeting of peaceable citizens! With what intention? With the intention of murdering them, or as many of them as they could. . . .

Look upon the economic battlefields! Behold the carnage and plunder of the Christian patricians! . . . And then tell me whether this order has in it any moral principle for which it should be preserved. I say that the preservation of such an order is criminal—is murderous.

It means the preservation of the systematic destruction of children and women in factories. It means the preservation of enforced idleness of large armies of men, and their degradation. It means the preservation of intemperance, and sexual as well as intellectual prostitution. It means the preservation of misery, want, and servility on the one hand, and the dangerous accumulation of spoils, idleness, voluptuousness, and tyranny on the other. It means the preservation of vice in every form. And last, but not least, it means the preservation of the class struggle, of strikes, riots, and bloodshed. That is your "order," gentlemen. Yes, and it is worthy of you to be the champions of such an order. You are eminently fitted for that role. You have my compliments!

5. Samuel Gompers Urges Clemency for the Haymarket Anarchists, 1887

To the Governor of Illinois:

I have differed all my life with the principles and methods of the condemned, but know no reason why I should not ask the Governor to interpose and save condemned men from the gallows. The execution would not be one of justice; not to the interest of the great state of Illinois; not to the interests of the country; nor the workingmen. I come as a representative of the New York Central Labor Union and as president of the American Federation of Labor, organizations opposed to anarchy.

If these men are executed it would simply be an impetus to this so-called revolutionary movement which no other thing on earth can give. These men would, apart from any consideration of mercy or humanity, be looked upon as martyrs. Thousands and thousands of labor men all over the world would consider that these men had been executed because they were standing up for free speech and free press. . . .

The working people have long begged for justice and very frequently not in vain. They arise now and ask in the name of mercy, in the name of humanity, in the name of progress, not to allow this execution to take place, but, sir, to stand between these men and death, and as I in a letter and dispatch sent to you have said, you will not only be blessed by the country but the unborn thousands that come after us.

I want to say to you, sir, I am not desirous of going into the details of the question. I don't believe I am competent to do so; but I believe that in some measure, however remote, the police of Chicago have been somewhat responsible for this trouble.

6. Leonora M. Barry Describes Obstacles to the Organization of Women, 1887

I reached Pittsburgh, June 11, by invitation of L.A. 7228. Here would be a good place for some to come who are constantly talking of *women's sphere*. Women are employed in the manufacturing of barbed wire, under-ground cable, cork works, pickle factories, bakeries, sewing of all kinds and all the other branches of business at which women are employed, elsewhere. I visited a large establishment, a part of which is to be fitted for the manufacturing of nails, at which women are to be employed. There are also many laundries here in which women are compelled to work, . . . ten hours per day. . . . Also, in a tailoring establishment here I found that whatever wages are made by the employee, she must pay her employer 50 cents per week for the steam-power which runs the machines. There is but little organization here among the women, consequently their condition is similar to that of all others who are unprotected—small pay for hard labor and long hours. While the cause of their lack of interest in organized labor is largely due to their own ignorance of the importance of this step, yet much blame can be attached to the neglect and indifference of their brother toilers within the jurisdiction of D.A. 3, who seem to lose sight of one important fact, that organization can never do the work it was intended to do until every competitor in the labor market can be taught its principles.

7. An AFL Perspective on Women in the Work Force, 1897

The invasion of the crafts by women has been developing for years amid irritation and injury to the workman. The right of the woman to win honest bread is accorded on all sides, but with craftsmen it is an open question whether this manifestation is of a healthy social growth or not.

The rapid displacement of men by women in the factory and workshop has to be met sooner or later, and the question is forcing itself upon the leaders and thinkers among the labor organizations of the land.

Is it a pleasing indication of progress to see the father, the brother and the son displaced as the bread winner by the mother, sister and daughter? . . .

The growing demand for female labor is not founded upon philanthropy, as those who encourage it would have sentimentalists believe; it does not spring from the milk of human kindness. It is an insidious assault upon the home; it is the knife of the assassin, aimed at the family circle—the divine injunction. It debars the man through financial embarrassment from family responsibility, and physically, mentally and socially excludes the woman equally from nature's dearest impulse. Is this the demand of civilized progress; is it the desire of Christian dogma? . . .

To combat these impertinent inclinations, dangerous to the few, the old and well-tried policy of divide and conquer is invoked, and to our own shame, it must be said, one too often renders blind aid to capital in its warfare upon us. The employer in the magnanimity of his generosity will give employment to the daughter, while her two brothers are weary because of their daily tramp in quest for work. The father, who has a fair, steady job, sees not the infamous policy back of the flattering propositions. Somebody else's daughter is called in in the same manner, by and by, and very soon the shop or factory is full of women, while their fathers have the option of working for the same wages or a few cents more, or take their places in the large army of unemployed. . . .

The wholesale employment of women in the various handicrafts must gradually unsex them, as it most assuredly is demoralizing them, or stripping them of that modest demeanor that lends a charm to their kind, while it numerically strengthens the multitudinous army of loafers, paupers, tramps and policemen, for no man who desires honest employment, and can secure it, cares to throw his life away upon such a wretched occupation as the latter.

The employment of women in the mechanical departments is encouraged because of its cheapness and easy manipulation, regardless of the consequent perils; and for no other reason. The generous sentiment enveloping this inducement is of criminal design, since it comes from a thirst to build riches upon the dismemberment of the family or the hearthstone cruelly dishonored. . . .

But somebody will say, would you have women pursue lives of shame rather than work? Certainly not; it is to the alarming introduction of women into the mechanical industries, hitherto enjoyed by the sterner sex, at a wage uncommandable by them, that leads so many into that deplorable pursuit.

Chapter 18:
Document Set 2 References

1. A. C. Buell Accounts for the Violence of the Railroad Strike, 1877
   A. C. Buell, special correspondent, New York, July 30, 1877, *New Orleans Daily Democrat*, August 4, 1877.

2. Terence V. Powderly Defines the Knights of Labor, 1878, 1889
   T. V. Powderly, *Thirty Years of Labor: 1859–1889* (Columbus, Ohio, 1889), pp. 242–271.

3. "Eight Hour Day," ca. 1880s
   "Eight Hour Day" in *Annals of America* (Chicago: Encyclopaedia Britannica, Inc., 1968), Vol. 11, p. 122.

4. August Spies Comments on the Haymarket Incident, 1886
   The Chicago Martyrs (San Francisco: Free Society Press, 1899), pp. 1–16.

5. Samuel Gompers Urges Clemency for the Haymarket Anarchists, 1887
   AFL History, Encyclopedia, and Reference Book (Washington, D.C.: American Federation of Labor, 1924), p. 73.

6. Leonora M. Barry Describes Obstacles to the Organization of Women, 1887
   Pamphlet, Sophia Smith collection (Women's History Archive), Smith College, Northampton, Mass.

7. An AFL Perspective on Women in the Work Force, 1897
   Edward O'Donnell, "Women as Bread Winners—The Error of the Age," *American Federationist*, Vol. 4, No. 8, October 1897.

CHAPTER 18

DOCUMENT SET 3
The Rise of the New South: New Opportunities in a Changing Economy

The growth of industrialism is the central theme in the textbook treatment of economic change after the Civil War. An important aspect of American economic development in this period involved the rise of the New South, including the early, tentative steps taken toward diversification. Although agriculture remained the heart of the southern economy, the expansion of iron and steel production and the proliferation of cotton textile mills signaled the inauguration of a new stage in the region's economic history.

The following documents focus on the South's changing economic base and its implications for social and human relations. As you analyze the evidence, be aware of the racial composition of the southern workforce in this period of transition. Compare Booker T. Washington's vision of race relations with that of Augustus Straker. Account for any differences you may detect.

The textbook's discussion of the southern mill economy makes it apparent that the intense labor-capital conflict that plagued the North and the Midwest was less evident in the piedmont South. Use the text to frame an explanation of the contrast between northern and southern laborers and their expectations.

By the early twentieth century, Henry W. Grady's hopes for southern industrial growth had been only partially realized. When Progressive journalist Ray Stannard Baker published his perceptive analysis of the race question in the South, he suggested that the region's industrializing economy was weakened by a labor problem. What did he mean by this observation? Examine Baker's comments against the textbook background on the New South's work force.

As you review the evidence, try to connect the photographic record of work and the work place in the New South with the labor question and southern solutions to the problem. By 1910, southern entrepreneurs had begun to reshape the regional labor system to meet the demands of a changing economy. How is the new system reflected in the visual evidence? Think about the human consequences and social implications of an economic system in transition.

Questions for Analysis

1. What was "new" about the New South? What were the economic goals of the New South promoters, publicists, and investors? To what extent were their objectives realized? What were the impediments to industrial development? Account for the results of these efforts as of the early twentieth century.

2. T. Thomas Fortune, Booker T. Washington, and D. Augustus Straker were all African American observers of the New South in its formative years. How would you explain their conflicting analyses of the South's social and economic problems? How did their views compare with those of Ray Stannard Baker? Account for any differences you identify.

3. Who were the greatest beneficiaries of New South industrial development efforts? What interests were most directly benefitted by investment in the southern economy? Which groups within the South were best able to advance socially and economically? Why?

4. Examine the photographs in Document 7. What social and economic meanings can be drawn from them? Does the camera merely record the "truth" or "facts"? What precautions must be taken in analyzing such documents? What do the photographs reveal about the labor system of the New South? What social and economic problems were created by the changes taking place in the southern economy? What solutions were advanced?

1. T. Thomas Fortune Predicts a Class Struggle in the South, 1884

As I have said elsewhere, the future struggle in the South will be, not between white men and black men but between capital and labor, landlord and tenant. Already the cohorts are marshaling to the fray; already the forces are mustering to the field at the sound of the slogan.

The same battle will be fought upon Southern soil that is in preparation in other states where the conditions are older in development but no more deep-seated, no more pernicious, no more blighting upon the industries of the country and the growth of the people.

It is not my purpose here to enter into an extended analysis of the foundations upon which our land system rests, nor to give my views as to how matters might be remedied. I may take up the question at some future time. It is sufficient for my purpose to have indicated that the social problems in the South, as they exfoliate more and more as resultant upon the war, will be found to be the same as those found in every other section of our country; and to have pointed out that the questions of "race," "condition," "politics," etc., will all properly adjust themselves with the advancement of the people in wealth, education, and forgetfulness of the unhappy past.

The hour is approaching when the laboring classes of our country, North, East, West, and South, will recognize that they have a *common cause,* a *common humanity,* and a *common enemy;* and that, therefore, if they would triumph over wrong and place the laurel wreath upon triumphant justice, without distinction of race or of previous condition, *they must unite!* And unite they will, for "a fellow feeling makes us wond'rous kind." When the issue is properly joined, the rich, be they black or be they white, will be found upon the same side; and the poor, be they black or be they white, will be found on the same side.

Necessity knows no law and discriminates in favor of no man or race.

2. Henry W. Grady's Vision of a New South, 1886–1887

The South found her jewel in the toad's head of defeat. The shackles that had held her in narrow limitations fell forever when the shackles of the negro slave were broken. Under the old regime the negroes were slaves to the South; the South was a slave to the system. The old plantation, with its simple police regulations and feudal habit, was the only type possible under slavery. Thus was gathered in the hands of a splendid and chivalric oligarchy the substance that should have been diffused among the people, as the rich blood, under certain artificial conditions is gathered at the heart, filling that with affluent rapture but leaving the body chill and colorless.

The old South rested everything on slavery and agriculture, unconscious that these could neither give nor maintain healthy growth. The new South presents a perfect democracy, the oligarchs leading in the popular movement—a social system compact and closely knitted, less splendid on the surface, but stronger at the core—a hundred farms for every plantation, fifty homes for every palace—and a diversified industry that meets the complex needs of this complex age.

The new South is enamored of her new work. Her soul is stirred with the breath of a new life. The light of a grander day is falling fair on her face. She is thrilling with the consciousness of growing power and prosperity. As she stands upright, full-statured and equal among the people of the earth, breathing the keen air and looking out upon the expanded horizon, she understands that her emancipation came because through the inscrutable wisdom of God her honest purpose was crossed, and her brave armies were beaten.

3. D. Augustus Straker's Prescription for Southern Racial Harmony, 1888

It is well known that free labor has produced more cotton in the South than slave labor ever did, and yet one class of people, the consumer, is poorer today as a class—not a race—than before the war. The poor white and the Negro laborer find it impossible, as a class of laborers, to "get ahead" in the South at the present time. We must not look at the exception to prove this rule of statement. It is not because some of the laboring class have succeeded to accumulate a competency that this class is not suffering from an unjust relationship between capital and labor, as is most strikingly seen between production and the price of consumption. . . .

Why is the cost of a yard of cloth today as dear, or dearer, than it was before the war, and this while the consumer before the war and at its close had twenty-five cents for every pound of cotton wherewith to buy his yard of cloth, and has now but seven or eight cents to do so with. This is the true cause of discontent and restlessness in the South today among the laboring classes, black and white. This difference is the true cause of the exodus, and not politics only. It is true that blind prejudice, the result of social distinction made by slavery, which causes one man to think his brother inferior to him because of color, manifests itself in lynching and wanton murders in the South. The true reason for this trouble is social disparity in condition, and not color, although the perpetrators of these cruel deeds themselves think it otherwise. . . .

But after all of these reflections and observations which I have made on this topic, its causes and effects, I have not only the hope, but the certain evidence, of rapid changes even in the social condition of the South. Capital, industry, morality, develop-

ment, experience, contact, the extinguishment of old animosities, are all doing the work of producing a more harmonious condition among the two races. God speed the hour. . . .

. . . If you wish the Negro to be industrious, open the doors of your factories, your stores of merchandise, your counting house and other places of industry to him. If you wish him to be cultivated, drive him not from the contact of social manners; put him not in "Jim Crow" cars, as is done in the South; relegate him not to the rear in your theatres or churches or other places of social contact. If you would have him be honest, be honest yourselves towards him. Give him wages according to his merit, and not his color. This must all be done before the colored citizen can reach the high social, political, moral and industrial plane in life required of him by the hard taskmaster, who demands bricks without straw from the laborer. . . .

The industrial development of the South, as shown in the former pages, gives great hope for a "New South" in the future. The millstone around its neck is its own method of solving its race and political difficulties. Contact is the method of assimilation unless the forces be repellent; hence the South, in its industrial progress by the introduction of Northern men and Northern money, must lose its old identity in its "New South," and in the next quarter of a century the "Old South" will disappear. Brotherly love will be its practice; equality of rights its trade mark, politically; friendship, its practice among all men and women of all races. This is a consummation devoutly wished for by the author of these pages, and nothing less will build up a "New South."

4. The Atlanta Compromise as a Blueprint for African American Economic Progress, 1895

[I]t is well to bear in mind that whatever other sins the South may be called to bear, when it comes to business, pure and simple, it is in the South that the Negro is given a man's chance in the commercial world, and in nothing is this Exposition more elo-

quent than in emphasizing this chance. Our greatest danger is that in the great leap from slavery to freedom we may overlook the fact that the masses of us are to live by the productions of our hands, and fail to keep in mind that we shall prosper in proportion as we learn to dignify and glorify common labour and put brains and skill into the common occupations of life; shall prosper in proportion as we learn to draw the line between the superficial and the substantial, the ornamental gewgaws of life and the useful. No race can prosper till it learns that there is as much dignity in tilling a field as in writing a poem. It is at the bottom of life we must begin, and not at the top. Nor should we permit our grievances to overshadow our opportunities.

To those of the white race who look to the incoming of those of foreign birth and strange tongue and habits for the prosperity of the South, were I permitted I would repeat what I say to my own race, "Cast down your bucket where you are." Cast it down among the eight millions of Negroes whose habits you know, whose fidelity and love you have tested in days when to have proved treacherous meant the ruin of your firesides. Cast down your bucket among these people who have, without strikes and labour wars, tilled your fields, cleared your forests, builded your railroads and cities, and brought forth treasures from the bowels of the earth, and helped make possible this magnif-

icent representation of the progress of the South. Casting down your bucket among my people, helping and encouraging them as you are doing on these grounds, and to education of head, hand, and heart, you will find that they will buy your surplus land, make blossom the waste places in your fields, and run your factories. While doing this, you can be sure in the future, as in the past, that you and your families will be surrounded by the most patient, faithful, law-abiding, and unresentful people that the world has seen. . . .

The wisest among my race understand that the agitation of questions of social equality is the extremest folly, and that progress in the enjoyment of all the privileges that will come to us must be the result of severe and constant struggle rather than an artificial forcing. No race that has anything to contribute to the markets of the world is long in any degree ostracized. It is important and right that all privileges of the law be ours, but it is vastly more important that we be prepared for the exercises of these privileges. The opportunity to earn a dollar in the factory just now is worth infinitely more than the opportunity to spend a dollar in an opera-house.

5. Ray Stannard Baker Analyzes the Southern Labor Problem, 1908

The South has been and is today dependent on a single labour supply—the Negro. Now Negroes, though recruited by a high birth rate, have not been increasing in any degree as rapidly as the demand for labour incident to the development of every sort of industry, railroads, lumbering, mines, to say nothing of the increased farm area and the added requirements of growing cities. With this enormous increased demand for labour the Negro supply has, relatively, been decreasing. Many have gone North and West, many have bought farms of their own, thousands, by education, have became professional men, teachers, preachers, and even merchants and bankers—always draining away the best and most industrious men of the race and reducing by so much the available supply of common labour. . . .

What has been the result? Naturally a fierce contest between agriculture and industry for the limited and dwindling supply of the only labour they had. . . .

Many cotton mills, indeed, employ agents whose business it is to go out through the country urging

the white farmers to come to town and painting glowing pictures of the possibilities of life there. I have visited a number of mill neighbourhoods and talked with the operatives. I found the older men sometimes homesick for free life of the farm. . . .

But nothing would persuade the women and children to go back to the old hard life. Hawkinsville has a small cotton mill and just such a community of white workers around it. Owing to the scarcity of labour, wages in the mills have been going up rapidly all over the South, during the last two or three years, furnishing a still more potent attraction for country people.

All these various tendencies are uniting to produce some very remarkable conditions in the South. A natural segregation of the races is apparently taking place. I saw it everywhere I went in the black belt. The white people were gravitating toward the towns or into white neighbourhoods and leaving the land, even though still owned by white men, more and more to the exclusive occupation of Negroes. Many black counties are growing blacker while not a few white counties are growing whiter. . . .

One of the most significant things I saw in the South—and I saw it everywhere—was the way in which the white people were torn between their feeling of race prejudice and their downright economic needs. Hating and fearing the Negro as a race (though often loving individual Negroes), they yet want him to work for them; they can't get along without him. In one impulse a community will rise to mob Negroes or to drive them out of the country because of Negro crime or Negro vagrancy, or because the Negro is becoming educated, acquiring property and "getting out of his place"; and in the next impulse laws are passed or other remarkable measures taken to keep him at work—because the South can't get along without him. . . .

And here are extracts from a remarkable letter from a Southern white working man signing himself Forrest Pope and published in the Atlanta *Georgian*, October 22, 1906:

When the skilled negro appears and begins to elbow the white man in the struggle for existence, don't you know the white man rebels and won't have it so? If you don't it won't take you long to find it out; just go out and ask a few of them, those who tell you the whole truth, and see what you will find out about it.

All the genuine Southern people like the Negro as a servant, and so long as he remains the hewer of wood and carrier of water, and remains strictly in what we choose to call his place, everything is all right, but when ambition, prompted by real education, causes the Negro to grow restless and he bestir himself to get out of that servile condition, then there is, or at least there will be, trouble, sure enough trouble. . . . Take a young Negro of little more than ordinary intelligence, even, get hold of him in time, train him thoroughly as to books, and finish him up with a good industrial education, send him out into the South with ever so good intentions both on the part of his benefactor and himself, send him to take my work away from me and I will kill him. . . .

I am, I believe, a typical Southern white workingman of the skilled variety, and I'll tell the whole world, including Drs. Abbott and Eliot, that I don't want any educated property-owning Negro around me. The Negro would be desirable to me for what I could get out of him in the way of labour that I don't want to have to perform myself, and I have no other uses for him.

One illustration more and I am through. I met at Montgomery, Alabama, a lawyer named Gustav Frederick Mertins. We were discussing the "problem," and Mr. Mertins finally made a striking remark, not at all expressing the view that I heard from some of the strongest citizens of Montgomery, but excellently voicing the position of many Southerners.

"It's a question," he said, "who will do the dirty work. In this country the white man won't: the Negro must. There's got to be a mudsill somewhere. If you educate the Negroes they won't stay where they belong; and you must consider them as a race, because if you let a few rise it makes the others discontented."

6. Workers in the New South

A. Youthful Worker in Carolina Cotton Mill, 1908

Photograph by Lewis W. Hine. Courtesy George Eastman House.

B. Workers at Home, Alexandria, Virginia, 1911

C. The National Child Labor Committee
Focuses on the Southern Mills, ca. 1910

Chapter 18:
Document Set 3 References

1. T. Thomas Fortune Predicts a Class Struggle in the South, 1884
   T. Thomas Fortune, *Black and White: Land, Labor, and Politics in the South* (New York: Fords, Howard, and Hulbert, 1884), pp. 241–242.

2. Henry W. Grady's Vision of a New South, 1886–1887
   Henry W. Grady, "The New South," December 21, 1886; "The South and Her Problems," October 26, 1887, in Edna Henry Lee Turpin, ed., *The New South and Other Addresses by Henry Woodfin Grady* (New York: Turpin, Maynard, Merrill, and Co., 1904), pp. 37–38, 75–81.

3. D. Augustus Straker's Prescription for Southern Racial Harmony, 1888
   D. Augustus Straker, *The New South Investigated* (Detroit: Ferguson Printing Company, 1888), pp. 104–105, 107, 132, 229–230.

4. The Atlanta Compromise as a Blueprint for African American Economic Progress, 1895

Booker T. Washington, *Up from Slavery* (Garden City: Doubleday, Page & Co., 1910), pp. 218–225.

5. Ray Stannard Baker Analyzes the Southern Labor Problem, 1908
   Ray Stannard Baker, *Following the Color Line* (New York: Doubleday, Page & Co., 1908; rep. Harper & Row, Inc., 1964), pp. 56–57, 70, 81, 84–85.

6. Workers in the New South
   A. Youthful Worker in Carolina Cotton Mill, 1908
      Photo by Lewis W. Hine. Courtesy of George Eastman House.
   B. Workers at Home, Alexandria, Virginia, 1911
      Photo by Lewis W. Hine. Milwaukee Art Museum.
   C. The National Child Labor Committee Focuses on the Southern Mills, ca. 1910
      Exhibition panel by Lewis W. Hine. Milwaukee Art Museum.

Chapter 18:
Document Set 3 Credits

6. A. Photograph by Lewis W. Hine. Courtesy George Eastman House
   B. Photograph by Lewis W. Hine, "Family Portrait Outside Home," 1911. Silverprint 4-9/16″ × 6-9/16″. Milwaukee Art Museum, Gift of Robert Mann

C. "Why This Double Standard?" Silverprint 6-2/16″ × 3-1/4″. Milwaukee Art Museum, Gift of Robert Mann

CHAPTER 19

Life in the City: Coping with the New Urban Environment

Chapter 19 focuses on the problems and opportunities Americans faced as a result of rapid urbanization following the Civil War. Stressing both physical changes in the urban landscape and the social problems confronted by city governments, your textbook explores the impact of economic and political modernization on the people of the nation's major urban industrial centers. Although the social experience of all groups is examined, special emphasis is placed on the world of the immigrant working class. The following documents probe deeply into the lives of the poor in an urbanizing society.

As an introduction to the urban environment of the Gilded Age, a speech by renowned landscape architect Frederick Law Olmsted surveys the chaotic living conditions and formidable challenges to city leaders inherent in the stresses of modernization. Olmsted's statement, made in 1870 when many social problems were emerging, remains optimistic about the potential in urban planning.

Cosmopolitan New York provides a vivid example of the populous eastern cities. Extensive excerpts from reformer Jacob Riis's hard-hitting *How the Other Half Lives* (1890) dramatize the plight of the city's impoverished slum dwellers, including many of the social problems that festered in the urban environment. Himself a Danish immigrant, Riis called attention to the ethnic character of New York's tenement districts, as well as the exploitation and suffering of the inhabitants. As you review his writings, try to determine what the author's motives and goals were. In addition, evaluate his evidence, including the statistical support provided in the appendix to his study.

These documents will enable you to contrast the New York urban landscape of 1870 with the scene in 1890. You will be able to judge whether Olmsted's optimism was justified. As you identify the underlying concerns in Riis's work, your analysis should lead to an evaluation of urbanization's impact on those who inhabited the nineteenth-century city.

Questions for Analysis

1. Using Olmsted's remarks on the consequences of urban growth as a resource, identify the major problems confronted by city governments in the Gilded Age. To what extent had progress been made toward their solution by 1890? What problems did Olmsted fail to foresee?

2. In what ways can the problems discussed by Jacob Riis be distinguished from Olmsted's concerns? How would you account for their differences in perspective? What was the significance of class in the observer's perception of urban problems?

3. As you review the materials relating to the world of the immigrant, do you find common problems in the experiences of the separate immigrant groups? In what ways were their adjustment strategies similar/different? What do the documents suggest about the relationship among immigrant groups? How did Riis explain such differences? What do his responses reveal about his own values?

4. How did Riis account for the immigrant's susceptibility to disease, alcoholism, family violence, crime, or other disruptions of family life? What light does the statistical evidence shed on these problems? Does Riis provide any remedies for the problems uncovered?

5. Define the term *tenement* as used in the Riis account of urban poverty in New York. How did urban reformers propose to deal with the housing problem? Using Riis as your main source, try to identify the heart of the problem.

1. Frederick Law Olmsted Accepts the Urban Challenge, 1870

We began experimentally with street railways twenty years ago. At present, in New York, one pair of horses serves to convey one hundred people, on an average, every day at a rate of fare about one-fiftieth of the old hackney coach rates; and the total number of fares collected annually is equal to that of the population of the United States. And yet thousands walk a number of miles every day because they cannot be seated in the cars. It is impossible to fix a limit to the amount of travel which really ample, convenient, and still cheap means of transportation for short distances would develop. . . .

See how rapidly we are really gaining and what we have to expect. Two recent inventions give us the means of reducing by a third, under favorable circumstances, the cost of good McAdam roads. There have been sixteen patents issued from one office for other new forms of perfectly smooth and nearly noiseless street pavement, some of which, after two or three years' trial, promise so well as to render it certain that some improvement will soon come by which more than one of the present special annoyances of town life will be abated. An improvement in our sewer system seems near at hand, also, which will add considerably to the comparative advantages of a residence in towns, and especially the more open town suburbs.

Experiments indicate that it is feasible to send heated air through a town in pipes like water; and that it may be drawn upon; and the heat which is taken, measured and paid for according to quantity required. Thus may come a great saving of fuel and trouble in a very difficult department of domestic economy. No one will think of applying such a system to farmhouses.

Again, it is plain that we have scarcely begun to turn to account the advantages offered to townspeople in the electric telegraph; we really have not made a beginning with those offered in the pneumatic tube, though their substantial character has been demonstrated. . . .

As railroads are improved, all the important stations will become centers or subcenters of towns, and all the minor stations suburbs. For most ordinary, everyday purposes, especially housekeepers' purposes, these will need no very large population before they can obtain urban advantages. . . .

The construction of good roads and walks, the laying of sewer, water, and gas pipes, and the supplying of sufficiently cheap, rapid, and comfortable conveyances to town centers is all that is necessary to give any farming land in a healthy and attractive situation the value of town lots. . . .

It is hardly a matter of speculation, I am disposed to think, but almost of demonstration that the larger a town becomes because simply of its advantages for commercial purposes, the greater will be the convenience available to those who live in and near it for cooperation, as well with reference to the accumulation of wealth in the higher forms—as in seats of learning, of science, and of art—as with reference to merely domestic economy and the emancipation of both men and women from petty, confining, and narrowing cares.

It also appears to be nearly certain that the recent rapid enlargement of towns and withdrawal of people from rural conditions of living is the result mainly of circumstances of a permanent character.

2. Jacob Riis Describes Immigrant Life in the New York City Tenements, 1890

To-day, what is a tenement? The law defines it as a house "occupied by three or more families, living independently and doing their cooking on the premises; or by more than two families on a floor, so living and cooking and having a common right in the halls, stairways, yards, etc." That is the legal meaning, and includes flats and apartment-houses, with which we have nothing to do. In its narrower sense the typical tenement was thus described when last arraigned before the bar of public justice: "It is generally a brick building from four to six stories high on the street, frequently with a store on the first floor which, when used for the sale of liquor, has a side opening for the benefit of the inmates and to evade the Sunday law; four families occupy each floor, and a set of rooms consists of one or two dark closets, used as bedrooms, with a living room twelve feet by ten. The staircase is too often a dark well in the centre of the house, and no direct through ventilation is possible, each family being separated from the other by partitions. Frequently the rear of the lot is occupied by another building of three stories high with two families on a floor." The picture is nearly as true to-day as ten years ago, and will be for a long time to come. The dim light admitted by the air-shaft shines upon greater crowds than ever. Tenements are still "good property," and the poverty of the poor man his destruction. A barrack down town where he *has to live* because he is poor brings in a third more rent than a decent flat house in Harlem. The statement once made a sensation that between seventy and eighty children had been found in one tenement. It no longer excites even passing attention, when the sanitary police report counting 101 adults and 91 children in a Crosby Street house, one of twins, built together. The children in the other, if I am not mistaken, numbered 89, a total of 180 for two tenements! ...

When once I asked the agent of a notorious Fourth Ward alley how many people might be living in it I was told: One hundred and forty families, one hundred Irish, thirty-eight Italian, and two that spoke the German tongue. Barring the agent herself, there was not a native-born individual in the court. The answer was characteristic of the cosmopolitan character of lower New York, very nearly so of the whole of it, wherever it runs to alleys and courts. One may find for the asking an Italian, a German, a French, African, Spanish, Bohemian, Russian, Scandinavian, Jewish, and Chinese colony.... The one thing you shall vainly ask for in the chief city of America is a distinctively American community. There is none; certainly not among the tenements. Where have they gone to, the old inhabitants? ...

They are not here. In their place has come this queer conglomerate mass of heterogeneous elements, ever striving and working like whiskey and water in one glass, and with the like result: final union and a prevailing taint of whiskey. The once unwelcome Irishman has been followed in his turn by the Italian, the Russian Jew, and the Chinaman, and has himself taken a hand at opposition, quite as bitter and quite as ineffectual, against these later hordes. Wherever these have gone they have crowded him out, possess-ing the block, the street, the ward with their denser swarms. But the Irishman's revenge is complete. Victorious in defeat over his recent as over his more ancient foe, the one who opposed his coming no less than the one who drove him out, he dictates to both their politics, and, secure in possession of the offices, returns the native his greeting with interest, while collecting the rents of the Italian whose house he has bought with the profits of his saloon. ...

The poorest immigrant comes here with the purpose and ambition to better himself and, given half a chance, might be reasonably expected to make the most of it. To the false plea that he prefers the squalid homes in which his kind are housed there could be no better answer. The truth is, his half chance has too long been wanting, and for the bad result he has been unjustly blamed. ...

Life in the tenements in July and August spells death to an army of little ones whom the doctor's skill is powerless to save. When the white badge of mourning flutters from every second door, sleepless mothers walk the streets in the gray of the early dawn, trying to stir a cooling breeze to fan the brow of the sick baby. There is no sadder sight than this patient devotion striving against fearfully hopeless odds. ...

Under the most favorable circumstances, an epidemic, which the well-to-do can afford to make light of as a thing to be got over or avoided by reasonable care, is excessively fatal among the children of the poor, by reason of the practical impossibility of isolating the patient in a tenement. The measles, ordinarily a harmless disease, furnishes a familiar example. Tread it ever so lightly on the avenues, in the tenements it kills right and left. Such an epidemic ravaged three crowded blocks in Elizabeth Street on the heels of the grippe last winter, and, when it had spent its fury, the death-maps in the Bureau of Vital Statistics looked as if a black hand had been laid across those blocks.... The track of the epidemic through these teeming barracks was as clearly defined as the track of a tornado through a forest district. There were houses in which as many as eight little children had died in five months. The records showed that respiratory diseases, the common heritage of the grippe and the measles, had caused death in most cases, discovering the trouble to be, next to the inability to check the contagion in those crowds, in the poverty of the parents and the wretched home conditions that made proper care of the sick impossible. ...

Turn and twist it as we may, over against every bulwark for decency and morality which society erects, the saloon projects its colossal shadow, omen of evil wherever it falls into the lives of the poor.

Nowhere is its mark so broad or so black. To their misery it sticketh closer than a brother, persuading them that within its doors only is refuge, relief. It has the best of the argument, too, for it is true, worse pity, that in many a tenement-house block the saloon is the one bright and cheery and humanly decent spot to be found. It is a sorry admission to make, that to bring the rest of the neighborhood up to the level of the saloon would be one way of squelching it; but it is so. Wherever the tenements thicken, it multiplies. Upon the direst poverty of their crowds it grows fat and prosperous, levying upon it a tax heavier than all the rest of its grievous burdens combined. . . . The dramshop yawns at every step, the poor man's club, his forum and his haven of rest when weary and disgusted with the crowding, the quarrelling, and the wretchedness at home. With the poison dealt out there he takes his politics, in quality not far apart. . . .

The law prohibiting the selling of beer to minors is about as much respected in the tenement-house districts as the ordinance against swearing. Newspaper readers will recall the story, told little more than a year ago, of a boy who after carrying beer a whole day for a shopful of men over on the East Side, where his father worked, crept into the cellar to sleep off the effects of his own share in the rioting. It was Saturday evening. Sunday his parents sought him high and low; but it was not until Monday morning, when the shop was opened, that he was found killed and half-eaten by the rats that overran the place. . . .

For the corruption of the child there is no restitution. . . .

What, then, are the bald facts with which we have to deal in New York?

I. That we have a tremendous, ever swelling crowd of wage-earners which it is our business to house decently.

II. That it is not housed decently.

III. That it must be so housed *here* for the present, and for a long time to come, all schemes of suburban relief being as yet utopian, impracticable.

IV. That it pays high enough rents to entitle it to be so housed, as a right.

V. That nothing but our own slothfulness is in the way of so housing it, since "the condition of the tenants is in advance of the condition of the houses which they occupy" (Report of Tenement-house Commission).

VI. That the security of the one no less than of the other half demands, on sanitary, moral, and economic grounds, that it be decently housed.

VII. That it will pay to do it. As an investment, I mean, and in hard cash. This I shall immediately proceed to prove.

VIII. That the tenement has come to stay, and must itself be the solution of the problem with which it confronts us. . . .

The sea of a mighty population, held in galling fetters, heaves uneasily in the tenements. Once already our city, to which have come the duties and responsibilities of metropolitan greatness before it was able to fairly measure its task, has felt the swell of its resistless flood. If it rise once more, no human power may avail to check it. The gap between the classes in which it surges, unseen, unsuspected by the thoughtless, is widening day by day. No tardy enactment of law, no political expedient, can close it. Against all other dangers our system of government may offer defence and shelter; against this not.

3. A Statistical Snapshot of the Tenement Population, 1890

Population of tenements in New York in 1869[*] (census)	468,492
Population of tenements in New York in 1888[†] (census)	1,093,701
Population of tenements in New York in 1888 under five years of age	143,243
Population of New York in 1880 (census)	1,206,299
Population of Manhattan Island in 1880 (census)	1,164,673

[*]In 1869, a tenement was a house occupied by four families or more.

[†]In 1888, a tenement was a house occupied by three families or more.

Population of Tenth Ward in 1880 (census)	47,554
Population of Eleventh Ward in 1880 (census)	68,778
Population of Thirteenth Ward in 1880 (census)	37,797
Population of New York in 1890 (census)	1,513,501
Population of Manhattan Island in 1890 (census)	1,440,101
Population of Tenth Ward in 1890 (census)	57,514
Population of Eleventh Ward in 1890 (census)	75,708
Population of Thirteenth Ward in 1890 (census)	45,882
Density of population to the square mile in 1880, New York City (census)	30,976
Density of population to the square mile in 1880, Manhattan Island (census)	41,264
Density of population to the square mile in 1880, Tenth Ward (census)	276,672
Density of population to the square mile in 1880, Eleventh Ward (census)	224,576
Density of population to the square mile in 1880, Thirteenth Ward (census)	226,048
Density of population to the square mile in 1890, New York City (census)	28,451
Density of population to the square mile in 1890, Manhattan Island (census)	73,299
Density of population to the square mile in 1890, Tenth Ward (census)	334,080
Density of population to the square mile in 1890, Eleventh Ward (census)	246,040
Density of population to the square mile in 1890, Thirteenth Ward (census)	274,432
Number of persons to a dwelling in New York, 1880 (census)	16.37
Number of persons to a dwelling in London, 1881 (census)	7.9
Number of persons to a dwelling in Philadelphia, 1880 (census)	5.79
Number of persons to a dwelling in Brooklyn, 1880 (census)	9.11
Number of persons to a dwelling in Boston, 1880 (census)	8.26
Death-rate of New York, 1889	25.19
Death-rate of London, 1889	17.4
Death-rate of Philadelphia, 1889	19.7
Death-rate of Brooklyn, 1889	22.5
Death-rate of Boston, 1889	24.42
Death-rate in tenements in New York, 1869	28.35
Death-rate in tenements in New York, 1888	22.71
Number of burials in city cemetery (paupers), New York, 1889	3,815
Percentage of such burials on total	9.64
Immigrants landed at Castle Garden in 20 years, ending with 1889	5,335,396
Immigrants landed at Castle Garden in 1889	349,233
Immigrants from England landed at Castle Garden in 1889	46,214
Immigrants from Scotland landed at Castle Garden in 1889	11,415

Immigrants from Ireland landed at Castle Garden in 1889   43,090

Immigrants from Germany landed at Castle Garden in 1889   75,458

	1883	*1884*	*1885*	*1886*	*1887*	*1888*	*1889*
Italy	25,485	14,076	16,033	29,312	44,274	43,927	28,810
Russia Poland	7,577	12,432	16,578	23,987	33,203	33,052	31,329
Hungary	13,160	15,797	11,129	18,135	17,719	12,905	15,678
Bohemia	4,877	7,093	6,697	4,222	6,449	3,982	5,412

Number of tenements in New York, December 1, 1888   32,390

Number built from June 1, 1888, to August 1, 1890   3,733

Rear tenements in existence, August 1, 1890   2,630

Total number of tenements, August 1, 1890   37,316

Estimated population of tenements, August 1, 1890   1,250,000

Estimated number of children under five
years in tenements, 1890   163,712

Chapter 19:
Document Set 1 References

1. Frederick Law Olmsted Accepts the Urban Challenge, 1870
   Frederick Law Olmsted, "Public Parks and the Enlargement of Towns," *Journal of Social Science,* No. 3 (1871).

2. Jacob Riis Describes Immigrant Life in the New York City Tenements, 1890

   Jacob Riis, *How the Other Half Lives,* 1890 (New York: Sagamore Press, rep. 1957), pp. 13–16, 18, 124–126, 159, 162, 215, 226.

3. A Statistical Snapshot of the Tenement Population, 1890
   Riis, "Appendix: Statistics Bearing on the Tenement Problem," in Riis, pp. 228–231.

CHAPTER 19

Responses to the Urban Challenge: Social Innovation

The preceding document set provided a graphic portrayal of the city in transition and the social disorganization that accompanied rapid urbanization. As your textbook indicates, city planners and government officials reacted to a chaotic environment with imagination, launching such innovations as modernized police systems, expanded public services, and the "city beautiful" movement. Equally challenging was the human misery and social dislocation caused by uncontrolled urban expansion and dramatic shifts in population distribution. The following documents explore some of the more significant responses to what came to be called "the social question."

No reaction was more intense than the new religious consciousness of social evil, detailed in your textbook's treatment of the Social Gospel movement. As you review the evidence, be aware of the link between Christian commitment and social reform. This relationship is evident in several of the documents, beginning with the strong sense of Christian moralism in Jacob Riis's introduction to *How the Other Half Lives*. Although expressed in the novelist's format, a similar militance can be found in the words of the Reverend Charles M. Sheldon's protagonist, Harry Maxwell, who spoke for a troubled generation. Finally, compare Sheldon's fictional account with the Reverend Walter Rauschenbusch's definition of the social crisis and its remedy. Try to identify the sources of their concern.

Another approach to the urban crisis lay in private philanthropy. The 1881 report of Boston philanthropist Robert Treat Paine to the American Social Science Association reveals the potential as well as the limita-

tions of private giving. Be particularly conscious of the charity worker's definition of success; it reveals the philanthropist's perspective on reform and the poor.

A related attack on poverty and working-class problems grew out of the rising social-settlement movement described in your textbook. Not only did the settlements grapple with urban problems, but the entire movement influenced a broad range of social movements and institutions. The excerpt from Jane Addams's lecture entitled "The Objective Necessity for Social Settlements" states the goals and philosophy of the movement. Try to assess her purposes, as well as the relationship of the movement to the religious currents of the period.

One such theme stressed a renewed social commitment to moral purity. The purity crusade, as described in your textbook, attempted to counter governmental plans to regulate prostitution and evolved into a drive to elevate the moral consciousness of the entire community. The excerpts from the Reverend J. J. Fleharty's treatise, *Social Impurity* (1875), include several possible responses to moral degradation. As you analyze Fleharty's argument, try to determine his motives, concerns, and proposed solution to the problem of social imperfection.

As you search the documents for evidence of urbanization's social impact, be conscious of similarities in the varied responses to social change. The intensification of social criticism in the late nineteenth century may be directly related to the successes of the nascent Progressive generation.

Questions for Analysis

1. What was the relationship between religion and class? How were the exhortations of the reformers related to class fears and concerns? How are these fears reflected in the evidence?

2. How did proponents of the Social Gospel justify their commitment to reform? What do the documents reveal about their reasoning? In what way was renewed religious faith related to the rise of the city?

3. How would you explain the moral purity movement's apparent obsession with sex and sexuality? What do their words reveal about the social environment in which its supporters functioned? What were their goals and methods?

4. What was the ethnic and cultural character of the new urban population? What were the religious implications of this new social mix? Do the documents reveal

any relationship between changes in the makeup of the urban population and the intensification of the Social Gospel movement? Explain.

5. How do the documents reflect nineteenth-century attitudes toward women's roles in American society? What evidence distinguishes between working-class and middle-class values with reference to women's status?

1. Jacob Riis Appeals to Christian Conscience, 1890

The complaint was universal among the tenants that they were entirely uncared for, and that the only answer to their requests to have the place put in order by repairs and necessary improvements was that they must pay their rent or leave. The agent's instructions were simple but emphatic: "Collect the rent in advance, or, failing, eject the occupants." Upon such a stock grew this upas-tree. Small wonder the fruit is bitter. The remedy that shall be an effective answer to the coming appeal for justice must proceed from the public conscience. Neither legislation nor charity can cover the ground. The greed of capital that wrought the evil must itself undo it, as far as it can now be undone. Homes must be built for the working masses by those who employ their labor; but tenements must cease to be "good property" in the old, heartless sense. "Philanthropy and five per cent." is the penance exacted.

If this is true from a purely economic point of view, what then of the outlook from the Christian standpoint? Not long ago a great meeting was held in this city, of all denominations of religious faith, to discuss the question how to lay hold of these teeming masses in the tenements with Christian influences, to which they are now too often strangers. Might not the conference have found in the warning of one Brooklyn builder, who has invested his capital on this plan and made it pay more than a money interest, a hint worth heeding: "How shall the love of God be understood by those who have been nurtured in sight only of the greed of man?"

2. Jesus as a Model for Personal Conduct, 1898

"What would be the result, if in this city every church member should begin to do as Jesus would do? It is not easy to go into details of the result. But we all know that certain things would be impossible that are now practiced by church members. What would Jesus do in the matter of wealth? How would He spend it? What principle would regulate His use of money? Would He be likely to live in great luxury and spend ten times as much on personal adornment and entertainment as He spent to relieve the needs of suffering humanity? How would Jesus be governed in the making of money? Would He take rentals from saloon and other disreputable property, or even from tenement property that was so constructed that the inmates had no such thing as a home and no such possibility as privacy or cleanliness?

"What would Jesus do about the great army of unemployed and desperate who tramp the streets and curse the church, or are indifferent to it, lost in the bitter struggle for the bread that tastes bitter when it is earned, on account of the desperate conflict to get it. Would Jesus care nothing for them? Would He go His way in comparative ease and comfort? Would He say it was none of His business? Would He excuse Himself from all responsibility to remove the causes of such a condition?

"What would Jesus do in the center of a civilization that hurries so fast after money that the very girls employed in great business houses are not paid enough to keep soul and body together without fearful temptations, so great that scores of them fall and are swept over the great, boiling abyss; where the demands of trade sacrifice hundreds of lads in a business that ignores all Christian duties towards them in the way of education and moral training and personal affection? Would Jesus, if He were here today, as a part of our age and commercial industry, feel nothing, do nothing, say nothing, in the face of these facts which every business man knows? . . .

But if our definition of being a Christian is simply to enjoy the privileges of worship, be generous at no expense to ourselves, have a good, easy time surrounded by pleasant friends and by comfortable things, live respectably, and at the same time avoid the world's great stress of sin and trouble because it is too much pain to bear it—if this is our definition of Christianity, surely we are a long way from following the steps of Him who trod the way with groans and tears and sobs of anguish for a lost humanity, who sweat, as it were, great drops of blood, who cried out on the upreared cross, 'My God! My God! Why hast thou forsaken me.'

"Are we ready to make and live a new discipleship? Are we ready to reconsider our definition of a Christian? What is it to be a Christian? It is to imitate Jesus. It is to do as He would do. It is to walk in His steps."

3. Walter Rauschenbusch Outlines the New Social Gospel, 1907

A minister mingling with both classes can act as an interpreter to both. He can soften the increasing class hatred of the working class. He can infuse the spirit of moral enthusiasm into the economic struggle of the dispossessed and lift it to something more than a "stomach question." On the other hand, among the well-to-do, he can strengthen the consciousness that the working people have a real grievance and so increase the disposition to make concessions in practical cases and check the inclination to resort to force for the suppression of discontent. If the ministry would awaken among the wealthy a sense of social compunction and moral uneasiness, that alone might save our nation from a revolutionary explosion. . . .

The spiritual force of Christianity should be turned against the materialism and mammonism of our industrial and social order.

If a man sacrifices his human dignity and self-respect to increase his income, or stunts his intellectual growth and his human affections to swell his bank account, he is to that extent serving mammon and denying God. Likewise if he uses up and injures the life of his fellow-men to make money for himself, he serves mammon and denies God. But our industrial order does both. It makes property the end, and man the means to produce it. . . .

Pastor Stöcker . . . said: "We have put the question the wrong way. We have asked: How much child and female labor does industry need in order to flourish, to pay dividends, and to sell goods abroad? Whereas we ought to have asked: How ought industry to be organized in order to protect and foster the family, the human individual, the Christian life?" That simple reversal of the question marks the difference between the Christian conception of life and property and the mammonistic. . . .

It is the function of religion to teach the individual to value his soul more than his body, and his moral integrity more than his income. In the same way it is the function of religion to teach society to value human life more than property, and to value property only in so far as it forms the material basis for the higher development of human life. When life and property are in apparent collision, life must take precedence. This is not only Christian but prudent. . . . Religious men have been cowed by the prevailing materialism and arrogant selfishness of our business world. They should have the courage of religious faith and assert that "man liveth not by bread alone," but by doing the will of God, and that the life of a nation "consisteth not in the abundance of things" which it produces, but in the way men live justly with one another and humbly with their God.

4. Robert Treat Paine, Jr., Reports the Results of Private Philanthropy, 1881

I have here the report of a lady placed in charge of some large tenement house properties, in the worst section of New York, belonging to a Society, which takes them with the benevolent aim, not only to renovate them, but to prove how much may be done to help even drunken and degraded tenants to a better life. This also, is a successful business operation. A few extracts will show the missionary spirit in which Mrs. Miles has taken up this work, and what she has achieved. . . .

Mr. Cutting and a friend visited the "court" with me, yesterday. Mr. Cutting was thoroughly disappointed, and so was I (but agreeably so), there was really so little left of the "Gotham court," as you and I had seen it, a month ago. In house "B," you will remember the shattered windows on the first floor, and the dreadful room, in which Mrs. Burke was, also, Mrs. Moore, Mrs. Sullivan, and the woman McGuire,—Mrs. Burke, who had not been sober for six weeks when you saw her, on the day of her baby's funeral; you will also recollect a curious bundle in the corner of the room, which, upon investigation, proved to be Mrs. Burke, who is since dead. She promised the priest and myself, upon our visit, that she would drink no more; the poor thing was faithful to her promise, and went to the hospital, where, doubtless, the sudden total abstinence hastened her death. The neighbors say, "God's blessing will be upon me, because I was the means of her dying *sober.*"

That the people have been lifted and morally elevated in the course of the year, there can be no doubt. Your remark upon the occasion of your visit, "Where are the poor people?" was to me the most satisfactory proof that this result had been obtained. That they have never grown restless under the constant supervision, my knowledge that on several occasions my people had been offered rooms at *less money,* but preferred remaining where they were, and the fact that Mulberry street (where the rule is *more* stringent) has now never a vacant apartment, are all proofs positive to me, that these people do appreciate this movement in their behalf. As a missionary, I have at all times been a welcome visitor, and they are always ready and glad to hear "the word"; and, when trouble comes to them, I am the first one to whom they apply.

5. Jane Addams Defines the Social-Settlement Movement, 1892

I believe that there is a distinct turning among many young men and women toward this simple acceptance of Christ's message. They resent the assumption that Christianity is a set of ideas which belong to the religious consciousness, whatever that may be. They insist that it cannot be proclaimed and instituted apart from the social life of the community and that it must seek a simple and natural expression in the social organism itself. The Settlement movement is only one manifestation of that wider humanitarian movement which throughout Christendom, but preeminently in England, is endeavoring to embody itself, not in a sect, but in society itself. . . .

Certain it is that spiritual force is found in the Settlement movement, and it is also true that this force must be evoked and must be called into play before the success of any Settlement is assured. There must be the overmastering belief that all that is noblest in life is common to men as men, in order to accentuate the likenesses and ignore the differences which are found among the people whom the Settlement constantly brings into juxtaposition. . . .

The Settlement, then, is an experimental effort to aid in the solution of the social and industrial problems which are engendered by the modern conditions of life in a great city. It insists that these problems are not confined to any one portion of a city. It is an attempt to relieve, at the same time, the overaccumulation at one end of society and the destitution at the other; but it assumes that this overaccumulation and destitution is most sorely felt in the things that pertain to social and educational advantages. From its very nature it can stand for no political or social propaganda. It must, in a sense, give the warm welcome of an inn to all such propaganda, if perchance one of them be found an angel. The one thing to be dreaded in the Settlement is that it lose its flexibility, its power of quick adaptation, its readiness to change its methods as its environment may demand. It must be open to conviction and must have a deep and abiding sense of tolerance. It must be hospitable and ready for experiment. It should demand from its residents a scientific patience in the accumulation of facts and the steady holding of their sympathies as one of the best instruments for that accumulation. It must be grounded in a philosophy whose foundation is on the solidarity of the human race, a philosophy which will not waver when the race happens to be represented by a drunken woman or an idiot boy. Its residents must be emptied of all conceit of opinion and all self-assertion, and ready to arouse and interpret the public opinion of their neighborhood. They must be content to live quietly side by side with their neighbors, until they grow into a sense of relationship and mutual interests. Their neighbors are held apart by differences of race and language which the residents can more easily overcome. They are bound to see the needs of their neighborhood as a whole, to furnish data for legislation, and to use their influence to secure it. In short, residents are pledged to devote themselves to the duties of good citizenship and to the arousing of the social energies which too largely lie dormant in every neighborhood given over to industrialism. They are bound to regard the entire life of their city as organic, to make an effort to unify it, and to protest against its over-differentiation.

It is always easy to make all philosophy point to one particular moral and all history adorn one particular tale; but I may be forgiven the reminder that the best speculative philosophy sets forth the solidarity of the human race; that the highest moralists have taught that without the advance and improvement of the whole, no man can hope for any lasting improvement in his own moral or material individual condition; and that the subjective necessity for Social Settlements is therefore identical with that necessity, which urges us on toward social and individual salvation.

6. Reverend J. J. Fleharty Explains the Moral Purity Crusade, 1875

Recklessness in the treatment of the "social question," by either pulpit or Christian press, would be a calamity. To write in an indefinite way on a subject so delicate is folly. The issue is upon us. The horizon is darkening with the storm which now threatens our social institutions. The crisis is at hand, and to be silent is treason "against God and virtue." . . .

The American press seems to take especial pride in heralding over the land every departure from the rules of civilized life. The divorces and the new developments of social impurity are all eagerly chronicled, as if best adapted to the public palate. This indicates the direction in which we would surely drift if not awakened to the danger that threatens us. This crime has not been confined to any class of society. It invades the holy state of matrimony, and severs its bond of union. It destroys youthful purity, and drags down the good and beautiful into its vortex of ruin. It transforms the timid girl into a gaping sensualist. Even boys and girls are corrupted by the tide of obscenity that sweeps through city, village, and country. . . .

Fœticide increases the chances for social impurity, greatly deadens the conscience, and leads to indulgence in secret socialism. It is a dead weight on Protestantism in the United States, and Catholics have some ground for accusing Protestants of this fearful crime. . . .

This fearful sin, fœticide, is much more frequent than is generally supposed; and in some cases so-called Christians boast of their skill in the bloody work. They are not Christians, unless they have repented of the dreadful deed so skillfully performed. They are guilty of murder, the murder of their own offspring. . . .

Young people thirst for a knowledge of sexuality. They are hurried into public life at a tender age. Misses give parties and have beaux. Boys, scarce in their teens, boast of their "girls," are jealous of rivals, and escort their misses to proper or improper places at unseasonable hours. Through various means, frequently unnoticed by parents, children are, to some extent, demoralized before they reach their teens. Unfaithful women, mothers of families, above suspicion perhaps, instigate mere boys to the performance of the adulterous act. Bad men likewise initiate girls into the secrets of marital pleasure. Thus the young are corrupted, and the seed sown soon yields an abundant harvest. . . .

A knowledge *of the cause of social impurity.* Many of the most prominent causes have already been pointed out. The use of ardent spirits is also a prominent cause. Stimulus of every kind tends to inflame the passions. . . . The saloon-keeper is largely responsible for the existence of vile dens of infamy, where impurity reaches its climax and exhausts its vitality in the early deaths of its withered victims. Banish strong drinks, and thousands will be saved from this fearful destiny. Many who are unsuspected, through the use of stimulants, sometimes drugged, have been led on to commit the adulterous act.

The influence of alcohol on the social morals of our people can not easily be overestimated. A drunken person has neither conscience nor reason left; but the flame of passion burns all the brighter in the drunkard's heart when thus kindled by alcohol. The saloon is the strong ally of the brothel, and constantly feeds it. It corrupts husbands, and degrades the wife and children and forces them into the ranks of the vicious. The sin of intemperance sooner or later leads to social impurity. If the saloons were blotted out of existence to-day, a long stride would be taken toward the rescue of the masses from social ruin. . . .

Another great cause was found by Dr. Sanger to be *"destitution."* He found that five hundred and twenty-five out of two thousand women had reached their low condition by destitution. For this, in many cases, personal friends are to blame; but society is more to blame for its wicked injustice in refusing to pay women for their labor. Girls, doing the same work performed by boys, usually receive about half as much pay. This is a burning shame. Women's work is not as well paid for as men's, yet they are the weaker sex. Even civil law discriminates in favor of men. . . .

Ministers of the Gospel should point out the causes of this social depravity [lust], so wide-spread. Physicians should point out the consequences of social sin. Legislators should enact laws more fully protecting and fostering social morality. Benevolent societies should rescue the poor and unprotected from ruin. . . .

The world demands a religion that purifies man's moral nature, his whole being. Christ's religion does just this by "renewing us in righteousness," justification and regeneration, "and true holiness," sanctification. Many of the grossest of men and women have been converted, and then wholly sanctified, and freed from all desire to commit social sin. The desire for strong drink is utterly taken away by the grace of God. Anger, pride, the love of the world, are removed from the heart. Man's moral being may be healed of all its maladies by the blood of Christ.

Chapter 19:
Document Set 2 References

1. Jacob Riis Appeals to Christian Conscience, 1890
   Jacob Riis, *How the Other Half Lives,* 1890 (New York: Sagamore Press, rep. 1957), p. 4.

2. Jesus as a Model for Personal Conduct, 1898
   Charles M. Sheldon, "What Would Jesus Do?," *In His Steps* (Chicago: Advance Publishing Company, 1898), pp. 272–276.

3. Walter Rauschenbusch Outlines the New Social Gospel, 1907
   Walter Rauschenbusch, *Christianity and the Social Crisis* (New York: Macmillan, 1907), pp. 367–372.

4. Robert Treat Paine, Jr., Reports the Results of Private Philanthropy, 1881
   Robert T. Paine, Jr., "Homes for the People," *Journal of Social Science,* 15(1882).

5. Jane Addams Defines the Social-Settlement Movement, 1892
   Jane Addams, *Twenty Years at Hull House,* 1910 (New York: Macmillan, rep. 1949), pp. 123–127.

6. Reverend J. J. Fleharty Explains the Moral Purity Crusade, 1875
   J. J. Fleharty, *Social Impurity: The Sin of the World in All Ages, the Causes and the Remedy* (Cincinnati: Privately published, 1875), pp. 5, 41, 102, 116–117, 139–141, 161–162, 166, 168–169.

CHAPTER 20

The Cult of Domesticity and the Reaction: True Women and New Women

Women in Victorian America lived within an atmosphere of emotional, economic, political, and intellectual confinement, limited to roles and activities consistent with the concept of true womanhood. The dominant value structure of the era dictated that the female sphere be bounded by the family, home, and church, where women could fulfill a loving and nurturing function. As the following documents suggest, the social sanctions that enforced this code were strong, but not accepted by all women as binding. Your analysis of these materials should focus on the origins of the cult of domesticity, its impact on women's self-image, and the personal responses of those who questioned its validity.

An excellent illustration of the code's crippling influence on the human spirit may be found in the memoir of journalist Jane Grey Swisshelm, whose words document the suppression of her own creative energies. Note the relationship between the doctrine of "separate spheres" and the development of female self-image, as revealed in Swisshelm's regrets over paths not taken.

The deeper roots of prevailing assumptions about woman's sphere are evident in several assertions by male commentators, including social reformer Orestes Brownson, Senator George Vest of Missouri, and former president Grover Cleveland. All present the prevailing masculine viewpoint on the place of women in Victorian society. As you examine their arguments, be alert to common assumptions and shared concerns. Try to determine what motivated their interest in the maintenance of separate spheres. Connect their ideas with the Supreme Court's reasoning in its denial of Myra Bradwell's appeal of an Illinois Supreme Court decision barring her from the practice of law. Consider popular beliefs about women's nature in your effort to account for the acceptance of Victorian standards.

An important clue to traditional assumptions can be found in the ideas of Laura Curtis Bullard, Charlotte Perkins Gilman, and Grover Cleveland. As you review their remarks, look for an explanation of increasing male uncertainty in the late nineteenth century. Compare the views of Bullard and Gilman with the half-hidden assumptions in Jane Swisshelm's personal recollection of movement from sphere to sphere. In the final analysis, these documents should increase your awareness of a growing gender conflict that had surfaced by the early twentieth century.

The documents reflect one of the most important social assumptions made by nineteenth-century Americans. Relate your conclusions to the textbook discussion of the transition from Victorian lady to new woman.

Questions for Analysis

1. Define the concept of "true womanhood" in nineteenth-century terms. How do the documents reflect nineteenth-century beliefs concerning the place of women in society? Compare these assumptions with your textbook's description of the "new woman." How do the documents illustrate the basic components of this concept?

2. What was the intellectual, social, cultural, and economic basis of the cult of domesticity? Who established the outlines for the accepted social assumptions of Victorian America? Why were males so involved in the development of an intellectual rationale for these values? How do the documents clarify the motivations, fears, and concerns of those who defended the social-sexual status quo?

3. How were the cultural ideals of the Victorian era based on feminine values? What do the documents imply about women's power as social influences? What do the documents reveal about the avenues through which women were assumed to exert their influence? Evaluate the importance of women's influence on values and public policy in the nineteenth century.

4. What do the documents tell us about the significance of the cult of domesticity in shaping the lives, goals, and aspirations of women? How would you account for the acceptance of the prevailing social assumptions by so many women? Use evidence drawn from the documents to support your argument.

5. What solution did rebellious women offer to the apparently underdeveloped self-awareness of American women? Do the documents shed light on the answer provided by female activists? What was the typical male response to feminist arguments? In what way did the words of Vest and Cleveland reflect underlying currents of social change?

1. Jane Swisshelm's Personal Crisis, ca. 1850

During all my girlhood I saw no pictures, no art gallery, no studio, but had learned to feel great contempt for my own efforts at picture-making. A traveling artist stopped in Wilkinsburg and painted some portraits; we visited his studio, and a new world opened to me. . . .

Bard, the wagon-maker, made me a stretcher, and with a yard of unbleached muslin, some tacks and white lead, I made a canvas. In the shop were white lead, lampblack, king's yellow and red lead, with oil and turpentine. I watched Bard mix paints, and concluded I wanted brown. Years before, I heard of brown umber, so I got umber and some brushes and began my husband's portrait. . . . The figure was correct, and the position in the chair, and, from the moment I began it, I felt I had found my vocation. . . . I forgot God, and did not know it; forgot philosophy, and did not care to remember it; but alas! I forgot to get Bard's dinner, and, although I forgot to be hungry, I had no reason to suppose he did. He would willingly have gone hungry, rather than give any one trouble; but I had neglected a duty. Not only once did I do this, but again and again, the fire went out or the bread ran over in the pans, while I painted and dreamed.

My conscience began to trouble me. Housekeeping was "woman's sphere," although I had never then heard the words, for no woman had gotten out of it to be hounded back; but I knew my place and scorned to leave it. I tried to think I could paint without neglect of duty. It did not occur to me that painting was a duty for a married woman! Had the passion seized me before marriage, no other love could have come between me and art; but I felt that it was too late, as my life was already devoted to another object—housekeeping. . . .

I put away my brushes; resolutely crucified my divine gift, and while it hung writhing on the cross, spent my best years and powers cooking cabbage. . . .

Where are the pictures I should have given to the world? . . . Is that Christianity which has so long said to one-half of the race, "Thou shalt not use any gift of the Creator, if it be not approved by thy brother; and unto man, not God, thou shalt ever turn and ask, 'What wilt thou have me to do?'"

It was not only my art-love which must be sacrificed to my duty as a wife, but my literary tastes must go with it. "The husband is the head of the wife." To be head, he must be superior. An uncultivated husband could not be the superior of a cultivated wife. I knew from the first that his education had been limited, but thought the defect would be easily remedied as he had good abilities, but I discovered he had no love for books. His spiritual guides derided human learning and depended on inspiration. My knowledge stood in the way of my salvation, and I must be that odious thing—a superior wife—or stop my progress, for to be and appear were the same thing. I must be the mate of the man I had chosen; and if he would not come to my level, I must go to his. So I gave up study, and for years did not read one page in any book save the Bible.

2. Orestes A. Brownson Defines Woman's Sphere, 1873

Woman was created to be a wife and a mother; that is her destiny. To that destiny all her instincts point, and for it nature has specially qualified her. Her proper sphere is home, and her proper function is the care of the household, to manage a family, to take care of children, and attend to their early training.

For this she is endowed with patience, endurance, passive courage, quick sensibilities, a sympathetic nature, and great executive and administrative ability. She was born to be a queen in her own household, and to make home cheerful, bright, and happy.

We do not believe women, unless we acknowledge individual exceptions, are fit to have their own head. The most degraded of the savage tribes are those in which women rule, and descent is reckoned from the mother instead of the father. Revelation asserts, and universal experience proves that the man is the head of the woman, and that the woman is for the man, not the man for the woman; and his greatest error, as well as the primal curse of society is that he abdicates his headship, and allows himself to be governed, we might almost say, deprived of his reason, by woman. It was through the seductions of the woman, herself seduced by the serpent, that man fell, and brought sin and all our woe into the world. She has all the qualities that fit her to be a help-meet of man, to be the mother of his children, to be their nurse, their early instructress, their guardian, their life-long friend; to be his companion, his comforter, his consoler in sorrow, his friend in trouble, his ministering angel in sickness; but as an independent existence, free to follow her own fancies and vague longings, her own ambition and natural love of power, without masculine direction or control, she is out of her element, and a social anomaly, sometimes a hideous monster, which men seldom are, excepting through a woman's influence. This is no excuse for men, but it proves that women need a head, and the restraint of father, husband, or the priest of God.

3. Senator George Vest Endorses the Protection of Women in Their Sphere, 1887

I pity the man who can consider any question affecting the influence of woman with the cold, dry logic of business. What man can, without aversion, turn from the blessed memory of that dear old grandmother, or the gentle words and caressing hand of that dear blessed mother gone to the unknown world, to face in its stead the idea of a female justice of the peace or township constable? For my part I want when I go to my home—when I turn from the arena where man contends with man for what we call the prizes of this paltry world—I want to go back, not to be received in the masculine embrace of some female ward politician, but to the earnest, loving look and touch of a true woman. I want to go back to the jurisdiction of the wife, the mother; and instead of a lecture upon finance or the tariff, or upon the construction of the Constitution, I want those blessed, loving details of domestic life and domestic love.

. . . I speak now respecting women as a sex. I believe that they are better than men, but I do not believe they are adapted to the political work of this world. I do not believe that the Great Intelligence ever intended them to invade the sphere of work given to men, tearing down and destroying all the best influences for which God has intended them. . . .

Women are essentially emotional. It is no disparagement to them they are so. It is no more insulting to say that women are emotional than to say that they are delicately constructed physically and unfitted to become soldiers or workmen under the sterner, harder pursuits of life.

What we want in this country is to avoid emotional suffrage, and what we need is to put more logic into public affairs and less feeling. There are spheres in which feeling should be paramount. There are kingdoms in which the heart should reign supreme. That kingdom belongs to woman. The realm of sentiment, the realm of love, the realm of the gentler and the holier and kindlier attributes that make the name of wife, mother, and sister next to that of God himself.

I would not, and I say it deliberately, degrade woman by giving her the right of suffrage. I mean the word in its full signification, because I believe that woman as she is to-day, the queen of the home and of hearts, is above the political collisions of this world, and should always be kept above them. . . .

It is said that the suffrage is to be given to enlarge the sphere of woman's influence. Mr. President, it would destroy her influence. It would take her down from that pedestal where she is today, influencing as a mother the minds of her offspring, influencing by her gentle and kindly caress the action of her husband toward the good and pure.

4. The Supreme Court Reinforces the Cult of Domesticity, 1873

The claim that, under the fourteenth amendment of the Constitution, which declares that no State shall make or enforce any law which shall abridge the privileges and immunities of citizens of the United States, the statute law of Illinois, or the common law prevailing in that State, can no longer be set up as a barrier against the right of females to pursue any lawful employment for a livelihood (the practice of law included), assumes that it is one of the privileges and immunities of women as citizens to engage in any and every profession, occupation, or employment in civil life.

It certainly cannot be affirmed, as an historical fact, that this has ever been established as one of the fundamental privileges and immunities of the sex. On the contrary, the civil law, as well as nature herself, has always recognized a wide difference in the respective spheres and destinies of man and woman. Man is, or should be, woman's protector and defender. The natural and proper timidity and delicacy which belongs to the female sex evidently unfits it for many of the occupations of civil life. The constitution of the family organization, which is founded in the divine ordinance, as well as in the nature of things, indicates the domestic sphere as that which properly belongs to the domain and functions of womanhood. The harmony, not to say identity, of interests and views which belong, or should belong, to the family institution is repugnant to the idea of a woman adopting a distinct and independent career from that of her husband. So firmly fixed was this sentiment in the founders of the common law that it became a maxim of that system of jurisprudence that a woman had no legal existence separate from her husband, who was regarded as her head and representative in the social state; and, notwithstanding some recent modifications of this civil status, many of the special rules of law flowing from and dependent upon this cardinal principle still exist in full force in most States. One of these is, that a married woman is incapable, without her husband's consent, of making contracts which shall be binding on her or him. This very incapacity was one circumstance which the Supreme Court of Illinois deemed important in rendering a married woman incompetent fully to perform the duties and trusts that belong to the office of an attorney and counsellor.

It is true that many women are unmarried and not affected by any of the duties, complications, and incapacities arising out of the married state, but these are exceptions to the general rule. The paramount destiny and mission of woman are to fulfill the noble and benign offices of wife and mother. This is the law of the Creator. And the rules of civil society must be adapted to the general constitution of things, and cannot be based upon exceptional cases.

5. Laura Curtis Bullard on the Enslavement of Women, 1870

One of the saddest spectacles in our present social condition of man as master, and woman as slave, is the unconsciousness of the majority of women of their humiliating position; their indifference, so long as they themselves are comfortable, to the sufferings of others; their horror of those among them who, stung by a sense of their degradation, dare to demand freedom for themselves and for their class. . . .

To this day, the most civilized nations of the world believe as firmly as did the early Semitic races, in the barbaric ages, that woman was made for man. The advance of civilization has changed her position somewhat. She is less the drudge, and more the plaything, or the companion of man. But it has never yet been acknowledged by any but a few of the noblest of men that she was created by God an independent being, with individual duties and individual rights, and no more made merely as a companion for man than was man made merely for a companion to woman.

Men and women were created for each other, but not alone for each other. Upon both, their Maker has imposed the duty of individual development, and it is only because their mutual companionship and association is necessary for this great end, that it can be truly said that they were made for each other. This great truth has been only half understood; and men have taught, and women have accepted, the theory that man is the central figure in creation, and woman simply an accessory. In consequence of this error men and women have suffered alike. The degradation of one-half the human race has not left the other half unharmed. . . .

The pettiness of women, and the distortion of their characters, which is produced by the confinement to one limited circle which the pressure of public opinion forces upon them, must have its effects, not only upon themselves, but on their children, their husbands, their brothers—in short, upon all the men with whom they are associated.

In the interests of the race it is most important that women should be roused to a sense of their subject condition, and to the humiliation which it involves. They should no longer accept the ideal of womanly character which society offers them, but rise to the conception of the free and independent being that God intended a true woman to be. They should no longer tamely submit to the bondage in which custom and education have for ages held them, but break off the shackles which bind them. They should demand a freedom of thought and a freedom of action equal to that which man demands for himself, and which God designed as the true means for the development of both sexes.

The enfranchisement of woman is the germ from which shall spring the reorganization of society.

6. Charlotte Perkins Gilman Indicts the American Home, 1903

We have made great progress in the sense of justice and fair play; yet we are still greatly lacking in it. What is the contribution of domestic ethics to this mighty virtue? In the home is neither freedom nor equality. There is ownership throughout; the dominant father, the more or less subservient mother, the utterly dependent child; and sometimes that still lower grade—the servant. Love is possible, love deep and reciprocal; loyalty is possible; gratitude is possible; kindness, to ruinous favouritism, is possible; unkindness, to all conspiracy, hate, and rebellion is possible; justice is not possible.

Justice was born outside the home and a long way from it; and it has never even been adopted there. . . .

The home, in its arbitrary position of arrested development, does not properly fulfill its own essential functions—much less promote the social ones. Among the splendid activities of our age it lingers on, inert and blind, like a clam in a horse-race.

It hinders, by keeping woman a social idiot, by keeping the modern child under the tutelage of the primeval mother, by keeping the social conscience of the man crippled and stultified in the clinging grip of the domestic conscience of the woman. It hinders by its enormous expense; making the physical details of daily life a heavy burden to mankind; whereas, in our stage of civilisation, they should have been long since reduced to a minor incident.

7. Grover Cleveland's Defense of True Womanhood, 1905

Woman's Clubs Not Only Harmful, But a Menace

I am persuaded that without exaggeration of statement we may assume that there are woman's clubs whose objects and intents are not only harmful, but harmful in a way that directly menaces the integrity of our homes and the benign disposition and character of our wifehood and motherhood. . . . I believe that it should be boldly declared that the best and safest club for a woman to patronize is her home. American wives and American mothers, as surely as "the hand that rocks the cradle is the hand that rules the world," have, through their nurture of children and their influence over men, the destinies of our Nation in their keeping to a greater extent than any other single agency. It is surely not soft-hearted sentimentalism which insists that, in a country where the people rule, a decisive share in securing the perpetuity of its institutions falls upon the mothers who devote themselves to teaching their children who are to become rulers, lessons of morality and patriotism and disinterested citizenship. Such thoughts suggest how supremely great is the stake of our country in woman's unperverted steadfastness, and enjoin the necessity of its protection against all risks and all temptations.

The Real Path of True Womanhood

I am in favor of according to women the utmost social enjoyment; and I am profoundly thankful that this, in generous and sufficient measure, is within their reach without encountering the temptations or untoward influences so often found in the surroundings of woman's clubs.

For the sake of our country, for the sake of our homes, and for the sake of our children, I would have our wives and mothers loving and devoted, though all others may be sordid and heedless; I would have them disinterested and trusting, though all others may be selfish and cunning; I would have them happy and contented in following the Divinely appointed path of true womanhood, though all others may grope in the darkness of their own devices.

Chapter 20:
Document Set 1 References

1. Jane Swisshelm's Personal Crisis, ca. 1850
   Jane Swisshelm, *Half a Century* (Chicago: Jansen, McClurg & Co., 1880), pp. 47–50.

2. Orestes A. Brownson Defines Woman's Sphere, 1873
   Orestes A. Brownson, "The Woman Question. Article II [a review of Horace Bushnell, *Woman's Suffrage: The Reform Against Nature* (New York: 1869), from *Brownson's Quarterly Review,* October 1873]," in Henry F. Brownson, ed., *The Works of Orestes A. Brownson,* Vol. XVIII (Detroit, 1885), p. 403.

3. Senator George Vest Endorses the Protection of Women in Their Sphere, 1887
   Congressional Record, 49th Cong., 2nd Sess., January 25, 1887, p. 986.

4. The Supreme Court Reinforces the Cult of Domesticity, 1873
   Bradwell v. State of Illinois, 83 U.S. 130 (1873).

5. Laura Curtis Bullard on the Enslavement of Women, 1870
   The Revolution, October 6, 1870.

6. Charlotte Perkins Gilman Indicts the American Home, 1903
   Charlotte Perkins Gilman, *The Home, Its Work and Influence* (New York: McClure, Phillips, 1903), pp. 171–172, 315.

7. Grover Cleveland's Defense of True Womanhood, 1905
   Grover Cleveland, "Woman's Mission and Woman's Clubs" *Ladies Home Journal,* Vol. 22 (May 1905).

CHAPTER 20

The Trend Toward a Consumer Society: Advertising and Popular Taste

The late Victorian years witnessed dramatic social and economic changes that led to an altered class structure and new patterns of consumption as Americans spent the wealth created by a modern industrial economy. Reacting to this opportunity, business developed creative distribution systems to exploit markets as yet untouched. Among the ideas introduced were large-scale, mail-order sales; the proliferation of department stores; and the acceleration of advertising to reach a new mass market. The marketing innovations of the late nineteenth and early twentieth centuries played an important role in the creation of modern mass culture. The following documents record the transition, as reflected in the advertising appeals made to American consumers whose buying habits changed drastically in reaction to the new social ethic of consumption. Your analysis of advertising should focus on the target audiences and the approaches adopted by advertisers bent on creating a market. Be aware of advertisers' perceptions of consumer fantasies as an important factor in shaping marketing strategies.

The first document contains census figures on annual earnings by industry and occupation, 1890–1926. Study these statistics for evidence on income levels in relation to consumption potential. As you review the documents that follow, try to determine which social and economic classes were targeted by most advertisers.

The advertising copy and illustrations included in this document set emphasize household items, clothing, medical remedies, and luxury goods. Consider the products stressed as evidence of evolving tastes and newly available consumer goods. What do they reveal about changing American lifestyles, home lives, and patterns of leisure? Note also the variation in appeals made to male and female consumers.

Another important index to the social significance of advertising is the forum in which messages are delivered. The documents include materials drawn from middle-class magazines, trading cards, and the 1897 Sears catalog. Observe how different messages are projected toward different audiences. Determine what the documents reveal about the perceived needs, interests, and resources of the targeted group.

Finally, concentrate on the style, appearance, and decorative character of the products displayed. Evaluate these features as indications of the social and economic ethic of late-nineteenth-century America. Relate the ornate decorative styles to the rise of conspicuous consumption in the late nineteenth century. As you consider the social meaning of the new spending, reflect on the displacement of deferred gratification by a more modern consumer ethic.

Questions for Analysis

1. To which sexes were particular advertisements addressed? How did appeals to women differ from those intended for men? What assumptions did advertisers make concerning the needs, interests, preferences, and roles of men and women?

2. Examine the consumer items displayed in the advertisements, paying particular attention to the uses, purposes, and cost of the products. What do the documents reveal about changes in American class structure, lifestyles, and the social aspirations of consumers? Compare the Sears ads with those that appeared in middle-class magazines or as trading cards. How does the evidence reflect the values of particular consumer groups?

3. In what way do the documents reflect changes in American business methods between 1880 and 1917? On what basis did Sears market its goods? What advantages did the Sears system offer consumers? What was the significance of Sears's success in this period?

4. How did advertisers appeal to consumers with both direct and indirect messages? Was advertising based on hope, fear, acquisitiveness, or all of these?

What traditional values and habits were called into question by the new consumer ethic of the twentieth century?

5. As you review the income data, consider the relationship between consumer resources and prevailing price levels. How did the business and marketing systems resolve the problem implied by the data? What evidence do the documents offer that links early-twentieth-century consumer society with modern marketing methods and buyer behavior?

Group 1. Personal Income, 1890–1926

Year	All industries – Including farm labor	All industries – Excluding farm labor	Wage earners, manufacturing	Wage earners, steam railroads	Street railways	Telephones	Telegraphs	Gas and electricity	Clerical workers, mfg. and steam railroads	Bituminous coal mining	Farm labor	Federal employees	Postal employees	Public school teachers	Ministers
	603	604	605	606	607	608	609	610	611	612	613	614	615	616	617
1926	$1,376	$1,473	$1,309	$1,613	$1,566	$1,117	$1,215	$1,477	$2,310	$1,247	$593	$1,809	$2,128	$1,277	$1,826
1925	1,336	1,434	1,280	1,597	1,565	1,108	1,161	1,448	2,239	1,141	587	1,776	2,051	1,263	1,769
1924	1,303	1,402	1,240	1,570	1,544	1,104	1,150	1,436	2,196	1,120	574	1,708	1,934	1,247	1,678
1923	1,299	1,393	1,254	1,585	1,493	1,069	1,133	1,355	2,126	1,246	572	1,658	1,870	1,224	1,620
1922	1,201	1,305	1,149	1,591	1,436	1,064	1,110	1,343	2,067	954	508	1,625	1,844	1,188	1,622
1921	1,233	1,349	1,180	1,632	1,539	1,038	1,159	1,364	2,134	1,013	522	1,593	1,870	1,082	1,556
1920	1,407	1,489	1,358	1,817	1,608	980	1,145	1,432	2,160	1,386	810	1,648	1,844	936	1,428
1919	1,201	1,272	1,158	1,509	1,387	844	967	1,291	1,914	1,097	706	1,520	1,618	810	1,238
1918	1,047	1,115	980	1,424	1,111	690	831	1,092	1,697	1,211	604	1,380	1,339	689	1,186
1917	830	887	774	989	872	616	769	853	1,477	976	481	1,295	1,207	648	1,069
1916	708	765	651	867	798	567	806	679	1,359	750	388	1,211	1,175	605	1,017
1915	633	687	568	815	748	529	792	644	1,267	589	355	1,152	1,162	578	984
1914	627	682	580	795	737	476	742	651	1,257	543	351	1,140	1,157	564	938
1913	621	675	578	760	704	438	717	661	1,236	631	360	1,136	1,124	547	899
1912	592	646	550	721	674	438	669	641	1,209	614	348	1,128	1,091	529	879
1911	575	629	537	705	685	419	670	648	1,213	553	338	1,116	1,071	509	856
1910	574	630	558	677	681	417	649	622	1,156	558	336	1,108	1,049	492	802
1909	543	594	518	644	671	430	622	618	1,136	524	328	1,106	1,021	476	831
1908	516	563	475	667	650	420	639	595	1,111	487	324	1,102	987	455	833
1907	542	595	522	661	658	412	635	623	1,091	580	319	1,094	944	431	831
1906	520	569	506	607	662	412	592	581	1,074	537	315	1,084	921	409	773
1905	503	554	494	589	646	401	581	543	1,076	500	302	1,072	935	392	759
1904	490	540	477	600	610	392	601	556	1,056	470	290	1,066	931	377	759
1903	489	543	486	593	582	397	573	....	1,037	522	277	1,067	928	358	761
1902	467	519	473	562	576	408	544	....	1,025	490	264	1,061	934	346	737
1901	454	508	456	549	601	....	....	615	1,009	465	255	1,047	936	337	730
1900	438	490	435	548	604	....	....	620	1,011	438	247	1,033	925	328	731
1899	428	480	426	543	591	....	....	612	1,004	379	239	1,017	924	318	722
1898	417	468	412	542	558	....	....	698	1,010	316	228	1,025	939	306	739
1897	411	462	408	543	552	....	....	703	970	270	224	1,057	950	298	750
1896	411	462	406	544	531	....	....	665	954	282	220	1,084	944	294	764
1895	415	468	416	546	509	....	....	640	941	307	216	1,104	935	289	787
1894	400	448	386	546	508	....	....	670	928	292	214	1,110	919	283	824
1893	430	480	420	563	526	....	....	627	923	383	232	1,101	902	276	809
1892	445	495	446	563	535	....	....	625	885	393	238	1,096	899	270	793
1891	438	487	442	554	529	....	....	587	882	377	236	....	894	264	786
1890	438	486	439	560	557	....	....	687	848	406	233	....	878	256	794

Group 2. The Built Environment, 1885–1898

A. Bronner and Company, Clothiers, New York, 1885

B. Palliser's *American Architecture*

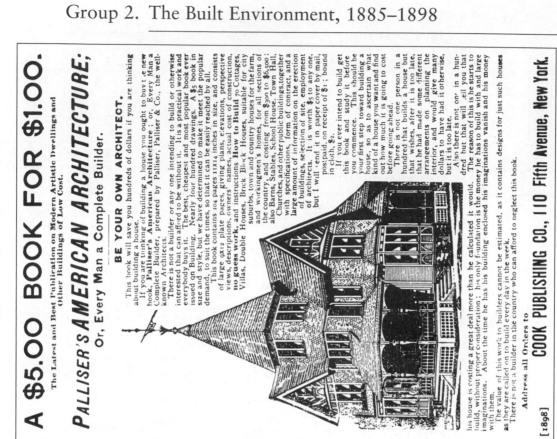

Group 3. Inside the Home, 1885

A. The Conqueror Wringer, 1885

B. American Machine Company Irons and Fluting Machines, 1885

Group 4. Female Concerns, 1880–1902

A. "Fibre Chamois," 1896

For EASTER GOWNS that bouffant and stylish effect in sleeves and skirt will be secured by the use of FIBRE CHAMOIS INTERLINING. Nothing else so fully meets the demands of lightness, keeping the garment in its original shape and style, and in giving body to the thinnest material. ❦ ❦

REDFERN Uses It — LILLIAN RUSSELL Wears It — JENNESS MILLER Recommends It.

Three weights: No. 10, Light; No. 20, Medium; No. 30, Heavy.   Width 64 inches.

Beware of worthless imitations.   See that what you buy is stamped   **Fibre Chamois.**   To be had at the Lining Counter of all Dry Goods Stores.

C. Dr. Kilmer's Female Remedy, 1885

B. Dr. and Madame Strong's Corsets, 1885

D. A "Positive Cure," 1880

LYDIA E. PINKHAM'S
VEGETABLE COMPOUND
IS A POSITIVE CURE
For all those painful Complaints and Weaknesses so common to our best female population.

It will cure entirely the worst form of Female Complaints, all Ovarian troubles, Inflammation, Ulceration, Falling and Displacements of the Womb and the consequent Spinal Weakness, and is particularly adapted to the Change of Life.

It will dissolve and expel Tumors from the uterus in an early stage of development. The tendency to cancerous humors there is checked very speedily by its use. It removes faintness, flatulency, destroys all craving for stimulants, and relieves weakness of the stomach. It cures Bloating, Headaches, Nervous Prostration, General Debility, Sleeplessness, Depression and Indigestion.

That feeling of bearing down, causing pain, weight and backache is always permanently cured by its use.

It will at all times and under all circumstances act in harmony with the laws that govern the female system. For the cure of Kidney Complaints of either sex, this Compound is unsurpassed.

LYDIA E. PINKHAM'S VEGETABLE COMPOUND is prepared at 283 and 235 Western Avenue, Lynn, Mass. Price, $1.00. Six bottles for $5.00. Sent by mail in the form of pills, also in the form of lozenges, on receipt of price, $1 00 per box, for either. Send for pamphlet. All letters of inquiry promptly answered. Address as above.

No family should be without *LYDIA E. PINKHAM'S LIVER PILLS.* They cure constipation, biliousness, and torpidity of the liver, 25¢. per box

Sold by all Druggists.

COMPLIMENTS OF

Group 5. Outside Interests, 1886–1907

**A. Advertisement for the Pierce Arrow
   Automobile, 1907**

B. Cadillac Advertisement, 1903

The Cadillac Runabout

The Cadillac

The Automobile that Solves the Problem

Until the CADILLAC was made, all automobile construction was more or less experimental—no one had made an entirely satisfactory motor vehicle.   This machine is made on a new system developed from the experiences of all previous makers: the faults and weaknesses of the old methods have been avoided and a new ideal of motor travel developed that gives a perfect vehicle for comfort, speed, absolute safety, greatest durability, simplicity of operation, wide radius of travel, and reliability under all conditions of roads.   There is no other automobile that can be compared to the Cadillac in any particular of speed, stability, ease of operation or convenience of use.   You should not buy before examining this wonderful new machine.   Price f.o.b. at factory, $750.

The new tonneau attachment, at an extra cost of $100, gives a combination of light carriage for city streets and substantial touring car for country roads—practically two motor vehicles in one, with a seating capacity of two or four, as required—a very graceful effect in either use.   Write for new illustrated booklet.

CADILLAC AUTOMOBILE COMPANY, Detroit, Mich.

With detachable tonneau

C. Eastman Kodak Co., 1898

Holidays are Kodak Days.

Folding
Pocket
Kodak
$10.

Folding
Pocket
Kodak
$10.

Indoors and Out the holiday season is a delightful one for amateur photography, making the Kodak an especially welcome **Christmas Gift.**

The Christmas tree, groups of friends at the dinner table or at the card party are all fascinating subjects for the flash-light and the winter days give ample opportunity for indoor portraiture, while outside, the barren, wind swept fields, or the trees covered with their feathery mantles of white offer unlimited possibilities to the amateur artist.

Flash-light pictures and daylight pictures are easy with a Kodak.

KODAKS $5.00 to $35.00.

EASTMAN KODAK CO.

Rochester, N. Y

Catalogues free at the dealers or by mail.

[1898]

D. Western Wheel Works, New York, 1886

Group 6. The Sears Wish Book, 1897

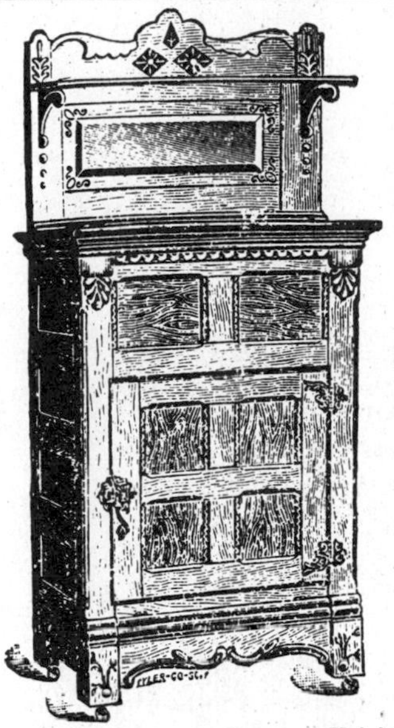

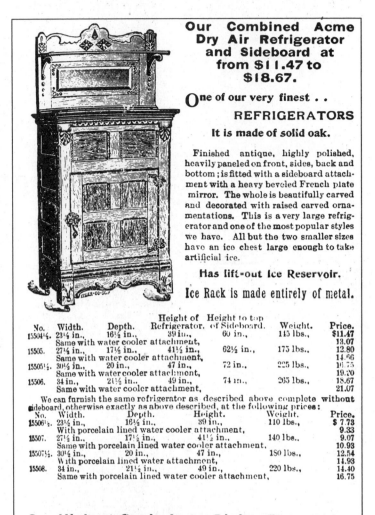

Our Combined Acme Dry Air Refrigerator and Sideboard at from $11.47 to $18.67.

One of our very finest . .

REFRIGERATORS

It is made of solid oak.

Finished antique, highly polished, heavily paneled on front, sides, back and bottom; is fitted with a sideboard attachment with a heavy beveled French plate mirror. The whole is beautifully carved and decorated with raised carved ornamentations. This is a very large refrigerator and one of the most popular styles we have. All but the two smaller sizes have an ice chest large enough to take artificial ice.

Has lift-out Ice Reservoir.

Ice Rack is made entirely of metal.

No.	Width.	Depth.	Height of Refrigerator.	Height to top of Sideboard.	Weight.	Price.
15504½.	23½ in.,	16½ in.,	39 in.,	60 in.,	145 lbs.,	$11.47
	Same with water cooler attachment,					13.07
15505.	27½ in.,	17½ in.,	41½ in.,	62½ in.,	175 lbs.,	12.80
	Same with water cooler attachment,					14.66
15505½.	30½ in.,	20 in.,	47 in.,	72 in.,	225 lbs.,	16.75
	Same with water cooler attachment,					19.20
15506.	34 in.,	20½ in.,	49 in.,	74 in.,	265 lbs.,	18.67
	Same with water cooler attachment,					21.07

We can furnish the same refrigerator as described above complete without sideboard, otherwise exactly as above described, at the following prices:

No.	Width.	Depth.	Height.	Weight.	Price.
15506½.	23½ in.,	16½ in.,	39 in.,	110 lbs.,	$ 7.73
	With porcelain lined water cooler attachment,				9.33
15507.	27½ in.,	17½ in.,	41½ in.,	140 lbs.,	9.07
	Same with porcelain lined water cooler attachment,				10.93
15507½.	30½ in.,	20 in.,	47 in.,	180 lbs.,	12.54
	With porcelain lined water attachment,				14.93
15508.	34 in.,	21½ in.,	49 in.,	220 lbs.,	14.40
	Same with porcelain lined water cooler attachment,				16.75

Our Highest Grade Acme Dining Room Sideboard and Refrigerator Combined, $50.00.

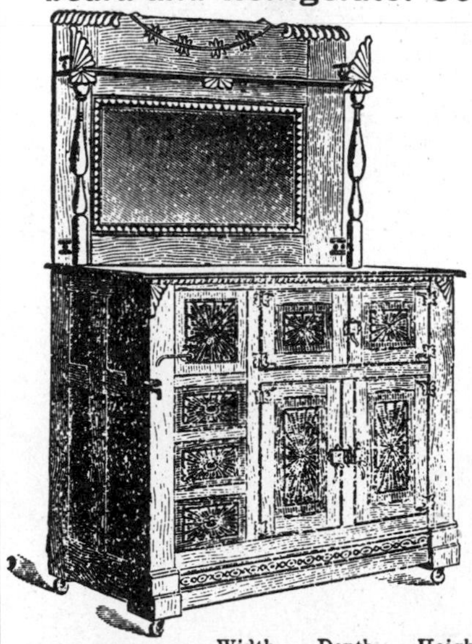

During the past several years our customers have asked us to make a combined sideboard and refrigerator suitable for a well furnished dining room, consequently we have designed and made one, as shown by the illustration. They are a combination of sideboard, refrigerator and water cooler. They are made of selected kiln dried quarter sawed oak, rubbed and polished. The refrigerator is entirely separated from the tank for ice water, and the drawers behind have a double partition lined with non-conducting material. It contains all the improvements of our celebrated Acme, and is one of the handsomest pieces of dining room furniture furnished in the country. It is not only highly polished but is heavily paneled, beautifully carved, decorated and ornamented. It is fitted with a very large beveled edge French plate mirror, trimmed throughout with heavy solid bronze trimmings, old copper finish, and is the handsomest thing in the way of a refrigerator ever produced.

	Width.	Depth.	Height.	Shipping Weight.	Price.
No. 15509¼.......	56 inches.	26 inches.	27 inches.	500 lbs.	$50.00

Please observe that our price of **$50.00** is the price for this refrigerator when shipped by freight C. O. D., subject to examination on receipt of a sufficient deposit to cover freight charges both ways. If you will send as your order with enough to cover freight charges both ways we will send the refrigerator to you by freight C. O. D. subject to examination. You can examine it at your freight depot, and if found perfectly satisfactory and exactly as represented, pay the freight agent the balance and freight charges. Three per cent. discount allowed if cash in full accompanies your order. If you send the full amount of cash with your order you may deduct 3 per cent., when **$48.50** pays for the refrigerator.

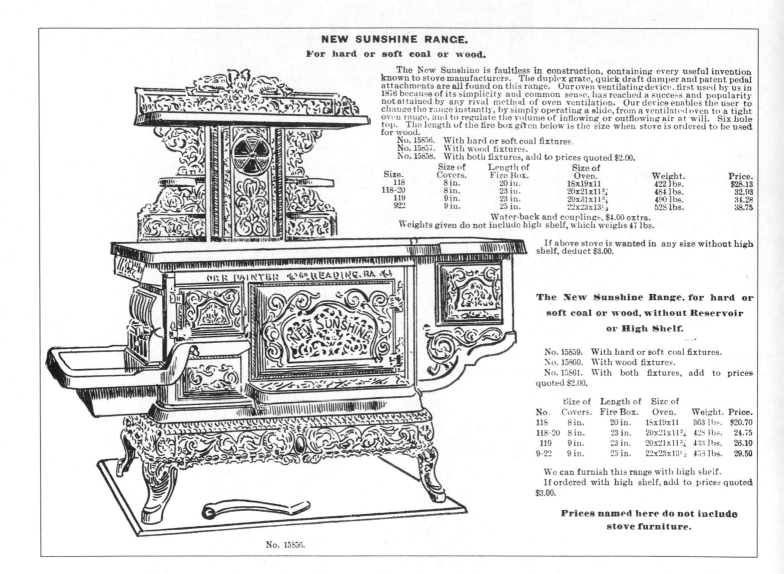

NEW SUNSHINE RANGE.
For hard or soft coal or wood.

The New Sunshine is faultless in construction, containing every useful invention known to stove manufacturers. The duplex grate, quick draft damper and patent pedal attachments are all found on this range. Our oven ventilating device, first used by us in 1876 because of its simplicity and common sense, has reached a success and popularity not attained by any rival method of oven ventilation. Our device enables the user to change the range instantly, by simply operating a slide, from a ventilated oven to a tight oven range, and to regulate the volume of inflowing or outflowing air at will. Six hole top. The length of the fire box given below is the size when stove is ordered to be used for wood.

No. 15856. With hard or soft coal fixtures.
No. 15857. With wood fixtures.
No. 15858. With both fixtures, add to prices quoted $2.00.

Size.	Size of Covers.	Length of Fire Box.	Size of Oven.	Weight.	Price.
118	8 in.	20 in.	18x19x11	422 lbs.	$28.13
118-20	8 in.	23 in.	20x21x11¾	484 lbs.	32.93
119	9 in.	23 in.	20x31x11¾	490 lbs.	34.28
922	9 in.	25 in.	22x23x13½	528 lbs.	38.75

Water-back and couplings, $4.00 extra.
Weights given do not include high shelf, which weighs 47 lbs.

If above stove is wanted in any size without high shelf, deduct $3.00.

The New Sunshine Range, for hard or soft coal or wood, without Reservoir or High Shelf.

No. 15859. With hard or soft coal fixtures.
No. 15860. With wood fixtures.
No. 15861. With both fixtures, add to prices quoted $2.00.

No.	Size of Covers.	Length of Fire Box.	Size of Oven.	Weight.	Price.
118	8 in.	20 in.	18x19x11	363 lbs.	$20.70
118-20	8 in.	23 in.	20x21x11¾	428 lbs.	24.75
119	9 in.	23 in.	20x21x11¾	433 lbs.	26.10
9-22	9 in.	25 in.	22x23x13½	453 lbs.	29.50

We can furnish this range with high shelf.
If ordered with high shelf, add to prices quoted $3.00.

Prices named here do not include stove furniture.

No. 15856.

A $50.00 PARLOR SUIT FOR $33.00.

No. 9505 It is difficult to imagine a more beautiful and artistic suit than the one which we show in the illustration. Our artist has endeavored to draw the different pieces so that you can get an idea of the handsome design. It is one of the richest and most stylish appearing parlor suits made for the season of 1897. It is after a design executed by **expert artists in this line,** and the manufacturers are taking particular pains that the suit shall be not only perfect in detail and handsome in outline, but thoroughly substantial and durable in every respect. It is a suit that **will last a lifetime** and a suit that you will never become tired of. It is made with a **solid oak frame** or a frame made of **curly birch with imitation mahogany finish.** Either wood is decidedly handsome and thoroughly substantial. The frames are beautifully carved after the most stylish pattern, and the suit as a whole has the appearance of one which would retail frequently at from **$75.00** to **$80.00. It consists of 6 pieces,** a large sofa, a large divan, large easy rocker, large arm chair and two parlor chairs. We upholster this suit in five different styles of upholstering. D. E. F. G and H. D is a very fine blocaline crush plush; E is an **elegant silk tapestry;** F a superb Wilton rug; G a choice grade of silk brocatell and H a very handsome and durable satin damask. You have your choice of upholstering. In all grades the patterns are the very latest designs, and in coloring you will have your choice of all the popular shades. We recommend, however, that you leave the matter of coloring in general to our designer, as we make these parlor suits specially to order and will upholster the various pieces in the latest popular shades, all harmonizing perfectly. The weight of the suit when packed very carefully for shipment is 300 lbs. We pack each of these pieces with the utmost care, covering all parts with burlap so that they will reach you in perfect condition. Casters free.

Our special price for above 6 piece Parlor Suit, upholstered in grade D or E..$33.00

Same Suit, upholstered in grade F, our special price 37.00

Same Suit, upholstered in grade G or H, our special price........... 38.00

The demand the past season from professional men such as **clergymen, doctors, lawyers** and the other professions, for something we could guarantee, and sell at a price in keeping with our general rock bottom prices, has induced us to make quite extensive preparations for the coming season. **We have contracted for quite a quantity** of extra fine material for this class of goods, have arranged for special cutters and special tailors, and will be able to furnish these suits in **Styles 8 or 9** as illustrated above made up thoroughly first class, and at less than one half the price charged by local tailors. **Regular sizes will run from 34 to 42 inches** chest measure. Extra sizes sizes can be had at 20 percent. extra. Orders will be accepted the same as for any other suits on receipt of $1.00 as a guarantee of good faith, balance and express charges to be paid at the express office. A discount of 3 per cent. allowed if cash in full accompanies your order. **Sample of cloth free on application.**

No. 4548. Our $18.00 Clerical or Professional Suit, made in either style, single breasted Prince Albert or standing collar clerical, as desired. Made from a very fine quality imported English clay worsted, one of the finest English weaves, elegantly lined, trimmed and finished, and warranted in every respect. **Our Special Price, Style 8 or 9.................$18.00**

No. 4549. Our $22.00 Professional Suit, in either style. These suits are made from the very finest imported black clay worsted, one of the finest English weaves, in weight suitable for year around wear, elegantly lined, trimmed and fully warranted. **Our Special Price, Style 8 or 9. $22.00**

No. 4350. Our $23.00 Broadcloth Professional Suit in either style, just the suit for ministers, physicians and other professional men. Your tailor would charge you $40.00 for such a suit. Made from fine imported smooth finished black broadcloth, elegantly trimmed with the finest material made, and made by the best workmen. Every garment fully warranted. Our facilities for furnishing these suits are second to none, and if you will favor us with an order we will convince you that we can give you such values as can be had from no other concern.

Ladies Spring and Summer Wraps.
Sears, Roebuck and Co. Inc.

24934 $11.00.

24910 $3.98

24913 $4.85

24912 $4.50

24935 $13.50

24933 $11.50

24914 $6.00

24911 $4.12

24936 $14.75

24910 Very Stylish Ladies' Cape, braided all around with soutache braid, lined throughout with fancy lining, satin ribbon, rouching around collar and long streamers in front. Colors, black, blue, green or Havana. Well worth $6.00. Our price only...$3.98

24911 Sicilian Silk, Ladies' Cape, elaborately embroidered with jet. lined throughout with changeable taffeta silk, lace trimming on collar and gros grain satin ribbon around collar and down front.
A very nobby garment for...$4.12

24912 A Neat, Full Sweep Ladies' Cape, of very fine imported black, clay worsted richly beaded and braided with jet and tinsel all around bottom, lace around collar and satin ribbon streamers in front, collar and fronts faced with silk serge. Would be cheap at $8.00.
Our price...$4.50

24913 This is the Exact Copy of a Parisian Cape, made of fancy silk brilliantine, lined throughout with changeable silk, very full sweep, collar trimmed with very fine black lace and satin ribbon. Can not be duplicated for less than $7.50. Our price...$4.85

24914 A Very Nobby Ladies' Cape, made of fine tan broadcloth, entire cape overlaid with straps and trimmed with small pearl buttons, two bows in front and one in back, stitched all around with silk. An exquisite $10.00 cape for...$6.00

24933 Fine Tan Kersey Jacket Tailor Made, fly front, trimmed with fancy pearl buttons, fronts lined with plaid taffeta silk, entire jacket stitched with silk, sleeves and lapels are of the very newest style.
Our price...$11.50

24934 A Very Genteel Double Breasted Reefer Jacket, made of tan imported covert cloth, four white pearl buttons in front and eight on sleeves, lined throughout with fancy figured silk. A real $15.00 jacket for.....$11.00

24935 Imported English Covert Cloth Jacket, in either gray or tan, fly front, coat back, very newest lapels and sleeves, two rows of silk stitching all around, six rows around sleeves, lined throughout with plaid taffeta silk. A very nobby jacket. Our price.......$13.50

24936 Ladies' Tailor Made Jacket, very latest style made of fine Kersey, in black, tan, blue or green lapels; and sleeves are the very newest shape, pointed cuffs, fancy pocket flaps, lined throughout with brocaded silk, stitched all around with silk. Any retailer would ask at least $22.00 for this jacket, we sell it for...$14.75

Chapter 20:
Document Set 2 References

Group 1. Personal Income, 1890–1926
"Average Annual Earnings in All Industries and in Selected Industries and Occupations: 1890 to 1926," *Statistical History of the United States, Colonial Times to the Present* (Stamford: Fairfield Publishers, Inc., 1965), pp. 91–92.

Group 2. The Built Environment, 1885–1898
A. Bronner and Company, Clothiers, New York, 1885
Robert Jay, *The Trade Card in Nineteenth Century America* (Columbia: University of Missouri Press, 1987), p. 79.
B. Palliser's *American Architecture.*
Palliser's *American Architecture,* Edgar R. Jones, *Those Were the Good Old Days: A Happy Look at American Advertising, 1880–1930* (New York: Simon and Schuster, 1959), p. 94.

Group 3. Inside the Home, 1885
A. The Conqueror Wringer, 1885
Jay, p. 89.
B. American Machine Company Irons and Fluting Machines, 1885
Jay, p. 89.

Group 4. Female Concerns, 1880–1902
A. "Fibre Chamois," 1896
Jones, p. 88.

B. Dr. and Madame Strong's Corsets, 1885
Jay, p. 86.
C. Dr. Kilmer's Female Remedy, 1885
Jay, p. 86.
D. A "Positive Cure," 1880
Jay, p. 45.

Group 5. Outside Interests, 1886–1907
A. Advertisement for the Pierce Arrow Automobile, 1907
John M. Blum *et al., The National Experience: A History of the United States* (San Diego: Harcourt, Brace, Jovanovich, 1988), "Past and Its Presence," III.
B. Cadillac Advertisement, 1903
The Saturday Evening Post Treasury (New York: Simon and Schuster, 1954), p. 176.
C. Eastman Kodak Co., 1898
Jones, p. 78.
D. Western Wheel Works, New York, 1886
Jones, p. 101.

Group 6. The Sears Wish Book, 1897
Fred Israel, ed., *1897 Sears Roebuck Catalogue* (New York: Chelsea House, rep. 1968), frontispiece, pp. 105, 123, 164, 171, 273.

Chapter 20:
Document Set 2 Credits

2. A. The Warshaw Collection of Business Americana, Archives Center, National Museum of American History, Smithsonian Institution
B. From Edgar R. Jones, *Those Were The Good Old Days: A Happy Look at American Advertising, 1880–1930* (New York: Simon and Schuster, 1979, page 84)

3. A. The Warshaw Collection of Business Americana, Archives Center, National Museum of American History, Smithsonian Institution

4. A. The Warshaw Collection of Business Americana, Archives Center, National Museum of American History, Smithsonian Institution
B. The Warshaw Collection of Business Americana, Archives Center, National Museum of American History, Smithsonian Institution

C. Collection of The New York Historical Society
D. From Robert Jay, *The Trade Card in 19th Century America* (Columbia: University of Missouri Press, 1987, page 45). From the author's collection. Reprinted by permission of The University of Missouri Press.

5. A. Corbis-Bettman
B. *The Saturday Evening Post Treasury* (New York: Simon and Schuster, 1954, page 176)
C. The Warshaw Collection of Business Americana, Archives Center, National Museum of American History, Smithsonian Institution
D. The Warshaw Collection of Business Americana, Archives Center, National Museum of American History, Smithsonian Institution

6. Courtesy of Sears, Roebuck and Company

CHAPTER 20

DOCUMENT SET 3
Ethnicity in the Graphic Arts: Middle-Class Notions of Immigrant Life

The textbook describes a vigorous assault by the middle class on urban working-class culture. The campaign aimed at restraining what the well-to-do regarded as essentially immoral activities. Among those most affected by this attack were the immigrants who peopled the cities of late-nineteenth-century America. Particularly alarming to middle-class citizens were alcohol abuse, political immorality, immigrant religion, and flirtation with radical ideology. Taken together, these perceived deficiencies in immigrant behavior constituted what seemed to many native-born critics an intolerable threat to traditional American institutions.

One expression of middle-class concern may be found in the graphic arts of the late nineteenth century, especially the political cartoon. Political cartoons and other such illustrations had long been employed as a formidable weapon in partisan discourse. Since the days of the early Republic, graphic artists had used their skills to advance the causes of their favored public figures. With the advent of Thomas Nast on the journalistic scene in the 1860s, however, political satire reached new heights as a politically charged art form.

The following documents provide vivid evidence of the cartoonists' art as well as the effectiveness of the political illustration as a potent weapon. The work of Nast, Joseph Keppler, and other graphic artists of the late nineteenth century, which often appeared in middle-class magazines, clearly documents the values, fears, prejudices, and views of both the artists and their publishers. The evidence in this document set offers a vivid reminder of the strength of nativism and the assumptions made by native-born Americans about immigrant working-class culture.

As you review the evidence, be especially aware of the middle-class moral standards that prevailed in Victorian America. Reflect on the textbook's discussion of "middle-class society and culture" and "manners and morals" as crucial context for analysis of the messages projected in the illustrations. Be sure to think about ethnic and racial stereotyping as you attempt to extract hidden (and not-so-hidden) meanings from the cartoonists' work.

Finally, consider the fact that two of the most prominent illustrators included in this document set were themselves immigrants, although they belonged to the old immigration of the mid-nineteenth century. Both Thomas Nast and Joseph Keppler were German-born. Yet by the 1870s their cartoons reflected several stereotypes of immigrant groups. Think about differences among immigrant groups and the separate identities of various immigrant cultures. On another level, ask what the work of Nast and Keppler may reflect about the process of becoming American. What light do these documents shed on the entire debate over the alternative concepts of assimilation and ethnic survival? And what do they reveal about middle-class attitudes with regard to working-class culture in Victorian America?

Questions for Analysis

1. Define the term *stereotype.* How does the evidence illustrate the presence of ethnic stereotyping in nineteenth-century America? Can you identify the origins of any modern ethnic stereotypes in the documents?

2. What were the origins of the middle-class fears expressed in the visual evidence? Relate the concerns of the artists to the changes taking place in late-nineteenth-century cities. What was the connection between the illustrators' works and urban social reality?

3. Relying on your textbook, consider the character of immigrant working-class leisure in the American city. What do the documents reveal about middle-class attitudes toward those leisure activities?

4. Since Thomas Nast and Joseph Keppler were themselves immigrants, how would you account for the ideas expressed in their work from the 1870s

on? What does their art reveal about the process of acculturation and assimilation? And what did their ideas reflect about the distinction between the old and the new immigration?

5. Compare the responses to immigrant culture found in the documents with modern reactions to the new immigrants of late-twentieth-century America. What similarities and/or differences may be observed? How would you account for them?

Group 1. The Irish Menace

A. Erin's Own, 1867

B. The New Slavery, 1870

Group 2. The Imperial Church

A. The Promised Land, 1870

[99]

October 1, 1870

B. Sectarianism Unleashed, 1870

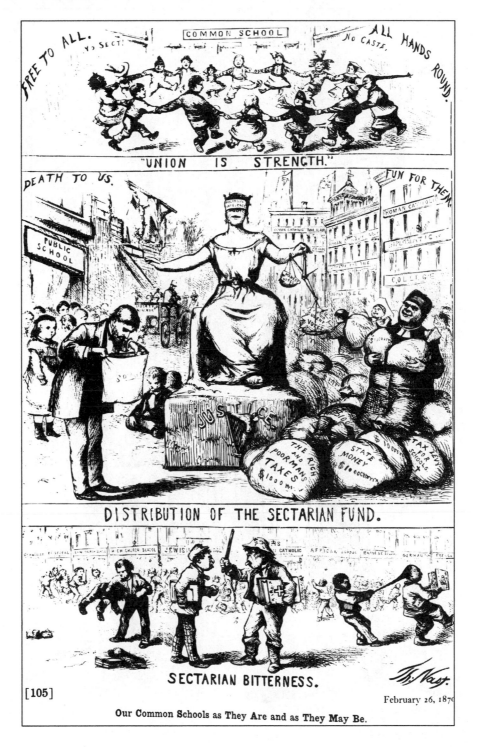

[105]

Our Common Schools as They Are and as They May Be.

Group 3. The Vulnerable Worker

A. The Union Menace, 1871

[73]   May 20, 1871

The Workingman's Mite.

B. The Lure of the Commune, 1874

[74]   February 7, 1874

C. The Assault on Capital, 1878

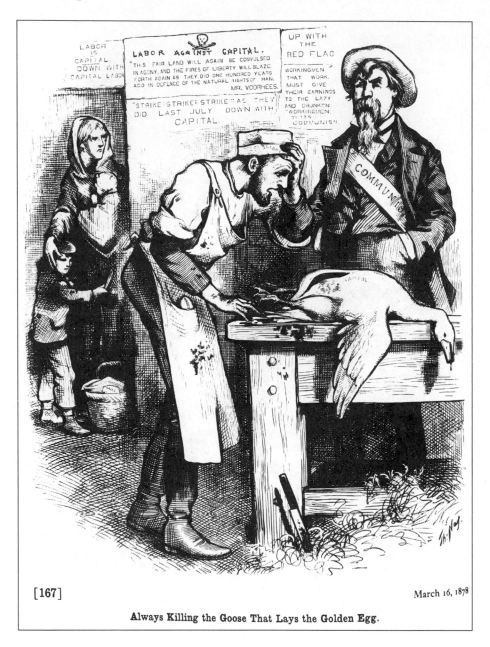

[167]   March 16, 1878

Always Killing the Goose That Lays the Golden Egg.

Group 4. The Unwelcome Asian

A. The Closing Door, 1882

[145] April 1, 1882

E Pluribus Unum (Except the Chinese).

B. An Answer to Chinese Avarice, 1895

Group 5. The Immigrant Threat

A. Disinterested Americanism, 1877

[186]   April 14, 1877

Reform Is Necessary in the Foreign Line.

B. A Threat to Social Order, 1909

Chapter 20:
Document Set 3 References

Group 1.   The Irish Menace
  A. Erin's Own, 1867
     Morton Keller, *The Art and Politics of Thomas Nast* (London: Oxford University Press, 1968), no. 103. Cartoon by Thomas Nast.
  B. The New Slavery, 1870
     Keller, no. 112. Cartoon by Thomas Nast.

Group 2.   The Imperial Church
  A. The Promised Land, 1870
     Keller, no. 99. Cartoon by Thomas Nast.
  B. Sectarianism Unleashed, 1870
     Keller, no. 105. Cartoon by Thomas Nast.

Group 3.   The Vulnerable Worker
  A. The Union Menace, 1871
     Keller, no. 73. Cartoon by Thomas Nast.
  B. The Lure of the Commune, 1874
     Keller, no. 74. Cartoon by Thomas Nast.

  C. The Assault on Capital, 1878
     Keller, no. 167. Cartoon by Thomas Nast.

Group 4.   The Unwelcome Asian
  A. The Closing Door, 1882
     Keller, no. 145. Cartoon by Thomas Nast.
  B. An Answer to Chinese Avarice, 1895
     Courtesy, Collection of Alan Gowans.

Group 5.   The Immigrant Threat
  A. Disinterested Americanism, 1877
     Keller, no. 186. Cartoon by Thomas Nast.
  B. A Threat to Social Order, 1909
     Life, April 8, 1909. Also available from Anti-Defamation League of B'nai B'rith, 315 Lexington Ave., New York, NY 10016, as part of the slide-tape collection "The Distorted Image: Stereotype and Caricature in American Popular Graphics, 1850–1922."

Chapter 20:
Document Set 3 Credits

1. A. Reproduced from Brandeis University Library collection of *Harper's Weekly,* April 6, 1867
   B. Reproduced from Brandeis University Library collection of *Harper's Weekly,* April 16, 1870

2. A. Reproduced from Brandeis University Library collection of *Harper's Weekly,* October 1, 1870
   B. Reproduced from Brandeis University Library collection of *Harper's Weekly,* February 26, 1870

3. A. Reproduced from Brandeis University Library collection of *Harper's Weekly,* May 20, 1871
   B. Reproduced from Brandeis University Library collection of *Harper's Weekly,* February 17, 1874
   C. Reproduced from Brandeis University Library collection of *Harper's Weekly,* March 16, 1878

4. A. Reproduced from Brandeis University Library collection of *Harper's Weekly,* April 1, 1882
   B. Collection of Alan Gowans

5. A. Reproduced from Brandeis University Library collection of *Harper's Weekly,* April 14, 1877

6. *LIFE,* April 8, 1909. Also available from Anti-Defamation league of B'nai B'rith, 823 United Nations Plaza, New York, NY 10017, as part of the slide-tape collection, "The Distorted Image: Stereotype and Caricature in American Popular Graphics, 1850–1922"

CHAPTER 21

DOCUMENT SET 1
Civil-Service Reform: A Curse or a Blessing?

Central to the political culture of urban, industrial America in the late nineteenth century was the political machine and the spoils system on which it was based (see Chapter 19 for full discussion of boss rule). Tracing its origins to the Jacksonian principle of rotation in office, the machine system sustained vigorous party organizations. At the same time it fulfilled a critical social function by aiding in the assimilation of a burgeoning immigrant population. Although boss rule brought a semblance of order to industrializing communities, elite social and political reformers argued that the moral price was excessive. Liberal critics of the prevailing political ethic fixed on nonpartisan civil service as an alternative to the rampant corruption that in their view undermined American government.

Building on your textbook's discussion of both the spoils system and the civil-service reform movement, the following documents explore the rationale behind the spoils system, the goals of critics and supporters, and the results of efforts to purify American politics. As you examine the evidence, be especially attentive to personal background as an indicator of each commentator's private opinions. Prepare to make a judgment on the strengths and weaknesses of the political machine.

The nature of the machine system is evident in the first group of readings, which includes the words of New York Republican Senator Roscoe Conkling and Tam-many Hall district leader George Washington Plunkitt. The purposes and values of the political machines are expressed by these two leaders, whose comments are refreshingly frank in their defense of the political status quo. Compare their remarks with the criticisms of congressional wife Julia Foraker.

The remarks of President Chester A. Arthur advance a solution to the problem. From his words try to identify the origins of the crisis, as well as the reasons action had been delayed. As you analyze the Pendleton Act's provisions, determine what the main targets of the legislation were. The concluding document evaluates the reformers' solution. Assessing the status of the reform movement eight years after enactment of reform legislation, George W. Curtis of the National Civil Service Reform League argued the case for the concept of civil service and its promise for the future. His comments, like those of Conkling and Plunkitt, tend toward exaggeration, but they advance an argument for the efficacy of reform. Comparing Curtis's views with those of Plunkitt, try to assess the reform movement and its outcome.

As you evaluate the liberal reform movement, consider the negative and positive aspects of machine government, including the varied functions of the political organization in an urbanizing society. Be aware also of the motivations behind reform activism and the outcomes of the drive for civic improvement.

Questions for Analysis

1. What do the documents reveal about the basis for party loyalty in late-nineteenth-century America? How widespread was support for political party organizations? How would you explain the interest they aroused in their supporters?

2. Do the socioeconomic backgrounds of political reformers shed light on the forces underlying the civil-service reform movement? Using your textbook and documents, demonstrate the relationship between social class and political preference.

3. Late-nineteenth-century politicians are often charged with responsibility for widespread corruption of government. How would supporters of the machine system have reacted to such attacks? Do the documents provide evidence to confirm or deny the charges? After reflecting on both textbook and documents, what is your assessment of the machine and the spoils system?

4. What was the civic reformers' primary solution to the problems created by machine government? Do the documents provide any evidence to confirm or deny their assumptions? How would you account for the divergent conclusions of Plunkitt and Curtis? Which source provides the most accurate evaluation of reform?

1. Roscoe Conkling Defends the Spoils System, 1877

Who are these men who, in newspapers and elsewhere, are cracking their whips over Republicans and playing school-master to the Republican party and its conscience and convictions? . . . Some of them are men who, when they could work themselves into conventions, have attempted to belittle and befoul Republican administrations and to parade their own thin veneering of superior purity. Some of them are men who, by insisting that it is corrupt and bad for men in office to take part in politics, are striving now to prove that the Republican party has been unclean and vicious all its life, and that the last campaign was venal and wrong and fraudulent, not in some of the States, but in all the States, North and South. For it is no secret that in all States office-holders, in committees, in organizations and everywhere, did all that men could fairly do to uphold the candidates of our party, and that they were encouraged and urged to do so. Some of these worthies masquerade as reformers. Their vocation and ministry is to lament the sins of other people. Their stock in trade is rancid, canting self-righteousness. They are wolves in sheep's clothing. Their real object is office and plunder. When Dr. Johnson defined patriotism as the last refuge of a scoundrel, he was unconscious of the then undeveloped capabilities and uses of the word "Reform."

2. George Washington Plunkitt Scorns Reform, 1905

Everybody is talkin' these days about Tammany men growin' rich on graft, but nobody thinks of drawin' the distinction between honest graft and dishonest graft. There's all the difference in the world between the two. Yes, many of our men have grown rich in politics. I have myself. I've made a big fortune out of the game, and I'm gettin' richer every day, but I've not gone in for dishonest graft—blackmailin' gamblers, saloonkeepers, disorderly people, etc.—and neither has any of the men who have made big fortunes in politics.

There's an honest graft, and I'm an example of how it works. I might sum up the whole thing by sayin': "I seen my opportunities and I took 'em."

Just let me explain by examples. My party's in power in the city, and it's goin' to undertake a lot of public improvements. Well, I'm tipped off, say, that they're going to lay out a new park at a certain place.

I see my opportunity and I take it. I go to that place and I buy up all the land I can in the neighborhood. Then the board of this or that makes its plan public, and there is a rush to get my land, which nobody cared particular for before.

Ain't it perfectly honest to charge a good price and make a profit on my investment and foresight? Of course, it is. Well, that's honest graft.

. . . This civil service law is the biggest fraud of the age. It is the curse of the nation. There can't be no real patriotism while it lasts. How are you goin' to interest our young men in their country if you have no offices to give them when they work for their party? Just look at things in this city today. There are ten thousand good offices, but we can't get at more than a few hundred of them. How are we goin' to provide for the thousands of men who worked for the Tammany ticket? It can't be done. These men were full of patriotism a short time ago. They expected to be servin' their city, but when we tell them that we can't place them, do you think their patriotism is goin' to last? Not much. They say: "What's the use of workin' for your country anyhow? There's nothin' in the game." And what can they do? I don't know, but I'll tell you what I do know. I know more than one young man in past years who worked for the ticket and was just overflowin' with patriotism, but when he was knocked out by the civil service humbug he got to hate his country and became an Anarchist. . . .

When the people elected Tammany, they knew just what they were doin'. We didn't put up any false pretenses. We didn't go in for humbug civil service and all that rot. We stood as we have always stood, for rewardin' the men that won the victory. They call that the spoils system. All right; Tammany is for the spoils system, and when we go in we fire every anti-Tammany man from office that can be fired under the law. It's an elastic sort of law and you can bet it will be stretched to the limit. . . .

Say, the people's voice is smothered by the cursed civil service law; it is the root of all evil in our government. You hear of this thing or that thing goin' wrong in the nation, the State or the city. Look down beneath the surface and you can trace everything wrong to civil service. I have studied the subject and I know. The civil service humbug is undermin' our institutions and if a halt ain't called soon this great republic will tumble down like a Park Avenue house when they were buildin' the subway, and on its ruins will rise another Russian government. . . .

First, this great and glorious country was built up by political parties; second, parties can't hold together if their workers don't get the offices when they win; third, if the parties go to pieces, the government they built up must go to pieces, too; fourth, then there'll be h--- to pay.

3. A Senator's Wife Recalls the Office Seekers, ca. 1870s

There is, I consider, but one real fly in the Washington amber. One is penetrated at first by the charm of everything. How fluid and colorful the life is! So much movement! Such delightful people from all over the world! And then, presto! as by a swarm of locusts the land is darkened. The office-seekers have come to town! Every four years this phenomenon turns our exquisite national capital into a merry-go-round with a hoarse-voiced, brand-new crowd clamoring for place. The first two weeks after Foraker took his seat in the Senate he received more than twenty-five hundred letters from men who wanted a

political office. This number was augmented, of course, by crowds of others at the official gates. . . .

An office-seeker is a man who can't do anything but hold office. And he never really quite gives up. I used to receive a great many begging letters, myself. One I remember was from a woman who wrote me that her husband had voted for my husband at every election; he had just died. Now would I send her "a widow's mourning outfit, complete and up-to-date, and send so that *I'll get same by Wednesday*, madam." The italics are hers. So you see, even after an office-seeker dies his widow carries on.

4. President Chester A. Arthur Endorses the Pendleton Act, 1882

In the early years of the administration of the Government the personal direction of appointments to the civil service may not have been an irksome task for the Executive, but now that the burden has increased fully a hundredfold it has become greater than he ought to bear, and it necessarily diverts his time and attention from the proper discharge of other duties no less delicate and responsible, and

which in the very nature of things can not be delegated to other hands.

In the judgment of not a few who have given study and reflection to this matter, the nation has outgrown the provisions which the Constitution has established for filling the minor offices in the public service.

But whatever may be thought of the wisdom or expediency of changing the fundamental law in this regard, it is certain that much relief may be afforded, not only to the President and to the heads of the Departments, but to Senators and Representatives in Congress, by discreet legislation. They would be protected in a great measure by the bill now pending before the Senate, or by any other which should embody its important features, from the pressure of personal importunity and from the labor of examining conflicting claims and pretensions of candidates. . . .

I declare my approval of such legislation as may be found necessary for supplementing the existing provisions of law in relation to political assessments.

In July last I authorized a public announcement that employees of the Government should regard themselves as at liberty to exercise their pleasure in making or refusing to make political contributions, and that their action in that regard would in no manner affect their official status.

In this announcement I acted upon the view, which I had always maintained and still maintain, that a public officer should be as absolutely free as any other citizen to give or to withhold a contribution for the aid of the political party of his choice. It has, however, been urged, and doubtless not without foundation in fact, that by solicitation of official superiors and by other modes such contributions have at times been obtained from persons whose only motive for giving has been the fear of what might befall them if they refused. It goes without saying that such contributions are not voluntary, and in my judgment their collection should be prohibited by law.

5. The Pendleton Civil Service Act, 1883

Be it enacted by the Senate and House of Representatives of the United States of America in Congress assembled, That the President is authorized to appoint, by and with the advice and consent of the Senate, three persons, not more than two of whom shall be adherents of the same party, as Civil Service Commissioners, and said three commissioners shall constitute the United States Civil Service Commission. . . .

Sec. 2. That it shall be the duty of said commissioners:

First. To aid the President, as he may request, in preparing suitable rules for carrying this act into effect, and when said rules shall have been promulgated it shall be the duty of all officers of the United States in the departments and offices to which any such rules may relate to aid, in all proper ways, in carrying said rules, and any modifications thereof, into effect.

Second. And, among other things, said rules shall provide and declare, as nearly as the conditions of good administration will warrant, as follows:

First, for open, competitive examinations for testing the fitness of applicants for the public service now classified or to be classified hereunder. Such examinations shall be practical in their character, and so far as may be shall relate to those matters which will fairly test the relative capacity and fitness of the persons examined to discharge the duties of the service into which they seek to be appointed.

Second, that all the offices, places, and employments so arranged or to be arranged in classes shall be filled by selections according to grade from among those graded highest as the results of such competitive examinations.

Third, appointments to the public service aforesaid in the departments at Washington shall be apportioned among the several States and Territories and the District of Columbia upon the basis of population as ascertained at the last preceding census. . . .

Fifth, that no person in the public service is for that reason under any obligations to contribute to any political fund, or to render any political service, and that he will not be removed or otherwise prejudiced for refusing to do so.

Sixth, that no person in said service has any right to use his official authority or influence to coerce the political action of any person or body. . . .

Sec. 11. That no Senator, or Representative, or Territorial Delegate of the Congress, or Senator, Representative, or Delegate elect, or any officer or employee of either of said houses, and no executive, judicial, military, or naval officer of the United States, and no clerk or employee of any department, branch or bureau of the executive, judicial, or military or naval service of the United States, shall, directly, or indirectly, solicit or receive, or be in any manner concerned in soliciting or receiving, any assessment, subscription, or contribution for any political purpose whatever, from any officer, clerk, or employee of the United States, or any department, branch, or bureau thereof, or from any person receiving any salary or compensation from moneys derived from the Treasury of the United States.

6. George W. Curtis Cites the Reform Record, 1891

The National Civil Service Reform League was organized at Newport, R.I., on the 11th of August, 1881. It was the result of a conference among members of civil service reform associations that had spontaneously arisen in various parts of the country for the purpose of awakening public interest in the question, like the clubs of the Sons of Liberty among our fathers, and the anti-slavery societies among their children. The first act of the League was a resolution of hearty approval of the bill then pending in Congress, known as the Pendleton bill. . . .

The passage of the law was the first great victory of the ten years of the reform movement. The second is the demonstration of the complete practicability of reform attested by the heads of the largest offices of administration in the country. In the Treasury and Navy departments, the New York Custom House and Post Office, and other important custom houses and post offices, without the least regard to the wishes or the wrath of that remarkable class of our fellow citizens, known as political bosses, it is conceded by officers, wholly beyond suspicion of party independence, that, in these chief branches of the public service, reform is perfectly practicable and the reformed system a great public benefit. And, although as yet these offices are by no means thoroughly reorganized upon reform principles, yet a quarter of the whole number of places in the public service to which the reformed methods apply are now included within those methods. . . .

Upon a survey even so general as this of the progress of civil service reform within the ten years of the existence of this League, it is idle to deny the prodigious advance which it has made, both in public opinion and in practical application. . . . The League has represented not party strategy to carry an election, but public conviction to reform an acknowledged evil of administration. If it had done nothing more its service would be great in having forced the spoils system to its defence. The political pirates are at last driven to show the black flag and defiantly to declare that at every election the whole public service in every detail, with all its emoluments and opportunities, shall be made the prize of a vast struggle of greed and intrigue, of bribery and dishonesty of every kind, all inflamed to fury by party spirit. We demand that all public business, which is not political, shall be kept free from politics and shall be transacted upon the simple principles which are approved by universal private experience. . . . Those who would use the patronage of public employment as the vast bribery fund of a party are on one side. Washington and Lincoln, patriotism and good sense, the wisdom of age, the instinct of youth, are on the other. Let all good men choose their part. We have chosen ours.

Chapter 21:
Document Set 1 References

1. Roscoe Conkling Defends the Spoils System, 1877
   A. R. Conkling, *The Life and Letters of Roscoe Conkling* (New York: Charles R. Webster, 1889), pp. 538–541, 546–547.

2. George Washington Plunkitt Scorns Reform, 1905
   William L. Riordon, ed., *Plunkitt of Tammany Hall, 1905* (New York: E. P. Dutton, rep. 1963), pp. 3, 11–13.

3. A Senator's Wife Recalls the Office Seekers, ca. 1870s
   Julia B. Foraker, *I Would Live It Again: Memories of a Vivid Life* (New York: Harper and Brothers, 1932), pp. 215–217.

4. President Chester A. Arthur Endorses the Pendleton Act, 1882
   Chester A. Arthur, "Annual Message," 1882, James D. Richardson, ed., *A Compilation of the Messages and Papers of the Presidents, 1798–1908* (Washington, D.C.: Bureau of National Literature and Art, 1909), Vol. VIII, pp. 145–147.

5. The Pendleton Civil Service Act, 1883
   United States Statutes at Large, Ch. 27, 47th Cong., 2nd Sess., pp. 403–404, 406.

6. George W. Curtis Cites the Reform Record, 1891
   George W. Curtis, "Ten Years of Reform," Address Delivered at the Tenth Annual Meeting of National Civil Service Reform League, Sept. 29–30, 1891, in George W. Curtis, *Orations and Addresses of George W. Curtis,* Charles Eliot Norton, ed. (New York: Harper and Brothers, 1894), Vol. 2, pp. 454–455, 474–476.

CHAPTER 21

DOCUMENT SET 2

Expansionism and Its Consequences: Developing a Strategy for Empire

A substantial portion of Chapter 21 is devoted to late-nineteenth-century foreign policy, including American expansion in Latin America and the Pacific. As your textbook indicates, American expansionism reached a climax in the 1890s with the adoption of colonialism in the wake of the Spanish American War. By this time scholars, business interests, agriculturalists, politicians, and military strategists had developed a cogent intellectual rationale for imperialism.

The following documents provide evidence of the imperial rhetoric that dominated foreign-policy debate in the McKinley era. Your task is to separate rhetoric from reality as you review the public statements of business and political figures. Comparing the assertions in the documents with the economic and political environment described in your text, determine whether expansionist fears of a saturated home market were justified. In making this analysis, consider the bases on which individual and institutional actions normally rest, including the prevailing perception of reality.

The urgency of foreign-policy debate was evident in the words of naval theorist Alfred Thayer Mahan and Indiana Republican Senator Albert J. Beveridge, both proponents of an expansionist program. As you analyze their arguments, be conscious of ways in which political and institutional backgrounds may have influenced their views. Equally important were contemporary American social and economic assumptions.

A narrower focus characterizes the next group of documents, which concentrate on China policy. As you review the writings of former minister to China Charles Denby and of South Carolina Senator John McLaurin, try to identify common strains in their arguments for an aggressive Far Eastern policy. Relate their positions to the thinking that led to the establishment of the American Asiatic Association, a pressure group for American business interests in China.

With the acquisition of the Philippines, the threat of partition in China, and the consensus on the necessity for expansion, a long-term strategy for empire became an urgent policy question. By 1900, the tradition of the Open Door had emerged as the answer to this strategic problem. Examine the excerpt from Secretary of State John Hay's first Open Door note in order to identify the American policy goal and the business/government proposal to achieve it.

Finally, Democratic party presidential candidate William Jennings Bryan expresses the views of the anti-imperialist minority on the consequences of expansionism. As you evaluate Bryan's argument, be alert to his overall objectives for the United States. How did Bryan regard the broad goals of imperial planners? The new strategic calculus shaped the future role of the United States in world affairs, and Open Door expansionism was to become the central feature in the birth of the modern American empire.

Questions for Analysis

1. Define the term *imperialism*. What were the origins of the term, and what were its implications? Compare nineteenth-century European imperialism with the American variety. What do the documents reveal about American perceptions of the benefits of empire?

2. To what extent do the documents clarify the forces behind the endorsement of colonialism and empire between 1898 and 1900? Which factors were most significant in explaining the Spanish-American War, Philippine annexation, and adoption of the Open Door Policy?

3. In what way was the Open Door Policy a strategy for empire? What was the long-term purpose behind the first and second Open Door notes? To what extent were American goals achieved? With what consequences?

4. What do the documents reveal about the dominant ideas in late-nineteenth-century strategic thought? How did modern technology influence the naval theories propounded by Mahan and others?

5. As you review references to the internal political debate over imperialism, what evidence do you find of disagreement? To what extent did Bryan's position contradict

the goals pursued by supporters of empire? How did Bryan's solution in the 1900 presidential campaign relate to the strategy of empire?

6. What evidence of nineteenth-century racial theories can be found in the documents? Can you identify a relationship between racism, colonialism, and the management of indigenous populations? What were the implications of the Filipino Rebellion?

1. Alfred Thayer Mahan Defines Security in Terms of Sea Power, 1897

The interesting and significant feature of this changing attitude is the turning of the eyes outward, instead of inward only, to seek the welfare of the country. To affirm the importance of distant markets, and the relation to them of our own immense powers of production, implies logically the recognition of the link that joins the products and the markets,—that is, the carrying trade; the three together constituting that chain of maritime power to which Great Britain owes her wealth and greatness. Further, is it too much to say that, as two of these links, the shipping and the markets, are exterior to our own borders, the acknowledgment of them carries with it a view of the relations of the United States to the world radically distinct from the simple idea of self-sufficingness? We shall not follow far this line of thought before there will dawn the realization of America's unique position, facing the older worlds of the East and West, her shores washed by the oceans which touch the one or the other, but which are common to her alone....

Despite a certain great original superiority conferred by our geographical nearness and immense resources,—due, in other words, to our natural advantages, and not to our intelligent preparations,—the United States is woefully unready, not only in fact but in purpose to assert in the Caribbean and Central America a weight of influence proportioned to the extent of her interests. We have not the navy, and, what is worse, we are not willing to have the navy, that will weigh seriously in any disputes with those nations whose interests will conflict there with our own. We have not, and we are not anxious to provide the defence of the seaboard which will leave the navy free for its work at sea. We have not, but many other powers have, positions, either within or on the borders of the Caribbean....

Yet, were our sea frontier as strong as it now is weak, passive self-defence, whether in trade or war, would be but a poor policy, so long as the world continues to be one of struggle and vicissitude. All around us now is strife; "the struggle of life," "the race of life," are phrases so familiar that we do not feel their significance till we stop to think about them. Everywhere nation is arrayed against nation; our own no less than others. What is our protective system but an organized warfare?

2. Albert J. Beveridge Endorses Imperialism, 1898

The opposition tells us that we ought not to govern a people without their consent. I answer: The rule of liberty, that all just government derives its authority from the consent of the governed, applies only to those who are capable of self-government....

They ask us how we will govern these new possessions. I answer: Out of local conditions and the necessities of the case methods of government will grow. If England can govern foreign lands, so can America. If

Germany can govern foreign lands, so can America. If they can supervise protectorates, so can America....

[T]oday we are raising more than we can consume. Today we are making more than we can use. Today our industrial society is congested; there are more workers than there is work; there is more capital than there is investment. We do not need more money—we need more circulation, more employment. Therefore we must find new markets for our produce, new occupation for our capital, new work for our labor. And so, while we did not need the territory taken during the past century at the time it was required [acquired?], we do need what we have taken in 1898, and we need it now. . . .

Ah! as our commerce spreads, the flag of liberty will circle the globe and the highways of the ocean—carrying trade to all mankind—be guarded by the guns of the republic. And as their thunders salute the flag, benighted peoples will know that the voice of liberty is speaking, at last, for them; that civilization is dawning, at last, for them—liberty and civilization, those children of Christ's gospel, who follow and never precede the preparing march of commerce. . . .

Fellow Americans, we are God's chosen people. Yonder at Bunker Hill and Yorktown His providence was above us. At New Orleans and on ensanguined seas His hand sustained us. Abraham Lincoln was His minister, and His was the Altar of Freedom the boys in blue set on a hundred battlefields. His power directed Dewey in the East, and delivered the Spanish Fleet into our hands on the eve of Liberty's natal day, as He delivered the elder Armada into the hands of our English sires two centuries ago. His great purposes are revealed in the progress of the flag, which surpasses the intentions of congresses and cabinets, and leads us like a holier pillar of cloud by day and pillar of fire by night into situations unforeseen by finite wisdom and duties unexpected by the unprophetic heart of selfishness.

The American people cannot use a dishonest medium of exchange; it is ours to set the world its example of right and honor. We cannot fly from our world duties; it is ours to execute the purpose of a fate that has driven us to be greater than our small intentions. We cannot retreat from any soil where Providence has unfurled our banner; it is ours to save that soil for liberty and civilization. For liberty and civilization and God's promise fulfilled, the flag must henceforth be the symbol and the sign to all mankind—the flag!

3. Charles Denby's Argument for the Retention of the Philippines, 1898

Dewey's victory has changed our attitude before the world. We took no part in international questions. We had no standing in the councils of the nations. We were a *quantité négligeable*. . . .

The position of absolute indifference to what is happening in the world is difficult of maintenance; and when it is maintained it is humiliating. . . .

We have a great commerce to take care of. We have to compete with the commercial nations of the world in far-distant markets. Commerce, not politics, is king. The manufacturer and the merchant dictate to diplomacy and control elections. The art of arts is the extension of commercial relations—in plain language, the selling of native products and manufactured goods. . . .

I am in favor of holding the Philippines because I cannot conceive of any alternative to our doing so, except the seizure of territory in China; and I prefer to hold them rather than to oppress further the helpless government and people of China. I want China to preserve her autonomy, to become great and prosperous; and I want these results, not for the interests of China but for our interests. I am not the agent or attorney of China; and, as an American, I do not look to the promotion of China's interests, or Spain's, or any other country's, but simply of our own.

The whole world sees in China a splendid market for our native products—our timber, our locomotives, our rails, our coal oil, our sheetings, our mining plants, and numberless other articles. We are closer to her than any other commercial country except Japan. There is before us a boundless future which will make the Pacific more important to us than the Atlantic. . . .

The Philippines are a foothold for us in the Far East. Their possession gives us standing and influence. It gives us also valuable trade both in exports and imports.

Should we surrender the Philippines, what will become of them? Will Spain ever conquer the insurgents, and, should she do so, will she retain the islands? To her they will be valueless; and if she sells them to any continental power she will, by that act, light the torches of war. . . .

There is, perhaps, no such thing as manifest destiny; but there is an evident fitness in the happening of events and a logical result of human action.

Dewey's victory is an epoch in the affairs of the Far East. We hold our heads higher. We are coming to our own. We are stretching out our hands for what nature meant should be ours. We are taking our proper rank among the nations of the world. We are after markets, the greatest markets now existing in the world. Along with these markets will go our beneficent institutions, and humanity will bless us.

4. Senator John McLaurin Demands an Open Door in China, 1899

The "open-door policy" is what we need and want. This has heretofore been secured by "treaty rights," which have been respected by other nations only to the extent to which it conduced to their trade interest. While ostensibly recognizing these "treaty rights," other nations, in violation of them, have acquired territory and excluded therefrom our legitimate commerce. Russia has gradually absorbed Manchuria and is building a railroad across Siberia to command the trade of China. Germany has been active and waiting in expectancy to obtain the Philippines. Japan has given Russia all the fruits of her victory of 1895. France has been the willing tool of Russia, and England has been passive in her fear to assail her. . . .

In the vicissitudes and good fortune of a war with Spain, and without any intention of doing so, the United States has acquired the possession of the Philippines, which gives to her paramount political and commercial advantages.

My judgment is that the control of them, or at least of some portions, is the only safeguard for our trade interests in the East. The abandonment of them means the dismemberment of China, its partition among the European powers, and the inevitable loss of our Chinese trade. . . .

I do not favor the adoption by this country of a colonial policy, because of the vexed and threatening problems growing out of it, but I do think that, if possible, the United States should maintain sufficient interests in the islands to command equal trade rights with other nations in China. This will prevent for a long time the dismemberment of this vast empire. England and Japan favor the integrity of the empire, but they alone cannot guarantee it against the other European powers. With the weight of the influence of the United States thrown against dismemberment, it would be rendered impossible. . . .

There is much political rot in the constant parading of the term "imperialism." It is a misnomer, intended to confuse and deceive. It involves the idea of the incorporation into our body politic as American citizens millions of the semi-barbarous inhabitants of a tropical country. I do not believe such a thing is intended, possible or desirable; nor is such a result necessary to secure such commercial expansion as we want. I think the dictates of common sense will govern the American people, and the ghost "imperialism," sprung for political effect, will not prevent them from gathering the full fruits of the victory so easily won, and treading the path so plainly blazed out by an overruling Providence. . . .

It will be observed, therefore, that the question of our trade in the East involves both political and commercial consequences. Upon its settlement, in my judgment, depends the future welfare of our people in maintaining equality of opportunity in the Eastern markets. A mere superficial view will not reveal its transcendent importance. To the Southern people it is fraught with momentous consequences. Cotton manufacturing in the South has grown in a few years with phenomenal rapidity. Millions of dollars are now invested in mills.

The product of these have found remunerative markets in China and other countries of the East, our cotton goods being peculiarly adapted for clothing the teeming millions of that warm climate. Their trade is the hope of this great manufacturing industry of the South. If it is cut off by other nations, not only the manufacturer, but the producer of raw cotton will suffer.

5. The American Asiatic Association Organizes Businessmen in Support of an Aggressive China Policy, 1899, 1905

June 10, 1899

The present number of the Journal of The American Asiatic Association is issued for the purpose of presenting in a compact and intelligible form the reasons why the future of China is a question of supreme moment to the United States. Till the importance of that question is appreciated by the American people, it is useless to expect on the part of our Government a policy as vigorous and resolute as the occasion demands. Since free access to the greatest undeveloped market in the world touches the interests of every one engaged in productive industry or distributive commerce throughout the United States, it is highly desirable that the circulation of this issue of the Journal should be as wide as the country....

Extract from the Constitution of the Association:

ARTICLE II.

OBJECTS AND PURPOSES.

The objects and purposes of this Association are:

1. To foster and safeguard the trade and commercial interests of the citizens of the United States, and others associated therewith, in the Empires of China, Japan, and Korea, and in the Philippine Islands, and elsewhere in Asia or Oceania;

2. To secure the advantages of sustained watchfulness and readiness for action, attainable by union and permanent organization, in respect of such Asiatic trade, and as well in matters of legislation, or treaties affecting the same;

3. To promote the creation and maintenance of a consular service of the United States in Asia and in Oceania, which shall be founded upon the principles of uniform selection for proved fitness, of regular promotion, security of tenure during good service, and adequate compensation;

4. To provide for convenient ascertainment and distribution of information affecting the interests of its members;

5. And, generally to promote a beneficial acquaintance and association of those having interests and pursuits in common concerned with such trade or commerce....

February, 1905

... The returns elsewhere given of the exports of American cotton cloths to China for the eight months ending with February bring out very clearly the vital importance of this trade to the prosperity of the entire cotton textile industry of the United States. Last year, up to the same date, our whole exports of cotton cloths amounted to $9,865,434, while for two-thirds of the current fiscal year they amount to $23,966,430. The difference of $14,000,000 is almost entirely accounted for by the growth in the exports to the Chinese Empire, and but for this growth tens of thousands of spindles in southern mills would have been either standing still or engaged in turning out a product calculated to increase the destructive competition for the possession of the home market. It is quite true that the domestic market absorbs ten times as much as the whole foreign outlet for these goods, but the fractional surplus which goes to China marks, nevertheless, the difference between a prosperous industry and one that is demoralized by an absence of fixed price and enough of over production to make the domestic buyer master of the situation.

6. Secretary of State John Hay Presents a Coherent Strategy for Empire, 1899

Earnestly desirous to remove any cause of irritation and to insure at the same time to the commerce of all nations in China the undoubted benefits which should accrue from a formal recognition by the various powers claiming "spheres of interest" that they shall enjoy perfect equality of treatment for their commerce and navigation within such "spheres," the Government of the United States would be pleased to see His German Majesty's Government give formal assurances, and lend its cooperation in securing like assurances from the other interested powers, that each, within its respective sphere of whatever influence—

First. Will in no way interfere with any treaty port or any vested interest within any so-called "sphere of interest" or leased territory it may have in China.

Second. That the Chinese treaty tariff of the time being shall apply to all merchandise landed or shipped to all such ports as are within said "sphere of interest" (unless they be "free ports"), no matter to what nationality it may belong, and that duties so leviable shall be collected by the Chinese Government.

Third. That it will levy no higher harbor dues on vessels of another nationality frequenting any port in such "sphere" than shall be levied on vessels of its own nationality, and no higher railroad charges over lines built, controlled, or operated within its "sphere" on merchandise belonging to citizens or subjects of other nationalities transported through such "sphere" than shall be levied on similar merchandise belonging to its own nationals transported over equal distances.

7. Bryan's Solution to the Philippine Problem, 1900

When I say that the contest of 1900 is a contest between Democracy on the one hand and plutocracy on the other I do not mean to say that all our opponents have deliberately chosen to give to organized wealth a predominating influence in the affairs of the Government, but I do assert that on the important issues of the day the Republican party is dominated by those influences which constantly tend to substitute the worship of mammon for the protection of the rights of man. . . .

There is an easy, honest, honorable solution of the Philippine question. It is set forth in the Democratic platform and it is submitted with confidence to the American people. This plan I unreservedly indorse. If elected, I will convene congress in extraordinary session as soon as inaugurated and recommend an immediate declaration of the nation's purpose, first, to establish a stable form of government in the Philippine Islands, just as we are now establishing a stable form of government in Cuba; second, to give independence to the Cubans; third, to protect the Filipinos from outside interference while they work out their destiny, just as we have protected the republics of Central and South America, and are, by the Monroe doctrine, pledged to protect Cuba.

A European protectorate often results in the plundering of the ward by the guardian. An American protectorate gives to the nation protected the advantage of our strength, without making it the victim of our greed. For three-quarters of a century the Monroe doctrine has been a shield to neighboring republics and yet it has imposed no pecuniary burden upon us. After the Filipinos had aided us in the war against Spain, we could not honorably turn them over to their former masters; we could not leave them to be the victims of the ambitious designs of European nations, and since we do not desire to make them a part of us or to hold them as subjects, we propose the only alternative, namely, to give them independence and guard them against molestation from without.

When our opponents are unable to defend their position by argument they fall back upon the assertion that it is destiny, and insist that we must submit to it, no matter how much it violates our moral precepts and our principles of government. This is a complacent philosophy. It obliterates the distinction between right and wrong and makes individuals and nations the helpless victims of circumstance.

Chapter 21:
Document Set 2 References

1. Alfred Thayer Mahan Defines Security in Terms of Sea Power, 1897
   Alfred Thayer Mahan, *The Interest of America in Sea Power* (New York: Harper and Brothers, 1897), pp. 3–27.

2. Albert J. Beveridge Endorses Imperialism, 1898
   Albert J. Beveridge, Speech, September 16, 1898, *Modern Eloquence*, Thomas B. Reed, ed., Vol. 11 (Philadelphia: John D. Morris and Co., 1903), pp. 224–243.

3. Charles Denby's Argument for the Retention of the Philippines, 1898
   Charles Denby, "Shall We Keep the Philippines?" *Forum* (November 1898).

4. Senator John McLaurin Demands an Open Door in China, 1899
   "Southern Trade in China," *Manufacturers' Record,* October 20, 1899.

5. The American Asiatic Association Organizes Businessmen in Support of an Aggressive China Policy, 1899, 1905
   Journal of the American Asiatic Association, I (June 10, 1899), p. 1; V (February 1905), p. 66.

6. Secretary of State John Hay Presents a Coherent Strategy for Empire, 1899
   William M. Malloy, ed., *Treaties, Conventions, International Acts, Protocols and Agreements Between the United States and Other Powers, 1776–1909* (Washington, D.C.: Government Printing Office, 1910), Vol. 1, pp. 246–247.

7. Bryan's Solution to the Philippine Problem, 1900
   William Jennings Bryan, "Imperialism, Being the Speech of William Jennings Bryan in Response to the Committee Appointed to Notify Him of His Nomination to the Presidency of the United States Delivered at Indianapolis, August 8, 1900," in *Bryan on Imperialism* (New York: 1900, rep. Arno Press, 1970), pp. 69, 90.

CHAPTER 21

DOCUMENT SET 3

The Farmers' Alliance and the People's Party: Populism as a Product of a Movement Culture

As a result of the dramatic downward trend in farm prices during the last quarter of the nineteenth century, southern and western agriculture was confronted by an unprecedented economic and social crisis. By the late 1880s, farmers were flocking to the banner of the Farmers' Alliance, an organization that committed itself to economic cooperation and political mobilization as solutions to the problems that threatened to overwhelm them. The intensity and comprehensiveness of their response have led historians to view the Farmers' Alliance movement and the People's Party of the 1890s as the first steps in an effort to create a cooperative commonwealth that would unite urban and rural producers in a challenge to the two-party system and the corporate interests that dominated it.

The following documents address the question of this movement's substance and character. Study the statements of Alliance and Populist leaders with an eye to their economic and social assumptions, as well as their proposed remedies. The textbook discussion of agrarian discontent and the election of 1896 provides background and context for your review of the evidence. How did the Alliance and People's Party define the origins of the farm problem and identify the producers' enemies?

As you examine the evidence, pay particular attention to the rhetoric employed by the rebels. Consider the contemporary meaning of such terms as *producer, radical, revolution,* and *class.* By placing these words in their historical context and comparing their meanings with modern definitions, you will gain insight into the language of labor and its centrality to a movement culture. Try to determine what farm leaders meant by their words, including the wider effect they were intended to have.

While the People's Party met defeat in the climactic election of 1896, the Populists' significance lies as much in the cultural protest they represented as in their modest political successes, for Populism expressed a dramatic alternative vision of America's future that differed sharply from the world view of corporate capitalism. Agrarian radicals embraced a counterculture that assumed worker cooperation and an equitable distribution of the wealth created by America's producers. Your analysis should include an assessment of the goals they set and their proposals to achieve them. What did these objectives reveal about the social and ideological assumptions accepted by the Alliance and the People's Party?

The social ideas expressed by the rebels are evident in several of the documents. Review these materials with special emphasis on the problems of race relations and gender equity within the Farmers' Alliance. Ask yourself what made these issues so controversial, and consider their significance as evidence of counterthemes in the history of American politics, racial dialogue, and gender relations.

Your analysis of race and gender questions will underscore the striking differences between the agrarian radicals and the mainstream politicians of their era. Equally dramatic was the Populists' willingness to raise class issues often de-emphasized in American politics. As you try to account for these departures from traditional political discourse, think about the reasons for Populist boldness. Be especially aware of the socioeconomic composition of the party's base. Since not all farmers endorsed their program, it is important that you explore the characteristics of those who found the Populist message appealing. Finally, try to assess the significance of a lost cause that expressed a social and economic consciousness not shared by most Americans of the late nineteenth century. What was the legacy of the farm rebellion for the generations that followed?

Questions for Analysis

1. What is the meaning of the term *radical*? In what sense, if any, were the Farmers' Alliance and the People's Party radical? Analyze the use made of language by the agrarian rebels of the 1890s. What insights into the essential character of Populism may be gained through careful analysis of the movement's rhetoric? What was the significance of its emphasis on cooperation?

2. Does the evidence suggest that the Farmers' Alliance and the People's Party looked to the past or the future? Identify the key issues that drew their attention, and determine whether their solutions were practical and realistic.

3. What are the attributes of a social or political "movement"? To what extent does the farm rebellion of the late nineteenth century fit your definition? What was new about the goals established by the Alliance and the Populists, and why did their assertions so alarm the mainstream political leadership of the United States?

4. What has been the historical function of third parties in the American political system? To what extent did the People's Party fulfill that function? How? With what results, short term and long? By what standard may we judge the failure or success of a political movement?

5. Explain the class analysis adopted by spokespersons for the agrarian rebels of the late nineteenth century. What did they mean by "producers," and how did they define their enemies?

6. What was the role of women and blacks in the farm rebellion of the late nineteenth century? How was the movement's incorporation of these groups related to the rhetoric and practices of the Farmers' Alliance and the People's Party?

1. The Farmers' Alliance Proposes a Cooperative Commonwealth, 1889

Co-operation is the distinctive feature of the Farmers' Alliance. The objects are fully and clearly set forth in the Declaration of Purposes. Its principles are founded upon equity and justice. It has entered the conflict against monopoly, and on its banners is inscribed its motto: "In things essential, unity; in all things, charity." It can not afford to turn back. It is in the fight. Its position is exposed. The enemy's guns are trained upon every vulnerable point. It will not do to stand still. Nothing but an aggressive warfare will win. Monopoly and privileged classes are intrenched behind fortifications which the farmers have builded for them. The fight on the one side is waged to retain the privilege to rob and plunder. On the other hand it is made to regain constitutional rights. The fight on the part of the farmer is being made, not only for himself but for generations yet unborn. It is a fight for liberty, equality and a just reward for his labor. To lose is to be dependent, poor and miserable. To win is to be free, comfortable and happy. To banish monopoly of every description is to give new vitality to every industry, and strengthen the foundations of government. To fail, is to drift into centralization, where money and aristocracy will rule and land monopoly be the prevailing system.... Upon the part of the producers a mighty and almost universal effort is being made to free themselves from the iron grasp of privileged classes. It is the final struggle for the peaceful solution of the great issue between the people and Shylock. If this effort, this last hope, more sweet than the grapes of Eschol, fail; if it burn to ashes upon fallen altars, nothing short of a desperate revolution will ever save the Republic. It is the duty of every citizen to do all in his power to avert such a dreadful catastrophe. We must press forward. Our numbers are overwhelmingly in our favor if we can only extend our organization and secure the co-operation of our brethren....

Laboring men of America! The voice of Patrick Henry and the fathers of American Independence rings down through the corridors of time and tells you to strike. Not with glittering musket, flaming sword and deadly cannon; but with the silent, potent and all-powerful ballot, the only vestige of liberty left. Strike from yourselves the shackles of party slavery, and exercise independent manhood.

Strike at the foundation of the evils which are threatening the existence of the Republic.

Strike for yourselves, your families, your fellow man, your country and your God.

Strike from the face of the land the monopolies and combinations that are eating out the heart of the Nation.

Let the manhood of the Nation rise up in defense of liberty, justice and equality. Let the battle go on until all the people, from North to South and East to West, shall join in one loud acclaim, "Victory is ours, and the people are free!"

2. Political and Economic Cooperation as the Solution to the Race Problem, 1891

The Race Problem

By J. H. Turner, National Secretary-Treasurer of the National Farmers' Alliance and Industrial Union

The white farmers of the South, while they are more reluctant to cut loose from party, are perfectly willing and ready to take the negro by the hand and say to him: We are citizens of the same great country; we have the same foes to face, the same ills to bear; therefore our interests as agriculturists are one, and we will co-operate with you, and defend and protect you in all your rights.

In proof of the above, I will simply submit the agreement entered into by the National Farmers' Alliance and Industrial Union and the Colored National Farmers' Alliance and Co-operative Union, at their meetings in the city of Ocala, Florida, on the second day of December, 1890, which is as follows:—

Your committee on above beg leave to report that we visited the Colored Farmers' National Alliance and Co-operative Union Committee, and were received with the utmost cordiality, and after careful consultation it was mutually and unanimously agreed to unite our orders upon the basis adopted December 5, 1890, a basis between the National Farmers' Alliance

and Industrial Union and the Farmers' Mutual Benefit Association; . . . and hereby pledge ourselves to stand faithfully by each other in the great battle for the enfranchisement of labor and the laborers from the control of corporate and political rings; each order to bear its own members' expense on the Supreme Council, and be entitled to as many votes as they have legal voters in their organization. We recommend and urge that equal facilities, educational, commercial, and political, be demanded for colored and white Alliance men alike, competency considered, and that a free ballot and a fair count will be insisted upon and had, for colored and white alike, by every true Alliance man in America. We further recommend that a plan of district Alliances, to conform to district Alliances provided for in this body, be adopted by every order in confederation, with a district lecturer, and county Alliances organized in every county possible, and that the lecturers and officers of said district and counties co-operate with each other in conventional, business, educational, commercial, and political matters.

3. Bettie Gay Views the Alliance as an Opportunity for Women, 1891

The Influence of Women in the Alliance

By Mrs. Bettie Gay, Columbus, Texas

[T]his is a new era in human progress, when woman demands an equal opportunity in every department of life. She is no longer to be considered a tool, a mere plaything, but a human being, with a soul to save and a body to protect. Her mind must be cultivated, that she may be made more useful in the reform movement and the development of the race. It is an acknowledged principle in science that cultivated and intelligent mothers produce brainy children, and the only means by which the minds of the human race can be developed is to strengthen, by cultivation, the intellectual capacities of the mothers, by which means a mentally great race may be produced. When I look into the hard and stolid faces of many of the mothers of the present, and know that they have been deprived of the opportunities which would have improved them, I am not surprised that we are surrounded by people who are the advocates of a system but little better than cannibalism. . . .

If I understand the object of the Alliance, it is organized not only to better the financial condition of the people, but to elevate them socially, and in every other way, and make them happier and better, and to make this world a fit habitation for man, by giving to the people equal opportunities. Every woman who has at heart the welfare of the race should attach herself to some reform organization, and lend her help toward the removal of the causes which have filled the world with crime and sorrow, and made outcasts of so many of her sex. It is a work in which all may engage, with the assurance that they are entering upon a labor of love, in the interest of the downtrodden and disinherited; a work by which all mankind will be blessed, and which will bless those who are to come after for all time. . . .

What we need, above all things else, is a better womanhood, —a womanhood with the courage of conviction, armed with intelligence and the greatest virtues of her sex, acknowledging no master and accepting no compromise. When her enemies shall have laid down their arms, and her proper position in society is recognized, she will be prepared to take upon herself the responsibilities of life, and civilization will be advanced to that point where intellect instead of brute force will rule the world. When this work is accomplished, avarice, greed, and passion will cease to control the minds of the people, and we can proclaim, "Peace on earth, good will toward men."

4. The Alliance's Vision of Community, 1891

These ideas have gained such a hold upon public opinion, that they bid fair to cause a complete change in our form of government, as far as its industrial conditions are concerned, during the next quarter of a century. It looks as though, before that period was passed, the government would assume control and ownership of all means of transportation in the form of railroads; that the government would adopt a system of issuing money to the people without the aid of banking institutions, and that a larger volume per capita would be in circulation than ever before in the history of any government in the world; that the local governments of cities and towns would assume control and complete ownership of all street railroads, gas and water works. In fact, it bids fair to be a radical revolution in the industrial affairs of government. It looks as though the days of individualism and corporations were doomed, and that the next step in the line of human advancement would be the adoption of the socialistic state of society.

5. Tom Watson Indicts Corporate Plunder, 1892

The corporation is a convenient cloak for the rascality of the individual. It is also his protection. His share in the profits has no limits save the amount of the profits; while his share of the losses is confined to the stock he subscribed for. . . .

These Corporations are the Feudal Barons of this Century. Their Directors live in lordly Palaces and Castles. Their Yachts are on the sea; their Parlor Cars on the rails. They spread feasts that would feed a starving factory town. They throw away on the decorations of a Ball Room enough to clothe the children of a city. They keep bands of Militia to do their fighting. In Pennsylvania it is called the "Coal and Iron Police." In New York and Illinois it is called "The Pinkerton Detective Agency." At the word of command these hireling assassins shoot down men, women and children. Time and again they have made the streets run red with the blood of innocent people.

The murderers are never punished. They are spirited away on the trains.

Not only do the Corporations keep armed Retainers: they keep oily and servile Courtiers to do their bidding in other walks of life. Their paid Lobby bribes the voter. Their paid editor feeds the public with lies. Their corrupt Lawyers and Judges peddle out justice to the highest bidder. Their Attorneys go on the Bench or into Senates to vote the will of their Masters.

The ambitious young men fear them: their power is so terribly great. The pulpit fears them: for the plush-covered Pew is the seat of the millionaire. The Pew overawes the Sacred Desk. . . .

To restore the liberties of the people, the rule of the people, the equal rights of the people is our purpose; and to do it, the revolution in the old systems must be complete. . . .

The hot-beds of crime and vice to-day are at the two extremes of Society. One is among the class who have all the work and no money; the other is with the class who have all the money and no work. The one class is driven to crime and vice by hardships, despair, desperation. The other class chooses crime and vice because of their surplus of money, their lack of purpose, their capacity to live in idleness and gratify sensual pleasures. . . .

Any system which increases the Moneyed Class where there is all money and no work, debauches Society. . . . Any System which increases the class where there is all work and no money debauches and endangers Society. Any system which will add to the great Middle Class where there is reasonable work and fair reward, secures to Society the best results of which humanity is capable. Every principle advocated by the People's Party seeks that end and logically leads to it.

Why the Third Party is Necessary in the South

1. A third party is absolutely necessary in the South because, under present conditions, neither of the old parties can afford our people any relief. The Republican party is composed of a few whites and the negroes. They hate the name of Democrat. Under the present organization of their party, no aid can come from them because they are absolutely controlled from the North under a platform and under a leadership which repudiates our demands for reform.

The Democratic party, on the other hand, is composed of the whites and a few negros. They hate the name Republican. Under the present organization no aid can come from them because they are likewise controlled from the North under a platform and a leadership which repudiates our demands for reform. . . .

2. The Southern people were always supporters of the Jeffersonian theory of government. They always believe in preserving the rights of the individual citizen and the maintenance of civil equality. They always dreaded the Hamiltonian idea of a moneyed aristocracy with national banks, unbridled corporations and the class rule of the few. . . .

3. It offers the only solution of the color question. Under our generous treatment of the negro in the South he is becoming rapidly educated. He can fully appreciate an argument addressed to his interest as a farmer and as a laborer. I have found them quick to understand the reform measures we advocate. As a body they are laborers, not capitalists. What is more natural than that they should feel a deep personal interest in this movement. They do feel it. They will as a rule vote with us on it, leaving their party for the very same reasons that we leave ours. Thus the two races will dwell side by side in political harmony instead of political discord. There are those who profess to see great danger of negro supremacy. I do not share in this alarm. I cannot see how the colored people can be more dangerous to us when they agree with us and vote with us than when they differ from us and vote against us. We assume a singularly absurd attitude when we say that white people shall never have good laws just because the colored people are going to help us get them.

4. Because it is the death of sectionalism.

6. The Omaha Platform, 1892

The conditions which surround us best justify our co-operation: we meet in the midst of a nation brought to the verge of moral, political, and material ruin. Corruption dominates the ballot-box, the legislatures, the Congress, and touches even the ermine of the bench. The people are demoralized; most of the States have been compelled to isolate the voters at the polling-places to prevent universal intimidation or bribery. The newspapers are largely subsidized or muzzled; public opinion silenced; business prostrated; our homes covered with mortgages; labor impoverished; and the land concentrating in the hands of the capitalists. The urban workmen are denied the right of organization for self-protection; imported pauperized labor beats down their wages; a hireling standing army, unrecognized by our laws, is established to shoot them down, and they are rapidly degenerating into European conditions. The fruits of the toil of millions are boldly stolen to build up colossal fortunes for a few, unprecedented in the history of mankind; and the possessors of these, in turn, despise the republic and endanger liberty. From the same prolific womb of governmental injustice we breed the two great classes—tramps and millionaires. . . .

[B]elieving that the forces of reform this day organized will never cease to move forward until every wrong is remedied, and equal rights and equal privileges securely established for all the men and women of this country.

We declare, therefore,—

First. That the union of the labor forces of the United States this day consummated shall be permanent and perpetual; may its spirit enter all hearts for the salvation of the republic and the uplifting of mankind!

Second. Wealth belongs to him who creates it, and every dollar taken from industry without an equivalent is robbery. "If any will not work, neither shall he eat." The interests of rural and civic labor are the same; their enemies are identical.

Third. We believe that the time has come when the railroad corporations will either own the people or the people must own the railroads; and, should the government enter upon the work of owning and managing all railroads, we should favor an amendment to the Constitution by which all persons engaged in the government service shall be placed under a civil service regulation of the most rigid character, so as to prevent the increase of the power of the national administration by the use of such additional government employees.

First, *Money.* We demand a national currency, safe, sound, and flexible, issued by the general government only, a full legal tender for all debts, public and private, and that, without the use of banking corporations, a just, equitable, and efficient means of distribution direct to the people, at a tax not to exceed two percent per annum, to be provided as set forth in the sub-treasury plan of the Farmers' Alliance, or a better system; also, by payments in discharge of its obligations for public improvements.

(a) We demand free and unlimited coinage of silver and gold at the present legal ratio of sixteen to one.

(b) We demand that the amount of circulating medium be speedily increased to not less than fifty dollars per capita.

(c) We demand a graduated income tax.

(d) We believe that the money of the country should be kept as much as possible in the hands of the people, and hence we demand that all state and national revenues shall be limited to the necessary expenses of the government economically and honestly administered.

(e) We demand that postal savings banks be established by the government for the safe deposit of the earnings of the people and to facilitate exchange.

Second, *Transportation.* Transportation being a means of exchange and public necessity, the government should own and operate the railroads in the interest of the people.

(a) The telegraph and telephone, like the post-office system, being a necessity for the transmission of news, should be owned and operated by the government in the interest of the people.

Third, *Land.* The land, including all the natural sources of wealth, is the heritage of the people, and should not be monopolized for speculative purposes, and alien ownership of land should be prohibited. All land now held by railroads and other corporations in excess of their actual needs, and all lands now owned by aliens, should be reclaimed by the government and held for actual settlers only.

Chapter 21:
Document Set 3 References

1. The Farmers' Alliance Proposes a Cooperative Commonwealth, 1889
   W. Scott Morgan, *History of the Wheel and Alliance and the Impending Revolution* (Fort Scott, Kansas: J. H. Rice & Sons, 1889), pp. 351–352.

2. Political and Economic Cooperation as the Solution to the Race Problem, 1891
   J. H. Turner, "The Race Problem," in N. A. Dunning, ed., *The Farmers' Alliance History and Agricultural Digest* (Washington, D.C.: Alliance Publishing Company, 1891), pp. 272, 278.

3. Bettie Gay Views the Alliance as an Opportunity for Women, 1891
   Bettie Gay, "The Influence of Women in the Alliance," in Dunning, pp. 308, 311–312.

4. The Alliance's Vision of Community, 1891
   Dunning, p. 326.

5. Tom Watson Indicts Corporate Plunder, 1892
   Thomas E. Watson, *The People's Party Campaign Book, 1892: Not a Revolt: It Is a Revolution* (Washington, D.C.: National Watchman Publishing Company, 1892), pp. 206–207, 220–221, 249–250.

6. The Omaha Platform, 1892
   The National Economist, July 9, 1892.

DOCUMENT SET 1

Muckraking: The Novel as a Force for Social Change

As noted in the textbook, the social, economic, and political changes of the Progressive Era were preceded by a sweeping intellectual revolution that produced a new concept of the government's role as protector of the public interest. While scholars rejected Social Darwinism, another group of popular writers began to address social issues through novels and magazines aimed at a broad middle-class audience. Perhaps the best known of these literary works was *The Jungle*, Upton Sinclair's dramatic exposé of corruption in the Chicago stockyards at the turn of the century. The following documents examine the novel as a force for reform. As you review the extensive excerpts from Sinclair's work, as well as Roosevelt's remarks on consumer-protection legislation, be conscious of both the novelist's agenda and the president's goals.

Roosevelt's statements as well as the political cartoon suggest that *The Jungle* was not the only factor behind reform legislation. Try to determine what larger progressive themes surfaced in the drive for the Meat Inspection and Pure Food and Drug acts.

As you read the excerpts from *The Jungle*, think about the popular sensation produced by its publica-tion and account for the widespread interest in Sinclair's novel. Consider also the novelist's personal political background and his primary objectives as a writer. As you do so, define the term *propaganda* and evaluate the book as a propaganda tract.

By analyzing Roosevelt's comments, make a judgment about the president's perception of the written word as an influence for social change. Determine what his words reveal about his political position in 1906 and his perspective on the work of the muckraking writers of the early twentieth century. Relying on your textbook as well as the documents, try to determine the relationship between popular literature, public opinion, and legislative reform in the Progressive Era.

Finally, these documents suggest a relationship between industrialization and a wide range of social problems. Identify the social consequences of industrialization and their long-term implications. Evaluate the solutions advanced to address the problems that emerged in the new industrial society, and explain why a new political consensus developed.

Questions for Analysis

1. What does *The Jungle* stress as the social result of industrialization? What was Sinclair's explanation for the existence of these social problems? What was his solution? How did liberal and radical political solutions for the ills of an industrial society differ? Compare Roosevelt's and Sinclair's goals.

2. The textbook quotes Sinclair as saying that "I aimed at the nation's heart but hit it in the stomach." What was the meaning of this remark? How does it reflect the state of the national political consensus of Progressive America?

3. What were the origin and meaning of the term *muckraking*? By examining Roosevelt's comments on the muckrakers, can you determine what the president's evaluation of their work was? What do Roosevelt's remarks suggest about the limits and extent of his commitment to reform?

4. What do the excerpts from *The Jungle* reveal about immigrant life in the early twentieth century? What was the impact of the industrial system on individuals and families?

5. Typically, historians have established a direct link between *The Jungle* and the enactment of consumer-protection legislation in 1906. Do the documents provide evidence to confirm, refute, or modify that widely held assumption? What aspects of the beef trust does the political cartoon attack? What does this focus suggest about the influence of Sinclair's work?

6. Define *progressivism*, using your textbook as a resource. What themes of the movement are evident in the issues raised by *The Jungle*? What aspects of the worker experience are mirrored in the novel and in the president's words?

1. The Beef Trust Exploits the Public, 1902

2. Upton Sinclair's Attack on the Meat Packers, 1906

And then there was the condemned meat industry, with its endless horrors. The people of Chicago saw the government inspectors in Packingtown, and they all took that to mean that they were protected from diseased meat; they did not understand that these hundred and sixty-three inspectors had been appointed at the request of the packers, and that they were paid by the United States government to certify that all the diseased meat was kept in the state. They had no authority beyond that; for the inspection of meat to be sold in the city and state the whole force in Packingtown consisted of three henchmen of the local political machine! . . .

There were the men in the pickle rooms, for instance, where old Antanas had gotten his death; scarce a one of these that had not some spot of horror on his person. Let a man so much as scrape his finger pushing a truck in the pickle rooms, and he might have a sore that would put him out of the world; all the joints of his fingers might be eaten by the acid, one by one. Of the butchers and floorsmen, the beef boners and trimmers, and all those who used knives, you could scarcely find a person who had the use of his thumb; time and time again the base of it had been slashed, till it was a mere lump of flesh against which the man pressed the knife to hold it. The hands of these men would be criss-crossed with cuts, until you could no longer pretend to count them or to trace them. They would have no nails,—they had worn them off pulling hides; their knuckles were swollen so that their fingers spread out like a fan. There were men who worked in the cooking rooms, in the midst of steam and sickening odors, by artificial light; in these rooms the germs of tuberculosis might live for two years, but the supply was renewed every hour. There were the beef luggers, who carried two-hundred-pound quarters into the refrigerator cars, a fearful kind of work, that began at four o'clock in the morning, and that wore out the most powerful men in a few years. There were those who worked in the chilling rooms, and whose special disease was rheumatism; the time limit that a man could work in the chilling rooms was said to be five years. There were the wool pluckers, whose hands went to pieces even sooner than the hands of the pickle men; for the pelts of the sheep had to be painted with acid to loosen the wool, and then the pluckers had to pull out this wool with their bare hands, till the acid had eaten their fingers off. There were those who made the tins for the canned meat, and their hands, too, were a maze of cuts, and each cut represented a chance for blood poisoning. Some worked at the stamping machines, and it was very seldom that one could work long there at the pace that was set, and not give out and forget himself, and have a part of his hand chopped off. There were the "hoisters," as they were called, whose task it was to press the lever which lifted the dead cattle off the floor. They ran along upon a rafter, peering down through the damp and the steam, and as old Durham's architects had not built the killing room for the convenience of the hoisters, at every few feet they would have to stoop under a beam, say four feet above the one they ran on, which got them into the habit of stooping, so that in a few years they would be walking like chimpanzees. Worst of any, however, were the fertilizer men, and those who served in the cooking rooms. These people could not be shown to the visitor—for the odor of a fertilizer man would scare away any ordinary visitor at a hundred yards, and as for the other men, who worked in tank rooms full of steam, and in some of which there were open vats near the level of the floor, their peculiar trouble was that they fell into the vats; and when they were fished out, there was never enough of them left to be worth exhibiting—sometimes they would be overlooked for days, till all but the bones of them had gone out to the world as Durham's Pure Leaf Lard! . . .

There was never the least attention paid to what was cut up for sausage; there would come all the way back from Europe old sausage that had been rejected, and that was mouldy and white—it would be dosed with borax and glycerine, and dumped into the hoppers, and made over again for home consumption. There would be meat that had tumbled out on the floor, in the dirt and sawdust, where the workers had tramped and spit uncounted billions of consumption germs. There would be meat stored in great piles in rooms; and the water from leaky roofs would drip over it, and thousands of rats would race about on it. It was too dark in these storage places to see well, but a man could run his hand over these piles of meat and sweep off handfuls of the dried dung of rats. These rats were nuisances, and the packers would put poisoned bread out for them, they would die, and then rats, bread, and meat would go into the hoppers together. This is no fairy story and no joke; the meat would be shovelled into carts, and the man who did the shoveling would not trouble to lift out a rat even when he saw one—there were things that went into the sausage in comparison with which a poisoned rat was a tidbit. There was no place for the men to wash their hands before they ate their dinner, and so they made a practice of washing them in the water that was to be ladled into the sausage. There were the butt-ends of smoked meat, and the scraps of corned beef, and all the odds and ends of the waste of the plants, that would be dumped into old barrels in the cellar and left there. Under the system of rigid economy which the packers enforced, there were some jobs that it only paid to do once in a long time, and among these was the cleaning out of the waste barrels. Every spring they did it; and in the barrels would be dirt and rust and old nails and stale water—and cart load after cart load of it would be taken up and dumped into the hoppers with fresh meat, and sent out to the public's breakfast. Some of it they would make into "smoked" sausage—but as the smoking took time, and was therefore expensive, they would call upon their chemistry department, and preserve it with borax and color it with gelatine to make it brown. All of their sausage came out of the same bowl, but when they came to wrap it they would stamp some of it "special," and for this they would charge two cents more a pound. . . .

And then Schliemann went on to outline some of the wastes of competition: the losses of industrial warfare; the ceaseless worry and friction; the vices—such as drink, for instance, the use of which had nearly doubled in twenty years, as a consequence of the intensification of the economic struggle; the idle and unproductive members of the community, the frivolous rich and the pauperized poor; the law and the whole machinery of repression; the wastes of social ostentation, the milliners and tailors, the hairdressers, dancing masters, chefs and lackeys. "You understand," he said, "that in a society dominated by the fact of commercial competition, money is necessarily the test of prowess, and wastefulness the sole criterion of power. So we have, at the present moment, a society with, say, thirty per cent of the population occupied in producing useless articles, and one per cent occupied in destroying them. . . .

And then there were official returns from the various precincts and wards of the city itself! Whether it was a factory district or one of the "silk-stocking" wards seemed to make no particular difference in the increase; but one of the things which surprised the [Socialist] party leaders most was the tremendous vote that came rolling in from the stockyards.

Packingtown comprised three wards of the city, and the vote in the spring of 1903 had been five hundred, and in the fall of the same year, sixteen hundred. Now, only a year later, it was over sixty-three hundred—and the Democratic vote only eighty-eight hundred! There were other wards in which the Democratic vote had been actually surpassed, and in two districts, members of the state legislature had been elected. Thus Chicago now led the country; it has set a new standard for the party, it had shown the workingmen the way!

—So spoke an orator upon the platform; and two thousand pairs of eyes were fixed upon him, and two thousand voices were cheering his every sentence. The orator had been the head of the city's relief bureau in the stockyards, until the sight of misery and corruption had made him sick. He was young, hungry-looking, full of fire; and as he swung his long arms and beat up the crowd, to Jurgis he seemed the very spirit of the revolution. "Organize! Organize! Organize!"—that was his cry. He was afraid of this tremendous vote, which his party had not expected, and which it had not earned. "These men are not Socialists!" he cried. "This election will pass, and the excitement will die, and people will forget about it; and if you forget about it, too, if you sink back and rest upon your oars, we shall lose this vote that we have polled today, and our enemies will laugh us to scorn! It rests with you to take your resolution—now, in the flush of victory, to find these men who have voted for us, and bring them to our meetings, and organize them and bind them to us! We shall not find all our campaigns as easy as this one. Everywhere in the country tonight the old party politicians are studying this vote, and setting their sails by it; and nowhere will they be quicker or more cunning than here in our own city. Fifty thousand Socialist votes in Chicago means a municipal-ownership Democracy in the spring! And then they will fool the voters once more, and all the powers of plunder and corruption will be swept into office again! But whatever they may do when they get in, there is one thing they will not do, and that will be the thing for which they were elected! They will not give the people of our city municipal ownership—they will not mean to do it, they will not try to do it; all that they will do is give our party in Chicago the greatest opportunity that has ever come to Socialism in America! We shall have the sham reformers self-stultified and self-convicted; we shall have the radical Democracy left without a lie with which to cover its nakedness! And then will begin the rush that will never be checked, the tide that will never turn till it has reached its flood—that will be irresistible, overwhelming—the rallying of the outraged workingmen of Chicago to our standard! And we shall organize them, we shall drill them, we shall marshal them for the victory! We shall bear down the opposition, we shall sweep it before us—and Chicago will be ours! *Chicago will be ours!* CHICAGO WILL BE OURS!"

The End

3. Theodore Roosevelt Describes the Muckrakers, 1906

In Bunyan's "Pilgrim's Progress" you may recall the description of the Man with the Muck-rake, the man who could look no way but downward, with the muck-rake in his hand; who was offered a celestial crown for his muck-rake, but who would neither look up nor regard the crown he was offered, but continued to rake to himself the filth of the floor.

In "Pilgrim's Progress" the Man with the Muck-rake is set forth as the example of him whose vision is fixed on carnal instead of on spiritual things. Yet he also typifies the man who in this life consistently refuses to see aught that is lofty, and fixes his eyes with solemn intentness only on that which is vile and debasing. Now, it is very necessary that we should not flinch from seeing what is vile and debasing. There is filth on the floor, and it must be scraped up with the muck-rake; and there are times and places where this service is the most needed of all the services that can be performed. But the man who never does anything else, who never thinks or speaks or writes, save of his feats with the muck-rake, speedily becomes, not a help to society, not an incitement to good, but one of the most potent forces for evil.

There are, in the body politic, economic and social, many and grave evils, and there is urgent necessity for the sternest war upon them. There should be relentless exposure of and attack upon every evil man whether politician or business man, every evil practice, whether in politics, in business, or in social life. I hail as a benefactor every writer or speaker, every man who, on the platform, or in book, magazine, or newspaper, with merciless severity makes such attack, provided always that he in his turn remembers that the attack is of use only if it is absolutely truthful.

4. Roosevelt Insists on Regulatory Legislation, 1906

I have recently had an investigation made by Commissioner Neill of the Labor Bureau and Mr. J. B. Reynolds, of the situation in Chicago packing houses. It is hideous, and it must be remedied at once. I was at first so indignant that I resolved to send in the full report to Congress. As far as the beef packers themselves are concerned I should do this now with a clear conscience, for the great damage that would befall them in consequence would be purely due to their own actions. But the damage would also come to all the stock growers of the country and the effect of such a report would undoubtedly be well-nigh ruinous to our export trade in meat for the time being, and doubtless the damaging effect would be apparent long after we had remedied the wrongs. I am therefore going to withhold the report for the time being, and until I can also report that the wrongs have been remedied, provided that without making it public I can get the needed legislation; that is, provided we can have the meat inspection amendment that has been put on in the Senate in substance enacted into law. Of course what I am after is not to do damage even to the packers, still less to the stockmen and farmers. What I want is the immediate betterment of the dreadful conditions that prevail, and moreover the providing against a possible recurrence of these conditions. The beef packers have told me through Mr. Louis Swift that if I will not make this report public they will guarantee to remedy all the wrongs which we have found or may find to exist. This is good as far as it goes, but it does not go far enough, and it is absolutely necessary that we shall have legislation which will prevent the recurrence of these wrongs. I should not make the report public with the idea of damaging the packers. I should do it only if it were necessary in order to secure the remedy.

Chapter 22:
Document Set 1 References

1. The Beef Trust Exploits the Public, 1902
   "Nursery Rhymes for Infant Industries," in Frederick Opper, "Alphabet of Joyous Trusts," No. 2, *New York Journal,* September 24, 1902.

2. Upton Sinclair's Attack on the Meat Packers, 1906
   Upton Sinclair, *The Jungle,* 1906 (New York: New American Library, rep. 1960), pp. 98, 101–102, 136–137, 332, 340–341.

3. Theodore Roosevelt Describes the Muckrakers, 1906
   Theodore Roosevelt, Address, April 14, 1906, in Theodore Roosevelt, *The Autobiography of Theodore Roosevelt, Condensed from the Original Edition, Supplemented by Letters, Speeches, and Other Writings,* Wayne Andrews, ed. (New York: Charles Scribner's Sons, 1913, rep. 1958), pp. 246–247.

4. Roosevelt Insists on Regulatory Legislation, 1906
   Roosevelt, *Autobiography,* pp. 244–245.

Chapter 22:
Document Set 1 Credits

1. A. From "Nursery Rhymes for Infant Industries," in Frederik Opper's "Alphabet of Joyous Trusts," No. 2, *New York Journal,* September 24, 1902

CHAPTER 22

The Rise of Women's Activism: New Responsibilities

The documents in this set link several themes in the textbook's discussion of the Progressive Era, including moral reform, women's suffrage, and the role of female activists in the public sphere. Confronted with the reality of harsh working conditions in the nation's factories and mills, socially conscious middle-class women's organizations enlisted in a crusade against industrial exploitation of women and children that drew them into the political struggle. As the following documents suggest, it was a short distance from moral uplift and social concern to an all-consuming emphasis on the great reform—the drive for female suffrage.

One critical vehicle for women's influence on social and economic life was the increasingly active General Federation of Women's Clubs. As described in your text, these organizations moved from an early educational function to a new role as proponents of social justice. As you examine the writings of Martha E. D. White and Rheta Childe Dorr, try to determine why this shift in emphasis occurred and what assumptions about the unique nature of women prevailed. Be aware of the writers' backgrounds as they relate to the class base of the women's movement at this time.

Building on their sense of social responsibility, women expended great energy on such issues as protective legislation for female workers. The next group of documents focuses on the landmark Supreme Court case of *Muller* v. *Oregon* (1908), described in your textbook as evidence of a moderating judicial climate. As you review the excerpts from the legal brief of counsel Louis D. Brandeis in support of Oregon's restrictive law, compare its assumptions with those of Justice David J. Brewer, writing for the majority that affirmed the state legislation. Finally, read Dorr's description of the National Consumers' League role in the *Muller* case. Note the League's efforts as a part of the new women's activism. Be also aware of the result of its activity, including the wider effect of the *Muller* decision. Finally, consider the long-term implications of the "special protection" approach endorsed.

Even though the impact of middle-class women's organizations on protective legislation was substantial, their social activism had broader implications. The final group of documents illustrates the link between women's emphasis on social justice and the ultimately successful suffrage movement. Both Dorr and reformer Jane Addams explore the importance of suffrage to the achievement of social reform. Relate their arguments to the long-standing disagreement over the idea of "separate spheres" for men and women. These documents clearly reveal a relationship among women as domestic beings, social reformers, and political activists.

Questions for Analysis

1. How do the Brandeis brief and the Brewer opinion in the *Muller* case justify the Supreme Court's decision to approve protective legislation for women? What forms of evidence are presented in the brief? What was the significance of the *Muller* case for the overall cause of social justice?

2. What was the long-term significance of the *Muller* decision for the future of women's rights? What were the implications of the legal precedent established? How did suffrage activists strengthen their case for voting rights in the Progressive Era? What do the documents reveal about the relationship between social reform and the drive for political equality?

3. What were the original purposes of the women's clubs? What do the documents suggest with regard to the evolution of women's organizations and their goals? How did their objectives change after 1900? With what results?

4. What themes are evident in your textbook's discussion of progressivism? In what way were the concerns of the women's movement consistent with Progressive ideology and legislative activity? What evidence do the documents provide of a female contribution to the achievement of Progressive goals?

5. What was the class composition of the women's club movement? How does the socioeconomic makeup of women's organizations compare with that of other elements in the Progressive coalition? How would you account for the class base

of the social-justice movement? What were its implications for reform, including the suffrage campaign?

6. What do the careers of women like Jane Addams and Rheta Childe Dorr reveal about the changing roles of women in early-twentieth-century America? What was new about the "New Woman" and her contribution to the extension of social justice in the United States? How did female social reformers deal with the traditional concept of "separate spheres"?

1. Women in the U.S. Labor Force for Selected Years, 1890–1930

Year	Women in labor force (000's)	% women in total labor force	Women in labor force as % of total women of working age	% of women in labor force		
				Single	Married	Widowed or divorced
1890	3,712	17.0	18.9	68.2	13.9	17.9
1900	4,997	18.1	20.6	66.2	15.4	18.4
1910[a]	7,640	—	25.4	60.2	24.7	15.0
1920	8,347	20.4	23.7	77.0[b]	23.0	—
1930	10,632	21.9	24.8	53.9	28.9	17.2

[a]Data not comparable with later or earlier censuses due to difference in basis of enumeration.
[b]Includes widowed and divorced.

2. The Women's Clubs Embrace Reform, 1904

Outwardly, for twenty years, the woman's club remained an institution for the culture and pleasure of its members; but within, the desire for a larger opportunity was gradually strengthening. Parliamentary practice gave women confidence in their ability to lead larger issues to a successful conclusion. The inherent longing for power, coupled with confidence in the wisdom and beneficence of whatever woman should do, brought the leaders of the club movement to a conception of social service. To effect this, further organization was necessary. It was then, in 1890, that a union of individual clubs was formed into a chartered body, known as the General Federation of Women's Clubs. . . .

Securing the passage of laws is the extreme instance of what organized women have accomplished through the medium of public opinion. Many other concrete illustrations drawn from local conditions might be given; but they would all serve to illustrate that the woman's club is determining the mind of the community in its relation to many educational, philanthropic, and reformatory questions. . . .

The federation of one of the more enlightened states has recently undertaken to enter the field of direct politics. I quote the advice it gives to its constituents:—

"Before senators and representatives are even nominated, it is very essential that club women look up the record of the various candidates in their districts, and satisfy themselves as to their position regarding women upon boards of control of state institutions. Find out how they voted last year. Information will be gladly furnished by members of this committee. Then strive to create a sufficient public sentiment in your own locality to defeat, at the party caucus, any nominee known to oppose women representatives upon Boards of Control.". . .

Six years ago the General Federation undertook to help the solution of certain industrial problems, notably to further organization among working-women; to secure and enforce child labor legislation where needed; to further attendance at school; and to secure humane conditions under which labor is performed. State federations have acted in accordance with the General Federation's plans to appoint standing industrial committees, procure investiga-tions, circulate literature, and create a public senti-ment in favor of these causes. In Illinois this indirect power was of much aid in securing a Child Labor Law. In other communities something has been accomplished by way of enacting new laws or enforcing existing ones, showing that organized women readily avail themselves of the chance for indirect service in promoting the intelligent efforts of the federations.

3. Rheta Childe Dorr Recalls the Shift to Social Activism, 1904, 1905

[A]t the national Biennial Convention held in St. Louis in 1904, the whole club movement took a tremendous spurt forward. Not only did the program include a discussion, pro and con, of suffrage, but a woman voter was elected president of the General Federation. This was Sarah Platt Decker of Denver, a truly great woman, highly educated, widely traveled, experienced in politics, a woman whose sex alone kept her from being a United States Senator from Colorado. . . .

With all the power of her strong personality she painted a picture of the social and political problems which were troubling the world, and she made a plea to the women to drop their pleasant little essay-writing activities and to get into the struggle for a better civilization. Mrs. Decker made a clean sweep of all the committees, appointing able and energetic women to chairmanships. She created a few new committees, and to my surprise she called me from my place at the reporters' table to be chairman of the Committee on Industrial Conditions of Women and Children. She had had no direct contacts with working conditions, she told me, but she had read my articles in the *Evening Post* and she felt that the club women and the industrial workers must make common cause. Of course I accepted, and with the help of Mary McDowell of Chicago, May Alden Ward of Boston, and others who joined my committee, I set out to enlighten the club women. With the help of my colleagues I prepared reading lists, and through letters, circular and personal, I urged on the women the duty of informing themselves of local factory conditions, and of standing by factory workers in righteous trade disputes. . . . In 1905, with leaders in the Women's Trade Union League and the Association of Social Settlements, I was instrumental in securing the first official investigation into conditions of working women in the United States.

4. The Brandeis Brief States the Case for Protective Legislation, 1908

1. The Dangers of Long Hours

A. *Causes*

(1) Physical Differences Between Men and Women

The dangers of long hours for women arise from their special physical organization taken in connection with the strain incident to factory and similar work.

Long hours of labor are dangerous for women primarily because of their special physical organization. In structure and function women are differenti-ated from men. Besides these anatomical and physio-logical differences, physicians are agreed that women are fundamentally weaker than men in all that makes for endurance: in muscular strength, in nervous energy, in the powers of persistent attention and application. Overwork, therefore, which strains endurance to the utmost, is more disastrous to the health of women than of men, and entails upon them more lasting injury. . . .

B. *Bad Effect of Long Hours on Health*

The fatigue which follows long hours of labor becomes chronic and results in general deterioration of health. Often ignored, since it does not result in immediate disease, this weakness and anæmia undermines the whole system; it destroys the nervous energy most necessary for steady work, and effectually predisposes to other illness. The long hours of standing, which are required in many industries, are universally denounced by physicians as the cause of pelvic disorders. . . .

C. *Bad Effect of Long Hours on Safety*

Accidents to working women occur most frequently at the close of the day, or after a long period of uninterrupted work. The coincidence of casualties and fatigue due to long hours is thus made manifest. . . .

D. *Bad Effect of Long Hours on Morals*

The effect of overwork on morals is closely related to the injury to health. Laxity of moral fibre follows physical debility. When the working day is so long that no time whatever is left for a minimum of leisure or home-life, relief from the strain of work is sought in alcoholic stimulants and other excesses. . . .

E. *Bad Effect of Long Hours on General Welfare*

The experience of manufacturing countries has illustrated the evil effect of overwork upon the general welfare. Deterioration of any large portion of the population inevitably lowers the entire community physically, mentally, and morally. When the health of women has been injured by long hours, not only is the working efficiency of the community impaired, but the deterioration is handed down to succeeding generations. Infant mortality rises, while the children of married working-women, who survive, are injured by inevitable neglect. The overwork of future mothers thus directly attacks the welfare of the nation. . . .

VI. The Reasonableness of the Ten-Hour Day

Factory inspectors, physicians, and working women are unanimous in advocating the ten-hour day, wherever it has not yet been established. Some indeed consider ten hours too long a period of labor; but as opposed to the unregulated or longer day, there is agreement that ten hours is the maximum number of working hours compatible with health and efficiency. . . .

Conclusion

We submit that in view of the facts above set forth and of legislative action extending over a period of more than sixty years in the leading countries of Europe, and in twenty of our States, it cannot be said that the Legislature of Oregon had no reasonable ground for believing that the public health, safety, or welfare did not require a legal limitation on women's work in manufacturing and mechanical establishments and laundries to ten hours in one day.

5. Justice David J. Brewer Affirms the Oregon Law, 1908

CURT MULLER, Plff. in Err.,

v.

STATE OF OREGON.

Constitutional law—regulating hours of women employees.

Rights under the 14th Amendment to the Federal Constitution are not infringed by the limitation of the hours of labor of women employed in laundries to ten hours daily which is made by Oregon Laws 1903, p. 148, although like legislation affecting male employees may be invalid. . . .

That woman's physical structure and the performance of maternal functions place her at a disadvantage in the struggle for subsistence is obvious. This is especially true when the burdens of motherhood are upon her. Even when they are not, by abundant testimony of the medical fraternity continuance for a long time on her feet at work, repeating this from day to day, tends to injurious effects upon the body, and, as healthy mothers are essential to vigorous offspring, the physical well-being of woman becomes an object of public interest and care in order to preserve the strength and vigor of the race. . . .

Though limitations upon personal and contractual rights may be removed by legislation, there is that in her disposition and habits of life which will operate against a full assertion of those rights. She will still be where some legislation to protect her seems necessary to secure a real equality of right. Doubtless there are individual exceptions, and there are many respects in which she has an advantage over him; but looking at it from the viewpoint of the effort to maintain an independent position in life, she is not upon an equality. Differentiated by these matters from the other sex, she is properly placed in a class by herself, and legislation designed for her protection may be sustained, even when like legislation is not necessary for men, and could not be sustained. . . . The limitations which this statute places upon her contractual powers, upon her right to agree with her employer as to the time she shall labor, are not imposed solely for her benefit, but also largely for the benefit of all. Many words cannot make this plainer. The two sexes differ in structure of body, in the functions to be performed by each, in the amount of physical strength, in the capacity for long-continued labor, particularly when done standing, the influence of vigorous health upon the future well-being of the race, the self-reliance which enables one to assert full rights, and in the capacity to maintain the struggle for subsistence. This difference justifies a difference in legislation, and upholds that which is designed to compensate for some of the burdens which rest upon her.

We have not referred in this discussion to the denial of the elective franchise in the state of Oregon, for while that may disclose a lack of political equality in all things with her brother, that is not of itself decisive. The reason runs deeper, and rests in the inherent difference between the two sexes, and in the different functions in life which they perform.

For these reasons, and without questioning in any respect the decision in Lochner v. New York, we are of the opinion that it cannot be adjudged that the act in question is in conflict with the Federal Constitution, so far as it respects the work of a female in a laundry, and the judgment of the Supreme Court of Oregon is affirmed.

6. Dorr Describes the National Consumers' League Role in the *Muller* Case, 1908

The case was appealed, and appealed again, by the laundrymen, and finally reached the Supreme Court of the United States. Then the Consumers' League took a hand.

The brief for the State of Oregon . . . was prepared by Louis S. Brandeis, of Boston, assisted by Josephine Goldmark, one of the most effective workers in the League's New York Headquarters. This brief is probably one of the most remarkable legal documents in existence. It consists of one hundred and twelve printed pages, of which a few paragraphs were written by the attorney for the State. All the rest was contributed, under Miss Goldmark's direction, from the Consumers' League's wonderful collection of reasons why women workers should be protected. . . . The Consumers' League convinced the Supreme Court of the United States, and the Oregon ten-hour law was upheld. . . .

Waitresses' Union, Local No. 484, of Chicago, led by a remarkable young working woman, Elizabeth Maloney . . . drafted, and introduced into the Illinois Legislature, a bill providing an eight-hour working day for every woman in the State. . . .

The "Girls' Bill," as it immediately became known, was the most hotly contested measure passed by the Illinois Legislature during the session. Over 500 manufacturers appeared at the public hearing on the bill . . . presenting the business aspect of the question; the girls showed the human side. . . .

"I am a waitress," said Miss Maloney, "and I work ten hours a day. In that time a waitress who is tolerably busy *walks* ten miles, and the dishes she carries back and forth aggregate in weight 1,500 to 2,000 pounds. Don't you think eight hours a day is enough for a girl to walk?"

Only one thing stood in the way of the passage of the bill after that day. The doubt of its constitutionality proved an obstacle too grave for the friends of the workers to overcome. It was decided to substitute a ten-hour bill, an exact duplicate of the "Oregon Standard" established by the Supreme Court of the United States. The principle of limitation upon the hours of women's work once established in Illinois, the workers could proceed with their fight for an eight-hour day.

7. Jane Addams Links the Vote with Social Reform, 1906

Insanitary housing, poisonous sewage, contaminated water, infant mortality, the spread of contagion, adulterated food, impure milk, smoke-laden air, ill-ventilated factories, dangerous occupations, juvenile crime, unwholesome crowding, prostitution and drunkenness are the enemies which the modern cities must face and overcome would they survive. Logically, its electorate should be made up of those who can bear a valiant part in this arduous contest, those who in the past have at least attempted to care for children, to clean houses, to prepare foods, to isolate the family from moral dangers, those who have traditionally taken care of that side of life which inevitably becomes the subject of municipal consideration and control as soon as the population is congested. To test the elector's fitness to deal with this situation by his ability to bear arms is absurd. These problems must be solved, if they are solved at all, not from the military point of view, not even from the industrial point of view, but from a third which is rapidly developing in all the great cities of the world—the human welfare point of view.

8. A Feminist Argument for Suffrage and Social Justice, 1910

I am persuaded that the time is at hand when this sentimental, half contemptuous attitude of half the population towards the other half will have to be abandoned. I believe that the time has arrived when self-interest, if other motive be lacking, will compel society to examine the ideals of women. . . .

Not only in the United States, but in every constitutional country in the world the movement towards admitting women to full political equality with men is gathering strength. In half a dozen countries women are already completely enfranchised. In England the opposition is seeking terms of surrender. In the United States the stoutest enemy of the movement acknowledges that woman suffrage is ultimately inevitable. The voting strength of the world is about to be doubled, and the new element is absolutely an unknown quantity. Does anyone question that this is the most important political fact the modern world has ever faced?. . .

Women, since society became an organized body, have been engaged in the rearing, as well as the bearing of children. They have made the home, they have cared for the sick, ministered to the aged, and given to the poor. The universal destiny of the mass of women trained them to feed and clothe, to invent, manufacture, build, repair, contrive, conserve, economize. They lived lives of constant service, within the narrow confines of a home. Their labor was given to those they loved, and the reward they looked for was purely a spiritual reward.

A thousand generations of service, unpaid, loving, intimate, must have left the strongest kind of a mental habit in its wake. Women, when they emerged from the seclusion of their homes and began to mingle in the world procession, when they were thrown on their own financial responsibility, found themselves willy-nilly in the ranks of the producers, the wage earners; when the enlightenment of education was no longer denied them, when their responsibilities ceased to be entirely domestic and became somewhat social, when, in a word, women began to *think*, they naturally thought in human terms. They couldn't have thought otherwise if they had tried.

They might have learned, it is true. In certain circumstances women might have been persuaded to adopt the commercial habit of thought. But the circumstances were exactly propitious for the encouragement of the old-time woman habit of service. The modern thinking, planning, self-governing, educated woman came into a world which is losing faith in the commercial ideal, and is endeavoring to substitute in its place a social ideal. She came into a generation which is reaching passionate hands towards democracy. She became one with a nation which is weary of wars and hatreds, impatient with greed and privilege, sickened of poverty, disease, and social injustice. The modern, free-functioning woman accepted without the slightest difficulty these new ideals of democracy and social service. Where men could do little more than theorize in these matters, women were able easily and effectively to act.

Chapter 22:
Document Set 2 References

1. Women in the U.S. Labor Force for Selected Years, 1890–1930
   "Women in the U.S. Labor Force for Selected Years, 1890–1977," U.S. Bureau of Census, *Historical Statistics of the United States, Colonial Times to 1970* (Washington, D.C.: Government Printing Office, 1975), Vol. I, pp. 132–133; *Statistical Abstract of the United States Census: 1978,* pp. 398, 404.

2. The Women's Clubs Embrace Reform, 1904
   Martha E. D. White, "Work of the Women's Club," *Atlantic Monthly,* Vol. 93 (May 1904).

3. Rheta Childe Dorr Recalls the Shift to Social Activism, 1904, 1905
   Rheta Childe Dorr, *A Woman of Fifty* (New York: Funk and Wagnalls, 1924), pp. 118–120.

4. The Brandeis Brief States the Case for Protective Legislation, 1908
   Louis D. Brandeis, "Brief for the State of Oregon," in *Women in Industry* (New York: Reprinted for National Consumers' League, 1908), pp. 18, 28, 42, 44, 47, 92, 113.

5. Justice David J. Brewer Affirms the Oregon Law, 1908
   Muller v. *Oregon,* Supreme Court, *United States Reports,* 208 U.S. 412 (1908).

6. Dorr Describes the National Consumers' League Role in the *Muller* Case, 1908
   Rheta Childe Dorr, *Women's Demand for Humane Treatment of Women Workers in Shop and Factory* (New York: Consumers' League of the City of New York, 1909), reprinted from *Hampton's Magazine* (December 1909).

7. Jane Addams Links the Vote with Social Reform, 1906
   Jane Addams, "Jane Addams Declares Ballot for Women Made Necessary by Changed Conditions," *Chicago Sunday Record-Herald,* April 1, 1906.

8. A Feminist Argument for Suffrage and Social Justice, 1910
   Rheta Childe Dorr, *What Eight Million Women Want* (Boston: Small, Maynard and Co., 1910), pp. 2–6.

DOCUMENT SET 3

A Commitment to the Environment: Conservation as a Political Issue

The fledgling conservation movement that first appeared in the 1870s had produced only modest gains by the late nineteenth century. As your textbook indicates, the preservationist drive took on new momentum in the first decade of the new century. By the time the Progressive movement came to dominate American politics, new pressure organizations had begun to insist that politicians act to safeguard the nation's remaining wilderness areas for the use of future generations. No political figure was more responsive to this call to action than President Theodore Roosevelt, himself an ardent conservationist since his years as governor of New York. As a result, conservation moved to the forefront of domestic politics during Roosevelt's eventful presidency.

The following documents record the emergence of conservation as a controversial political issue. As you review the evidence, notice the nuances and gradations in opinion among supporters of the wilderness idea. The textbook devotes substantial attention to the tension between preservationists like John Muir and resource managers like Gifford Pinchot. As the debates of the Roosevelt Era unfolded, it became increasingly clear that contradictory tendencies within the conservation movement had developed. You should try to identify those differences.

No question was more hotly debated than the controversial plan to flood the Hetch Hetchy Valley in Yosemite National Park. The problem of water re-sources and their preservation became a central issue in the political discourse of Progressive America. This document set includes the words of Muir, Pinchot, and Roosevelt, as well as the arguments advanced by several persons committed to full exploitation of the nation's resources. Try to determine what caused people to become conservationist and how their commitment to the earth translated into political action.

As you examine the evidence, think about the concentration on water resources and try to determine why access to water was becoming such a crucial problem. How did the perspectives of Martin Dies and George Knapp differ from those of the conservationists? As you search for an explanation of their views, be aware of the witnesses' backgrounds as a factor in the positions they expressed. Evaluate the arguments made by those who urged the development of the Hetch Hetchy water resource.

The textbook "Place in Time" section on John Muir and the Hetch Hetchy controversy provides essential background for your analysis of the evidence. Try to determine why Muir's position was rejected by Congress in spite of an outpouring of support from preservationists. Be alert to the interests at stake in this battle and the arguments that ultimately prevailed. As you examine this early confrontation between developers and conservationists, consider its implications for the future. In what ways is the debate of the Roosevelt Era related to the modern struggle over the environment?

Questions for Analysis

1. What were the origins of Theodore Roosevelt's commitment to conservation and environmental protection? In what ways did he exercise presidential leadership on the issue? With what results?

2. Using the documents as your basic resource, distinguish between the differing approaches to conservation evident in the debate over the use, waste, and preservation of the nation's natural resources. What was the distinction between resource management and preservationism? What were the advantages and disadvantages of each? Do modern environmentalists owe anything to the Progressive conservationists?

3. Why did the conflict over Hetch Hetchy become such a divisive controversy? Why do you think it was possible to generate such widespread protest over this issue? What were the most persuasive arguments for damming the Hetch Hetchy? How did they relate to changes in American population distribution? Who were the proponents of full development, and what was the relationship between their regional/political backgrounds and their endorsement of resource exploitation?

4. How were the issues raised by conservationists related to the overriding themes of the Progressive movement? What did Roosevelt and Pinchot mean by the "public interest"? What do the documents reveal about the tension between private interests and the general welfare? How were the Progressives limited by their own assumptions? What was their legacy to the environmentalists of the future?

5. Why was the idea of conservation, which was first raised in the 1870s, not adopted by large numbers of American citizens until the early twentieth century? What does the available evidence tell us about the reasons for a new sensitivity to environmental concerns in the Roosevelt Era?

1. Theodore Roosevelt Recalls an Early Commitment to Conservation, 1913

When Governor of New York, as I have already described, I had been in consultation with Gifford Pinchot and F. H. Newell, and had shaped my recommendations about forestry largely in accordance with their suggestions. Like other men who had thought about the national future at all, I had been growing more and more concerned over the destruction of the forests.

While I had lived in the West I had come to realize the vital need of irrigation to the country, and I had been both amused and irritated by the attitude of Eastern men who obtained from Congress grants of National money to develop harbors and yet fought the use of the Nation's power to develop the irrigation work of the West. Major John Wesley Powell the explorer of the Grand Cañon, and Director of the Geological Survey, was the first man who fought for irrigation, and he lived to see the Reclamation Act passed and construction actually begun. . . . But Gifford Pinchot is the man to whom the nation owes most for what has been accomplished as regards the preservation of the natural resources of our country. He led, and indeed during its most vital period embodied, the fight for the preservation through the use of our forests. He played one of the leading parts in the effort to make the National Government the chief instrument in developing the irrigation of the arid West. He was the foremost leader in the great struggle to coördinate all our social and governmental forces in the effort to secure the adoption of a rational and farseeing policy for securing the conservation of all our national resources. He was already in the

Government service as head of the Forestry Bureau when I became President; he continued throughout my term, not only as head of the Forest service, but as the moving and directing spirit in most of the conservation work, and as counsellor and assistant on most of the other work connected with the internal affairs of the country. . . .

The result of all the work outlined above was to bring together in the Bureau of Forestry, by the end of 1904, the only body of forest experts under the Government, and practically all of the first-hand information about the public forests which was then in existence. In 1905, the obvious foolishness of continuing to separate the foresters and the forests, reënforced by the action of the First National Forest Congress, held in Washington, brought about the Act of February 1, 1905, which transferred the National Forests from the care of the Interior Department to the Department of Agriculture, and resulted in the creation of the present United States Forest Service.

The men upon whom the responsibility of handling some sixty million acres of National Forest lands was thus thrown were ready for the work, both in the office and in the field, because they had been preparing for it for more than five years. Without delay they proceeded, under the leadership of Pinchot, to apply to the new work the principles they had already formulated. One of these was to open all the resources of the National Forest to regulated use. Another was that of putting every part of the land to that use in which it would best serve the public. Following this principle, the Act of June 11, 1906, was drawn, and its passage was secured from Congress. This law throws open to settlement all land in the National Forests that is found, on examination, to be chiefly valuable for agriculture. Hitherto all such land had been closed to the settler.

The principles thus formulated and applied may be summed up in the statement that the rights of the public to the natural resources outweigh private rights, and must be given its first consideration. Until that time, in dealing with the National Forests, and the public lands generally, private rights had almost uniformly been allowed to overbalance public rights. The change we made was right, and was vitally necessary; but, of course, it created bitter opposition from private interests.

2. Gifford Pinchot Urges the Management of Water Resources, 1907

The conception that water is, on the whole, the most important natural resource has gained firm hold in the irrigated West, and is making rapid progress in the humid East. Water, not land, is the primary value in this Western country, and its conservation and use to irrigate land is the first condition of prosperity. The use of our streams for irrigation and for domestic and manufacturing uses is comparatively well developed. Their use for power is less developed, while their use for transportation has only begun. The conservation of inland waterways of the United States for these great purposes constitutes, perhaps, the greatest single task which now confronts the Nation. The maintenance and increase of agriculture, the supply of clear water for domestic and manufacturing use, the development of electrical power, transportation and lighting, and the creation of a system of inland transportation by water whereby to regulate freight rates by rail and to move the bulkier commodities cheaply from place to place, is a task upon whose successful accomplishment the future of the Nation depends in a peculiar degree. This is the problem to which the Inland Waterways Commission, recently appointed by President Roosevelt, has begun to address itself.

We are accustomed, and rightly accustomed, to take pride in the vigorous and healthful growth of the United States and in its vast promise for the future. Yet we are making no preparation to realize what we so easily and glibly foresee and predict. The vast possibilities of our great future will become realities only if we make ourselves, in a sense, responsible for that future. The planned and orderly development and conservation of our natural resources is the first duty of the United States. It is the only form of insurance that will certainly protect us against disasters that lack of foresight has repeatedly brought down on nations since passed away.

3. The National Conservation Commission's Analysis of Wasted Resources, 1909

The duty of man to man, on which the integrity of nations must rest, is no higher than the duty of each generation to the next; and the obligation of the nation to each actual citizen is no more sacred than the obligation to the citizen to be, who, in turn, must bear the nation's duties and responsibilities. . . .

In the growth of the country and gradual development of the natural resources there have been three noteworthy stages. The first stage was that of individual enterprise for personal and family benefit. It led to the conquest of the wilderness.

The next stage was that of collective enterprise, either for the benefit of communities or for the profit of individuals forming the communities. It led to the development of cities and States, and too often to the growth of great monopolies.

The third stage is the one we are now entering. Within it the enterprise is collective and largely cooperative, and should be directed toward the larger benefit of communities, States, and the people generally.

In the first stage the resources received little thought. In the second they were wastefully used. In the stage which we are entering wise and beneficial uses are essential, and the checking of waste is absolutely demanded. . . .

. . . The most reprehensible waste is that of destruction, as in forest fires, uncontrolled flow of gas and oil, soil wash, and abandonment of coal in the mines. This is attributable, for the most part, to ignorance, indifference, or false notions of economy, to rectify which is the business of the people collectively.

Nearly as reprehensible is the waste arising from misuse, as in the consumption of fuel in furnaces and engines of low efficiency, of loss of water in floods, the employment of ill-adapted structural materials, the growing of ill-chosen crops, and the perpetuation of inferior stocks of plants and animals, all of which may be remedied.

Reprehensible in less degree is the waste arising from nonuse. Since the utilization of any one resource is necessarily progressive and dependent on social and industrial conditions and the concurrent development of other resources, nonuse is sometimes unavoidable. It becomes reprehensible when it affects the common welfare and entails future injury. Then, it should be rectified in the general interest.

For the prevention of waste the most effective means will be found in the increase and diffusion of knowledge, from which is sure to result an aroused public sentiment demanding prevention. The people have the matter in their own hands. They may prevent or limit the destruction of resources and restrain misuse through the enactment and enforcement of appropriate state and federal laws.

4. John Muir Calls for the Preservation of Yosemite, 1908

I am anxious that the Yosemite National Park may be saved from all sorts of commercialism and marks of man's work other than the roads, hotels, etc., required to make its wonders and blessings available. For as far as I have seen there is not in all the wonderful Sierra, or indeed in the world, another so grand and wonderful and useful a block of Nature's mountain handiwork.

There is now under consideration, as doubtless you well know, an application of San Francisco supervisors for the use of the Hetch-Hetchy Valley and Lake Eleanor as storage reservoirs for a city water supply. This application should, I think, be denied, especially the Hetch-Hetchy part, for this Valley, as you will see by the inclosed description, is a counterpart of Yosemite, and one of the most sublime and beautiful and important features of the Park, and to dam and submerge it would be hardly less destructive and deplorable in its effect on the Park in general than would be the damming of Yosemite itself. For its falls and groves and delightful camp-grounds are surpassed or equaled only in Yosemite, and furthermore it is the hall of entrance to the grand Tuolumne Cañon, which opens a wonderful way to the magnificent Tuolumne Meadows, the focus of pleasure travel in the Park and the grand central camp-ground. If Hetch-Hetchy should be submerged, as proposed, to a depth of one hundred and seventy-five feet, not only would the Meadows be made utterly inaccessible along the Tuolumne, but this glorious cañon way to the High Sierra would be blocked.

I am heartily in favor of a Sierra or even a Tuolumne water supply for San Francisco, but all the water required can be obtained from sources outside the Park, leaving the twin valleys, Hetch-Hetchy and Yosemite, to the use they were intended for when the Park was established. . . .

These sacred mountain temples are the holiest ground that the heart of man has consecrated, and it behooves us all faithfully to do our part in seeing that our wild mountain parks are passed on unspoiled to those who come after us, for they are national properties in which every man has a right and interest.

5. The Conservation Movement Under Attack, 1910

I propose to speak for those exiles in sin who hold that a large part of the present "conservation" movement is unadulterated humbug. That the modern Jeremiahs are as sincere as was the older one, I do not question. But I count their prophecies to be baseless vaporings, and their vaunted remedy worse than the fancied disease. I am one who can see no warrant of law, of justice, nor of necessity for that wholesale reversal of our traditional policy which the advocates of "conservation" demand. I am one who does not shiver for the future at the sight of a load of coal, nor view a steel-mill as the arch-robber of posterity. I am one who does not believe in a power trust, past, present or to come; and who, if he were a capitalist seeking to form such a trust, would ask nothing better than just the present conservation scheme to help him. I believe that a government bureau is the worst imaginable landlord; and that its essential nature is not changed by giving it a high-sounding name, and decking it with home-made haloes. I hold that the present forest policy ceases to be a nuisance only when it becomes a curse.

6. Muir's Plea to Save Hetch Hetchy, 1912

That anyone would try to destroy such a place seems incredible; but sad experience shows that there are people good enough and bad enough for anything. The proponents of the dam scheme bring forward a lot of bad arguments to prove that the only righteous thing to do with the people's parks is to destroy them bit by bit as they are able. Their arguments are curiously like those of the devil, devised for the destruction of the first garden—so much of the very best Eden fruit going to waste; so much of the best Tuolumne water and Tuolumne scenery going to waste. Few of their statements are even partly true, and all are misleading.

Thus, Hetch Hetchy, they say, is a "low-lying meadow." On the contrary, it is a high-lying natural landscape garden, as the photographic illustrations show.

"It is a common minor feature, like thousands of others." On the contrary it is a very uncommon feature; after Yosemite, the rarest and in many ways the most important in the National Park. . . .

These temple destroyers, devotees of ravaging commercialism, seem to have a perfect contempt for Nature, and, instead of lifting their eyes to the God of the mountains, lift them to the Almighty Dollar.

Dam Hetch Hetchy! As well dam for water tanks the people's cathedrals and churches, for no holier temple has ever been consecrated by the heart of man.*

---

*When the Raker Act was passed by Congress and signed by President Woodrow Wilson in December, 1913, Muir had lost his long campaign to preserve Hetch Hetchy Valley. The City of San Francisco began construction activities the next year. O'Shaughnessy Dam was completed and water storage commenced in 1923. The reservoir fills the former valley and backs into the canyon above, fluctuating seasonally. Public access by auto ends at the dam, and promised recreational facilities have never been developed. [From Duke Frederick *et al.*, *Destroy to Create* (Dryden Press, 1972), p. 154.]

7. Martin Dies Endorses Resource Development at Hetch Hetchy, 1913

I am awfully glad my friends from California and elsewhere are getting tired of this conservation hobby, because, Mr. Chairman, I think it is one of the delusions of the age in which we live. . . .

I sympathize with my friends in California who want to take a part of the public domain now, notwithstanding all their declamations for conservation of resources. I am willing to let them have it. I am willing to let them have it when they take it in California and San Francisco for the public good.

That is what the great resources of this country are for. They are for the American people. I want them to open the coal mines in Alaska. I want them to open the reservations in this country. I am not for reservations and parks. I would have the great timber and mineral and coal resources of this country opened to the people, and I only want to say, Mr. Chairman, that your Pinchots and your conservationists generally are theorists who are not, in my humble judgment, making propaganda in the interest of the American people.

Let California have it, and let Alaska open her coal mines. God Almighty has located the resources of this country in such a form as that His children will not use them in disproportion, and your Pinchots will not be able to controvert and circumvent the laws of God Almighty.

Chapter 22:
Document Set 3 References

1. Theodore Roosevelt Recalls an Early Commitment to Conservation, 1913
   Theodore Roosevelt, *An Autobiography* (New York: Macmillan, 1913), pp. 428–461.

2. Gifford Pinchot Urges the Management of Water Resources, 1907
   Gifford Pinchot, "The Conservation of Natural Resources," *The Outlook,* Vol. 87 (October 12, 1907).

3. The National Conservation Commission's Analysis of Wasted Resources, 1909
   National Conservation Commission, *Report of the National Conservation Commission, February, 1909,* in U.S. Congress, Senate Document 676, 60th Cong., 2nd Sess. (Washington, D.C.: Government Printing Office, 1909), pp. 13–15.

4. John Muir Calls for the Preservation of Yosemite, 1908
   John Muir to Roosevelt, April 21, 1908, in William Frederick Bade, *The Life and Letters of John Muir* (Boston: Houghton Mifflin & Co., 1924), Vol. II, pp. 417–420.

5. The Conservation Movement Under Attack, 1910
   George L. Knapp, "The Other Side of Conservation," *North American Review,* Vol. CXCI, No. 653 (April 1910).

6. Muir's Plea to Save Hetch Hetchy, 1912
   John Muir, *The Yosemite* (New York: Century, 1912), pp. 260–262.

7. Martin Dies Endorses Resource Development at Hetch Hetchy, 1913
   Congressional Record, 63rd Cong., 1st Sess., August 30, 1913, pp. 4003–4004.

DOCUMENT SET 1
Total War and the Boundaries of Dissent:
The Response from the Heartland

Chapter 23 describes the origins of World War I and the role of the United States in determining its outcome. Extensive attention is devoted to the impact of the war on American institutions. The following documents stress the problem of dissent, with emphasis on the resistance mounted by both anti-war Socialists and German Americans. Moreover, they explore the enforcement of conformity in the name of national unity. Using these materials you can reconstruct the social environment of a nation at war.

Beginning with the words of songwriter George M. Cohan's popular *Over There* (1917), the documents reveal the enthusiasm and militance of the popular response to President Woodrow Wilson's leadership. Yet your textbook acknowledges that the administration confronted a recently isolationist nation less unified than the popular rhetoric implied. The documents therefore include samples of the government propaganda drive, including sharp visual images of the enemy.

In no area was the perception of a threat greater than in the nation's midwestern heartland, where German Americans actively resisted the pressure for political conformity and cultural unity. As the docu-

ments indicate, Socialism was one means of expressing resentment against the widespread criticism of all things German. Clear evidence of the social climate is found in Socialist Oscar Ameringer's biting reminiscences of rural Wisconsin "patriots." Note Ameringer's emphasis on class differences in his description of the wartime bond drives. Examine the activities of such citizen groups as the Wisconsin Defense League in the context of total war.

Finally, the last group of documents reveals the limits of dissent in a society at war. The first statement is an excerpt from Socialist leader Eugene V. Debs's Canton, Ohio, address (1918), which ultimately resulted in its author's imprisonment for violation of the Espionage Act. As a follow-up, review the Supreme Court's landmark Schenck decision (1919) with regard to the boundaries of wartime dissent.

As you review these materials, consider the impact of total war, including the pressure exerted against traditional civil liberties. Analyze the documents as evidence of governmental mobilization of public opinion, and note the consequences of the Wilson administration's actions.

**Questions for
Analysis**

1. What evidence do these documents provide concerning the political impact of total war? How were traditional constitutional rights and civil liberties affected by World War I? What justification was offered for the limits placed on dissent?

2. How did government agencies portray the enemy, allies, and Americans in materials disseminated throughout the United States? What evidence of government image-making can be found in these documents? What were the social consequences of government efforts to mobilize public opinion?

3. What did the activities of the Wisconsin Defense League reveal about the impact of war? What was the relationship between government agencies such as the Committee on Public Information and citizen volunteer organizations?

4. What do these documents reveal about the influence of ethnic and cultural factors in American politics from 1914 to 1919?

5. What evidence of class differences can be found in these documents? What do the illustrations from *The Masses* reveal about left-wing criticism of the war? Why were government critics so concerned about the class impact of the war?

6. Why are song titles, lyrics, and illustrations particularly revealing as evidence of public perceptions of World War I? What special insights can be gained from such documents?

1. A Musical Call to Arms from George M. Cohan, 1917

OVER THERE

Johnnie get your gun, get your gun, get your gun,
Take it on the run, on the run, on the run;
Hear them calling you and me;
Every son of liberty.
Hurry right away, no delay, go today,
Make your daddy glad, to have had such a lad,
Tell your sweetheart not to pine,
To be proud her boy's in line.

Chorus:
Over there, over there,
Send the word, send the word over there,
That the Yanks are coming, the Yanks are coming,
The drums rum-tumming everywhere.

So prepare, say a prayer,
Send the word, send the word to beware,
We'll be over, we're coming over,
And we won't come back till it's over over there.

Johnnie get your gun, get your gun, get your gun,
Johnnie show the Hun, you're a son-of-a-gun,
Hoist the flag and let her fly,
Like true heroes do or die.
Pack your little kit, show your grit, do your bit,
Soldiers to the ranks from the towns and the tanks,
Make your mother proud of you,
And to liberty be true.

2. Friendly Words for the Foreign Born, 1917

There is no such thing as half treason. Any treason is all treason. And let no foreign-born man, who is today in the United States, comfort himself that, because he has not become a naturalized citizen, he owes no allegiance to the United States, and that he cannot be punished for treason to the United States. That is not the case, and it is well for us all—whether native-born, naturalized or unnaturalized—to understand just where we each stand with relation to the Government in the crime of treason. . . .

And every one who owes allegiance to the Government can be guilty of treason; the *native-born* man, because he was born here; the *naturalized* man, because he took an oath of allegiance; the *unnaturalized* or alien man, because he lives here for the time being. . . .

My advice, therefore, to every foreign-born man and woman who is staying in the United States today is to keep clear of any disloyalty; keep clear of any one who counsels or advises it. Indeed, any one, native, naturalized, or alien, who knows of such disloyal plans, purposes, or schemes is already on dangerous ground, although he may not himself have done a thing; for as your friend I should tell you that there is not only treason which consists of overt acts, but there is a lesser treason which consists in knowing of treason by others against the United States and not making it known.

Let me make that very plain, for it may save some people trouble. If a man or woman knows of treason against the United States, and keeps it to himself, it is like receiving stolen goods. So it is with treason, for to conceal treason is to commit treason. Now here is what the law provides about this lesser treason, or "misprison of treason," as it is called, and *it applies to all persons living in the United States, whether native-born, naturalized, or not naturalized, for they all owe allegiance.* . . .

So in these times the safe path for native-born, naturalized, and alien is not only to avoid treason one's self, but, if one learns of it, to either go in person or write some of the officers named in this statute and tell him what one knows.

It is not necessary for me to tell you the many forms treason may take, for treason will always find a hundred different secret ways in which it can give aid and sympathy to the enemy. But right can take but one plain course. Be loyal, true, straight, and square to the Government, and you will be sure you are not committing treason. I am not trying to tell people how near they can approach the line of treason without crossing it. I am telling them how far they can keep from the line by simply being loyal to the flag and to America.

When a man is driving along a precipice, he tries to drive as far away from the edge as he can. My advice to every foreign-born man who comes to me will be: Put a flag at your door, another on your coat, and above all keep one in your heart. If you do, you will stand four-square as countrymen of Washington and Lincoln, and no nation has ever loved any leader, be he King or Kaiser, Sultan or Czar, as all nations to-day love George Washington and Abraham Lincoln. In following their loyal footsteps no man of any race can go astray.

THIS PAMPHLET IS AVAILABLE IN BOHEMIAN, POLISH, GERMAN, ITALIAN, HUNGARIAN AND RUSSIAN

3. The Visual Image of the Enemy, ca. 1917–1918

4. The Wisconsin Defense League Urges a Loyalty Pledge, ca. 1917

TO THE CITIZENS OF WISCONSIN

THE WISCONSIN DEFENSE LEAGUE

Endorses the following

DECLARATION

TO THE PRESIDENT OF THE UNITED STATES:

As an American faithful to American ideals of justice, liberty and humanity, and confident that the Government has exerted its most earnest efforts to keep us at peace with the world, I hereby declare my absolute and unconditional loyalty to the Government of the United States, and pledge my support to you in protecting American rights against unlawful violence upon land and sea, in guarding the Nation against hostile attacks, and in upholding international right.

If you endorse these sentiments sign here:

Name

Address

Do you stand willing to back your country in case of need? If you do fill out the blank below.

Show Uncle Sam where you stand.
This is not an Enlistment.   It is your pledge of loyalty.

Present Occupation:

Age: Weight: Height:

General Health: Married or Single:

Previous Naval or Military Experience:

1. Are you a Machinist:
2. " " " Stenographer:
3. " " " Chauffeur:
4. Can you drive a Motorcycle
5. Are you a Locomotive or Marine Engineer:
6. " " " an Electrician:
7. " " " a Cook or Baker:
8. " " " " Plumber, Carpenter, Coppersmith or Boilermaker:
9. " " " " Horse Shoer:
10. " " " " Packer:
11. " " " " Teamster:
12. " " " " Yachtsman or Boatman:
13 " " " " Aviator:
14. " " " " Blacksmith

Will you volunteer for service in any of the military branches of the United States in case of war:

Indicate the branch of service you prefer:

U. S. ARMY   **U. S. NAVY**
U. S. MARINE CORPS   **NATIONAL GUARD**

Mail to Army and Navy Recruiting Office, Plankinton Arcade, Milwaukee

5. George Creel Recalls the "World's Greatest Adventure in Advertising," 1920

How We Advertised America

1. The "Second Lines"

It was in this recognition of Public Opinion as a major force that the Great War differed most essentially from all previous conflicts. The trial of strength was not only between massed bodies of armed men, but between opposed ideals, and moral verdicts took on all the value of military decisions. Other wars went no deeper than the physical aspects, but German *Kultur* raised issues that had to be fought out in the hearts and minds of people as well as on the actual firing-line. The approval of the world meant the steady flow of inspiration into the trenches; it meant the strengthened resolve and the renewed determination of the civilian population that is a nation's second line. The condemnation of the world meant the destruction of morale and the surrender of that conviction of justice which is the very heart of courage.

The Committee on Public Information was called into existence to make this fight for the "verdict of mankind," the voice created to plead the justice of America's cause before the jury of Public Opinion.... *In no degree was the Committee an agency of censorship, a machinery of concealment or repression. It's emphasis throughout was on the open and the positive. At no point did it seek or exercise authorities under those war laws that limited the freedom of speech and press.* In all things, from first to last, without halt or change, it was a plain publicity proposition, a vast enterprise in salesmanship, the world's greatest adventure in advertising....

The President went before Congress, a state of war was accepted formally, and even as one army gathered in the cantonments, another went out over the land to watch, to search, to listen. The Department of Justice had already in the field a large, intelligent, and well-trained organization; there was also the Secret Service of the Treasury Department and into being swiftly sprang Military Intelligence, Naval Intelligence, Shipping Board Intelligence, etc.; and, by way of climax, the American Protective League, an organization of *two hundred and fifty thousand* "citizen volunteers" formed with the sanction of the Attorney-General and operated under the direction of the Bureau of Investigation.

Never was a country so thoroughly contra-espionaged! Not a pin dropped in the home of any one with a foreign name but that it rang like thunder on the inner ear of some listening sleuth! And with what result? . . .

As for criminal prosecutions, 1,532 persons were arrested under the provisions of the Espionage Act prohibiting disloyal utterance, propaganda, etc.; 65 persons for threats against the President; 10 persons for sabotage; and under the penal code, with relation to conspiracy, 908 indictments were returned, the last group including the I. W. W. cases. Even this does not spell guilt in every instance, for there have been acquittals as well as convictions, and many trials are yet to be held. . . .

The State Councils of Defense did splendid work, as a rule, and the country owes much to them, but there were exceptions that aroused far more anger than loyalty, conducting themselves in a manner that would have been lawless in any other than a "patriotic" body. During Liberty Loan drives, for instance, it became a habit, in certain sections, to compel a regular income return from the foreign-born and the poorer classes. Men, claiming authority, would visit these homes, insist upon a statement of earnings, expenditures, savings, etc., and then calmly announce the amount of the contribution that the dazed victims were expected to make. Anything in the nature of resistance was set down as "slacking" and "disloyalty," and some of the penalties visited were expulsion from the community, personal ill treatment, or a pleasant little attention like painting the house yellow. Of all the bitternesses and disaffections reported to us, the majority proceeded from this sort of terrorism, and it had results that will be felt for years to come. . . .

The loyalty of "our aliens," however, splendid as it was, had in it nothing of the spontaneous or the accidental. Results were obtained only by hard, driving work. The bitterness bred by years of neglect and injustice were not to be dissipated by any mere war-call, but had to be burned away by a continuous educational campaign. The *real* America had to be revealed to these foreign-language groups—its drama of hope and struggle, success and blunders—and their minds had to be filled with the tremendous truth that the fight against Germany was a fight for all that life has taught decent human beings to hold dear.

6. *The Masses* Interprets the Great Crusade, 1916–1917

A. "At Last a Perfect Soldier!"
   The Masses, August 1916

Drawn by Robert Minor, July 1916

CAL EXAMINER: "At last a perfect soldier!"

B. Having Their Fling,
The Masses, September 1917

Having Their Fling

C. Come on In, The Blood's Fine!
   The Masses, June 1917

Drawn by R. Kempf, June 1917

7. Oscar Ameringer Recalls the "Terror" in the Wisconsin Hinterlands, ca. 1917–1918

When war came it was the small-town and county-seat people that became the "real patriots," while the old-line German farmers were decidedly hostile to the mess. This situation provided the latecomers with a fine opportunity to show the original settlers who the true Americans were. In the pursuit of this worthy aim the riff-raff of the towns organized themselves into "Home Defense Guards," "County Councils of Defense," snoopers, and Liberty-loan strong-arm squads. The leaders in these patriotic drives were the bankers, naturally. It is said that the mortality rate of bankers during that war was even lower than that of generals, and that's saying a lot, because only one of our generals was wounded in action—by the premature explosion of a champagne bottle.

Now the Teutonic ruralists were not against licking [defeating] the kaiser. . . . In the matter of Liberty bonds they always bought their quota and better. You see, the patriotic bankers who headed the Liberty-bond drives knew almost to a penny what those hyphenated Americans were worth.

They'd say, "Mr. Spiegelmeyer, you are down for five hundred dollars. So no back talk. I looked up your account before I came out here." Or, "Mr. Scheibenschieber, your share is seven hundred dollars. I know you haven't the cash on hand, because you have just bought the forty adjoining your place. But don't let that worry you. Just sign this six-per-cent note for the seven hundred dollars and I'll keep your four-per-cent Liberty bond for security. I know you are perfectly good for the note and so are the Liberty bonds." Or, "Mr. Rauschenbauer, your quota is three hundred dollars. I know you've only got a hundred dollars in my bank. So give me your check for one hundred and sign this six-per-cent note for the balance and I'll see to it the bonds are safe in my safe." In the latter instance, if the balance of two hundred was not paid, as happened in many cases, the banker had the three-hundred-dollar bond and the hundred-dollar down payment of the buyer. In case the buyer had paid in full for the bond or bonds and got hard pressed for money, the bankers would always accommodate the customer by taking his bond or bonds back, at first for sixty-five cents on the dollar and toward the end at ninety-six cents on the dollar. It pays to be a patriot.

In cases where the prospect refused to buy Liberty bonds he would be visited by strong-arm salesmen who brought ropes with them to help the prospect see his duty toward his government. Quite frequently his house was painted yellow to proclaim just what kind of a dog lived there.

8. A Socialist Critique of the War by Eugene V. Debs, 1918

When the Bolsheviki came into power and went through the archives they found and exposed the secret treaties—the treaties that were made between the Czar and the French Government, the British Government and the Italian Government, proposing, after the victory was achieved, to dismember the German Empire and destroy the Central Powers. These treaties have never been denied nor repudiated. Very little has been said about them in the American press. I have a copy of these treaties, showing that the purpose of the Allies is exactly the purpose of the Central Powers, and that is the conquest and spoliation of the weaker nations that has always been the purpose of war. . . .

The master class has always declared the wars; the subject class has always fought the battles. The master class has had all to gain and nothing to lose, while the subject class has had nothing to gain and all to lose—especially their lives. . . .

And here let me emphasize the fact—and it cannot be repeated too often—that the working class who fight all the battles, the working class who make the supreme sacrifices, the working class who freely shed their blood and furnish the corpses, have never yet had a voice in either declaring war or making peace. It is the ruling class that invariably does both. They alone declare war and they alone make peace. . . .

What a compliment it is to the Socialist movement to be persecuted for the sake of the truth! The truth alone will make the people free. And for this reason the truth must not be permitted to reach the people. The truth has always been dangerous to the rule of the rogue, the exploiter, the robber. So the truth must be ruthlessly suppressed. That is why they are trying to destroy the Socialist movement; and every time they strike a blow they add a thousand new voices to the hosts proclaiming that Socialism is the hope of humanity. . . .

Do not worry over the charge of treason to your masters, but be concerned about the treason that involves yourselves. Be true to yourself and you cannot be a traitor to any good cause on earth.

Yes, in good time we are going to sweep into power in this nation and throughout the world. We are going to destroy all enslaving and degrading capitalist institutions and recreate them as free and humanizing institutions. The world is daily changing before our eyes. The sun of capitalism is setting; the sun of Socialism is rising. It is our duty to build the new nation and the free republic. We need industrial and social builders. We Socialists are the builders of the beautiful world that is to be. We are all pledged to do our part. We are inviting—aye challenging you in the name of your own manhood and womanhood to join us and do your part.

In due time the hour will strike and this great cause triumphant—the greatest in history—will proclaim the emancipation of the working class and the brotherhood of all mankind.

9. The Supreme Court Limits Free Speech in Wartime, 1919

Holmes, J.: . . . According to the testimony Schenck said he was general secretary of the Socialist party and had charge of the Socialist headquarters from which the documents were sent. He identified a book found there as the minutes of the Executive Committee of the party. The book showed a resolution of August 13, 1917, that 15,000 leaflets should be printed on the other side of one of them in use, to be mailed to men who had passed exemption boards, and for distribution. Schenck personally attended to the printing. . . .

The document in question upon its first printed side recited the first section of the Thirteenth Amendment, said that the idea embodied in it was violated by the Conscription Act and that a conscript is little better than a convict. In impassioned language it intimated that conscription was despotism in its worse form and a monstrous wrong against humanity in the interest of Wall Street's chosen few. It said, "Do not submit to intimidation," but in form at least confined itself to peaceful measures such as a petition for the repeal of the act. The other and later printed side of the sheet was headed "Assert Your Rights." It stated reasons for alleging that any one violated the Constitution when he refused to recognize "your right to assert your opposition to the draft." . . . Of course the document would not have been sent unless it had been intended to have some effect, and we do not see what effect it could be expected to have upon persons subject to the draft except to influence them to obstruct the carrying of it out. The defendants do not deny the jury might find against them on this point.

But it is said, suppose that that was the tendency of this circular, it is protected by the First Amendment to the Constitution. . . . We admit that in many places and in ordinary times the defendants in saying all that was said in the circular would have been within their constitutional rights. But the character of every act depends upon the circumstances in which it is done. . . . The most stringent protection of free speech would not protect a man in falsely shouting fire in a theatre and causing a panic. . . . The question in every case is whether the words used are used in such circumstances and are of such a nature as to create a clear and present danger that they will bring about the substantive evils that Congress has a right to prevent. It is a question of proximity and degree. When a nation is at war many things that might be said in time of peace are such a hindrance to its effort that their utterance will not be endured so long as men fight and that no Court could regard them as protected by any constitutional right. It seems to be admitted that if an actual obstruction of the recruiting service were proved, liability for words that produced that effect might be enforced. The statute of 1917 in §4 punishes conspiracies to obstruct as well as actual obstruction. If the act, (speaking, or circulating a paper,) its tendency and the intent with which it is done are the same, we perceive no ground for saying that success alone warrants making the act a crime. . . .

Judgments affirmed.

Chapter 23:
Document Set 1 References

1. A Musical Call to Arms from George M. Cohan, 1917
   George M. Cohan, "Over There," Copyright 1917, Renewed 1945 by Leo Feist, Inc.

2. Friendly Words for the Foreign Born, 1917
   Joseph Buffington, "Friendly Words to the Foreign Born," in Committee on Public Information, Loyalty Leaflets, 1917, No. 1, pp. 4–8.

3. The Visual Image of the Enemy, ca. 1917–1918
   "Destroy this Mad Brute," U.S. Army.

4. The Wisconsin Defense League Urges a Loyalty Pledge, ca. 1917
   Wisconsin Defense League, "To the Citizens of Wisconsin," ca. 1917, Broadside, State Historical Society of Wisconsin.

5. George Creel Recalls The "World's Greatest Adventure in Advertising," 1920
   George Creel, *How We Advertised America* (New York: Harper and Brothers, 1920; rep. 1972), pp. 3–4, 168–169, 180–181, 184.

6. *The Masses* Interprets the Great Crusade, 1916–1917
   A. By Robert Minor, *The Masses,* August 1916.
   B. By Art Young, *The Masses,* September 1917.
   C. By R. Kempf, *The Masses,* June 1917.

7. Oscar Ameringer Recalls the "Terror" in the Wisconsin Hinterlands, ca. 1917–1918
   Oscar Ameringer, *If You Don't Weaken: The Autobiography of Oscar Ameringer.* New Edition Copyright © 1983 by the University of Oklahoma Press, pp. 327–329.

8. A Socialist Critique of the War by Eugene V. Debs, 1918
   Eugene V. Debs, "Speech," June 16, 1918, Canton, Ohio (New York: Oriole Chapbooks, n.d.), pp. 10–12, 22.

9. The Supreme Court Limits Free Speech in Wartime, 1919
   Schenck v. *U.S., United States Reports, Supreme Court,* 249 U.S. 47 (1919).

Chapter 23:
Document Set 1 Credits

3. U.S. Army

4. A Wisconsin Defense League broadside, ca. 1917, State Historical Society of Wisconsin.

5. Excerpts from *How We Advertised America* by George Creel. Copyright 1920, 1947 by George Creel. Reprinted by permission of HarperCollins Publishers.

6. A. Robert Minor, *The Masses,* August 1916
   B. Art Young, *The Masses,* September 1917
   C. C. R. Kempf, *The Masses,* June 1917

7. From *If You Don't Weaken: The Autobiography of Oscar Ameringer.* New edition copyright © 1983 by the University of Oklahoma Press.

CHAPTER 23

DOCUMENT SET **2**

The Social Impact of Total War: World War I as a Catalyst for Change

World War I changed American society and politics in many ways. The following documents focus on several of the war's most significant consequences. As you review these materials, be conscious of their implications for the political and social future of the United States. In addition, use the evidence to improve your understanding of the immediate postwar problems that plagued American citizens.

No change had greater long-term social impact than war-related population movement, particularly the "great migration" of blacks to the urban areas of the North. The motives and aspirations behind this movement are evident in the letter from a hopeful migrant to Emmet J. Scott.

Another important aspect of the black wartime experience was life in the armed forces. Refer to your textbook for a full discussion of black participation in the AEF and the impact of military service on those involved. As you examine the editorial from *Crisis*, be conscious of the role played by the militant W. E. B. Du Bois in shaping the magazine's editorial policy. Your evaluation of the editorial's argument should reflect an awareness of the war's influence on black veterans.

Similarly, Woodrow Wilson's plea to Congress for a woman suffrage amendment records the importance of the war as a catalyst, in this instance for progressive reform. Rely on your textbook for details on wartime reform and women's contributions to the war effort. Be especially aware of the president's own linkage of the two in his call for women's suffrage.

As a result of labor's wartime growth, the labor question assumed prominence after the armistice. It was reinforced by another indirect result of the war, the rise of Bolshevism in Russia. Probe Samuel Gompers's remarks on the Soviets for evidence of rising concern within the American labor movement over the war's impact on workers. Gompers's wartime stance, relations with the Wilson administration, and personal ideology should be considered in your analysis of his concerns. Further evidence of the explosive social and political environment of postwar America can be found in Socialist Victor Berger's analysis of his own persecution at the hands of the House of Representatives. Your textbook places the Berger incident in the context of the hysteria and intolerance that were the by-products of total war. Both Berger's and Gompers's remarks reveal concerns over the unanticipated consequences of war.

Finally, the last pair of documents addresses the most significant outcomes of World War I, the Treaty of Versailles and the League of Nations. Your textbook provides a valuable context for the profound differences reflected in the *New Republic* article and Wilson's St. Louis speech. Account for this clash between the two voices of liberalism and extract from their disagreement evidence of the state of opinion in postwar America.

Questions for Analysis

1. What do the documents reveal about the relationship between the pressures of total war and the prospects for liberal reform?

2. What was the impact of World War I on black Americans? In what way did their lives and ideas change as a result of mobilization for war? What do the documents imply about black self-image, achievements, problems, and aspirations?

3. How would you account for the emergence of the Red Scare of 1919? Do the documents provide insight into the underlying concerns that troubled American citizens and leaders? What do the remarks of Samuel Gompers and Victor Berger reveal about the social and political consequences of total war?

4. One of Wilson's stated goals when the United States intervened in World War I was to "make the world safe for democracy." Extracting evidence from the documents, evaluate the results of the president's efforts to achieve that goal. Was *America* safe for democracy?

5. In what ways were women affected by World War I? What were the positive and negative results? What evidence of change do the documents reveal?

1. A Black Migrant's Reasons for Relocation, 1917

Dapne, Ala., 4/20/17

Sir: I am writing you to let you know that there is 15 or 20 familys wants to come up there at once but cant come on account of money to come with and we cant phone you here we will be killed they dont want us to leave here & say if we dont go to war and fight for our country they are going to kill us and wants to get away if we can if you send 20 passes there is no doubt that every one of us will com at once. we are not doing any thing here we cant get a living out of what we do now some of these people are farmers and som are cooks barbers and black smiths but the greater part are farmers & good worker & honest people & up to date the trash pile dont want to go no where These are nice people and respectable find a place like that & send passes & we all will come at once we all wants to leave here out of this hard luck place if you cant use us find some place that does need this kind of people we are called Negroes here. I am a reader of the Defender and am delighted to know how times are there & was glad to, know if we could get some one to pass us away from here to a better land. We work but cant get scarcely any thing for it & they dont want us to go away & there is not much of anything here to do & nothing for it Please find some one that need this kind of people & send at once for us. We dont want anything but our wareing and bed clothes & have not got no money to get away from here with & beging to get away before we are killed and hope to here from you at once. We cant talk to you over the phone here we are afraid to they dont want to hear one say that he or she wants to leave here if we do we are apt to be killed. They say if we dont go to war they are not going to let us stay here with their folks and it is not any thing that we have done to them.

2. *The Crisis* Views the War as a Stimulus to Black Activism, 1919

We are returning from war! The Crisis and tens of thousands of black men were drafted into a great struggle. For bleeding France and what she means and has meant and will mean to us and humanity and against the threat of German race arrogance, we fought gladly and to the last drop of blood; for America and her highest ideals, we fought in far-off hope; for the dominant southern oligarchy entrenched in Washington, we fought in bitter resignation. For the America that represents and gloats in lynching, disfranchisement, caste, brutality and devilish insult—for this, in the hateful upturning and mixing of things, we were forced by vindictive fate to fight also.

But today we return! We return from the slavery of uniform which the world's madness demanded us to don to the freedom of civil garb. We stand again to look America squarely in the face and call a spade a spade. We sing: This country of ours, despite all its better souls have done and dreamed, is yet a shameful land.

It *lynches*. . . .

It *disfranchises* its own citizens. . . .

It encourages *ignorance*. . . .

It *steals* from us. . . .

It *insults* us. . . .

This is the country to which we Soldiers of Democracy return. This is the fatherland for which we fought! But it is *our* fatherland. It was right for us to fight. The faults of *our* country are *our* faults. Under similar circumstances, we would fight again. But by the God of Heaven, we are cowards and jackasses if now that that war is over, we do not marshal every ounce of our brain and brawn to fight a sterner, longer, more unbending battle against the forces of hell in our own land.

> We *return*.
> We *return from fighting*.
> We *return fighting*.

Make way for Democracy! We saved it in France, and by the Great Jehovah, we will save it in the United States of America, or know the reason why.

3. Anna Howard Shaw Urges Equality of Sacrifice, 1917

We must remember that more and more sacrifices are going to be demanded but I want to say to you women, do not meekly sit down and make all the sacrifices and demand nothing in return. It is not that you want pay but we all want an equally balanced sacrifice. The Government is asking us to conserve food while it is allowing carload after carload to rot on the side tracks of railroad stations and great elevators of grain to be consumed by fire for lack of proper protection. If we must eat Indian meal in order to save wheat, then the men must protect the grain elevators and see that the wheat is saved. We must demand that there shall be conservation all along the line.... [W]hile we are asked to have meatless days and wheatless days, I have never yet seen a demand for a smokeless day! They are asking through the newspapers that we women shall dance, play bridge, have charades, sing and do everything under the sun to raise money to buy tobacco for the men in the trenches, while the men who want us to do this have a cigar in their mouth at the time they are asking it! I said that if men want the soldiers to have tobacco, let them have smokeless days and furnish it! ...

There is no end to the things that women are asked to do. I know this is true because I have read the newspapers for the last six months to get my duty before me. The first thing we are asked to do is to provide the enthusiasm, inspiration and patriotism to make men want to fight, and we are to send them away with a smile! That is not much to ask of a mother! We are to maintain a perfect calm after we have furnished all this inspiration and enthusiasm, "keep the home fires burning," keep the home sweet and peaceful and happy, keep society on a level, look after business, buy enough but not too much and wear some of our old clothes....

The Woman's Committee of the Council of National Defense now asks for your cooperation, that we may be what the Government would have us be, soldiers at home, defending the interests of the home, while the men are fighting with the gallant Allies who are laying down their lives that this world may be a safe place and that men and women may know the meaning of democracy, which is that we are one great family of God. That, and that only, is the ideal of democracy for which our flag stands.

4. President Woodrow Wilson Appeals for Women's Suffrage as a War Measure, 1918

I regard the concurrence of the Senate in the constitutional amendment proposing the extension of the suffrage to women as vitally essential to the successful prosecution of the great war of humanity in which we are engaged. I have come to urge upon you the considerations which have led me to that conclusion. It is not only my privilege, it is also my duty to apprise you of every circumstance and element involved in this momentous struggle which seems to me to affect

its very processes and its outcome. It is my duty to win the war and to ask you to remove every obstacle that stands in the way of winning it....

We have made partners of the women in this war; shall we admit them only to a partnership of suffering and sacrifice and toil and not to a partnership of privilege and right? This war could not have been fought, either by the other nations engaged or by America, if it had not been for the services of the women,—services rendered in every sphere,—not merely in the fields of effort in which we have been accustomed to see them work, but wherever men have worked and upon the very skirts and edges of the battle itself. . . .

The women of America are too noble and too intelligent and too devoted to be slackers whether you give or withhold this thing that is mere justice; but I know the magic it will work in their thoughts and spirits if you give it them. I propose it as I would pro-

pose to admit soldiers to the suffrage, the men fighting in the field for our liberties and the liberties of the world, were they excluded. The tasks of the women lie at the very heart of the war, and I know how much stronger that heart will beat if you do this just thing and show our women that you trust them as much as you in fact and of necessity depend upon them. . . .

I tell you plainly that this measure which I urge upon you is vital to the winning of the war and to the energies alike of preparation and of battle.

5. Samuel Gompers Attacks Bolshevism, 1921

While the labor movement of the world is gradually but steadily shaking itself free of the illusion that the Soviets are a workingmen's government—the first workingmen's government—conservative powers are beginning to give them commercial and political support and a part of the press is engaged in finding virtuous reasons for this policy. . . .

The Soviets may or may not reach a common understanding of real practical importance with cynical imperialists and capitalistic adventurers. There is no possible common ground between Bolshevism and organized labor. Nor will the proposed economic alliance between Bolshevism and Reaction be able to force labor to compromise with the Soviets. In the long run this alliance will help to make still more clear to the wage-earners the true character of Bolshevism. But its first result is to re-inforce the already formidable Bolshevist propaganda.

I must take this opportunity to point out that the hostility of the Bolshevists to the American Federation of Labor is of the same degree of intensity

and of the same general character as the hostility of a large group of reactionary employers—a group to be found in all countries, but at the present moment far more aggressive and powerful in the United States than in any other nation of the globe. So closely identical are the anti-labor-union policies of the Bolshevists and Reactionaries that a number of instances have already arisen of deliberate cooperation to destroy organized labor. But even when there is no definite alliance the similarity of the purposes and methods of the two groups bring it about that they spread an identical propaganda. The Reactionary, therefore, does not disguise the delight with which he reads of the Bolshevist attacks on organized labor, nor do the Bolshevists disguise their joy at the victories of Reaction. Nor is this the only way by which Reaction aids Bolshevism; in its refusal to grant reasonable economic concessions and to cede to reasonable demands for political and legislative reforms, the Reactionaries inevitably drive the thoughtless and impatient into the arms of Bolshevism.

6. Victor Berger Challenges Congress, 1919

Mr. Chairman and gentlemen of the committee—this is not the time for fine phrases. This committee is making history. It is not Victor Berger's seat in the National House of Representatives alone that is in the balance—representative government as such is in the balance.

I was told that the cards are stacked against me, that arguments are useless, that the Milwaukee Socialist is to be unseated in obedience to the dictates of certain capitalist influences because he is a Socialist and because he is of German extraction. . . .

While I am well aware that the capitalist octopus in America is frightened by what is going on in Europe—particularly in Russia—while I know that there is a great deal of prejudice against Socialists, and especially against Socialists of German descent, I refuse to believe that sane men—and members of Congress at that—who favor a democratic form of government would deliberately try to destroy that kind of government. . . .

I repeat that I have nothing to retract from the articles that I have written or from the speeches I have made. All my predictions have come true. And a great deal more will come true than I have predicted.

This was the worst imperialistic war ever known in the history of the world. Every honest man who has any brains admits it now. . . .

As for America in particular—what have we gained in this war and by this war? What has America gained except billions of debts and a hundred thousand of cripples? And we have lost most of our political democracy. Can anybody think of a single thing, worth while, that we have gained through this war? And even a casual reader of the daily newspaper will admit that an imperialistic peace of the worst kind is the result of the much-heralded peace conference in Paris. All the predictions of the Socialists—and especially my predictions in *The Milwaukee Leader*—have come true, I am sorry to say.

And because I am a student of the world's history, because I can see clearly, because I warned my fellowmen, my countrymen, of the events that were bound to happen if we pursued a certain course, therefore I was indicted, found guilty, and sentenced to serve 20 years in the penitentiary.

This incident of being found guilty in Judge Landis' court for exercising my constitutional right of free speech and a free press should have nothing to do, however, with my being seated in the House of Representatives. . . .

Gentlemen, it may depend upon your decision in this case to a great extent whether the common people are to lose all faith in political elections and representative government—whether they are to turn to "direct action" and "soviets."

The tendency manifest among workmen of our country today is decidedly against "politics" and in favor of "direct action." The only "politics" the workingmen know in this country (with the exception of very few places in the Middle West and the Northwest) is capitalistic politics. And this "politics" is so discredited that even the Boston policemen will not trust the promises of politicians, but prefer "direct action" and the strike. . . .

In one instance after the other, labor unions are showing their willingness to accept the strike, and especially the general strike, as their sole weapon, and they are willing to use this weapon to enforce all of their demands, political and economic. . . .

To sum up: I have always been proud of the Socialist record of observance of law. I have always tried to change or repeal such laws as, in my opinion, were harmful. My work was always constructive. I have always striven to conserve what is best in capitalist civilization as an inheritance for coming generations.

The law under which suppression of free speech and of free press was enforced is a flat denial of rights guaranteed every citizen by the Constitution of the United States. The manner in which that unjust and inherently unconstitutional law was used to procure my conviction for a crime which I never in word, deed, or spirit contemplated, was a travesty upon justice.

My case is still pending in the courts on an appeal. I am confident that the verdict will be reversed by the higher tribunal. I believe that the higher court will hold that I was within my constitutional rights in printing these editorials. A man can not be considered guilty, especially in a political case of this kind, until the highest court in the land has spoken. And in the opinion of real democrats, he will not be considered guilty at any time.

The Fifth District of the State of Wisconsin is entitled to be represented by the man of its own choice. I say again, it is not the personal case of Victor Berger—representative government is on trial.

And the particular question now is: Does the National House of Representatives desire to unseat the regularly elected and regularly certified representative of the Fifth District of Wisconsin because he stood honestly and loyally by his principles?

7. Images of Social Ferment, 1917–1918

A. **"True Blue,"** ca. 1918

B. Women Pull Their Weight, ca. 1918

C. A Critique of Traditional
   Gender Roles, 1917

Chapter 23:
Document Set 2 References

1. A Black Migrant's Reasons for Relocation, 1917
   Letter, Dapne, Ala., 4/20/17, Emmet J. Scott, ed., "Letters of Negro Migrants of 1916–1918," *Journal of Negro History,* 4 (July 1, 1919), pp. 290–340.

2. *The Crisis* Views the War as a Stimulus to Black Activism, 1919
   The Crisis, 18 (May 1919).

3. Anna Howard Shaw Urges Equality of Sacrifice, 1917
   Anna Howard Shaw, NAWSA Convention, 1917, in Mari Jo and Paul Buhle, eds., *The Concise History of Woman Suffrage* (Champaign: University of Illinois Press, 1978), pp. 438–440.

4. President Woodrow Wilson Appeals for Women's Suffrage as a War Measure, 1918
   Woodrow Wilson, "Appeal for Woman Suffrage: Address Delivered in the Senate of the United States," September 30, 1918.

5. Samuel Gompers Attacks Bolshevism, 1921
   Samuel Gompers and William English Walling, *Out of Their Own Mouths: A Revolution and an Indictment of Sovietism* (New York: E. P. Dutton, 1921), pp. v–ix.

6. Victor Berger Challenges Congress, 1919
   Victor L. Berger, *Voice and Pen of Victor L. Berger: Congressional Speeches and Editorials* (Milwaukee: The Milwaukee Leader, 1929), pp. 577–589, 592–603.

7. Images of Social Ferment, 1917–1918
   A. "True Blue," ca. 1918, National Archives, Record Group 28, Records of the Office of Solicitor, Records of the Espionage Act of World War I, File B–584.
   B. Women Pull Their Weight, ca. 1918
   Chandler Christy, "The Motor Corps of America," 1918. Reprinted in Bevis Hillier, *Posters* (London: Weidenfeld and Nicolson, 1969).
   C. A Critique of Traditional Gender Roles, 1917
   Maurice Becker, "They Ain't Our Equals Yet!" *The Masses* 9 (January 1917), p. 18. Courtesy of Tamiment Institute Library, New York University.

Chapter 23:
Document Set 2 Credits

2. From *The Crisis,* May 19, 1919—W. E. B. DuBois editorial. Reprinted by permission of Crisis Publishing Company.

7. A. National Archives
   B. Poster by Howard Chandler Christy/Philip Granville (Lords Gallery)
   C. From *The Masses,* January 1917. Courtesy of The Tamiment Institute Library, New York University

CHAPTER 23

War and Peace: Justifications and Outcomes

When the nations of Europe slipped into what became World War I in 1914, Woodrow Wilson and the American public recoiled in horror and disbelief. The president's subsequent proclamation of neutrality undoubtedly expressed the sentiments of most Americans whose doubts about the belligerents' war aims reinforced the widely held assumption that the United States ought to remain uninvolved in the European conflict. Review your textbook coverage of the period 1914–1917 to identify the reasons so many American citizens supported a policy of neutrality. Against this background, analyze Woodrow Wilson's proclamation to determine whether any hidden issues were likely to complicate the administration's announced intentions.

The documents will help you to understand how, less than three years later, Wilson's policy could be reversed with the support of majority opinion in the United States. Your task is to uncover the reasons such a dramatic shift in attitudes occurred. Examine the Zimmermann telegram and Wilson's war message for evidence of both overt causes and public explanations for the decision to intervene, as well as the underlying forces that propelled the United States into the war.

As you consider the impact of the Zimmermann telegram and the implications of unrestricted submarine warfare, assess President Wilson's role in shaping events. Evaluate the evenhandedness of the American neutrality policy. Consider the impact of economic and technological factors on the policy-making process. To what extent was Wilson actually able to control the course of events?

Once the United States entered the war, American opinion makers became engaged in an effort to remold public opinion (see Document Set 1). As liberal ideology took hold, the war's objectives took center stage and Wilsonion idealism loomed large as the president intensified his efforts to define the war and shape the peace. Use the documents to gain a clear understanding of the purposes for which Americans believed they fought. From Wilson's point of view, what would have constituted a just peace?

Given American expectations and international political realities, it was inevitable that the Treaty of Versailles would disappoint many observers. Think about the conflicting assessments of the peace that were widely expressed in 1919. As you reflect on the war's outcome, try to evaluate Wilson's performance as a war leader and shaper of the peace. Assess his vision of a new world order and his proposed framework for maintaining the peace. What was Wilson's legacy?

Questions for Analysis

1. To what extent was it possible to maintain American neutrality? What do the documents reveal about the obstacles to long-term neutrality after 1914? How would you account for the dramatic shift in American opinion about intervention between 1914 and 1917? In what way did changing world events and the evolving American perception of the issues at stake influence the character and intensity of American belligerency once the United States intervened?

2. Contrast the conflicting evaluations of the peace settlement made at Paris. To what extent were critics fair in their assessment of Wilson's statecraft? How did the war's outcome compare with the war aims articulated in the Fourteen Points speech? Were the results worth a war?

3. What do the documents suggest concerning the interplay between idealism and realism in the conduct of foreign policy? To what extent was it possible to reconcile principle and pragmatism in dealing with the problems of neutralism and peacemaking?

4. In what ways did the Zimmermann telegram change the course of history? What other events of 1916 and 1917 magnified its impact? With what results?

1. Woodrow Wilson Outlines American Neutrality Policy, 1914

Proclamation of August 4, 1914

WHEREAS a state of war unhappily exists between Austria-Hungary and Serbia and between Germany and Russia and between Germany and France:

And WHEREAS the United States is on terms of friendship and amity with the contending powers, and with the persons inhabiting their several dominions;

And WHEREAS there are citizens of the United States residing within the territories or dominions of each of the said belligerents and carrying on commerce, trade, or other business or pursuits therein;

And WHEREAS there are subjects of each of the said belligerents residing within the territory or juristiction of the United States, and carrying on commerce, trade, or other business or pursuits therein;

And WHEREAS the laws and treaties of the United States, without interfering with the free expression of opinion and sympathy, or with the commercial manufacture or sale of arms or munitions of war, nevertheless impose upon all persons who may be within their territory and jurisdiction the duty of an impartial neutrality during the existence of the contest;

And WHEREAS it is the duty of a neutral government not to permit or suffer the making of its waters subservient to the purposes of war;

Now, Therefore, I, WOODROW WILSON, President of the United States of America, in order to preserve the neutrality of the United States . . . do hereby declare and proclaim. . . .

That the statutes and the treaties of the United States and the law of nations alike require that no person, within the territory and jurisdiction of the United States, shall take part, directly or indirectly, in the said wars, but shall remain at peace with all of the said belligerents, and shall maintain a strict and impartial neutrality. . . .

2. The Zimmermann Telegram Alters the Debate, 1917

TELEGRAM RECEIVED.

FROM   2nd from London # 5747.

"We intend to begin on the first of February
unrestricted submarine warfare. We shall endeavor
in spite of this to keep the United States of
America neutral. In the event of this not succeeding, we make Mexico a proposal of alliance on the
following basis: make war together, make peace
together, generous financial support and an understanding on our part that Mexico is to reconquer
the lost territory in Texas, New Mexico, and
Arizona. The settlement in detail is left to you.
You will inform the President of the above most
secretly as soon as the outbreak of war with the
United States of America is certain and add the
suggestion that he should, on his own initiative,
~~invite~~ Japan to immediate adherence and at the same
time mediate between Japan and ourselves. Please
call the President's attention to the fact that
the ruthless employment of our submarines now
offers the prospect of compelling England in a
few months to make peace." Signed, ZIMMERMANN.

3. Wilson Asks for a Declaration of War, 1917

On the third of February last I officially laid before you the extraordinary announcement of the Imperial German Government that on and after the first day of February it was its purpose to put aside all restraints of law of humanity and use its submarines to sink every vessel that sought to approach either the ports of Great Britain and Ireland or the western coasts of Europe or any of the ports controlled by the enemies of Germany within the Mediterranean. That had seemed to be the object of the German submarine warfare earlier in the war, but since April of last year the Imperial Government had somewhat restrained the commanders of its undersea craft in conformity with its promise then given to us that passenger boats should not be sunk and that due warning would be given to all other vessels which its submarines might seek to destroy, when no resistance was offered or escape attempted, and care taken that their crews were given at least a fair chance to save their lives in their open boats. The precautions taken were meagre and haphazard enough, as was proved in distressing instance after instance in the progress of the cruel and unmanly business, but a certain degree of restraint was observed. The new policy has swept every restriction aside. Vessels of every kind, whatever their flag, their character, their cargo, their destination, their errand, have been ruthlessly sent to the bottom without warning and without thought of help or mercy for those on board, the vessels of friendly neutrals along with those of belligerents. . . .

I am not now thinking of the loss of property involved, immense and serious as that is, but only of the wanton and wholesale destruction of the lives of noncombatants, men, women, and children, engaged in pursuits which have always, even in the darkest periods of modern history, been deemed innocent and legitimate. Property can be paid for; the lives of peaceful and innocent people cannot be. The present German submarine warfare against commerce is a warfare against mankind.

It is a war against all nations. American ships have been sunk, American lives taken, in ways which it has stirred us very deeply to learn of, but the ships and people of other neutral and friendly nations have been sunk and overwhelmed in the waters in the same way. There has been no discrimination. The challenge is to all mankind. Each nation must decide for itself how it will meet it. The choice we make for ourselves must be made with a moderation of counsel and a temperateness of judgment benefiting our character and our motives as a nation. We must put excited feeling away. Our motive will not be revenge or the victorious assertion of the physical might of the nation, but only the vindication of right, of human right, of which we are only a single champion. . . .

With a profound sense of the solemn and even tragical character of the step I am taking and of the grave responsibilities which it involves, but in unhesitating obedience to what I deem my constitutional duty, I advise that the Congress declare the recent course of the Imperial Government to be in fact nothing less than war against the government and people of the United States; that it formally accept the status of belligerent which has thus been thrust upon it; and that it take immediate steps not only to put the country in a more thorough state of defense but also to exert all its power and employ all its resources to bring the Government of the German Empire to terms. . . .

Our object now, as then, is to vindicate the principles of peace and justice in the life of the world as against selfish and autocratic power and to set up amongst the really free and self-governed peoples of the world such a concert of purpose and of action as will henceforth ensure the observance of those principles. Neutrality is no longer feasible or desirable where the peace of the world is involved and the freedom of its peoples, and the menace to that peace and freedom lies in the existence of autocratic governments backed by organized force which is controlled wholly by their will, not by the will of their people. . . .

One of the things that has served to convince us that the Prussian autocracy was not and could never be our friends is that from the very outset of the present war it has filled our unsuspecting communities and even our offices of government with spies and set criminal intrigues everywhere afoot against our national unity of counsel, our peace within and without, our industries and our commerce. . . . That it means to stir up enemies against us at our very doors the intercepted note to the German Minister at Mexico City is eloquent evidence.

We are accepting this challenge of hostile purpose because we know that in such a government, following such methods, we can never have a friend; and that in the presence of its organized power, always lying in wait to accomplish we know not what purpose, there can be no assured security for the democratic governments of the world. We are now about to accept gauge of battle with this natural foe to liberty and shall, if necessary, spend the whole force of the nation to check and nullify its pretensions and its power. We are glad, now that we see the facts with no veil of false pretence about them, to fight thus for the ultimate peace of the world and for the liberation of its peoples, the German peoples included: for the rights of nations great and small and the privilege of men everywhere to choose their way of life and of obedience. The world must be made safe for democracy. . . .

There are, it may be, many months of fiery trial and sacrifice ahead of us. It is a fearful thing to lead this great peaceful people into war, into the most terrible and disastrous of all wars, civilization itself seeming to be in the balance. But the right is more precious than peace, and we shall fight for the things which we have always carried nearest our hearts, — for democracy, for the right of those who submit to authority to have a voice in their own governments, for the rights and liberties of small nations, for a universal dominion of right by such a concert of free peoples as shall bring peace and safety to all nations and make the world itself at last free. To such a task we can dedicate our lives and our fortunes, everything that we are and everything that we have, with the pride of those who know that the day has come when America is privileged to spend her blood and her might for the principles that gave her birth and happiness and the peace which she has treasured. God helping her, she can do no other.

4. Wilson's Fourteen Points Clarify Liberal War Aims, 1918

The program of the world's peace, therefore, is our program; and that program, the only possible program, as we see it, is this:

I. Open covenants of peace, openly arrived at, after which there shall be no private international understandings of any kind but diplomacy shall proceed always frankly and in the public view.

II. Absolute freedom of navigation upon the seas, outside territorial waters, alike in peace and in war, except as the seas may be closed in whole or in part by international action for the enforcement of international covenants.

III. The removal, so far as possible, of all economic barriers and the establishment of an equality of trade conditions among all the nations consenting to the peace and associating themselves for its maintenance.

IV. Adequate guarantees given and taken that national armaments will be reduced to the lowest point consistent with domestic safety.

V. A free, open-minded, and absolutely impartial adjustment of all colonial claims, based upon a strict observance of the principle that in determining all such questions of sovereignty the interests of the populations concerned must have equal weight with the equitable claims of the government whose title is to be determined.

VI. The evacuation of all Russian territory and such a settlement of all questions affecting Russia as will secure the best and freest coöperation of the other nations of the world in obtaining for her an unhampered and unembarrassed opportunity for the independent determination of her own political development and national policy and assure her of a sincere welcome into the society of free nations under institutions of her own choosing; and, more than a welcome, assistance also of every kind that she may need and may herself desire. The treatment accorded Russia by her sister nations in the months to come will be the acid test of their good will, of their comprehension of her needs as distinguished from their own interests, and of their intelligent and unselfish sympathy.

VII. Belgium, the whole world will agree, must be evacuated and restored, without any attempt to limit the sovereignty which she enjoys in common with all other free nations. No other single act will serve as this will serve to restore confidence among the nations in the laws which they have themselves set and determined for the government of their relations with one another. Without this healing act the whole structure and validity of international law is forever impaired.

VIII. All French territory should be freed and the invaded portions restored, and the wrong done to France by Prussia in 1871 in the matter of Alsace-Lorraine, which has unsettled the peace of the world for nearly fifty years, should be righted, in order that peace may once more be made secure in the interest of all.

IX. A readjustment of the frontiers of Italy should be effected along clearly recognizable lines of nationality.

X. The peoples of Austria-Hungary, whose place among the nations we wish to see safeguarded and assured, should be accorded the freest opportunity of autonomous development.

XI. Rumania, Serbia, and Montenegro should be evacuated; occupied territories restored; Serbia accorded free and secure access to the sea; and the relations of the several Balkan states to one another determined by friendly counsel along historically established lines of allegiance and nationality; and international guarantees of the political and economic independence and territorial integrity of the several Balkan states should be entered into.

XII. The Turkish portions of the present Ottoman Empire should be assured a secure sovereignty, but the other nationalities which are now under Turkish rule would be assured an undoubted security of life and an absolutely unmolested opportunity of autonomous development, and the Dardanelles should be permanently opened as a free passage to the ships and commerce of all nations under international guarantees.

XIII. An independent Polish state should be erected which should include the territories inhabited by indisputably Polish populations, which should be assured a free and secure access to the sea, and whose political and economic independence and territorial integrity should be guaranteed by international covenant.

XIV. A general association of nations must be formed under specific covenants for the purpose of affording mutual guarantees of political independence and territorial integrity to great and small states alike.

5. *The New Republic* Expresses Liberal Criticism of the Versailles Treaty, 1919

A government may sign this peace, but it will never be altogether executed. For the trouble with the treaty is that it gives the Germans too many good reasons for feeling themselves thoroughly abused. Their imperial power is destroyed, that of others is increased; the principle of nationality is worked against them; the armistice is flatly violated in the Saar; Mr. Wilson's general principles about the removal of economic barriers, of special alliances within the general family of the League of Nations, the implied promise to admit Germany to the League, all seem to have gone down the wind. With all these things done to them, it will be exceedingly difficult to keep German workingmen and Germans who were boys during the war convinced that they are suffering justly for the sins of the Hohenzollerns.

Not only will they be less and less convinced; they will be increasingly angry and vindictive. And in their anger they will have the growing sympathy of labor throughout Europe, and currents will be set up which will shake the whole edifice of European society. Looked at from the purely American point of view, on a cold calculation of probabilities, we do not see how this treaty is anything but the prelude to quarrels in a deeply divided and hideously embittered Europe.

However much the words of the Fourteen Points may be invoked to justify this treaty, one thing is so plain as to seem beyond argument. The world which will result from the document can by no stretch of language be made to agree with the picture which the President had in mind when he went to Paris, or when he spoke in the days of his glory of what was to be accomplished. His own inner disillusionment is only too apparent in the after-dinner speech which he delivered in Paris the other night. By the standards of which he himself was the most eloquent spokesman he has failed. The treaty is the work of the European governments, mitigated at a few points no doubt by Mr. Wilson. But the settlement which we are now asked to guarantee in all its detail, to underwrite with the lives and the resources of America, is one made by European government in the spirit of the traditional diplomacy of Europe. In the meshes of that diplomacy it would be reckless folly for a nation placed as ours is to entangle itself. Therefore, assuming that the document becomes the law of Europe, the immediate task for Americans is to decide coolly just how they will limit their obligations under the Covenant. That they must be limited seems to us an inescapable conclusion.

6. Wilson Defends the Treaty and the League, 1919

The essential matter, my fellow citizens, is this: This League will include all the fighting nations of the world, except Germany. The only nations that will not be admitted into it promptly are Germany and Turkey. All the fighting nations of the world are in it, and what do they promise? This is the center of the document. They promise that they never will go to war without first either submitting the question at issue to arbitration and absolutely abiding by the decision of the arbitrators, or, if they are not willing to submit it to arbitration, submitting it to discussion by the council of the League; that they will give the council of the League six months in which to consider it, and that if they do not like the opinion of the council, they will wait three months after the opinion is rendered before going to war. And I tell you, my fellow citizens, that any nation that is in the wrong and waits nine months before it goes to war never will go to war. . . .

This Nation went into this war to see it through to the end, and the end has not come yet. This is the beginning, not of the war but of the processes which are going to render a war like this impossible. There are no other processes than those that are proposed in this great treaty. It is a great treaty, it is a treaty of justice, of rigorous and severe justice, but do not forget that there are many other parties to this treaty than Germany and her opponents. There is rehabilitated Poland. There is rescued Bohemia. There is redeemed Jugo-Slavia. There is the rehabilitated Rumania. All the nations that Germany meant to crush and reduce to the status of tools in her hands have been redeemed by this war and given the guarantee of the strongest nations of the world that nobody shall invade their liberty again. If you do not want to give them that guarantee, then you make it certain that without your guarantee the attempt will be made again, and if another war starts like this one, are you going to keep out of it? If you keep out of this arrangement, that sort of war will come soon. If you go into it, it never will come. We are in the presence, therefore, of the most solemn choice that this people was ever called upon to make. That choice is nothing less than this: Shall America redeem her pledges to the world? America is made up of the peoples of the world. All the best bloods of the world flow in her veins, all the old affections, all the old and sacred traditions of peoples of every sort throughout the wide world circulate in her veins, and she has said to mankind at her birth: "We have come to redeem the world by giving it liberty and justice." Now we are called upon before the tribunal of mankind to redeem that immortal pledge.

7. Conflicting Visions of the Versailles Treaty, 1920

A. "The Accuser"

THE ACCUSER

KIRBY, *WORLD JOURNAL TRIBUNE*

B. "Interrupting the Ceremony"

INTERRUPTING THE CEREMONY

McCUTCHEON, CHICAGO TRIBUNE–NEW YORK NEWS SYNDICATE, INC.

Chapter 23:
Document Set 3 References

1. Woodrow Wilson Outlines American Neutrality Policy, 1914
   Woodrow Wilson, "Proclamation of the President," August 4, 1914, in Woodrow Wilson, *The New Democracy: Presidential Messages, Addresses, and Papers (1913–1917)*, Ray Stannard Baker and William E. Dodd, eds. (New York: Harper and Brothers, 1926), Vol. 1, pp. 151–152, 155.

2. The Zimmermann Telegram Alters the Debate, 1917
   Zimmermann Telegram (photocopy of original decoded telegram), January 2, 1917, National Archives, Record Group 59, General Records of Department of State, Decimal File No. 862.2012/69 (1910–1929).

3. Wilson Asks for a Declaration of War, 1917
   Wilson, "For Declaration of War Against Germany," April 2, 1917, in Woodrow Wilson, *War and Peace; Presidential Messages, Addresses, and Public Papers, 1917–1924*, Baker and Dodd, eds., Vol. 1, pp. 6–8, 9, 11, 13–14, 16.

4. Wilson's Fourteen Points Clarify Liberal War Aims, 1918
   Wilson, "The Fourteen Points Speech," January 8, 1918, in Baker and Dodd, *War and Peace*, Vol. 1, pp. 159–161.

5. *The New Republic* Expresses Liberal Criticism of the Versailles Treaty, 1919
   "Europe Proposes," *The New Republic*, Vol. 19 (May 17, 1919).

6. Wilson Defends the Treaty and the League, 1919
   Wilson, Speech, St. Louis, Mo., September 5, 1919, in Baker and Dodd, eds., *War and Peace*, Vol. 1, pp. 642, 644–645.

7. Conflicting Visions of the Versailles Treaty, 1920
   A. "The Accuser," Kirby, *World Journal Tribune*, ca. 1920.
   B. "Interrupting the Ceremony," McCutcheon, *Chicago Tribune–New York News Syndicate*, ca. 1920.

Chapter 23:
Document Set 3 Credits

2. National Archives
7. A. Kirby, *World Journal Tribune*, 1920
   B. © Chicago Tribune Company. All rights reserved. Used with permission.

CHAPTER 24

DOCUMENT SET 1
The Business Values of the 1920s: Promise and Reality

The economic development described in your textbook was accompanied by a widespread endorsement of business values as the key to long-term stability and social progress. The following documents examine the popularity enjoyed by business leaders in the 1920s, as well as common perceptions of their outlook. Moreover, they explore the social consequences of the national commitment to the business system. As you review these materials, determine whether the new corporate ethic promoted the common good.

The first group of documents outlines the world view of the business elite, as well as the broad community acceptance of its value system. Frederick Lewis Allen's retrospective provides a penetrating critique of the public adulation heaped on businesspeople at the peak of their influence. Be aware of the historical context in which Allen's account appeared.

Equally revealing is efficiency analyst Edward Purington's description of the business creed of the 1920s. Purington's enthusiasm for free enterprise theology is evident in his sweeping embrace of the business argument, which borders on a religious commitment. A more thoughtful expression of the business,

political, and economic outlook is found in Republican presidential candidate Herbert Hoover's confession of faith in liberal individualism. Both documents should be interpreted in light of the social, political, and economic milieu at the time of their publication. Use your textbook account of the new economic order as a resource for understanding the social power of business values.

An important analytical question will center on the validity of Purington's argument. Other contemporary observers advanced a different interpretation of business claims. Focusing on the new order's benefits to workers, these accounts attempt to assess the social consequences of unbridled business enterprise. Evangelist/author Kirby Page argued in *Atlantic Monthly* that the beneficence of the United States Steel Corporation had limits. Compare Page's view of welfare capitalism with business claims of social stewardship. Account for the contrast in interpretation and try to evaluate the business argument, analyzing the documents against the background of the textbook's treatment of labor problems, business response, and the ideology of utopian capitalism.

Questions for Analysis

1. How would you account for Herbert Hoover's endorsement of individualism? To what extent was Hoover sincere in his argument that social benefits would be the result of unrestrained enterprise? What do the documents reveal about Hoover's social assumptions?

2. Why did the American public respond positively to the arguments of business spokespersons of the 1920s? Do the documents reveal any assumptions rooted in the past experience of the American people?

3. What were the broad social consequences of corporate decisions concerning social welfare, wage levels, and the distribution of wealth? How did the commentators differ in interpreting these results?

4. What evidence do the documents provide of the extent to which the business ethic penetrated all levels of American society and thought in the 1920s? How would you account for the widespread acceptance of business values by American intellectual and religious leaders?

1. Frederick Lewis Allen Recalls the Business Ethos of the New Era, 1931

Business itself was regarded with a new veneration. Once it had been considered less dignified and distinguished than the learned professions, but now people thought they praised a clergyman highly when they called him a good business man. College alumni, gathered at their annual banquets, fervently applauded the banker trustees who spoke of education as one of the greatest American industries and compared the president and the dean to business executives. The colleges themselves organized business courses and cheerfully granted credit to candidates for degrees in the arts and sciences for their work in advertising copy-writing, marketing methods, elementary stenography, and drug-store practice. Even Columbia University drew men and women into its home-study courses by a system of follow-up letters worthy of a manufacturer of refrigerators, and sent out salesmen to ring the door bells of those who expressed a flicker of interest; even the great University of Chicago made use of what André Siegfried has called "the mysticism of success" by heading an advertisement of its correspondence courses with the admonition to "develop power at home, to investigate, persevere, achieve." . . . The Harvard Business School established annual advertising awards, conferring academic *éclat* upon well-phrased sales arguments for commercial products. It was not easy for the churches to resist the tide of business enthusiasm. The Swedish Immanuel Congregational Church in New York, according to an item in the *American Mercury*, recognized the superiority of the business to the spiritual appeal by offering to all who contributed one hundred dollars to its building fund "an engraved certificate of investment in preferred capital stock in the Kingdom of God." And a church billboard in uptown New York struck the same persuasive note: "Come to Church. Christian Worship Increases Your Efficiency. Christian F. Reisner, Pastor." . . .

Indeed, the association of business with religion was one of the most significant phenomena of the day. When the National Association of Credit Men held their annual convention at New York, there were provided for the three thousand delegates a special devotional service at the Cathedral of St. John the Divine and five sessions of prayer conducted by Protestant clergymen, a Roman Catholic priest, and a Jewish rabbi; and the credit men were uplifted by a sermon by Dr. S. Parkes Cadman on "Religion in Business." Likewise the Associated Advertising Clubs, meeting in Philadelphia, listened to a keynote address by Doctor Cadman on "Imagination and Advertising," and at the meeting of the Church Advertising Department the subjects discussed included "Spiritual Principles in Advertising" and "Advertising the Kingdom through Press-Radio Service." The fact that each night of the session a cabaret entertainment was furnished to the earnest delegates from 11:30 to 2 and that part of the Atlantic City Beauty Pageant was presented was merely a sign that even men of high faith must have their fun.

2. Edward Purington's Endorsement of Business Values, 1921

Among the nations of the earth today America stands for one idea: *Business*. National opprobrium? National opportunity. For in this fact lies, potentially, the salvation of the world.

Thru business, properly conceived, managed and conducted, the human race is finally to be redeemed. How and why a man works foretells what he will do, think, have, give and be. And real salvation is in doing, thinking, having, giving and being—not in sermonizing and theorizing. . . .

What is the finest game? Business. The soundest science? Business. The truest art? Business. The fullest education? Business. The fairest opportunity? Business. The cleanest philanthropy? Business. The sanest religion? Business.

You may not agree. That is because you judge business by the crude, mean, stupid, false imitation of business that happens to be located near you.

The finest game is business. The rewards are for everybody, and all can win. There are no favorites—

Providence always crowns the career of the man who is worthy. And in this game there is no "luck"—you have the fun of taking chances but the sobriety of guaranteeing certainties. The speed and size of your winnings are for you alone to determine; you needn't wait for the other fellow in the game—it is always your move. And your slogan is not "Down the Other Fellow!" but rather "Beat Your Own Record!" or "Do It Better Today!" or "Make Every Job a Masterpiece!" The great sportsmen of the world are the great business men.

The soundest science is business. All investigation is reduced to action, and by action proved or disproved. The idealistic motive animates the materialistic method. Hearts as well as minds are open to the truth. Capital is furnished for the researches of "pure science"; yet pure science is not regarded pure until practical. Competent scientists are suitably rewarded—as they are not in the scientific schools.

The truest art is business. The art is so fine, so exquisite, that you do not think of it as art. Language, color, form, line, music, drama, discovery, adventure—all the components of art must be used in business to make it of superior character.

The fullest education is business. A proper blend of study, work and life is essential to advancement. The whole man is educated. Human nature itself is the open book that all business men study; and the mastery of a page of this educates you more than the memorizing of a dusty tome from a library shelf. In the school of business, moreover, you teach yourself and learn most from your own mistakes. What you learn here you live out, the only real test.

The fairest opportunity is business. You can find more, better, quicker chances to get ahead in a large business house than anywhere else on earth. The biographies of champion business men show how they climbed, and how you can climb. Recognition of better work, of keener and quicker thought, of deeper and finer feeling, is gladly offered by the men higher up, with early promotion the rule for the man who

justifies it. There is, and can be, no such thing as buried talent in a modern business organization.

The cleanest philanthropy is business. By "clean" philanthropy I mean that devoid of graft, inefficiency and professionalism, also of condolence, hysterics and paternalism. Nearly everything that goes by the name of Charity was born a triplet, the other two members of the trio being Frailty and Cruelty. Not so in the welfare departments of leading corporations. Savings and loan funds; pension and insurance provisions; health precautions, instructions and safeguards; medical attention and hospital care; libraries, lectures and classes; musical, athletic and social features of all kinds; recreational facilities and financial opportunities—these types of "charitable institutions" for employees add to the worker's self-respect, self-knowledge and self-improvement, by making him an active partner in the welfare program, a producer of benefits for his employer and associates quite as much as a recipient of bounty from the company. I wish every "charity" organization would send its officials to school to the heads of the welfare departments of the big corporations; the charity would mostly be transformed into capability, and the minimum of irreducible charity left would not be called by that name.

The sanest religion is business. Any relationship that forces a man to follow the Golden Rule rightfully belongs amid the ceremonials of the church. A great business enterprise includes and presupposes this relationship. I have seen more Christianity to the square inch as a regular part of the office equipment of famous corporation presidents than may ordinarily be found on Sunday in a verbalized but not vitalized church congregation. A man is not wholly religious until he is better on weekdays than he is on Sunday. The only ripened fruits of creeds are deeds. You can fool your preacher with a sickly sprout or a wormy semblance of character, but you can't fool your employer. I would make every business house a consultation bureau for the guidance of the church whose members were employees of the house.

3. Herbert Hoover Embraces Individualism, 1928

Liberalism is a force truly of the spirit, a force proceeding from the deep realization that economic freedom cannot be sacrificed if political freedom is to be preserved. Even if governmental conduct of business could give us more efficiency instead of less efficiency, the fundamental objection to it would remain unal-

tered and unabated. It would destroy political equality. It would increase rather than decrease abuse and corruption. It would stifle initiative and invention. It would undermine the development of leadership. It would cramp and cripple the mental and spiritual energies of our people. It would extinguish equality and opportunity. It would dry up the spirit of liberty and progress. For these reasons primarily it must be resisted. For 150 years liberalism has found its true spirit in the American system, not in the European systems.

I do not wish to be misunderstood in this statement. I am defining a general policy. It does not mean that our government is to part with one iota of its national resources without complete protection to the public interest. I have already stated that where the government is engaged in public works for purposes of flood control, of navigation, of irrigation, of scientific research or national defense, or in pioneering a new art, it will at times necessarily produce power or commodities as a by-product. But they must be a by-product of the major purpose, not the major purpose itself.

Nor do I wish to be misinterpreted as believing that the United States is a free-for-all and devil-take-the-hindmost. The very essence of equality of opportunity and of American individualism is that there shall be no domination by any group or combination in this republic, whether it be business or political. On the contrary, it demands economic justice as well as political and social justice. It is no system of laissez faire. . . .

One of the great problems of government is to determine to what extent the government shall regulate and control commerce and industry and how much it shall leave it alone. No system is perfect. We have had many abuses in the private conduct of business. That every good citizen resents. It is just as important that business keep out of government as that government keep out of business.

Nor am I setting up the contention that our institutions are perfect. No human ideal is ever perfectly attained, since humanity itself is not perfect. . . .

By adherence to the principles of decentralized self-government, ordered liberty, equal opportunity, and freedom to the individual, our American experiment in human welfare has yielded a degree of well-being unparalleled in all the world. It has come nearer to the abolition of poverty, to the abolition of fear of want than humanity has ever reached before. Progress of the past seven years is the proof of it. This alone furnishes the answer to our opponents, who ask us to introduce destructive elements into the system by which this has been accomplished.

4. Kirby Page Assesses the Social Consequences of Corporate Labor Policies, 1922

What are the social consequences of current business policies? To what extent are human values subordinated in the effort to secure large returns on invested capital? Do the workers receive an adequate share of the proceeds of modern industry? How shall we determine an equitable adjustment of profits and wages? Wherein resides the dominant power in the control of modern business?

This study of one of our large corporations is an attempt to shed light upon such questions as these. The United States Steel Corporation was selected for this purpose because of its magnitude and the important part which it plays in one of our basic industries. . . .

First of all, let us inquire as to hours and working conditions. In his testimony before the United States Senate Investigating Committee, Judge Gary, chairman of the Steel Corporation, said: "Twenty-six and a half percent of all employees work the twelve-hour turn, and the number is 69,284." . . .

It does not require a vivid imagination to picture the consequences of the twelve-hour day.

Twelve hours at the mill, one-half hour going to and one-half hour coming from work, one-half hour for breakfast and one-half hour for supper, eight hours of sleep—add these up! A scant two hours are left for domestic duties, homelife, social and civic life, reading and study! What sort of a husband, father, and citizen is a twelve-hour worker likely to be? How much energy and interest is such a worker likely to have left for intellectual and spiritual matters?

Wages

Let us next analyze the wages paid by the Steel Corporation. Surely wages must be adequate if the average for all employees in 1920 was approximately $7 per day. There is no doubt that skilled labor is paid well in comparison with other industries. But how about unskilled labor? . . .

What are the facts at the present time? Three successive wage cuts during 1921 reduced the wages of unskilled labor in the employ of the Steel Corporation slightly more than 40 percent, the rate now being 30 cents per hour, with no extra pay for overtime. Eight hours a day, six days per week, at this rate amounts to $14.40 per week—$748.80 per year, if no time is lost from sickness or otherwise. Is this a partial explanation of the reluctance of the employees to give up the twelve-hour day, about which we hear so much? . . .

Causes of Low Wages and Long Hours

Why, then, does the corporation continue to pay its unskilled workers about $340 a year less than a minimum health and decency standard, and in normal times compel approximately 70,000 of its employees to work the twelve-hour day?

The first reason is because it follows the usual procedure of not basing wages upon the needs of the workers but upon the market rate. The market rate is paid for labor as for any material commodity. The size of the corporation enables it to play an important part in determining the market rate. . . .

The second reason is that, from the viewpoint of the management, it is more important to pay regular dividends and to build up a huge reserve than it is to pay workers in excess of the market rate, even though this rate is insufficient for the maintenance of a decent or comfortable standard of life. . . .

The third reason is that adequate pressure has not been brought to bear upon the Steel Corporation by the workers themselves or by public opinion. . . .

What is the labor policy of the corporation? On June 17, 1901, six weeks after the corporation was organized, the Executive Committee passed the following resolution:

That we are unalterably opposed to any extension of union labor, and advise subsidiary companies to take a firm position when these questions come up, and say that they are not going to recognize it—that is, any extension of unions in mills where they do not now exist; that great care should be used to prevent trouble, and that they promptly report and confer with this corporation.

This policy has been rigidly adhered to. . . .

Consequences of Anti-union Policy

In the light of the facts obtained, the Commission of Inquiry of the Interchurch World Movement summarized these consequences as follows:

Maintaining the nonunionism alternative entailed for the employers: (1) discharging workmen for unionism; (2) black lists; (3) espionage and the hiring of "labor detective agencies" operatives; (4) strikebreakers, principally Negroes. Maintaining the nonunionism alternative entailed for communities: (1) the abrogation of the right of assembly, the suppression of free speech, and the violation of personal rights (principally in Pennsylvania); (2) the use of state police, state troops, and (in Indiana) of the United States Army; (3) such activities on the part of constituted authorities and of the press and the pulpit as to make the workers believe that these forces oppose labor. In sum, the actual existent state of the steel industry is a state of latent war over rights of organization conceded by public opinion in other civilized countries.

Chapter 24:
Document Set 1 References

1. Frederick Lewis Allen Recalls the Business Ethos of the New Era, 1931
   Frederick Lewis Allen, *Only Yesterday: An Informal History of the Nineteen-Twenties* (New York: Harper and Row, 1931; rep. 1964), pp. 146–148.

2. Edward Purington's Endorsement of Business Values, 1921
   Edward Earl Purington, "Big Ideas from Big Business," *The Independent,* April 16, 1921.

3. Herbert Hoover Embraces Individualism, 1928
   Herbert C. Hoover, *The New Day: Campaign Speeches of Herbert Hoover* (Palo Alto: Stanford University Press, 1928), pp. 149–176.

4. Kirby Page Assesses the Social Consequences of Corporate Labor Policies, 1922
   Kirby Page, "The United States Steel Corporation," *Atlantic Monthly* (May 1922).

Chapter 24:
Document Set 1 Credits

DOCUMENT SET 2

Sources of Social Conflict: Reactions to Changing Moral Values

Caught between the values of a rural past and the urban future, Americans clashed in the 1920s over several social issues that challenged their most deeply held beliefs. These documents reflect some of the prominent social currents of the "New Era," with emphasis on the disagreements they generated. As you review these materials, try to determine why Americans were divided in a decade of apparent growth and prosperity.

No issue concerned White Anglo-Saxon Protestant America more than the altered ethnoreligious character of the population, a problem addressed in the first group of documents. Sociologist Henry Pratt Fairchild and Ku Klux Klan leader Hiram Wesley Evans spoke for different elements in the American social structure; examine their remarks for evidence of agreement. As a follow-up, search the words of convicted criminal Bartolomeo Vanzetti for the sources of discontent among native-born Americans in the 1920s.

Related to the issue of immigrant influence in the United States was the prohibition question. Evaluate the evidence in light of the textbook's assertion that the dry crusade was a symbolic expression of ethnocultural differences and urban-rural tension. Hiram Evans's declaration reveals the problems simmering beneath the surface of American politics, while Philadelphia court statistics reflect the difficulties of enforcing an unpopular law. The documents mirror social patterns described in your text, especially the predominant lifestyle of urban areas.

By contrast, an excerpt from William Jennings Bryan's diatribe against Darwin provides a glimpse of fundamentalist concern that modern science constituted a threat to traditional values. Relate Bryan's argument to the *Scopes* case, described in your textbook, and try to link his position with the views of Hiram Wesley Evans. As you assess the traditional viewpoint, be aware of the background and concerns brought to the debate by the main protagonists.

An important aspect of the new intellectual and social milieu involved a new sexual morality that included variations on the traditional moral code. The next pair of documents reflects shifting standards of sexual behavior. As you review Eleanor Wembridge's comments on college women's attitudes and Suzanne LaFollette's remarks on divorce, analyze the evidence with an eye to underlying values and assumptions about sex.

As you review this document set, reflect upon the wider implications of social change. Consider the relationship among politics, culture, and shifting social values.

Questions for Analysis

1. What were the origins of the prohibition experiment? What do the documents reveal about the consequences of prohibition's failure?

2. In what ways was the value system of rural, small-town America challenged in the 1920s? What were the social and political results? How do the documents reflect the clash in values?

3. To what extent did a "sexual revolution" occur in the 1920s? What was a "radical feminist," and what evidence exists to measure the changes in sexual behavior and attitudes toward women and the family?

4. What was the basis for the cultural conflict of the 1920s? Was the struggle essentially a clash between regions or value systems? What were the ideas and beliefs associated with the "new" and the "old" America?

5. Compare the textbook material on the immigration restriction movement with evidence in the documents relating to the influence of immigrants on American institutions. How would you explain the postwar shift in public opinion that resulted in the enactment of restrictionist legislation? What arguments were presented in favor of restrictionism? What "hidden agendas" lay behind these statements?

1. Henry Pratt Fairchild Questions the "Melting Pot" Theory, 1926

As far as the United States is concerned, the first and most direct effect of unrestricted immigration is a retardation, if not a definite lowering, of the standard of living of the common people. It is the search for a higher standard of living which, more than anything else, brings the immigrant here. The standard of the American is higher than his. He can raise his by coming. If in the process he lowers the standard of the American, that is no concern of his. . . .

The nature of the competition between standards of living is such that the lower pulls down the upper much more than it elevates itself. Each successively lower standard that is allowed to enter the competition reduces the level just so much more. The truth has long been recognized by students of the problem, and forcibly expressed by General Francis A. Walker, that the ultimate outcome of unrestricted immigration is a progressive deterioration of the standard until no "difference of *economic level* exists between our population and that of the most degraded communities abroad." Certainly the ideal of liberalism is not to be found in such a denouement as this. . . .

There can be only one conclusion. The eventual effect of an unrestricted immigration movement, governed only by the economic self-interest of the migrating individuals, must under modern conditions be a progressive depression of the standard of living of mankind as a whole. It is, therefore, contrary to the liberal spirit, and the label so vigorously exploited and so confidently flaunted in the face of the American public is found to have been falsely applied.

But there is more to the question than this. Other interests than the economic call for consideration.

It has been repeatedly stated that the consequence of nonassimilation is the destruction of [American] nationality. This is the central truth of the whole problem of immigration, and it cannot be overemphasized. An immigration movement that did not involve nonassimilation might be tolerated, though it might have other evil consequences which would condemn it. But an immigration movement that does involve nonassimilation—like the movement to the United States during the last fifty years at least—is a blow at the very heart of nationality and cannot be endured if nationality is conceived to have any value whatsoever.

2. Hiram W. Evans on the Ku Klux Klan Program, 1926

The Klan, therefore, has now come to speak for the great mass of Americans of the old pioneer stock. We believe that it does fairly and faithfully represent them, and our proof lies in their support. To understand the Klan, then, it is necessary to understand the character and present mind of the mass of old-stock Americans. The mass, it must be remembered, as distinguished from the intellectually mongrelized "Liberals."

These are, in the first place, a blend of various peoples of the so-called Nordic race, the race which, with all its faults, has given the world almost the whole of modern civilization. The Klan does not try to represent any people but these. . . .

[T]hese Nordic Americans for the last generation have found themselves increasingly uncomfortable, and finally deeply distressed. There appeared first confusion in thought and opinion, a groping and hesitancy about national affairs and private life alike, in sharp contrast to the clear, straightforward purposes of our earlier years. There was futility in religion, too, which was in many ways even more distressing. Presently we began to find that we were dealing with strange ideas; policies that always sounded well but somehow always made us still more uncomfortable.

Finally came the moral breakdown that has been going on for two decades. One by one all our traditional moral standards went by the boards or were so disregarded that they ceased to be binding. The sacredness of our Sabbath, of our homes, of chastity, and finally even of our right to teach our own children in our own schools fundamental facts and truths were torn away from us. Those who maintained the old standards did so only in the face of constant ridicule. . . .

The old-stock Americans are learning, however. They have begun to arm themselves for this new type of warfare. Most important, they have broken away from the fetters of the false ideals and philanthropy which put aliens ahead of their own children and their own race. . . .

One more point about the present attitude of the old-stock American: he has revived and increased his long-standing distrust of the Roman Catholic Church. It is for this that the native Americans, and the Klan as their leader, are most often denounced as intolerant and prejudiced. . . .

The Ku Klux Klan, in short, is an organization which gives expression, direction and purpose to the most vital instincts, hopes, and resentments of the old-stock Americans, provides them with leadership, and is enlisting and preparing them for militant, constructive action toward fulfilling their racial and national destiny. Madison Grant summed up in a single sentence the grievances, purpose, and type of membership of the Klan: "Our farmers and artisans . . . of American blood, to recognize and meet this danger." The Klan literally is once more the embattled American farmer and artisan, coordinated into a disciplined and growing army, and launched upon a definite crusade for Americanism! . . .

Thus the Klan goes back to the American racial instincts, and to the common sense which is their first product, as the basis of its beliefs and methods. . . .

There are three of these great racial instincts, vital elements in both the historic and the present attempts to build an America which shall fulfill the aspirations and justify the heroism of the men who made the nation. These are the instincts of loyalty to the white race, to the traditions of America, and to the spirit of Protestantism, which has been an essential part of Americanism ever since the days of Roanoke and Plymouth Rock. They are condensed into the Klan slogan: "Native, white, Protestant supremacy."

3. Bartolomeo Vanzetti's Last Court Statement, 1927

Now, I should say that I am not only innocent of all these things, not only have I never committed a real crime in my life—though some sins but not crimes—not only have I struggled all my life to eliminate crimes, the crimes that the official law and the official moral condemns, but also the crime that the official moral and the official law sanctions and sanctifies—the exploitation and the oppression of the man by the man, and if there is a reason why I am here as a guilty man, if there is a reason why you in a few minutes can doom me, it is this reason and none else. . . .

We were tried during a time that has now passed into history. I mean by that, a time when there was a hysteria of resentment and hate against the people of our principles, against the foreigner, against slackers. . . .

Well, I have already say that I not only am not guilty . . . but I never commit a crime in my life—I have never steal and I have never kill and I have never spilt blood, and I have fought against the crime, and I have fought and I have sacrificed myself even to eliminate the crimes that the law and the church legitimate and sanctify.

This is what I say: I would not wish to a dog or to a snake, to the most low and misfortunate creature of the earth—I would not wish to any of them what I have had to suffer for things that I am not guilty of. But my conviction is that I have suffered for things that I am guilty of. I am suffering because I am a radical and indeed I am a radical; I have suffered because I was an Italian, and indeed I am an Italian; I have suffered more for my family and for my beloved than for myself; but I am so convinced to be right that if you could execute me two times, and if I could be reborn two other times, I would live again to do what I have done already.

I have finished. Thank you.

4. Prohibition in Philadelphia, 1919–1925

Scope of Bootlegging

At this point it might be interesting to consider the scope of the profession of bootlegging in a community such as Philadelphia. Beginning with the year 1919, the era of prohibition, the Police Department of the City of Philadelphia made the following number of arrests for intoxication, intoxication and disorderly conduct, and habitual drunkenness. Intoxication and disorderly conduct are very closely allied. . . .

The statistics of the Police Department, beginning with the year 1919, follow:

1919	Total
Intoxication 16,819	
Intoxication and disorderly conduct 6,794	
Habitual drunkards 127	
	23,740

1920	
Intoxication 14,313	
Intoxication and disorderly conduct 6,097	
Habitual drunkards 33	
	20,443

1921	
Intoxication 21,850	
Intoxication and disorderly conduct 5,232	
Intoxicated drivers* 494	
Habitual drunkards 33	
	27,609

1922	
Intoxication 36,299	
Intoxication and disorderly conduct 7,925	
Intoxicated drivers 472	
Habitual drunkards 50	
	44,746

1923	Total
Intoxication 45,226	
Intoxication and disorderly conduct 8,076	
Intoxicated drivers 645	
Habitual drunkards 177	
	54,124

1924	
Intoxication 47,805	
Intoxication and disorderly conduct 6,404	
Intoxicated drivers 683	
Habitual drunkards 874	
	55,766

1925	
Intoxication 51,361	
Intoxication and disorderly conduct 5,522	
Intoxicated drivers 820	
Habitual drunkards 814	
	58,517

*Not classified previous to year 1921.

5. William Jennings Bryan Attacks Evolutionary Thought, 1922

The hypothesis to which the name of Darwin has been given—the hypothesis that links man to the lower forms of life and makes him a lineal descendant of the brute—is obscuring God and weakening all the virtues that rest upon the religious tie between God and man. . . .

I submit three propositions for the consideration of the Christians of the nation:

First, preachers who break the bread of life to lay members should believe that man has in him the breath of the Almighty, as the Bible declares—not the blood of the brute, as the evolutionists affirm. He should also believe in the virgin birth of the Saviour.

Second, none but Christians in good standing and with spiritual conception of life should be allowed to teach in Christian schools. Church schools are worse than useless if they bring students under the influence of those who do not believe in the religion upon which the Church and church schools are built. Atheism and agnosticism are more dangerous when hidden under the cloak of religion than when they are exposed to view.

Third, the tax-payers should prevent the teaching in the public schools of atheism, agnosticism, Darwinism, or any other hypothesis that links man in blood relationship with the brutes. Christians build their own colleges in which to teach Christianity; let atheists and agnostics build their own schools in which to teach their doctrines—whether they call it atheism, agnosticism, or a scientific interpretation of the Bible.

6. A Report on the New Moral Code, 1925

Last summer I was at a student conference of young women comprised of about eight hundred college girls from the middle western states. The subject of petting was very much on their minds, both as to what attitude they should take toward it with the younger girls, (being upperclassmen themselves) and also how much renunciation of this pleasurable pastime was required of them. If I recall correctly, two entire mornings were devoted to discussing the matter, two evenings, and another overflow meeting. . . .

Before the conference I made it my business to talk to as many college girls as possible. I consulted as many, both in groups and privately, as I had time for at the conference. And since it is all to be repeated in another state this summer, I have been doing so, when opportunity offered, ever since. . . .

One fact is evident, that whether or not they pet, they hesitate to have anyone believe that they do not. It is distinctly the *mores* of the time to be considered as ardently sought after, and as not too priggish to respond. As one girl said—"I don't particularly care to be kissed by some of the fellows I know, but I'd let them do it any time rather than think I wouldn't dare. As a matter of fact, there are lots of fellows I don't kiss. It's the very young kids that never miss a chance."

That petting should lead to actual illicit relations between the petters was not advised nor countenanced among the girls with whom I discussed it. They drew the line quite sharply. That it often did so lead, they admitted, but they were not ready to allow that there were any more of such affairs than there had always been. School and college scandals, with their sudden departures and hasty marriages, have always existed to some extent, and they still do. But only accurate statistics hard to arrive at, can prove whether or not the sex carelessness of the present day extends to an increase of sex immorality. . . .

I sat with one pleasant college Amazon, a total stranger, beside a fountain in the park, while she asked if I saw any harm in her kissing a young man whom she liked, but whom she did not want to marry. "It's terribly exciting. We get such a thrill. I think it is natural to want nice men to kiss you, so why not do what is natural?" There was no embarrassment in her manner. Her eyes and her conscience were equally untroubled. I felt as if a girl from the Parthenon frieze had stepped down to ask if she might not sport in the glade with a handsome faun. Why not indeed? Only an equally direct forcing of twentieth century science on primitive simplicity could bring us even to the same level in our conversation, and at that, the stigma of impropriety seemed to fall on me, rather than on her.

7. Suzanne LaFollette on Marriage and Divorce, 1929

The general acceptance of the idea of divorce at present is in great measure the result of woman's growing demand for reciprocity in her relations with men, and her refusal to be owned either economically or sexually. It may be regarded as an aspect of her general declaration of independence. That there are women who still make a profession of being owned, either in or out of wedlock, does not invalidate the general truth that as women have found themselves in a position to make their demands effective, they have insisted upon elevating marriage to a higher moral plane. Divorce has been one of the means to this end. No doubt it is a means often abused; but no institution has been more often abused by unscrupulous people than that of marriage, and no one ever thought the abuse an argument against the institution. It is largely due to the possibility of divorce that marriage now tends to be regarded as a voluntary partnership involving equal economic and spiritual obligations on both sides, and justly to be dissolved when those obligations have been violated by either party or have become onerous to either or to both.

8. Community Pressure for Cultural Conformity in Granite City, Illinois, 1920

9. Changing Moral Values: A Visual Essay

A. Art Young Comments on the Sexual Revolution, 1927

"Mother, when you were a girl, didn't you find it a bore to be a virgin?"

B. John Held, Jr., Portrays College Life, ca. 1920s

COMPARATIVE ANATOMY

ZOOLOGY

C. *New Yorker*'s Version of the "Flapper"
   Image, ca. Late 1920s

D. Hollywood Explores the New Value System, 1929

Chapter 24:
Document Set 2 References

1. Henry Pratt Fairchild Questions the "Melting Pot" Theory, 1926
   Henry Pratt Fairchild, *The Melting Pot Mistake* (Boston: Little, Brown, and Co., 1926), pp. 251–254.

2. Hiram W. Evans on the Ku Klux Klan Program, 1926
   Hiram W. Evans, in *North American Review* (March–April–May 1926).

3. Bartolomeo Vanzetti's Last Court Statement, 1927
   The Sacco-Vanzetti Case (New York: Henry Holt and Co., 1929), Vol. 5, pp. 4896–4904.

4. Prohibition in Philadelphia, 1919–1925
   Joseph K. Willing, "Profession of Bootlegging," *Annals of the American Academy of Political and Social Science* (May 1926).

5. William Jennings Bryan Attacks Evolutionary Thought, 1922
   William Jennings Bryan, *The Menace of Darwinism* (New York: Fleming H. Revell Co., 1922), pp. 15–17, 22–23, 49–51.

6. A Report on the New Moral Code, 1925
   Eleanor Rowland Wembridge, "Petting and the Campus," *Survey* (July 1, 1925).

7. Suzanne LaFollette on Marriage and Divorce, 1929
   Suzanne LaFollette, "Women in the Modern World," in Alvin Johnson *et al.*, eds. *Civilization and Enjoyment, Man and His World Series* (New York: D. Van Nostrand, 1929), pp. 58–60.

8. Community Pressure for Cultural Conformity in Granite City, Illinois, 1920
   "School for Americanization," 1920, National Archives, Record Group 85, Records of the Immigration and Naturalization Service, File 2767/44, Americanization Files.

9. Changing Moral Values: A Visual Essay
   A. Art Young Comments on the Sexual Revolution, 1927
      Art Young, *Colliers,* 1927.
   B. John Held, Jr., Portrays College Life, ca. 1920s
      John Held, Jr., *Life* magazine, reprinted in Paul Sann, *The Lawless Decade* (New York: Crown Publishers, Inc., 1957), p. 48.
   C. *New Yorker*'s Version of the "Flapper" Image, ca. Late 1920s
      Baskerville cartoon, reprinted in *The New Yorker Twenty-Fifth Anniversary Album* (New York: Harper and Brothers, 1950), insets.
   D. Hollywood Explores the New Value System, 1929
      Paramount poster for movie *Dangerous Curves,* reprinted in Leslie Halliwell, *Mountain of Dreams: The Golden Years of Paramount Pictures* (New York: Stonehill Publishing Company, 1976), p. 8.

Chapter 24:
Document Set 2 Credits

CHAPTER 24

**Labor Under Stress: Southern Workers
in the "New Era"**

Business hegemony in the 1920s meant that organized labor experienced a sharp decline. The problems confronting the union movement were complicated by rising real wages and the expansion of benefits as a result of the new "welfare capitalism." So significant were the gains made by semiskilled and skilled workers that the plight of the unskilled, who failed to share in the new prosperity, was all but ignored.

Overall economic expansion concealed alarming regional variations in workplace experience and worker compensation. As noted in the textbook, the most notable exception to the theme of improved wages and benefits was in the chronically low-wage South, where a rapidly developing textile industry grew dramatically by exploiting local economic conditions. The following documents suggest that the major losers in this competitive struggle were southern mill workers, who remained locked in a semifeudal social and economic system. An examination of their plight will enable you to glimpse the underside of an expanding industrial economy and to consider the price of economic progress.

Begin your analysis with a review of the statistical material dealing with increased tenancy and a shrinkage in personal income in the South. Compare these data with the assertions made in several other documents concerning the background of the labor force in the mill towns of the Piedmont. Think about the significance of this information as part of an explanation for the mixed success of labor organizers in appealing to southern workers in the 1920s.

As you explore the characteristics of the region's labor force, place the mill workers in their social context by studying the power structure in the communities they inhabited. Notice the recurrent use of the term *feudal* to describe the socioeconomic system that prevailed in the mill towns of the South. What are the implications of the feudal analogy for an understanding of everyday life in the "New" South? Your analysis of the evidence will underscore the fact that workplace activity is only part of the broader worker experience, which encompasses participation in a more comprehensive worker culture. Be especially alert to the backgrounds and motivations of those who advanced the comparison between industrial employment in a developing economy and the drudgery of medieval serfdom.

Your examination of southern work life and labor activism will reveal sectional differences not only in wage rates but also in receptivity to the appeals of labor organizers. Ask yourself why northern unionists and the United Textile Workers organization were so concerned about working and living conditions in southern industry. In what way was the southern labor problem a national problem for the union movement?

The bleakness of the mill towns and the harshness of the workplace drew the attention of the American Federation of Labor several times in the 1920s. In the late twenties, the southern labor problem also interested the Communist party, which viewed the region as an area of opportunity for radical organizing. One striking illustration of the radical initiative was the bitterly divisive labor confrontation in Gastonia, North Carolina, in 1929. The documents contain two accounts of the Gastonia strike, one a personal recollection by Communist Fred Beal and the other a scholarly account by Liston Pope of the Yale Divinity School. As you compare these analyses of the struggle, look for points of agreement and disagreement. What did the Gastonia crisis reveal about the predicament of southern workers and the appeal of radicalism in America?

**Questions for
Analysis**

1. Define the term *feudalism*. Employing the documents as your main resource, decide whether the social and economic system of the mill towns is aptly compared with that of medieval Europe. In what ways was the concept of feudalism relevant to an understanding of the lives of southern workers?

2. What was the reaction of southern workers to the problems and conditions they faced as they became part of the industrial work force? What light do the documents shed on the reasons for their response to their new work environment?

3. Which workers made up the bulk of the southern labor force in the 1920s? What do the documents reveal about their ethnocultural backgrounds, economic status, and social histories? Why did they migrate? How did their life experiences influence

their behavior and thinking once they became part of the worker culture of the mill towns?

4. Compare the labor movement in the northern textile industry with the union movement in the South during the 1920s. How would you account for the major differences? What was unique about union activity in the South? How would you account for the predominant attitudes of southern workers toward labor organizations?

5. How did the industrialization of southern communities affect family life? What roles were assumed by women and children as contributors to the family economy? What changes in attitudes and values may be detected from a careful review of the documentary evidence?

6. What is meant by "ideology"? What factors typically produce changes in ideological consciousness? What do the documents suggest about worker responses to ideological appeals in the mill towns of the 1920s?

1. Income and Farm Tenancy in the South, 1880–1920

A. Growth of White Farm Tenancy, 1890–1920 (Georgia and the Carolinas)

	All Tenants		Sharecroppers Only	
	Number	*% of All White Farmers*	*Number*	*% of All White Farmers*
1890	115,530	37.4		
1900	147,735	38.7	99,516	26.1
1910	182,316	41.8	121,353	27.8
1920	194,721	42.6	146,276	32.0

Sources: *Eleventh Census, 1890: Report of Farm and Home Ownership*, pp. 566–570; *Twelfth Census, 1900: Agriculture*, Pt. 1, pp. 69, 109, 119; *Thirteenth Census, 1910: Agriculture*, p. 172; *Fourteenth Census, 1920: Agriculture*, Pt. 2, pp. 226, 268, 292. Tenancy data in 1880 were not broken down by race. Separate data for sharecropping were not collected until 1900.

B. Estimated Personal Income per Capita (For Total Population)

	1880		1900		1920	
	Total ($)	*% of U.S. Average*	*Total ($)*	*% of U.S. Average*	*Total ($)*	*% of U.S. Average*
Georgia	86	49.1	86	42.3	348	52.9
North Carolina	64	36.6	72	35.5	354	53.8
South Carolina	72	41.1	74	36.5	336	51.1
United States	175		203		658	

Source: Richard A. Easterlin, "State Income Estimates," in Simon Kuznets and Dorothy S. Thomas (eds.), *Population Estimates and Economic Growth: United States, 1870–1950* (Philadelphia, 1957), Vol. I, p. 753.

2. "The Winnsboro Cotton Mill Blues," ca. 1930s

Old man Sargent, sitting at the desk,
The damn old fool won't give us a rest.
He'd take the nickels off a dead man's eyes
To buy Coca Cola and Eskimo pies.

> Chorus: I got the blues, I got the blues,
> I got the Winnsboro cotton mill blues,
> Lordy, Lordy, spoolin's hard;
> You know and I know, I don't have
> to tell,
> You work for Tom Watson, got to work
> like hell
> I got the blues, I got the blues,
> I got the Winnsboro cotton mill blues.

When I die, don't bury me at all,
Just hang me up on the spool-room wall;
Place a knotter in my hand,
So I can spool in the Promised Land.

When I die, don't bury me deep,
Bury me down on Six Hundred Street;
Place a bobbin in each hand
So I can doff in the Promised Land.

3. Organized Labor's View of Southern Industrial Conditions, 1927, 1929

Southern Industrial Conditions Menace the Life of Trade Unions

By Harvey O'Connor

Federated Press

WASHINGTON.—America's trade unionists had better look sharply to the south if they do not want a regime of open shop paternalism hitherto unequalled in labor history to spread northward, engulfing unionism as it goes. Even if the Dixie type of industrial feudalism does not spread, it is becoming each year a greater menace to the maintenance of union standards in organized northern industries. . . .

The mill owners are drawing their labor power from the vast reservoir of half-famished mountaineers whose standard of living is the lowest in the United States. From wretched huts in the Carolina hills, the "poor white trash" gladly troop down to the mill towns. So infinitely superior are these villages with the monotonous rows of four-room shacks, many of which have running water and even electricity, to the primitive cabins of the "hill-billies" that they willingly sacrifice freedom of action and submit to the baronial tyranny of their employer, who owns homes, school, church and the entire community.

Even the low wages paid in the mill seem princely to the mountaineer who hardly handled $100 in cash the year around. In addition his wife and children are privileged to toil in the same mill and so for the first time the family escapes the generation-old semistarvation of the hill regions.

Employers hire the village preachers, who in turn laud the mill owner and make religion the vehicle for feudal submission. Race pride is stirred by references to the "finest Anglo-Saxon strain in America" and enmity against the Negro is cultivated by veiled references that he will be brought in if ever the white workers lose their proper humility. With the nightmare of the hill life behind him and the terror of Negro competition before him, the southern textile operative is as nearly "union proof" as any worker in the land.

Are Southern Cotton Mill Villages Feudalistic?

Mercer G. Evans, Emory University

. . . (1) It is now well known that the mobility of labor is a matter of degree, dependent largely upon economic and trade resourcefulness. In no case is complete mobility possible. Before a child born into a cotton mill village can withdraw himself from cotton mill employment in later life, he must have training or capacity for other employment, and must have economic resources to support him while making the change. As a rule cotton mill children have no such resourcefulness . . . .

(2) With this background, then, when the child reaches manhood, there is no escape from the industry. The only trade he knows, the only society he can mingle with, his only world, is in the cotton mill village. . . .

(3) Contractual freedom depends upon one's resources. If a worker has no resources with which to maintain the life of himself and dependents, if he further has no capacities that can be sold to any other employers, he has no economic freedom to decline a contract presented by a cotton mill employer. Such is the case of most cotton mill employes. The laws place very little restriction upon the freedom of the employer to make the terms of the contract such as he sees fit. The employers have seen to it that no unions have come into existence to furnish resources to the worker while he demands changes in the terms of the contract. The employe himself, with his low wage and lack of other training, has no resources. Theoretically he is a free individual. Actually, he is quite unfree. . . .

Several strikes have occurred over the discrimination practiced by employers against union members, but all of them have been lost. In some cases, when attempts were made to form unions, the organizers were intimidated into leaving the community, and it appears that in all cases the employer either gave the employes reason to believe, or at any rate they did believe, that any association whatever with unionism would mean their economic destruction. . . . It is useless to claim either that the workers want or do not want unions. No free and fair opportunity has been offered them to show their wishes. In spite of this, however, a number of unions have from time to time been formed, and many abortive strikes have occurred in their defense. . . .

There seems, therefore, to be good justification for the use of the word "feudalism" as descriptive of the cotton mill villages of the South; it is only less valid as descriptive of the cotton mill communities located within towns and cities.

4. James Edmonds, Union Man, ca. 1930

But 1925 didn't bring much promise. It was to be my lot in that year to raise my voice against what I think is one of the most inhuman things that ever hit any industry. Hundreds of folks go to jail every year and spend the best part of their lives there for doing things not half as harmful to their fellow man as the stretch-out [mill workers' term for changes in work responsibilities that forced workers to tend more machines per person than had previously been required]. The Cone Company was one of the first in the country to begin it. The handwriting was on the wall early in the year, but it didn't reach a showdown till June. . . .

. . . I had seen women, one of them my own daughter, going all day long in that unbearable heat with their clothes stuck to their bodies like they had been dipped in a pool of water. Going up and down their alleys weeping, working, all day long, and though the company was gaining from the stretch-out by saving in wages it wasn't gaining a thing by using such awful heat. I've wove enough to know that cloth makes better with the temperature at 90 than it does when it's at 104.

When all the reorganization had finally took place, every fourth weaver had lost his job. . . .

. . . And it seemed to me that I could look out there in the years and see the awful misery ahead for working people. Thousands throwed out of jobs and the rest drove like machines till they died before their life was half over. When they was gone there'd be plenty others to take their place, young folks with hopes for living to be ground out until they had no life left, just to feed the selfishness and greed of people in power. And to me then the saddest part of it all was that the people, because of their lot in life, was too ignorant to protect themselves from what was being forced on them. It was like taking advantage of a child. I knew what a man was up against if he tried to point out some sort of way. I felt awful ignorant and not big enough for the job. But I had seen all I could stand.

I organized the weavers and set the day for a protest. Every man, woman, and child in the weave room promised to stick by me. . . .

A bunch of us, that realized the stretch-out hadn't been took half as far as the company meant to take it, got together to try to think of some way to help ourselves before it was too late. We decided to write to William Greene, president of the Federation of

Labor, and ask him if he'd send a representative to Greensboro to tell us about ways and means of organizing. They asked me to write the letter, and I did.

Mr. Greene sent a representative and I signed my union card on March 1, 1930. Sometime in May I was elected president of the local, and my son Percy was elected secretary.

Now and then talk reached my ears that I was being accused by company officials of being the cause of the union organizing in Greensboro. We was getting members pretty fast and I begin to have hopes that we'd soon be strong enough to check the stretch-out. On June 20 as I walked out of the mill at quitting time I was handed a little yellow slip. As each member of my family come out, they was give the same. The slips meant we'd all been fired.

I waited a few days trying to think what was the best thing to do and then I went to Frank Hopkins [a manager]. . . .

Frank twisted his watch chain a minute while he looked down at the floor in a deep study. Finally he turned toward me. "James, there's just one thing you have to do to get your job back," he said. "I can't tell you what it is but you ought to know."

"I think I know what you mean," I told Frank. "If I'll write a little piece for the *Textorion* [the company newsletter], the voice of the people, saying that I don't believe what I do believe, that I'm sorry I ever joined the union, that I think it would be impossible for a company to be better to its help, that no person to my knowing is overloaded with work in the mill, if I'd write them things I could get my job back, couldn't I, Frank? I want to go back to work; I don't know what's to become of me if I don't, but if I go it'll be as a free man. It ain't pride

or stubbornness that makes me hold out, it's a feeling that I'd rather starve to death than sell my soul for bread." . . .

. . . In a few months we had signed up 94 percent of the people working for the Cone Mills. I was a happy man because I could see a little light ahead for the cotton mill people.

The company, of course, hadn't been sleeping. It had done everything in its power to check us and finally used the one sure way of winning. Word was circulated around that every person who wouldn't disclaim the union would lose his job, and if the worst came to worst the Cones would close down their mills because they had enough money to live on anyway. So when they finally started questioning the people, they went to them one by one, and in their talking give them the impression that the most of the folks had already disclaimed the union. The people got confused and scared; they had no way of knowing how most of the rest was standing. They begin to reason, "What good will it do me to stick by my word unless the rest stick by theirs? My job is threatened, the job that means bread for my family." So, one by one, they give in, and all day long they come in groups of twenty, twenty-five, thirty led by a overseer, or sometimes by a preacher who'd stand witness they'd drawn out of the union. . . .

Though I'm not taking any active part in [the] union now I still have a interest in what it's doing. . . .

I had a belief that's the strongest kind of religion, and I was called on to pay the price for it. They almost starved me out, but they didn't change my way of thinking. I'm still certain I took the right road back there in 1930. Peace inside is worth a whole lot to a man.

5. Clara Williams: No Union for Her, Late 1930s

That strike last summer when the mill shut down for a week was what got us behind. There's always a few to make trouble for the rest. . . .

The first time I ever saw what labor unions done was in Danville. . . . What was the strikers doin'? Settin' out in the bitter cold weather around fires built in the street. I didn't like the looks of it and I've had no use for the union since. And they didn't get a God's thing to eat but pinto beans, I know, because that's what the folks had where I was stayin'. No, sir, no union for me.

The folks here at the Cone Mills ought to know to leave the unions alone. Didn't old man Caesar

Cone leave it in his will—well, I reckon it was his diary—anyhow, he wrote it down—that before he'd recognize a union he'd shut down all his mills? And Julius Cone has had it put down in black and white that he'll do the same thing. Folks can talk all they want to about their right to join a union but right don't count much when money is against you. The government can say it'll make the Cones let everybody that wants to join the union but the Cones is still totin' the keys to the mill. . . .

. . . [T]hem Cones is awful good where big things is concerned. It wasn't long, not more'n six months, anyhow, before the cut that they give us

$14,000 on our new church. Yessir, all we had to raise was $6,000. One of the Cones come down there and made a talk, sayin' that he knowed they was more able to give than us, and they was glad of the opportunity to help build our church. They understand it ain't easy for us to get along on what they can pay us. I've got nothin' to say against the Cones, and I'll have nothin' to do with no labor union.

6. George S. Mitchell Assesses Obstacles to Unionism, 1931

The company-owned mill village has given the employer two sets of defenses. In the first place, he has been able to influence opinion toward the exclusion of union propaganda by means of a subtle pressure exerted through his welfare work and by virtue of his dominant economic position; fear of running counter to the employer's wishes, bound up with his ownership of the operative's house, prevents free expression of "disloyal sentiments." In the second place, if these barriers are overleaped and a union is formed in a given village, the employer has extraordinary resources in the way of mill-paid deputies, in the right of eviction, prevention of trespass, influence over the churches through his monetary contributions to them, exclusion from welfare privileges, and control of meeting places.

Another obstacle to organization is the ignorance and farm background of most of the workers. Being relatively new to industry, large numbers of the operatives are still in the stage of reliance upon an employer rather than dependence upon autonomous collective action for economic safety. Contrary to much that has been said and printed, however, articulate loyalty to the employer is confined to a small group of influential villagers. Isolation on the farm and autocratic control in the mill villages have prevented the growth of the ordinary agencies of democratic participation in local affairs. This has meant unfamiliarity with the conduct of meetings, failure in estimating the quality of elected leaders, and difficulty in dealing collectively.

The reserve of labor on the farms, gradually pushing into factory employment, has kept the mills oversupplied with workers. This has been a manifest hindrance to union effort.

Poverty of the Southern operatives has been a principal discouragement. In the North the union has fought its dues up to a point where they now average about a dollar a month. This is a sum which the Southern operative can be induced to part with only in a cause devoutly believed in.

7. Fred E. Beal Recalls the Gastonia Strike of 1929

MINIMUM WEEKLY WAGE OF $20.
40-HOUR 5-DAY WORKING WEEK.
BETTER SANITARY CONDITIONS.
NO MORE HANK CLOCKS.
NO MORE PIECE WORK.
COMPANY HOUSES TO BE REPAIRED,
    SCREENS AND BATHTUBS ADDED.
CHEAPER RENTS AND LIGHTS.
RECOGNITION OF THE UNION.

These demands were presented to Superintendent J. A. Baugh of the Manville-Jenckes Mills by the Strike Committee.

"Now that I have read these demands," Mr. Baugh replied, "you realize that if we should comply with them it would mean that we would virtually give you the plant. You surely don't expect us to do that."

I considered the demands very moderate. But the manufacturers did not intend to let the strikers win even a few crumbs. As one of the mill owners put it: "Give in an inch and they'll demand the works." The Gaston County manufacturers met immediately in Gastonia and raised a huge fund to fight the strikers. The fund, it was reported, was to be used to pay off thugs, gunmen, newspaper editors, and other flunkeys of the mill owners.

George Pershing, representing the Young Communist League, thought it his Communist duty to give out red-hot statements. "I am here," he said to the anxious reporters, "for the purpose of organizing the Young Communist Workers' League. The principal view of the Communists is control of the country by the workers. Under Communist control the Loray Mill and every other mill would be operated by a general committee made up of one representative worker from each department, and they would elect a manager who would be responsible to this general committee." At this point, I broke in. I took George aside and told him that the struggle in Gastonia was to win the strike for its immediate benefits and not for forming Soviets. Hereafter I would give out all press reports. But the damage had been done. . . .

The police and deputies were doing everything within their power to antagonize the strikers. The minor skirmish with the cable was the excuse used by the mill owners for calling out the militia. . . . One of the soldiers started to push back a woman who stood her ground. She told him to stop pushing. She was willing to go away, but not to be driven. The soldier was not smart enough to take the hint. So Mrs. Bertha Tompkins cracked him over the head with a stick. It required four soldier boys to carry her from the field and deposit her in the calaboose. She was the mother of four children under five and earned only four dollars for three nights' work of eleven hours each. Small wonder certain unconventional ideas got into her head! . . .

The bringing in of the militia served one good purpose. It advertised our strike throughout the country, especially in the South. Workers came from every southern state. By foot, horse, and ramshackle car, they came to join the union.

8. Liston Pope Analyzes Gastonia's Meaning, 1942

The real issue in all the Southern strikes in 1929, so far as employers were concerned, was that of the right of workers to limit, through collective action, the control of the employers. In Gastonia, however, this issue assumed special significance in the fact of Communist leadership of the collective action. Employers fought trade unionism and collective bargaining wherever they appeared, but in no other situation did they fight so effectively, and with such complete victory, as at Gastonia. It was easy for employers there to convince the community that the strike represented not simply an effort at modification of the employers' power but a threat to the entire community as then conceived and organized. Whether or not employers at Gastonia regarded the Communist challenge as serious—there is considerable evidence that they did—they succeeded in provoking community reaction more violent in character than that found in any of the other Southern strikes. . . .

Strikers who persisted to the end of the 1929 strike at Loray disappeared almost completely from the community after the Communist leaders were expelled. From fragmentary data, they seem to have become distributed almost equally between mountain farms and cotton mills in neighboring towns and states. . . . Workers active in the strike are extremely reluctant to talk of their part in it or to identify other persons involved; the Loray management has not only refused to give them jobs (under the expert eye of its ex-spy employment manager) but has also refused to recommend them for employment elsewhere, and has actively attempted to stamp out seeds sown by the Communists among them. . . .

The Communist analysis of political realities, supported by the excesses to which policemen and deputy sheriffs went in suppressing the strike, stirred many workers to new thoughts. As one worker remembers, with a trace of bitterness, "that was the meanest law [i.e., law enforcement] I ever seen; us people didn't have no rights." The most somnolent mentality could easily deduce that justice in the North Carolina strikes of 1929 was Janus-faced, with violence by strikers always leading to conviction while violence against strikers issued without exception in acquittal. Similar suspicion was engendered in the minds of many workers concerning the impartiality of the press, the disinterested benevolence of welfare programs established by the employers, and the merits of traditional reliance upon individualism and good will for improvement of status. The "class struggle" probably came as near being a reality in Gastonia in 1929 as it has ever been in America, and though the majority of the workers were not ready to accept its sharp alternatives, the issues it posed were not quickly dismissed.

Chapter 24:
Document Set 3 References

1. Income and Farm Tenancy in the South, 1880–1920
   Eleventh Census, 1890; Report of Farm and Home Ownership, pp. 566–570; *Twelfth Census, 1900: Agriculture*, Part I, pp. 69, 109, 119; *Thirteenth Census, 1910, Agriculture*, p. 172; *Fourteenth Census, 1920: Agriculture*, Part 2, pp. 226, 268, 292, in I. A. Newby, *Plain Folk in the New South: Social Change and Cultural Persistence, 1880–1915* (Baton Rouge: Louisiana State University Press, 1989), pp. 573–574.

2. "The Winnsboro Cotton Mill Blues," ca. 1930s
   Lyrics anonymous. In Edith Fowke and Joe Glazer, *Songs of Work and Freedom* (Garden City, N.Y.: Doubleday & Company, Inc., 1960), pp. 74–76.

3. Organized Labor's View of Southern Industrial Conditions, 1927, 1929
   The Textile Worker, Vol. XV (August 1927), Vol. XVI (January 1929).

4. James Edmonds, Union Man, ca. 1930
   Tom E. Terrill and Jerrold Hirsch, eds., *Such as Us: Southern Voices of the Thirties* (Chapel Hill: University of North Carolina Press, 1987), pp. 178–180, 183–185, 187.

5. Clara Williams: No Union for Her, Late 1930s
   Terrill and Hirsch, pp. 188–189.

6. George S. Mitchell Assesses Obstacles to Unionism, 1931
   George Sinclair Mitchell, *Textile Unionism and the South* (Chapel Hill: University of North Carolina Press, 1931), pp. 84–85.

7. Fred E. Beal Recalls the Gastonia Strike of 1929
   Fred E. Beal, *Proletarian Journey: New England, Gastonia, Moscow* (New York: Hillman-Curl, Inc., 1937), pp. 136–139.

8. Liston Pope Analyzes Gastonia's Meaning, 1942
   Liston Pope, *Millhands and Preachers: A Study of Gastonia* (New Haven: Yale University Press, 1942), pp. 257, 311–312.

CHAPTER 25

DOCUMENT SET 1
Crisis in Dearborn: The Ford Hunger March

Chapter 25 begins with a sketch of America in the early stages of the Great Depression, including its staggering human toll. Among the topics addressed are protests such as the Farm Holiday and the Bonus March of 1932. Less well known but dramatic in its public impact was a bloody confrontation between the unemployed and various police groups that occurred on March 7, 1932, at the Ford plant in Dearborn, Michigan. The following documents describe the clash, which worker groups labeled the "Ford Massacre."

To focus public attention on the rise of unemployment, the Auto Workers Union and the Detroit Unemployed Council organized a mass march to the employment office at the Ford Motor Company's giant River Rouge plant. Although both groups were dominated by the Communist party, their efforts to dramatize the problem of joblessness drew the support of many nonaligned workers. After the marchers entered Dearborn, a violent clash occurred at the plant gate, where the demonstrators confronted units from the Detroit and Dearborn police departments and private police from the Ford Service Department. The result was five deaths and fifty injuries, as well as public revulsion at the brutal repression of the unemployed.

As you examine these documents on the Ford Hunger March, place them in the context of the desperate early depression years. Relate these events to the other protests described in your textbook, including the eviction of the bonus marchers from Washington, D.C. Try to determine the goals of both the leaders and the participants. When you consider the objectives of both the protesters and their targets, be particularly sensitive to their backgrounds.

Included in this unit are the later recollections of labor lawyer Maurice Sugar and Unemployed Council leader William (Bud) Reynolds, one a second-hand account and the other an eyewitness description. Equally instructive are the press reports, including headlines from local papers, observations by a *New York Times* correspondent, and the reflections of the liberal *Nation* magazine. Another local perspective may be found in the Republican prosecutor's reaction to the Dearborn incident, including his perception of its origins.

Your analysis of the evidence should center on the human impact of depression unemployment. Moreover, note that the documents reveal the outlines of American assumptions concerning the capitalist political economy, as well as the political and social implications of the economic crisis.

Questions for Analysis

1. What were the goals of the demonstration planners, such as the leaders of the Unemployed Council and the Auto Workers Union? What do the documents reveal about the organizers' assumptions?

2. Why did the leaders of the unemployed movement focus their attention on the Ford Motor Company? Since Henry Ford had pioneered the five-dollar-day wage scale, why did his holdings become a target for demonstrators?

3. How would you explain the initial press reaction to the events at Dearborn? What do the various press accounts, when compared with other observations, reveal about the nature of historical evidence? Which accounts of the incident are accurate? How do you know?

4. What do the "Ford Massacre," Bonus March, and Farm Holiday have in common as indicators of the national state of mind in 1932? What do the documents tell us about the hopes, fears, and beliefs of Americans in 1932? In what way do these documents reflect the social and political environment in the United States at that time?

5. How were civil liberties affected by the crisis in Dearborn? Did the marchers have a right to demonstrate and use the public streets as they did? Why or why not?

6. How would you assess responsibility for the outbreak of violence at the Ford plant? Use the documents to support your position.

1. Maurice Sugar's Reconstruction of the Ford Hunger March, 1980

The marchers proceeded across the Baby Creek Bridge and gathered at the corner of Fort Street and Miller Road in a dense throng around a waiting truck. They were still in Detroit. One of the marchers, Detroit Communist leader Albert Goetz, swung up on the truck and began to speak.

He restated the purpose of the march: to have a committee present their demands to the Ford Motor Company. He called on the workers to form an orderly and disciplined march. "We don't want any violence," he said sharply. "Remember, all we are going to do is to walk to the Ford employment office. No trouble. No fighting. Stay in line. Be orderly."

Goetz paused a moment. The crowd was silent. "I understand," he continued, "that the Dearborn police are planning to stop us. Well, we will try to get through somehow. But remember, no trouble."

A tremendous cheer greeted his remarks and the march began.

Eight abreast, singing and cheering, the marchers proceeded toward the Dearborn city limits, where about fifty Dearborn and Ford police in uniform were lined up across the road. The workers went forward.

An officer yelled, "Who are your leaders?"

"We are all leaders," the marchers shouted back.

"Stop or we'll shoot," threatened the cops, and immediately they fired large amounts of tear gas into the ranks of the workers.

The marchers hesitated. Blinded and choked by the gas, they retreated. Some ran up a railroad trestle on one side of the road. The officers now came forward and with their night sticks attacked others as they were standing, some alone, some in small groups.

The workers fought back. A group rescued one marcher from an officer on the trestle. One of the officers shot at the workers as they ran from the trestle . . . .

The workers, filling the air with a hail of stones, pushed the police back, and when the tear gas gave out, the police turned and ran.

For almost a half-mile the marchers continued down the highway toward the plant, the police retreating before them. Then they reached the first street intersection, where they were confronted with two fire engines equipped with ladders and hoses. The firemen were frantically attempting to make the hose connections. Before they had succeeded, the workers reached them, whereupon they joined the police in retreat. This retreat was continued for another half-mile, until the employment gate—Gate 3 of the plant—was reached.

At this point the fire department units made their water connections. About thirty feet above the road and extending across it, was a bridge used for the passage of workmen into the factory without interference by traffic. Stationed on the road below the bridge were a large number of police officers. From the top of the bridge the firemen poured powerful streams of icy water on the workers below. From the bridge and from the road below came a steady rain of tear gas bombs. According to the marchers, it was at this bridge that the Dearborn police were joined by a large number of Ford Motor Company private police, by a strong force of officers from the Detroit Police Department, and by the state police.

A regular siege developed. The workers, now grimy with sweat and dust, their eyes red from gas fumes, kept up a regular barrage with the stones they had carried from the field.

The police drew their pistols. Suddenly they began shooting into the crowd. It was here that nineteen-year-old Joe York was shot and killed, then Coleman Leny and Joe DeBlasio.

The police were shooting left and right. Besides the three fatalities, there were twenty-two workers known wounded by gunshot. Perhaps fifty more were hit, escaping to their homes or places of hiding for medical attention.

In the face of the downpour of icy water and the rain of bullets, almost all the marchers withdrew. It was then that the leaders of the union and the Unemployed Council decided to call off the demonstration. A speaker mounted the back of a car and said that the tear gassing, clubbing, and shooting were "Ford's bloody answer to the demands of the employed and unemployed Ford workers."

2. A Ford Executive Recalls the Dearborn Incident, 1956

The year 1932 brought a multitude of Communist-inspired big city demonstrations of unemployed. There had been a number of such manifestations in Detroit and some in front of our plant. With few exceptions there was no violence, and it was assumed that in case of any trouble the Dearborn police could handle it.

In March, ten days after our first V–8 came off the production line, a crowd of about five thousand formed ranks in Detroit. To this day, I am convinced there were no Ford employees among them. They were led by a group of open Communists. Mayor Frank Murphy granted them a parade permit and gave the marchers a police motorcycle escort to Detroit city limits.

That noon, while I was with Henry Ford at lunch at the roundtable at Dearborn Laboratories, I had a telephone call from my office. I was told there had been a riot near one of the gates, and Harry Bennett was so badly hurt that he was in the plant hospital. . . .

It seems that when the marchers reached the Dearborn city limits they were halted by a police line. When told they had no parade permit and were forbidden to go farther, they pushed forward. The Dearborn police pumped tear shells into their midst, but the wind changed abruptly and blew the gas back at the officers.

By the time the demonstrators reached the Rouge plant area on Miller Road, Bennett heard of the affair and drove up to the head of the line; he believed he could persuade the leaders to disband their followers. When he got out of his car, someone gave the order to get him. There was a tussle, and Bennett went down from a blow on the head. The police rushed in and began shooting, with the result that four men were killed and fifty went to the hospital.

3. The Press Reacts to the Violence, 1932

Revolvers and Clubs Used by Both Sides

Harry Bennett, Head of the Ford Police, Was Shot in the Head

Two Civilians and Four Policemen Were Reported Shot

Communists Inflamed by Foster Hurl Stones and Clubs in Prearranged Outbreak

Harry Bennett and Others in Hospital Following Battle Started When Agitator Fires Six Shots

A Howling Mob of 3,000 Jobless Men and Women Laid Siege Yesterday to Henry Ford's River Rouge Plant

Special to the New York Times.

Detroit, March 7.—Nearly 3,000 of Detroit's unemployed, with Communists in their midst, took part in a riot today at the gates of the Ford Motor Company's plant in Dearborn. Their demonstration culminated in a furious fight in which four men were killed and at least fifty others were injured.

The demonstration by the unemployed, who had planned to ask Ford company officials, through a committee, to give them work, started quietly, but before it was over, Dearborn pavements were stained with blood, streets were littered with broken glass and the wreckage of bullet-riddled automobiles and nearly every window in the Ford plant's employment building had been broken. . . .

One of those seriously injured was Harry Bennett, chief Ford detective. One report was that he had been hit on the head with a brick hurled at him from a short distance, but a conflicting report said that he had been wounded by a bullet. At the Ford Emergency Hospital in Dearborn, where he was taken, officials declined to divulge the nature of his injuries.

Bennett was injured as he attempted to drive through the mob in a closed car. He was recognized by some of the rioters, a score of whom showered the machine with stones, while someone else fired a shot. Bennett was rescued unconscious by the Ford company police.

Charles E. Sorensen, general manager of the Ford company, was riding in the car with Bennett, but he escaped injury, despite the fact that the car was overturned in the rush.

John Collins, Detroit manager of The New York Times Wide World Photograph Syndicate, was shot in the hand while taking a photograph of the scene.

A check-up of the injured at the various hospitals in the vicinity showed tonight that ten of them had been shot and that fifteen policemen had been clubbed or stoned. . . .

The change of front on the part of Detroit newspapers in the few days following the recent attack by Dearborn and Ford private police on a parade of 3,000 unemployed workers has already been noticed in these columns. On the day following the riot—Tuesday—the newspapers unanimously condemned the "Communist outrage." On Wednesday morning they had completely changed their tone and expressed regret for the "blunder" committed by the authorities, described the demonstration as "orderly," and discovered compassion for the marchers who had been killed or beaten. It is perhaps worth noting that all day Tuesday unemployed meetings were being held in various parts of the city; one hall which held 6,500 was crammed to the doors, every seat being taken and every possible spare inch being occupied, while an overflow meeting of many more thousands milled about in the street outside. On Tuesday night the business men of the city were reported as being thoroughly frightened, and since there is no great love for Henry Ford among them, the word was somehow passed to the newspapers. Next morning the change of tone began. Nor did the demonstrations end on Tuesday. The funeral of the four men killed by the police was held on Saturday, March 12. Ten thousand persons marched; 1,000 automobiles—by actual count—added to the procession; at the cemetery the attendant at one gate estimated that 20,000 persons were within; at another gate, nearer the place where the ceremonies were actually taking place, an attendant declared that at least 30,000 made up the close-packed mass of men and women.

4. William Reynolds Offers an Eyewitness Account in Retrospect, 1960

The March was under the auspices of the Detroit Unemployed Council, of which I was secretary-organizer. The March itself was under a committee composed of Al Goetz, Tony Gerlach, and myself. It formed at Fort and Miller Road or a road that runs into Miller Road, I'm not sure which, in Detroit, and, under the observance of a force of Detroit police, who made no effort to interfere in any way. The marchers consisted of about 3000, men, women and youth, and marched toward the Ford River Rouge plant, and were met at the Dearborn city line by Dearborn police, and perhaps by Ford special police, who tried to stop the march with clubs and tear gas. The march was proceeding between a nearby road and the River Rouge on our left. Tear gas was quickly resorted to, but because the strong west wind picked up the gas immediately, we were able, by crowding the river, to drive the police back with stones and bricks which we picked up from the filled ground by the many thousands. When we reached the vicinity of the plant, we were met by fire equipment, but were able to stone them into a retreat also, because we rushed them before they could get their lines laid, and they retreated with considerable damage to the equipment before they got a hose laid at all.

Our objective was the employment office, which sat back from Miller Road behind a high iron fence, somewhat short of Gate 3. We couldn't get in to the office, and the struggle had reached an intensity that precluded any formal negotiations through a committee. We stoned the employment office, which was a considerable distance back from the road. I knew that Autostroy, the Russian auto commission carrying out a contract with Ford, occupied the second floor above the employment office, so I gave the order, "Let them have it on the second floor!" I knew nobody would be hurt, and I wanted the Russians to have a taste of the American class struggle. Some time in this period—and the struggle in this vicinity must have lasted around an hour—Harry Bennett came into the road area, riding the running board of a service car. I recognized him, and as he had on a white muffler which was streaming out in the wind, it was easy to direct

[a] fire of stones at him, and he was sent to the hospital by quite a few stones finding their mark. . . .

Somewhere—I would say about midway in the period of the unemployment office vicinity struggle—the police opened fire with pistols, and several, especially of the young fellows, were shot point blank, and then the machine guns were turned loose. Many were wounded. At this point, Goetz and I decided that any further movement by us would meet with general slaughter, and we succeeded, in a period of perhaps ten minutes, in getting the general body of marchers back away from the building to the other side of the road where we consulted with the general body the best we could under the circumstances, and were confronted with quite a great determination to move forward and try to charge into the factory grounds. This we discouraged, and the marchers started to move toward Detroit and transportation. The body dispersed in groups large and small toward their respective areas, but mostly toward Detroit. . . .

The bodies lay in state at the Ferry Avenue hall, South Slav, and a large jar was placed at the door, and $4000 was dropped in by those who passed by, without any solicitation.

The march was held along Woodward Avenue, with a banner stretched from curb to curb saying, "Ford-Bennett-Murphy, murderers." You understand, of course, that Murphy's actions were technically quite correct; the charge represented the general great anger and much unsatisfactory experience with Murphy in day-to-day dealings with the needs of the unemployed, as mayor of the city. As far as Bennett and Ford are concerned, I did then and do now subscribe 100% to the charges.

5. A Statement from the Wayne County Prosecutor, Harry Toy, 1932

Investigation of the rioting yesterday which was conducted by the office of the prosecuting attorney, together with the police of Dearborn and the Wayne County sheriff, gives me grounds for belief that this riot had been previously planned by a small group of plotters and agitators.

Investigation so far does not disclose that it was a "hunger march," not an unemployment march, but rather the evidence indicates that it was the result of acts of criminal syndicalism.

Criminal syndicalism is defined as the doctrine which advocates crime, sabotage, violence or unlawful methods of terrorism as a means of accomplishing industrial or political reform.

There is definite evidence which indicates that several persons, some of whom are at present unknown, openly incited the group toward a riot. Many of the witnesses interviewed refused to divulge this information, which information in my opinion will probably disclose these acts of inciting a riot or criminal syndicalism.

6. The American Civil Liberties Union Assesses the Damage, 1932

On the facts, the circulars of a week before and the public announcement of the intention to parade to Dearborn to present a petition and statement of demands to the Ford Motor Company should be borne in mind. Also, that the intention to parade for this purpose was announced at a mass meeting which was largely attended on March 6, 1932. The parade was organized lawfully in the City of Detroit and its leaders advised the participants to do nothing provocative and to remain peaceable. The purposes of the paraders were lawful and proper, including such political purposes as the representatives of a recognized and legal political party may have had.

Employing organizations as preeminent as the Ford Motor Company must expect people to look to it in times such as these. . . .

Such of the Ford and Dearborn police as were injured appear, without exception, to have been injured by stones. There are among the police no injuries whatsoever by any bullet or firearm.

The acts of violence by the paraders consisted of the use of sticks and stones, apparently in defense of what they regarded as their right to parade and demonstrate and in self defense.

The injuries of the paraders were inflicted by Company and City police. They consist of gun shot wounds almost without exception in the sides and backs of the paraders. We cannot too strongly emphasize this difference between the injuries sustained by the paraders and those admitted by the police. . . .

As a matter of public policy the highways of the state,—and Miller Road where this shooting occurred was a state highway—should be open to parades and demonstrations of this kind. The police should see that such a parade is not unnecessarily interfered with. On this occasion the police provoked such violence as the paraders resorted to by refusing to accord them their right to parade on a state highway and to present their petition to the Ford Motor Company. It appears that the demonstrators were peaceful until their rights were interfered with and they were attacked. . . .

This is the only demonstration in this country, so far as we can learn, which has resulted in shooting and killing the demonstrators. The loss of life and the injuries on this occasion were wholly unnecessary and could have been avoided by consulting the history of such matters and by following the policy of late years successfully adopted and continued in Detroit. Once again is illustrated the historic danger of use and reliance upon what are called company and private police and public police under their influence and domination.

So long as paraders resort to nothing more than the demonstrators did on this occasion, until they were resisted in the exercise of their rights, nothing more has occurred than can be expected under the circumstances.

The Detroit Branch of the American Civil Liberties Union will wholeheartedly, for the public good, enter the defense of any person indicted for speeches or opinions, it will assist in any suits growing out of this episode, and it will continue its attempt to reverse, humanize, and modernize the policy of the police and officials of Dearborn and of the Ford Motor Company by offering its services in protecting any further parades or demonstrations there.

AMERICAN CIVIL LIBERTIES UNION

By Roger N. Baldwin,
        Director

By Walter M. Nelsen
        Chairman, Detroit Branch

Dated: March 12, 1932.

Chapter 25:
Document Set 1 References

1. Maurice Sugar's Reconstruction of the Ford Hunger March, 1980
   Maurice Sugar, *The Ford Hunger March* (Berkeley: Meiklejohn Civil Liberties Institute, 1980), pp. 34–36.

2. A Ford Executive Recalls the Dearborn Incident, 1956
   Charles E. Sorensen, *My Forty Years with Ford* (New York: Collier, 1962), pp. 238–239.

3. The Press Reacts to the Violence, 1932
   Detroit Times, March 7, 1932; *Detroit Press,* March 8, 1932; *Detroit Mirror,* March 8, 1932; *New York Times,* March 8, 1932; *Nation,* March 30, 1932.

4. William Reynolds Offers an Eyewitness Account in Retrospect, 1960

Williams Reynolds, Personal Account, April 30, 1960, in Maurice Sugar Papers, Walter P. Reuther Archives of Labor and Urban Affairs, Wayne State University, Detroit, Michigan, Box 53.

5. A Statement from the Wayne County Prosecutor, Harry Toy, 1932
   Harry Toy, Statement, March 8, 1932, in Sugar, p. 56.

6. The American Civil Liberties Union Assesses the Damage, 1932
   Roger N. Baldwin and Walter M. Nelson, Report, March 12, 1932, in Henry Kraus Papers, Reuther Archives, Box 1.

Chapter 25:
Document Set 1 Credits

1. Excerpted from *The Ford Hunger March* by Maurice Sugar. Berkeley: Meiklejohn Civil Liberties Institute. Case Studies on Law and Social Change No. 1 (1980). Used by permission.

2, 3. "Four Killed in Riot at Main Ford Plant as 3,000 Idle Fight," March 8, 1932. Copyright © 1932 by The New York Times Company. Reprinted by permission.

4. William Reynolds, Personal Account, April 30, 1960. Archives of Labor and Urban Affairs, Wayne State University. Used with permission.

6. Roger N. Baldwin and Walter M. Nelsen, Report, March 12, 1932. Archives of Labor and Urban Affairs, Wayne State University. Used with permission.

CHAPTER 25

Assessing the New Deal: Franklin D. Roosevelt and the Limits of Liberalism

The unprecedented economic crisis of the Great Depression produced sharp reaction on the American political scene. The voluntarism of the Hoover administration gave way to a reluctant acceptance of limited government intervention in 1932, and the end result was a political change destined to have a profound impact on the American system. Although the New Deal was not a clearly defined program in 1933, the Roosevelt policies and reform measures were to make a permanent mark on American political, social, and economic institutions.

The following documents explore the nature and extent of institutional changes that resulted from the New Deal. As you review the evidence, relate political and economic innovations to the evolutionary stages of the New Deal. Using your textbook as a resource, try to account for the timing of reform legislation. In so doing, be sure to develop a clear definition of the term *reform*.

As you examine both contemporary evaluations and later recollections of New Dealers and critics, place particular emphasis on outcomes. The central issues to be addressed are the long-term significance of the Roosevelt program, the extent of its appeal to a variety of interests, and the ideological character of the New Deal.

You will encounter at least two basic forms of evidence. The first group of documents is composed of evaluations written *during* the Roosevelt years. The *New Republic* assessment and Raymond Moley's review give contrasting opinions of the New Deal's accomplishments; similarly, Labor Secretary Frances Perkins and Louisiana Senator Huey P. Long express sharply divergent views. Be alert to the commentators' respective backgrounds, political identifications, and ideological leanings as you analyze their arguments.

The second cluster of documents presents another interpretive problem. The oral history technique allows historians to tap the memories of those who made and experienced history. However, as you review the recollections of New Deal economists Gardner Means and Joe Marcus, as well as conservative Republican Hamilton Fish, you should take special precautions to ensure objectivity. Not only must you deal with the problem of selective memory, but it is also important to be aware of the interviewer's role in the process. Nonetheless, the excerpts from Studs Terkel's *Hard Times* will enable you to compare contemporary judgments with participant perspectives developed upon reflection over the years. Use evidence from the documents to support your own conclusions with regard to the short- and long-term impact of the Roosevelt program.

Questions for Analysis

1. Was the New Deal an evolutionary or revolutionary movement? Do either of these descriptions provide an adequate interpretive slant on the Roosevelt program? Use evidence drawn from the documents to support your position.

2. How would you evaluate Roosevelt as a crisis leader? Identify strengths and weaknesses reflected in the available evidence.

3. Was the New Deal a success or failure? To what extent did the New Deal achieve Roosevelt's primary economic goal? What, if any, viable alternatives existed? Why did Roosevelt's contemporaries differ so sharply in their evaluations of his presidency and policies?

4. Compare the New Deal described in the oral histories of the 1960s with the program reflected in the contemporary reactions of the 1930s. How would you account for differences or similarities?

5. What was the New Deal's legacy to future generations? What is the meaning of the term *reform*, and why is it important to an understanding of the New Deal's significance?

6. In the short run, which groups and interests in the United States were the primary beneficiaries of the New Deal? What was the social and political result of its economic impact?

1. *The New Republic* Reviews the New Deal's Accomplishments, 1940

One need only recall what conditions were in 1932 to realize the amazing change in our national thinking that has taken place in eight years. While there is still complaint about paternalism and centralized government (from the Republicans who were the great exponents of these ideas, applied under special circumstances, for the first seventy-five years of their party's life) it is obvious that even the critics are only half-hearted in what they say.

As a nation we have agreed, once and forever, that the individual must not bear the sole responsibility for his failure to cope with economic problems of unemployment or old age which are, quite obviously, beyond his power, and that society as a whole must take over a substantial part of the burden.

We have at last learned that laissez-faire has been dead for years; that the unguided lust of the business man for profit does not infallibly produce Utopia.

And finally, we have reaffirmed in these past eight years an early American doctrine that had been all but forgotten in preceding decades: that the country exists for the welfare and happiness of all its inhabitants;. . . .

The New Deal, even in its second term, has clearly done far more for the general welfare of the country and its citizens than any administration in the previous history of the nation. Its relief for underprivileged producers in city and country, though inadequate to the need, has been indispensable. Without this relief an appalling amount of misery would have resulted, and a dangerous political upheaval might have occurred. Since the expenditure of money for relief—even the insufficient amounts recently appropriated—has been the principal target of the administration's conservative enemies, this accomplishment alone would be sufficient reason for support of the New Deal. . . .

In addition, the New Deal in this second period has accomplished much of permanent benefit to the nation. Perhaps its most important achievement was the National Labor Relations Act, the result of which was to inhibit employers' opposition to union organization and true collective bargaining, so that trade-union membership was more than doubled. This was not a mere act of justice; it was the laying of a solid foundation for our society in the future. Without a strong, alert and independent labor movement a modern industrial nation is in constant danger from the enemies of political and social democracy. Second only to the strengthening of unions is the establishment of minimum labor standards. The fury with which reactionaries have attacked these two labor measures is an index of their importance.

Other permanent improvements are the impetus given to conservation of soil and forests, the many-sided TVA, a great road-building program, flood control, a good beginning at slum clearance and adequate housing for those not provided for by private construction, great hydroelectric projects, extension of electricity at reasonable rates through the Rural Electrification Administration, and the inauguration of insurance against unemployment and the other forms of social security.

The government as an instrument of democratic action in the future has also been strengthened and renovated. This is not merely a matter of the addition of many new agencies, but of the more efficient organization of the whole executive department—including a planning board under the President which so far has been relatively unimportant but is capable of future development. The Courts, too, have been revivified, partly by legislation, but principally by excellent new appointments, so that we now have a Supreme Court which is abreast of the times.

It is improbable that these more permanent changes will be or even can be destroyed by any new administration.

2. Raymond Moley Expresses Reservations on the New Deal, 1939

Roosevelt's administration has achieved much. It has outlawed many abuses. It has readjusted some of our lopsided economic relationships. It has established firmly in the nation's consciousness the principle of economic interdependence. There will remain, after Roosevelt has left office, a vastly changed philosophy of business enterprise, an improvement in the methods of social-welfare activities. Many of the New Deal measures, even those that have failed, have had an important educational value, for they have shown what will not work. These gains are incontestable.

But it is difficult to reconcile them with what they have cost. It is not alone that immense treasure has been spent for economic rehabilitation that has not materialized, that, after seven years, investment remains dormant, enterprise is chilled, the farmers' problem has not yet been solved, unemployment is colossal. It is that thousands of devoted men and women, who felt, as sincerely as Roosevelt, that we must redefine the aims of democratic government in terms of modern needs, have been alienated. They asked only that the repair work done upon the structure of policy follow a consistent pattern of architecture. They pointed out only that unskillful combinations of Gothic, Byzantine, and Le Corbusier defy the law of gravity, and invite ultimate collapse.

These men and women have been told that they are "yes-but" liberals, that they are "copperheads," that they must subscribe to either all or nothing. Their position on such perversions of progressive doctrine as the Court-packing plan has been made a test of personal loyalty. Often the fact of their employment as the managers of businesses has automatically subjected them to the suspicion of self-interest. Their enthusiasm and their energies have been lost.

They have been told, in these latter days, that their collaboration is no longer wanted.

Even the submerged third, whose interests the President has so persistently championed, have been thoughtlessly injured. Extravagant promises have raised expectations far beyond any reasonable hope of realization. Disillusionment must ultimately be the bitter harvest of such planting.

But perhaps the most serious injury that has been done the cause of orderly progress has been the impairment of the nation's unity by the repeated suggestion that benefits can come to one group only at the expense of others. Progressivism depends upon cooperation, not upon conflict. It looks to the creation of an increasingly large number of shared values, not to the establishment of "an economy of maintenance" which can do no more than redistribute the wealth that already exists.

Roosevelt has never condemned businessmen or newspaper publishers as a whole. He has always qualified his denunciations with reference to the "small, bad" minority in those groups. But the fact that he has limited himself to denunciation of the "small, bad" minority in these specific groups and ignored the "small, bad" minority in all other groups has been just as effective in developing class antagonism as a general denunciation. An administration that leaves more rather than less consciousness of class has done the country a disservice.

3. Frances Perkins Describes Roosevelt's Ideology, 1946

A superficial young reporter once said to Roosevelt in my presence, "Mr. President, are you a Communist?"

"No."

"Are you a capitalist?"

"No."

"Are you a Socialist?"

"No," he said, with a look of surprise as if he were wondering what he was being cross examined about.

The young man said, "Well, what is your philosophy then?"

"Philosophy?" asked the President, puzzled. "Philosophy? I am a Christian and a Democrat—that's all."

Those two words expressed, I think, just about what he was. They expressed the extent of his politi-

cal and economic radicalism. He was willing to do experimentally whatever was necessary to promote the Golden Rule and other ideals he considered to be Christian, and whatever could be done under the Constitution of the United States and under the principles which have guided the Democratic party. . . .

He believed in leadership from the office of the President, a leadership based upon the immense sources of information and analysis which the Executive Department had and which were available to the President. He fully recognized, however, the importance of Congress and the desirability of maintaining the strength of our congressional system. . . .

Roosevelt was not very familiar with economic theory. He thought of wealth in terms of the basic wealth in agriculture, transportation, and services which were the familiar pattern of his youth. He recognized or took for granted the changes that had come about in our economy in his own lifetime: the shift in emphasis from agriculture to industry and distribution, the importance of the financial elements. Honorable methods in all business matters seemed to him imperative and to be insisted upon, by changes in the law if necessary. And under "honorable" he instinctively included wages and working conditions of the best, together with friendly, fair industrial relations. But, he had, I am sure, no thought or desire to impose any overall economic or political change on the United States. . . .

The objective of all these plans was to make human life on this planet in this generation more decent. "Decent" was the word he often used to express what he meant by a proper, adequate, and intelligent way of living.

If the application of these and similar ideas constitute revolution, then the phrase "Roosevelt revolution," used half in jest, may be correct. If such it was, it was a social revolution—a revolution in living—not an economic or a political revolution.

Radicals were always getting angry at Roosevelt for not being interested in overall economic and political changes. For him, the economic and political measures were not the end but the means. He was not even a vigorous anti-monopolist. Big enterprises, if morally and socially responsible, seemed entirely all right. Efficiency interested him only as it produced more comforts for more people and a better standard of living. Bigness did not frighten him as it did many people. He would insist on moral and social responsibility for all the institutions of human life; for the school, for the family, for business and industry, for labor, for professional services, for money management, for government—yes, even for the Church. . . .

What he cared about was improvement in people's lives. If economic changes were necessary, he would make them, but only to do a specific task. When he said of himself that he was "a little to the left of center" he described accurately his thinking and feeling in political and economic matters.

4. Huey P. Long's Criticism of the Roosevelt Program, 1936

Now, my friends, when this condition of distress and suffering among so many millions of our people began to develop in the Hoover administration, we knew then what the trouble was and what we would have to do to correct it. I was the first man to say publicly—but Mr. Roosevelt followed in my tracks a few months later and said the same thing. We said that all of our trouble and woe was due to the fact that too few of our people owned too much of our wealth. We said that in our land, with too much to eat, and too much to wear, and too many houses to live in, too many automobiles to be sold, that the only trouble was that the people suffered in the land of abundance because too few controlled the money and the wealth and too many did not have money with which to buy the things they needed for life and comfort.

So I said to the people of the United States in my speeches which I delivered in the United States Senate in the early part of 1932 that the only way by which we could restore our people to reasonable life and comfort was to limit the size of the big man's fortune

and guarantee some minimum to the fortune and comfort of the little man's family.

I said then, as I have said since, that it was inhuman to have food rotting, cotton and wool going to waste, houses empty, and at the same time to have millions of our people starving, naked, and homeless because they could not buy the things which other men had and for which they had no use whatever. So we convinced Mr. Franklin Delano Roosevelt that it was necessary that he announce and promise to the American people that in the event he were elected President of the United States he would pull down the size of the big man's fortune and guarantee something to every family—enough to do away with all poverty and to give employment to those who were able to work and education to the children born into the world.

Mr. Roosevelt made those promises; he made them before he was nominated in the Chicago convention. He made them again before he was elected in November, and he went so far as to remake those promises after he was inaugurated President of the United States. And I thought for a day or two after he took the oath as President, that maybe he was going through with his promises. No heart was ever so saddened; no person's ambition was ever so blighted, as was mine when I came to the realization that the President of the United States was not going to undertake what he had said he would do, and what I knew to be necessary if the people of America were ever [to be] saved from calamity and misery.

5. A New Deal Economist Portrays Roosevelt as a Friend of Capital, 1970

Were there questions in Washington about the nature of our society?

I don't think revolution as a topic of the day existed. The fact that people acted as they did, in violation of law and order, was itself a revolutionary act. People suddenly heard there was a Communist Party. It was insignificant before then. Suddenly, the more active people, the more concerned people, were in one way or another exposed to it. It never did command any real popular support, though it had influence in key places. This was a new set of ideas, but revolution was never really on the agenda.

F.D.R. was very significant in understanding how best to lead this sort of situation. Not by himself, but he mobilized those elements ready to develop these programs.

There are some who say F. D. R. saved this society. . . .

There's no question about it. The industrialists who had some understanding recognized this right away. He could not have done what he did without the support of important elements of the wealthy class. They did not sabotage the programs. Just the opposite. . . .

It was a very unusual Depression in the history of societies. It lasted so long and went so deep. Usually, when you get a depression—even a severe one—you get two, three years of decline and in another two, three years, you're back where you were. But *ten* years. . . . Just think, in 1939, we were back to the industrial production of '29. And you had a ten-year increase in population. If it weren't for the war orders from France and England, there's a question if we would ever have hit that point. The war did end the Depression. That doesn't mean that something else might not have ended it.

6. Gardner Means Recalls the New Deal as a Breakthrough, 1970

At the beginning of the New Deal, they called it a revolution. Then they began to say it wasn't a revolution. Our institutions were being shored up and maintained. What really happened was a revolution in point of view. We backed into the Twentieth Century describing our actual economy in terms of the small enterprises of the Nineteenth Century.

We were an economy of huge corporations, with a high degree of concentrated control. It was an economy that was in no sense described by classical theory. What Roosevelt and the New Deal did was to turn about and face the realities.

It was this which produced the yeastiness of experimentation that made the New Deal what it was. A hundred years from now, when historians look back on it, they will say a big corner was turned. People agreed that old things didn't work. What ran through the whole New Deal was finding a way to make things work. . . .

Most important, laissez faire in the Nineteenth Century manner was ended. The Government had a role to play in industrial activity. We didn't move into a fascist kind of governmental control, because we continued to use the market mechanism. In the two years of the NRA, the index of industrial production went up remarkably.

Things had been going downgrade—worse, worse, worse. More than anything else, the NRA changed the climate. It served its purpose. Had it lasted longer, it would not have worked in the public interest. Although toward the end, the consumer group was making progress.

Had the NRA continued, it would have meant dangerously diminishing the role of the market in limiting prices. You see, there was little Governmental regulation of the NRA. The Government handed industry over to industry to run, and offered some minor protection to others in the form of Labor and Consumer Advisory Boards. Industry became scared of its own people. Too much power was being delegated to the code authorities. It was business' fear of business rather than business' fear of Government, though they wouldn't quite put it that way. You might say, NRA's greatest contribution to our society is that it proved that self-regulation by industry doesn't work.

Laissez faire as such certainly did not come to an end with the New Deal. We still have a tremendous amount of freedom of decision-making in the individual corporate enterprise. The new element is the government's positive responsibility for making our economy run.

As for those first New Deal days, much of the excitement came from improvisation. Nothing was fully set in the minds of the people there. They were open to fresh ideas. Always. We wouldn't have been where we are now, were it not for Washington improvisations.

7. Hamilton Fish Expresses a Conservative's Recollection of Roosevelt, 1970

As soon as Roosevelt got in, he changed. He trampled his platform, brought into Washington a whole lot of young, socialistic, radical brain trusters, who sought to change the whole ideology of the United States. He had become finally an extremist.

During the first hundred days, I voted for practically every recommendation made by Roosevelt. The real break between me and my constituent was on the recognition of Soviet Russia. He recognized Soviet Russia without any support whatsoever in Congress. All former Presidents, everybody was against recognizing Soviet Russia at that time. But he went ahead and did it by himself. . . .

I broke with him, and began to be one of the leaders of opposition to the socialism of the New Deal and this big spending. There were ten million people unemployed all the time during the New Deal. That history has not been brought out clearly. Most of your historians of that period were New Dealers on the payroll. . . .

Roosevelt would have gone down in history as a great President after the first two terms. But he made a mistake, going for the third term. Jim Farley and all the rest fought it. His tragic mistake was when he was a sick and dying man, caved in, mentally and physically, and he insisted on a fourth term. "I'm the indispensable man." All that bunk.

He had all this fanatical, radical legislation introduced. They were not based on American customs. They were all Socialistic, and Socialism always fails. I know as much about this as anybody, 'cause I debated Norman Thomas, whom I have a very high idea of, at least ten different times.

Of course, Socialism has tremendous ideals. If everybody was an angel, Socialism would be wonderful. If everybody worked for everybody else and for themselves and for the country, it might work. But it's never worked in any big country. Maybe a small country of five million.

Chapter 25:
Document Set 2 References

1. *The New Republic* Reviews the New Deal's Accomplishments, 1940
   The New Republic, Vol. 102 (May 20, 1940).

2. Raymond Moley Expresses Reservations on the New Deal, 1939
   Raymond Moley, *After Seven Years* (New York: Harper and Brothers, 1939), pp. 398–400.

3. Frances Perkins Describes Roosevelt's Ideology, 1946
   Frances Perkins, *The Roosevelt I Knew* (New York: Harper and Row, 1946), pp. 330–333.

4. Huey P. Long's Criticism of the Roosevelt Program, 1936
   New York Times, January 26, 1936.

5. A New Deal Economist Portrays Roosevelt as a Friend of Capital, 1970
   "Joe Marcus," in Studs Terkel, *Hard Times: An Oral History of the Great Depression* (New York: Pantheon, 1970), pp. 268–269.

6. Gardner Means Recalls the New Deal as a Breakthrough, 1970
   "Gardner Means," in Terkel, pp. 247–250.

7. Hamilton Fish Expresses a Conservative's Recollection of Roosevelt, 1970
   "Colonel Hamilton Fish," in Terkel, pp. 291–292.

Chapter 25:
Document Set 2 Credits

CHAPTER 25

DOCUMENT SET 3
Environmental Disaster: Images of Human Error and Hope for the Future

Few issues were closer to Roosevelt's personal interests than the problems created by the ecological disaster that struck the Great Plains in the 1930s. Humanity's helplessness before nature was evident in the plight of thousands of Dust Bowl refugees who abandoned their blown-out farms for the uncertainties of migrant labor on the West Coast. Your textbook describes the environmental questions of the thirties and the New Deal's response to these new challenges. The following documents focus on one creative approach to public education on the need for a new relationship between the land and its human occupants.

The Roosevelt administration actively pursued a public-information program intended to familiarize voters with the New Deal. One of the most innovative dimensions of this effort was an experiment in documentary film production undertaken by the Resettlement Administration, then under the leadership of Rexford Tugwell. The first of these films, *The Plow that Broke the Plains* (1936), attempted to explain the agency's goals and alert the public to the need for land-use planning and conservation measures. Written and directed by film critic Pare Lorentz, *The Plow* stands as an important document that recorded the New Deal's social vision and commitment to the conservation of natural resources.

As you review the evidence, be aware of the function of film as historical document. Look for clues to the charged political context in which *The Plow* was produced and later watched by viewers. Try to determine what the filmmaker's objectives were and the reasons

the Roosevelt administration chose to support those goals.

Your examination of the documents will reveal that the film produced a sharp political reaction. Some of the letters included indicate that politicians were alarmed by what they saw. So controversial was *The Plow* that in 1940 it was banned by a congressional committee and withdrawn from circulation until 1962. Think about the possible reasons for the suppression of a film widely acknowledged to be an artistic achievement that raised a significant policy question. Why were some western members of Congress aligned against the Resettlement Administration's effort to raise public consciousness of an important national issue?

To answer this question, you will need to examine the synopsis of the film carefully for hints of potential controversy. As you examine the correspondence, try to determine what the film communicated to 1930s audiences. Be especially alert to American consciousness of land-use history and the culpability of users in the environmental crime committed on the Great Plains. As you think about the outcome in the "dirty thirties," attempt to understand the economic and social forces that had led to an ecologic nightmare.

When you reflect on this episode in governmental film production, consider the arguments for and against such activity. How do the efforts of Lorentz, Tugwell, and the Resettlement Administration mesh with your own definition of the proper functions of government?

Questions for Analysis

1. Review the synopsis of *The Plow that Broke the Plains* and the original Resettlement Administration proposal to make the film. Does the film content itself provide any clues to explain why the film became controversial?

2. Does the film contain any point of view concerning responsibility for the Dust Bowl crisis of the 1930s? What do the documents reveal about the reaction to the thesis developed by Pare Lorentz in *The Plow*? Why did political critics object to the film's analysis of the economic and social roots of the environmental problem?

3. Using your textbook as a resource, consider the New Deal's agricultural policies. What is the relationship between *The Plow* and the Roosevelt agricultural program?

4. Speculate on the place of *The Plow that Broke the Plains* in the history of documentary filmmaking in the United States. What are the components of an effective documentary film? To what extent were they present in Lorentz's work? What dangers and opportunities lay in the government's use of motion pictures as instruments of public education?

1. The Resettlement Administration Proposes an Educational Film, 1935

Comptroller General McCarl to the Administrator, Resettlement Administration,
August 19, 1935:

There has been received your letter of August 12, 1935, as follows:

The RA proposes to have a motion picture with sound accompaniment made at an estimated expense of $6,000, which will have for its subject matter the extent and richness of the western plain lands before their abuse, the settlements thereon, the beginning of misuse, such as overgrazing, overproduction, mechanized farming by absentee owners, etc., and the results thereof, such as wind and soil erosion, drought, dust storms, floods, worn land and poverty. There will also be animated maps showing the area of lands now unfit for profitable farming, and the areas where farmers must be supported, rehabilitated or moved, and animation showing soil areas which can be farmed scientifically and profitably.

In carrying out its function of dealing with soil erosion and other similar problems mentioned in the Executive Order creating the RA, the Administrator is faced with the necessity of educating its employees and the employees of cooperating agencies of the government with respect to these problems. . . . A moving picture of the character described above will be one of the most effective, quick, and inexpensive means of explaining some of these problems of the Administration to its employees and to the employees of these agencies. . . .

In short, the primary object of the motion picture is to help the Resettlement Administration and its employees to visualize and understand better the problems confronting them, and to aid them in the prevention of the results of soil erosion and related problems. The expense is a necessary one to the accomplishment of the objectives of the Emergency Relief Appropriations Act of 1935.

2. *The Plow that Broke the Plains:* A Synopsis, 1936

General Summary

"The Plow that Broke the Plains," America's first documentary motion picture, is a saga of the land of the Great Plains area of the United States.

Reproduced in ten principal sequences, the film traces the story of the plains country from that period in American history when the territory was a great windswept continent of grass peopled only by the aborigines and native fauna to the present day. From the days when the buffalo roamed the Great Plains through the successive invasions of range cattle, the homesteader and the large scale wheat farmer

to the present time when dust storms whip across once fertile acres carrying away the fertile topsoil and bringing tragedy and disaster to the Plains people in this saga of the soil.

As an addendum to the picture the producers have added sequences of narration and pictorial explanation of the work of the Resettlement Administration and other federal agencies in reconstruction of land and in the resettlement of impoverished farmers giving them new hope and a better chance to wrest a living from the good earth.

Synopsis by Sequences

Sequence 1: *Grass*

The Great Plains country was once an uncharted range, an unfenced and inexhaustible pasture a thousand miles long.

Sequence 2: *Cattle*

It was a cattlemen's paradise with southern plains for winter grazing and mountain sweeps for summer grazing. Fortunes were made in beef as the railroads brought the markets to the edge of the plains. Cattle syndicates and land speculators followed the steers to the grasslands and by 1866 hardly an acre was unclaimed. After the cattle came the sheepman and the dirt farmer.

Sequence 3: *The Homesteader*

The homesteader came to find a new land in the great fervor of national expansion. As the fence was strung and the first posts driven, America saw the last of the free range. The homesteader began to plow the range, ripping the grass cover that held the loose topsoil. With the homesteader came modern machinery and with it, increased culture of the soil bringing bounty in the good years there were rains. And still the homesteaders came impelled by land companies and offers of 320 acres of government land.

Sequence 4: *Warning*

But when the rains failed, homesteaders failed. Nature brought forceful retribution for breaking the sod of the plains. The homesteaders moved onward—there was plenty of land.

Sequence 5: *War*

When the World War came, new life came to the plains. Highgeared machinery, combines, night harvesting, additional farmers—all hands turned to the plains to answer the appeal that "Wheat will win the war! Plant wheat!" With a martial background the Great Plains yielded broad acres of wheat for the Allied cause.

Sequence 6: *Speculation*

But speculation always comes and with it the highest order of power machinery is thrown immediately into use. The world was our market! We had the land, the manpower and modern machinery. We welcomed the golden harvest of wheat and money as the rains held forth. Speculation was rife. The days of bouncing prosperity and of jazz age pleasure were here. The ticker tape sent stocks to a new high until the market, topheavy with its own distortion, toppled as the crash of 1929, wreaking financial and economic havoc throughout the nation.

Sequence 7: *Drought*

But when the rains held off, acres of once fertile land were left baking under the hot plains sun. Machinery rusted and in 1930 came the worst drought in our history, 1931, 1932, 1933 more drought and winds swept across the once verdant grasslands.

Sequence 8: *Dust Storm*

Striking with a stirring fury, the winds came and swept away the good earth imperilling life, wrecking hopes, bringing chaos and disaster.

Sequence 9: *Devastation*

For six years the people of the plains fought drought and dust. Most of their livestock starved or were choked by sandstorms. Many people left, but many stayed when everything was gone—all but life itself. But the misery and devastation of drought and dust swept a tide of invasion westward once again—toward the West Coast. In 1935 more than 30,000 refugees hit the trail out of the drought country every month. Homeless, penniless, bewildered, they joined the luckless army of the highway. As the emigres swept into California, historians pondered the problem of the plains and saw that in 50 years America had turned the grasslands into a great dust bowl—almost into a veritable desert waste.

Sequence 10: *Conclusion*

But the Federal Government is attacking the plains problem on two broad fronts. Congress has appropriated millions for drought relief to save farmers from starvation and dire poverty. On the second front the Government is carrying forward a program of permanent reconstruction of the land. Sod, seeds, and trees are being put into the plains. The Forestry Service, Soil Conservation Service, cooperating with the Department of Agriculture are uniting efforts to restore damaged lands. Farmers are being taught best methods of farming to prevent erosion.

The Resettlement Administration is taking title to 5,000,000 acres of land in the Great Plains and turning it back to grass and its natural uses. The Resettlement Administration has moved three divisions into the field and has loaned money for seed, feed, equipment for those who can stay and is moving thousands of others out, giving them a new chance to make a living. It is establishing farmstead communities where they can have advantage of public services, technical advice and assistance and an opportunity to secure homes and farms on long term credit.

But the sun still bakes the land and the winds still sweep across broad acres. It is the job of all agencies, private, state and federal to cooperate in reconstruc- tion to prevent the Great Plains from becoming a desert—we must all cooperate in a battle to save our greatest natural resource—the soil.

3. Congressman Fred Hildebrand Senses the Political Potential of the Motion Picture, 1936

June 15, 1936

Dr. Rexford G. Tugwell,
Resettlement Administration,
910 – 17th Street, N.W.,
Washington, D.C.

My dear Dr. Tugwell:

"The Plow that Broke the Plains," which I saw the other day in the Belasco Theater here, impressed me so much that I wish it might be exhibited in the schools of my district, and for that matter, throughout South Dakota.

Could not the Resettlement Administration make some provision to this end?

The film is distinctly educational and also the most effective possible propaganda for the New Deal—propaganda that is non-political insofar as the picture is concerned, for it confines itself strictly to facts, yet these facts are more convincing than any partisan appeal could possibly be. I am sure that showing this movie in South Dakota, as well as other states with similar agricultural problems, would be of great benefit from every standpoint.

Awaiting with interest your reply and with kind personal regards, I am

Sincerely yours,

Fred H. Hildebrand

4. Defensive Reaction on the High Plains, 1936

July 2, 1936

Dr. R. G. Tugwell,   Personal Attention
Administrator,
Resettlement Administration,
Washington, D.C.

Dear Dr. Tugwell:

Today a group of workers from the Regional and State Resettlement Offices attended a private showing of "The Plow that Broke the Plains." After the showing a conference was held in my office at which time we discussed the film and the advisability of having it shown throughout the State of Texas at the present time. I am simply writing you the observations and judgment of the group as expressed and agreed upon in this conference.

We recognize the possible value of the film particularly in other parts of the United States and we do not feel that there is justification for serious criticism of the film. However, the showing of the film in Texas at the present time would arouse controversy and rather bitter criticism of the Resettlement Administration. It is the judgment of our group that the showing of the film would serve no particularly good purpose at this time and it is our judgment that any good purpose which it might serve would be more than offset by the controversy and criticism which would be aroused.

. . . In view of the situation, it is the judgment of the 20 or 25 Resettlement staff members in this region who witnessed the film that it should not be released in Texas at the present time and for that reason we are requesting authorization to withhold the film from circulation. . . .

(1) The film greatly overdraws and unduly magnifies the true situation in the western plains. . . .

(2) The film only presents the distressing side of the situation without offering any solution. The con-

clusion which a great many people would naturally draw from seeing the film would be that it was a mistake in the beginning for people to settle in that area and that the only solution lies in the complete evacuation of the entire area. . . .

(3) The film includes in the dry and windswept area a great deal of country, in Texas at least, where no such conditions exist anywhere as those portrayed in the film. . . .

(4) The film fails to point out some of the natural advantages which exist in that country and which for many years have made it possible for farmers to endure the hazards and still prosper. . . .

I hope you will understand our point of view in suggesting that the film be withheld from circulation in this region at the present time and I believe that if you and your associates were in touch with local conditions and attitudes as we are in the region, you would agree with us in this suggestion. We feel that it would be unfortunate to arouse the controversy and criticism which would result. I shall be glad to have your reaction to these suggestions.

Sincerely yours,

D. P. Trent,
Regional Director

5. A Photographic Record of the "Dirty Thirties"

A. Dust Storm, Baca County, Colorado, 1930s

B. A Texas Homestead, ca. 1930s

C. Woman of the High Plains, Texas Panhandle, 1938

Chapter 25:
Document Set 3 References

1. The Resettlement Administration Proposes an Educational Film, 1935
Comptroller General McCarl to Administrator, Resettlement Administration, August 19, 1935, in Robert L. Snyder, *Pare Lorentz and the Documentary Film* (Norman: University of Oklahoma Press, 1968), pp. 202–203.

2. *The Plow that Broke the Plains:* A Synopsis, 1936
"The Plow that Broke the Plains," Synopsis attached to Rexford G. Tugwell to William L. Brown, April 2, 1936, Copyright Office, Department of Motion Pictures, Broadcasted and Recorded Sound, Library of Congress.

3. Congressman Fred Hildebrand Senses the Political Potential of the Motion Picture, 1936

Fred H. Hildebrand to Tugwell, June 15, 1936, Resettlement Administration Papers, National Archives.

4. Defensive Reaction on the High Plains, 1936
D. P. Trent to Tugwell, July 2, 1936, Resettlement Administration Papers.

5. A Photographic Record of the "Dirty Thirties"
A. Dust Storm, Baca County, Colorado, 1930s
Library of Congress.
B. A Texas Homestead, c. 1930s
USDA photo.
C. Woman of the High Plains, Texas Panhandle, 1938
Farm Security Administration, Library of Congress.

Chapter 25:
Document Set 3 Credits

5. A. Library of Congress
B. USDA Photo
C. Library of Congress

CHAPTER 26

Coping with Adversity: The Great Depression as a Memory Trip

For many Americans who survived the ordeal, the Great Depression of the 1930s was a formative experience. By examining daily life in depression America, your textbook captures the essence of the human response to the economic collapse. To reinforce your "feel" for the period, the following documents probe the reactions of representative Americans to the crisis. As you examine these materials, concentrate on the impact of the depression on the individual's world view and future life.

Because the Great Depression is a relatively recent event, students and scholars may take advantage of human memory as a historical source. Oral history, a valuable approach to the study of the recent past, presents many opportunities but also requires interpretative caution. As an analyst, you must be aware of such pitfalls as fading memory, selective memory, and personal bias.

The interviews chosen emphasize the depression's influence on workers, women, and minority groups, whose general experiences may be reviewed in the textbook account of the American people in the 1930s. Beginning with depression transient Ed Paulsen's memory of rootlessness, these memoirs reveal a sense of profound personal dislocation. Note the hints of alienation. Symptoms of this malaise also may be found in the recollections of the African American and Mexican American experiences by Clifford Burke, Miles Langston, and César Chávez. As you compare

their accounts of depression life, try to explain the black response to the crisis and to the New Deal.

Perhaps no group was more affected by the economic upheaval than the millions of American workers who embraced unionism in the 1930s. Several documents touch on the lives of working people. Bob Stinson's reconstruction of the dramatic General Motors sitdown strike at Flint exemplifies the significance of the depression as an opportunity for labor. As you analyze Stinson's words, consider the meaning of the Wagner Act to American workers. In sharp contrast to labor's success at Flint was the Memorial Day tragedy at Republic Steel in the same year, recalled by Dr. Lewis Andreas. How would you explain the outcome of organizational activity in South Chicago? Compare the goals of the two campaigns, and account for the divergent results.

Finally, the introspective memoirs of three women help us analyze the Great Depression's psychological impact. Assess the recollections of Jane Yoder, Peggy Terry, and Virginia Durr, all intensely personal reactions of depression victims to the loss of autonomy, economic independence, and self-esteem.

Throughout these oral histories runs a common thread: the power of the Great Depression to shape one's consciousness of the present, as well as future, attitudes. Determine how the lives of depression survivors were permanently changed as a result of the great national experience of the 1930s.

Questions for Analysis

1. Did "ordinary" Americans perceive the Great Depression as a positive or negative experience? Or a blend of both? How would you account for their retrospective impressions?

2. What was the impact of joblessness, rootlessness, and economic despair on the depression's victims? How did they assess blame or responsibility for their circumstances?

3. To what extent did the economic crisis of the 1930s produce a revolutionary situation? How dramatic was the change in social and political consciousness during the Great Depression? Use evidence from the documents to support your position. How would you explain Americans' political/ideological response to adversity?

4. What do the documents reveal about the significance of race, class, and gender in shaping a witness's perception of the depression experience? How did persons react to each other across racial and class lines? How were the lives of workers and minority citizens changed as a consequence of the depression?

5. What was the "typical" depression experience for a person in any one of the groups represented in the documents? Is it responsible or possible to use the concept of "typical" experience in interpreting the Great Depression? Why or why not?

6. What do the documents reveal about the impact of the Great Depression on the American concept of government responsibility for social welfare? How did public expectations of government change during the 1930s? How would you account for those changes? What were the long-term implications?

1. Ed Paulsen Describes the Transient Life, ca. 1934

We catch a train into Kansas City, Kansas, that night. At the stops, colored people were gettin' on the trains and throwin' off coal. You could see people gatherin' the coal. You could see the railroad dicks were gettin' tough.

Hal and I are ridin' on the top of the boxcar, it's a fairly nice night. All of a sudden, there's a railroad dick with a flashlight that reaches a thousand miles. Bam! Bam! He starts shooting. We hear the bullets hitting the cars, bam! like that. I throw my hands up and start walking towards that light. Hal's behind me. The guy says, "Get off." I said, "Christ, I can't." This thing's rollin' fifty miles an hour or more. He says, "Jump." I says, "I can't." He says, "Turn around and march ahead." He marches us over the top. There's a gondola, about eight feet down. He says, "Jump." So I jumped and landed in wet sand, up to my knees.

We come to a little town in Nebraska, Beatrice. It's morning. I'm chilled to the bone. We crawl into a railroad sandbox, almost frozen to death. We dry out, get warmed up, and make the train again. We pull into Omaha. It's night. All of a sudden, the train is surrounded by deputies, with pistols. The guy says, "Get in those trucks." I said, "What for? We haven't done anything." He said, "You're not going to jail. You're going to the Transient Camp." . . .

It wasn't a big thing, but it created a coyote mentality. You were a predator. You had to be. The coyote is crafty. He can be fantastically courageous and a coward at the same time. He'll run, but when he's cornered, he'll fight. I grew up where they were hated, 'cause they'd kill sheep. They'll kill a calf, get in the chicken pen. They're mean. But how else does a coyote stay alive? He's not as powerful as a wolf. He has a small body. He's in such bad condition, a dog can run him down. He's not like a fox. A coyote is nature's victim as well as man's. We were coyotes in the Thirties, the jobless.

No, I don't see the Depression as an ennobling experience. Survivors are still ridin' with the ghost— the ghost of those days when things came hard.

2. César Chávez Recalls an Eviction, 1934

Oh, I remember having to move out of our house. My father had brought in a team of horses and wagon. We had always lived in that house, and we couldn't understand why we were moving out. When we got to the other house, it was a worse house, a poor house. That must have been around 1934. I was about six years old.

It's known as the North Gila Valley, about fifty miles north of Yuma. My dad was being turned out of his small plot of land. He had inherited this from his father, who had homesteaded it. I saw my two, three other uncles also moving out. And for the same reason. The bank had foreclosed on the loan. . . .

But this had quite an impact on my father. He had been used to owning the land and all of a sudden there was no more land. What I heard . . . what I made out of conversations between my mother and my father—things like, we'll work this season and then we'll get enough money and we'll go and buy a piece of land in Arizona. Things like that. Became like a habit. He never gave up hope that some day he would come back and get a little piece of land.

I can understand very, very well this feeling. These conversations were sort of melancholy. I guess my brothers and my sisters could also see this very sad look on my father's face.

That piece of land he wanted ... ?

No, never. It never happened. He stopped talking about that some years ago. The drive for land, it's a very powerful drive. . . .

Labor strikes were everywhere. We were one of the strikingest families, I guess. My dad didn't like the conditions, and he began to agitate. Some families would follow, and we'd go elsewhere. Sometimes we'd come back. We couldn't find a job elsewhere, so we'd come back. Sort of beg for a job. Employers would know and they would make it very humiliating. . . .

Did these strikes ever win?

Never.

We were among these families who always honored somebody else's grievance.

3. Clifford Burke Comments on the African American Experience, Depression, ca. 1932

The Negro was born in depression. It didn't mean too much to him, The Great American Depression, as you call it. There was no such thing. The best he could be is a janitor or a porter or a shoeshine boy. It only became official when it hit the white man. If you can tell me the difference between the depression today and the Depression of 1932 for a black man, I'd like to know it. Now, it's worse, because of the prices. Know the rents they're payin' out here? I hate to tell ya. . . .

Why did these big wheels kill themselves? They weren't able to live up to the standards they were accustomed to, and they got ashamed in front of their women. You see, you can tell anybody a lie, and he'll agree with you. But you start layin' down the facts of real life, he won't accept it. The American white man has been superior so long, he can't figure out why he should come down. . . .

I made out during that ... *Great* Depression. (Laughs.) Worked as a teamster for a lumber yard. Forty cents an hour. Monday we'd have a little work. They'd say come back Friday. There wasn't no need to look for another job. The few people working, most all of them were white.

So I had another little hustle. I used to play pool pretty good. And I'd ride from poolroom to poolroom on this bicycle. I used to beat these guys, gamble what we had. . . . Everybody was out trying to beat the other guy, so he could make it. It was pathetic.

4. Roosevelt Remembered, from an African American Perspective, ca. 1936

Roosevelt touched the temper of the black community. You did not look upon him as being white, black, blue or green. He was President Roosevelt. He had tremendous support through his wife. Yet the immediate image is "Great White Father."

The WPA and other projects introduced black people to handicrafts and trades. It gave Negroes a chance to have an office to work out of with a typewriter. It made us feel like there was something we could do in the scheme of things. I don't remember any serious black opposition to Roosevelt. When you see a blithe spirit, naturally you're attracted to it.

I think the powers-that-be missed the boat, during the Depression. There was a kind of integration of poverty. But even though everybody was poor, we still had this stiff-collar, white-shirted Puritanical Wilson thing going. So even though we were all in the same boat, I'm still white and you're still black, and so we don't need to get together.

5. Bob Stinson's Memory of the Flint Sit-Down, 1936–1937

The Flint sit-down happened Christmas Eve, 1936. I was in Detroit, playing Santa Claus to a couple of small nieces and nephews. When I came back, the second shift had pulled the plant. It took about five minutes to shut the line down. The foreman was pretty well astonished. (Laughs.)

The boys pulled the switches and asked all the women who was in Cut-and-Sew to go home. They informed the supervisors they could stay, if they stayed in their office. They told the plant police they could do their job as long as they didn't interfere with the workers.

We had guys patrol the plant, see that nobody got involved in anything they shouldn't. If anybody got careless with company property—such as sitting on an automobile cushion without putting burlap over it—he was talked to. You couldn't paint a sign on the wall or anything like that. You used bare springs for a bed. 'Cause if you slept on a finished cushion, it was no longer a new cushion.

Morale was very high at the time. It started out kinda ugly because the guys were afraid they put their foot in it and all they was gonna do is lose their jobs. But as time went on, they begin to realize they could win this darn thing, 'cause we had a lot of outside people comin' in showin' their sympathy.

Time after time, people would come driving by the plant slowly. They might pull up at the curb and roll down the window and say, "How you guys doin'?" Our guys would be lookin' out the windows, they'd be singin' songs and hollerin'. Just generally keeping themselves alive.

Sometimes a guy'd come up to you on the street and say, "How the guys doin'?" You say, "They're doin' all right." Then he'd give ya a song and dance: "I hear the boys at Chevrolet are gonna get run out tonight."* I'd say, "Hogwash." He'd end with sayin': "Well, I wish you guys the best of luck because, God damn, when I worked there it was a mess." The guy'd turn around and walk away. . . .

The men sat in there for forty-five days. Governor Murphy—I get emotional over him (laughs)—was trying to get both sides to meet on some common ground. I think he lost many a good night's sleep. We wouldn't use force. Mr. Knudsen was head of General Motors and, of course, there was John L. Lewis. . . .

John L. was as close to a Shakespearean actor as any I've ever listened to. He could get up there and damn all the adversaries—he had more command of language. He made a speech that if they shoot the boys out at the plant, they'd have to shoot him first.

There were a half a dozen false starts at settlement. Finally, we got the word: The thing is settled. My God, you had to send about three people, one right after the other, down to some of those plants because the guys didn't believe it. Finally, when they did get it, they marched out of the plants with the flag flyin' and all that stuff. . . .

When Mr. Knudsen put his name to a piece of paper and says that General Motors recognizes the UAW–CIO—until that moment, we were nonpeople, we didn't even exist. (Laughs.) That was the big one. (His eyes are moist.)

---

*Several other General Motors plants in Flint were the scenes of similar sit-downs.

6. The Memorial Day Massacre, as Seen by Lewis Andreas, 1937

The Wagner Act had become the law—the right of labor to picket, to organize. Professionals, social workers, theological students—all kinds of people got into the thing. Some of the workers didn't like this. They must have wondered what we were doing there. But they didn't mind me, because I was a doctor and trouble was brewing.

A few days before Memorial Day, 1937, some steel workers picketed Republic Steel on the Far South Side. I received a call: "We've got a very nasty situation here. There're probably going to be some injuries. There's not a hospital for miles around, not even a drugstore. Would you come and get a few first aid stations started?"

There was a tavern called Sam's Place. I took a few supplies and got a first aid station started. The men who picketed that day got clobbered. There were a few split skulls and a few fractures. Everybody got mad and then decided to try it again on Memorial Day. . . .

The police were standing in line in front of Republic Steel, quite a distance from the others. It was a hell of a hot day, about ninety. They had their winter uniforms on. The sun was strong, and all I could see were their stars glittering. . . .

I stayed behind. All of a sudden, I heard some popping going on and a blue haze began rising. I said: My God, tear gas. What do you do for that? I couldn't remember what the medical books said. I ran back to Sam's Place. About three minutes later, they started bringing in the wounded, shot. There were about fifty shot. Ten of them died. One little boy was shot in the heel. I took care of him. One

woman was shot in the arm. They were lying there, bleeding bullet wounds in the belly, in the leg and all over. All sorts of fractures, lacerations. . . . I had absolutely no preparation at all for this. . . .

I made charts of these gun shots. A great majority of them were shot from behind. Mel Coughlin, the assistant state's attorney, asked me, "Can you define the back?" In the courtroom, I just got up and turned around and said, "What you're looking at now—that's the back."

What happened was this: There were a few rocks thrown at the police when the shooting started. Or even before. They all turned and ran. I said in my testimony before the La Follette Committee: like the shutters of a Venetian blind. As they were running, the police shot into them.

The police weren't all bad. Some of them quit the force because of the incident. They couldn't stand what happened. I know this as a fact because some of the guys came up here as patients and told me. . . .

It's the tableau I remember: people walking out on the prairie and the police shooting them down.

7. A Child's Recollection of Class Distinctions, by Jane Yoder, ca. 1936–1939

I can think of the WPA . . . my father immediately got employed in this WPA. This was a godsend. This was the greatest thing. It meant food, you know. Survival, just survival.

How stark it was for me to come into nurses' training and have the girls—one of them, Susan Stewart, lived across the hall from me, her father was a doctor—their impressions of the WPA. How it struck me. Before I could ever say that my father was employed in the WPA, discussions in the bull sessions in our rooms immediately was: these lazy people, the shovel leaners. I'd just sit there and listen to them. I'd look around and realize: sure, Susan Stewart was talking this way, but her father was a doctor, and her

mother was a nurse. Well, how nice. They had respectable employment. In my family, there was no respectable employment. I thought, you don't know what it's like.

How can I defend him? I was never a person who could control this. It just had to come out or I think I'd just blow up. So I would say, "I wonder how much we know until we go through it. Just like the patients we take care of. None of them are in that hospital by choice." I would relate it in abstractions. I think it saved me from just blowing up.

I would come back after that and I'd just say: Gee, these are just two separate, separate worlds.

8. Peggy Terry on Shame and Dignity, ca. 1937

I first noticed the difference when we'd come home from school in the evening. My mother'd send us to the soup line. And we were never allowed to cuss. If you happened to be one of the first ones in line, you didn't get anything but water that was on top. So we'd ask the guy that was ladling out the soup into the buckets—everybody had to bring their own bucket to get the soup—he'd dip the greasy, watery stuff off the top. So we'd ask him to please dip down to get some meat and potatoes from the bottom of the kettle. But he wouldn't do it. So we learned to cuss. We'd say: "Dip down, God damn it." . . .

It's different today. People are made to feel ashamed now if they don't have anything. Back then, I'm not sure how the rich felt. I think the rich were as contemptuous of the poor then as they are now. But among the people that I knew, we all had an understanding that it wasn't our fault. It was something that had happened to the machinery. Most people blamed Hoover, and they cussed him up one side and down the other—it was all his fault. I'm not saying he's blameless, but I'm not saying either it was all his fault. Our system doesn't run by just one man, and it doesn't fall by just one man, either.

You don't recall at any time feeling a sense of shame?

I remember it was fun. It was fun going to the soup line. 'Cause we all went down the road, and we laughed and we played. The only thing we felt is that we were hungry and we were going to get food. Nobody made us feel ashamed. There just wasn't any of that.

9. Virginia Durr Reflects on the Depression's Lessons, ca. 1930s

Oh, no, the Depression was not a romantic time. It was a time of terrible suffering. The contradictions were so obvious that it didn't take a very bright person to realize something was terribly wrong.

Have you ever seen a child with rickets? Shaking as with palsy. No proteins, no milk. And the companies pouring milk into gutters. People with nothing to wear, and they were plowing up cotton. People with nothing to eat, and they killed the pigs. If that wasn't the craziest system in the world, could you imagine anything more idiotic? This was just insane.

And people blamed themselves, not the system. They felt they had been at fault: . . . "if we hadn't bought that old radio" . . . "if we hadn't bought that old secondhand car." Among the things that horrified me were the preachers—the fundamentalists. They would tell the people they suffered because of their sins. And the people believed it. God was punishing them. Their children were starving because of their sins.

People who were independent, who thought they were masters and mistresses of their lives, were all of a sudden dependent on others. Relatives or relief. People of pride went into shock and sanitoriums. My mother was one.

Up to this time, I had been a conformist, a Southern snob. I actually thought the only people who amounted to anything were the very small group which I belonged to. The fact that my family wasn't as well off as those of the girls I went with—I was vice president of the Junior League—made me value even more the idea of being well-born. . . .

What I learned during the Depression changed all that. I saw a blinding light like Saul on the road to Damascus. (Laughs.) It was the first time I had seen the other side of the tracks. The rickets, the pellagra—it shook me up. I saw the world as it really was. . . .

The Depression affected people in two different ways. The great majority reacted by thinking money is the most important thing in the world. Get yours. And get it for your children. Nothing else matters. Not having that stark terror come at you again. . . .

And there was a small number of people who felt the whole system was lousy. You have to change it. The kids come along and they want to change it, too. But they don't seem to know what to put in its place. I'm not so sure I know, either. I do think it has to be responsive to people's needs. And it has to be done by democratic means, if possible. Whether it's possible or not—the power of money is such today, I just don't know. Some of the kids call me a relic of the Thirties. Well, I am.

Chapter 26:
Document Set 1 References

Note: All documents appear in Studs Terkel, *Hard Times: An Oral History of the Great Depression* (New York: Pantheon, 1970).

1. Ed Paulsen Describes the Transient Life, ca. 1934

2. César Chávez Recalls an Eviction, 1934

3. Clifford Burke Comments on the African American Experience, ca. 1932

4. Roosevelt Remembered, from an African American Perspective, ca. 1936

5. Bob Stinson's Memory of the Flint Sit-Down, 1936–1937

6. The Memorial Day Massacre, as Seen by Lewis Andreas, 1937

7. A Child's Recollection of Class Distinctions, by Jane Yoder, ca. 1936–1939

8. Peggy Terry on Shame and Dignity, ca. 1937

9. Virginia Durr Reflects on the Depression's Lessons, ca. 1930s

Chapter 26:
Document Set 1 Credits

1–9. From *Hard Times: An Oral History of the Great Depression* by Studs Terkel. Copyright © 1970 by Studs Terkel. Reprinted by permission of Pantheon Books, a division of Random House, Inc.

CHAPTER 26

Trouble on the Land: Images of the Dispossessed

For American farmers the 1920s had been troubled times; in the 1930s the bottom simply fell out. The Roosevelt administration's response to a collapsed agricultural economy was the Agricultural Adjustment Administration with its emphasis on forced scarcity. For some it brought relief, but for those on the bottom rail, the result was further dislocation. The following documents focus on rural problems as a theme of the depression years, revealing a clear relationship between literature and social problems.

Setting a tone for what follows, South Dakota farm activist Emil Loriks recalls agrarian distress on the Great Plains as potentially revolutionary in its implications. Compare his description with the textbook's analysis of rural radicalism (see Chapters 25 and 26). A tendency toward political consciousness also was evident in the Works Progress Administration's cultural projects. An excerpt from the Federal Theatre Project's "Triple A Plowed Under" illustrates the left-wing leanings of its employees, reflected in a reference to Communist party leader Earl Browder. This scene juxtaposed Browder and Thomas Jefferson in an expression of outrage at the Supreme Court's invalidation of AAA.

Social consciousness also penetrated journalist James Agee's uncompromising account of life among Alabama sharecroppers. An excerpt from *Let Us Now Praise Famous Men* records Agee's observations on a rural graveyard in words that capture the pathos of a life that was both hard and short. Agee's work was part of what your textbook interprets as an affirmative cultural mood evident in the literary output of the late depression years.

Try to compare Agee's reactions with the militance of Socialist H. L. Mitchell's autobiographic account of the Southern Tenant Farmers Union. This union was a center of controversy as a result of its organizational work among Arkansas sharecroppers in 1935 and 1936. Try to determine why STFU provoked such heavy resistance from the planters and politicians. Finally, make a comparison of Mitchell and Agee with John Steinbeck's celebration of a resilient people, *The Grapes of Wrath,* watching also for evidence of political and social militance. Look for a line of continuity and relate it to themes in the social environment of the 1930s.

Questions for Analysis

1. Define the term *collectivism.* What evidence do you find in the documents that collectivistic themes surfaced in the 1930s? Which groups and classes expressed such ideas?

2. How would you describe the ideological persuasion of the American intellectual elite in the 1930s? How did the character of American cultural and literary life change during the course of the decade? How would you account for shifting ideas?

3. Why were rural problems and the land prominent in the literature of the Great Depression? Can you identify common themes in the documents? Explain.

4. What were the unique problems experienced by sharecroppers and tenant farmers in the 1930s? What solutions were offered to address their concerns? Why did organizational efforts to aid farmers on the bottom rail generate a negative planter reaction? What evidence do the documents provide to clarify this response?

1. A Farm Activist Recalls Rebellion on the Great Plains, ca. 1932

Oh, the militancy then! At Milbank, during a farm sale, they had a sheriff and sixteen deputies. One of them got a little trigger-happy. It was a mistake. The boys disarmed him so fast, he didn't know what happened. They just yanked the belts off 'em, didn't even unbuckle 'em. They took their guns away from 'em. After that, we didn't have much trouble stopping sales.

Thirteen highways to Sioux Falls were blocked. They emptied the stockyards there in a day or two. There was some violence, most of it accidental.

I'll never forget a speech by a Catholic priest at a Salem meeting, straight south of here about forty miles. It was the most fiery I ever heard. He said, "If you men haven't got the guts to picket the roads and stop this stuff from going to market, put on skirts and get in the kitchen and let your wives go out and do the job." (Laughs.) The boys used the police stations as their headquarters. (Laughs.) The police couldn't do much. The sheriffs and deputies just had to go along.

That judge situation in Iowa was a warning. In Brown County, farmers would crowd into the courtroom, five or six hundred, and make it impossible for the officers to carry out the sales. (Laughs.)

Deputies would come along with whole fleets of trucks and guns. One lone farmer had planks across the road. They ordered him to remove them. They came out with guns. He said, "Go ahead and shoot, but there isn't one of you S.O.B.'s getting out of here alive." There were about fifteen hundred farmers there in the woods. The trucks didn't get through. It was close in spirit to the American Revolution.

2. The Federal Theatre Project Interprets the Fall of AAA, 1938

Voice of Living Newspaper (over loudspeaker):
  January 6, 1936. . . . Supreme Court invalidates AAA in Hoosac Mills case.
Voice (also over loudspeaker):
  The majority opinion—Justice Roberts.
(As travelers open from rear, projection of Constitution is thrown on glass curtain. Discovered in shadow against projection are Justice Stone, three other justices, then Justice Roberts, and the four remaining justices, right. Roberts rises to one-foot platform directly in front of him. Five justices who concurred in his opinion, turn in profile as he begins to speak.)
Justice Roberts:
  . . . Beyond cavil the sole objective of the legislation is to restore the purchasing price of agricultural products to a parity with that prevailing in an earlier day; to take money from the processor and bestow it on the farmers. The Constitution is the supreme law of the land, ordained and established by the people. All legislation must conform to the principles it lays down. The power to confer or withhold unlimited benefits is the power to coerce or destroy. This is coercion by economic pressure. The judgment is affirmed. . . .
Thomas Jefferson:
  There must be an arbiter somewhere. True, there must. But does that prove it is either the Congress or the Supreme Court? The ultimate arbiter is the people of the Union, assembled by their deputies in convention at the call of Congress or two-thirds of the States.
(Travelers slowly close, with Jefferson remaining standing on platform, center.)
Voice over Loudspeaker:
  Farmers voted, by more than 6 to 1, for continuance of Triple-A.
(Men start crossing stage in front of travelers, from right to left.)
First Man:
  The AAA is dead. . . . (Exits left.)
Second Man:
  No more allotment checks. . . . (Exits left.)
Third Man:
  What the hell're we agoin' to do this winter?(Exits left.)

A Woman:
How're we goin' t' get coal? (Exits left.)
Fourth Man:
They say the people wrote the Constitution. . . .
(Exits left.)

Fifth Man:
Them people have been dead a long time. . . .(Also exits.)

Blackout

3. James Agee Describes the Grave of a Tenant Farmer's Child, 1936

Just beside it there is a large square white-painted church, which we got into. Bare benches of heavy pine, a lot of windows, partition-curtains of white sheeting run on wires, organ, chairs, and lectern.

The graveyard is about fifty by a hundred yards inside a wire fence. There are almost no trees in it: a lemon verbena and a small magnolia; it is all red clay and very few weeds. . . .

I think these would be graves of small farmers.

There are others about which there can be no mistake: they are the graves of the poorest of the farmers and of the tenants. Mainly they are the graves with the pine headboards; or without them. . . .

The boards at some of the graves have fallen slantwise or down; many graves seem never to have been marked except in their own carefully made shape. These graves are of all sizes between those of giants and of newborn children; and there are a great many, so many they seem shoals of minnows, two feet long and less, lying near one another; and of these smallest graves, very few are marked with any wood at all, and many are already so drawn into the earth that they are scarcely distinguishable. . . . On the graves of children there are still these pretty pieces of glass and china, but they begin to diminish in size and they verge into the forms of animals and into homuncular symbols of growth; . . . and of these I knew, when Louise told me how precious her china dogs were to her and her glass lace dish, where they would go if she were soon drawn down, and of many other things in that home, to whom they would likely be consigned; . . . in the buying in what daintiness it will a little while adorn her remembrance when the heaviness has sufficiently grown upon her and she has done the last of her dancing: for it will only be by a fortune which cannot be even hoped that she will live much longer; and only by great chance that they can do for her what two parents have done here for their little daughter: not only a tea set, and a coca-cola bottle, and a milk bottle, ranged on her short grave, but a stone at the head and a stone at the foot, and in the headstone her six month image as she lies sleeping dead in her white dress, the head sunken delicately forward, deeply and delicately gone, the eyes seamed, as that of a dead bird, and on the rear face of this stone the words:

We can't have all things to please us,
Our little Daughter, Joe An, has gone to Jesus.

. . . [L]et us then hope better of our children, and of our children's children; let us know, let us *know* there is cure, there is to be an end to it, whose beginnings are long begun, and in slow agonies and all deceptions clearing; and in the teeth of all hope of cure which shall pretend its denial and hope of good use to men, let us most quietly and in most reverent fierceness say, not by its captive but by its utmost meanings:

Our father, who art in heaven, ...

4. H. L. Mitchell Remembers the Southern Tenant Farmers Union, 1936

The Union had won a signal victory in the strike of 1935 when the cotton pickers demanded $1.00 per hundred pounds for picking the crop, and had accepted 75 cents or the equivalent of $1.50 per day, winning a wage increase of 50 percent. The union membership grew to 25,000. The organizers in the field, the local secretaries, and above all, the newly liberated women leaders, were determined to win a wage increase for the six weeks work in the spring of 1936 and force the planters to sign contracts with the union. . . .

A new kind of picketing started spontaneously. There were long lines of men, women, and children marching down the roads. . . . The planters also took to the roads, riding in cars day and night. Bands of men with guns and baseball bats began to attack the peaceful marchers. Near Earle, Arkansas, Paul D. Peacher and Everett Hood led a mob in an attack on black and white marchers. Among those almost beaten to death was one of the eighteen men who had founded the movement two years before, Jim Reese, the white sharecropper who was so amazed when Norman Thomas first came to Arkansas in early 1934 and spoke at the Tyronza High School auditorium. A black woman, Eliza Nolden, was so badly beaten that she died of her injuries. Frank Weems, a black man, was beaten to the ground. Weems disappeared. . . .

I sent a telegram to Reverend Claude C. Williams, who then lived in Little Rock and was conducting something he called "New Era Schools." . . . I asked Williams to go to Earle and conduct Frank Weems' funeral.

The next day Claude Williams arrived in Memphis to get information as to the persons to contact. While waiting in the outer office to see me, Williams was joined by Willie Sue Blagden who, hearing of his mission in Arkansas, asked to join him on the trip. I told Williams how to get to the leading union members in Earle, and he asked if he should allow Willie Sue to accompany him. He felt that the presence of a white woman might be some protection; southern chivalry was still presumably alive even in Arkansas. . . . Stopping at a drugstore in town for a

Coca-Cola, they were apprehended by a band of planters and taken out to a woods. Williams was roughly handled, called a Yankee agitator, and severely beaten with harness straps. Willie Sue was given only two or three hard licks. About sundown, she arrived back at the railway station in Memphis and called me. She was hysterical. . . .

The beating of a white woman and a white minister became a nationwide human interest story. No attention was paid to Eliza Nolden, a black woman soon to die from the effects of a severe beating, nor to the serious condition of white sharecropper Jim Reese, injured for life, or to the fact that Frank Weems, a black sharecropper, had presumably been beaten to death. After all, these three people were just sharecroppers. . . .

The most revolutionary idea ever advanced in American agriculture was the proposal of the Southern Tenant Farmers Union for collectivization of cotton production on the huge plantations of eastern Arkansas. . . . [T]he mere introduction of legislation to confiscate large landholdings raised a specter to haunt the planters in eastern Arkansas, as well as the banks and insurance companies in every state where farm tenancy existed. They were concerned that this fundamental proposal of the scarcely noticed movement of black and white sharecroppers could become the wave of the future in American agriculture. While the Communist Party sponsored the Alabama Sharecroppers Union, and greatly influenced the Farm Holiday movement in the midwest, the party never considered such a radical departure as a new farm system. As soon as the STFU's land program became known, nightriders responded with a reign of terror unequalled in the South until the civil rights confrontations of the 1960s.

The Southern Tenant Farmers Union, composed as it was of people at the bottom of the economic heap, was striking at the heart of the power structure. In a sense, we presented a greater threat than did the civil rights movement nearly thirty years later. The land collectivization proposal may have been the most significant contribution of the Southern Tenants Farmers Union.

5. Images of the Dust Bowl Migration from John Steinbeck, 1939

The Western States nervous under the beginning change. Texas and Oklahoma, Kansas and Arkansas, New Mexico, Arizona, California. A single family moved from the land. Pa borrowed money from the bank, and now the bank wants the land. The land company—that's the bank when it has land—wants tractors, not families on the land. . . .

One man, one family driven from the land; this rusty car creaking along the highway to the west. I lost my land, a single tractor took my land. I am alone and I am bewildered. And in the night one family camps in a ditch and another family pulls in and the tents come out. The two men squat on their hams and the women and children listen. Here is the node, you who hate change and fear revolution. Keep these two squatting men apart; make them hate, fear, suspect each other. Here is the anlage of the thing you fear. This is the zygote. For here "I lost my land" is changed; a cell is split and from its splitting grows the thing you hate—"We lost *our* land." The danger is here, for two men are not as lonely and perplexed as one. And from this first "we" there grows a still more dangerous thing: "I have a little food" plus "I have none." If from this problem the sum is "We have a little food," the thing is on its way, the movement has direction. Only a little multiplication now, and this land, this tractor are ours. The two men squatting in a ditch, the little fire, the side-meat stewing in a single pot, the silent, stone eyed women; behind, the children listening with their souls to words their minds do not understand. The night draws down. The baby has a cold. Here, take this blanket. It's wool. It was my mother's blanket—take it for the baby. This is the thing to bomb. This is the beginning—from "I" to "we."

If you who own the things people must have could understand this, you might preserve yourself. If you could separate causes from results; if you could know that Paine, Marx, Jefferson, Lenin, were results, not causes, you might survive. But that you cannot know. For the quality of owning freezes you forever into "I," and cuts you off forever from the "we."

The Western States are nervous under the beginning of change. Need is the stimulus to concept, concept to action. A half-million people moving over the country; a million more restive, ready to move; ten million more feeling the first nervousness.

And tractors turning the multiple furrows in the vacant land. . . .

And in Kansas and Arkansas, in Oklahoma and Texas and New Mexico, the tractors moved in and pushed the tenants out.

Three hundred thousand in California and more coming. And in California the roads full of frantic people running like ants to pull, to push, to lift, to work. For every manload to lift, five pairs of arms extended to lift it; for every stomachful of food available, five mouths open.

And the great owners, who must lose their land in an upheaval, the great owners with access to history, with eyes to read history and to know the great fact: when property accumulates in too few hands it is taken away. And that companion fact: when a majority of the people are hungry and cold they will take by force what they need. And the little screaming fact that sounds through all history: repression works only to strengthen and knit the repressed. The great owners ignored the three cries of history. The land fell into fewer hands, the number of dispossessed increased, and every effort of the great owners was directed at repression. The money was spent for arms, for gas to protect the great holdings, and spies were sent to catch the murmuring of revolt so that it might be stamped out. The changing economy was ignored, plans for the change ignored; and only means to destroy revolt were considered, while the causes of revolt went on.

The tractors which throw men out of work, the belt lines which carry loads, the machines which produce, all were increased; and more and more families scampered on the highways, looking for crumbs from the great holdings, lusting after the land beside the roads. The great owners formed associations for protection and they met to discuss ways to intimidate, to kill, to gas. And always they were in fear of a principal—three hundred thousand—if they ever move under a leader—the end. Three hundred thousand, hungry and miserable; if they ever know themselves, the land will be theirs and all the gas, all the rifles in the world won't stop them. And the great owners, who had become through their holdings both more and less than men, ran to their destruction, and used every means that in the long run would destroy them. Every little means, every violence, every raid on a

Hooverville, every deputy swaggering through a ragged camp put off the day a little and cemented the inevitability of the day. . . .

In the West there was panic when the migrants multiplied on the highways. Men of property were terrified for their property. Men who had never been hungry saw the eyes of the hungry. Men who had never wanted anything very much saw the flare of want in the eyes of the migrants. And the men of the towns and of the soft suburban country gathered to defend themselves; and they reassured themselves that they were good and the invaders bad, as a man must do before he fights. They said, These goddamned Okies are dirty and ignorant. They're degenerate, sexual maniacs. These goddamned Okies are thieves. They'll steal anything. They've got no sense of property rights.

And the latter was true, for how can a man without property know the ache of ownership? And the defending people said, They bring disease, they're filthy. We can't have them in the schools. They're strangers. How'd you like to have your sister go out with one of 'em? . . .

And the migrants streamed in on the highways and their hunger was in their eyes, and their need was in their eyes. They had no argument, no system, nothing but their numbers and their needs. When there was work for a man, ten men fought for it— fought with a low wage. If that fella'll work for thirty cents, I'll work for twenty-five. . . .

And the companies, the banks worked at their own doom and they did not know it. The fields were fruitful, and starving men moved on the roads. The granaries were full and the children of the poor grew up rachitic, and the pustules of pellagra swelled on their sides. The great companies did not know that the line between hunger and anger is a thin line. And money that might have gone to wages went for gas, for guns, for agents and spies, for blacklists, for drilling. On the highways the people moved like ants and searched for work, for food. And the anger began to ferment.

Chapter 26:
Document Set 2 References

1. A Farm Activist Recalls Rebellion on the Great Plains, ca. 1932
   "Emil Loriks," in Studs Terkel, *Hard Times: An Oral History of the Great Depression* (New York: Pantheon, 1970), p. 227.

2. The Federal Theatre Project Interprets the Fall of AAA, 1938
   "Triple A Plowed Under," by the Staff of the Living Newspaper, *Federal Theatre Plays* (New York: Random House, 1938), pp. 44–47.

3. James Agee Describes the Grave of a Tenant Farmer's Child, 1936
   James Agee and Walker Evans, *Let Us Now Praise Fa-mous Men* (New York: Ballantine, 1941; rep. 1960), pp. 395–399.

4. H. L. Mitchell Remembers the Southern Tenant Farmers Union, 1936
   H. L. Mitchell, *Mean Things Happening in This Land: The Life and Times of H. L. Mitchell, Co-Founder of the Southern Tenant Farmers Union* (Montclair, N.J.: Allan-held, Osmun, 1979), pp. 86–89, 124, 126–127.

5. Images of the Dust Bowl Migration from John Steinbeck, 1939
   John Steinbeck, *The Grapes of Wrath* (New York: Viking, 1939; rep. Penguin, 1986), pp. 193–195, 306–307, 363–365.

Chapter 26:
Document Set 2 Credits

CHAPTER 26

Mass Culture and Social Crisis: Music, Film, and the Mood of Depression America

The textbook's discussion of the American cultural scene in the 1930s notes that as the decade wore on, a shift in tone occurred when the shapers of mass culture discovered resilience in the people. After the Roosevelt administration had grasped the reins of power, the public began to find strength in governmental institutions that only a few short months before had seemed paralyzed in the wake of the economic collapse. One barometer of public mood can be seen in the period's motion pictures, popular songs, and other forms of public entertainment. The following documents assume that film scripts are valid records of the latent media messages projected at audiences struggling to understand a rapidly changing economy and society.

Feature films were very close to the center of the nation's consciousness in the troubled thirties. Film was central to the national temper, which shifted from the despair of the Hoover years to the cautious hopefulness of the early Roosevelt era. In a capitalist society, it is naturally important that a film speak to the audience for which it is intended. Hence an examination of the themes in motion pictures will help to delineate the hopes and fears of the public that absorbed the images projected on the screen. By focusing on two films of the early depression, you will be able to transport yourself intellectually to another time and place.

As an introduction to the disillusionment of the late Hoover era, consider the dark mood of the concluding scene of *I Am a Fugitive from a Chain Gang* (1932). As a wrongly convicted fugitive, Paul Muni's James Allen must exist outside the law and escape into the bleak uncertainty of depression America. Society is locked in debilitating paralysis.

James Allen's alienation contrasts sharply with the buoyant optimism of the teen-aged transients in *Wild Boys of the Road* (1933), who escape punishment after a violent incident and an unjustified arrest. Although the issues of homelessness and economic despair are addressed as the youthful vagrants wander the countryside, a Rooseveltian judge provides the ultimate solution to their problem under the watchful eye of the NRA blue eagle on the courtroom wall. Review the dialogue in the script for evidence of the film maker's political message. Pay particular attention to the *original* ending as well as the "happy ending" finally selected by director Mervyn LeRoy.

As you analyze the rhetoric of *Wild Boys of the Road*, including the film's conclusion, think about the New Deal connections of the Warners, as noted in the textbook, and try to relate politics to the Hollywood product. In evaluating the film as a historical document, use the personal recollections of liberal journalist and writer Robert Bendiner as contextual background against which the film script may be analyzed.

Through the popular sources used in this document set, you can recapture the perceptual experience of average Americans groping for answers to the social and economic problems that had disrupted their world. By approaching the evidence from a scholarly perspective, you will gain insight into everyday life in the depression era, as well as the emotions and concerns of the mass audience that made the movies the central entertainment medium of the 1930s.

Questions for Analysis

1. Compare and contrast the conclusions of *Wild Boys of the Road* (1933) and *I Am a Fugitive from a Chain Gang* (1932). To what extent do these films seriously confront the social problems of the early 1930s? On what level do they reveal deeper meanings relating to the state of political and social consensus in 1932 and 1933?

2. What is the relationship between the two endings proposed for *Wild Boys of the Road*? What factors typically influence decisions with regard to the predominant messages and themes conveyed through feature films? What did the decision to use the second ending indicate about the motivations and beliefs of the producers, director, and studio management? What did it reveal about the attitudes assumed to be present in the mass audience?

3. Robert Bendiner's memoir refers to the "gloomy depression" of Herbert Hoover and the "exhilarating depression" of Franklin D. Roosevelt. What do you think he

meant by the use of these phrases? How does the evidence support or refute Bendiner's thesis?

4. In what way do politics intrude on film making? What evidence of political influence or posturing do you find in the film scripts?

5. In what ways were motion pictures important to the American mass audience of the 1930s? What was the social function of the mass media? How did the needs and desires of consumers affect the products of Hollywood and the theater?

6. What is the meaning of the term *social injustice*? To what extent did social justice become a concern for the purveyors of mass culture in the 1930s? At what historical moments do such matters engage public attention? Why? With what results?

1. E. Y. Harburg's Bitter Memories, 1932

E. Y. (Yip) Harburg

Song lyricist and writer of light verse. Among the works in which his lyrics were sung are: Finian's Rainbow, The Bloomer Girl, Jamaica, The Wizard of Oz, *and* Earl Carroll's Vanities.

We thought American business was the Rock of Gibraltar. We were the prosperous nation, and nothing could stop us now. A brownstone house was forever. You gave it to your kids and they put marble fronts on it. There was a feeling of continuity. If you made it, it was there forever. Suddenly the big dream exploded. The impact was unbelievable.

I was walking along the street at that time, and you'd see the bread lines. The biggest one in New York City was owned by William Randolph Hearst. He had a big truck with several people on it, and big cauldrons of hot soup, bread. Fellows with burlap on their shoes were lined up all around Columbus Circle, and went for blocks and blocks around the park, waiting.

There was a skit in one of the first shows I did, *Americana*. This was 1930. In the sketch, Mrs. Ogden Reid of the *Herald Tribune* was very jealous of Hearst's beautiful bread line. It was bigger than her bread line. It was a satiric, volatile, show. We needed a song for it.

On stage, we had men in old soldiers' uniforms, dilapidated, waiting around. And then into the song. We had to have a title. And how do you do a song so it isn't maudlin? Not to say: my wife is sick, I've got six children, the Crash put me out of business, hand me a dime. I hate songs of that kind. I hate songs that are on the nose. I don't like songs that describe a historic moment pitifully.

The prevailing greeting at that time, on every block you passed, by some poor guy coming up, was: "Can you spare a dime?" Or: "Can you spare something for a cup of coffee?" . . . "Brother, Can You Spare a Dime?" finally hit on every block, on every street. I thought that could be a beautiful title. If I could only work it out by telling people, through the song, it isn't just a man asking for a dime.

This is the man who says: I built the railroads. I built that tower. I fought your wars. I was the kid with the drum. Why the hell should I be standing in line now? What happened to all this wealth I created?

I think that's what made the song. Of course, together with the idea and meaning, a song must have poetry. It must have the phrase that rings a bell. The art of song writing is a craft. Yet, "Brother, Can You Spare a Dime?" opens up a political question. Why should this man be penniless at any time in his life, due to some fantastic thing called a Depression or sickness or whatever it is that makes him so insecure?

In the song the man is really saying: I made an investment in this country. Where the hell are my dividends? Is it a dividend to say: "Can you spare a dime?" What the hell is wrong? Let's examine this thing. It's more than just a bit of pathos. It doesn't reduce him to a beggar. It makes him a dignified human, asking questions—and a bit outraged, too, as he should be.

Everybody picked the song up in '30 and '31. Bands were playing it and records were made. When Roosevelt was a candidate for President, the Republicans got pretty worried about it. Some of the network radio people were told to lay low on the song. In some cases, they tried to ban it from the air. But it was too late. The song had already done its damage.

2. Warner Brothers Dissects a Sick Society, 1932

FADE IN

SERIES OF INSERTS OF NEWSPAPER HEADLINES—

1. CONVICT MAKES SECOND ESCAPE

2. JAMES ALLEN AT LARGE AGAIN
   Desperate Convict, Denied
   Pardon, Escapes Second Time,
   Dynamites Bridge.

3. GUNMAN ESCAPES
   Authorities Confident of
   Allen's Recapture.

DISSOLVE TO:

351. Closeup

of a U.S. map. The camera moves from one spot to another, hesitating,—then jumping here, there and everywhere. Superimposed is a hodge-podge of trains, boats and automobiles. Superimposed on this map are the pages of a calendar—turning—turning—turning. Finally the camera stops IRISED on Chicago.

DISSOLVE TO:

352. An Alley

A row of garages facing the alley, behind a large apartment house. A Ford coupe turns into the alley, and into the open door of one of the garages. After a moment a girl comes out.

MAN'S VOICE:

Helen—

She stops and turns. Allen appears out of the darkness, slinking along the edge of the building for protection. He has on a suit that was once good but is now old and worn. He looks like a bum. Helen stares at him a moment, then gasps as she recognizes him. He draws her back into the shadows.

HELEN:

(her voice choking)
Jim!—Jim—why haven't you come before?—
ALLEN:
I couldn't! I was afraid to.
HELEN:
You could have written. It's been almost a year since you escaped!

ALLEN:

(with bitter laugh)
I haven't escaped—they're still after me. They'll always be after me. I've had jobs but I can't keep them—something happens—someone turns up—I hide in rooms all day and travel by night—no friends—no rest—no peace—
HELEN:

(clutching him)
Jim!—
ALLEN:
Keep moving! That's all that's left for me—
HELEN:

(clinging to him)
No—please! I can't let you go like this. It was all going to be so different. . . .
ALLEN:

(with a hollow laugh)
I hate everything but you. . . . I had to take a chance tonight to see you . . . and say goodbye . . .

Helen gazes at him with tears streaming down her face; then she throws her arms about his neck impulsively, and kisses him. They cling together fiercely. There is the sound of a police siren approaching—then fading away. Allen is startled then starts away.

HELEN:

(following him)
Can't you tell me where you're going?—
(he shakes his head)
Will you write?
(he shakes his head)
Do you need any money?

(he shakes his head again,
still backing away)
But you must, Jim! How do you live?

A car is heard approaching, Allen backs into the dark shadows of the alley.
ALLEN:
I steal. . . .

Helen stands watching, an expression of infinite suffering and pity on her face, as Allen disappears into the darkness.

DISSOLVE TO:

353. Closeup

of map as in previous scene with camera jumping north—south—east—west—and finally

DISSOLVING INTO:

354. The Brow of a Hill at Dawn

In the shot is a sign which reads—
U.S. BORDER
The figure of Allen, in silhouette, is seen trudging slowly up and over the brow of the hill . . . a broken, defeated, beaten figure of a man . . . a hunted animal . . . a fugitive. Over this comes the words:

THE END

3. Robert Bendiner Recalls Two Depressions, 1932–1933

The Gloomy Depression

Certainly those pre-Roosevelt days of the Thirties, so discouraging to a Coolidge, were far from invigorating for any of us, and the most rampant collector of nostalgia cannot want to see their return. But they did provide the darkness that was to make bright the dawn, when the real story of the Thirties begins. There is hardly a doubt that the brilliance of the Roosevelt day, when it came, was enhanced by the blackness of the Hoover night that preceded it. . . .

President Hoover was by no means insensitive to the chaos around him, and when his face appeared in the newsreels there were in it visible signs of strain. But so far had American capitalism carried him personally, from Iowa farm boy to cosmopolitan millionaire, that he could not bring himself to tamper with it in any serious way, even to save it from its own worst defects. . . .

His alternative to such programs was not total inaction, but it might just as well have been, for the actions he favored were no more effective than a parasol in a typhoon. He leaned heavily on the psychological approach, and from time to time would call business leaders to the White House so they could tell reporters on the lawn afterward that conditions were "fundamentally sound," a better description of the interviews than it was of conditions. . . .

Almost as soon as the nomination was safely in Roosevelt's hands, however, he moved to change the atmosphere dramatically. Violating the hoary protocol that a nominee had to wait for a delegation to solemnly apprise him of his selection before he could open his mouth, Roosevelt flew out to the convention in Chicago to symbolize a fresh approach to the country's dire problems: "Let it be from now on the task of our party to break foolish traditions." In his acceptance speech the "forgotten man" was thoroughly remembered, dwelt upon, and courted, and for the first time we heard the promise of a "new deal." The beaming self-confidence that was gradually to warm a shaken people in the campaign, the cigarette holder titled at an angle that was to convey the verve of the man in countless newspaper photographs and newsreels, the vibrant voice that was to make of radio a first-class political weapon, the gallantry with which he minimized his physical affliction, and, above all, the pledges to deal specifically and from above with all the country's agonies—all these burst on a nation starving for leadership and imagination. It would be months before St. George could be duly vested with power to take on the dragon, and meanwhile things could and would get worse. But, all the same, bands across the country were playing "Happy Days Are Here Again," and even if they weren't quite here yet, there was a widespread disposition to believe they were on the way.

The Exhilarating Depression of Franklin Roosevelt

[T]here was . . . a feeling that a great turning point had come, that with a bold new President entering the White House that very week—only a kindly fate could have brought about this happy coincidence—an end had come to the long period of wretched deterioration. What would follow was bound to be better and offered besides all the prickly pleasure of the unknown. The *New Yorker's* Reporter at Large, writing from Washington, found the air "charged with the excitement of action. Things were being done. . . . "

Everywhere, it seemed, newspapers and radio were singing the President's praises. And when he shortly afterward moved to restore beer to the people as well as banks, his popularity was enough to bring tears to the eyes of his bodyguard. The chief of the Secret Service, who had served four years with Herbert Hoover, was so overcome at having his charge greeted everywhere with cheers and applause that he unprofessionally whispered to reporters, "Gosh, but it sounds good to hear that again." . . .

The mingling of relief, admiration, and excitement in that first week was infectious. It set the national tone for the next year or so, even if the plight of a great many individuals was not to be soon or greatly changed. Suddenly, after years of bucolic languor under Coolidge and chilled remoteness under Hoover, Washington had become the swirling, raucous, highly personal center of American life.

4. *Wild Boys* [and Girls] *of the Road* Domesticated, 1933

JUDGE WHITE:
 (becoming grave)
 I've tried to make you realize this is serious business. Every one of you face being held in custody.
 (to Eddie)
 Eddie, you're in the worst spot of all. Your record and your age will compel me to send you to a reformatory! You're an enemy to society and I've got to keep you off the street. Now have you got anything to say?

EDDIE:
 (suddenly rising and bursting out emotionally)
 Sure I've got something to say! I knew all that stuff about you helping us was baloney!
 (he leans over the desk dramatically)
 I'll tell you why we can't go home! Because our folks are poor! They're sick with worry! They can't get jobs! There isn't enough to eat! What good will it do you to send us home to starve!
 (his voice starts to choke up)
 You say you have to send us to jail to keep us off the streets. That's a lie! You're locking us up because you don't want to *see* us! You want to forget us!

 (he shrieks hysterically)
 But you can't! I'm not the only one—there's six hundred thousand more kids like me! And there's more hitting the road every day!

The Judge is gazing sorrowfully at Eddie. One of the commissioners makes a move as though to stop Eddie, but the Judge holds him back and lets Eddie continue with his passionate plea.

EDDIE:
 (choking up)
 You read in the papers about giving people help! The banks get it—the soldiers get it—the breweries get it—and they're always yelling about giving it to the farmers! But what about *us*? We're kids!
 (tears suddenly starting
 to roll down his cheeks)
 I'm not a bad boy! Neither is Tommy! Us three kids have been only traveling around the country looking for work! You don't think we *like* the road, do you?
 (bitterly—choking back a sob)
 I had a job this morning. All I needed was a coat! I had to have it—do you hear—I *had* to have it! We

were broke and I went out to beg for some nickels! When a guy gave me a chance to make five dollars—sure I took it! Wouldn't you? Wouldn't *anybody*! How did I know what a mess it was going to get us in!
>   (choking back sobs)
> I only did it for a coat! I only did it for a job! I only did it because I wanted to go to work and it meant everything to us!
>   (suddenly—defiantly)
> But what's the use? You're not going to believe me and I don't care whether you do or not!
>   (dramatically)
> Go ahead! Put me in a cell—lock me up! I'm sick of being hungry and cold! I'm sick of freight trains! Jail *can't* be any worse than the street—so give it to me!

Suddenly Eddie can go on no longer. He sinks into his chair and buries his face in his hands, sobbing. Tommy and Sally are too embarrassed and touched by his plea to offer Eddie any comfort. He wouldn't want it anyway. For a second the only sound in the court room that can be heard is Eddie's stifled sobs. The attendants are all very much moved. The stenographer nervously blows her nose. Judge White's hand trembles a little as he picks up three petitions resting in front of him.

JUDGE WHITE:
>   (in a voice that sounds like a death knell)
> Sally Clark. House of Correction. One year—ten months.

He stamps and hands the petition over to a commissioner who starts filling out commitment papers.

JUDGE WHITE:
> Thomas Gordon. Country Farm. Eligible for probation in one year.

He stamps and hands this petition also over to the commissioner and then gazes at Eddie.

Eddie rises quickly, drying his eyes and squaring his chin. Once more he is bitter.

EDDIE:
>   (grimly)
> Aw, come on—get it over with—

JUDGE WHITE:
>   (steeling himself for the ordeal)
> Edward, the law compels me to send you to the State Reformatory. You will be confined there until you reach your twenty-first birthday. I'm sorry to do this—but the law leaves me no other alternative.

He gravely stamps the petition and hands it over to the commissioner, then rises and steps down from the bench. As he starts to pass Eddie he pauses for a second, softens, and stops. He squeezes Eddie's arm, turns and quickly walks down the aisle toward his chambers.

ATTENDANT:
>   (taking Eddie's arm)
> Come on, Eddie.

EDDIE:
>   (sneeringly)
> All right, all right. Let me get my hat—

Eddie picks up his hat and walks out of the court room with the attendant.
>   CUT TO:

288. Int. Judge's Chamber

Judge White enters. He stops thoughtfully beside his desk and gazes at a framed photograph. It is a picture of a clean-cut, attractive boy of about fifteen. In one corner, in boy's handwriting, is autographed "To Dad from Billy."

The Judge walks over to a window, removes his glasses, wipes his eyes and stares down at the street below.
>   CUT TO:

289. Ext. Street

A Juvenile Hall police car, with seats running along the side, and heavy wire mesh surrounding the upper part, is parked at the curb. The attendant brings three kids out of the Court Building and ushers them into the waiting car. They are Eddie, Sally and Tommy. They climb into the police car. . . .

295. Int. Judge's Chambers

The Judge is looking sadly down at the Juvenile Hall police car on the street. His secretary enters. She steps over to the Judge's side and gazes down at the car with the Judge. The car starts to move off down the street.

SECRETARY:
>   (thoughtfully)
> There was an awful lot of truth in what that kid said.

JUDGE:
>   (sadly—gazing down at the street below)
> I'm sorry for one thing—

SECRETARY:
> What?

JUDGE:

> (indicating the street below)
> —that *they* didn't hear it.

> CUT TO:

296. Crowds

of men and women, bustling and hustling from subway entrances, stores and cars, jamming the streets and sidewalks—all going busily on about their business . . . .

> FADE OUT.

THE END

Alternate Ending
(Happy)
for
Wild Boys of the Road

JUDGE WHITE:

> (quietly—after a second of silence)
> Edward.

Eddie doesn't lift his head. He is trying his best to choke back his sobs. Tommy and Sally, moved and embarrassed, do not look at him. Judge White gravely picks up the petitions and steps down from the bench. He crosses over to the three kids.

JUDGE WHITE:

> (quietly)
> Edward—I'm going to dismiss your case.

EDDIE:

> (looking up, surprised)
> You're going to what?

JUDGE WHITE:

I'm going to release you. Furthermore, I'm going to help you. I'm going to personally phone the personnel manager of the place who gave you that job and see that you go back to work tomorrow morning. You'll get your coat and pants—but you've got to make me one promise. I want you to drop in occasionally and tell the probation officer how you are making out. Will you do it?

EDDIE:

> (rising—too full of emotion to speak)
> Gee, Judge—

JUDGE WHITE:

> (turning to Sally and Tommy)

As for you, Sally, I'm sure we can place you in some private home where perhaps you can do a little housework in return for your board. Perhaps some arrangements can be made for you to attend school part of the day. Tommy, we'll have more of a problem with you, but I'll promise you one thing—we'll find a spot for you and you'll be given a chance.

The kids are too full of emotion to speak. They stand silently looking at the Judge through misty eyes.

JUDGE WHITE:

> (curtly)
> That's all. Now go over to Juvenile Hall and they'll give you your release papers. Everything else will be taken care of.

Judge White squeezes Tommy's arm, abruptly turns and walks quickly back towards his chambers. An attendant steps forward and taps Eddie on the arm.

ATTENDANT:

> (brusquely)
> Come on—let's go.

The kids turn and silently follow the attendant out of the court room.

> CUT TO:

288. Int. Judge's Chambers

Judge White enters. He stops thoughtfully beside his desk and gazes at a framed photograph. It is a picture of a clean-cut, attractive boy of about fifteen. In one corner, in boy's handwriting, is autographed "To Dad from Billy." The Judge walks over to a window, removes his glasses, wipes his eyes and stares down at the street below.

> CUT TO:

289. Ext. Street

A Juvenile Hall police car, with seats running along the side, and heavy wire mesh surrounding the upper part, is parked at the curb. The attendant brings three kids out of the Court Building and ushers them into the waiting car. They are Eddie, Sally and Tommy. They climb into the police car.

> CUT TO:

290. Eddie, Sally and Tommy—Pan Shot

as they sit down in one corner of the police car. Eddie wipes his eyes on his sleeve. Tommy feels awkward. Sally quietly slips her arm around Eddie's.

TOMMY:

(awkwardly)
Well? Why don't somebody say something?

SALLY:
I—I can't.

EDDIE:

(his eyes starting to shine)
Gee, isn't he a marvelous guy?

SALLY:
I bet he likes kids. . . .

The car suddenly starts and pulls the kids away from the CAMERA. We PAN on it and HOLD as it disappears down the street.

FADE OUT.

THE END

5. Images of Depression America from Hollywood

A. Movie Still from *I Am a Fugitive from a Chain Gang*, 1932

B. Movie Still from *Wild Boys of the Road*, 1933

Chapter 26:
Document Set 3 References

1. E. Y. Harburg's Bitter Memories, 1932
   Oral History, E. Y. Harburg, in Studs Terkel, *Hard Times: An Oral History of the Great Depression* (New York: Pantheon, 1970), pp. 34–36.

2. Warner Brothers Dissects a Sick Society, 1932
   Howard J. Green, Brown Holmes, and Sheridan Gibney, *I Am a Fugitive from a Chain Gang,* Screenplay (Final), July 7, 1932, United Artists Collection, Madison, State Historical Society of Wisconsin, Record Group I, Series 1.2, Box 190.

3. Robert Bendiner Recalls Two Depressions, 1932–1933
   Robert Bendiner, *Just Around the Corner: A Highly Selective History of the Thirties* (New York: E. P. Dutton, 1967), pp. 3, 18–19, 28–30, 36–37.

4. *Wild Boys* [and Girls] *of the Road,* Domesticated, 1933
   Earl Baldwin, *Wild Boys of the Road,* Screenplay (Final), June 1, 1933, United Artists Collection, State Historical Society of Wisconsin, Record Group I, Series 1.2, Box 437.

5. Images of Depression America from Hollywood
   Still Negatives, State Historical Society of Wisconsin, Wisconsin Center for Films and Theater Research.

Chapter 26:
Document Set 3 Credits

CHAPTER 27

Hollywood's Foreign Policy: Interventionism in American Films, 1939–1940

The first section of Chapter 27 is devoted to the final stage of the neutrality period. From 1939 on, American public opinion shifted toward a more activist role in support of the democracies' struggle against fascism. Your text notes the increasing interest in interventionist literature and radio programming at this time, but equally significant were feature films, some of them addressing the escalating crisis in Europe. The following documents focus on two motion pictures, one produced in 1939 and one in 1940, that show how feature films can shed light on both popular and elite cultures.

In September 1941, isolationist Senator Gerald Nye of North Dakota charged that in the nation's movie capital, "one speaks not of the foreign policy of the United States but of the foreign policy of Hollywood." His rhetoric reflected the reality that some movie producers had entered the national foreign policy debate with topical films containing a strong interventionist bias.

An important cinematic breakthrough occurred in 1939, when Warner Brothers declared war on Germany with *Confessions of a Nazi Spy*, a strident exposé of the pro-fascist German-American Bund. Alerted to the activities of a Nazi spy ring by Roosevelt, Jack Warner decided to use the film to call attention to the potential for German subversion in the United States. Review the excerpt from screenwriter Milton Krims's shooting script for an indication of the film's political bias, and search Pare Lorentz's review for clues to critical and public reactions to the film.

The second group of documents focuses on the Walter Wanger–Alfred Hitchcock thriller, *Foreign Correspondent* (1940). Review the textbook account of the escalating German offensive of spring 1940, which provides the historical context in which this film was produced. Try to determine Wanger's intent in producing this film at this time. As you consider the public impact of *Foreign Correspondent*, review the letter from Wanger's friend, Marcus Rebock.

Political reaction to Hollywood's new stance was sharp and quick, as revealed in Montana Senator Burton K. Wheeler's letters to Paramount News and movie czar Will Hays. Isolationist anxieties reached a climax in Nye's St. Louis speech, which detailed the charges against the film industry. Examine these remarks to gain the isolationists' perspective on the forces at work on American public opinion in 1941. The end result, a Senate investigation of movie propaganda, revealed substantial antiwar sentiment as the nation edged toward intervention.

Reacting to the Senate attacks, the movie producers engaged former presidential candidate Wendell Willkie as defense counsel for the hearings. Willkie's letter to the investigating committee not only revealed his own interventionist bias (see textbook account of the 1940 campaign) but also indicated Hollywood's belief in its educational role and public responsibility. As you evaluate Willkie's remarks, reflect on the significance of film content as an expression of the movie industry's perception of popular values. Your analysis of the evidence should focus on the state of American opinion concerning intervention as well as on government and media roles in shaping public attitudes.

Questions for Analysis

1. As you review the film script excerpts, can you determine why Senators Nye and Wheeler were so concerned about the film industry in 1941? To what extent were their fears and suspicions justified? Explain.

2. What were the backgrounds of Jack Warner, Walter Wanger, Alfred Hitchcock, and some of the other Hollywood figures active in the effort to incorporate topical subject material into films produced between 1939 and 1941? To what extent did personal background and political affiliation influence Hollywood productions?

3. In what way can a motion picture be understood as a historical document? Do films reflect popular values and attitudes? Or do they influence public opinion in a particular direction? Defend your position, using the evidence from the film scripts and textbook background as you develop your case.

4. What larger issues were raised by Nye's attack on the motion picture industry? Using Willkie's letter as a primary source, explain what the producers and studio heads believed to be at stake in 1941. Which position was most persuasive? Why?

5. The final version of *Foreign Correspondent*, released in August 1940, was set in London. How would you account for this revision of the final shooting script of June 5, 1940?

6. The term *propaganda* appears frequently in the documents. How would you define the term? If Walter Wanger believed in the interventionist position, why did he object to the term being applied to his work, including *Foreign Correspondent*? Do you think the term applies to the films coming out of Hollywood between 1939 and 1941? Why or why not?

1. Warner Brothers Declares War on the German American Bund, 1939

CONFESSIONS OF A NAZI SPY

by
Milton Krims
and
John Wexley
Based on the articles of
Leon G. Turrou
Directed
by
Anatole Litvak

Supervisor, Lord

328. Newspaper Headlines

U.S. ATTORNEY DEMANDS INDICTMENT HIGH NAZI OFFICIALS!!

German Naval Intelligence Chief Indicted in U.S. Spy Ring

Grand Jury Indicts Eighteen Including Nazi Officials

NAZI SPY TRIAL STARTS TOMORROW!!!

331. Close Shot Kellog Another Angle

KELLOG:

...In simple language, the indictment means that this group of defendants conspired to secure secret information about our national defense and to transmit this information to the advantage of a foreign government—namely, Germany!

332. Full Shot Court

Commotion and hubbub of voices. Jury reacting. Reporters reacting big. Messengers rushing out.

KELLOG'S VOICE:

(deliberately)

I wish to make it perfectly clear—that this conspiracy was conceived in and operated directly by the present German Government.

333. Close Shot Kellog Another Angle

KELLOG:

(continuing)

...It has been suggested that the roles of these four defendants are inconsequential. That is true—but therein lies their precise value—their personal unimportance. They have been but little cogs in a vast and intricate machine ... A worldwide spy network whose organized efficiency leaps all oceans and boundaries ... A vicious network whose complex fabric weaves inevitably through the Naval Intelligence Offices in Bremen and Hamburg—through many German-American organizations here—through the War and Propaganda Ministries in Berlin to the inner sanctums of present Germany's highest officialdom ...

338. Int. Berlin Office Med. Shot

very modern, very luxurious. At one end hangs a large silk swastika banner—at the other end a picture of Hitler. The whole side wall is a huge map of the world. A man stands with his back to CAMERA. Several men in the uniforms of high-ranking Nazis, including Von Eichen, Straubel and Huber, stand facing him. The Man speaks—and CAMERA SLOWLY MOVES IN to follow his finger.

MAN'S VOICE:

Our power increases from day to day. All of Europe is at our mercy, on its knees, begging us not to destroy it. Austria is part of Greater Germany. Czechoslovakia is through. Italy is with us and safeguards Jugo-Slavia. Japan is our ally. Hungary is practically ours. Our agents are succeeding in Rumania, Poland and Lithuania. Franco will soon have all Spain. France will be isolated from all sides.

MAN'S VOICE:

(moves pointer to U.S.)

But now, since our glorious victory at Munich, all our efforts must be directed at the strongest remaining democracy—the United States. Here we must repair the few petty mistakes that have recently been made . . .

(points to South America)

In order to dominate completely the countries of South America—all excellent markets for our manufactured goods, all superb sources of raw materials—

(points to U.S.)

—we must paralyze the influence of the United States by using every instrument of propaganda at our command.—Furthermore we must know every military and naval secret it possesses. . . .

339. Insert Headlines

"NAZI SPY CASE GOES TO JURY TODAY!!

U.S. ATTORNEY KELLOG FINISHES SUMMATION!"

340. Int. Court Room Long Shot (Kellog in B.G.)

KELLOG:

. . . It has been suggested that the information these defendants have obtained for Germany is of small moment—but as we have endeavored to bring out during the course of this trial—we have only scratched the surface of the Nazi espionage network. We cannot calculate the extent of this spyring that has penetrated every nerve and tissue of this nation, together with its propaganda and religious hatred.

(picks up large chart)

Here, on this chart . . .

341. Insert Chart

KELLOG:

(continuing—OVER chart)

. . . We can see the amazing system of sinister forces at work in this country. . . .

DISSOLVE THRU TO:

342. News Headlines

double exposed on chart, in b.g.

NAZI SPIES FOUND GUILTY! JURY CONVICTS GERMAN SPIES! JUDGE TO PRONOUNCE SENTENCE!

WIPE TO:

343e. Closeup Kellog

speaking directly into CAMERA.

KELLOG:

And some still say there is nothing to fear—that we are immune—that we are separated by vast oceans from the bacteria of aggressive Dictatorships and Totalitarian states. But we know, and have seen the mirror of history in Europe's last year.

343f. Montage Over Kellog's Closeup

Over Kellog's closeup, we see: Bund meetings—American Legion fight—Camp Horst Wessel meetings—drilling—pamphlet distribution—Hitler screaming—Kassel screaming, etc.

KELLOG:

And we know this bacteria can slowly poison the organism of our civilized society and dull its common sense and reason—working insidiously through its Bunds and training camps—where its spies take over and where it diligently trains its youth to seize power. . . .

344. Superimposed Shots of American Bund Order Service

marching, are replaced by row on row of grim, robot-like German troops marching with full battle equipment. . . .

2. Pare Lorentz Assesses the Warner Brothers' Attack, 1939

If you needed to be convinced that we have a free screen, one look at *Confessions of a Nazi Spy* should convince you, because the Warner Brothers have declared war on Germany in this one. Although it is hysterical, vicious, ill-contrived, and peculiarly ambiguous, I do not object to the picture because it will be a notable one in many ways; a direct assault on the rulers of a foreign nation, a direct accusation of espionage in this country on the part of Germany, it at least is a political movie that pulls no punches. It is, however, wild-eyed in itself.

It is based on a series of articles written by a G-man who is not, I am told by officials, held in great repute by the Department of Justice, for whom he worked. It is further based on as fishy a trial as I ever read about—a trial that involved an army deserter who wrote to a German newspaper, "I want to be a spy," and who copied military information out of a book he found in the New York Public Library. From the petty and almost burlesque facts of the trial, the Warners claim that the Germans are, through the German-American Bunds, attempting to organize a Nazi group in this country that eventually hopes to seize control of the government. . . .

[W]hether it annoys you or frightens you, *Confessions of a Nazi Spy* is an important picture. From now on we should see some action on the screen; with this precedent there is no possible way any producer could argue against dramatizing any social or political theme on the grounds that he's afraid of domestic or foreign censorship. Everybody duck.

3. Walter Wanger and Alfred Hitchcock Call for Preparedness, 1940

As Johnny steps up to the microphone, the announcer steps back out of picture. Johnny holds a manuscript in his hand, from which he reads:

JOHNNY:
> (*quietly, his eyes on the manuscript*)
> Hello, America. I have been watching a part of the world being blown to pieces. A part of the world as nice as Vermont and Ohio, Virginia, California and Illinois, lies ripped up and bleeding like a steer in a slaughter house.

Through the foregoing comes the sound of sirens. Johnny glances around a second towards where Carol is sitting, then continues above the noise.

JOHNNY:
> And I've seen things that make the history of the savages read like Pollyanna legends. I've seen—

An official steps quickly forward to Johnny.

OFFICIAL:
> (*with a slight accent*)
> Pardon. They are coming. We will have to postpone the broadcast.

JOHNNY:
> Postpone, my eye! Let's talk while we've still got a chance.

Carol has risen. She comes to stand beside him. The sound of the sirens increases.

ANOTHER FRENCH OFFICIAL:
> The Nazis! The bombers! (to Carol) Madam, we have a shelter downstairs!

VARIOUS VOICES:
> Lights out! They're in the sky! Out—downstairs, every one!

Johnny puts his arm around Carol.

JOHNNY:
> How about it, Carol?

CAROL:
> They're listening in America, Johnny.

The lights go out, leaving Johnny's and Carol's faces alone, dimly lit. Behind them we can hear the general exodus—various officials darting about, etc.

JOHNNY:

O.K., we'll tell 'em then.

He looks down at his manuscript, grins and throws it away. He turns back to the microphone.

JOHNNY:

I can't read the rest of the speech I had because all the lights have gone out so I'll have to just talk off the cuff. All that noise you hear isn't static. It's death coming to Paris. Yes, they're coming here now. You can hear the bombs now, falling on the streets, cafes and homes. Don't turn me out. Hang on a while.

This is a big story—and you're part of it. It's too late to do anything here except stand in the dark and let them come. It feels like all the lights are out everywhere—except in America. Keep those lights burning there. Cover them with steel, ring them with guns. Build a canopy of battleships and bombing planes around them.—Hello, America! Hang onto your lights. They're the only light left in the world!

FADE OUT.

THE END

4. A Friend Supports Wanger's Use of Propaganda in Films, 1940

129 Greenaway Rd.,
Eggertsville, N.Y.
Sept. 19, 1940

Dear Walter:

Glad to hear that you are reading THE EAGLES GATHER, and hope that they have awakened your enthusiasm, and the interest I also hope I aroused in you during our conversation in New York.

My wife and I saw FOREIGN CORRESPONDENT. You did an excellent job, and in Buffalo, at least, it was received with excitement and enthusiasm. The story is not only vital, but retains interest all along, reaching a fine patriotic climax.

True to your belief, the picture does more than deliver a mere message. It cannot be stressed too

much these days. The idea that people may get tired of propaganda is ridiculous. People like it if given to them in an entertaining form. Through that medium, not only will they listen, but will enjoy the message. It is therefore my belief that taking my suggestion as a lead, I am sure that joining THE EAGLES with DYNASTY, you will be able to produce a magnificent film which can stress the necessity for preparedness, and rearmament.

Sincerely,

Marcus Rebock

5. Burton K. Wheeler Takes Aim at Hollywood, 1941

UNITED STATES SENATE
Committee on Interstate Commerce

January 13, 1941

Mr. Will Hays
28 West 44th Street
New York City

My dear Mr. Hays:

I have just sent the following letter to Paramount News at Washington, D.C.:

"... The propaganda for war that is being waged by the motion picture companies of this country is reaching a point at which I believe legislation will have to be enacted regulating the industry in this respect unless the industry itself displays a more impartial attitude."

Many complaints are coming to me and to other members of Congress to the effect that the motion picture industry is carrying on a violent propaganda campaign intending to incite the American people to the point where they will become involved in this war. As you well know, the motion picture and news reel is one of the great agencies for molding public opinion of this country and if we are going to preserve this nation as a democratic republic, it is highly essential that both sides of each question be presented.

I sincerely hope that you will call this to the attention of your people as I am fast coming to the con- clusion that legislation should be enacted to remedy the present situation.

Yours respectfully,

(sgd) B. K. Wheeler

6. Gerald P. Nye Attacks Propaganda in Films, 1941

To carry on propaganda you must have money. But you also must have the instruments of propaganda. And one of the most powerful, if not the most powerful, instrument of propaganda is the movies. In Germany, Italy, and in Russia—the dictator countries—the government either owns or completely controls and directs the movies. And they are used as instruments of government propaganda. In this country the movies are owned by private individuals. But, it so happens that these movie companies have been operating as war propaganda machines almost as if they were being directed from a single central bureau.

We all go to the movies. We know how, for too long now, the silver screen has been flooded with picture after picture designed to rouse us to a state of war hysteria. Pictures glorifying war. Pictures telling about the grandeur and the heavenly justice of the British Empire. Pictures depicting the courage, the passion for democracy, the love of humanity, the tender solicitude for other people, by the generals and trade agents and the proconsuls of Great Britain, while all the peoples who are opposed to her, including even courageous little Finland now, are drawn as course, bestial, brutal scoundrels. . . .

Why do they do this? Well, because they are interested in foreign causes. You cannot doubt that. Go to Hollywood. It is a raging volcano of war fever. The place swarms with refugees. It also swarms with British actors. In Hollywood they call it the "British Army of Occupation." The leaders are almost all heavy contributors to the numerous committees of all sorts organized, under the guise of relief to Britain, Greece, or Russia, to propagandize us into war.

Why do they want to push us into war? Well, they have all sorts of interests. But here is one I can give you: One of the leading Wall Street investment houses made a study of these movie industries only a few months ago. It told its clients that if Britain loses, seven of the eight leading companies will be wiped out. . . .

What I would like to know is this: Are the movie moguls doing this because they like to do it, or has the Government of the United States forced them to become the same kind of propaganda agencies that the German, Italian, and Russian film industries have become? I have excellent reason to believe that this governmental influence has prevailed. . . .

Americans, we want to be strong and ready always to effectively defend ourselves against the worst that any part of the world might choose to bring against us, of course. We want to leave no stone unturned that will aid in guaranteeing such a defense.

But, likewise, we ought to want freedom from foreign influence in times like these. Let's have courageous American thinking, not the kind which finds us waiting for the cue that Churchill gives; not the kind that has to be painted and pictured by propagandists or by forces whose profits are dependent upon foreign causes.

Let's be Americans because of and for causes that are American. Let us bury forever the thought that real Americanism is determined only by those who both hate Hitler most and love Britain best. Let us be giving larger thought to what is best for America. . . .

This is a wonderful hour for more America-first thinking; for a fine, clean expression by all our people of determination to stay out of these never-ending foreign wars, to keep faith with ourselves and with those who 150 years ago, won for us divorcement from the hates, the wars, and the power politics of Europe.

7. Wendell Willkie Defends Freedom of the Screen, 1941

Willkie, Owen, Otis & Bailly,
Washington, D.C., September 8, 1941.

United States Senator D. Worth Clark,
Senate Office Building, Washington, D.C.

My Dear Senator Clark: You are beginning an investigation of the motion-picture industry. My firm has been asked to represent it as counsel. We assume the charges against the industry are contained in Resolution 152, introduced in but not yet passed by the United States Senate, and in the speech of Senator Nye, coauthor of the resolution, which was delivered by him in St. Louis on the day the resolution was introduced.

After reading the resolution and Senator Nye's speech with care, I have come to the conclusion that your subcommittee intends to inquire whether or not the motion-picture industry, as a whole, and its leading executives, as individuals, are opposed to the Nazi dictatorship in Germany. If this is the case, there need be no investigation.

The motion-picture industry and its executives are opposed to the Hitler regime in Germany; they have watched with horror the destruction of a free life within Germany and the ruthless invasions of other countries by Nazis. On behalf of the motion-picture industry and its personnel, I wish to put on the record this simple truth: We make no pretense of friendliness to Nazi Germany nor to the objectives and goals of this ruthless dictatorship. We abhor everything which Hitler represents. . . .

The motion-picture industry has no wish to flout the authority or the position of your committee. But the industry has instructed me to say that it intends to continue to present to the American people a truthful and accurate portrayal of their defense effort. However, when Senator Nye says that the industry is doing this work on the demand of the administration, we emphatically and indignantly deny his charge. The administration has made no such demand, and frankly, the motion-picture industry would be ashamed if it were not doing voluntarily what it is now doing in this patriotic cause. . . .

The resolution charges that the motion-picture business is in the hands of groups interested in involving the United States in war. The co-author, Senator Nye, explains this allegation on the basis of the individual opinions of the executives of the business, their racial and geographic backgrounds, and their mercenary motives. This charge should be supported by cold facts. We know that your committee will want to discuss only facts, so, in brief, I will present them for your record.

Of the more than 1,100 feature pictures produced since the outbreak of the present war, only some 50 have had anything to do with the issues involved in the war or with the ideological beliefs of the participants. Some of these 50, we are glad to admit, do portray nazi-ism for what it is—a cruel, lustful, ruthless, and cynical force. We know that this is an accurate portrayal of nazi-ism. . . .

The pictures portraying England and Germany do not purport to tell the American people what they should do about nazi-ism, save as the knowledge of the true facts may, as it always has, influence the judgment of right-thinking men and women. We believe that it is the truth which makes and keeps men free and that it is the suppression of the truth which is a menace to human liberty wherever it occurs. . . .

I cannot let pass this opportunity to warn of the very genuine dangers involved in the type of investigation which you are now proposing to start. The radio business is already included in the original resolution. From the motion-picture and radio industries, it is just a small step to the newspapers, magazines, and other periodicals. And from the freedom of the press, it is just a small step to the freedom of the individual to say what he believes. The United States, with England and its allies, remain the bulwark of the rights of the individual in the world today. The rights of the individual mean nothing if freedom of the press and freedom of speech are destroyed. There can be no disunity within the United States on this principle, and I know there is none.

In conclusion, we insist that your committee is proceeding with doubtful legal authority in the conduct of the proposed hearings on the subjects contained in the original resolution and amplified in Senator Nye's speech. Furthermore, the manner of the committee's creation does not establish the impression of impartiality. And, as I have said above, the investigation and harassment of free expression in the United States, is a procedure, once accepted, that may be applied to the theater, to newspapers and magazines, to the radio, to publications of all kinds and finally to the right of public officials and private citizens to speak freely. As American citizens, we protest this as vigorously as possible.

Chapter 27:
Document Set 1 References

1. Warner Brothers Declares War on the German-American Bund, 1939
   Milton Krims and John Wexley, *Confessions of a Nazi Spy,* Script, 1939 (Including Revisions), in John Wexley Papers, Madison, State Historical Society of Wisconsin, Box 1.

2. Pare Lorentz Assesses the Warner Brothers' Attack, 1939
   Pare Lorentz, "Confessions of a Nazi Spy," in *Lorentz on Film* (New York: Hopkinson and Blake, 1975), pp. 168–169.

3. Walter Wanger and Alfred Hitchcock Call for Preparedness, 1940
   "Shooting Script," June 5, 1940, *Foreign Correspondent,* in Walter Wanger Papers, Madison, State Historical Society of Wisconsin, Box 78.

4. A Friend Supports Wanger's Use of Propaganda in Films, 1940
   Marcus Rebock to Walter Wanger, September 19, 1940, in Wanger Papers, Box 77.

5. Burton K. Wheeler Takes Aim at Hollywood, 1941
   Burton K. Wheeler to Will Hays, January 13, 1941, in United Artists Collection, Madison, State Historical Society of Wisconsin, Monroe Greenthal File, Box 4.

6. Gerald P. Nye Attacks Propaganda in Films, 1941
   Gerald P. Nye, "Our Madness Increases as Our Emergency Shrinks," Extension of Remarks of Hon. Gerald P. Nye of North Dakota in the Senate of the United States, Monday, August 4, 1941, in Gerald P. Nye Papers, West Branch, Herbert Hoover Presidential Library, Box 58.

7. Wendell Willkie Defends Freedom of the Screen, 1941
   Wendell Willkie to D. Worth Clark, September 8, 1941, in United States Congress, Senate, Propaganda in Motion Pictures, Hearings Before a Subcommittee of the Committee on Interstate Commerce, United States Senate, 77th Cong., 1st session, pp. 18–21.

Chapter 27:
Document Set 1 Credits

1. Text from Milton Krims and John Wexley, *Confessions of a Nazi Spy,* Script, 1939 (including revisions), in John Wexley Papers. The State Historical Society of Wisconsin.

3. "Shooting Script," June 5, 1940, *Foreign Correspondent* in Walter Wanger Papers, The State Historical Society of Wisconsin.

4. Marcus Rebock to Walter Wanger, Sept. 19, 1940, in Wanger Papers. The State Historical Society of Wisconsin.

5. Burton K. Wheeler to Will Hays, Jan. 13, 1941, in United Artists Collection. The State Historical Society of Wisconsin.

CHAPTER 27

War and Society: Outsiders on the Inside

World War II resulted in revolutionary changes in American society and the national economy. Chapter 27 concentrates on this social transformation and examines the long-term consequences of total war for the future of the United States. Among the groups most directly affected by wartime changes were American women and the black community. The following documents explore their social and economic experiences, revealing the catalytic effects of war.

The first three documents focus on the black response to wartime opportunity. Beginning with black labor leader A. Philip Randolph's remarks on the March on Washington Movement's goals, these materials reflect the heightened militancy of black activists who sought to infuse the war with social meaning. Relate the urgency of his comments and Grant Reynolds's outrage to the new social mobility described in your textbook. Similarly, Walter White's reflections on the economic background of the Detroit riot in 1943 should be read in conjunction with the textbook section on black economic advances. Note the relationship between the authors' backgrounds, their forums, and the views expressed. Search the documents for evidence of war as a stimulus to social change.

No less affected by the war's unsettling influence were American women, who entered the labor force in unprecedented numbers. Seizing the opportunity to combine patriotism and financial gain, women responded to wartime propaganda appeals that stressed common sacrifice. As you review the remaining documents, try to determine what motives propelled women into the work force.

In the first two selections, the Labor Department's Women's Bureau details the entry of women into the steel industry and the shipyards. Examine these descriptions for evidence of the government's long-term intentions with regard to the future sexual division of labor. Moreover, be aware of workplace problems unique to female workers. The Women's Bureau's Mary Elizabeth Pidgeon provided useful analysis of women's work concerns as the war drew to a close.

The final selections include a sample of black and female recollections of the changes wrought by World War II and a set of illustrations focusing on some of the issues surrounding the changing character of the workplace. Drawn from Studs Terkel's *The Good War,* the oral history accounts reflect mature judgments concerning the social meaning of war. Always be cautious about the possibility of selective memory as you compare wartime accounts and later recollections of the wartime experience.

As you analyze the documents, be aware of continuities and contrasts in the black/female historical experiences. Try to judge the long-term effects of World War II on blacks and women, relating the documents to your textbook's account of the war as a destabilizing force.

Questions for Analysis

1. How do the goals, demands, and experiences of blacks and women in the 1940s compare with the ideas expressed during World War I (see document sets for Chapter 23)? Do you find evidence that the social environment had changed?

2. What do the documents reveal about government appeals to attract women into the labor force? What was the result of these appeals? Why did women enter the work force?

3. Review the White report and the textbook account for clues to the causes behind the Detroit riot of 1943. What does the evidence reveal about the origins of the clash?

4. What was the meaning of World War II to African Americans? What do the documents reveal about their goals for the war? What problems were present for them in the work force and military service?

5. What problems did women encounter in the workplace? In what ways were these concerns unique to female workers? To what extent was unionism helpful in dealing with the problems of women workers?

1. A. Philip Randolph States African American Goals, 1942

When the defense program began and billions of the taxpayers' money were appropriated for guns, ships, tanks, and bombs, Negroes presented themselves for work only to be given the cold shoulder. North as well as South, and despite their qualifications, Negroes were denied skilled employment. Not until their wrath and indignation took the form of a proposed protest march on Washington, scheduled for July 1, 1941, did things begin to move in the form of defense jobs for Negroes. The march was postponed by the timely issuance (June 25, 1941) of the famous Executive Order No. 8802 by President Roosevelt. But this order and the President's Committee on Fair Employment Practice, established thereunder, have as yet only scratched the surface by way of eliminating discriminations on account of race or color in war industry. Both management and labor unions in too many places and in too many ways are still drawing the color line.

It is to meet this situation squarely with direct action that the March on Washington Movement launched its present program of protest mass meetings. Twenty thousand were in attendance at Madison Square Garden, June 16; 16,000 in the Coliseum in Chicago, June 26; 9,000 in the city Auditorium of St. Louis, August 14. Meetings of such magnitude were unprecedented among Negroes. . . .

By fighting for their rights now, American Negroes are helping to make America a moral and spiritual arsenal of democracy. Their fight against the poll tax, against lynch law, segregation, and Jim Crow, their fight for economic, political, and social equality, thus becomes part of the global war for freedom.

2. African American Doubts About the War for Democracy, 1944

For the past two years and ten months I have been a Chaplain on active duty with the United States Army. I have found Negro soldiers bitterly resentful of their lot in this war. . . .

Out on the Pacific Coast I found young Negroes holding key positions in the industries—the airplane industry to be exact—which produce the most difficult of weapons to master, the army bomber. Other young Negroes are now flying these planes. Still other young Negroes are now prepared to be their navigators. Now it is a commonly accepted fact among honest men and women that no racial group has cornered the market on either intelligence or native ability. This is what the celebrated pamphlet *The Races of Mankind* would have told a few thousand army officers had it not been banned by stupid people who refuse to recognize the obvious. All Negro soldiers are not graduate engineers. Nor are all white soldiers. All Negro soldiers were not born in that section of the nation, which because it seeks to keep the Negro in the educational gutter, directs that white youth too must wallow in the pig sty of ignorance. But the Honorable Secretary of War has not claimed that white soldiers cannot master the techniques of modern weapons of war. His blanket statement about the Negro soldier's inability in this respect not only insults the thousands of intelligent Negro youth in our armed forces from all sections of the country, but by indirection it classifies them as morons incapable of attaining the intelligence level of the most ignorant southern cracker. What does the Negro soldier think about this? He considers it a vicious attack upon his manhood. And what is more he thinks that the Administration continues to insult him as long as such men are allowed to control his destiny in this war. The Negro soldier will not give his life for the perpetuation of this outright lynching of his ability, nor for the right of domestic Nazis to make of him a military scapegoat.

3. Walter White Describes Racial Tension in Wartime Detroit, 1944

In 1916 there were 8,000 Negroes in Detroit's population of 536,650. In 1925 the number of Negroes in Detroit had been multiplied by ten to a total of 85,000. In 1940, the total had jumped to 149,119. In June, 1943, between 190,000 and 200,000 lived in the Motor City. . . .

Jobs

Early in July, 1943, 25,000 employees of the Packard Plant, which was making Rolls-Royce engines for American bombers and marine engines for the famous PT boats, ceased work in protest against the upgrading of three Negroes. Subsequent investigation indicated that only a relatively small percentage of the Packard workers actually wanted to go on strike. The UAW-CIO bitterly fought the strike. But a handful of agitators charged by R.J. Thomas, president of the UAW-CIO, with being members of the Ku Klux Klan, had whipped up sentiment particularly among the Southern whites employed by Packard against the promotion of Negro workers. During the short-lived strike, a thick Southern voice outside the plant harangued a crowd shouting, "I'd rather see Hitler and Hirohito win than work beside a nigger on the assembly line." The strike was broken by the resolute attitude of the union and of Col. George E. Strong of the United States Aircraft Procurement Division, who refused to yield to the demand that the three Negroes be down-graded. . . . The racial hatred created, released, and crystallized by the Packard strike played a considerable role in the race riot which was soon to follow. It also was the culmination of a long and bitter fight to prevent the employment of Negroes in wartime industry. There had been innumerable instances, unpublicized, in the Detroit area of work stoppages and slow downs by white workers, chiefly from the South, and of Polish and Italian extraction. Trivial reasons for these stoppages had been given by the workers when in reality they were in protest against unemployment or promotion of Negroes. . . .

Detroit Labor Unions and the Negro

One of the most extraordinary phenomena of the riot was the fact that while mobs attacked Negro victims outside some of the industrial plants of Detroit, there was not only no physical clash inside any plant in Detroit but not as far as could be learned even any verbal clash between white and Negro workers. This can be attributed to two factors: first, a firm stand against discrimination and segregation of Negro workers by the UAW-CIO, particularly since the Ford strike of 1941. The second factor is that when the military took over, the armed guards in the plants were ordered by the Army to maintain order at all costs and to prevent any outbreak within the plants. . . .

The Detroit riot brought into sharp focus one of the most extraordinary labor situations in the United States. Prior to the Ford strike of 1941 many Negroes in Detroit considered Ford their "great white father" because the Ford plant almost alone of Detroit industries employed Negroes. When the UAW-CIO and the UAW-AFL sought to organize Ford workers, their approach at the beginning was a surreptitious one. The unions felt that the very high percentage of Southern whites in Detroit would refuse to join the Union if Negroes were too obviously participating. But when the strike broke, far-sighted Negro leaders in Detroit took an unequivocal position in behalf of the organization of workers. A serious racial clash was averted by the intercession of thoughtful whites and Negroes. Following the winning of the NLRB election by the union, it began to take a broader and more unequivocal position that all workers and union members should share in the benefits of union agreements irrespective of race, creed, or color.

4. The Women's Bureau Recommends Improved Conditions for Female Shipyard Workers, 1944

Times have changed with lightning speed. By late 1943, thousands of women along both coasts and on the Gulf, Great Lakes, and inland waterways were actively engaged in almost every phase of ship building and repair work, and it is anticipated that it will be necessary to recruit thousands more before the war is over. Though the introduction of women into the shipyards did not begin in earnest until the fall of 1942, by January 1943 as many as 4 per cent of all the production wage earners in the industry were women. The proportion had risen to a little over 5 per cent by March, and by September to 9.5 per cent. In January 1944 it was 10 per cent. These figures include the 8 navy yards engaged in ship construction and repair, in which women have made extensive gains and comprised in September nearly one-fourth of the women wage earners in the industry. . . .

It is clear, then, that the shipyards are charting new seas in the utilization of the woman labor force, and the mistakes or successes that result may have a profound effect not only on the production and repair of ships, but on the cost and efficiency of such production and the health, work, and life histories of thousands of women. It is important to take stock now. Misconceptions should be dispelled, well-founded facts pooled, and the fund of information available from industries with longer histories in the employment of women disseminated. It is with these objects in view that the present report is submitted. It is the aim of the Women's Bureau through the recommendations and suggestions made here to promote conditions for the woman shipyard worker conducive to her most efficient and productive employment and her well-being as a member of society and the labor force. . . .

1. Secure the cooperation of men supervisors and workers.
2. Select and place women carefully.
3. Employ women only in jobs found to be suitable.
4. Pay women and upgrade them on the same basis as men.
5. Schedule an 8-hour day and a 48-hour 6-day week; allow a lunch period of at least 30 minutes, and rest periods of 10 to 15 minutes in each work spell of as much as 4 hours. Rotate shifts no more frequently than every two months.
6. Set up an effective woman employee counselor system.
7. Give new women workers preliminary induction into the work and environment of the shipyard before putting them on the job.
8. Provide personal-service, food, and medical facilities that meet approved standards of adequacy and quality.
9. Study and expand the safety program to adapt it to women workers, and instruct women thoroughly in safe work practice.

5. The Women's Bureau's Assessment of Women's Progress in the Workplace, 1944

In the past the opportunity given women workers to learn and to exercise skills has been narrower in range than men's has been. In consequence, very large numbers of women were little thought of in connection with other types of work, and so they continued to be given little opportunity to develop additional skills. The war situation has changed that considerably. With shortages of men workers, women have been employed in a greater variety of occupations than before. . . .

Unfortunately, there are many cases where women still have been given far too little chance to be upgraded to their highest skills. In 1943, the National Industrial Conference Board analyzed reports from some 130 plants, chiefly in heavier metal industries, plants that had employed relatively few women or none. In nearly 60 percent of these plants there were no plans for advancing women from the top production jobs they held at the time of reporting to more highly skilled jobs. Moreover, numerous instances are reported of the placement of women in jobs that are not in the usual line for the job progression; in such blind-alley jobs neither proficiency nor length of service can bring these women beyond a limited early stage of work. If this situation continues, it will be a great disadvantage to women after the war, and in fact government agencies are finding promotional discrimination against them as one of the major reasons why women quit jobs in war plants. . . .

Plant seniority practices under the clauses of many union agreements give women workers very inadequate protection. For example, some agreements

definitely provide that women's occupation of jobs formerly held by men shall be for the duration only. Some agreements give women employed at time of signing the agreement full seniority rights with men, but for women employed after that time set up a list for women separate from that for men. Some agreements provide for the seniority of women as "separate and distinct from the seniority of men." Agreements fixing seniority by department only may affect women and men quite differently. Other agreements are so vaguely worded as to permit interpretations that are of disadvantage to women.

6. Dellie Hahne Recalls the War's Impact on Women's Attitudes, ca. 1945

There was *one* good thing came out of it. I had friends whose mothers went to work in factories. For the first time in their lives, they worked outside the home. They realized that they were capable of doing something more than cook a meal. I remember going to Sunday dinner one of the older women invited me to. She and her sister at the dinner table were talking about the best way to keep their drill sharp in the factory. I had never heard anything like this in my life. It was just marvelous. I was tickled.

But even here we were sold a bill of goods. They were hammering away that the woman who went to work did it temporarily to help her man, and when he came back, he took her job and she cheerfully leaped back to the home.

There was a letter column in which some woman wrote to her husband overseas: "This is an exact picture of our dashboard. Do we need a quart of oil?" Showing how dependent we were upon our men. Those of us who read it said, This is pure and simple bullshit. 'Cause if you don't know if you need a quart of oil, drive the damn thing to the station and have the man show you and you'll learn if you need a quart of oil. But they still wanted women to be dependent, helpless.

I think a lot of women said, Screw that noise. 'Cause they had a taste of freedom, they had a taste of making their own money, a taste of spending their own money, making their own decisions. I think the beginning of the women's movement had its seeds right there in World War Two.

7. Memories of War as Opportunity, ca. 1942–1945

The war started and jobs kinda opened up for women that the men had. I took a job at a shoe-repair place on Wilshire Boulevard. Cleanin' shoes and dyin' shoes, the same thing that men did. They started takin' applications at Douglas, to work in a defense plant. I was hired.

I didn't want a job on the production line. I heard so many things about accidents, that some girls got their fingers cut off or their hair caught in the machines. I was frightened. All I wanted to do was get in the factory, because they were payin' more than what

I'd been makin'. Which was forty dollars a week, which was pretty good considering I'd been makin' about twenty dollars a week. When I left Tennessee I was only makin' two-fifty a week, so that was quite a jump. . . .

They [other women workers] weren't interested in the war. Most of them were only interested in the money. Most of us was young and we really didn't know. All we were after was that buck. I didn't care about the money. That was a big salary for me, I was satisfied with that. . . .

I do know one thing, this place was very segregated when I first come here. Oh, Los Angeles, you just couldn't go and sit down like you do now. You had certain places you went. You had to more or less stick to the restaurants and hotels where black people were. It wasn't until the war that it really opened up. 'Cause when I come out here it was awful, just like bein' in the South. . . .

I really didn't know what the war was about. I was in the house one day and all of a sudden they started yellin' about the war, war, war. Roosevelt had declared war. Well, they know that when there's a war, somebody's gonna get a job. This was during the Depression, so I think people were kinda glad the war had started. So right away they started hirin'. I think the war had kind of a pleasure. People didn't realize the seriousness of the war. All they were thinkin' about is they had lived in these Depression days. It was so hard to come by a dollar.

Those who had to go, that was the sad part. I had a brother that went to war, my youngest. He come back. The war helped some people because they come back, they took trades, learned to do things. My brother come back and now he is very successful. I think the army really made a man out of him. He works at Rockwell in the missile department and he's a supervisor. He wouldn't have known what to do if he hadn't gone in the army. . . .

They didn't mix the white and black in the war. But now it gives you a kind of independence because they felt that we gone off and fought, we should be equal. Everything started openin' up for us. We got a chance to go places we had never been able to go before.

In ways it was too bad that so many lives were lost. But I think it was for a worthy cause, because it did make a way for us. And we were able to really get out.

8. Images of the War at Home: Women as a National Resource, 1942–1945

A. Answers to Women's Questions about War Work, 1943

B. New Workers Create New Problems, ca. 1943

C. New Opportunities for African American Welders, ca. 1944

E. The Government Appeals to Women's Patriotism, ca. 1943

D. A UAW Woman, 1944

Chapter 27:
Document Set 2 References

1. A. Philip Randolph States African American Goals, 1942
   A. Philip Randolph, "Why Should We March?" *Survey Graphic* (November 1942).

2. African American Doubts About the War for Democracy, 1944
   Grant Reynolds, "What the Negro Thinks of This War," *The Crisis,* Vol. 51 (September 1944).

3. Walter White Describes Racial Tension in Wartime Detroit, 1944
   Walter White, "What Caused the Detroit Riots?" Part I in *What Caused the Detroit Riots?* by Walter White and Thurgood Marshall (New York: NAACP, 1943), pp. 5–16.

4. The Women's Bureau Recommends Improved Conditions for Female Shipyard Workers, 1944
   Dorothy K. Newman, "Employing Women in the Shipyards," *Bulletin of the Women's Bureau,* no. 192–196 (Washington, D.C.: Government Printing Office, 1944), pp. 1–6.

5. The Women's Bureau's Assessment of Women's Progress in the Workplace, 1944
   Mary Elizabeth Pidgeon, "A Preview as to Women Workers in Transition from War to Peace," Special Bulletin No. 18 of the Women's Bureau (Washington, D.C.: Government Printing Office, March 1944).

6. Dellie Hahne Recalls the War's Impact on Women's Attitudes, ca. 1945
   "Dellie Hahne," in Studs Terkel, *"The Good War": An Oral History of World War II* (New York: Pantheon, 1984), p. 122.

7. Memories of War as Opportunity, ca. 1942–1945
   "Sarah Killingworth," in Terkel, pp. 113–116.

8. Images of the War at Home: Women as a National Resource, 1942–1945
   A. Answers to Women's Questions about War Work, 1943
      "Answers to Questions Women Ask about War Work," National Archives, Records of the War Manpower Commission, Record Group 211.
   B. New Workers Create New Problems, ca. 1943
      "It's Either That . . . ," National Archives, Records of the Federal Works Agency, Record Group 162.
   C. New Opportunities for African-American Welders, ca. 1944
      Photograph, National Archives, Records of the Office of War Information, Record Group 208.
   D. A UAW Woman, 1944
      Women Work, Women Vote, Special Supplement to *Ammunition,* 2 (August 1944), cover.
   E. The Government Appeals to Women's Patriotism, ca. 1943
      "Soldiers Without Guns," U.S. Army poster, in Nancy Hewitt, ed., *Women, Families and Communities* (Glenview, Ill.: Scott, Foresman and Company, 1990), p. 193.

Chapter 27:
Document Set 2 Credits

1. From "What the Negro Thinks of This War," *The Crisis,* Vol. 51 (Sept. 1944). Reprinted by permission of Crisis Publishing Company.

3. From Walter White, "What Caused the Detroit Riots?" Part I in *What Caused the Detroit Riots* by Walter White and Thurgood Marshall, NAACP, 1943. Reprinted with permission of NAACP.

8. A. National Archives
   B. National Archives
   C. National Archives
   D. United Automobile Workers Union
   E. National Archives

CHAPTER 27

Coalition Warfare: New Friends in a Grand Alliance

Your textbook emphasizes the interrelationship between the home front, the military effort, and the diplomacy of coalition warfare. These linkages were evident in the Roosevelt administration's concerted effort to build domestic support for America's partners in the grand coalition against fascism. Roosevelt and his advisors were convinced that an important dimension of the struggle for a free world lay in the creation of public opinion in the United States that was favorable to the Allies.

To achieve this goal, the administration moved in December 1941 to regulate the media through an Office of Censorship that managed the news in a manner consistent with the national interest. In June 1942 Roosevelt established the Office of War Information (OWI) in an effort to influence public opinion and promote an awareness of the issues of the war. The following documents highlight the images projected at an American public whose attitudes toward the Allies were still in the process of transformation.

It was unquestionably the Soviet Union that presented the greatest challenge to government image makers. After signing the shocking Nazi-Soviet Pact of August 1939, the Soviets invaded Finland, ostensibly for security reasons. Search the documents for evidence of American public reaction to Soviet behavior. *The New Republic* editorial and Roosevelt's comments suggest that liberals in particular struggled as they reflected on Soviet policy. Think about the reasons for liberal discomfort.

The remaining documents reveal that the Roosevelt administration took extraordinary steps to reshape the image of Joseph Stalin and the Soviet Union in the United States. By sanctioning former ambassador Joseph Davies' publication of a memoir of his years in the prewar Soviet Union and by acquiescing in the production of a movie derived from the story, Roosevelt took a long step toward the dissemination of home-front propaganda. As you review the excerpt from the film script, the OWI reaction to the film, and the public response from Dwight MacDonald and other intellectuals, think about the significance of the film and the controversy it generated in relation to the war aims of a democratic state.

An examination of the film script, posters, photographs, and other visual images contained in this document set will heighten your awareness of the powerful social impact of total war. Consider the limits of government power in a democratic nation and the implications of wartime pressures for the preservation of democratic ideals and institutions. As you review the public opinion polls, do you observe any measurable effect of the government information program? Account for the public debate that surrounded the film *Mission to Moscow,* which was only moderately successful as a box office attraction. Your analysis of the furor wrought by this Hollywood production should help you to understand the American aversion to propaganda, as well as the process of opinion formation in a nation at war.

Questions for Analysis

1. Compare the opinions recorded in the *Fortune* survey with the attitudes expressed by Roosevelt and the *New Republic* editorialists in 1939 and 1940. How would you explain the divergent views?

2. Examine the visual images presented as part of the document set. Do you identify any distinction between the subliminal messages projected in *Time's* 1939 man-of-the-year cover and the visual imagery contained in materials produced after 1941? In what way do the movie posters, portraits, and photographs shed light on the impact of total war on American perceptions of the Allies?

3. What was the source of the controversy generated by the production of the film *Mission to Moscow*? Why were the critics so upset by a film that had received the endorsement of OWI? To what extent were the criticisms justified?

4. Elmer Davis, director of the Office of War Information, was on record in support of a public information program that pursued a "strategy of truth." Based on the evidence available to you, do you believe that the OWI's Bureau of Motion Pictures was successful in the achievement of his goal? Why or why not?

5. What is the meaning of the term *propaganda*? With what nations was the idea of propaganda most closely associated in the 1930s and 1940s? In view of the evidence, would you say that those assumptions were accurate?

1. The Soviet Invasion of Finland Shocks American Liberals, 1939

There never has been a clearer case of calculated and unprovoked aggression by a large power against a small neighbor than the invasion of Finland by the Soviet Union. There never has been one more universally denounced by persons of all classes and of all shades of belief, the world around. . . .

The *New Republic* in the past has pointed out that Stalin's action had been immensely successful in terms of power politics but that a final judgment on his shrewdness would have to be reserved, for it was possible that he would overplay his hand. This he has done, in a most blatant and obvious way, in Finland. By a brutal assault on a well governed, intelligent nation that had won the admiration of the world for its sturdy and progressive culture, the Soviet Union has unleashed the dogs of hate that were already straining to tear it to pieces. It has made defense of its action impossible on the part of those who were friendly or were willing to reserve judgment. It has provided a strong moral case for those who wish to destroy communism and all its works. It has diverted against itself much of the hostility that had hitherto been concentrated on its greatest and nearest political enemy. This is a disaster, not only for Finland but also and more certainly for world communism and the Soviet state itself.

2. Roosevelt Denounces Soviet Dictatorship, 1940

More than twenty years ago, while most of you were pretty young children, I had the utmost sympathy for the Russian people. In the early days of Communism I recognized that many leaders in Russia were bringing education and better health and, above all, better opportunity to millions who had been kept in ignorance and serfdom under the imperial regime. . . .

And I, with many of you, hoped that Russia would work out its own problems and their government would eventually become a peace-loving, popular government with free ballot, a government that would not interfere with the integrity of its neighbors.

That hope is today either shattered or is put away in storage against some better day. The Soviet Union, as a matter of practical fact, as everybody knows, who has got the courage to face the fact, the practical fact known to you and known to all the world, is run by a dictatorship, a dictatorship as absolute as any other dictatorship in the world.

It has allied itself with another dictatorship and it has invaded a neighbor so infinitesimally small that it could do no conceivable, possible harm to the Soviet Union, a small nation that seeks only to live at peace as a democracy and a liberal forward looking democracy at that.

3. Joseph E. Davies Defends the Soviet Union as a Reliable Ally, 1942

Now that the United States and the U.S.S.R. find themselves at war against a common enemy, what sort of relations can we expect between the two countries? The traditional relationship between the American and Russian peoples has been one of friendship and good will. As continental powers we have no clashing interests abroad. We both stand to gain from peace, to lose from war. We have no territorial ambitions, no vast overseas commitments. And there is also a positive bond. American engineers have already played an important part in building the new Russia; they can play a bigger part in building and rebuilding postwar Russia. We have always depended on Russia for some of our manganese, chrome, potash and mercury; Russia has imported copper from the United States, and in the postwar period will certainly increase its purchases of plant equipment and industrial goods. . . .

These questions of Communism in America and Russian aid against Japan go back to two fundamental aspects of this war. We cannot hope to win unless we have complete faith in our own institutions and full confidence in our allies. To worry about Russian Communism in America is to give way to defeatism before we have even begun to fight. And to expect the Russians to carry the fight to Japan after they have given Hitler his first real setback is to demand that other nations do all the bleeding, fighting and dying. Every one of us is in this war up to his ears. President Roosevelt has warned us to expect bad news at first, but he has set a course that will lead to victory. Our immediate task is to hold our faith—in ourselves and in those fighting beside us. The record the Russians have written on the scorched earth of their own land should fortify our confidence in our friends and in our cause.

4. OWI Endorses Warner Brothers' *Mission to Moscow*, 1943

MISSION TO MOSCOW is a magnificent contribution to the Government's motion picture program as a means of communicating historical and political material in a dramatic way. As the picture unfolds the whole field of international relations, Axis intrigue and the shameful role of the appeasers of the Axis in the past decade is illuminated for us. The presentation of the Moscow trials is a high point in the picture and should do much to bring understanding of Soviet international policy in the past years and dispel the fears which many honest persons have felt with regard to our alliance with Russia. . . .

The producers of this picture are to be congratulated for the forthright courage and honesty which

made its production possible. Not only is it a great contribution to the war program in itself but it may well affect Hollywood's war product. Especially remarkable is the use of documentary footage in this picture, not simply as material for transitional montage or a background for narration but as the very warp and woof of the story itself. The result is to give the picture as a whole the immediacy of a vivid personal experience. It is to be hoped that MISSION TO MOSCOW will have immediate release and the widest possible distribution. The picture presents no problems from the point of view of either domestic or overseas distribution.

5. *Mission to Moscow* Presents the Soviet Case, 1943

DAVIES:

Well, you see, Mr. Molotov, I've done what my president sent me to do. My end of the job is finished.

MOLOTOV:

No one could have been more conscientious in respect to both our countries.

There is the SOUND of a door opening and shutting at the far end of the room. Molotov stops, looks off-scene. The others follow his gaze.

241. Med. Long Shot   Stalin

from their angle as he walks toward the camera. (*Note*: In his book, Mr. Davies describes Stalin as follows: "His demeanor is kindly, his manner almost deprecatingly simple, his personality and expression of reserved strength and poise very marked." In the writer's opinion these characteristics for the part are even more important than physical verisimilitude.)

242. Med. Shot   The Group

as Stalin walks directly to Davies, dispensing with the formality of an introduction. The two men shake hands.

STALIN:

Mr. Davies, I am happy to know you.

DAVIES:

Thank you, Mr. Stalin. This is a great pleasure for me . . . (smiles) also considerable of a surprise.

They all smile at this frankness and the ice is broken.

KALININ:

Gentlemen, won't you please have chairs?

STALIN (as they are seated):

Besides your work here in Moscow, I understand you have visited many other sections of the Soviet Union.

DAVIES:

And I've been deeply impressed by what I've seen—your industrial plants, the development of your natural resources, and the work being done to improve living conditions everywhere in your country. I believe history will record you as a great builder for the benefit of common men.

STALIN (with sincere modesty):

It is not my achievement, Mr. Davies. Our five-year plans were conceived by Lenin and carried out by the people themselves.

DAVIES:

Well, the result has been a revelation to me. I confess I wasn't prepared for all I've found here. (With a smile.) You see, Mr. Stalin, I'm a capitalist, as you probably know.

STALIN (laughingly):

Yes, we know you are a capitalist—there can be no doubt about that.

They all join in the laughter.

KALININ:

We also know this about you, Mr. Davies—the worst things you've had to say, you have said to our faces, the best things you have said to our enemies.

STALIN:

We want you to realize that we feel more friendly toward the government of the United States than any other nation. If there are any matters that are not settled between us, please take them up with Molotov. . . .

293. Med. Shot   President Roosevelt's Study   Night

Davies and the president are leaning over a small map that rests on the desk under a lamp. The rest of the room is dark. Except for his hands on the map, the president is mostly in the shadow. Unlike the first scene, whose atmosphere was easy and relaxed, this is one of tension and repressed excitement. As Davies talks, his finger is on the map.

DAVIES:

. . . I was in Smolensk in '38. The city is an important rail center. It will be a serious blow if the Germans take it.

ROOSEVELT:

I don't see how it can hold out with pincers closing in on both sides.

DAVIES:

Well, losing a city—or ten cities—isn't losing the war. The Russians will take their losses and go on fighting.

ROOSEVELT:

How about Moscow? The military experts say it will fall within six weeks.

DAVIES:

I can only say that I think they're wrong, Boss. I predict the Red Army will amaze the world.

ROOSEVELT:

I'm glad to hear you say that, Joe. I'm going to ask Congress to extend Lend-Lease aid to Russia. That means, if we're wrong, the stuff will fall into German hands.

DAVIES:

It's worth the risk. For the first time in months I feel there's a chance of beating Hitler.

ROOSEVELT:

If only more of our people realized that! There's been so much prejudice stirred up about the Soviet Union that the public haven't been given a chance to know the truth. . . .

DISSOLVE TO:

295. Stock Shot   German Footage

A wave of German tanks breaks over Soviet positions. Red Army troops fight desperately but give ground under the sheer weight of the attack. (Again no music—only harsh, mechanized sounds.)

FIRST ISOLATIONIST'S VOICE (OVER SCENE):

Why, Russia's as good as licked! She'll never last out the summer.

296. Close-up   First Isolationist

FIRST ISOLATIONIST:

And then what will happen to the war supplies we're sending her?

297. Stock Shot   Crowd

listening to the isolationist's words.

FIRST ISOLATIONIST'S VOICE (OVER SCENE):

Supplies that *you're* paying for, my fellow citizens, out of your hard-earned taxes.

298. Close Shot   Second Isolationist

SECOND ISOLATIONIST:

. . . Another thing about this Joe Stalin. He might change color overnight—from Bolshevik red to the black swastika.

299. Long Shot   Davies

speaking from a platform, SHOUTING OVER the backs of an audience. (*Note:* At the beginning, let Davies speak at a distance as though his voice were at first a small one that grows in volume as his cause gathers strength.)

DAVIES:

The plain answer is that Premier Stalin and the Soviet government have solemnly pledged they will fight to the end and make no separate peace with Hitler.

300. Stock Shot   Russian Artillery

firing at the invaders. The Soviet gun crews working with feverish speed.

DAVIES' VOICE (OVER SCENE):

And the Soviet Union keeps its word!

301. Close Shot   Third Isolationist

THIRD ISOLATIONIST (with gesticulations):

If I had to choose between Hitler and Stalin, I'd a thousand times rather live in a world dominated by a Nazi Hitler than by Red Stalin.

302. Map of Europe

The German borders have engulfed most of Europe and are slowly swallowing the vast territory of Russia.

FOURTH ISOLATIONIST'S VOICE (OVER SCENE; speaking in a hollow, prophetic voice):

We have seen France fall, England bruised and helpless, and now Russia reeling toward defeat. Why throw good money after bad?

303. Med. Shot   Davies

DAVIES (pleading):

Russia needs tanks and planes. Russia needs food and strategic metals. Russia needs understanding and encouragement.

304. Stock Shots   Of Heroic Russian Resistance

Civilians digging breastworks in their streets. Guerrilla snipers shooting Germans from behind trees. Soviet airmen shooting down German bombers.

Russian demolition squads blowing up one of their own dams and scorching the earth before the invaders.

DAVIES' VOICE (OVER SCENE):

The Russian people will defend their cities. They will fight in their streets, in their forests, behind the German lines and over them in the air. They will scorch the earth and level their vast projects . . . but they will yield nothing to the invader but death.

305. Close-up   Second Isolationist

SECOND ISOLATIONIST (sarcastically):

And I ask you, what business is all this of ours? No nation is threatening us.

306. An Audience Listening

SECOND ISOLATIONIST'S VOICE:

Would you tell me how any aggressor could possibly molest our country—a country that by the blessing of Providence is isolated from attack by two vast oceans?

307. Med. Shot   Davies

DAVIES:

As I read of beleaguered Moscow and Leningrad and of Germany striking into the depth of Russian industries, then I say to myself and I say to you—

308. Stock Shot   An Immense Audience (Madison Square Garden or Similar Hall)

DAVIES' VOICE:

"There, but for the grace of God, goes America." . . .

334. Final Sequence

As the last SHOT in the preceding MONTAGE, we see the Nazi army in Russia in headlong retreat. Now for smooth continuity we match this SHOT'S general effect with a SHOT of our own, showing German infantrymen retreating through a gray fog or ground mist, twenty or thirty men in ragged formation, partly obscured by the fog. The sounds of battle continue faintly in the distance.

DAVIES' VOICE:

And now slowly but surely the tide of evil forces recedes across the earth, leaving in its wake the next great task of rebuilding a free world . . .

Now the German soldiers are swallowed up in the fog as they move on out of the scene, and for a few feet the screen reveals only the swirling fog, mixed with the smoke of battle. It slowly begins to lift and dispel during the following commentation.

DAVIES' VOICE:

In faith and justice to the heroes of all nations who have given their lives in this, the people's war . . .

The fog has now blown away and we see the bleak corner of a Russian battlefield, covered with swirling snow. Row on row of plain wooden crosses mark the graves of the Russian dead, and a Soviet sentinel is standing guard over them, holding his bayoneted rifle with its butt against the ground.

DAVIES' VOICE:

—we, the living, say to you: Wherever you may hallow the ground in which you lie . . .

DAVIES' VOICE:

. . . know you all that we, the free men and women of the earth, will never again permit that you shall have died in vain . . .

As the soldier [an American marine] looks up slowly toward the sky, we

PAN UP TO:

339. Long Shot   The Sky

Slowly the clouds of war sweep away to reveal the bright sky of a new day and a new world, and CAMERA REMAINS on this inspiring symbol to the end, as the music builds powerfully with the closing words, spoken with great and moving sincerity.

DAVIES' VOICE:

And to you, the unborn generations yet to come, we pledge that whatever else our victory shall bring, it will first and forever make an end of war—so that you to whom the great future belongs, shall be able to live, not as fighting beasts, but with the spirit of God in your souls—free, happy, and secure in an everlasting peace.

FADE OUT

THE END

6. *Mission to Moscow* Attacked as Propaganda, 1943

We make three main charges:

"Mission to Moscow" falsifies history and even distorts the very book on which it is based.

One of the chief purposes of the film is to present the Moscow Trials of 1936–1938 as the just punishment of proved traitors. These trials were generally regarded, at the time they took place, as brutal travesties of justice. Most of the American press, like the rest of the civilized world, considered them to be frame-ups of Stalin's personal and political opponents....

"Mission to Moscow" glorifies the Stalin dictatorship and its methods.

It may seem curious that Warner Brothers should be so anxious to re-educate the American public on the Moscow Trials, an issue long since past and one which might seem of interest today chiefly to those who are supporting Stalin's straight party line.... [I]t is quite simply official propaganda on behalf of the present government of Russia. It corresponds in every detail with what the Kremlin would like the American people to think about its domestic and foreign policies....

"Mission to Moscow" has the most serious implications for American democracy.

Throughout the film there is a deliberate confusion of Soviet and American policy, so that critics of the one at any time in the past few years are presented as necessarily opposing the other. The Kremlin and the White House are practically brought under the same roof. All opponents of Roosevelt's pre-Pearl Harbor foreign policy are smeared as either fascists or dupes of fascism; Congress is slanderously portrayed and President Roosevelt is correspondingly exalted as all-seeing and all-wise. These "amalgam" techniques, this deification of The Leader are methods hitherto more characteristic of totalitarian propaganda than of our own.... The Kremlin's values are not our values, its political methods are not our methods, and we are deeply disturbed by quasi-official propaganda designed to prove the contrary.

7. The American Perception of the Soviet Ally, 1945

1. Survey on Russia

In the mind of the U.S. public, there is little doubt of the importance of friendly relations with Russia. The following attitude scale shows the Russophobes in a minority of less than 10 per cent, those cool toward Russia a mere 11 per cent—both together about balanced by those who say it is important to keep on friendly terms with Russia. But most significantly, the scale shows that the largest segment of the public wants to put a stop-loss order on its endorsement of Russia's importance. Success or failure of the relationship is looked on as a joint responsibility of the two countries.

With which one of these four statements do you come closest to agreeing?

It is going to be very important to keep on friendly terms with Russia after the war, and we should make every possible effort to do so.	22.7%
It is important for the U.S. to be on friendly terms with Russia after the war, but not so important that we should make too many concessions to her.	49.2
If Russia wants to keep on friendly terms with us after the war, we shouldn't discourage her, but there is no reason why we should make any special effort to be friendly.	11.3

We shall be better off if we have just as little as possible to do
with Russia after the war.................................... 9.3
Don't know.. 7.5

Hopes for success are down a little from last January and "don't know" answers have increased, probably because of V-E strains, but hope still predominates.

Thinking back for a moment to our relations with Russia a few years before the war, do you think we will get along better with Russia in the future than we did in the past, not so well, or about the same?

	January	This survey
Better	48.3%	42.4%
Not so well	22.0	19.1
About the same	20.1	23.5
Don't know	9.6	15.0

Do you feel that most of the common people in Russia are now pretty friendly toward the U.S., or not so friendly, or that most of them don't have any feeling one way or the other?

Friendly toward U.S.	52.7%
Not so friendly	7.0
Not one way or other	22.0
Don't know	18.3

A good part of the U.S. public apparently assumes friendship on the part of the Russians because it has a clear conscience—whether justified or not—on its own behavior toward Russia. Asked if the U.S. had done anything since the last war that may have given the Russians reason to doubt our friendship, 73.7 per cent answered that there was nothing they could think of.

8. Images of the Soviets and Their Leadership, 1939–1945

A. Soviet Brutality in Finland, ca. 1939

Talburt, New York World-Telegram

Peace!

C. Stalin as a Clear-Eyed Man of Determination, 1943

B. A Ruthless "Man of the Year," 1940

D. Studio Card, *Mission to Moscow,* **1943**

Chapter 27:
Document Set 3 References

1. The Soviet Invasion of Finland Shocks American Liberals, 1939
   "Stalin Spreads the War," *New Republic,* Vol. CI (December 13, 1939).

2. Roosevelt Denounces Soviet Dictatorship, 1940
   Franklin D. Roosevelt, Speech, American Youth Councils, February 10, 1940, in Benson L. Grayson, ed., *The American Image of Russia, 1917–1977* (New York: Frederick Ungar Publishing Co., 1978), pp. 151–152.

3. Joseph E. Davies Defends the Soviet Union as a Reliable Ally, 1942
   Joseph E. Davies, "What We Didn't Know About Russia," *Reader's Digest,* Vol. XL (March 1942).

4. OWI Endorses Warner Brothers' *Mission to Moscow,* 1943
   Report, Hollywood Office, Bureau of Motion Pictures, Office of War Information, April 29, 1943, Box 1434, Entry 264, Record Group 208, Office of War Information Records, Archives Branch, Washington National Records Center, Suitland, Md.

5. *Mission to Moscow* Presents the Soviet Case, 1943
   Film script, *Mission to Moscow,* in David Culbert, ed., *Mission to Moscow* (Madison: University of Wisconsin Press, 1980), pp. 189–91, 210–211, 214–216, 222–224.

6. *Mission to Moscow* Attacked as Propaganda, 1943
   Form Letter, Dwight MacDonald *et al.* to "Dear Friend," May 12, 1943, NAACP Papers, Washington, D.C., Manuscript Division, Library of Congress.

7. The American Perception of the Soviet Ally, 1945
   "U.S. Opinion on Russia," *Fortune,* Vol. XXXII (September 1945).

8. Images of the Soviets and Their Leadership, 1939–1945
   A. Soviet Brutality in Finland, ca. 1939
      Talburt, "Peace," *New York World-Telegram,* n.d., in Peter G. Filene, ed., *American Views of Soviet Russia, 1917–1965* (Homewood, Ill.: Dorsey Press, 1968), p. 138.
   B. A Ruthless "Man of the Year," 1940
      Time, January 1, 1940.
   C. Stalin as a Clear-Eyed Man of Determination, 1943
      Time (January 4, 1943).
   D. Studio Card, *Mission to Moscow,* 1943
      David Culbert, ed., *Mission to Moscow,* p. 53.

Chapter 27:
Document Set 3 Credits

CHAPTER 28

The Greek Crisis and the Truman Doctrine: Origins of Containment

Perhaps no historical problem has been more controversial than the origins of the Cold War after World War II. Acknowledging its importance to an understanding of recent American foreign policy, your textbook devotes a substantial portion of Chapter 28 to anticommunism and containment. The following documents focus on a pivotal incident of the early Cold War, the Greek crisis of 1947, and the Truman Doctrine as evidence of the postwar confrontation between the United States and the Soviet Union. As you examine these materials, be conscious of the conflicting world views that gave rise to the clash. Try also to relate the debates of 1947 to foreign-policy problems that plagued the United States into the 1980s.

The first two documents contain the Truman administration's analysis of the issues at stake when Great Britain withdrew from Greece. Examine Acting Secretary of State Dean Acheson's and President Truman's assumptions as they moved to forge the Truman Doctrine into a broad commitment to the containment of communism. As you evaluate the argument, compare their position with the Soviet perspective on Truman's message to Congress, as reflected in the *Soviet News* editorial. How did the Soviet and American views of the Greek situation differ? Use the textbook account

as a guide to Washington's policy assumptions and sense of urgency.

Once Truman settled on the containment program, his most serious problem involved persuading the Congress (and the public) that the new departure was necessary. The result was a hard-sell campaign that convinced important Republicans, such as Senate Foreign Relations Committee Chairman Arthur Vandenberg of Michigan, that resistance to an expansive communist movement was essential. Vandenberg's letter to a constituent reveals his own beliefs and motives for embracing bipartisanship in foreign policy. Equally significant were the signs of future danger inherent in Truman's approach. Determine why Vandenberg was concerned about the foreign-policy crisis.

A final group of documents explores the intellectual rationale for a firm anti-Soviet stance in American foreign policy. Transcending the immediate Greek problem, George Frost Kennan's well-known essay, "Sources of Soviet Conduct," established a broad framework for Soviet-American relations in the future.

As you review the concluding document, drawn from Kennan's memoirs, assess the author's reservations about the Truman Doctrine. Try to relate Kennan's and Vandenberg's concerns to the evolution and extension of the containment policy in subsequent years.

Questions for Analysis

1. What do the documents reveal about the origins of the Greek crisis in 1946–1947? How did American and Soviet analysts interpret the roots of conflict?

2. What were the underlying purposes of the Truman Doctrine? How did the Truman administration implement its plan? With what results, both short and long term?

3. Define containment as Kennan intended the policy to operate. What do the documents reveal about the assumptions held by Kennan, Acheson, and Truman? What was the logic of Kennan's argument, and what did he hope to achieve through the policies advanced in the "Sources of Soviet Conduct"?

4. What were the criticisms of the Kennan-Truman position, in both the United States and the Soviet Union? On what basis did Kennan himself later fault the Truman administration's adaptation of his ideas?

5. Democratic Senator Walter George of Georgia responded to the Truman Doctrine by saying: ". . . when we make a policy of this kind we are irrevocably committing ourselves to a course of action, and there is no way to get out of it next

week or next year. You go down to the end of the road." Where was the end of the road? What do the documents suggest about the future implications of the decisions of 1947–1948?

6. In what way do the documents contribute to an understanding of the origins of the Cold War? What light do they shed on the issue of responsibility for the breakdown in Soviet-American relations, 1945–1948? Is there any reason to believe that the Cold War could have been avoided?

1. Dean Acheson Explains the Truman Doctrine, 1947

On February 24 of this year the British Ambassador, in a note dated February 21, informed the Department of State that as of March 31 the British Government would be obliged to discontinue the financial, economic, and advisory assistance which it has been giving to Greece and Turkey. Within a week the President informed congressional leaders of this situation and advised with them on the course of action which the Government should take. On March 12, the President informed Congress and the Nation of the situation and recommended that this Government extend aid to Greece and Turkey.

On March 3 we received from the Greek Government an urgent appeal for financial, economic, and expert assistance. Assistance is imperative, the Greek Government says, if Greece is to survive as a free nation. . . .

[I]t is necessary only to glance at the map to realize that the survival and integrity of Greece is of grave importance in a much wider situation. The inexorable facts of geography link the future of Greece and Turkey. Should the integrity and independence of Greece be lost or compromised, the effect upon Turkey is inevitable. . . .

I need not emphasize to you what would more than likely be the effect on the nations in the Middle East of a collapse in Greece and Turkey, and the installation of totalitarian regimes there. Both from the point of view of economics and morale, the effects upon countries to the east would be enormous, especially if the failure in Greece and Turkey should come about as the result of the failure of this great democracy to come to their aid. On the other hand, I ask you to consider the effects on their morale and their internal development should Greece and Turkey receive a helping hand from the United States, the country with which they closely associate the principles of freedom. It is not too much to say that the outcome in Greece and Turkey will be watched with deep concern throughout the vast area from the Dardanelles to the China Sea.

It is also being watched with deepest anxiety by the peoples to the west, particularly the peoples of Europe who, as the President said, are struggling against great difficulties to maintain their freedom and independence while they repair the damage of war. . . .

The present parliament of Greece was democratically elected in an election which foreign observers agreed was fair. There can be no doubt that it represents the majority of the Greek people. The present Greek Cabinet contains representatives of 85 percent of the members of the Greek Parliament. The mere fact that Greece has a king does not necessarily make Greece's form of government less democratic than that of other countries, as is shown for instance by the governments of Norway, of Sweden, of Denmark, of the Netherlands and of Great Britain. . . .

In Greece today we do not have a choice between a perfect democracy and an imperfect democracy. The question is whether there shall be any democracy at all. If the armed minorities that now threaten Greece's political and economic stability were to gain control, free institutions and human freedoms would disappear, and democratic progress would come to an abrupt halt.

It is not claimed that all persons involved in the present armed challenge to the Greek Government are Communists. There are among them many persons who honestly, but in our opinion, mistakenly, support the Communist-led forces because they do not like the present Greek Government. The political amnesty offered by the Greek Government offers to all the opportunity to cooperate in making democratic Greek institutions work.

We are planning aid to Greece with the hope and intention that conditions will be created in which the Greek Government can achieve more efficient administration and perfect its democratic processes.

2. Harry S Truman Outlines a Program for Greece and Turkey, 1947

The peoples of a number of countries of the world have recently had totalitarian regimes forced upon them against their will. The Government of the United States has made frequent protests against coercion and intimidation, in violation of the Yalta agreement, in Poland, Rumania, and Bulgaria. I must also state that in a number of other countries there have been similar developments.

At the present moment in world history nearly every nation must choose between alternative ways of life. The choice is too often not a free one.

One way of life is based upon the will of the majority, and is distinguished by free institutions, representative government, free elections, guarantees of individual liberty, freedom of speech and religion, and freedom from political oppression.

The second way of life is based upon the will of a minority forcibly imposed upon the majority. It relies upon terror and oppression, a controlled press and radio, fixed elections, and the suppression of personal freedoms.

I believe that it must be the policy of the United States to support free peoples who are resisting attempted subjugation by armed minorities or by outside pressures.

I believe that we must assist free peoples to work out their own destinies in their own way.

I believe that our help should be primarily through economic and financial aid which is essential to economic stability and orderly political processes.

The world is not static, and the *status quo* is not sacred. But we cannot allow changes in the *status quo* in violation of the Charter of the United Nations by such methods as coercion, or by such subterfuges as political infiltration. In helping free and independent nations to maintain their freedom, the United States will be giving effect to the principles of the Charter of the United Nations.

It is necessary only to glance at a map to realize that the survival and integrity of the Greek nation are of grave importance in a much wider situation. If Greece should fall under the control of an armed minority, the effect upon its neighbor, Turkey, would be immediate and serious. Confusion and disorder might well spread throughout the entire Middle East.

Moreover, the disappearance of Greece as an independent state would have a profound effect upon those countries in Europe whose peoples are struggling against great difficulties to maintain their freedoms and their independence while they repair the damages of war.

It would be an unspeakable tragedy if these countries, which have struggled so long against overwhelming odds, should lose that victory for which they sacrificed so much. Collapse of free institutions and loss of independence would be disastrous not only for them but for the world. Discouragement and possibly failure would quickly be the lot of neighboring peoples striving to maintain their freedom and independence. . . .

We must take immediate and resolute action.

I therefore ask the Congress to provide authority for assistance to Greece and Turkey in the amount of $400,000,000 for the period ending June 30, 1948. In requesting these funds, I have taken into consideration the maximum amount of relief assistance which would be furnished to Greece out of the $350,000,000 which I recently requested that the Congress authorize for the prevention of starvation and suffering in countries devastated by the war.

In addition to funds, I ask the Congress to authorize the detail of American civilian and military personnel to Greece and Turkey, at the request of those countries, to assist in the tasks of reconstruction, and for the purpose of supervising the use of such financial and material assistance as may be furnished. I recommend that authority also be provided for the instruction and training of selected Greek and Turkish personnel.

3. The Soviet Reaction to the Truman Doctrine, 1947

The pathetic appeal of the Tsaldaris Government to the U.S.A. is clear evidence of the bankruptcy of the political regime in Greece. But the matter does not lie solely with the Greek Monarchists and their friends, now cracked up to American Congressmen as the direct descendants of the heroes of Thermopylae: it is well known that the real masters of Greece have been and are the British military authorities.

British troops have been on Greek territory since 1944. On Churchill's initiative, Britain took on herself the responsibility for "stabilising" political conditions in Greece. The British authorities did not confine themselves to perpetuating the rule of the reactionary, anti-democratic forces in Greece, making no scruple in supporting ex-collaborators with the Germans. The entire political and economic activities under a number of short-lived Greek Governments have been carried on under close British control and direction.

Today we can see the results of this policy—complete bankruptcy. British troops failed to bring peace and tranquility to tormented Greece. The Greek people have been plunged into the abyss of new sufferings, of hunger and poverty. Civil war takes on ever fiercer forms.

Was not the presence of foreign troops on Greek territory instrumental in bringing about this state of affairs? Does not Britain, who proclaimed herself the guardian of Greece, bear responsibility for the bankruptcy of her charge?

. . . Truman did not even consider it necessary to wait for the findings of the Security Council Commission specially sent to Greece to investigate the situation on the spot.

Truman, indeed, failed to reckon either with the international organisation or with the sovereignty of Greece. What will be left of Greek sovereignty when the "American military and civilian personnel" gets to work in Greece by means of the 250 million dollars brought into that country? The sovereignty and independence of Greece will be the first victims of such singular "defense." . . .

Henry Wallace and several other leading American figures came out with a sharply negative response to Truman's message.

We are now witnessing a fresh intrusion of the U.S.A. into the affairs of other states. American claims to leadership in international affairs grow parallel with the growing appetite of the American quarters concerned. But the American leaders, in the new historical circumstances, fail to reckon with the fact that the old methods of the colonizers and die-hard politicians have out-lived their time and are doomed to failure. In this lies the chief weakness of Truman's message.

4. Senator Arthur H. Vandenberg, Jr., Justifies a Bipartisan Foreign Policy, 1947

May 12, 1947

You ask me whether there is any "precedent" for the action we are taking in Greece and Turkey. Of course, there are many partial precedents in respect to relief for stricken countries and even for "military missions." But I doubt whether there is any over-all "precedent." But I am afraid we cannot rely upon "precedents" in facing the utterly unprecedented condition in the world today.

Certainly there is no "precedent" for today's world-wide cleavage between democracy and communism. Perhaps, however, there is something of a "parallel" in remembering what occurred prior to a similar cleavage between democracy and naziism when we surely learned that we cannot escape trouble by trying to run away from it and when "appeasement" proved to be a fatal investment. Of course, we shall never know whether history would have been different if we had all stood up to the aggressor at Munich. But at least we know what it cost to "lie down." Perhaps this is a "precedent." . . .

Greece must be helped or Greece sinks permanently into the communist order. Turkey inevitably follows. Then comes the chain reaction which might sweep from the Dardanelles to the China sea. . . . I do not know whether our new American policy can succeed in arresting these subversive trends (which ultimately represent a direct threat to us). I can only say that I think the adventure is worth trying as an alternative to another "Munich" and perhaps to another war (against the occurrence of which every human effort must be made).

March 24, 1947

The trouble is that these "crises" never reach Congress until they have developed to a point where Congressional discretion is pathetically restricted. When things finally reach a point where a President asks us to "declare war" there usually is nothing left except to "declare war." In the present instance, the overriding fact is that the President has made a long-delayed statement regarding Communism on-the-march which must be supported if there is any hope of ever impressing Moscow with the necessity of paying any sort of peaceful attention to us whatever. If we turned the President down—after his speech to the joint Congressional session—we might as well either resign ourselves to a complete Communist encirclement and infiltration or else get ready for World War No. Three.

5. Mr. "X" on the Sources of Soviet Conduct, 1947

[I]t will be clearly seen that the Soviet pressure against the free institutions of the Western world is something that can be contained by the adroit and vigilant application of counter-force at a series of constantly shifting geographical and political points, corresponding to the shifts and maneuvers of Soviet policy, but which cannot be charmed or talked out of existence. The Russians look forward to a duel of infinite duration, and they see that already they have scored great successes. . . .

It is clear that the United States cannot expect in the foreseeable future to enjoy political intimacy with the Soviet regime. It must continue to regard the Soviet Union as a rival, not a partner, in the political arena. It must continue to expect that Soviet policies will reflect no abstract love of peace and stability, no real faith in the possibility of a permanent happy coexistence of the Socialist and capitalist worlds, but rather a cautious, persistent pressure toward the disruption and weakening of all rival influence and rival power.

Balanced against this are the facts that Russia, as opposed to the Western world in general, is still by far the weaker party, the Soviet policy is highly flexible, and that Soviet society may well contain deficiencies which will eventually weaken its own total potential. This would of itself warrant the United States entering with reasonable confidence upon a policy of firm containment, designed to confront the Russians with unalterable counter-force at every point where they show signs of encroaching upon the interests of a peaceful and stable world. . . .

It would be an exaggeration to say that American behavior unassisted and alone could exercise a power of life and death over the Communist movement and bring about the early fall of Soviet power in Russia. But the United States has it in its power to increase enormously the strains under which Soviet policy must operate, to force upon the Kremlin a far greater degree of moderation and circumspection than it has had to observe in recent years, and in this way to promote tendencies which must eventually find their outlet in either the break-up or the gradual mellowing of Soviet power.

6. George F. Kennan Recalls an Early Response to the Truman Doctrine, 1947

I accepted the conclusion, to which many others in the government had arrived, that (and I use the words of the War College presentation) "if nothing were done to stiffen the backs of the non-Communist elements in Greece at this juncture the Communist elements would soon succeed in seizing power and in establishing a totalitarian dictatorship along the lines already visible in other Balkan countries." . . . Communist rule, I thought, "would probably be successfully consolidated in the long run and might some day have most unfortunate strategic consequences from the standpoint of any military adversary of the Soviet Union." And more important still were the probable repercussions which such a development would have on neighboring areas. . . .

So much for the reasons for our limited intervention in Greece. Why, then, approving this action, did I take exception to the language of the President's message?

I took exception to it primarily because of the sweeping nature of the commitments which it implied. The heart of the message and the passage that has subsequently been most frequently quoted was this:

I believe it must be the policy of the United States to support free peoples who are resisting subjugation by armed minorities or by outside pressures.

I believe that we must assist free peoples to work out their own destinies in their own way.

This passage, and others as well, placed our aid to Greece in the framework of a universal policy rather than in that of a specific decision addressed to a specific set of circumstances. It implied that what we had decided to do in the case of Greece was something we would be prepared to do in the case of any other country, provided only that it was faced with the threat of "subjugation by armed minorities or by outside pressures."

It seemed to me highly uncertain that we would invariably find it in our interests or within our means to extend assistance to countries that found themselves in this extremity. The mere fact of their being in such a plight was only one of the criteria that had to be taken into account in determining our action. The establishment of the existence of such a threat was only the beginning, not the end, of the process of decision. I listed, in my presentation to the War College, three specific considerations that had supported our decision to extend assistance to Greece:

A. The problem at hand is one within our economic, technical, and financial capabilities.

B. If we did not take such action, the resulting situation might redound very decidedly to the advantage of our political adversaries.

C. If, on the other hand, we do take the action in question, there is good reason to hope that the favorable consequences will carry far beyond the limits of Greece itself.

These considerations, I pointed out, did not necessarily apply to all other regions. I doubted, for example, that any of them would fully apply in the case of China: the first most definitely would not.

Nevertheless, the misapprehension already conveyed was, as I see it, never entirely corrected. Throughout the ensuing two decades the conduct of our foreign policy would continue to be bedeviled by people in our own government as well as in other governments who could not free themselves from the belief that all another country had to do, in order to qualify for American aid, was to demonstrate the existence of a Communist threat. Since almost no country was without a Communist minority, this assumption carried very far. And as time went on, the firmness of understanding for these distinctions on the part of our own public and governmental establishment appeared to grow weaker rather than stronger. In the 1960s so absolute would be the value attached, even by people within the government, to the mere existence of a Communist threat, that such a threat would be viewed as calling, in the case of Southeast Asia, for an American response on a tremendous scale, without serious regard even to those main criteria that most of us in 1947 would have thought it natural and essential to apply.

7. Joseph Stalin Eats Greek Crow, 1947

TODAY'S SPECIALTY, WITH TRUMAN DOCTRINE DRESSING

Smith Cartoon reprinted by permission of Newspaper Enterprise Association, Inc.

Chapter 28:
Document Set 1 References

1. Dean Acheson Explains the Truman Doctrine, 1947
"Statement by Acting Secretary of State Dean Acheson Before the Committee on Foreign Relations on an Explanation of the Truman Doctrine," March 24, 1947, Raymond Dennet and Robert Turner, eds., *Documents on American Foreign Relations* (Princeton: Princeton University Press, 1949), Vol. 9, 1947, pp. 650–658.

2. Harry S Truman Outlines a Program for Greece and Turkey, 1947
Harry S Truman, Speech, March 12, 1947, *Public Papers of the Presidents, Harry S Truman, 1947* (Washington, D.C.: Government Printing Office, 1963), pp. 176–180.

3. The Soviet Reaction to the Truman Doctrine, 1947
Soviet News, 2 (March 15, 1947).

4. Senator Arthur H. Vandenberg, Jr., Justifies a Bipartisan Foreign Policy, 1947
Arthur H. Vandenberg, Jr., to R. F. Moffett, May 12, March 24, 1947, in Arthur H. Vandenberg, Jr. (with the Collaboration of Joe Alex Morris), ed., *The Private Papers of Senator Vandenberg* (Boston: Houghton Mifflin, 1952), pp. 341–342.

5. Mr. "X" on the Sources of Soviet Conduct, 1947
"X," "The Sources of Soviet Conduct," *Foreign Affairs,* 25 (July 1947).

6. George F. Kennan Recalls an Early Response to the Truman Doctrine, 1947
George F. Kennan, *Memoirs, 1925–1950* (Boston: Little, Brown, 1967), pp. 316, 319–320, 322.

7. Joseph Stalin Eats Greek Crow, 1947
Dorman H. Smith, "Today's Specialty, with Truman Doctrine Dressing," 1947 (Newspaper Enterprise Association), in Foreign Policy Association, eds., *A Cartoon History of United States Foreign Policy Since World War I* (New York: Vintage, 1967), p. 81.

Chapter 28:
Document Set 1 Credits

DOCUMENT SET 2
The Great Fear Unleashed: The Cold War Comes Home

Postwar tensions with the Soviet Union bred a climate of fear and suspicion in the United States as Americans adjusted to peacetime conditions. The Truman administration's rigidity and militance in foreign policy were matched by the president's commitment to anticommunism at home. Beset by mounting evidence of subversive activity, Truman moved to strengthen internal security amidst conservative charges of laxity, himself contributing to the rising paranoia. The result was an atmosphere of intolerance, described in your textbook as a scramble to find scapegoats for the nation's domestic and foreign problems. Before the hysteria subsided, American political culture became homogenized, while civil liberties suffered their most serious setback since the Great Red Scare of 1919. The documents that follow provide vivid evidence of the link between a Cold War foreign policy and intolerance on the home front.

It was not coincidental that nine days after the declaration of the Truman Doctrine, the president issued a loyalty order intended to root out subversives in government service. As you review his order, focus on Truman's justification for action and the grounds established for a person's removal from government employment.

Your textbook indicates that anticommunism had long been present in Congress, where the House Un-American Activities Committee became the focal point for efforts to explore subversion. A dramatic illustration is provided by the 1947 HUAC hearings described in your textbook. Although labor unions and political dissenters drew the committee's fire, its attack on the entertainment industry caught the public imagination as did few others. The documents explore the ramifications of HUAC's interest in the motion picture industry. Review FBI Director J. Edgar Hoover's analysis of alleged communist infiltration of the media and its significance. An excerpt from the autobiography of film director Edward Dmytryk, who refused to cooperate with the committee in 1947 but changed his mind in 1951, reveals not only the presence of political radicals in Hollywood but also the constitutional issue raised by the Hollywood resisters. Both Dmytryk's recollection and the personal memoir of screenwriter/playwright Lillian Hellman document the insidious blacklist that was the film industry's response to anticommunist political pressure. Notice what these documents reveal about the personal, constitutional, and political implications of the anticommunist crusade.

The concluding documents record the climax of the Red Scare in the unparalleled demagoguery of Wisconsin Senator Joseph R. McCarthy. As you review the excerpts from his Wheeling speech (1950) and sweeping attack on Secretary of Defense George C. Marshall (1951), identify the targets of the senator's criticism. Be also aware of the close linkage between foreign policy and domestic politics in the age of the Cold War. Try to assess the relationship between anticommunist hysteria and the Democratic party's decline, described in your textbook as the end of an era.

Questions for Analysis

1. What were the sources of anticommunism in the postwar United States? What evidence do the documents provide to explain domestic support for Joseph McCarthy and his predecessors? What was the basis for the anticommunist appeal?

2. What were the similarities and differences between the Red Scare of 1919 and the anticommunism of the Truman years? Consider the instigators, targets, duration, and implications of the two movements.

3. Using the loyalty program as a point of departure, evaluate the Truman administration as a carrier of the liberal social, economic, and political tradition. How did the demands of the Cold War domestic environment influence the prospects for reform? What did "liberalism" mean in the immediate postwar years, and how was it affected by the anticommunist crusade?

4. Why did American opponents of communism focus their attention on the motion picture industry between 1947 and 1951? In what way did the House Un-American Activities Committee hearings document the charges against Hollywood?

5. What were the constitutional and civil liberties issues at stake during the second Red Scare? What evidence of these concerns can be found in the documents? How did the accused respond to the assault against them? With what results?

1. President Truman's Loyalty Order, 1947

Executive Order 9835
Prescribing Procedures for the Administration of an Employees Loyalty Program in the Executive Branch of the Government

Whereas each employee of the government of the United States is endowed with a measure of trusteeship over the democratic processes which are the heart and sinew of the United States; and

Whereas it is of vital importance that persons employed in the federal service be of complete and unswerving loyalty to the United States; and

Whereas, although the loyalty of by far the overwhelming majority of all government employees is beyond question, the presence within the government service of any disloyal or subversive person constitutes a threat to our democratic processes; and

Whereas maximum protection must be afforded the United States against infiltration of disloyal persons into the ranks of its employees, and equal protection from unfounded accusations of disloyalty must be afforded the loyal employees of the government:

Now, therefore, by virtue of the authority vested in me by the Constitution and statutes of the United States, . . . it is hereby, in the interest of the internal management of the government, ordered as follows:

Part I—Investigation of Applicants

1. There shall be a loyalty investigation of every person entering the civilian employment of any department or agency of the executive branch of the federal government. . . .

Part V—Standards

1. The standard for the refusal of employment or the removal from employment in an executive department or agency on grounds relating to loyalty shall be that, on all the evidence, reasonable grounds exist for belief that the person involved is disloyal to the government of the United States.

2. Activities and associations of an applicant or employee which may be considered in connection with the determination of disloyalty may include one or more of the following:

a. Sabotage, espionage, or attempts or preparations therefor, or knowingly associating with spies or saboteurs;

b. Treason or sedition or advocacy thereof;

c. Advocacy of revolution or force or violence to alter the constitutional form of government of the United States;

d. Intentional, unauthorized disclosure to any person, under circumstances which may indicate disloyalty to the United States, of documents or information of a confidential or nonpublic character obtained by the person making the disclosure as a result of his employment by the government of the United States;

e. Performing or attempting to perform his duties, or otherwise acting, so as to serve the interests of another government in preference to the interests of the United States;

f. Membership in, affiliation with, or sympathetic association with any foreign or domestic organization, association, movement, group, or combination of persons, designated by the attorney general as totalitarian, fascist, communist, or subversive, or as having adopted a policy of advocating or approving the commission of acts of force or violence to deny other persons their rights under the Constitution of the United States, or as seeking to alter the form of government of the United States by unconstitutional means.

2. J. Edgar Hoover Notes the Communist Interest in Hollywood, 1947

The party has departed from depending upon the printed word as its medium of propaganda and has taken to the air. Its members and sympathizers have not only infiltrated the airways but they are now persistently seeking radio channels.

The American Communists launched a furtive attack on Hollywood in 1935 by the issuance of a directive calling for a concentration in Hollywood. The orders called for action on two fronts: (1) an effort to infiltrate the labor unions; (2) infiltrate the so-called intellectual and creative fields.

In movie circles, Communists developed an effective defense a few years ago in meeting criticism. They would counter with the question, "After all, what is the matter with communism?" It was effec-

tive because many persons did not possess adequate knowledge of the subject to give an intelligent answer.

Some producers and studio heads realized the possibility that the entire industry faces serious embarrassment because it could become a springboard for Communist activities. Communist activity in Hollywood is effective and is furthered by Communists and sympathizers using the prestige of prominent persons to serve, often unwittingly, the Communist cause. The party is content and highly pleased if it is possible to have inserted in a picture a line, a scene, a sequence conveying the Communist lesson and, more particularly, if they can keep out anti-Communist lessons.

3. Edward Dmytryk Recalls the Hollywood Ten in Washington, 1947

Since *Crossfire* was a worldwide smash, my attack, as well as Adrian's, centered on the committee's ethnic bias and its attempts to limit freedom of speech in the area of national self-criticism. But none of our lawyers really expected that we would be heard, and the strategy was say nothing, hide under the possible cover of the First Amendment, and hope for a favorable verdict from the Supreme Court. "Taking the Fifth" was never considered, though it would have kept us out of jail; the implication of guilt was considered too dangerous. . . .

With all the public feeling in our favor, Bart Crum suggested that Adrian and I should testify freely, which we were perfectly willing to do. We felt it might serve to pull the committee's fangs. You'd have thought we were offering to atomize the Kremlin. The unanimity rule was invoked, and that was that. From their point of view, they were absolutely right. If we had answered any substantive questions at all, we would have been legally required to give names if we were asked to. If we refused to name party members, as, at that time, we certainly would have done, we would still be cited for contempt. If we had given the names, the other members of our group

would have been in the soup. Eventually, that's where we wound up anyway, but at this point the battle had barely begun and our eyes were fixed on a liberal Supreme Court. With no argument, we put our suggestion aside and on the 27th of October, entered the chamber prepared to face the inquisitors.

The chamber was crowded; the real fun was about to begin. . . . Dore Schary sat beside me as we watched John Howard Lawson being sworn in. He was the leader and would set the tone of our attack. Unfortunately, Lawson was tone-deaf.

It started with the usual identification by name and address. Then Lawson requested permission to read a statement. After a bit of bickering, Thomas asked to look at it before making his decision. He was, as they say in court, making a record. The statement was handed over to the chairman, who made only a slight pretense of reading it, then ruled that it was irrelevant. Lawson started to argue; Thomas banged his gavel. The exchange got so hot that the chairman nearly forgot to ask what came to be called "the sixty-four dollar question": "Are you now or have you ever been a member of the Communist party?"

Now Lawson started shouting in earnest, trying to enumerate his reasons for refusing to answer the question. Between gavel poundings, the chairman screamed, "Answer yes or no!" Shouting and banging—banging and shouting. It was a miserable scene. I was hit by a feeling I had had once before, when a car skidded into me across a wet street. "This is it," I thought. I scrunched down in my seat and turned to Dore.

"What are my chances at the studio now?" I asked.

"You have an ironclad contract," he replied.

And so it went for the rest of the hearing. I could literally feel the listeners' sympathies oozing away with each shout from one of our group. Thomas had made a ridiculous show of himself with his shouting and free use of the gavel; now we were matching him shout for shout—it was a fight we couldn't win. . . .

We made it back to Hollywood, basking for a short time in the light of what our leftist friends assured us was a fine and glorious victory, but the decision that would affect our lives was being made at the Waldorf-Astoria Hotel in New York. There, on November 27, 1947, the representatives of the motion-picture industry formally decided to fire any accused worker who would not freely answer all questions asked by the Un-American Activities Committee and who could not clear himself of charges that he was or had been a member of the Communist party. The following day, since Dore refused to be the hatchet man, N. Peter Rathvon called Scott and me into his office and asked us once more to recant and to purge ourselves. With hardly any sense of martyrdom at all, we refused. In that case, he informed us, we were no longer employees of RKO. So much for ironclad contracts.

4. Lillian Hellman Defies HUAC, 1952

May 19, 1952

Honorable John S. Wood
Chairman
House Committee on Un-American Activities
Room 226 Old House Office Building
Washington 25, D.C.

Dear Mr. Wood:

As you know, I am under subpoena to appear before your Committee on May 21, 1952.

I am most willing to answer all questions about myself. I have nothing to hide from your Committee and there is nothing in my life of which I am ashamed. I have been advised by counsel that under the Fifth Amendment I have a constitutional privilege to decline to answer any questions about my political opinions, activities and associations, on the grounds of self-incrimination. I do not wish to claim this privilege. I am ready and willing to testify before the representatives of our Government as to my own opinions and my own actions, regardless of any risks or consequences to myself.

But I am advised by counsel that if I answer the Committee's questions about myself, I must also answer questions about other people and that if I refuse to do so, I can be cited for contempt. My counsel tells me that if I answer questions about myself, I will have waived my rights under the Fifth Amendment and could be forced legally to answer questions about others. This is very difficult for a layman to understand. But there is one principle that I do understand: I am not willing, now or in the future, to bring bad trouble to people who, in my past association with them, were completely innocent of any talk or any action that was disloyal or subversive. I do not like subversion or disloyalty in any form and if I had ever seen any I would have considered it my duty to have reported it to the proper authorities. But to hurt innocent people whom I knew many years ago in order to save myself is, to me, inhuman and indecent and dishonorable. I cannot and will not cut my conscience to fit this year's fashions, even though I long ago came to the conclusion that I was not a political person and could have no comfortable place in any political group.

I was raised in an old-fashioned American tradition and there were certain homely things that were taught to me: to try to tell the truth, not to bear false witness, not to harm my neighbor, to be loyal to my country, and so on. In general, I respected these ideals of Christian honor and did as well with them as I knew how. It is my belief that you will agree with these simple rules of human decency and will not expect me to violate the good American tradition from which they spring. I would, therefore, like to come before you and speak of myself.

I am prepared to waive the privilege against self-incrimination and to tell you anything you wish to know about my views or actions if your Committee will agree to refrain from asking me to name other people. If the Committee is unwilling to give me this assurance, I will be forced to plead the privilege of the Fifth Amendment at the hearing.

A reply to this letter would be appreciated.

Sincerely yours,

Lillian Hellman

The letter that I sent the Committee on May 19, 1952, had been refused by letter on May 20. It was, therefore, necessary for me to do what I did not want to do: take the Fifth Amendment. The Fifth Amendment is, of course, a wise section of the Constitution: you cannot be forced to incriminate yourself. But the amendment has difficulties that are hard for a layman to understand. . . .

The opening questions were standard: what was my name, where was I born, what was my occupation, what were the titles of my plays. It didn't take long to get to what really interested them: my time in Hollywood, which studios had I worked for, what periods of what years, with some mysterious emphasis on 1937. (My time in Spain, I thought, but I was wrong.)

Had I met a writer called Martin Berkeley? (I had never, still have never, met Martin Berkeley, although Hammett told me later that I had once sat at a lunch table of sixteen or seventeen people with him in the old Metro-Goldwyn-Mayer commissary.) I said I must refuse to answer that question. . . .

Was I a member of the Communist Party, had I been, what year had I stopped being? How could I harm such people as Martin Berkeley by admitting I had known them, and so on. At times I couldn't follow the reasoning, at times I understood full well that in refusing to answer questions about membership in the Party I had, of course, trapped myself into a seeming admission that I once had been.

But in the middle of one of the questions about my past, something so remarkable happened that I am to this day convinced that the unknown gentleman who spoke had a great deal to do with the rest of my life. A voice from the press gallery had been for at least three or four minutes louder than the other voices. (By this time, I think, the press had finished reading my letter to the Committee and were discussing it.) The loud voice had been answered by a less loud voice, but no words could be distinguished. Suddenly a clear voice said, "Thank God somebody finally had the guts to do it."

5. Joseph R. McCarthy's Wheeling Speech, 1950

Five years after a world war has been won, men's hearts should anticipate a long peace, and men's minds should be free from the heavy weight that comes with war. But this is not such a period—for this is not a period of peace. This is a time of the "cold war." This is a time when all the world is split into two vast, increasingly hostile armed camps. . . .

The reason why we find ourselves in a position of impotency is not because our only powerful potential enemy has sent men to invade our shores, but rather because of the traitorous actions of those who have been treated so well by this Nation. It has not been the less fortunate or members of minority groups who have been selling this Nation out, but rather those who have had all the benefits that the wealthiest nation on earth has had to offer—the finest homes, the finest college education, and the finest jobs in Government we can give.

This is glaringly true in the State Department. There the bright young men who are born with silver spoons in their mouths are the ones who have been the worst. . . . In my opinion the State Department, which is one of the most important government departments, is thoroughly infested with Communists.

I have in my hand 57 cases of individuals who would appear to be either card carrying members or certainly loyal to the Communist Party, but who nevertheless are still helping to shape our foreign policy. . . .

As you know, very recently the Secretary of State proclaimed his loyalty to a man guilty of what has always been considered as the most abominable of all crimes—of being a traitor to the people who gave him a position of great trust. The Secretary of State in attempting to justify his continued devotion to the man who sold out the Christian world to the atheistic world, referred to Christ's Sermon on the Mount as a justification and reason therefor, and the reaction of the American people to this would have made the heart of Abraham Lincoln happy.

When this pompous diplomat in striped pants, with a phony British accent, proclaimed to the American people that Christ on the Mount endorsed communism, high treason, and betrayal of a sacred trust, the blasphemy was so great that it awakened the dormant indignation of the American people.

He has lighted the spark which is resulting in a moral uprising and will end only when the whole sorry mess of twisted, warped thinkers are swept from the national scene so that we may have a new birth of national honesty and decency in government.

6. McCarthy Attacks George C. Marshall, 1951

How can we account for our present situation unless we believe that men high in this Government are concerting to deliver us to disaster? This must be the product of a great conspiracy, a conspiracy on a scale so immense as to dwarf any previous such venture in the history of man. A conspiracy of infamy so black that, when it is finally exposed, its principals shall be forever deserving of the maledictions of all honest men.

Who constitutes the highest circles of this conspiracy? About that we cannot be sure. We are convinced that Dean Acheson, who steadfastly serves the interests of nations other than his own, the friend of Alger Hiss, who supported him in his hour of retribution, who contributed to his defense fund, must be high on the roster. The President? He is their captive. I have wondered, as have you, why he did not dispense with so great a liability as Acheson to his own and his party's interests. It is now clear to me. In the relationship of master and man, did you ever hear of man firing master? Truman is a satisfactory front. He is only dimly aware of what is going on. . . .

What can be made of this unbroken series of decisions and acts contributing to the strategy of defeat? They cannot be attributed to incompetence. If Marshall were merely stupid, the laws of probability would dictate that part of his decisions would serve this country's interest. If Marshall is innocent of guilty intention, how could he be trusted to guide the defense of this country further? We have declined so precipitously in relation to the Soviet Union in the last 6 years. How much swifter may be our fall into disaster with Marshall at the helm? Where will all this stop? That is not a rhetorical question: Ours is not a rhetorical danger. Where next will Marshall carry us? It is useless to suppose that his nominal superior will ask him to resign. He cannot even dispense with Acheson.

What is the objective of the great conspiracy? I think it is clear from what has occurred and is now occurring: to diminish the United States in world affairs, to weaken us militarily, to confuse our spirit with talk of surrender in the Far East and to impair our will to resist evil. To what end? To the end that we shall be contained, frustrated and finally fall victim to Soviet intrigue from within and Russian military might from without. . . .

It is the great crime of the Truman administration that it has refused to undertake the job of ferreting the enemy from its ranks. I once puzzled over that refusal. The President, I said, is a loyal American; why does he not lead in this enterprise? I think that I know why he does not. The President is not master in his own house. Those who are master there not only have a desire to protect the sappers and miners—they could not do otherwise. They themselves are not free. They belong to a larger conspiracy, the world-wide web of which has been spun from Moscow. It was Moscow, for example, which decreed that the United States should execute its loyal friend, the Republic of China. The executioners were that well-identified group headed by Acheson and George Catlett Marshall.

Chapter 28:
Document Set 2 References

1. President Truman's Loyalty Order, 1947
   Harry S Truman, Executive Order 9835, in *Code of Federal Regulations,* Title 3—The President, 1943–1948 Compilation (Washington, D.C.: Government Printing Office, 1957), pp. 627–631.

2. J. Edgar Hoover Notes the Communist Interest in Hollywood, 1947
   J. Edgar Hoover, Testimony, *Investigation of Un-American Propaganda Activities in the United States, Hearings Before the Committee on Un-American Activities, House of Representatives,* 80th Cong., 1st Sess., Washington, D.C.: Government Printing Office, 1947, part 2, pp. 33–50.

3. Edward Dmytryk Recalls the Hollywood Ten in Washington, 1947

   Edward Dmytryk, *It's a Hell of a Life But Not a Bad Living* (New York: Times Books, 1978), pp. 98–99, 103.

4. Lillian Hellman Defies HUAC, 1952
   Lillian Hellman, *Scoundrel Time* (New York: Bantam, 1976), pp. 89–91, 96, 101–102, 105–106.

5. Joseph R. McCarthy's Wheeling Speech, 1950
   Joseph R. McCarthy, Remarks, *Congressional Record,* 81st Cong., 2nd Sess., pp. 1954–1957.

6. McCarthy Attacks George C. Marshall, 1951
   Joseph R. McCarthy, Speech, June 14, 1951, *Congressional Record,* 82nd Cong., 1st Sess., 1951, pp. 6556–6603.

Chapter 28:
Document Set 2 Credits

3. From *It's a Hell of a Life But Not a Bad Living* by Edward Dmytryk. Copyright © 1979 by Edward Dmytryk. Reprinted by permission of Times Books, a division of Random House, Inc.

4. From *Scoundrel Time* by Lillian Hellmann, copyright © 1976 by Lillian Hellman. By permission of Little, Brown and Company.

CHAPTER 28

DOCUMENT SET 3
Korea: The Forgotten War

Against the background of an escalating Cold War abroad and the rise of domestic anticommunism, the Truman administration faced its most serious foreign policy challenge in June 1950, when Soviet-backed North Korean troops poured across the 38th parallel in a full-scale invasion of the Republic of Korea. Viewing the North Korean attack as a test of the containment policy, President Harry S Truman responded by committing American troops to the defense of South Korea and securing United Nations support. What followed was a sometimes frustrating attempt to wage a limited war that was poorly understood by an American public schooled in the philosophy of total victory.

As you review the following documents, try to gain a clear impression of the war's origins. Assess the regime of Syngman Rhee and consider President Truman's reservations about his leadership. Think about Truman's consciousness of history as he formulated American military and foreign policy during the Korean crisis.

Your analysis should focus on the definition of American goals in Korea and the debate over the proper means to achieve them. From the beginning,

Truman's policies were controversial. Ask yourself why the president was so bitterly attacked, especially by conservatives. Be sure to develop a working definition of the term "limited warfare."

These policy disagreements cannot be divorced from the words and deeds of the brilliant but egocentric American theater commander in Korea, General Douglas MacArthur. Relying upon the documents, explore his differences with the administration over strategy, tactics, and objectives. As you evaluate MacArthur's position, place the controversy over his actions within the broader context of American constitutional tradition and the history of civil-military relations. Determine why Truman and his military advisers concluded that MacArthur had to be relieved of command.

Finally, think about the public response to the president's decision, and relate it to the public's attitude toward a war entering a second, inconclusive year. Why were Americans so concerned about Truman's action? Was their dissatisfaction tied to the unique characteristics of the Korean conflict and the new international realities of the Cold War era?

Questions for Analysis

1. To what extent was President Truman justified in the decision to intervene in Korea in June 1950? How was his action influenced by history? What constitutional issues did the president's orders raise?

2. What were the intentions and capabilities of the North Koreans and how were they related to the mission of United Nations forces? What were the objectives of American intervention?

3. What was the basis of the disagreement between Truman and MacArthur? Which of them bore heaviest responsibility for the rift in civil-military relations? Was it unavoidable? What issues did it raise?

4. What was "limited war" and what limitations did it impose on belligerents? Were American policies justified? Is a democratic society capable of the restraints assumed in the theory of "limited war"?

5. Why do you think the Korean conflict has not gained greater public attention? In what way do the documents help you to answer this question?

1. President Harry S Truman Recalls the Origins of the Korean Conflict, 1950

We knew, however, that the Russians had built up a "People's Army" in North Korea. We knew that Communist infiltration into South Korea was considerable. We knew that the new government of Syngman Rhee would find it difficult to resist effectively if it were attacked. However, a careful estimate had been made by our experts of the chances of survival of the new Republic of Korea, and the conclusion had been reached that "its prospects for survival may be considered favorable as long as it can continue to receive large-scale aid from the U.S.". . . .

To bolster Korea's military position, I approved a defense agreement, which was signed on January 26, 1950. We continued, however, to be concerned over the internal and economic situation in South Korea. One of the reasons, though a minor one, why I had approved the policy of troop withdrawal was the danger that we might be able to escape involvement in the political arguments of the young state. President Syngman Rhee is a man of strong convictions and has little patience with those who differ with him. From the moment of his return to Korea in 1945, he attracted to himself men of extreme right-wing attitudes and disagreed sharply with the political leaders of more moderate views, and the withdrawal of military government removed restraints that had prevented arbitrary actions against his opponents. I did not care for the methods used by Rhee's police to break up political meetings and control political enemies, and I was deeply concerned over the Rhee government's lack of concern about the serious inflation that swept the country. Yet we had no choice but to support Rhee. . . .

June 27, 1950

Statement by the President

In Korea the Government forces, which were armed to prevent border raids and to preserve internal security, were attacked by invading forces from North Korea. The Security Council of the United Nations called upon the invading troops to cease hostilities and to withdraw to the 38th parallel. This they have not done, but on the contrary have pressed the attack. The Security Council called upon all members of the United Nations to render every assistance to the United Nations in the execution of this resolu-tion. In these circumstances I have ordered United States air and sea forces to give the Korean Government troops cover and support.

The attack upon Korea makes it plain beyond all doubt that Communism has passed beyond the use of subversion to conquer independent nations and will now use armed invasion and war. It has defied the orders of the Security Council of the United Nations issued to preserve international peace and security. In these circumstances the occupation of Formosa by Communist forces would be a direct threat to the security of the Pacific area and to United States forces performing their lawful and necessary functions in that area.

Accordingly I have ordered the Seventh Fleet to prevent any attack upon Formosa. As a corollary of this action I am calling upon the Chinese Government on Formosa to cease all air and sea operations against the mainland. The Seventh Fleet will see that this is done. The determination of the future status of Formosa must await the restoration of security in the Pacific, a peace settlement with Japan, or consideration by the United Nations.

I have also directed that United States Forces in the Philippines be strengthened and that military assistance to the Philippine Government be accelerated.

I have similarly directed acceleration in the furnishing of military assistance to the forces of France and the Associated States in Indo-China and the dispatch of a military mission to provide close working relations with those forces.

I know that all members of the United Nations will consider carefully the consequences of this latest aggression in Korea in defiance of the Charter of the United Nations. A return to the rule of force in international affairs would have far-reaching effects. The United States will continue to uphold the rule of law.

I have instructed Ambassador Austin, as the representative of the United States to the Security Council, to report these steps to the Council.

Our allies and friends abroad were informed through our diplomatic representatives that it was our feeling that it was essential to the maintenance of peace that this armed aggression against a free nation be met firmly. We let it be known that we considered the Korean situation vital as a symbol of the strength and determination of the West. Firmness now would be the only way to deter new actions in other portions of the world. Not only in Asia but in Europe, the Middle East, and elsewhere the confidence of peoples in countries adjacent to the Soviet Union would be very adversely affected, in our judgment, if we failed to take action to protect a country established under our auspices and confirmed in its freedom by action of the United Nations. If, however, the threat to South Korea was met firmly and successfully, it would add to our successes in Iran, Berlin, and Greece, a fourth success in opposition to the aggressive moves of the Communists. And each success, we suggested to our allies, was likely to add to the caution of the Soviets in undertaking new efforts of this kind. Thus the safety and prospects for peace of the free world would be increased.

2. General Douglas MacArthur Outlines His Objectives in Korea, 1951

General Headquarters,
Supreme Commander for the Allied Powers,
Tokyo, Japan, March 20, 1951

Hon. Joseph W. Martin, Jr.,
House of Representatives, Washington, D.C.

Dear Congressman Martin:

I am most grateful for your note of the 8th forwarding me a copy of your address of February 12. The latter I have read with much interest, and find that with the passage of years you have certainly lost none of your old-time punch.

My views and recommendations with respect to the situation created by Red China's entry into war against us in Korea have been submitted to Washington in most complete detail. Generally these views are well known and clearly understood, as they follow the conventional pattern of meeting force with maximum counterforce, as we have never failed to do in the past. Your view with respect to the utilization of the Chinese forces on Formosa is in conflict with neither logic nor this tradition.

It seems strangely difficult for some to realize that here in Asia is where the Communist conspirators have elected to make their play for global conquest, and that we have joined the issue thus raised on the battlefield; that here we fight Europe's war with arms while the diplomats there still fight it with words; that if we lose the war to communism in Asia the fall of Europe is inevitable, win it and Europe most probably would avoid war and yet preserve freedom. As you pointed out, we must win. There is no substitute for victory.

With renewed thanks and expressions of most cordial regard, I am

Faithfully yours,

Douglas MacArthur

3. Truman Relieves MacArthur, 1951

I felt compelled to have Joseph Short, my press secretary, call a special news conference for 1 A.M., April 11, which was as quickly as it was possible to have the orders, in their slightly changed form, reproduced.

The reporters were handed a series of papers, the first being my announcement of General MacArthur's relief.

"With deep regret," this announcement read, "I have concluded that General of the Army Douglas MacArthur is unable to give his wholehearted support to the policies of the United States Government and of the United Nations in matters pertaining to his official duties. In view of the specific responsibilities imposed upon me by the Constitution of the United States and the added responsibility which has been entrusted to me by the United Nations, I have decided that I must make a change of command in the Far East. I have, therefore, relieved General MacArthur of his commands and have designated Lieutenant General Matthew B. Ridgway as his successor.

"Full and vigorous debate on matters of national policy is a vital element in the constitutional system of our free democracy. It is fundamental, however, that military commanders must be governed by the policies and directives issued to them in the manner provided by our laws and Constitution. In time of crisis, the consideration is particularly compelling."

4. General Omar N. Bradley Warns Against Global War, 1951

The fundamental military issue that has arisen is whether to increase the risk of a global war by taking additional measures that are open to the United States and its allies. We now have a localized conflict in Korea. Some of the military measures under discussion might well place the United States in the position of responsibility for broadening the war and at the same time losing most if not all of our allies.

General MacArthur has stated that there are certain additional measures which can and should be taken, and that by so doing no unacceptable increased risk of global war will result. . . .

Korea, in spite of the importance of the engagement, must be looked upon with proper perspective. It is just one engagement, just one phase of this battle that we are having with the other power center in the world which opposes us and all we stand for. For 5 years this "guerrilla diplomacy" has been going on. In each of the actions in which we have participated to oppose this gangster conduct, we have risked world war III. But each time we have used methods short of total war. As costly as Berlin and Greece and Korea may be, they are less expensive than the vast destruction which would be inflicted upon all sides if a total war were to be precipitated.

I am under no illusion that our present strategy of using means short of total war to achieve our ends and oppose communism is a guarantee that a world war will not be thrust upon us. But a policy of patience and determination without provoking a world war, while we improve our military power, is one which we believe we must continue to follow.

As long as we keep the conflict within its present scope, we are holding to a minimum the forces we must commit and tie down.

The strategic alternative, enlargement of the war in Korea to include Red China, would probably delight the Kremlin more than anything else we could do. It would necessarily tie down additional forces, especially our seapower and our airpower, while the Soviet Union would not be obliged to put a single man into the conflict.

Under present circumstances we have recommended against enlarging the war. The course of action often described as a "limited war" with Red China would increase the risk we are taking by engaging too much of our power in an area that is not the critical strategic prize.

Red China is not the powerful nation seeking to dominate the world. Frankly, in the opinion of the Joint Chiefs of Staff, this strategy would involve us in the wrong war, at the wrong place, at the wrong time, and with the wrong enemy.

5. A Grieving Parent Charges the Administration with Appeasement, 1951

Senator Harry P. Cain,
Senate Office Building, Washington, D.C.

Dear Senator Cain:

May I appear before your committee to speak for my son; like the 17,000 other sons killed in Korea he fought well; his brother marines have told me how well he died.

His service to his country did not stop with his dying for he left a $5,000 policy, directing it to be used to develop an engine of revolutionary design and great promise he invented. When it is developed and patented I am directed to turn it over, not to his relatives, not to his estate, but to the Navy for the benefit of his country.

Do you think that this unselfishness and that of the other 17,000 entitles them to a small favor from their country? Do you think that it entitles them to be heard by your committee, even if only through the consciences of their fathers, consciences which now trouble them because they did not fight until too late for their sons, fight against the action of our leaders in abandoning American traditions of courage and sending our sons out to die, shackled by appeasement? . . .

To rob our sons of the sweetness and the greatness of life is bad enough, but to cap it by appeasing, by paying blackmail with their lives is to add the final indignity of cheating them in their dying.

We must not allow those who have yet to die to be thus cheated. Having changed the rules by lowering and degrading the things for which Americans are being expected to die, we must in all fairness change the rules by which we send our sons out to do the dying. Having turned from the old American ideals of courage to this alien thing, appeasement and fear, we must no longer deceive them into thinking they will die for the one when it is really the other.

We must either return to the American traditions of honor or revert to the voluntary system of recruiting, or if that fails we should hire mercenaries. Every boy who comes to offer his life should be frankly informed of these new and sadly changed standards of honor. If with his eyes open he desires to go, all right. If he wants no part of a bloody one-hand-tied-behind-the-back stalemate in a bull pen with no hope for victory, he should have the option of declining. I want to urge legislation to implement such an option.

You have listened to witnesses in defense of the President and his Secretaries of Defense and State; in defense of our top military leaders who suffer on their high level from the same foxhole funk or paralysis as the GI does on his level; in defense of the British and those few terrified and tawdry Americans who prefer to see our fighting men keep on dying with one hand tied rather than to share with them whatever risk there may be to those at home by letting our men fight with both hands. I ask that you listen to a witness on behalf of my dead son and the other sons who would themselves cry out against their betrayal had their voices not been stilled forever.

6. Dean Acheson Justifies Personal Sacrifice in Limited Warfare, 1951

Our country, which has risen to a position of unprecedented power and eminence in the world, is seeking to use that power in such a way as to help bring about a peaceful international order. This means that we have to be doing two things at once: while we move ahead in our efforts to build the kind of a world in which we can all live together peacefully and in common helpfulness, we are at the same time protecting ourselves from being over-run by the tyranny which is run from Moscow. I have sometimes compared this two-pronged effort as being like the way our ancestors had to have some men drilling and keeping watch from the block-houses, while others went on, tilling the fields.

In a sense, we are standing with one foot in the world of our hopes for a future order among nations, and the other foot in the world of power. Both of these are part of the present reality. Unless we are strong enough — we and the other free nations — to prevent the Soviet rulers from extending their control over the entire world, then we shall never have the chance to help build the kind of a world we all want.

There are many terrible heartbreaks in this course of action, but there is no easier way to a peaceful world. Your son asks in his letter whether Korea proves anything. That he is heartsick over the loss of life and the destruction in Korea is right and good, and reflects what must be the instinctively humane feelings of good men everywhere. But I hope he will come to see that Korea proves — has already proved — a great deal. In Korea, the men and the nations who love freedom and who believe in the United Nations have made it clear that they are willing to fight for these things. By standing firm against aggression in Korea, we are doing our best to prevent the world from following the road which led us, twice in recent times, to World War. The heroic sacrifices which are now being made in Korea may enable the world to pass through this time of hostility and tension without the catastrophe, the greater destruction and the immeasurably greater sacrifices of a world conflict.

7. Differing Views of the Korean Conflict, 1950–1951

A. "Starting Something?"

STARTING SOMETHING?

MARCUS, © 1950 BY THE NEW YORK TIMES COMPANY.
REPRINTED BY PERMISSION.

B. "Build a Better Mousetrap . . . "

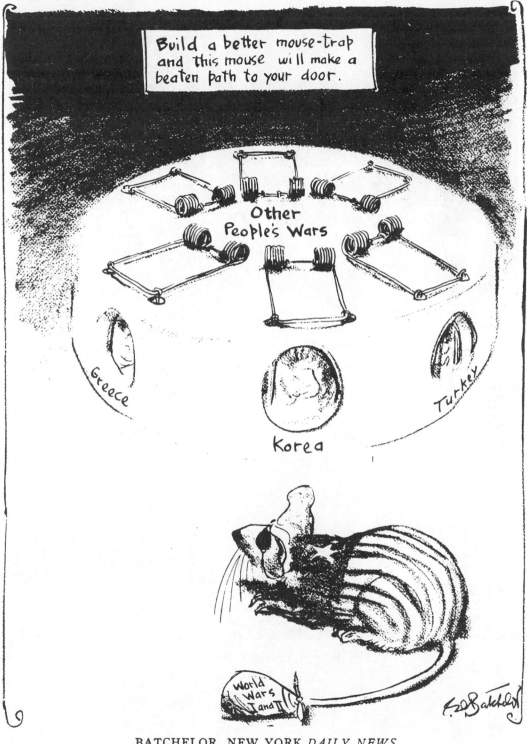

BATCHELOR, NEW YORK *DAILY NEWS*

C. "Hemmed In"

Chapter 28:
Document Set 3 References

1. President Harry S Truman Recalls the Origins of the Korean Conflict, 1950
   Harry S Truman, *Memoirs by Harry S Truman, Years of Trial and Hope,* Vol. 2 (New York: Signet, 1956), pp. 374, 375, 385–387.

2. General Douglas MacArthur Outlines His Objectives in Korea, 1951
   Douglas MacArthur to Hon. Joseph W. Martin, March 20, 1951, *Hearings before the Joint Senate Committee on Armed Services and Foreign Relations, Congressional Record,* 82nd Cong., 1st Sess. (Washington, D.C.: Government Printing Office, 1951), p. 3182.

3. Truman Relieves MacArthur, 1951
   Truman, *Memoirs,* p. 509.

4. General Omar N. Bradley Warns Against Global War, 1951
   Omar M. Bradley, Chairman of the Joint Chiefs of Staff, Testimony, *Hearings,* pp. 730–734.

5. A Grieving Parent Charges the Administration with Appeasement, 1951

Eugene R. Guild to Sen. Harry P. Cain, June 18, 1951, *Hearings,* pp. 3095–3096.

6. Dean Acheson Justifies Personal Sacrifice in Limited Warfare, 1951
   Dean Acheson to Clarence E. Moulette, February 23, 1951, in Acheson, *It Has Fallen to Us* (Washington, D.C.: Government Printing Office, 1951), Publication 4144, General Foreign Policy Series 45, pp. 1–7.

7. Differing Views of the Korean Conflict, 1950–1951
   A. "Starting Something?", Marcus, 1950, by *New York Times Company,* in Editors, Foreign Policy Association, *A Cartoon History of United States Foreign Policy* (New York: Vintage, 1967), p. 101.
   B. "Build a Better Mousetrap . . .", Batchelor, New York *Daily News,* ca. 1951, in *Cartoon History,* p. 103.
   C. "Hemmed In," Reg Manning, McNaught Syndicate, Inc., ca. 1951, in *Cartoon History,* p. 104.

Chapter 28:
Document Set 3 Credits

CHAPTER 29

DOCUMENT SET 1
Changing Times: The Origins of the Modern Civil Rights Movement, 1954–1956

Although your textbook emphasizes President Dwight Eisenhower's moderation and centrist politics, it is evident that in at least one area of social policy dramatic changes were under way during the 1950s. Due in part to the Supreme Court's initiative and in part to heightened militancy among African Americans, an essentially conservative decade witnessed significant advances in the area of civil rights. The following documents record the rise of a new activism in a highly conscious, politicized African American community that rejected the "separate but equal" doctrine that had previously defined the African American place in American society. As you review these materials, be aware of the concerns, self-images, and convictions that led African American citizens to demand their share of the American dream.

The textbook emphasizes the liberalized Warren Court as an important stimulus to change. As you focus on the problem of equal educational facilities for all Americans, examine the watershed *Brown* decision (1954) to gain an understanding of the court's reasoning. Be aware of not only the rationale for overturning *Plessy* v. *Ferguson,* but also the wide implications of the principle asserted.

Although the court was unanimous in its decision, Eisenhower was slow to execute the ruling. As noted in your textbook, the president's lack of enthusiasm encouraged southern whites to resist implementation. Herbert Sass's frank discussion of the southern position reveals some of the fears that lay behind the traditional resistance to integrated education.

In 1957 the crucial test came when Arkansas Governor Orval E. Faubus attempted to block the inte-

gration of Little Rock Central High School. Examine Eisenhower's reasons for finally using federal authority to force compliance with the *Brown* decision. Eisenhower's speech to the national television audience reflects the state of moderate opinion in the nation as the president moved to assert federal supremacy and the primacy of the Supreme Court.

Education was the main civil rights battleground of the 1950s, but as noted in your textbook, the ripple effect of *Brown* v. *Topeka* spilled over into other areas of social contact. The remaining documents explore the importance of a second watershed incident of the early civil rights movement, the Montgomery bus boycott of 1955, which symbolically challenged the entire Jim Crow system and ended in the emergence of a new national civil rights leader, Martin Luther King, Jr.

Examine the extended excerpt from King's account of the origins of the Montgomery protest. As you analyze King's words, be aware of the deeper forces and feelings that lay behind Rosa Parks's action and the decisions of the Montgomery Improvement Association. As you evaluate his interpretation of these important events, compare it with the interview with civil rights activist Jo Ann Robinson and try to distinguish between underlying causes, planned actions, and precipitating events.

These documents provide evidence that social tensions underlay the consensus of the quiet fifties. Use them to assess the importance of ideas, organizations, and individuals as agents for social and political change.

Questions for Analysis

1. What was the basic rationale for the *Plessy* v. *Ferguson* decision of 1896? How did the *Brown* decision address the traditional argument for "separate but equal" educational facilities? What sort of evidence supported the Supreme Court's new position?

2. What do the documents reveal about the motives behind southern resistance to desegregation of the public schools? How does the Sass argument compare with the rationale implied in President Eisenhower's television speech? As you review the evidence, decide which motives were uppermost in the thinking of the resistance.

3. What was the relationship between the *Brown* decision and the forces that led to the Montgomery bus boycott? Do the documents shed light on the reasons resistance to segregation became so firm in Montgomery in 1955?

4. What evidence do the documents provide concerning the origins of the modern civil rights movement? Did the drive toward desegregation and the removal of discrimination reflect situational problems, such as personal crises and ad hoc responses? What other factors are evident in the rise of the demand for social and political justice?

5. How did the civil rights crisis of the 1950s reflect traditional political and constitutional issues? What did the clashes at Little Rock and Montgomery indicate about the evolution of American federalism? Why do you believe Eisenhower chose to intervene in Little Rock? Support your position with evidence drawn from the documents.

6. Using evidence from the documents, support or refute the "great man" theory of history as an explanation for the acceleration of the civil rights movement in the 1950s. What alternative hypotheses can be offered to explain the quickening of the reform impulse on the issue of race relations?

1. The Supreme Court Reverses the "Separate but Equal" Doctrine, 1954

We come then to the question presented: Does segregation of children in public schools solely on the basis of race, even though the physical facilities and other "tangible" factors may be equal, deprive the children of the minority group of equal educational opportunities? We believe that it does. . . .

To separate them from others of similar age and qualifications solely because of their race generates a feeling of inferiority as to their status in the community that may affect their hearts and minds in a way unlikely ever to be undone. The effect of this separation on their educational opportunities was well stated by a finding in the Kansas case by a court which nevertheless felt compelled to rule against the Negro plaintiffs:

Segregation of white and colored children in public schools has a detrimental effect upon the colored children. The impact is greater when it has the sanction of the law; for the policy of separating the races is usually interpreted as denoting the inferiority of the Negro group. A sense of inferiority affects the motivation of a child to learn. Segregation with the sanction of law, therefore, has a tendency to retard the educational and mental development of Negro children and to deprive them of some of the benefits they would receive in a racially integrated school system.

Whatever may have been the extent of psychological knowledge at the time of *Plessy v. Ferguson,* this finding is amply supported by modern authority. Any language in *Plessy v. Ferguson* contrary to this finding is rejected.

We conclude that in the field of public education the doctrine of "separate but equal" has no place. Separate educational facilities are inherently unequal. Therefore, we hold that the plaintiffs and others similarly situated for whom the actions have been brought are, by reason of the segregation complained of, deprived of the equal protection of the laws guaranteed by the Fourteenth Amendment. This disposition makes unnecessary any discussion whether such segregation also violates the Due Process Clause of the Fourteenth Amendment.

Because these are class actions, because of the wide applicability of this decision, and because of the great variety of local conditions, the formulation of decrees in these cases presents problems of considerable complexity. On reargument, the consideration of appropriate relief was necessarily subordinated to the primary question—the constitutionality of segregation in public education. We have now announced that such segregation is a denial of the equal protection of the laws.

2. A Southern Defense of Segregated Education, 1956

[I]f the small children of the two races in approximately equal numbers—as would be the case in a great many of the South's schools—were brought together intimately and constantly and grew up in close association in integrated schools under teachers necessarily committed to the gospel of racial integration, there would be many in whom race preference would not develop. This would not be, as superficial thinkers might suppose, a good thing, the happy solution of the race problem in America. It might be a solution of a sort, but not one that the American people would desire. It would inevitably result, beginning with the least desirable elements of both races, in a great increase of racial amalgamation, the very process which throughout our history we have most sternly rejected. For although to most persons today the idea of mixed mating is disagreeable or even repugnant, this would not be true of the new generations brought up in mixed schools with the desirability of racial integration as a basic premise. Among those new generations mixed matings would become commonplace, and a greatly enlarged mixed-blood population would result.

That is the compelling reason, though by no means the only reason, why the South will resist, with all its resources of mind and body, the mixing of the races in its public schools. It is a reason which, when its validity is generally recognized, will quickly enlist millions of non-Southerners in support of the South's position. The people of the North and West do not favor the transformation of the United States into a nation composed in considerable part of mixed bloods any more than the people of the South do. Northern support of school integration in the South is due to the failure to realize its inevitable biological effect in regions of large Negro population. If Northerners did realize this, their enthusiasm for mixed schools in the South would evaporate at once.

3. President Dwight Eisenhower Enforces the *Brown* Decision in Little Rock, 1957

My Fellow Citizens. . . . I must speak to you about the serious situation that has arisen in Little Rock. . . . In that city, under the leadership of demagogic extremists, disorderly mobs have deliberately prevented the carrying out of proper orders from a federal court. Local authorities have not eliminated that violent opposition and, under the law, I yesterday issued a proclamation calling upon the mob to disperse.

This morning the mob again gathered in front of the Central High School of Little Rock, obviously for the purpose of again preventing the carrying out of the court's order relating to the admission of Negro children to that school.

Whenever normal agencies prove inadequate to the task and it becomes necessary for the executive branch of the federal government to use its powers and authority to uphold federal courts, the President's responsibility is inescapable.

In accordance with that responsibility, I have today issued an Executive Order directing the use of troops under federal authority to aid in the execution of federal law at Little Rock, Arkansas. This became necessary when my Proclamation of yesterday was not observed, and the obstruction of justice still continues. . . .

A foundation of our American way of life is our national respect for law.

In the South, as elsewhere, citizens are keenly aware of the tremendous disservice that has been done to the people of Arkansas in the eyes of the nation, and that has been done to the nation in the eyes of the world.

At a time when we face grave situations abroad because of the hatred that communism bears toward a system of government based on human rights, it would be difficult to exaggerate the harm that is being done to the prestige and influence, and indeed to the safety, of our nation and the world.

Our enemies are gloating over this incident and using it everywhere to misrepresent our whole nation. We are portrayed as a violator of those standards of conduct which the peoples of the world united to proclaim in the Charter of the United Nations. There they affirmed "faith in fundamental human rights" and "in the dignity and worth of the human person" and they did so "without distinction as to race, sex, language or religion."

And so, with deep confidence, I call upon the citizens of the State of Arkansas to assist in bringing to an immediate end all interference with the law and its processes. If resistance to the federal court orders ceases at once, the further presence of federal troops will be unnecessary and the City of Little Rock will return to its normal habits of peace and order and a blot upon the fair name and high honor of our nation in the world will be removed.

Thus will be restored the image of America and of all its parts as one nation, indivisible, with liberty and justice for all.

4. Martin Luther King, Jr., Remembers the Montgomery Boycott, 1955–1956

On December 1, 1955, an attractive Negro seamstress, Mrs. Rosa Parks, boarded the Cleveland Avenue Bus in downtown Montgomery. She was returning home after her regular day's work in the Montgomery Fair—a leading department store. Tired from long hours on her feet, Mrs. Parks sat down in the first seat behind the section reserved for whites. Not long after she took her seat, the bus operator ordered her, along with three other Negro passengers, to move back in order to accommodate boarding white passengers. By this time every seat in the bus was taken. This meant that if Mrs. Parks followed the driver's command she would have to stand while a white male passenger, who had just boarded the bus, would sit. The other three Negro passengers immediately complied with the driver's request. But Mrs. Parks quietly refused. The result was her arrest.

There was to be much speculation about why Mrs. Parks did not obey the driver. Many people in the white community argued that she had been "planted" by the NAACP in order to lay the groundwork for a test case, and at first glance that explanation seemed plausible, since she was a former secretary of the local branch of the NAACP. So persistent and persuasive was this argument that it convinced many reporters from all over the country. Later on, when I was having press conferences three times a week—in order to accommodate the reporters and journalists who came to Montgomery from all over the world—the invariable first question was: "Did the NAACP start the bus boycott?"

But the accusation was totally unwarranted, as the testimony of both Mrs. Parks and the officials of the NAACP revealed. Actually, no one can understand the action of Mrs. Parks unless he realizes that eventually the cup of endurance runs over, and the human personality cries out, "I can take it no longer." Mrs. Parks's refusal to move back was her intrepid affirmation that she had had enough. It was an individual expression of a timeless longing for human dignity and freedom. She was not "planted" there by the NAACP, or any other organization; she was planted there by her personal sense of dignity and self-respect. She was anchored to that seat by the accumulated indignities of days gone by and the boundless aspirations of generations yet unborn. She was a victim of both the forces of history and the forces of destiny. She had been tracked down by the *Zeitgeist*—the spirit of the time. . . .

I decided that I had to face the challenge head on, and attempt to combine two apparent irreconcilables. I would seek to arouse the group to action by insisting that their self-respect was at stake and that if they accepted such injustices without protesting, they would betray their own sense of dignity and the eternal edicts of God Himself. But I would balance this with a strong affirmation of the Christian doctrine of love. By the time I had sketched an outline of the speech in my mind, my time was up. Without stopping to eat supper (I had not eaten since morning) I said good-by to Coretta and drove to the Holt Street Church. . . .

Then came my closing statement. "If you will protest courageously, and yet with dignity and Christian love, when the history books are written in future generations, the historians will have to pause and say, 'There lived a great people—a black people—who injected new meaning and dignity into the veins of civilization.' This is our challenge and our overwhelming responsibility." As I took my seat the people rose to their feet and applauded. I was thankful to God that the message had gotten over and that the task of combining the militant and the moderate had been at least partially accomplished. The people had been as enthusiastic when I urged them to love as they were when I urged them to protest. . . .

Now the time had come for the all-important resolution. Ralph Abernathy read the words slowly and forcefully. The main substance of the resolution called upon the Negroes not to resume riding the buses until (1) courteous treatment by the bus operators was guaranteed; (2) passengers were seated on a first-come, first-served basis—Negroes seated from the back of the bus toward the front while whites seated from the front toward the back; (3) Negro bus operators were employed on predominantly Negro routes. At the words "All in favor of the motion stand," every person to a man stood up, and those who were already standing raised their hands. Cheers began to ring out from both inside and outside. The motion was carried unanimously. The people had expressed their determination not to ride the buses until conditions were changed. . . .

Many will inevitably raise the question, why did this event take place in Montgomery, Alabama, in 1955? Some have suggested that the Supreme Court decision on school desegregation, handed down less than two years before, had given new hope to eventual justice to Negroes everywhere, and fired them with the necessary spark of encouragement to rise against their oppression. But although this might help to explain why the protest occurred when it did, it cannot explain why it happened in Montgomery.

Certainly, there is a partial explanation in the long history of injustice on the buses of Montgomery. The bus protest did not spring into being full grown as Athena sprang from the head of Zeus; it was the culmination of a slowly developing process. Mrs. Parks's arrest was the precipitating factor rather than the cause of the protest. The cause lay deep in the record of similar injustices. Almost everybody could point to an unfortunate episode that he himself had experienced or seen.

But there comes a time when people get tired of being trampled by oppression. There comes a time when people get tired of being plunged into the abyss of exploitation and nagging injustice. The story of Montgomery is the story of 50,000 such Negroes who were willing to substitute tired feet for tired souls, and walk the streets of Montgomery until the walls of segregation were finally battered by the forces of justice. . . .

The day of days, Monday, December 5, 1955, was drawing to a close. We all prepared to go to our homes, not yet fully aware of what had happened. The deliberations of that brisk, cool night in December will not be forgotten. That night we were starting a movement that would gain national recognition; whose echoes would ring in the ears of people of every nation; a movement that would astound the oppressor, and bring new hope to the oppressed. The night was Montgomery's moment in history.

5. Jo Ann Robinson Recalls the Background of Direct Action in Montgomery, 1955–1956

The Women's Political Council was an organization begun in 1946 after dozens of black people had been arrested on the buses. We witnessed the arrests and humiliations and the court trials and the fines paid by people who just sat down on empty seats. We knew something had to be done. . . .

The evening that Rosa Parks was arrested, Fred Gray called me and told me that her case would be [heard] on Monday. As president of the main body of the Women's Political Council, I got on the phone and called all the officers of the three chapters. I told them that Rosa Parks had been arrested and she would be tried. They said, "You have the plans, put them into operation." . . .

After we had circulated those 35,000 circulars, we went by the church. That was about 3:30 in the afternoon. We took them to the minister. . . . The [ministers] agreed to meet that night to decide what should be done about the boycott after the first day. You see, the Women's Council planned it only for Monday, and it was left up to the men to take over after we had forced them really to decide whether or not it had been successful enough to continue, and how long it was to be continued.

They had agreed at the Friday night meeting that they would call this meeting at Holt Street Church and they would let the audience determine whether or not they would continue the bus boycott or end it in one day.

Monday night, the ministers held their meeting. . . . When they got through reporting that very few people had ridden the bus, that the boycott was really a success—I don't know if there was one vote that said "No, don't continue that boycott"—they voted unanimously to continue the boycott. And instead of it lasting one day as the Women's Council had planned it, it lasted for thirteen months. . . .

Now when you ask why the courts had to come in, they had to come in. You get 52,000 people in the streets and nobody's showing any fear, something had to give. So the Supreme Court had to rule that segregation was not the way of life.

Chapter 29:
Document Set 1 References

1. The Supreme Court Reverses the "Separate but Equal" Doctrine, 1954
   Brown v. *Board of Education of Topeka, United States Reports,* 347 U.S. 483 (1954).
2. A Southern Defense of Segregated Education, 1956
   Herbert Ravenel Sass, *Atlantic Monthly* (November 1956).
3. President Dwight Eisenhower Enforces the *Brown* Decision in Little Rock, 1957
   New York Times, September 25, 1957.
4. Martin Luther King, Jr., Remembers the Montgomery Boycott, 1955–1956
   Martin Luther King, Jr., *Stride Toward Freedom: The Montgomery Boycott* (New York: Harper and Row, 1958), pp. 43–46, 48–54.
5. Jo Ann Robinson Recalls the Background of Direct Action in Montgomery, 1955–1956
   Jo Ann Robinson, Interview, in Juan Williams *et al., Eyes on the Prize: America's Civil Rights Years, 1954–1965* (New York: Penguin, 1988), pp. 70–71.

DOCUMENT SET 2

Eisenhower, Dulles, and Hemispheric Security: Intervention in Guatemala

Your textbook emphasizes Eisenhower's role in improving Soviet-American relations and limiting the American commitment in Vietnam. It is clear, however, that the president and his militant anticommunist secretary of state, John Foster Dulles, were equally committed to a policy of sometimes brutal interventionism in the Third World. In no instance was their determination more evident than in the case of Guatemala, where in 1954 the left-leaning but independent regime of Colonel Jacob Arbenz-Guzman defied the American-controlled United Fruit Company and challenged the hemispheric dominance of the United States. The following documents explore the Eisenhower-Dulles rationale for dislodging the democratically elected Arbenz government. As you analyze the evidence, be especially aware of the assumptions and motivations behind American policy.

The first document, the often-quoted "duck test" for the legitimacy of suspect regimes, establishes continuity between the conservative anticommunism of the Eisenhower administration and the Cold War liberalism of the Truman era. Former U.S. Ambassador Richard C. Patterson, the author of these remarks, remained outspoken in his public warnings of a communist threat following his recall from Guatemala in 1949.

Subtler but equally alarmed was President Eisenhower, who was determined to prevent the establishment of a Soviet beachhead in Central America. Like Dulles, the president viewed the Arbenz regime as a threat to hemispheric security. The excerpt from his memoirs clearly reveals his reason for approving CIA efforts to overthrow the elected government of Guatemala. Even more outspoken was Secretary Dulles, who addressed the American public in June 1954 in an effort to justify American intervention. Note the Eisenhower-Dulles interpretation of democracy and popular will. Try to determine where they place blame for the crisis.

In sharp contrast to the administration position is Professor Philip B. Taylor's account of the events in Guatemala, written only a few months after the American intervention. Taylor, a professor of political science at Michigan State University, published his version of the counterrevolution in the *American Political Science Review.* Be aware of Taylor's background as you assess his interpretation of historical events, and compare his interpretation with the administration's view.

Try to determine how the successful intervention in Guatemala was related to other policies of the Eisenhower administration. Be sensitive to the administration's overall approach to challenges in the developing world, as described in the textbook. Finally, think about the relationship between Guatemala in 1954 and subsequent American policies in dealing with hemispheric problems.

Questions for Analysis

1. What were the Eisenhower administration's basic assumptions about the nature of the Arbenz regime in Guatemala? What do the documents tell us about Eisenhower's and Dulles's ideologies? How did their personal beliefs influence their handling of the crisis?

2. What were the desires of the Guatemalan people in 1954? What was the meaning of Dulles's assertion that the United States would maintain its support for the "just aspirations of the Guatemalan people"? How would the legitimacy of those aspirations be determined in the future? By whom?

3. Compare the Dulles-Eisenhower view of the historical origins of the crisis with Philip B. Taylor's account of the same events. How are the authors of these documents using history? How would you account for their conflicting interpretations of the evidence?

4. What was the American response to Third World revolution in the 1950s? How would you account for that attitude? In what way did the Guatemalan incident exemplify weaknesses or strengths in the foreign policy of the Eisenhower administration?

5. What do the documents reveal concerning the motivations behind U.S. Latin American policies in the 1950s? How does the evidence clarify the geopolitical reasons for the actions of Eisenhower and Dulles? What were the economic, political, ideological, and strategic influences on the development of administration policy?

1. Ambassador Richard C. Patterson Devises the "Duck Test," 1949

Many times it is impossible to prove legally that a certain individual is a communist; but for cases of this sort I recommend a practical method of detection—the "duck test." The duck test works this way: suppose you see a bird walking around in a farm yard. This bird wears no label that says "duck." But the bird certainly looks like a duck. Also he goes to the pond and you notice he swims like a duck. Then he opens his beak and quacks like a duck. Well, by this time you have probably reached the conclusion that the bird is a duck, whether he's wearing a label or not.

2. Eisenhower's Recollection of American Intervention in Guatemala, 1954

The troubles had been long-standing, reaching back nine years to the Guatemalan revolution of 1944, which had resulted in the overthrow of the dictator General Jorge Ubico. Thereafter, the Communists busied themselves with agitating and with infiltrating labor unions, peasant organizations, and the press and radio. In 1950 a military officer, Jacobo Arbenz Guzmán, came to power and by his actions soon created the strong suspicion that he was merely a puppet manipulated by Communists.

The American republics wanted no Communist regime within their midst. They recognized that subversion by Communism was only another form of aggression, even more evil than that achieved by naked military force. However, in unstable regions where revolutions and rioting were not uncommon, where some governments were being maintained by dictatorial means, where resentments against the United States were sometimes nurtured by groups other than Communist cells, it was difficult to differentiate positively between Communist influence and uncontrolled and politically rebellious groups. For example, on February 24, 1953, the Arbenz government announced its intention, under an agrarian reform law, to seize about 225,000 acres of unused United Fruit Company land. . . .

Expropriation in itself does not, of course, prove Communism; expropriation of oil and agricultural properties years before in Mexico had not been fostered by Communists. . . .

About that time [October 1953] a new ambassador, John E. Peurifoy, was appointed to Guatemala. He was familiar with the tactics of the Communists in Greece, where he had served. Peurifoy soon reached definite conclusions on the nature of the Arbenz government. . . .

Something had to be done quickly. The first task was to marshal and crystallize Latin American public opinion on the issue. The opportunity presented itself at the Tenth Inter-American Conference of the Organization of the American States (OAS) which met in Caracas, Venezuela, in March of 1954. At that meeting the United States urged the adoption of a joint condemnation of Communism, contending vigorously that it should not be permitted to control any state in the Western Hemisphere. Foster Dulles, representing the United States, argued that if Communism should succeed to this extent, it should be treated as a threat to the peace. On March 6 he introduced a draft resolution of a "Declaration of Solidarity for the Preservation of the Political Integrity of the American States against International Communist Intervention." . . .

On March 26, in a plenary session, the organization approved the resolution by a vote of seventeen to one, with Guatemala opposing, and Argentina and Mexico abstaining—Costa Rica was absent. As passed, it differed in only one respect from the draft; it called not for immediate action to meet the Communist threat but rather for a "meeting to consider the adoption of measures in accordance with existing treaties." . . .

In the two months from March to May, 1954, the agents of international Communism in Guatemala continued their efforts to penetrate and subvert their neighboring Central American states, using consular agents for their political purposes and fomenting political assassinations and strikes. In Guatemala itself the government answered protests by suspending constitutional rights, conducting mass arrests, and killing leaders in the political opposition.

In May things came to a head. On the 17th of that month Foster Dulles reported to the press that the United States had reliable information on a shipment of arms from behind the Iron Curtain. . . .

Meanwhile, in Guatemala, Arbenz had declared a state of siege and launched a reign of terror. Then on June 18 armed forces under Carlos Castillo Armas, an exiled former colonel in the Guatemalan Army, crossed the border from Honduras into Guatemala, initially with a mere handful of men—reportedly about two hundred. As he progressed he picked up recruits. Simultaneously three obsolete bombers, presumably under his direction, buzzed Guatemala City and bombed the ordinance depot. Things seemed to be going well for Castillo's small band until June 22. On that date Allen Dulles reported to me that Castillo had lost two of the three old bombers with which he was supporting his "invasion." . . .

"What do you think Castillo's chances would be," I asked Allen Dulles, "without the aircraft?"

His answer was unequivocal: "About zero."

"Suppose we supply the aircraft. What would the chances be then?"

Again the CIA chief did not hesitate: "About 20 per cent."

I considered the matter carefully. I realized full well that United States intervention in Central America and Caribbean affairs earlier in the century had greatly injured our standing in all of Latin America. On the other hand, it seemed to me that to refuse to cooperate in providing indirect support to a strictly anti-Communist faction in this struggle would be contrary to the letter and spirit of the Caracas resolution. I had faith in the strength of the inter-American resolve therein set forth. On the actual value of a shipment of planes, I knew from experience the important psychological impact of even a small amount of air support. In any event, our proper course of action—indeed my duty—was clear to me. We would replace the airplanes. . . .

The major factor in the successful outcome was the disaffection of the Guatemalan armed forces and the population as a whole with the tyrannical regime of Arbenz. The air support enjoyed by Castillo Armas, though meager, was important in relative terms; it gave the regular armed forces an excuse to take action in their own hands to throw out Arbenz. The rest of Latin America was not in the least displeased. . . .

By the middle of 1954 Latin America was free, for the time being at least, of any fixed outposts of Communism.

3. John Foster Dulles Reports on Guatemala, 1954

Tonight I should like to talk with you about Guatemala. It is the scene of dramatic events. They expose the evil purpose of the Kremlin to destroy the inter-American system, and they test the ability of the American States to maintain the peaceful integrity of this hemisphere.

For several years international communism has been probing here and there for nesting places in the Americas. It finally chose Guatemala as a spot which it could turn into an official base from which to breed subversion which would extend to other American Republics. . . .

In Guatemala, international communism had an initial success. It began 10 years ago, when a revolution occurred in Guatemala. The revolution was not without justification. But the Communists seized on it, not as an opportunity for real reform, but as a chance to gain political power.

Communist agitators devoted themselves to infiltrating the public and private organizations of Guatemala. They sent recruits to Russia and other Communist countries for revolutionary training and indoctrination in such institutions as the Lenin School at Moscow. Operating in the guise of "reformers" they organized the workers and peasants under Communist leadership. Having gained control of what they call "mass organizations," they moved on to take over the official press and radio of the Guatemalan Government. They dominated the social security organization and ran the agrarian reform program. Through the technique of the "popular front" they dictated to the Congress and the President. . . .

Guatemala is a small country. But its power, standing alone, is not a measure of the threat. The master plan of international communism is to gain a solid political base in this hemisphere, a base that can be used to extend Communist penetration to the other peoples of the other American Governments. It was not the power of the Arbenz government that concerned us but the power behind it.

If world communism captures any American State, however small, a new and perilous front is established which will increase the danger to the entire free world and require even greater sacrifices from the American people.

This situation in Guatemala had become so dangerous that the American States could not ignore it. At Caracas last March the American States held their Tenth Inter-American Conference. They then adopted a momentous statement. They declared that "the domination or control of the political institutions of any American State by the international Communist movement . . . would constitute a threat to the sovereignty and political independence of the American States, endangering the peace of America." . . .

Throughout the period I have outlined, the Guatemalan Government and Communist agents throughout the world have persistently attempted to obscure the real issue—that of Communist imperialism—by claiming that the United States is only interested in protecting American business. . . . But this issue is relatively unimportant. All who know the temper of the U.S. people and Government must realize that our overriding concern is that which, with others, we recorded at Caracas, namely the endangering by international communism of the peace and security of this hemisphere.

The people of Guatemala have not been heard from. Despite the armaments piled up by the Arbenz government, it was unable to enlist the spiritual cooperation of the people.

Led by Col. Castillo Armas, patriots arose in Guatemala to challenge the Communist leadership—and to change it. Thus, the situation is being cured by the Guatemalans themselves.

Last Sunday, President Arbenz of Guatemala resigned and seeks asylum. Others are following his example. . . .

The need for vigilance is not past. Communism is still a menace everywhere. But the people of the United States and of the other American Republics can feel tonight that at least one grave danger has been averted. Also an example is set which promises increased security for the future. The ambitious and unscrupulous will be less prone to feel that communism is the wave of their future.

In conclusion, let me assure the people of Guatemala. As peace and freedom are restored to that sister Republic, the Government of the United States will continue to support the just aspirations of the Guatemalan people. A prosperous and progressive Guatemala is vital to a healthy hemisphere.

4. An American Scholar Explains the Overthrow of the Arbenz Regime, 1954

There is little doubt that communism got its start in Guatemala under [Juan José] Arévalo [who was elected for the 1945–1951 presidential term]; Arévalo's successor, Lt. Col. Arbenz, who served from March, 1951, until his ouster in July, 1954, was quite sympathetic to Communist activities, but under the best of contrary circumstances the ouster of Communists from their positions in the government would have been extremely difficult and would have stripped the government of its trained, though not necessarily efficient, bureaucrats. . . .

Among the exiles forced from Guatemala by the operations of the Arévalo-Arbenz government was Lt. Colonel Carlos Castillo Armas, who had been condemned to death for his implication in an unsuccessful attempt against the government in late 1950. . . .

Events in Guatemala leading to the civil war seem to have commenced with the State Department announcement on May 17, 1954, that a shipment of arms totaling 1,900 tons had arrived at Puerto Barrios, Guatemala. . . .

The United States employed the shipment to arouse sympathy for its subsequent anti-Arbenz actions. It was also employed as the basis for a nearly unprecedented request to the other members of the North Atlantic Treaty Organization that they grant the United States the privilege of searching their merchant ships on the high seas for arms shipments to Guatemala. The request was rejected by all of the nations to which requests were made.

On May 20, the United States concluded a Mutual Security Treaty with Honduras (a similar treaty had been signed with Nicaragua on April 23), and on May 24 it was announced that the United States Air Force was airlifting war material to the two nations. . . .

Col. Castillo Armas' troops entered Guatemalan territory from Honduras on June 19. A period of somewhat desultory fighting followed. Arbenz resigned on June 27 after an all-day conference with his military leaders, and the Army Chief of Staff, Col. Enrique Díaz, established a short-lived provisional government composed of three officers. One of these, Colonel Elfego Monzón, replaced Díaz on the 29th, after the direct intervention of Ambassador Peurifoy. Peurifoy and a Marine bodyguard, both armed, were present in the conference room at the time power changed hands. . . .

In response to the urgent request of the Guatemalan representative on June 19, the U.N. Security Council met on the call of its president, United States representative Henry Cabot Lodge, on June 20. Guatemalan representative Eduardo Castillo-Arriola asked immediate U.N. investigation of his charge that the fighting had begun with the invasion of his country by forces stationed in Honduras and Nicaragua and backed by "foreign monopolies" with the knowledge of the United States State Department. . . .

The Council meeting [of June 25] voted to take no direct action until it had the opportunity to receive a report from the Peace Committee. The Guatemalan government, which prior to the second Council meeting had rejected O.A.S. Peace Committee investigation, now reconsidered and announced it would welcome it. The date was the afternoon of June 26. After confirming the Guatemalan change of attitude, the Committee on the 27th determined that it would send a five-member team to Guatemala, Honduras, and Nicaragua, starting the 28th.

It seems quite tenable to argue that the action [to request a special O.A.S. Council meeting] was intended as a smoke-screen rather than as a sincere request. . . . The question why the United States should have requested the investigation after the horse had fled the stable, rather than before, seems almost rhetorical under the circumstances. Investigation, or the proposal of a real study of the situation, prior to the outbreak of fighting, would have been sincere. . . .

The O.A.S. Council met in special session on July 2 to approve 18–1, with one abstention, the motion presented by Honduras and seconded by the United States that the July 7 meeting be postponed *sine die.* . . .

And, of course, the inspection team of the Peace Committee did not reach its destination either. It was in Mexico City when the Castillo-Monzón negotiations opened, and it remained there. At the urgent request of the Monzón *junta,* it canceled its trip at that point on July 2 and returned to Washington. The inaction of the U.N. Security Council and of the Inter-American Peace Committee (as agent for the O.A.S.) had combined with the successful operations of Castillo Armas to overthrow the Arbenz government. . . .

The shocked conscience of the world was probably represented best in the British House of Commons on July 14, 1954, by Clement Attlee, head of the Labor party, in foreign affairs debate:

"The fact is that this was a plain act of aggression, and one cannot take one line on aggression in Asia and another line in Central America. I confess that I was rather shocked at the joy and approval of the American Secretary of State on the success of this *putsch.*

" . . . [We] cannot pass this off as just a Central American squabble, of which there are so many. There was a principle involved and that principle was the responsibility of the United Nations. . . . Therefore, I am afraid that Guatemala has left a rather unpleasant taste in one's mouth because, to illustrate the theme I was putting, it seems in some instances that the acceptance of the principles of the United Nations is subordinated to a hatred of Communism. . . . "

[The] entire situation leads to the conclusion that the United States failed to give evidence of faith in the processes of the United Nations; that it dragged its feet regarding effective O.A.S. action beyond the point of reason; that it was intimately involved in a situation of subversion of a constitutional govern- ment; and that it did not at any time undertake to make the record clear to the people either of the United States or of Latin America.

Chapter 29:
Document Set 2 References

1. Ambassador Richard C. Patterson Devises the "Duck Test," 1949
   Richard C. Patterson, 1949, quoted in Walter LaFeber, *Inevitable Revolutions: The United States in Central America* (New York: W. W. Norton, 1984), p. 114.

2. Eisenhower's Recollection of American Intervention in Guatemala, 1954
   Dwight D. Eisenhower, *The White House Years: Mandate for Change, 1953–1956* (New York: Doubleday, 1963), pp. 421–427.

3. John Foster Dulles Reports on Guatemala, 1954
   John Foster Dulles, "Radio and Television Address by Secretary Dulles, on International Communism in Guatemala," June 30, 1954, Department of State Publi- cation 5596, Inter-American Series 48, Washington, D.C., 1954, pp. 30–34.

4. An American Scholar Explains the Overthrow of the Arbenz Regime, 1954
   Philip B. Taylor, Jr., "The Guatemalan Affair—A Cri- tique of U.S. Foreign Policy," *American Political Science Review,* Vol. 50 (September 1956).

Chapter 29:
Document Set 2 Credits

CHAPTER 30

Critical Decisions: "Waist-Deep in the Big Muddy"

Of the many divisive issues in the "turbulent sixties," none was more disruptive than the escalating American commitment in Vietnam. To understand the disillusionment that followed, it is important to be aware of the early decisions of the Kennedy and Johnson administrations that led to that escalation. The following documents review the origins of American involvement in Southeast Asia and explore the process by which significant policies are arrived at, in this instance the fateful choice to expand the war in 1965.

Setting the stage for escalation, the Kennedy administration increased the American presence in Vietnam, deploying American advisers in a counterinsurgency program consistent with the flexible response strategy described in your textbook. By September 1963, however, administration leaders had concluded that the American surrogate, Ngo Dinh Diem, was a liability. Newsman Walter Cronkite's interview with Kennedy revealed the president's concern about the ominous developments in Saigon. Following Diem's assassination in October, the weaknesses in his regime became painfully evident, as noted in Assistant Secretary of State Roger Hilsman's memoir of the Kennedy years.

One year later, the deteriorating situation in South Vietnam forced President Lyndon B. Johnson to give serious attention to a change in American policy. Armed with the sweeping authority granted by the Gulf of Tonkin Resolution, Johnson prepared for escalation in early 1965. Examine National Security Adviser McGeorge Bundy's policy paper against the background provided by the Defense Department's John T. McNaughton in his memo of November 1964. Determine why Bundy recommended a major escalation, implemented by Johnson in February 1965.

The president's approval of a substantial bombing program aimed at North Vietnam reflected rising anxiety within the administration over the failure of ARVN forces to mount an effective resistance to Viet Cong guerrilla activities in the south. As you examine the February decision, be especially aware of the administration's interpretation of the war's origins.

In July the American military requested a significant increase in American troop commitment, resulting in a thorough policy review in Washington. The dynamics of the White House decision-making process are revealed in Jack Valenti's account of the internal debate over a decision that would result in the Americanization of the war. Consider the reasoning of all parties in the discussion.

Johnson's agreement with the majority recommendation was to have tragic consequences. As you examine the president's personal justification for a firm American commitment, be alert to the factors uppermost in his mind. Think about the policy process as well as personal experience as factors in a decision with grave implications for Asians and Americans alike.

Questions for Analysis

1. Using the textbook material on Kennedy's foreign-policy ideas, develop an explanation for the deepening American involvement in Vietnam during his administration. What do the documents reveal about his intentions at the time of his death? Do you find him optimistic or pessimistic? What was the basis for his views?

2. What was the American interpretation of the origins of the Vietnam War? Why was this problem such an important issue for American policymakers? What is your assessment of the American analysis?

3. One interpretation of the Vietnam War is the "quagmire thesis," which suggests that the United States slipped accidentally or unknowingly into a commitment from which it could not extricate itself. In view of the evidence from the documents, does this explanation of American involvement seem accurate? Why or why not?

4. In February 1965, President Johnson authorized a significant escalation in the war by approving air strikes in North Vietnam. How was the new policy defended? Was it a responsive action or a preplanned measure? Do the documents reveal the intent of the new bombing policy? Explain.

5. Perhaps the crucial decision of the early war years came in July 1965, when the Johnson administration decided on a major increase in American troop commitment in South Vietnam. The documents contain a record of policy discussions held on July 21–22, 1965, during which the proposed escalation was debated, together with the dissenting recommendation of Under Secretary of State George W. Ball. What were the issues at stake? Why did President Johnson ultimately approve the new troop limits?

6. As you review the chain of events from September 1963 to July 1965, do you draw from the documents any conclusions with regard to the reasons for the ultimate failure of American policy in Vietnam? What were the prospects for victory by 1965? How was the term *victory* defined? Was there any fatal flaw in American policy? Explain.

1. President John F. Kennedy's Analysis of Prospects for the Diem Regime, 1963

MR. CRONKITE: Mr. President, the only hot war we've got running at the moment is of course the one in Viet-Nam, and we have our difficulties here, quite obviously.

PRESIDENT KENNEDY: I don't think that unless a greater effort is made by the Government to win popular support that the war can be won out there. In the final analysis, it is their war. They are the ones who have to win it or lose it. We can help them, we can give them equipment, we can send our men out there as advisers, but they have to win it—the people of Viet-Nam—against the Communists. We are prepared to continue to assist them, but I don't think that the war can be won unless the people support the effort, and, in my opinion, in the last 2 months the Government has gotten out of touch with the people.

The repressions against the Buddhists, we felt, were very unwise. Now all we can do is to make it very clear that we don't think this is the way to win. It is my hope that this will become increasingly obvious to the Government, that they will take steps to try to bring back popular support for this very essential struggle.

. . . [I]n the final analysis it is the people and the Government itself who have to win or lose this struggle. All we can do is help, and we are making it very clear. But I don't agree with those who say we should withdraw. That would be a great mistake. I know people don't like Americans to be engaged in this kind of an effort. Forty-seven Americans have been killed in combat with the enemy, but this is a very important struggle even though it is far away.

We took all this—made this effort to defend Europe. Now Europe is quite secure. We also have to participate—we may not like it—in the defense of Asia.

2. Roger Hilsman Recalls a Realistic Evaluation of the Situation in South Vietnam, 1963

The Viet Cong took advantage of the preoccupation of the new regime with matters in Saigon to consolidate their holdings in the countryside and move into new ones. The new regime also set about to replace the incompetent and politically dangerous among the Diem-

Nhu political appointees at the district and province levels and to reward its own men—and the Viet Cong also made the most of the resulting confusion. . . .

[T]he greatest shocks were not how effectively the Viet Cong moved to take advantage of the Diem-

Nhu regime's past mistakes but the discovery of just how wild the statistics really were on which the United States had based so much optimism. On October 22, 1963, before the coup, the Bureau of Intelligence and Research had analyzed the statistics and concluded, not only that the trend was downhill, but that the statistics had started downhill in July, before the attack on the pagodas. . . .

But when the coup drew back the curtain, both sides of the argument were amazed at what the true picture really was. First, the Viet Cong had not really been "compressed" into the delta, but were merely lying low in the other regions while they concentrated on infiltrating strategic hamlets and gaining control from within. . . .

Second, a high percentage of attacks initiated by the government—the statistic on which so much American optimism had been based—had been mounted against "targets" where the Viet Cong were known *not* to be, as a means of inflating the statistics without risk of the casualties that would rouse Diem's ire. . . .

Third, the statistics on the number of strategic hamlets and on the number of villages under effective government control were completely false. Vice-President Nguyen Ngoc Tho, for example, informed us that of the 8600 strategic hamlets claimed under the Diem regime, only about 20 per cent actually met the standards. . . .

"*Ah, les statistiques!*" one of the Vietnamese generals exclaimed to an American friend. "Your Secretary of Defense loves statistics. We Vietnamese can give him all he wants. If you want them to go up, they will go up. If you want them to go down, they will go down."

3. Richard McNaughton's Assessment of Conditions in Vietnam, 1964

1. U.S. aims:

(a) To protect U.S. reputation as a counter-subversion guarantor.

(b) To avoid domino effect especially in Southeast Asia.

(c) To keep South Vietnamese territory from Red hands.

(d) To emerge from crisis without unacceptable taint from methods.

2. Present situation:

The situation in South Vietnam is deteriorating. Unless new actions are taken, the new government will probably be unstable and ineffectual, and the VC will probably continue to extend their hold over the population and territory. It can be expected that, soon (6 months? two years?), (a) government officials at all levels will adjust their behavior to an eventual VC take-over, (b) defections of significant military forces will take place, (c) whole integrated regions of the country will be totally denied to the GVN, (d) neutral and/or left-wing elements will enter the government, (e) a popular front regime will emerge which will invite the U.S. out, and (f) fundamental concessions to the VC and accommodations to the DRV will put South Vietnam behind the Curtain.

4. McGeorge Bundy Recommends "Sustained Reprisal," 1965

I. Introductory

We believe that the best available way of increasing our chance of success in Vietnam is the development and execution of a policy of *sustained reprisal* against North Vietnam—a policy in which air and naval action against the North is justified by and related to the whole Viet Cong campaign of violence and terror in the South.

While we believe the risks of such a policy are acceptable, we emphasize that its costs are real. It implies significant U.S. air losses even if no full air war is joined, and it seems likely that it would eventually require an extensive and costly effort against the whole air defense system of North Vietnam. U.S. casualties would be higher—and more visible to American feelings—than those sustained in the struggle in South Vietnam.

Yet measured against the costs of defeat in Vietnam, this program seems cheap. And even if it fails to turn the tide—as it may—the value of the effort seems to us to exceed its cost. . . .

III. Expected Effect of Sustained Reprisal Policy

1. We emphasize that our primary target in advocating a reprisal policy is the improvement of the situation in *South* Vietnam. Action against the North is usually urged as a means of affecting the will of Hanoi to direct and support the VC. We consider this an important but longer-range purpose. The immediate and critical targets are in the South—in the minds of the South Vietnamese and in the minds of the Viet Cong cadres.

2. Predictions of the effect of any given course of action upon the states of mind of people are difficult.

It seems very clear that if the United States and the Government of Vietnam join in a policy of reprisal, there will be a sharp immediate increase in optimism in the South, among nearly all articulate groups. The Mission believes—and our own conversations confirm—that in all sectors of Vietnamese opinion there is a strong belief that the United States could do much more if it would, and that they are suspicious of our failure to use more of our obviously enormous power. At least in the short run, the reaction to reprisal policy would be very favorable. . . .

8. We cannot assert that a policy of sustained reprisal will succeed in changing the course of the contest in Vietnam. It may fail, and we cannot estimate the odds of success with any accuracy—they may be somewhere between 25% and 75%. What we can say is that even if it fails, the policy will be worth it. At a minimum it will damp down the charge that we did not do all that we could have done, and this charge will be important in many countries, including our own. Beyond that, a reprisal policy—to the extent that it demonstrates U.S. willingness to employ this new norm in counter-insurgency—will set a higher price for the future upon all adventures of guerrilla warfare, and it should therefore somewhat increase our ability to deter such adventures. We must recognize, however, that that ability will be gravely weakened if there is failure for any reason in Vietnam.

5. A Major Policy Review, 1965

JOHNSON: Would you please begin, Bob. [McNamara summarized the Pentagon recommendation to plan to support 200,000 troops in Vietnam by the first of 1966 by calling up the same number of reserves. By mid-1966 approximately 600,000 additional men would be available.]

BALL: Isn't it possible that the VC will do what they did against the French—stay away from confrontation and not accommodate us?

WHEELER: Yes, that is possible, but by constantly harassing them, they will have to fight somewhere. . . .

BALL: Mr. President, I can foresee a perilous voyage, very dangerous. I have great and grave apprehensions that we can win under these conditions. But let me be clear. If the decision is to go ahead, I am committed.

JOHNSON: But, George, is there another course in the national interest, some course that is better

than the one McNamara proposes? We know it is dangerous and perilous, but the big question is, can it be avoided? . . .

BALL: Take what precautions we can, Mr. President. Take our losses, let their government fall apart, negotiate, discuss, knowing full well there will be a probable take-over by the Communists. This is disagreeable, I know. . . .

LODGE: There is not a tradition of a national government in Saigon. There are no roots in the country. Not until there is tranquility can you have any stability. I don't think we ought to take this government seriously. There is simply no one who can do anything. We have to do what we think we ought to do regardless of what the Saigon government does. . . .

BALL: We cannot win, Mr. President. This war will be long and protracted. The most we can hope for is a messy conclusion. There remains a great danger of intrusion by the Chinese. But the biggest problem is the problem of the long war. . . . As casualties increase, the pressure to strike at the very jugular of North Vietnam will become very great. I am concerned about world opinion. . . . If the war is long and protracted, as I believe it will be, then we will suffer because the world's greatest power cannot defeat guerrillas. Then there is the problem of national politics. Every great captain in history was not afraid to make a tactical withdrawal if conditions were unfavorable to him. The enemy cannot even be seen in Vietnam. He is indigenous to the country. I truly have serious doubt that an army of westerners can successfully fight orientals in an Asian jungle. . . . The least harmful way to cut losses in SVN is to let the government decide it doesn't want us to stay there. Therefore, we should put such proposals to the SVN that they can't accept. Then, it would move to a neutralist position. I have no illusions that after we were asked to leave South Vietnam, that country would soon come under Hanoi control. . . .

RUSK: If the Communist world finds out we will not pursue our commitment to the end, I don't know where they will stay their hand. I have to say I am more optimistic than some of my colleagues. I don't believe the VC have made large advances among the Vietnamese people. It is difficult to worry about massive casualties when we say we can't find the enemy. I feel strongly that one man dead is a massive casualty, but in the sense that we are talking, I don't see large casualties unless the Chinese come in.

LODGE: I feel there is a greater threat to start World War III if we don't go. Can't we see the similarity to our own indolence at Munich [the Munich conference of 1938 when Hitler, with the acquies-

cence of the West, seized part of Czechoslovakia]. I simply can't be as pessimistic as Ball. We have great seaports in Vietnam. We don't need to fight on roads. We have the sea. Let us visualize meeting the VC on our own terms. We don't have to spend all our time in the jungles. If we can secure our bases, the Vietnamese can secure, in time, a political movement to, one, apprehend the terrorist, and two, give intelligence to the government. . . . The Vietnamese have been dealt more casualties than, per capita, we suffered in the Civil War. The Vietnamese soldier is an uncomplaining soldier. He has ideas he will die for. . . .

JOHNSON: Doesn't it really mean that if we follow Westmoreland's requests we are in a new war? Isn't this going off the diving board?

MCNAMARA: If we carry forward all these recommendations, it would be a change in our policy. We have relied on the South to carry the brunt. Now we would be responsible for satisfactory military outcome. . . .

JOHNSON: But I don't know how we are going to get the job done. There are millions of Chinese. I think they are going to put their stack in. Is this the best place to do it? We don't have the allies we had in Korea. Can we get our allies to cut off supplying the North?

MCNAMARA: No, sir, we can't prevent Japan, Britain, and the others from chartering ships to Haiphong [the North Vietnamese port].

JOHNSON: Are we starting something that in two or three years we simply can't finish?

BROWN: It is costly to us to strangle slowly. But the chances of losing are less if we move in.

6. George Ball's Dissenting Opinion, 1965

(1) A Losing War: The South Vietnamese are losing the war to the Viet Cong. No one can assure you that we can beat the Viet Cong or even force them to the conference table on our terms, no matter how many hundred thousand *white, foreign* (U.S.) troops we deploy.

No one has demonstrated that a white ground force of whatever size can win a guerrilla war—which is at the same time a civil war between Asians—in jungle terrain in the midst of a population that refuses cooperation to the white forces (and the South Vietnamese) and thus provides a great intelligence advantage to the other side. . . .

(2) The Question to Decide: Should we limit our liabilities in South Vietnam and try to find a way out with minimal long-term costs?

The alternative—no matter what we may wish it to be—is almost certainly a protracted war involving an open-ended commitment of U.S. forces, mounting U.S. casualties, no assurance of a satisfactory solution, and a serious danger of escalation at the end of the road.

(3) Need for a Decision Now: So long as our forces are restricted to advising and assisting the South Vietnamese, the struggle will remain a civil war between Asian peoples. Once we deploy substantial

numbers of troops in combat it will become a war between the U.S. and a large part of the population of South Vietnam, organized and directed from North Vietnam and backed by the resources of both Moscow and Peiping.

The decision you face now, therefore, is crucial. Once large numbers of U.S. troops are committed to direct combat, they will begin to take heavy casualties in a war they are ill-equipped to fight in a non-cooperative if not downright hostile countryside.

Once we suffer large casualties, we will have started a well-nigh irreversible process. Our involvement will be so great that we cannot—without national humiliation—stop short of achieving our complete objectives. *Of the two possibilities I think humiliation would be more likely than the achievement of our objectives—even after we have paid terrible costs.*

7. President Lyndon Johnson's Defense of the American Presence in Vietnam, 1965

Three times in my lifetime, in two world wars and in Korea, Americans have gone to far lands to fight for freedom. We have learned at a terrible and brutal cost that retreat does not bring safety and weakness does not bring peace.

It is this lesson that has brought us to Viet-Nam. This is a different kind of war. There are no marching armies or solemn declarations. Some citizens of South Viet-Nam, at times with understandable grievances, have joined in the attack on their own government.

But we must not let this mask the central fact that this is really war. It is guided by North Viet-Nam, and it is spurred by Communist China. Its goal is to conquer the South, to defeat American power, and to extend the Asiatic dominion of communism.

There are great stakes in the balance.

Most of the non-Communist nations of Asia cannot, by themselves and alone, resist the growing might and the grasping ambition of Asian Communism.

Our power, therefore, is a very vital shield. If we are driven from the field in Viet-Nam, then no nation can ever again have the same confidence in American promise or in American protection.

In each land the forces of independence would be considerably weakened and an Asia so threatened by Communist domination would certainly imperil the security of the United States itself.

We did not choose to be the guardians at the gate, but there is no one else.

Nor would surrender in Viet-Nam bring peace, because we learned from Hitler at Munich that success only feeds the appetite of aggression. The battle would be renewed in one country and then another country, bringing with it perhaps even larger and crueler conflict, as we have learned from the lessons of history.

Moreover, we are in Viet-Nam to fulfill one of the most solemn pledges of the American nation. Three Presidents—President Eisenhower, President Kennedy, and your present President—over 11 years have committed themselves and have promised to help defend this small and valiant nation.

Strengthened by that promise, the people of South Viet-Nam have fought for many long years. Thousands of them have died. Thousands more have been crippled and scarred by war. We just cannot now dishonor our word, or abandon our commitment, or leave those who believed us and who trusted us to the terror and repression and murder that would follow.

This, then, my fellow Americans, is why we are in Viet-Nam.

8. A Cartoon Essay on the Johnson Escalation,
   1965–1966

**A. Escalation of the Air War as the
Solution, 1965**

Herblock, © 1965 *The Washington Post*. From *The Herblock Gallery* (Simon & Schuster, 1968)

B. Secretary of Defense Robert McNamara Sketches the Future for Johnson, 1965

C. A Hard Choice, 1966

THE STRATEGISTS

Mauldin, © 1966 *Chicago Sun Times*. Courtesy of Bill Mauldin and Wil-Jo Associates, Inc. Reprinted with special permission North America Syndicate.

D. The Consequences of Escalation, ca. 1966

Yardley, *The Sun* (Baltimore, Md.)

Chapter 30:
Document Set 1 References

1. President John F. Kennedy's Analysis of Prospects for the Diem Regime, 1963
CBS Interview, September 2, 1963, United States Senate, Committee on Foreign Relations, *Background Information Relating to Southeast Asia and Vietnam,* 90th Cong., 1st Sess. (Washington, D.C.: Government Printing Office, 1967), pp. 112–114.

2. Roger Hilsman Recalls a Realistic Evaluation of the Situation in South Vietnam, 1963
Roger Hilsman, *To Move a Nation* (New York: Delta, 1964, rep. 1967), pp. 521–522.

3. Richard McNaughton's Assessment of Conditions in Vietnam, 1964
Richard C. McNaughton, "Action for South Vietnam," 2nd Draft, November 6, 1964, in Neil Sheehan *et al.,* comp., *The Pentagon Papers* (New York: Bantam, 1971), p. 365.

4. McGeorge Bundy Recommends "Sustained Reprisal," 1965
McGeorge Bundy, "A Policy of Sustained Reprisal," Annex A to Memorandum to Lyndon B. Johnson, February 7, 1965, in Sheehan *et al., Pentagon Papers,* pp. 423, 425–426.

5. A Major Policy Review, 1965
Account of Meetings, July 21–22, 1965, in Jack Valenti, *A Very Human President* (New York: W. W. Norton, 1975), pp. 322–340, 340–353.

6. George Ball's Dissenting Opinion, 1965

George W. Ball, Memorandum, "A Compromise Solution in South Vietnam," July 1, 1965, in Sheehan *et al., Pentagon Papers,* pp. 449–450.

7. President Lyndon Johnson's Defense of the American Presence in Vietnam, 1965
Lyndon B. Johnson, Statement, Press Conference, July 28, 1965, Department of State Bulletin, Vol. 53 (August 16, 1965).

8. A Cartoon Essay on the Johnson Escalation, 1965–1966.
    A. Escalation of the Air War as the Solution, 1965 (Herblock, *Washington Post,* 1965), in Editors of the Foreign Policy Association, eds., *A Cartoon History of United States Foreign Policy Since World War I* (New York: Random House, 1967), p. 211.
    B. Secretary of Defense Robert McNamara Sketches the Future for Johnson, 1965
    Le Pelley, *Christian Science Monitor,* Christian Science Publishing Society, 1965, in *A Cartoon History,* p. 203.
    C. A Hard Choice, 1966
    Bill Mauldin, *Chicago SunTimes,* 1966, in *A Cartoon History,* p. 206.
    D. The Consequences of Escalation, ca. 1966
    Yardley, *The Sun* (Baltimore, Md.), ca. 1966, in *A Cartoon History,* p. 201.

Chapter 30:
Document Set 1 Credits

CHAPTER 30

DOCUMENT SET 2
Black Nationalism and Black Power: When the Singing Stopped

As the first phase of the civil rights revolution reached an emotional climax with the March on Washington in 1963, other voices emerged to test the nonviolent direct-action philosophy of Martin Luther King, Jr. Your textbook suggests an element of irony and confusion in the growth of black nationalism at the Second Reconstruction's moment of victory in 1965. These documents trace the rise and development of a militant Black Power movement and its challenge to the increasingly factionalized civil rights movement. When you examine the source material, ask why the new concept gained support in the mid-1960s.

Although black nationalism has been a theme throughout African American history, its earliest expression in the postwar era came from the separatist Nation of Islam. Led by an articulate young militant, Malcolm X, the black Muslims surfaced as an important force in the urban communities of the "turbulent sixties." Read the excerpt from Malcolm's New York speech with an eye to the reasons for both his personal appeal to northern blacks and the growth of the movement.

With the assassination of Malcolm X in 1965, the remnants of black nationalism veered toward the rising Black Power movement. Using the textbook coverage of urban disorder and African American militancy as background, read the early expressions of the Black Power argument by SNCC leader Stokely Carmichael and Charles V. Hamilton. In analyzing their position,

think about the reasons white Americans found it threatening. As you attempt to explain the white reaction, compare Carmichael's and Hamilton's ideas with the uncompromising platform and program of the Black Panther party, adopted in 1966. Trace the origins of Black Power and try to summarize its basic principles.

Stunned by the vivid rhetoric of black nationalism and the reality of urban rioting, President Johnson established the National Commission on Civil Disorders to investigate the causes and remedies for the violence. Review the excerpt from the commission's report for clues to the origins of the problems of cities. The conclusions can help you understand the textbook's explanation of the president's reaction.

By the end of the decade, some militants moved beyond rhetoric to make demands on the white power structure. Symptomatic of the change was the Black Manifesto drafted by James Forman and adopted by the National Black Economic Development Conference in 1969. Note its basic assumptions and determine why its authors chose to focus on the churches and synagogues.

The central theme of these documents is a new concept of black awareness. As you review the evidence, try to identify the common thread that links the sources and to relate that idea to the aspirations of the entire African American community.

Questions for Analysis

1. What is the unifying theme found in most of the documents? How would you account for the central argument expressed? Why did a portion of the community find the Black Power concept attractive?

2. Define the term *black nationalism*. What is the relationship between the principles of Islam and the nationalist argument? Why was Malcolm X such an electrifying and compelling leader for his followers? What was the relationship between his ideas and the development of the Black Power movement?

3. What was the perspective of Black Power supporters on the successes and failures of the old civil rights movement? How would you explain the views of the new militants? In what way did their prescriptions and methods depart from the existing traditions of the civil rights movement?

4. According to the findings of the National Commission on Civil Disorders, what were the sources of the rioting and violence in the summer of 1967? In what ways did these findings coincide with the social analysis of Black Power advocates? How did their proposed solutions compare? To what extent have conditions changed since 1967?

5. What do the documents reveal about the age and class composition of the Black Power movement? What elements in the African American population did its supporters represent? How would you explain that support? In what way do the documents supply evidence of the relationship between Black Power goals and the objectives and aspirations of the broader African American community in the United States?

1. Malcolm X Demands Black Liberation, 1964

Friends and enemies, tonight I hope that we can have a little fireside chat with as few sparks as possible being tossed around. . . . I hope that this little conversation tonight about the black revolution won't cause many of you to accuse us of igniting it when you find it at your doorstep. . . .

I'm still a Muslim but I'm also a nationalist, meaning that my political philosophy is black nationalism, my economic philosophy is black nationalism, my social philosophy is black nationalism. And when I say that this philosophy is black nationalism, to me this means that the political philosophy of black nationalism is that which is designed to encourage our people, the black people, to gain complete control over the politics and the politicians of our own community.

Our economic philosophy is that we should gain economic control over the economy of our own community, the businesses and the other things which create employment so that we can provide jobs for our own people instead of having to picket and boycott and beg someone else for a job.

And, in short, our social philosophy means that we feel that it is time to get together among our own kind and eliminate the evils that are destroying the moral fiber of our society, like drug addiction, drunkenness, adultery that leads to an abundance of bastard children, welfare problems. We believe that we should lift the level or the standard of our own society to a higher level wherein we will be satisfied and then not inclined toward pushing ourselves into other societies where we are not wanted. . . .

Why is America in a position to bring about a bloodless revolution? Because the Negro in this country holds the balance of power and if the Negro in this country were given what the Constitution says he is supposed to have, the added power of the Negro in this country would sweep all of the racists and the segregationists out of office. It would change the entire political structure of the country. It would wipe out the Southern segregationism that now controls America's foreign policy, as well as America's domestic policy.

And the only way without bloodshed that this can be brought about is that the black man has to be given full use of the ballot in every one of the 50 states. But if the black man doesn't get the ballot, then you are going to be faced with another man who forgets the ballot and starts using the bullet.

Revolutions are fought to get control of land, to remove the absentee landlord and gain control of the land and the institutions that flow from that land. The black man has been in a very low condition because he has had no control whatsoever over any land. He has been a beggar economically, a beggar politically, a beggar socially, a beggar even when it comes to trying to get some education. So that in the past the type of mentality that was developed in this colonial system among our people, today is being overcome. And as the young ones come up they know what they want. And as they listen to your beautiful preaching about democracy and all those other flowery words, they know what they're supposed to have.

So you have a people today who not only know what they want, but also know what they are supposed to have. And they themselves are clearing another generation that is coming up that not only will know what it wants and know what it should have, but also will be ready and willing to do whatever is necessary to see that what they should have materializes immediately. Thank you.

2. Stokely Carmichael's Assertion of Black Consciousness, 1966

For too many years, black Americans marched and had their heads broken and got shot. They were saying to the country, "Look, you guys are supposed to be nice guys and we are only going to do what we are supposed to do—why do you beat us up, why don't you give us what we ask, why don't you straighten yourselves out?" After years of this, we are at almost the same point—because we demonstrated from a position of weakness. We cannot be expected any longer to march and have our heads broken in order to say to whites: come on, you're nice guys. For you are not nice guys. We have found you out. . . .

Ultimately, the economic foundations of this country must be shaken if black people are to control their lives. The colonies of the United States—and this includes the black ghettoes within its borders, North and South—must be liberated. For a century, this nation has been like an octopus of exploitation, its tentacles stretching from Mississippi and Harlem to South America, the Middle East, southern Africa, and Vietnam; the form of exploitation varies from area to area but the essential result has been the same—a powerful few have been maintained and enriched at the expense of the poor and voiceless colored masses. This pattern must be broken. As its grip loosens here and there around the world, the hopes of black Americans become more realistic. For racism to die, a totally different America must be born.

This is what the white society does not wish to face; this is why that society prefers to talk about integration. But integration speaks not at all to the problem of poverty, only to the problem of blackness. Integration today means the man who "makes it," leaving his black brothers behind in the ghetto as fast as his new sports car will take him. It has no relevance to the Harlem wino or to the cottonpicker making $3 a day. As a lady I know in Alabama once said, "The food that Ralph Bunche eats doesn't fill my stomach." . . .

But our vision is not merely of a society in which all black men have enough to buy the good things of life. When we urge that black money go into black pockets, we mean the communal pocket. We want to see money go back into the community and used to benefit it. We want to see the cooperative concept applied in business and banking. We want to see black ghetto residents demand that an exploiting storekeeper sell them, at minimal cost, a building or a shop that they will own and improve cooperatively; they can back their demand with a rent strike, or a boycott, and a community so unified behind them that no one else will move into the building or buy at the store. . . .

As for white America, perhaps it can stop crying out against "black supremacy," "black nationalism," "racism in reverse," and begin facing reality. The reality is that this nation, from top to bottom, is racist; that racism is not primarily a problem of "human relations" but of an exploitation maintained—either actively or through silence—by the society as a whole. . . . We are just going to work, in the way *we* see fit, and on goals *we* define, not for civil rights but for all our human rights.

3. Carmichael and Hamilton Define Black Power, 1967

The adoption of the concept of Black Power is one of the most legitimate and healthy developments in American politics and race relations in our time. The concept of Black Power speaks to all the needs mentioned in this chapter. It is a call for black people in this country to unite, to recognize their heritage, to build a sense of community. It is a call for black people to begin to define their own goals, to lead their own organizations and to support those organizations. It is a call to reject the racist institutions and values of this society.

The concept of Black Power rests on a fundamental premise: *Before a group can enter the open society, it must first close ranks.* By this we mean that group solidarity is necessary before a group can operate effectively from a bargaining position of strength in a pluralistic society. Traditionally, each new ethnic group in this society has found the route to social and political viability through the organization of its own institutions with which to represent its needs within the larger society. Studies in voting behavior specifically, and political behavior generally, have made it clear that politically the American pot has not melted. Italians vote for Rubino over O'Brien; Irish for Murphy over Goldberg, etc. This phenomenon may seem distasteful to some, but it has been and remains today a central fact of the American political system. . . .

The point is obvious: black people must lead and run their own organizations. Only black people can convey the revolutionary idea—and it is a revolutionary idea—that black people are able to do things themselves. Only they can help create in the community an aroused and continuing black consciousness that will provide the basis for political strength. In the past, white allies have often furthered white supremacy without the whites involved realizing it, or even wanting to do so. Black people must come together and do things for themselves. They must achieve self-identity and self-determination in order to have their daily needs met. . . .

It does not mean *merely* putting black faces into office. Black visibility is not Black Power. Most of the black politicians around the country today are not examples of Black Power. The power must be that of a community, and emanate from there. The black politicians must start from there. The black politicians must stop being representatives of "downtown" machines, whatever the cost might be in terms of lost patronage and holiday handouts.

Black Power recognizes—it must recognize—the ethnic basis of American politics as well as the power-oriented nature of American politics. Black Power therefore calls for black people to consolidate behind their own, so that they can bargain from a position of strength. But while we endorse the *procedure* of group solidarity and identity for the purpose of attaining certain goals in the body politic, this does not mean that black people should strive for the same kind of rewards (i.e., end results) obtained by the white society. The ultimate values and goals are not domination or exploitation of other groups, but rather an effective share in the total power of the society.

4. The Black Panther Program, 1966

1. *We want freedom. We want power to determine the destiny of our Black Community.* . . .

2. *We want full employment for our people.* . . .

3. *We want an end to the robbery by the white man of our Black Community.* . . .

4. *We want decent housing, fit for shelter of human beings.* . . .

5. *We want education for our people that exposes the true nature of this decadent American society. We want education that teaches us our true history and our role in the present-day society.* . . .

6. *We want all black men to be exempt from military service.* . . .

7. *We want an immediate end to POLICE BRUTALITY and MURDER of black people.* . . .

8. *We want freedom for all black men held in federal, state, county and city prisons and jails.* . . .

9. *We want all black people when brought to trial to be tried in court by a jury of their peer group or people from their black communities, as defined by the Constitution of the United States.* . . .

10. *We want land, bread, housing, education, clothing, justice and peace. And as our major political objective, a United Nations-supervised plebiscite to be held throughout the black colony in which only black colonial subjects will be allowed to participate, for the purpose of determining the will of black people as to their national destiny.*

5. The Kerner Commission Report on the Causes of Civil Disorders, 1968

The summer of 1967 again brought racial disorders to American cities, and with them shock, fear and bewilderment to the nation.

The worst came during a two-week period in July, first in Newark and then in Detroit. Each set off a chain reaction in neighboring communities.

On July 28, 1967, the President of the United States established this Commission and directed us to answer three basic questions:

What happened?
Why did it happen?
What can be done to prevent it from happening again? . . .

This is our basic conclusion: Our nation is moving toward two societies, one black, one white—separate and unequal.

Reaction to last summer's disorders has quickened the movement and deepened the division. Discrimination and segregation have long permeated much of American life; they now threaten the future of every American.

This deepening racial division is not inevitable. The movement apart can be reversed. Choice is still possible. Our principal task is to define that choice and to press for a national resolution. . . .

Race prejudice has shaped our history decisively; it now threatens to affect our future.

White racism is essentially responsible for the explosive mixture which has been accumulating in our cities since the end of World War II. Among the ingredients of this mixture are:

- *Pervasive discrimination and segregation* in employment, education and housing, which have resulted in the continuing exclusion of great numbers of Negroes from the benefits of economic progress.
- *Black in-migration and white exodus,* which have produced the massive and growing concentrations of impoverished Negroes in our major cities, creating a growing crisis of deteriorating facilities and services and unmet human needs.
- *The black ghettos,* where segregation and poverty converge on the young to destroy opportunity and enforce failure. Crime, drug addiction, dependency on welfare, and bitterness and resentment against society in general and white society in particular are the result. . . .

Yet these facts alone cannot be said to have caused the disorders. Recently, other powerful ingredients have begun to catalyze the mixture:

- *Frustrated hopes* are the residue of the unfulfilled expectations aroused by the great judicial and legislative victories of the civil rights movement and the dramatic struggle for equal rights in the South.
- *A climate that tends toward approval and encouragement of violence* as a form of protest has been created by white terrorism directed against nonviolent protest; by the open defiance of law and federal authority by state and local officials resisting desegregation; and by some protest groups engaging in civil disobedience who turn their backs on nonviolence, go beyond the constitutionally protected rights of petition and free assembly, and resort to violence to attempt to compel alteration of laws and policies with which they disagree.
- *The frustrations of powerlessness* have led some Negroes to the conviction that there is no effective alternative to violence as a means of achieving redress of grievances, and of "moving the system." These frustrations are reflected in alienation and hostility toward the institutions of law and government and the white society which controls them, and in the reach toward racial consciousness and solidarity reflected in the slogan "Black Power."
- *A new mood* has sprung up among Negroes, particularly among the young, in which self-esteem and enhanced racial pride are replacing apathy and submission to "the system."
- *The police are not merely a "spark" factor.* To some Negroes police have come to symbolize white power, white racism and white repression. And the fact is that many police do reflect and express these white attitudes. The atmosphere of hostility and cynicism is reinforced by a widespread belief among Negroes in the existence of police brutality and in a "double standard" of justice and protection—one for Negroes and one for whites. . . .

The major goal is the creation of a true union—a single society and a single American identity. Toward that goal, we propose the following objectives for national action:

- Opening up opportunities to those who are restricted by racial segregation and discrimination and eliminating all barriers to their choice of jobs, education and housing.
- Removing the frustration of powerlessness among the disadvantaged by providing the means for them to deal with the problems that affect their own lives and by increasing the capacity of our public and private institutions to respond to these problems.

- Increasing communication across racial lines to destroy stereotypes, to halt polarization, end distrust and hostility and create common ground for efforts toward public order and social justice.

We propose these aims to fulfill our pledge of equality and to meet the fundamental needs of a democratic and civilized society—domestic peace and social justice.

6. James Forman's Black Manifesto, 1969

Brothers and Sisters:

We have come from all over the country, burning with anger and despair not only with the miserable economic plight of our people, but fully aware that the racism on which the Western world was built dominates our lives. . . .

We *HAVE* an ideology. Our fight is against racism, capitalism and imperialism and we are dedicated to building a socialist society inside the United States where the total means of production and distribution are in the hands of the State and that must be led by black people, by revolutionary blacks who are concerned about the total humanity of this world. And, therefore, we obviously are different from some of those who seek a black nation in the United States, for there is no way for that nation to be viable if in fact the United States remains in the hands of white racists. Then too, let us deal with some arguments that we should share power with whites. We say that there must be a revolutionary black Vanguard and that white people in this country must be willing to accept black leadership, for that is the only protection that black people have to protect ourselves from racism rising again in this country. . . .

Our seizure of power at this conference is based on a program and our program is contained in the following *Manifesto:*

TO THE WHITE CHRISTIAN CHURCHES
AND THE
JEWISH SYNAGOGUES
IN THE UNITED STATES OF AMERICA AND ALL
OTHER RACIST INSTITUTIONS

Black Manifesto

We the black people assembled in Detroit, Michigan, for the National Black Economic Development Conference are fully aware that we have been forced to come together because racist white America has exploited our resources, our minds, our bodies, our labor. For centuries we have been forced to live as colonized people inside the United States, victimized by the most vicious, racist system in the world. We have helped to build the most industrial country in the world.

We are therefore demanding of the white Christian churches and Jewish synagogues which are part and parcel of the system of capitalism, that they begin to pay reparations to black people in this country. We are demanding $500,000,000 from the Christian white churches and the Jewish synagogues. . . .

We do not intend to abuse our black brothers and sisters in black churches who have uncritically accepted Christianity. We want them to understand how the racist white Christian church with its hypocritical declarations and doctrines of brotherhood has abused our trust and faith. An attack on the religious beliefs of black people is not our major objective, even though we know that we were not Christians when we were brought to this country, but that Christianity was used to help enslave us. Our objective in issuing this Manifesto is to force the racist white Christian church to begin the payment of reparations which are due to all black people, not only by the church but also by private business and the U.S. government. We see this focus on the Christian church as an effort around which all black people can unite.

Our demands are negotiable, but they cannot be minimized, they can only be increased and the church is asked to come up with larger sums of money than we are asking. Our slogans are:

ALL ROADS MUST LEAD TO REVOLUTION

UNITE WITH WHOMEVER YOU CAN UNITE

NEUTRALIZE WHEREVER POSSIBLE

FIGHT OUR ENEMIES RELENTLESSLY

VICTORY TO THE PEOPLE

LIFE AND GOOD HEALTH TO MANKIND

RESISTANCE TO DOMINATION BY THE WHITE CHRISTIAN CHURCHES AND THE JEWISH SYNAGOGUES

REVOLUTIONARY BLACK POWER

WE SHALL WIN WITHOUT A DOUBT

Chapter 30:
Document Set 2 References

1. Malcolm X Demands Black Liberation, 1964
   Malcolm X, "The Black Revolution," April 8, 1964, *Two Speeches by Malcolm X* (New York: Merit, 1965), pp. 5, 14.

2. Stokely Carmichael's Assertion of Black Consciousness, 1966
   Stokely Carmichael, "What We Want," *New York Review of Books* (September 22, 1966).

3. Carmichael and Hamilton Define Black Power, 1967
   Stokely Carmichael and Charles V. Hamilton, *Black Power: The Politics of Liberation in America* (New York: Random House, 1967), pp. 44–47.

4. The Black Panther Program, 1966
   Black Panther Party Platform and Program, October 1966.

5. The Kerner Commission Report on the Causes of Civil Disorders, 1968
   Report of the National Advisory Commission on Civil Disorders (Washington, D.C.: Government Printing Office, 1968), pp. 1–13.

6. James Forman's Black Manifesto, 1969
   James Forman, "Black Manifesto," a speech delivered at the National Black Economic Development Conference in Detroit, Michigan, April 26, 1969, *Renewal*, Vol. 9, No. 6 (June 1969).

Chapter 30:
Document Set 2 Credits

CHAPTER 30

DOCUMENT SET 3
Huelga: Religion, Nonviolence, and the Rise of the UFW

Central to the history of the 1960s was the increased militance of minority groups seeking economic, political, and social equality in America. One of the most active freedom movements of this turbulent time resulted from the intensification of ethnic consciousness in the large Mexican American community of the Southwest. Inspired by the philosophy and example of Martin Luther King, Jr., and impressed by the advances made by African Americans, farmworker César Chávez worked to mobilize field laborers long exploited by Western agribusiness into the shock troops of a sweeping social movement.

Some of the most useful sources in the study of recent history are interviews conducted with the participants in the events that shaped modern American life. Among the documents contained in this unit are the recollections of two of the founders of the United Farmworkers Association, Jessie Lopez de la Cruz and Eugene Nelson. Note the differences in their accounts of the movement's development in the 1960s and account for the emphasis in each.

The documents offer insight into the character of unionism among the predominantly Mexican American workers who provided cheap labor in California and elsewhere in the Southwest. Be aware of the extent to which religious commitment became an important factor in the drive for social and economic justice. Note also the link between the churches and organized labor in the effort to improve the conditions and status of exploited workers. Assess the motivations of the organizations and institutions that committed themselves to the battle.

As you reflect upon the coalition that arose to support Chávez and the UFW, think about the fundamental nature of the struggle they had undertaken. Was it a labor movement? Was it a social movement? What is the difference? What was the outcome?

Finally, use these documents to evaluate the impact on history of personalities and the committed individual. Does the career of César Chávez support the "great man" theory of history? Would Chávez have considered himself a "great man"? How would you assess his role as an influence on the course of American social and economic history? Be sure to consider the impact of charisma on the course of great social movements. As you weigh the evidence, make your own judgment of Chávez's importance as a symbolic leader. In what ways did his life make a difference in the lives of his followers and supporters?

Questions for Analysis

1. What were the economic goals pursued by César Chávez and the UFW? What were his social goals? In what ways did the farmworkers' struggle display the characteristics of a social movement?

2. What were the most important influences on Chávez and the movement? How were they reflected in his policies, decisions, tactics, and actions?

3. In what ways does the evidence reflect the themes that dominated American social history in the 1960s? What do the documents reveal about the relationship between the civil rights movement and the other freedom struggles of the 1960s?

4. Chávez once said: "We want radical change. Nothing short of radical change is going to have any impact on our lives or our problems. We want sufficient power to control our own destinies." Assess his career and leadership in terms of his success or failure in achieving his goals.

1. Picket Captain Eugene Nelson Describes the Origins of the Delano Strike, 1965

As it nears its 100th day, the strike is going nationwide. The forgotten farm worker has made his voice heard at last. On December 12th the Student Nonviolent Coordinating Committee announces a cross-country boycott of Schenley products and Delano area grapes, and a few days later the boycott is to be joined by CORE, the United Auto Workers and other influential groups. Growers openly admit the boycott will hurt them, but stubbornly refuse to negotiate.

December 13th the most impressive group of church dignitaries ever to visit the Delano area arrives for a two-day inspection of the strike zone. The distinguished group includes Father James Vizzard, S.J., director of the National Catholic Rural Life Conference; Lester C. Hunt, executive assistant of the Bishops' Committee for the Spanish Speaking; Rabbi Erwin L. Herman of the Synagogue Council of America; Robert McAfee Brown, celebrated professor of religion at Stanford University; and seven other noted clergymen. The growers' ire and bad manners know no bounds, and they snub the distinguished clergymen after agreeing to a noon luncheon meet. Claiming a misunderstanding, they finally meet with them in the late afternoon for a chaotic and unproductive conference punctuated by insults to the visiting clerics.

The clergymen release a joint statement to the press, in which they affirm that "The right of churches and synagogues to engage in such action (studying the strike situation) is absolutely clear to us. We reject the heresy that churches and synagogues are to be concerned only with so-called 'spiritual' matters. We believe that this is God's world, which he not only made but continues to love. Consequently, whatever goes on in his world must be our concern, particularly when his will for the well-being of any of his children is being violated.". . .

Next day, in an incredible act of petty harassment, the local police refuse to renew our permit for the incinerators we use to warm ourselves by on all night picket duty in the freezing cold along the railroad tracks, and confiscate the containers. Our pickets are forced to stand out in below freezing weather.

But as often has been the case throughout the strike, the pettiness of our opponents is followed by a windfall for us. In this case it comes in the form of Walter Reuther of the United Auto Workers, and the endorsement of the AFL-CIO, which has just held a national convention in San Francisco. If we felt certain before that we ultimately would win the strike, now we are doubly certain.

Arriving on December 16th, the 100th day the FWA has been on strike, Reuther leads hundreds of workers on a march through the streets, proudly carrying a Huelga sign as he walks beside César Chávez of the FWA and Larry Itliong of the AWOC. Even now the growers cannot act civilized, and the march is marred when an intoxicated rancher is arrested for assaulting Migrant Ministers Dave Havens and Jim Drake.

Pandemonium breaks out as Reuther enters the crowded Filipino Hall; the large auditorium is overflowing with a standing-room-only crowd. César Chávez speaks to a tumultuous ovation, and then the applause of the crowd soars even louder as Reuther stands up to speak.

"This is not *your* strike, this is *our* strike," he begins, and the crowd erupts in wild applause, punctuated by choruses of "Huelga!" and "Viva Reuther!" "There is no power in the world like the power of free men working together in a just cause. If General Motors had to change *its* mind because of the auto workers, then the growers will have to change *their* mind, and the sooner they do, the better for them, the better for you and the better for the community. We will mobilize every weapon we have and fight back, we will put the full support of organized labor behind your boycott and this is a powerful economic weapon. You are leading history, and we march here together, fight here together and we will win here together."

... [I]t is a certainty that with the combined forces of organized labor, organized religion and the nation's civil rights groups behind the farm worker, the growers realize by now that they can wage at best nothing but a delaying battle. How long it will last, no one can say. . . .

Something remarkable has happened in the town of Delano, something which a scant few months ago no one foresaw. A pattern for a New America has emerged out of the chaos of a bitter labor dispute, the pattern of people of all races and backgrounds working and living together in perfect and unprecedented harmony. Idealistic people in other parts of America talk about this ideal; in Delano today it is working. When the strike began last September "Huelga" meant only that: "Strike." But something has happened along the way; "Huelga" has come to mean something more than "Strike"; it has come to mean cooperation, brotherhood, Love. The brotherly love of men working for a single high ideal; the healthy self-love of men fulfilling the dictates of their consciences. In Delano a new spirit is emerging, a spirit that may sweep over the earth, the spirit of brother-help-brother instead of dog-eat-dog. The growers or no one else can resist that spirit.

2. Jessie Lopez de la Cruz Offers a Woman's Perspective on *La Causa*, 1962–1970

It was very hard being a woman organizer. Many of our people my age and older were raised with the old customs in Mexico: where the husband rules, he is the king of his house. The wife obeys, and the children, too. So when we first started it was very, very hard. Men gave us the most trouble—neighbors there in Parlier! They were for the union, but they were not taking orders from women, they said. When they formed the ranch committee at Christian Brothers—that's a big wine company, part of it is in Parlier—the ranch committee was all men. We were working under our first contract in Fresno County. The ranch committee had to enforce the contract. If there are any grievances they meet with us and the supervisors. But there were no women on that first committee.

That year, we'd have a union meeting every week. Men, women, and children would come. Women would ask questions and the men would just stand back. I guess they'd say to themselves, "I'll wait for someone to say something before I do." The women were more aggressive than the men.

When the first contract was up, we talked about there being no women on the ranch committee. I suggested they be on it, and the men went along with this. And so women were elected. . . .

3. César Chávez Consolidates His Alliance with the Churches, 1968

To My Friends in the National Council of Churches:

I have just begun the seventh day of a personal fast of penance and hope. After so many months of struggle and slow progress, I have become fearful that our common commitment to non-violence is weakening and that we may take dangerous short-cuts to victory. I accept full responsibility for this temptation and for all of its possible negative results. Our hope is the same as it has always been: that farm workers here can work together to change unjust conditions and thus to serve their brothers throughout the land.

My fast is informed by my religious faith and by my deep roots in the Church. It is not intended as a pressure on anyone but only as an expression of my own deep feelings and my own need to do penance and to be in prayer. I know you will understand and I ask that you pray for me.

I regret that I cannot be with you in San Diego. My own weakness and the crucial importance of non-violence for our struggle are the only things that could have kept me from your meeting. Please forgive me.

I would like to express the thanks of all Delano strikers for the early and faithful support of the churches. You have been with us from the beginning and at cost and we shall not forget it.

Our struggle in Delano is not over. In some ways it becomes more difficult each day. Our success (or failure) here and the quality of the organization we build will help us to shape the future for farm workers everywhere in our country. We do not take this responsibility lightly. But we cannot be faithful to this responsibility without the participation of the Christian community. You can help us survive and win new victories; but because of who you represent you can also help us stay true to our intention to serve our fellow farm workers.

We need and want your continued presence and support.

Sincerely,

César Chávez
February 20, 1968

4. Chávez Defines the Character of the Movement, 1969

Dear Mr. Barr:

I am sad to hear about your accusations in the press that our union movement and table grape boycott have been successful because we have used violence and terror tactics. If what you say is true, I have been a failure and should withdraw from the struggle. But you are left with the awesome moral responsibility, before God and man, to come forward with what-

ever information you have so that corrective action can begin at once. . . .

By lying about the nature of our movement, Mr. Barr, you are working against non-violent social change. Unwittingly perhaps, you may unleash that other force that our union by discipline and deed, censure and education has fought to avoid; that panacean short cut: that senseless violence that honors no color, class or neighborhood.

You must understand—I must make you understand—that our membership and the hopes and aspirations of the hundreds of thousands of the poor and dispossessed that have been raised on our account, are above all, human beings, no better no worse than any other cross section of human society; we are not saints because we are poor but by the same measure neither are we immoral. We are men and women who have suffered and endured much and not only because of our abject poverty but because we have been kept poor. The color of our skins, the languages of our cultural and native origins, the lack of formal education, the exclusion from the democratic process, the numbers of our slain in recent wars—all these burdens generation after generation have sought to demoralize us, to break our human spirit. But God knows that we are not beasts of burden, we are not agricultural implements or rented slaves, we are men. And mark this well, Mr. Barr, we are men locked in a death struggle against man's inhumanity to man in the industry that you represent. And this struggle itself gives meaning to our life and ennobles our dying. . . .

For this is not to pretend that we have everywhere been successful enough or that we have not made mistakes. And while we do not belittle or underestimate our adversaries, for they are the rich and the powerful and possess the land, we are not afraid nor do we cringe from the confrontation. We welcome it! We have planned for it. We know that our cause is just, that history is a story of social revolutions, and that the poor shall inherit the land.

Once again, I appeal to you as the representative of your industry and as a man. I ask you to recognize and bargain with our union before the economic pressure of the boycott and strike takes an irrevocable toll; but if not, I ask you to at least sit down with us to discuss the safeguards necessary to keep our historical struggle free of violence. I make this appeal because as one of the leaders of our nonviolent movement, I know and accept my responsibility for preventing, if possible, the destruction of human life and property. . . .

We advocate militant nonviolence as our means for social revolution and to achieve justice for our people, but we are not blind or deaf to the desperate and moody winds of human frustration, impatience and rage that blow among us. Gandhi himself admitted that if his only choices were cowardice or violence, he would choose violence. Men are not angels and the time and tides wait for no man. Precisely because of these powerful human emotions, we have tried to involve masses of people in their own struggle. Participation and self-determination remain the best experience of freedom; and free men instinctively prefer democratic change and even protect the rights guaranteed to seek it. Only the enslaved in despair have need of violent overthrow.

This letter does not express all that is in my heart, Mr. Barr. But if it says nothing else it says that we do not hate you or rejoice to see your industry destroyed; we hate the agribusiness system that seeks to keep us enslaved and we shall overcome and change it not by retaliation or bloodshed but by a determined non-violent struggle carried on by those masses of farm workers who intend to be free and human.

Sincerely Yours,

César F. Chávez

5. A Symbol of Hope for California's Rural
   Underclass, ca. 1960s

Chapter 30:
Document Set 3 References

1. Picket Captain Eugene Nelson Describes the Origins of the Delano Strike, 1965
   Eugene Nelson, *Huelga* (Delano, Calif.: Farm Workers Press, 1966), pp. 120, 121–122.

2. Jessie Lopez de la Cruz Offers a Woman's Perspective on *La Causa,* 1962–1970
   Excerpted from an interview with Jessie de la Cruz in Ellen Cantarow, *Moving the Mountain: Women Working for Social Change* (Old Westbury, N.Y.: Feminist Press, 1978), p. 36.

3. César Chávez Consolidates His Alliance with the Churches, 1968
   César Chávez to National Council of Churches, February 20, 1968, in Winthrop Yinger, *César Chávez: The Rhetoric of Nonviolence* (Hicksville, N.Y.: Exhibition Press, 1975), pp. 108–109.

4. Chávez Defines the Character of the Movement, 1969
   Chávez to E. L. Barr, President California Grape and Tree Fruit League, April 23, 1969, in Yinger, pp. 112, 113, 114, 115.

5. A Symbol of Hope for California's Rural Underclass, ca. 1960s
   "Farmworkers, AFL–CIO," in George D. Horwitz, *La Causa: The California Grape Strike* (New York: Macmillan, 1970), frontispiece.

Chapter 30:
Document Set 3 Credits

CHAPTER 31

Vietnam and the Young: "Wild in the Streets"

Despite the optimism created by an economy of abundance, the 1960s produced unprecedented dissent and a new radicalism born of dissatisfaction with American affluence. Your textbook stresses the social disintegration of this troubled decade, which led to severe fragmentation by the 1970s. The key to the emergence of widespread social unrest was the maturation of a new generation of middle-class youth, the children of comfortable, college-educated parents. From these roots sprang the politically conscious New Left that did much to make the 1960s a period of turbulence and conflict.

The following documents trace the development of the New Left on college campuses, with emphasis on the disruptive and radicalizing impact of the war in Vietnam. As you review the evidence, watch for the issues that galvanized the protest movement, and think about the reasons they captured the imagination of militant youth. The first document, the Port Huron Statement adopted by Students for a Democratic Society in 1962, set the agenda for a generation of politicized youth. Compare this statement with the *Manifesto* drafted in 1969 by the Weatherman faction of the SDS, which measures the escalation of social tension that had occurred since 1962.

Several documents record events that helped radicalize activist student groups during the 1960s. Both the *New Republic* account of the University of Wisconsin Dow demonstrations and the Walker report on the police riot at the 1968 Democratic Convention reflect the generational conflict seething beneath the political surface as the Vietnam War escalated. Be aware of the social profile of the demonstrators, and analyze their motives.

The central place of the war in the "movement," particularly in the consciousness of the young, is evident in the music lyrics of the period. Pete Seeger's "Waist Deep in the Big Muddy" reflects concern over the divisive domestic- and foreign-policy issues of the day. As you analyze the words, think about the meaning of folk, rock, or other music as an expression of the values and concerns of the audience to whom they are addressed.

Given the rise in campus protest and street violence, it was not surprising that opposition to the New Left formed by the late 1960s. Against the background of the militant SDS *Manifesto*, evaluate the sources of conservative dissatisfaction. Review Tom Anderson's "Dear Brats" letter, which appeared in *American Opinion*, a conservative journal, for evidence of public reaction to student radicalism. Compare Anderson's tone to that of Vice President Spiro T. Agnew, whose attack on the Vietnam Moratorium demonstrations also recorded a political response to the antiwar movement. Assess these appeals to law and order in the context of themes evident in the Nixon administration, as described in the textbook coverage of the Silent Majority.

Questions for Analysis

1. Why were the college and university campuses the center of political and social dissent in the 1960s? What aspects of the campus environment described in the documents contributed to the development of the youth rebellion? What was the relationship between student radicalism and social class?

2. What were the sources of student discontent in the 1960s? Which issues seem to have been most significant in motivating students to become politically active? Why? How would you compare the political values of these students with those of your own generation? Explain.

3. In what way is popular music a measure of public political and social concerns? Using the lyrics from the song by Pete Seeger, explain how folk/rock music reflects the social environment in which it is produced and consumed. Using your textbook as a resource, relate the message in this song to the events occurring in 1967. Why did "Waist Deep in the Big Muddy" create a minor sensation when it was performed on national television? What are the limits of dissent in wartime? What did the popularity of such music reflect about the nature of the Vietnam War?

4. Whom did conservative critics hold responsible for the social disorder associated with campus radicalism and political dissent in the 1960s? Do the documents reveal common assumptions among the group described in your textbook (and by President Nixon) as the Silent Majority? How did conservatives think popular protest should be handled?

5. Compare the objectives evident in the Port Huron Statement with the ideas expressed in the *Manifesto* published by the SDS Weatherman faction in 1969. How had the assumptions and goals of the New Left evolved between 1962 and 1969? What factors explain the changes that had occurred?

6. Your textbook refers to generational continuities and generation gap. What do the documents reveal about the differences in values and assumptions between the postwar generation and the generation that had matured during World War II and the early Cold War years?

1. The Port Huron Statement Sets the Social Agenda for SDS, 1962

Introduction: Agenda for a Generation

We are people of this generation, bred in at least modest comfort, housed now in universities, looking uncomfortably to the world we inherit.

When we were kids the United States was the wealthiest and strongest country in the world; the only one with the atom bomb, the least scarred by modern war, an initiator of the United Nations that we thought would distribute Western influence throughout the world. Freedom and equality for each individual, government of, by, and for the people— these American values we found good, principles by which we could live as men. Many of us began maturing in complacency.

As we grew, however, our comfort was penetrated by events too troubling to dismiss. First, the permeating and victimizing fact of human degradation, symbolized by the Southern struggle against racial bigotry, compelled most of us from silence to activism. Second, the enclosing fact of the Cold War, symbolized by the presence of the Bomb, brought awareness that we ourselves, and our friends, and millions of abstract "others" we knew more directly because of our common peril, might die at any time.

We might deliberately ignore, or avoid, or fail to feel all other human problems, but not these two, for these were too immediate and crushing in their impact, too challenging in the demand that we as individuals take the responsibility for encounter and resolution.

While these and other problems either directly oppressed us or rankled our consciences and became our own subjective concerns, we began to see complicated and disturbing paradoxes in our surrounding America. The declaration "all men are created equal . . . " rang hollow before the facts of Negro life in the South and the big cities of the North. The proclaimed peaceful intentions of the United States contradicted its economic and military investments in the Cold War status quo.

. . . While two-thirds of mankind suffers undernourishment, our own upper classes revel amidst superfluous abundance. Although world population is expected to double in forty years, the nations still tolerate anarchy as a major principle of international conduct and uncontrolled exploitation governs the sapping of the earth's physical resources. Although mankind desperately needs revolutionary leadership, America rests in national stalemate, its goals ambiguous and tradition-bound instead of informed and clear, its democratic system apathetic and manipulated rather than "of, by, and for the people." . . .

Towards American Democracy

. . . 1 *America must abolish its political party stalemate.* . . .

2 *Mechanisms of voluntary association must be created through which political information can be imparted and political participation encouraged.* . . .

3 *Institutions and practices which stifle dissent should be abolished, and the promotion of peaceful dissent should be actively promoted.* . . .

4 *Corporations must be made publicly responsible.* . . .

5 *The allocation of resources must be based on social needs. A truly "public sector" must be established, and its nature debated and planned.* . . .

6 *America should concentrate on its genuine social priorities: abolish squalor, terminate neglect, and establish an environment for people to live in with dignity and creativeness.*

2. The Dow Demonstrations Polarize the University Community in Wisconsin, 1967

The faculty of the University of Wisconsin, said to run the place, has given the new Chancellor, William H. Sewell, a vote of confidence for the way he handled the peaceable student demonstration here. Sewell brought the Madison police riot squad onto campus to disperse 200 people sitting down outside a room where Dow Chemical Company representatives were holding job interviews. Dow makes napalm used by our forces in Vietnam.

Instead of clearing the building, the police clubbed, stomped and tear gassed those inside, as well as 1,500 students standing outside. . . .

On the morning of October 18, the demonstrators had proceeded in rag-tag formation to the Commerce Building, a few blocks from where the Dow men were conducting their interviews. The demonstration had an altogether festive air; reporters and cameramen clogged the entranceway to Commerce. The demonstrators had to push their way in. Finally some 200 got inside, solidly packing every bit of space on the main floor. During the morning Ralph Hansen, the campus police chief, called Chancellor Sewell and told him his force couldn't handle the demonstrators; Sewell told him to go ahead and call in the city police. Larry Silver, a graduate student in the Law School, was inside the Commerce Building and reports what happened next:

"Approximately at 12:30 Chief Hansen asked to see some of the leaders of the demonstration. He knew them by name. He talked to them and they said over a loudspeaker there was going to be a deal: If Dow would leave, the demonstrators would leave.

Everyone cheered with approval . . . the protest leaders then left to get confirmation of this offer from Chancellor Sewell. They returned; they announced that their meeting with the chancellor did not produce this result and that Dow would not leave. At this point Chief Hansen took the loudspeaker and addressed the noisy demonstrators: This is an unlawful assembly. If you wish to avoid arrest, leave now. The halls were so packed that there was no possibility of emptying them in less than 10 minutes. Within one minute of Chief Hansen's arrest warnings, at least 20 riot police, helmeted, with clubs swinging, charged the crowd. I could see several assaulted protestors falling. As they fell, police continued to beat them. . . . There was immediate panic among the protestors; there was no place to go; they were forced to face the police lines. When people tried to leave voluntarily, they were clubbed, tripped, and clubbed some more. . . . [A girl] wanted to get out. She tried to get up, but the police clubbed her to the floor with blows to the head and shoulders. At this point of the pandemonium, I was pushed back by the crowd which was trying to avoid the riot police." . . .

While this [faculty meeting the next day] was going on, Republicans who run the state legislature had whipped themselves into a frenzy. They thought Sewell was too lenient; a committee was set up to get the facts; it subpoenaed students to get the names of others. One representative suggested that future demonstrators deserved to be shot; others wanted the FBI to help find the students who had cut down an American flag from atop Bascom Hall.

Among both the faculty and legislators there is a growing conviction that the demonstration was part of a conspiracy masterminded by Students for a Democratic Society and the Du Bois Clubs. The only trouble with this theory is that people who have tried to find the local Du Bois Club chapter can't find it; and SDS was against the demonstration because its members, who at the hard core number perhaps 25, felt the protest did not reach to substantive issues.

3. Images of War in Folk Music: Pete Seeger Stirs Up Controversy, 1967

Waist Deep in the Big Muddy

Pete Seeger

It was back in nineteen forty two,
I was part of a good platoon.
We were on maneuvers in Loosiana,
One night by the light of the moon.
    The captain told us to ford a river,
    And that's how it all begun.
    We were knee deep in the Big Muddy,
    But the big fool said to push on. . . .

The sergeant said, "Sir, with all this equipment,
No man will be able to swim."
"Sergeant, don't be a nervous nellie,"
The Captain said to him.
    "All we need is a little determination;
    Men, follow me, I'll lead on."
    We were neck deep in the Big Muddy
    And the big fool said to push on.

All of a sudden, the moon clouded over,
We heard a gurgling cry.
A few seconds later, the captain's helmet
Was all that floated by.
    The sergeant said, "Turn around men,

I'm in charge from now on."
And we just made it out of the Big Muddy
With the captain dead and gone.

We stripped and dived and found his body
Stuck in the old quicksand.
I guess he didn't know that the water was deeper
Than the place he'd once before been.
    Another stream had joined the Big Muddy
    Just a half mile from where we'd gone.
    We'd been lucky to escape from the Big Muddy
    When the big fool said to push on.

Well, maybe you'd rather not draw any moral;
I'll leave that to yourself.
Maybe you're still walking and you're still talking
And you'd like to keep your health.
    But every time I read the papers
    That old feeling comes on:
    We're waist deep in the Big Muddy and
    The Big Fool says to push on. . . .

Waist deep! Neck deep!
Soon even a tall man'll be over his head!
Waist deep in the BIG MUDDY!
AND THE BIG FOOL SAYS TO PUSH ON!!

4. A Police Riot in the Streets of Chicago, 1968

During the week of the Democratic National Convention, the Chicago police were the targets of mounting provocation by both word and act. It took the form of obscene epithets, and of rocks, sticks, bathroom tiles and even human feces hurled at police by demonstrators. Some of these acts had been planned; others were spontaneous or were themselves provoked by police action. Furthermore, the police had been put on edge by widely published threats of attempts to disrupt both the city and the Convention.

That was the nature of the provocation. The nature of the response was unrestrained and indiscriminate police violence on many occasions, particularly at night.

That violence was made all the more shocking by the fact that it was often inflicted upon persons who had broken no law, disobeyed no order, made no threat. These included peaceful demonstrators, on-lookers, and large numbers of residents who were simply passing through, or happened to live in, the areas where confrontations were occurring.

Newsmen and photographers were singled out for assault, and their equipment deliberately damaged. Fundamental police training was ignored; and officers, when on the scene, were often unable to control their men. As one police officer put it: "What happened didn't have anything to do with police work." . . .

On August 18, 1968, the advance contingent of demonstrators arrived in Chicago and established their base, as planned, in Lincoln Park on the city's Near North Side. Throughout the week, they were joined by others—some from the Chicago area, some from states as far away as New York and California. On the weekend before the convention began, there were about 2,000 demonstrators in Lincoln Park; the crowd grew to about 10,000 by Wednesday.

There were, of course, the hippies—the long hair and love beads, the calculated unwashedness, the flagrant banners, the open lovemaking and disdain for the constraints of conventional society. In dramatic effect, both visual and vocal, these dominated a crowd whose members actually differed widely in physical appearance, in motivation, in political affiliation, in philosophy. . . .

To characterize the crowd, then, as entirely hippy-Yippie, entirely "New Left," entirely anarchist, or entirely youthful political dissenters is both wrong and dangerous. The stereotyping that did occur helps to explain the emotional reaction of both police and public during and after the violence that occurred.

Despite the presence of some revolutionaries, the vast majority of the demonstrators were intent on expressing by peaceful means their dissent either from society generally or from the administration's policies in Vietnam.

5. SDS Militants Endorse Revolution, 1969

The goal is the destruction of US imperialism and the achievement of a classless world: world communism. Winning state power in the US will occur as a result of the military forces of the US overextending themselves around the world and being defeated piecemeal; struggle within the US will be a vital part of this process, but when the revolution triumphs in the US it will have been made by the people of the whole world. For socialism to be defined in national terms within so extreme and historical an oppressor nation as this is only imperialist national chauvinism on the part of the "movement." . . .

There develops a "generation gap" and a "youth problem." Our heroes are no longer struggling businessmen, and we also begin to reject the ideal career of the professional and look to Mao, Che, the Panthers, the Third World, for our models, for motion. We reject the elitist, technocratic bullshit that tells us only experts can rule, and look instead to leadership from the people's war of the Vietnamese. Chuck Berry, Elvis, the Temptations brought us closer to the "people's culture" of Black America. The racist response to the civil rights movement revealed the depth of racism in America, as well as the impossibility of real change through American institutions. And the war against Vietnam is not "the

heroic war against the Nazis"; it's the big lie, with napalm, burning through everything we had heard this country stood for. Kids begin to ask questions: Where is the Free World? And who do the pigs protect at home? . . .

The most important task for us toward making the revolution, and the work our collectives should engage in, is the creation of a mass revolutionary movement, without which a clandestine revolutionary party will be impossible. . . .

This will be done at this stage principally among youth, through implementing the Revolutionary Youth Movement strategy discussed in this paper. It is practice at this, and not political "teachings" in the abstract, which will determine the relevance of the political collectives which are formed.

The strategy of the RYM for developing an active mass base, tying the city-wide fights to community and city-wide anti-pig movement, and for building a party eventually out of this motion, fits with the world strategy for winning the revolution, builds a movement oriented toward the power, and will become one division of the International Liberation Army, while its battlefields are added to the many Vietnams which will dismember and dispose of US imperialism. Long Live the Victory of People's War!

6. Conservative Tom Anderson Arraigns Student Radicals, 1969

"Dear Brats,"
Tom Anderson
June 1969

It is my annual custom at this time of year to write an inspiring message to America's militant youth. Since I always strive to make these messages sincere and "from the heart," I shall do my thing this year with that uppermost in mind:

Dear spoiled, deluded, and brainwashed brats:

I am sick of you. I am more sick of your professors, your administrators, your clergymen (if any), your parents, and others who have come very close to ruining an entire generation of young Americans....

You young militants, apparently brought up on the permissive nonreality of Dr. Spock, insist on running away from reality. You bemoan the world you "never made." What you fail to understand is that you must live in the world as it is and as it can be....

People keep telling me that the campus anarchists, pacifists, Marxists, pot addicts, and "fairies" are a very small minority. Very well, maybe so. But tell me why an overwhelming majority of decent young people will sit by supinely while its universities are being hijacked and burned. More appalling than the outrages perpetrated by the collegiate punks, pinks, and perverts is the spineless acquiescence of the student majority.

We are constantly told that only two percent of you students are disrupting the campuses. But that is not true. The cowardly, apathetic, and silent ninety-eight percent of you who are *uncommitted* are guilty of letting it happen....

When things are morally and legally wrong, you are right to rebel. But your rebellion must be moral, legal, and constructive, else *you* are wrong. Students don't have a moral or legal right to "take over" a building. They are violating property rights and the rights of other students, and they should be routed out with tear gas, arrested, and given jail sentences. That's the way it is in the real world!

The first requirement and obligation of the institution of learning is to build character. "Free speech" and "search for truth" do not include the right to promote subversion, insurrection, anarchy, arson, murder, and treason. Nor does "academic freedom" include the right publicly to push drugs, free sex, and Communism. Communism and other such perversions are like rape—they are not moot questions. Communism is not just another ideology or a political Party, but a criminal conspiracy to enslave the world. Communists should no more be given a collegiate platform than murderers, dope pushers, or smut peddlers.

Discipline, order and character are the foundation of learning, not permissiveness, anarchy, and perversion. The main purpose of a school, in my opinion, should be to build discipline and character. Chancellors, administrators, and teachers devoid of character cannot, of course, build character. This is where our educational system has failed. This is the explanation for revolutionary anarchy on the campus....

Millions of us are tired of the excess of tolerance become license, of trying to reason with unreason, of cant and Bolshevik clichés that were dated when your grandfather was in knickers. The academic leaders may be afraid of the militant young fascists and anarchists who are trying to turn our free Republic into a police state, but we the *people* are not.

7. Vice President Spiro Agnew's Perspective on Protest, 1969

I believe in legal protest within the Constitutional limits of free speech, including peaceful assembly and the right of petition. But I do not believe that demonstrations, lawful or unlawful, merit my approval or even my silence where the purpose is fundamentally unsound. In the case of the Vietnam Moratorium, the objective announced by the leaders—immediate unilateral withdrawal of all our forces from Vietnam—

was not only unsound but idiotic. The tragedy was that thousands who participated wanted only to show a fervent desire for peace, but were used by the political hustlers who ran the event. . . .

We have just such a group of self-proclaimed saviours of the American soul at work today. Relentless in their criticism of intolerance in America, they themselves are intolerant of those who differ with their views. In the name of academic freedom, they destroy academic freedom. Denouncing violence, they seize and vandalize buildings of great universities. Fiercely expressing their respect for truth, they disavow the logic and discipline necessary to pursue truth.

They would have us believe that they alone know what is good for America—what is true and right and beautiful. They would have us believe that their reflexive action is superior to our reflective action; that their revealed righteousness is more effective than our reason and experience.

Think about it. Small bands of students are allowed to shut down great universities. Small groups of dissidents are allowed to shout down political candidates. Small cadres of professional protestors are allowed to jeopardize the peace efforts of the President of the United States.

It is time to question the credentials of their leaders. And, if in questioning we disturb a few people, I say it is time for them to be disturbed. If, in challenging, we polarize the American people, I say it is time for a positive polarization.

. . . [O]n the eve of out nation's 200th birthday, we have reached the crossroads. Because at this moment totalitarianism's threat does not necessarily have a foreign accent. Because we have a homegrown menace, made and manufactured in the U.S.A. Because if we are lazy or foolish, this nation could forfeit its integrity, never to be free again.

I do not want this to happen to America. And I do not think that you do either. We have something magnificent here, something worth fighting for, and now is the time for all good men to fight for the soul of their country. Let us stop apologizing for our past. Let us conserve and create for the future.

Chapter 31:
Document Set 1 References

1. The Port Huron Statement Sets the Social Agenda for SDS, 1962
   Tom Hayden *et al.,* Port Huron Statement, mimeographed, Students for a Democratic Society, 1962, in Robert D. Marcus and David Burner, eds., *America Since 1945* (New York: St. Martin's Press, 1985), 4th ed., pp. 203–204, 215–217.

2. The Dow Demonstrations Polarize the University Community in Wisconsin, 1967
   James Ridgeway, "On Wisconsin," *The New Republic* (November 4, 1967).

3. Images of War in Folk Music: Pete Seeger Stirs Up Controversy, 1967
   Pete Seeger, "Waist Deep in the Big Muddy," 1967, Melody Trails, Inc., New York, N.Y.

4. A Police Riot in the Streets of Chicago, 1968
   Daniel Walker *et al., Rights in Conflict: Convention Week in Chicago, August 25–29, 1968,* A Report Submitted to the National Commission on the Causes and Prevention of Violence, pp. 29–33.

5. SDS Militants Endorse Revolution, 1969
   Karen Ashley *et al.,* "You Don't Need a Weatherman to Know Which Way the Wind Blows," mimeograph, 1969, in William H. Chafe and Harvard Sitkoff, eds., *A History of Our Time* (New York: Oxford University Press, 1983), pp. 236–238.

6. Conservative Tom Anderson Arraigns Student Radicals, 1969
   "Dear Brats," *American Opinion* (Belmont, Mass.), June 1969.

7. Vice President Spiro Agnew's Perspective on Protest, 1969
   Spiro T. Agnew, Address at Republican Dinner, October 8, 1969, *Speaking Freely* (Washington, D.C.: Public Affairs Press, 1970), pp. 16–24.

Chapter 31:
Document Set 1 Credits

CHAPTER 31

DOCUMENT SET 2

Subversion of the Political Process: The Watergate Crisis and the Constitutional System

The outcome of the 1972 presidential campaign was never in serious doubt; it was ironic, therefore, that the Watergate burglary attempt resulted in the downfall of the Nixon presidency, since Democratic candidate George McGovern was such a vulnerable candidate in his own right. McGovern's weakness did not dissuade the president and his staff from the fatal decision to conceal the White House connection with the accused burglars. The cover-up that followed ended in a congressional investigation that exposed massive abuses of power, as well as the moral failure of the president and those who advised him. As you review the following documents, arrive at your own judgment as to whether "the system worked," as many Americans believed it did when Richard Nixon resigned his office in 1974.

As you examine these materials, pay particular attention to the personal account contained in Richard Nixon's memoir and the narrative provided by White House Counsel John Dean. Try to determine the extent to which the president was personally engaged in the cover-up that occurred as his staff worked to control damage to the White House and the Nixon reelection campaign. As you consider the matter of presidential involvement, compare the Watergate affair with previous national scandals. Concentrate on the unique features of the Nixon administration's predicament and relate it to more recent government scandals.

Unlike either Warren Harding or U. S. Grant, Richard Nixon confronted impeachment proceedings once the full scope of the crisis became clear. Thus the early involvement of the Senate in the investigatory process is another topic for exploration. Think about the goals of congressional leaders and the underlying reasons for their vigilance in getting at the truth. Search the findings of the House Judiciary Committee for evidence of presidential malfeasance in office. Since Nixon resigned after the House committee adopted three articles of impeachment and was later pardoned by interim President Gerald Ford, the question of due process is also raised. Evaluate the success of the American constitutional system in responding to this unprecedented challenge. Compare the Watergate crisis to the Clinton impeachment proceedings of 1998–1999.

When you evaluate the conclusions of the House Judiciary Committee in Article I of the impeachment resolution and the committee's narrative of events between June and November 1972, look for the motivations that drove the Nixon White House toward self-destructive behavior. Compare the reasons cited in the congressional report with those that emerge in the Nixon and Dean recollections of the same events, making an effort to establish the historical "facts."

Finally, use your textbook and your analysis of the evidence to form an interpretation of Watergate's impact on the future of American politics. Speculate on the relationship between the paralysis of the late Nixon administration and the problems encountered in the American political process in the 1970s, 1980s, and 1990s. Think about the impact of Watergate on the development and management of impeachment during the Clinton years.

Questions for Analysis

1. What was the significance of the House Judiciary Committee's findings? Did the American constitutional process function as originally intended? Did the system "work"? What might have occurred if the tapes had not been uncovered or if John Dean had not chosen to testify? Would the system have "worked"?

2. Were there similarities or differences between the Watergate crisis and previous American political scandals? Does the evidence suggest any unique feature of Watergate that separates it from other instances of illegal activities at the highest level of government?

3. Focusing on the extent of presidential involvement, analyze the problem of responsibility for the Watergate scandal. What drove so many intelligent, highly

trained people to commit the acts that were perpetrated between 1970 and 1974, including the "Watergate horrors" associated with the White House plumbers group and the Committee to Reelect the President? Which sources do you trust as evidence of a truthful historical account of these events? Why?

4. Can you connect the Watergate disaster with any long-term trends in the development of the office of the presidency and the American political/constitutional system? How did President Nixon's exercise of executive authority compare with that of other modern presidents, especially since the 1930s? What light do the documents shed on changes in the balance of power in the American political process?

5. What research problems and opportunities are encountered in efforts to reconstruct the recent past? How do the documents reflect these limitations and opportunities? In what way do the witnesses and their backgrounds influence their accounts of historical events?

6. Compare the Watergate scandal with the Iran-contra affair and the Clinton scandals. Based on the evidence you have examined, can you draw lines of similarity or difference between the difficulties of the Nixon and Reagan administrations in coping with their respective internal crises? How do these crises compare with the problems confronted by President Clinton?

1. John Dean's Story of a White House Deception, 1972

I began my role in the cover-up as a fact-finder and worked my way up to idea man, and finally to desk officer. At the outset, I sensed no personal danger in what I was doing. In fact, I took considerable satisfaction from knowing that I had no criminal liability, and I consistently sought to keep it that way. I wanted to preserve my function as an "agent" of my superiors, taking no initiatives, always acting on orders. In the process, I often found myself searching for alternatives that would keep me from taking dangerous steps. When Ehrlichman suggested I "deep-six" the sensitive materials from Hunt's safe by throwing them into the Potomac River, for instance, I delayed for several days, searching for an alternative. I did not want to disappoint Ehrlichman, but I did not want to take responsibility for destroying potential evidence. Finally I came up with what I thought was a clever idea—to give the documents directly to L. Patrick Gray III, the acting FBI director

after Hoover's death. By this ruse, we could say we had turned all evidence over to "the FBI," and literally it would be true. . . .

On August 29, 1972, I was in San Clemente to report to Haldeman and Ehrlichman on cover-up matters. By then this seemed almost routine. The President was holding a news conference that day on the lawn of his Pacific estate. I was in my hotel room as it went on the networks, and I turned on my television set, listening with one ear as I worked. . . . My attention snapped into focus, however, when a reporter asked a very polite question about Watergate: "Mr. President, wouldn't it be a good idea for a special prosecutor, even from your standpoint, to be appointed to investigate the contribution situation and also the Watergate case?"

I shifted quickly to a bed in front of the television. The President explained that a special prosecutor was absolutely unnecessary, because there were no fewer than five investigations already under way.... I was stunned that the President had not ducked the question but had instead plowed into it with such bold lies. These investigations, plus several others, were precisely the ones I was spending most of my waking hours juggling and deflecting, containing them with stories and delay tactics. For a moment, I wondered whether the President might not *really know* what I was doing. My desire to believe any President, especially my own, was strong. No, I thought, Haldeman and Ehrlichman would never let him make such a strong statement without detailed discussions of its impact. This was hardball, it would probably work.

I damn near fell off the bed at what I heard next. "In addition to that," the President continued, "within our own staff, under my direction, the counsel to the President, Mr. Dean, has conducted a complete investigation of all leads which might involve any present members of the White House staff or anybody in the government. I can say categorically that his investigation indicates that no one in the White House staff, no one in this Administration, presently employed, was involved in this very bizarre incident." ...

In a daze, I listened to the President push coolly and brazenly on to bury the Watergate affair as a campaign issue. John Mitchell, he said, had launched his own intensive Watergate investigation before retiring as campaign chairman. Careful, I thought, that might be going *too* far. He added that Clark MacGregor, Mitchell's successor, was continuing the probe. All these investigations were laudable, said the President, because "we want all the facts brought out." Then he concluded, "What really hurts in matters of this sort is not the fact that they occur. What really hurts is if you try to cover it up."

I turned off the television. What a performance. That's what it takes to be on the first team. I thought of the millions of viewers who must have been nodding in agreement. What a reality warp. I knew its epic dimensions. I also knew that this knowledge was the key to my present success.

The fact that I had never heard of a "Dean investigation," much less conducted one, did not seem important then. I was basking in the glory of being publicly perceived as the man the President had turned to with a nasty problem like Watergate....

"Uh, the reason I thought we ought to talk this morning," I began [to President Nixon], "is because in our conversations, uh, I have the impression that you don't know everything I know." This opening was partly true and partly false. Like a good staff man, I wanted to give the President "deniability," just as I had been indoctrinated to do since my first day in the White House, even though most of what I was telling him now was not new. Also, I wanted to give him room to respond with shock and drastic action.

... "I think there's no doubt about the seriousness of the problem we've got," I said. "We have a cancer within—close to the Presidency—that's growing. It's growing daily. It's compounding. It grows geometrically now, because it compounds itself. Uh, that'll be clear as I explain, you know, some of the details of why it is. And it basically is because: one, we're being blackmailed; two, people are going to start perjuring themselves ... to protect other people and the like." I had my hands out in front of me, ticking these vulnerabilities off my fingers. Then I stopped. "And that is just ... And there is no assurance ... " I hesitated.

"That it won't bust," the President concluded for me.

"That it won't bust.". ...

I dispensed with [the subject of] Petersen, and quickly brought the President to the raw nerve—money: "All right, so arrangements were made through Mitchell, initiating it, in discussions that—I was present—that these guys had to be taken care of. Their attorneys' fees had to be done. Kalmbach was brought in. Kalmbach raised some cash. Uh, they were obvi—uh, you know ... " I was hesitating over whether I could be so blunt as to say that the defendants had clearly been going to blow if we didn't pay them. The President interrupted me.

"They put that under the cover of a Cuban Committee or something, didn't they?"

The question stunned me. The Cuban Committee was a technical part of only one of our payment schemes. A committee had been set up to collect defense funds for the Cuban defendants, and we had planned it; the committee would be flooded with anonymous cash. As it turned out, Hunt had preferred to have the money delivered directly to him and his wife, and the committee had never been used. ...

The President's cognizance of the committee, and his wish to keep it alive, punctured any hope that he would recoil in shock from whatever I might tell him. I tried to recover; if I couldn't impress him with details of the cover-up, I'd hammer in the implications. "And that's the most troublesome post thing," I went on, "because: one, Bob is involved in that; John is involved in that; I am involved in that; Mitchell is involved in that"—I was counting on my fingers again—"and that is an obstruction of justice."

The President sat back, as if I had breathed into his face. "In other words, the fact that, uh, you're, you're taking care of the witness."

"That's right," I stated.

2. The House Judiciary Committee's Analysis of the Cover-up, 1974

June 19, 1972–June 29, 1972

...At the meeting, on the morning of June 20, Kleindienst, Haldeman, Ehrlichman, Mitchell and Dean discussed the Watergate break-in. (Book II, 240–41)

On that same morning at 9:00 a.m. the President arrived in his Oval Office. While this meeting on Watergate took place one floor above among the President's chief of staff, his chief domestic adviser, his counsel, his Attorney General, and his campaign director, the President remained alone in the Oval Office (with the exception of a three-minute meeting with Butterfield from 9:01 to 9:04 a.m.) The President left the Oval Office at 10:20 a.m., and went to his EOB office. (Book II, 243)

At his EOB office, the President met with Ehrlichman from 10:25 until 11:20 a.m. (Book II, 243) The President did not discuss Watergate with Ehrlichman, even though the President had given Ehrlichman the highest level responsibility for investigation of the Watergate matter. (*In re Grand Jury,* Misc. 47–73, order, 12/19/73; Book II, 238: "Presidential Statements," 8/22/73, 45–46)

Starting at 11:26 a.m., during a meeting which lasted one hour and 19 minutes, the President did discuss Watergate with Haldeman....

In July, 1973, the tape recording of this June 20, 1972 meeting between the President and Haldeman was subpoenaed by the Special Prosecutor. The subpoena was resisted by the President on the grounds of executive privilege (Book II, 258) but upheld by the Court of Appeals. (Book IX, 748, 750–54) On November 26, 1973, when the President's lawyer finally produced the recording, it contained an eighteen and one-half minute erasure. The erasure obliterated that portion of the conversation which, according to Haldeman's notes, referred to Watergate. (Book II, 249–50) The obliteration was, in fact, caused by repeated manual erasures, which were made on the tape recorder used by the President's personal secretary Rose Mary Woods....

CONTAINMENT—JULY 1, 1972, TO ELECTION

I

PRESIDENTIAL PLAN FOR CONTAINMENT

From late June, 1972, until after the Presidential election in November, President Nixon through his close subordinates engaged in a plan of containment and concealment which prevented disclosures that might have resulted in the indictment of high CRP and White House officials; that might have exposed Hunt and Liddy's prior illegal covert activities for the White House; and that might have put the outcome of the November election in jeopardy. Two of the President's men, John Dean, Counsel to the President, a subordinate, and Herbert Kalmbach, personal attorney to the President, an agent, who had been assigned to carry out the cover-up, carried out their assignment. They did so with the full support of the power and authority of the President of the United States.

Tape recordings of Presidential conversations in the possession of the Committee establish that implementation of the plan prior to the election had the full approval of the President.... On the morning of March 21, 1973, Dean told the President regarding his investigation after the break-in, "I was under pretty clear instructions [laughs] not to really to investigate this, that this was something that just could have been disastrous on the election if it had—all hell had broken loose, and I worked on a theory of containment." The President replied, "Sure." (HJCT 88) During the same conversation, Dean said of the cover-up, "We were able to hold it for a long time."

The President's reply was, "Yeah, I know." (HJCT 101–02) Dean said that some bad judgments, some necessary judgments had been made before the election, but that at the time, in view of the election, there was no way.

The President said, "We're all in on it." . . .

On August 29, 1972, the President held a news conference. He discussed various pending investigative proceedings in connection with Watergate. . . .

In fact, Dean had conducted no investigation. He had been acting to narrow and frustrate investigation by the FBI. He had reached no conclusion that no one in the White House had been involved in

Watergate. He had made no report of such an investigation. . . .

The President and his staff had not "cooperated completely" with the investigatory agencies. The evidence, rather, shows clearly and convincingly that the President and his closest aides acted to obstruct and impede the investigations.

The President's statements on August 29 themselves were designed to delay, impede and obstruct the investigation of the Watergate break-in; to cover up, conceal, and protect those responsible and to conceal the existence and scope of other unlawful covert activities.

3. The Judiciary Committee's Conclusion on Impeachment Resolution, Article I, 1974

Conclusion

After the Committee on the Judiciary had debated whether or not it should recommend Article I to the House of Representatives, 27 of the 38 Members of the Committee found that the evidence before it could only lead to one conclusion: that Richard M. Nixon, using the powers of his high office, engaged, personally and through his subordinates and agents, in a course of conduct or plan designed to delay, impede, and obstruct the investigation of the unlawful entry, on June 17, 1972, into the headquarters of the Democratic National Committee; to cover up, conceal and protect those responsible; and to conceal the existence and scope of other unlawful covert activities.

This finding is the only one that can explain the President's involvement in a pattern of undisputed acts that occurred after the break-in and that cannot otherwise be rationally explained.

1. The President's decision on June 20, 1972, not to meet with his Attorney General, his chief of staff, his counsel, his campaign director, and his assistant John Ehrlichman, whom he had put in charge of the investigation—when the subject of their meeting was the Watergate matter.

2. The erasure of that portion of the recording of the President's conversation with Haldeman, on June 20, 1972, which dealt with Watergate—when the President stated that the tapes had been under his "sole and personal control."

3. The President's public denial on June 22, 1972, of the involvement of members of the Committee for the Re-election of the President or of the White House staff in the Watergate burglary, in spite of having discussed Watergate, on or before June 22, 1972, with Haldeman, Colson, and Mitchell—all persons aware of that involvement.

4. The President's directive to Haldeman on June 23, 1972, to have the CIA request the FBI to curtail its Watergate investigation.

5. The President's refusal, on July 6, 1972, to inquire and inform himself what Patrick Gray, Acting Director of the FBI, meant by his warning that some of the President's aides were "trying to mortally wound" him.

6. The President's discussion with Ehrlichman on July 8, 1972, of clemency for the Watergate burglars, more than two months before the return of any indictments.

7. The President's public statement on August 29, 1972, a statement later shown to be untrue, that an investigation by John Dean "indicates that no one in the White House staff, no one in the Administration, presently employed, was involved in this very bizarre incident."

8. The President's statement to Dean on September 15, 1972, the day that the Watergate indictments were returned without naming high CRP and White House officials, that Dean had handled his

work skillfully, "putting your fingers in the dike every time that leaks have sprung here and sprung there," and that "you just try to button it up as well as you can and hope for the best." . . .

In addition to this evidence, there was before the Committee the following evidence:

. . . Beginning immediately after June 17, 1972, the involvement of each of the President's top aides and political associates, Haldeman, Mitchell, Ehrlichman, Colson, Dean, LaRue, Mardian, Magruder, in the Watergate coverup. . . .

Finally, there was before the Committee a record of public statements by the President between June 22, 1972, and June 9, 1974, deliberately contrived to deceive the courts, the Department of Justice, the Congress, and the American people.

President Nixon's course of conduct following the Watergate break-in, as described in Article I, caused action not only by his subordinates but by the agencies of the United States, including the Department of Justice, the FBI, and the CIA. It required perjury, destruction of evidence, obstruction of justice, all crimes. But, most important, it required deliberate, contrived, and continuing deception of the American people.

President Nixon's actions resulted in manifest injury to the confidence of the nation and great prejudice to the cause of law and justice, and was subversive of constitutional government. His actions were contrary to his trust as President and unmindful of the solemn duties of his high office. It was this serious violation of Richard M. Nixon's constitutional obligations as President, and not the fact that violations of Federal criminal statutes occurred, that lies at the heart of Article I.

The Committee finds, based upon clear and convincing evidence, that this conduct, detailed in the foregoing pages of this report, constitutes "high crimes and misdemeanors" as that term is used in Article II, Section 4 of the Constitution. Therefore, the Committee recommends that the House of Representatives exercise its constitutional power to impeach Richard M. Nixon.

4. Nixon Recalls Damage Control, 1972

[June 20, 1972]

I am confident that our discussion about the break-in covered much the same points at 11:26 in the morning as it did just five hours later at 4:35 in the afternoon: that any of our own people, at any level, had embroiled us in such an embarrassing situation; and that the investigations and depositions, if they went too far in pursuing all the angles available, would hand the Democrats a major campaign issue. . . .

In our conversation that afternoon Haldeman ran through some of the other information he had picked up during the day. Haldeman said that, as he understood it, McCord was going to say that he was working with the Cubans, who had been putting in the bug for their own political reasons. Haldeman told me that Howard Hunt had either disappeared or was in the process of doing so, but he would come back if wanted. Haldeman indicated that the appearance of Hunt's name in the address book would be explained on the basis of his ties to the Cubans; he told me, as Colson had, that Hunt had been involved in the Bay of Pigs operation while he was in the CIA; in fact Haldeman had learned that one of the Cubans had been Hunt's deputy for the operation. Haldeman said that our people were making an effort to keep the incident tied to the motive of Cuban nationalism. . . .

[June 21, 1972]

In our conversation on Wednesday morning, June 21, Haldeman told me that Gordon Liddy was "the guy who did this." I asked who Liddy was, and Haldeman said he was the counsel for the finance committee at CRP. When I said I thought McCord was the man responsible for the break-in, Haldeman said no, it was Liddy; we didn't know what McCord's position was, but everyone seemed to think he would hang tight.

Ehrlichman had come up with the idea of having Liddy confess; he would say he did it because he wanted to be hero at the CRP. This would have several advantages: it would cut off the Democrats' civil suit and minimize their ability to go on fishing expeditions in the depositions connected with it; it would divert some of the press and political attacks by establishing guilt at a low level instead of letting it be imputed to a high one; . . . .

I said that after all this was not a hell of a lot of crime and in fact if someone asked me about Ziegler's statement that it was a "third-rate burglary," I was going to say no, it was only a "third-rate *attempt* at burglary." Haldeman said the lawyers all felt that if

Liddy and the arrested men entered a guilty plea they would get only fines and suspended sentences since apparently they were all first offenders.

I said I was for Erlichman's plan. . . .

Haldeman said that what he considered to be the real problem for the White House had nothing to do with the Watergate break-in itself, but concerned what he called "other involvements"—things that an investigative fishing expedition into the break-in could uncover and exploit politically. That was what made the Democrats' civil suit the biggest problem for the White House. . . .

[June 23, 1972]

On Friday, June 23, 1972, . . . Haldeman came in as he did every morning, unhurried, ready to begin the day.

We talked about the schedule for Kissinger's return from China that afternoon and about plans for a meeting with Rogers. Then we turned to what Haldeman referred to as the "Democratic break-in thing."

All the good news of the previous day had gone bad, and we were back in what Haldeman called "the problem area." The FBI, he said, was not under control because Acting Director Pat Gray did not know how to control it, and the investigation was leading into some productive areas. In particular, the FBI was apparently going to be able to trace the money after all. "And it goes in some directions we don't want it to go," Haldeman said. As I understood it, unless we could find some way to limit the investigation the trail would lead directly to the CRP, and our political containment would go by the boards.

Haldeman said that Mitchell and John Dean had come up with an idea on how to deal with this problem. Dean was a bright young man who had worked at the Justice Department until 1970, when he succeeded Ehrlichman as White House Counsel. In this capacity Dean had the responsibility for keeping track of and attending to any legal problems affecting the President or the White House.

As Haldeman explained it, General Vernon Walters, the Deputy Director of the CIA, was to call Pat Gray and tell him to "stay the hell out of this . . . business here. We don't want you to go any further on it." The FBI and the CIA had a long-standing agreement not to interfere in each other's secret operations. Haldeman said that this call would not be unusual. . . .

After this half-hour meeting with Haldeman I held a ninety-minute session on the economy and then conducted several brief ceremonial meetings. When I had finished, I buzzed for Haldeman to come in again. I wanted him to understand that I was not interested in concealing Hunt's involvement in Watergate from Helms and Walters or even from the FBI; in fact, I said that he should level with Helms and Walters and tell them that we knew Hunt had been involved in Watergate. But then he should point out that the whole Cuban involvement in Watergate would make the CIA and Hunt look bad; and the whole thing might possibly reopen the Bay of Pigs controversy, and that would be bad for the CIA, for the country, and for American foreign policy. I also did not want Helms and Walters to get the idea that our concern was political—which, of course, it was.
. . .

Haldeman said he made it clear to Helms that he was not going to get specifics but rather generalities. It had been left that Walters would go to see Gray and take care of the matter. It seemed that our intervention had worked easily. As far as I was concerned, this was the end of our worries about Watergate.

5. Herblock on the Course of Justice, 1973

From *Herblock Special Report* (W. W. Norton & Co, 1974) l-r, H. R. Haldeman, John
Erlichman, President Richard M. Nixon

6. A Skeptic's View of the President's Involvement
in the Cover-up, 1973

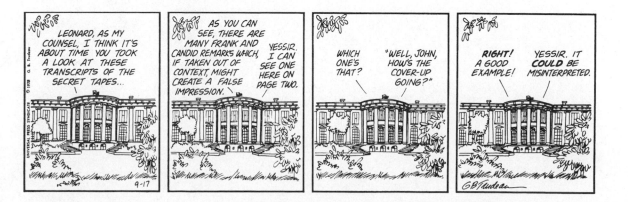

Gary Trudeau, "Doonesbury." September 17, 1973. Doonesbury copyright 1973 G. B. Trudeau. Reprinted with permission of Universal Press Syndicate.
All rights reserved.

Chapter 31:
Document Set 2 References

1. John Dean's Story of a White House Deception, 1972
   John Dean, *Blind Ambition* (New York: Simon & Schuster, 1976), pp. 117, 124–125, 200, 202–203.

2. The House Judiciary Committee's Analysis of the Cover-up, 1974
   U.S. Congress, House, Committee on the Judiciary, *Impeachment of Richard M. Nixon, President of the United States,* Report No. 93-1305, 93rd Cong., 2nd Sess., 1974, pp. 45–46, 55, 59–60.

3. The Judiciary Committee's Conclusion on Impeachment Resolution, Article I, 1974
   "Conclusion," Article I, Impeachment Resolution, House Report No. 93-1305, pp. 133, 135–136.

4. Nixon Recalls Damage Control, 1972
   Richard M. Nixon, *RN: The Memoirs of Richard Nixon* (New York: Grosset and Dunlap, 1978), pp. 632–633, 635–636, 639–640, 642.

5. Herblock on the Course of Justice, 1973
   Herbert Block, "Tape Job," in Gary B. Nash *et al.,* eds., *The American People: Creating a Nation and a Society* (New York: Harper-Row, 1986), p. 961a.

6. A Skeptic's View of the President's Involvement in the Cover-up, 1973
   Gary Trudeau, "Doonesbury," September 17, 1973, Universal Press Syndicate.

CHAPTER 31

A Changed Army for a Changed War: A View of Vietnam from the Participants

The response to the Vietnam War at all levels of American society provides a central theme in the textbook's treatment of the Nixon era. No policy adopted by the new administration was more controversial than the president's approach to the Indochina conflict. After campaigning on a pledge to remove the United States from the war through a secret plan, President Nixon revealed in 1969 that he would accomplish this goal by gradually withdrawing American troops while strengthening South Vietnamese forces.

The new policy of Vietnamization actually originated in the last year of the Johnson Administration. However, as withdrawal began, it became clear that pulling back meant that the United States would alter its initial commitment to halt the spread of communism by American military engagement. As the implications of the new Nixon Doctrine became clear, the character of the war began to change dramatically, as did the attitudes that prevailed among American troops in Vietnam.

The following documents attempt to capture the personal responses of American veterans to the intense emotional impact of mortal combat. Their reactions also record the growing cynicism and disillusionment that resulted from a new form of warfare. Probe the sources for evidence of changing perceptions of the war's purposes, as well as the long-term consequences of service in an unpopular cause.

These documents allow you to take advantage of participants' observations as primary source material. As you evaluate the evidence, be aware of the pitfalls in the use of oral histories as source material. What special precautions are needed in forming historical judgments? Consider the personal backgrounds and cultural baggage brought to the analysis by each witness. Try to uncover whatever truth may be filtered through the prism of personal experience.

As you review these accounts, formulate a hypothesis concerning the effect of changing political leadership on the course of the war. Moreover, assess Vietnamization as a policy and as a military strategy. As you do so, also consider the impact of Vietnamization on the men and women who were called on to execute government policy.

Finally, use the evidence to shape your own understanding of changing American attitudes toward the war. What was the effect of combat experience on those who returned to relate their stories to Americans on the home front? Be aware of the new consensus on the wisdom of American involvement in Vietnam and the reasons behind the shift in public opinion.

Questions for Analysis

1. To what extent was service in Vietnam different from duty in other wars? Use the documents to support your response.

2. Define the term *Vietnamization*. What was its ultimate goal? In what ways do the documents shed light on American success or failure in achieving that goal? How did the advent of a new administration and a new strategy change the character of military service?

3. What do the documents reveal about the failure of American policy in Vietnam? Why were the United States and South Vietnam unable to prevent an eventual communist victory?

4. How would you characterize the attitudes of American veterans toward the war in Vietnam? How would you account for their responses?

5. What was the long-term impact of service in Vietnam? How were the postwar lives of veterans affected by their wartime experience?

1. Philip Caputo's Recollection of Rage and Doubt, 1965–1966

When I walked into the mess for the evening meal, Chaplain Ryerson and the medical officer, Milsovic, stopped eating and looked at me. Putting my tray on the plywood table, I sat down. The Chaplain, who was as thin and cheerless as the doctor was heavyset and jolly, slid along the bench to sit across from me. . . .

"Maybe you could explain what we're doing over here. You've been a platoon commander. When we got here, we were just supposed to defend the airfield for a while and then go back to Okinawa. Now we're in the war to stay and nobody has been able to explain to me what we're doing. I'm no tactician, but the way it looks to me, we send men out on an operation, they kill a few VC, or the VC kill them, and then pull out and the VC come right back in. So we're back where we started. That's the way it looks to me. I think these boys are getting killed for nothing."

I held up my hands. "Chaplain, what do you want me to say? Maybe you're right. I don't know, I'm just a second lieutenant. Anyway, it's not that bad a war. We've taken only eighty-four casualties since the end of April, and only twelve of those have been KIA. Hell, in World War Two an outfit like this would take eighty-four casualties in five minutes."

"What's that supposed to mean? This isn't World War Two."

"What I mean is that twelve KIAs in two months isn't bad."

Ryerson's face reddened and his voice got strident. "That's twelve wrecked homes. *Twelve wrecked homes,* lieutenant." He pointed a finger at me. "Twelve KIA is pretty bad for the families of those dead marines." I didn't say anything. My food was getting cold in the tray. A few senior officers had turned around, to see what the chaplain's outburst was all about. . . .

Leaving the mess, I went back to my desk. It was difficult to work. The tent was stifling, and I felt confused. The chaplain's morally superior attitude had rankled me, but his sermon had managed to plant doubt in my mind, doubt about the war. Much of what he had said made sense: our tactical operations did seem futile and directed toward no apparent end. There were other doubts, aroused by the events of that day, which had made a mockery of all the Catholic theology the Dominican and Jesuit priests had preached to me in high school and college. . . .

Twelve wrecked homes. The chaplain's words echoed. *That's twelve wrecked homes. The doctor and I think in terms of human suffering, not statistics.* I thought about Sullivan again. He was one of the statistics, just like the four enemy soldiers killed that morning. The only difference was that they were in different columns on the colonel's scoreboard. *Twelve wrecked homes.* . . .

In the middle of November, at my own request, I was transferred to a line company in 1st Battalion. My convictions about the war had eroded almost to nothing; I had no illusions, but I had volunteered for a line company anyway. There were a number of reasons, of which the paramount was boredom. There was nothing for me to do but count casualties. I felt useless and a little guilty about living in relative safety while other men risked their lives. I cannot deny that the front still held a fascination for me. The rights or wrongs of the war aside, there was a magnetism about combat. You seemed to live more intensely under fire. Every sense was sharper, the mind worked clearer and faster. Perhaps it was the tension of opposites that made it so, an attraction balanced by revulsion, hope that warred with dread. You found yourself on a precarious emotional edge, experiencing a headiness that no drink or drug could match. . . .

Finally, there was hatred, a hatred buried so deep that I could not then admit its existence. I can now, though it is still painful. I burned with a hatred for the Viet Cong and with an emotion that dwells in most of us, one closer to the surface than we care to admit: a desire for retribution. I did not hate the enemy for their politics, but for murdering Simpson, for executing that boy whose body had been found in the river, for blasting the life out of Walt Levy. Revenge was one of the reasons I volunteered for a line company. I wanted a chance to kill somebody. . . .

The planes came in for another bombing run. There was a great roar, and the forms of the men in front of me blurred for an instant, as if a filmy, wavering curtain had dropped between us. While the planes bombed, we clawed our way through hedgerows and smoke toward the hill whose serene, pale-green crest we could see rising from the trees ahead. We had advanced a few hundred yards, but the hill did not look any closer. The noise of the battle was constant and maddening, as maddening as the barbed hedges and the heat of the fire raging just behind us.

Then it happened. The platoon exploded. It was a collective emotional detonation of men who had been pushed to the extremity of endurance. I lost control of them and even of myself. Desperate to get to the hill, we rampaged through the rest of the village, whooping like savages, torching thatch huts, tossing grenades into the cement houses we could not burn. In our frenzy, we crashed through the hedgerows without feeling the stabs of the thorns. We did not feel anything. We were past feeling anything for ourselves, let alone for others. We shut our ears to the cries and pleas of the villagers. One elderly man ran up to me, and, grabbing me by the front of my shirt, asked, "Tai Sao? Tai Sao?" Why? Why?

"Get out of my goddamned way," I said, pulling his hands off. I took hold of his shirt and flung him down hard, feeling as if I were watching myself in a movie. The man lay where he fell, crying, "Tai Sao? Tai Sao?" I plunged on toward the foot of the hill, now only a short distance away.

Most of the platoon had no idea of what they were doing. One marine ran up to a hut, set it ablaze, ran on, turned around, dashed through the flames and rescued a civilian inside, then ran on to set fire to the next hut. We passed through the village like a wind; by the time we started up Hill 52, there was nothing left of Ha Na but a long swath of smoldering ashes, charred tree trunks, their leaves burned off, and heaps of shattered concrete. Of all the ugly sights I saw in Vietnam, that was one of the ugliest: the sudden disintegration of my platoon from a group of disciplined soldiers into an incendiary mob.

. . . We had relieved our own pain by inflicting it on others. But that sense of relief was inextricably mingled with guilt and shame. Being men again, we again felt human emotions. We were ashamed of what we had done and yet wondered if we had really done it. The change in us, from disciplined soldiers to unrestrained savages and back to soldiers, had been so swift and profound as to lend a dreamlike quality to the last part of the battle. Despite the evidence to the contrary, some of us had a difficult time believing that we were the ones who had caused all that destruction. . . .

I could analyze myself all I wanted, but the fact was we had needlessly destroyed the homes of perhaps two hundred people. All the analysis in the world would not make a new village rise from the ashes. It could not answer the question that kept repeating itself in my mind nor lighten the burden of my guilt. The usual arguments and rationalizations did not help, either. Yes, the village had obviously been under enemy control; it had been a VC supply dump as much as it had been a village. Yes, burning the cache was a legitimate act of war and the fire resulting from it had been accidental. Yes, the later deliberate destruction had been committed by men *in extremis;* war was a state of extremes, and men often did extreme things in it. But none of that conventional wisdom relieved my guilt or answered the question: "Tai Sao?" Why?

2. Wallace Terry Recalls the African American Experience in Vietnam, 1968–1969

I learned a lot about people in my platoon. I learned you have to take a person for what he feels, then try to mold the individual into the person you would like to be with. Now my platoon had a lot of Southerners, as well as some Midwesterners. Southerners at the first sign of a black officer being in charge of them were somewhat reluctant. But then, when they found that you know what's going on and you're trying to keep them alive then they tried to be the best damn soldiers you've got. Some of the black soldiers were the worse I had because they felt that they had to jive on me. They wanted to let me know, Hey, man. Take care of me, buddy. You know I'm your buddy. That's bull. . . .

I dream about how the kids in my platoon would come to talk to you and say things about their families. Their families would be upset when they heard I was black. But then some guy would give me a picture of his sister. He would say, "She's white, but you'd still like her. Look her up when you get back to the States." And there would be the ones who did not get a letter that day. Or never got a letter their whole tour. In those cases, I would turn around and write them letters and send them back to Vandergrift.

And you dream about those that you lost. You wonder if there was something you could have done to save them. I only lost two kids. Really. . . .

It seemed like everyday somebody got hurt. Sometimes I would walk point. Everybody was carrying the wounded. We had 15 wounded in my platoon alone. And the water was gone.

Then on the twelfth day, while we were following this trail through the jungle, the point man came running back. He was all heated up. He said, "I think we got a tank up there." I told him, "I don't have time for no games." The enemy had no tanks in the South.

Then the trail started converging into a really well-camouflaged road, about 12 feet wide and better made than anything I had ever seen in Vietnam. Then I saw the muzzle of this gun. It was as big as anything we had. And all hell broke open. It was like the sun was screaming. . . .

Well, I ordered a perimeter drawn. And since I never ask my men to do something I don't do, I joined the perimeter. Then this sniper got me. Another RPG [rocket-propelled grenade]. I got it in the back. I could barely raise myself up on one elbow. I felt like shit, but I was trying to give a command. The guys just circled around me like they were waiting for me to tell them something. I got to my knees.

And it was funny. They had their guns pointed at the sky.

I yelled out, "I can walk. I can walk."

Somebody said, "No, sir. You will *not* walk."

I slumped back. And two guys got on my right side. Two guys got on my left side. One held me under the head. One more lifted my feet. Then they held me high above their shoulders, like I was a Viking or some kind of hero. They formed a perimeter around *me*. They told me [my] feet would never touch ground there again. And they held me high up in the air until the chopper came.

I really don't know what I was put in for. I was told maybe the Navy Cross. Maybe the Medal of Honor. It came down to the Silver Star. . . .

One day I wore my uniform over to Howard University in Washington to help recruit officer candidates. Howard is a black school, like the one I went to in Texas, Jarvis Christian College. I thought I would feel at home. The guys poked fun at me, calling me Uncle Sam's flunky. They would say the Marine Corps sucks. The Army sucks. They would say their brother or uncle got killed, so why was I still in. They would see the Purple Heart and ask me what was I trying to prove. The women wouldn't talk to you either.

I felt bad. I felt cold. I felt like I was completely out of it.

3. Gayle Smith's Private War, 1970–1971

I came into Vietnam at Long Binh. There was a replacement camp there, Camp something-or-other, I can't remember the name of it. On the bus from the airport to this camp, the first thing I saw was some Vietnamese guy peeing on the side of the road. And I thought, "Oh, geez, this is a backward country." And the next thing I saw was Coca-Cola signs. I thought, "This is very strange. This is a very unusual mixture." I saw barbed wire all over the city.

The first night I was there, the compound next to ours was shelled. A couple of guys were killed. I went over and there was a big hole in the barracks and it just dawned on me that . . . this was it. I was here, in the middle of a war. It was all around me. That day I went down to Binh Thuy and it was probably the first and last time I cried. I realized I was halfway around the world from home and I couldn't go home if I wanted to. I thought to myself, "What have I done? Here I am in the middle of this godforsaken country. I might get killed. I can't see my parents." I have to say I did cry a couple of times after that, but it mostly was because of my patients. It was when they died.

Boy, I remember how they came in all torn up. It was incredible. The first time a medevac came in, I got right into it. I didn't have a lot of feeling at that time. It was later on that I began to have a lot of feeling about it, after I'd seen it over and over and over again.

But an interesting thing happened in that it was very painful for me to keep seeing the same thing happen. And instead of doing I don't know what, I got *to* it. I turned that pain into anger and hatred and placed it onto the Vietnamese. You know what your head does, the way you think to survive . . . is different. I did not consider the Vietnamese to be people. They were human, but they weren't people. They weren't like us, so it was okay to kill them. It was okay to hate them. I see now that they're people just like us. But at that moment. . . .

I knew my patients were shooting up. They would come in and we would have to rule out gastroenteritis or appendicitis because they were sick from heroin or were withdrawing from it, so we had to be careful. And so I told them. I got to that point. I never thought I would care or not if somebody was on drugs, but it got to that point. I said to them, "I have enough to worry about with patients who have been wounded in battle or have had accidents without worrying about whether you are going to run out the back door and take heroin. You want to do it, just don't do it in this ward, because frankly I don't give a damn whether you die or not. If you do, that's your problem; if you OD, that's your problem, not my problem. I can't afford to worry about it. That costs me too much emotionally." I had too much invested in other people to divide myself with something like that.

. . . Then you would hear of things going on in the Vietnamization program—like an American pilot trying to teach a Vietnamese pilot how to fly. I heard of one case where the Vietnamese pilot did something wrong and the American swore at him and the Vietnamese pulled a gun out and put it to the pilot's head and said, "Fly us home." Then there were cases that came to our hospital from dust-off ships called into a hot landing zone to pull out wounded Vietnamese. We got them to our hospital and pulled off their bandages and there was nothing wrong with them. And when you see stuff like that it makes you want to put them back on the ship and throw them

out at about one thousand feet. And I'm not sure that didn't happen.

. . . I knew there was something wrong, but I couldn't put my finger on it. There was something wrong with me, but I didn't know what it was. And it was in a Vietnam veterans group that I realized that all my hatred for the Vietnamese and my wanting to kill them was really a reflection of all the pain that I had felt for seeing all those young men die and hurt . . . and how much I cared about them and how much I would stand there and look at them and think to myself, "You've just lost your leg for no reason at all." Or "You're going to die and it's for nothing." For nothing. I would never, never say that to them, but they knew it. . . .

Over and over and over. I used to see these people — they'd come in and give them Purple Hearts on the ward. And I'd look at them as they'd get their Purple Heart. At that point, it looked like it might be meaningful to them, so I didn't say anything. I never said anything, never said anything about what a waste it was. I would never dream of doing that, because they knew it and it would hurt like hell if they heard it anyway. But I would watch this ridiculous little ceremony, and they'd get a Purple Heart for what was left of them, and I'd think, "You're getting this? What are you getting this for? It's not going to get your leg back. It's not going to get your looks back. It's not going to make you avoid all the pain you're going to have to face when you go home and see your family and get back into society. It's all sitting in front of you and you're going to have to deal with it . . . and nothing will make up for that."

4. John Kerry Questions a War Gone Wrong, 1971

We found that not only was it a civil war, an effort by a people who had for years been seeking their liberation from any colonial influence whatsoever, but also we found that the Vietnamese whom we had enthusiastically molded after our own image were hard put to take up the fight against the threat we were supposedly saving them from.

We found most people didn't even know the difference between communism and democracy. They only wanted to work in rice paddies without helicopters strafing them and bombs with napalm burning their villages and tearing their country apart. They wanted everything to do with the war, particu-

larly with this foreign presence of the United States of America, to leave them alone in peace, and they practiced the art of survival by siding with whichever military force was present at a particular time, be it Viet Cong, North Vietnamese or American.

We found also that all too often American men were dying in those rice paddies for want of support from their allies. We saw first hand how monies from American taxes were used for a corrupt dictatorial regime. We saw that many people in this country had a one-sided idea of who was kept free by our flag, and blacks provided the highest percentage of casualties. We saw Vietnam ravaged equally by American bombs and search and destroy missions, as well as by Viet Cong terrorism, and yet we listened while this country tried to blame all of the havoc on the Viet Cong.

We rationalized destroying villages in order to save them. We saw America lose her sense of morality as she accepted very coolly a My Lai and refused to give up the image of American soldiers who hand out chocolate bars and chewing gum.

We learned the meaning of free fire zones, shooting anything that moves, and we watched while America placed a cheapness on the lives of orientals.

We watched the United States falsification of body counts, in fact the glorification of body counts. We listened while month after month we were told the back of the enemy was about to break. We fought using weapons against "oriental human beings." We fought using weapons against those people which I do not believe this country would dream of using were we fighting in the European theater. We watched while men charged up hills because a general said that hill has to be taken, and after losing one platoon or two platoons they marched away to leave the hill for reoccupation by the North Vietnamese. We watched pride allow the most unimportant battles to be blown into extravaganzas, because we couldn't lose, and we couldn't retreat, and because it didn't matter how many American bodies were lost to prove that point, and so there were Hamburger Hills and Khe Sanhs and Hill 81s and Fire Base 6s, and so many others.

5. Truong Nhu Tang Explains the Viet Cong Commitment, 1965, 1969–1970

For us, the escalation of American military involvement and the heightened activity of the United States government were signs that pointed ominously toward intervention by American ground forces. To the NLF [National Liberation Front], this eventuality was a living nightmare. No one, as 1965 dawned, had any illusions about our ability to gain a military decision against the immensely powerful American war machine. Thoughts of direct intervention filled us with sick anticipation of a prolonged and vastly more brutal war.

It was not a question of any lack of determination or confidence in our ultimate victory. But the war we were fighting in South Vietnam we saw at that point chiefly as a political struggle with a subordinate military dimension. Our strategy was to achieve a political revolution. To this end, armed violence was a means, but the political front was primary. . . .

Against this background, several factors stood out. First, time was very short. Second, although the balance of military forces between ourselves and the regime was steadily improving, our true strength and the enemy's true weakness was on the political front. Nothing illustrated that better than the events that had plagued Saigon since Diem's overthrow. The unrestrained irresponsibility and incompetence of the generals had led to apathy and disgust among people at every level. South Vietnam was a society without leadership and without direction—and these essentials the Americans could not provide. They could not impose order on chaos. And without a government in Saigon that could claim at least some tatters of legitimacy and effectiveness, how could the United States dare commit its troops and its all-important prestige? Overt anarchy in Saigon might force the Americans to look once again at their assumptions, to begin thinking about what they might salvage in Vietnam instead of how they might win.

. . . Although the guerrillas were short of food and often sick, they maintained the kind of esprit and comradeship that animates people who are fighting for a common purpose in which they believe with all their hearts. They got on, under horrendous conditions, through mutual support and a rough but genuine love for each other. Ironically, when faced with the disillusioning realities of postwar life, many of the former guerrillas looked back on the common life they shared in the Maquis [bush] as an idyllic period, a time to be especially treasured because it would not come again.

Chapter 31:
Document Set 3 References

1. Philip Caputo's Recollection of Rage and Doubt, 1965–1966
   Philip Caputo, *A Rumor of War* (New York: Ballantine Books, 1977), pp. 168, 169, 170, 218, 219, 287–288, 289–290.

2. Wallace Terry Recalls the African-American Experience in Vietnam, 1968–1969
   Wallace Terry, "Bloods: An Oral History of the Vietnam War by Black Veterans" in Andrew J. Rotter, ed., *Light at the End of the Tunnel* (New York: St. Martin's Press, 1991), pp. 306, 307, 309, 310.

3. Gayle Smith's Private War, 1970–1971
   "The Nurse with the Round Eyes," in Albert Santoli, *Everything We Had: An Oral History of the Vietnam War by Thirty-Three American Soldiers Who Fought It* (New York: Ballantine Books, 1984), pp. 126, 128–129, 130, 131.

4. John Kerry Questions a War Gone Wrong, 1971
   John Kerry, "Statement," April 23, 1971, Senate Committee on Foreign Relations, *Legislative Proposals Relating to the War in Southeast Asia: Hearings*, April 20, 21, 22, 28, 1971 (Washington, D.C.: Government Printing Office, 1971), pp. 180–210.

5. Truong Nhu Tang Explains the Viet Cong Commitment, 1965, 1969–1970
   Truong Nhu Tang, *A Vietcong Memoir* (New York: Vintage Books, 1985), pp. 58, 59, 173–174.

Chapter 31:
Document Set 3 Credits

1. Excerpts from *A Rumor of War* by Philip Caputo. Copyright © 1977 by Philip Caputo. Reprinted by permission of Henry Holt and Co., Inc.

2. From "Bloods: An Oral History of the Vietnam War" by Wallace Terry. Copyright © by Wallace Terry. Reprinted by permission of Random House, Inc.

3. Excerpts from *Everything We Had* by Albert Santoli. Copyright © 1981 by Albert Santoli and Vietnam Veterans of America. Used by permission of Random House, Inc.

5. Excerpts from *A Vietnam Memoir*, © 1985 by Truong Nhu Tang, David Chanoff and Doan Van Toai. Reprinted by permission of Harcourt Brace & Company.

CHAPTER 32

The Modern Women's Movement: The Equal Rights Amendment and Uncertain Equality

Your textbook asserts that one significant legacy of the tumultuous 1960s was a revitalized women's movement and the modification of women's status in the contemporary United States. However, by the 1980s, the future position of American women seemed less certain as a new conservatism swept over the social and political landscape. An important setback for feminism occurred when the heavily lobbied Equal Rights Amendment failed to achieve ratification by the 1982 deadline. The following documents examine the forces behind ERA, the reasoning of its proponents, and the antifeminist backlash that doomed the amendment. As you weigh the evidence, relate the outcome to the dominant political trends in modern America.

ERA traced its roots to the agitation of Alice Paul and the Women's Party of the 1920s. In 1972 the National Organization of Women and an influential feminist lobby persuaded Congress to enact the amendment, and by 1975, thirty-four states had ratified. Review the arguments of feminist Gloria Steinem in favor of a constitutional change. Examine the evidence for clues to the impact of the modern women's movement on the thinking of American women.

Many reasons for the failure of ERA have been identified by historians and feminists. For one, the early elitist bias of the early feminist movement played into the hands of the amendment's opponents. Search the Steinem argument for ideas and assumptions relevant to the concerns of most American women. Were the critics correct? As you analyze the sweeping statement adopted in 1975 by the broadly representative Women's Action Alliance, identify those aspects of its program which suggest changes in the social and economic base of the feminist movement. Compare this document with the National Organization of Women's Expanded Bill of Rights for the 21st Century.

Using your textbook as a resource, try to understand the cultural backlash that contributed to ERA's defeat. Consider the social values central to the resurgence of political conservatism in the 1980s, relating right-wing fears to the threat posed by the amendment. Phyllis Schlafly, cited by the textbook as a veteran conservative activist, argued in the *Radcliffe Quarterly* that ERA would bring alarming social change. As you evaluate her reasoning, try to link her views to the concerns and uncertainties that beset traditionalists in the 1970s and 1980s. Explore the connection between the rise of religious fundamentalism, political conservatism, and the fate of ERA.

An objective analysis of the documents will reveal the strengths, weaknesses, successes, and failures of modern feminism. Use them to better understand the social and political fragmentation of American society, as well as the ambivalence toward social change so evident on the modern political scene.

Questions for Analysis

1. Develop your own hypothesis to explain the failure to ratify the Equal Rights Amendment. How may the outcome of the debate be linked to prominent social trends in the 1980s?

2. What was the relationship between the social and political agendas of the modern conservative movement? How did ERA fit into the program of American conservatives? What evidence do the documents provide of a link between social uncertainty, fear of change, and the struggle against the amendment?

3. What was the social and economic basis of the modern feminist movement? To what extent was an "elitist" bias reflected in the goals of the movement? What were the implications of the movement's socioeconomic composition for the fate of ERA?

4. The Women's Action Alliance published an agenda of women's concerns in 1975 based on questionnaire responses from eighty women's organizations, including the Girl Scouts and radical feminist groups. As you review the program, do you find evidence of consensus or conflict among women's organizations? In what ways are the objectives in the NOW Expanded Bill of Rights for the 21st Century related to the WAA goals?

5. Why did some women oppose the Equal Rights Amendment? What aspects of feminism were perceived as a challenge to women and the family? Why? Compare the views of Gloria Steinem on the female response to the idea of constitutional guarantees with the outspoken assertions of Phyllis Schlafly.

1. The Equal Rights Amendment, 1972

Section 1. Equality of rights under the law shall not be denied or abridged by the United States or by any State on account of sex.

Section 2. The Congress shall have the power to enforce, by appropriate legislation, the provisions of this article.

Section 3. The amendment shall take effect two years after the date of ratification.

2. Gloria Steinem Argues the Case for Constitutional Change, 1970

I hope this committee will hear the personal, daily injustices suffered by many women—professionals and day laborers, women housebound by welfare as well as suburbia. We have all been silent for too long. We won't be silent anymore.

The truth is that all our problems stem from the same sex-based myths. We may appear before you as white radicals or the middle-aged middleclass or black soul sisters, but we are *all* sisters in fighting against these outdated myths. Like radical myths, they have been reflected in our laws. Let me list a few:

That Women Are Biologically Inferior to Men

In fact, an equally good case can be made for the reverse. Women live longer than men, even when the men are not subject to business pressures. . . .

However, I don't want to prove the superiority of one sex to another. That would only be repeating a male mistake. . . .

What we do know is that the difference *between* two races or two sexes is much smaller than the differences to be found *within* each group. Therefore, in spite of the slide show on female inferiorities that I understand was shown to you yesterday, the law makes much more sense when it treats individuals, not groups bundled together by some condition of birth. . . .

That Women Are Already Treated Equally in This Society

I'm sure there has been ample testimony to prove that equal pay for equal work, equal chance for advancement, and equal training or encouragement is obscenely scarce in every field, even those—like food and fashion industries—that are supposedly "feminine."

A deeper result of social and legal injustice, however, is what sociologists refer to as "Internalized Aggression." Victims of aggression absorb the myth of their own inferiority, and come to believe that their group is in fact second class.

Women suffer this second class treatment from the moment they are born. They are expected to *be* rather than achieve, to function biologically rather than learn. A brother, whatever his intellect, is more likely to get the family's encouragement and education money, while girls are often pressured to conceal ambition and intelligence, to "Uncle Tom."

Teachers, parents, and the Supreme Court may exude a protective, well-meaning rationale, but limiting the individual's ambition is doing no one a favor. Certainly not this country. It needs all the talent it can get.

That American Women Hold Great Economic Power

51% of all shareholders in this country are women. That's a favorite male-chauvinist statistic. However, the number of shares they hold is so small that the total is only 18% of all shares. Even those holdings are often controlled by men.

Similarly, only 5% of all the people in the country who receive $10,000 a year or more, earned or otherwise, are women. And that includes all the famous rich widows.

The constantly-repeated myth of our economic power seems less testimony to our real power than to the resentment of what little power we do have.

That Children Must Have Full-Time Mothers

American mothers spend more time with their homes and children than those of any other society we know about. . . .

The truth is that most American children seem to be suffering from too much Mother, and too little Father. Part of the program of Women's Liberation is a return of fathers to their children. . . .

As for the psychic health of the children, studies show that the quality of time spent by parents is more important than the quantity. The most damaged children were not those whose mothers worked, but those whose mothers preferred to work but stayed home out of a role-playing desire to be a "good mother."

That the Women's Movement Is Not Political, Won't Last, or Is Somehow Not "Serious"

. . . We are 51% of the population, we are essentially united on these issues across boundaries of class or race or age, and we may well end by changing this society more than the civil rights movement. That is an apt parallel. We, too, have our right wing and left wing, our separatists, gradualists, and Uncle Toms. But we are changing our own consciousness, and that of the country. . . .

I had deep misgivings about discussing this topic when National Guardsmen are occupying our campuses, the country is being turned against itself in a terrible polarization, and America is enlarging an already inhuman and unjustifiable war. But it seems to me that much of the trouble this country is in has to do with the Masculine Mystique; with the myth that masculinity somehow depends on the subjugation of other people. It is a bipartisan problem: both our past and current Presidents seem to be victims of this myth, and to behave accordingly.

Women are not more moral than men. We are only uncorrupted by power. But we do not want to imitate men, to join this country as it is, and I think our very participation will change it. Perhaps women elected leaders—and there will be many more of them—will not be so likely to dominate black people or yellow people or men; anybody who looks different from us.

After all, we won't have our masculinity to prove.

3. The Women's Action Alliance Agenda, 1975

I. *Fair Representation and Participation in the Political Process*

Encouragement for women to run for elective office, and provision of the necessary resources for women candidates; appointment of increased numbers of women to political positions.

Provision of opportunities for women and girls to develop and exercise leadership skills; systematic preparation and examination of all legislation, taking into account its effects on women; commitment to and enforcement of equal access and affirmative action rules within political parties. . . .

II. *Equal Education and Training*

Enforcement of laws which guarantee equal access to and treatment in all educational, vocational and athletic programs and facilities; equalization of financial aids, research opportunities and educational funds for girls and women.

Development of continuing education programs to meet the needs of varying life patterns, and to assess and give education credits for appropriate life experiences.

Increased numbers of women on faculties, administrations and policy making bodies, at all levels of educational systems.

Incorporation of women's issues into all areas of education curricula.

III. *Meaningful Work and Adequate Compensation*

Enforcement of legislation prohibiting discrimination at all levels of employment.

Extension of the basic workers' benefits to household workers, migrant and agricultural workers, and homemakers.

Economic and legal recognition of homemakers' work.

Recognition of pregnancy related disabilities as normal, temporary employment disabilities.

Attainment of equal pay for comparable work, that is, work frequently performed by women which is equivalent to work performed by men, but for which women receive less pay.

Review of widely used industrial designs and machinery which inhibit women's work production.

IV. *Equal Access to Economic Power*

A minimum standard of income for low income and disadvantaged persons.

Elimination of discrimination in income tax laws and the social security system, and introduction of coverage under S.S. for unpaid homemakers; elimination of discrimination against women in credit, insurance, and benefit and pension plans.

V. *Quality Child Care for All Children*

Creation of a comprehensive system of child care which includes parent involvement; child care as a tax deductible business expense.

VI. *Quality Health Care and Services*

Support for and expansion of medical and mental health services available without regard to ability to pay.

Implementation of the legal right of women to control their own reproductive systems.

Expansion of private and public health insurance to provide for women's special needs.

Increased attention to and support for research into new drugs and medical procedures which have special significance for women.

VII. *Adequate Housing*

VIII. *Just and Humane Treatment in the Criminal Justice System*

Repeal of laws which treat women and men differently within the criminal justice system; equalization of services for women and men offenders.

Achievement of expanded representation and participation of women in positions of authority in the criminal justice system.

Improved treatment of rape victims by personnel within the criminal justice system; re-examination of laws pertaining to victimless crimes.

IX. *Fair Treatment by and Equal Access to Media and the Arts*

X. *Physical Safety*

Recognition of and respect for the autonomy and dignity of the female person; recognition of rape as a violent and serious crime.

Reform of laws which made it unduly difficult to convict rapists and which place victims of rape in the role of the accused in the legal system; creation and expansion of support programs for rape victims.

XI. *Respect for the Individual*

Protection of the right to privacy of relationships between consenting adults.

Extension of all civil rights legislation to prohibit discrimination based on affectional or sexual preference.

End to prejudice and discrimination against women who wish to determine their own names.

Elimination of discrimination against women based on marital status.

Recognition that women are individuals with full rights to make the choices affecting their lives.

4. Phyllis Schlafly Attacks the ERA, 1982

All for Nothing

[F]or what benefit would our nation submit to the shame of having our constitutional process so compromised? For nothing. ERA offers absolutely no benefit to women, no new right, no new opportunity that we do not have now.

Of course, ERA will not give women any employment benefits, because ERA does not even apply to private industry. ERA prohibits sex discrimination only "by the United States and by any state." All federal employment laws are already sex neutral and prohibit sex discrimination in hiring, pay, and promotion. Under the Equal Employment Opportunity Act of 1972 and the Equal Employment Opportunity Commission it created, women have already won multi-million dollar back-pay settlements against the largest companies in our land.

ERA would require us to eliminate all sex bias from all federal and state laws and regulations. If the law is already sex neutral, as are the employment laws, ERA would have no effect.

ERA would have no effect on our tax laws because they are already sex neutral. Moreover, the new Economic Recovery Tax Act signed by President Ronald Reagan provides that all property held jointly by husbands and wives is to be treated as owned 50 percent by each, and that all transfers between husband and wife during life and at death can be tax free in unlimited amounts.

ERA would have no effect on our credit laws, because they are already sex neutral; the Equal Credit Opportunity Act of 1974 prohibits discrimination in credit because of sex. ERA would have no effect on Social Security; the Supreme Court made Social Security sex neutral in *Califano v. Goldfarb* (1977) and *Weinberger v. Weisenfeld* (1975)....

The Consequences

What, then, would ERA do? Plenty. In 1977 the US Commission on Civil Rights published a 230-page book written by the leading pro-ERA women lawyers, Ruth Bader Ginsburg (then a professor at Columbia Law School and now a judge on the US Court of Appeals for the District of Columbia) and Brenda Feigen-Fasteau (then a director of the Women's Rights Project for the American Civil Liberties Union and a frequent pro-ERA debater). This book, called *Sex Bias in the U.S. Code,* systematically identified the 800 federal laws that must be changed in order to eliminate all sex bias and conform to "the equality principle" of ERA. The list is very revealing; it ranges from the massively radical to the trivial.

1. Women must be drafted when men are drafted and assigned to military combat duty. "Supporters of the equal rights principle firmly reject draft or combat exemption for women, as Congress did when it refused to qualify the Equal Rights Amendment by incorporating any military service exemption." (p. 218) . . .

2. The breadwinner-husband and homemaker-wife concept must be eliminated. "Congress and the President should direct their attention to the concept that pervades the Code: that the adult world is (and should be) divided into two classes—independent men, whose primary responsibility is to win bread for a family, and dependent women, whose primary responsibility is to care for children and household. This concept must be eliminated from the Code if it is to reflect the equality principle." (p. 206)

3. The federal government must provide comprehensive child care. "The increasingly common two-earner family pattern should impel development of a comprehensive program of government-supported child care." (p. 214)

4. Single-sex schools and colleges, and single-sex school and college activities, must be sex integrated. All-boys' and all-girls' organizations must change the name of their organizations and become sex integrated because separate-but-equal organizations perpetuate stereotyped sex roles. This sex-integration mandate includes fraternities and sororities, Boy Scouts, Girl Scouts, Boys' Clubs, and 4-H Boys' and Girls' Clubs. (pp. 101, 219–220, 169, 145–148, 138)

5. A long list of language changes must be made to conform to ERA: "manmade" must be changed to "artificial," "mankind" to "humanity," "man" and "woman" to "person" or "human," "midshipman" to "midshipperson," "plainclothesman" to "plainclothesperson," "he" and "she" to "he/she," "her" and "him" to "her/him." . . .

Blank Check

In some areas, such as the draft and military combat duty, lawyers for both sides agree on the effect of ERA: ERA would require women to be drafted and sent into combat any time men are drafted and sent into combat. In other areas, such as ERA's effect on homosexual privileges, abortion funding, and financing government child care, prominent and responsible spokespersons can be found to say that ERA will or will not require those results. Who can give us the authoritative answer on the effect of ERA? Only the Supreme Court, and the Supreme Court will never tell us its decision unless and until ERA is ratified and an appropriate case is presented. That's why many people believe that ERA is a blank check to the federal courts, and that potential for mischief is sufficient reason for refusing to ratify it.

The American people have rejected ERA in the constitutional amendment process, and they have also rejected it in repeated democratic votes in statewide referenda. A proposal to put a state ERA in the state constitution was rejected overwhelmingly by the voters in Iowa in 1980, in Florida in 1978, in New York and New Jersey in 1975, and in Wisconsin in 1973. In 1978 the voters in Nevada also rejected the federal ERA in an advisory referendum.

ERA is an idea whose time will never come. It is an attempt to use the full power of the federal government to force the American people into a totally gender-neutral society in which we are absolutely denied our right to make reasonable differences of treatment between men and women. It is often called the "No Exceptions" Amendment because all attempts to mitigate the harsh and absolute effect of ERA were defeated by Congress in roll-call votes. Despite massive support from the media and millions of federal tax dollars improperly spent to force ERA upon us, ERA has been defeated. Requiescat in pace.

5. NOW Proposes an Expanded Bill of Rights, 1989

Expanded Bill of Rights for the 21st Century (1989)

Whereas, we are determined that an Equal Rights Amendment that bans sex discrimination in the United States Constitution is ratified; and

Whereas, the Supreme Court has begun to dismantle women's reproductive rights; and

Whereas, the Supreme Court has refused to grant the right to privacy on the basis of sexual preference; and

Whereas, the Supreme Court has dismantled affirmative action plans that fight institutional practices of race and sex discrimination; and

Whereas, the original Bill of Rights was passed in the year 1789 at a time when slavery was legal and women were considered legal chattel by our revolutionary founders; and

Whereas, it is time to complete the promise of liberty and justice under the law for all; and

Whereas, our nation faces new problems of catastrophic environmental conditions which could not have been conceived of by the country's founders;

Therefore be it resolved that it is time for an expanded Bill of Rights for the 21st Century which will ensure that all of the citizens of the United States enjoy basic, inalienable and indivisible human rights to which must be added:

1. the right to freedom from sex discrimination;
2. the right to freedom from race discrimination;
3. the right of all women to freedom from government interference in abortion, birth control and pregnancy and the right of indigent women to public funds for abortion, birth control and pregnancy services;
4. the right to freedom from discrimination on the basis of sexual orientation;
5. the right to freedom from discrimination based on religion, age, ongoing health condition, or a differently abled situation;
6. a right to a decent standard of living, including adequate food, housing, health care and education;
7. the right to clean air, clear water, safe toxic waste disposal and environmental protection; and
8. the right to be free from violence, including freedom from the threat of nuclear war.

Chapter 32:
Document Set 1 References

1. The Equal Rights Amendment, 1972
   Equal Rights Amendment, U.S. Congress, House of Representatives Joint Resolution 208, 92nd Cong., 1st Sess. (1971), pp. 1–3.

2. Gloria Steinem Argues the Case for Constitutional Change, 1970
   Testimony of Gloria Steinem, U.S. Congress, Senate Committee on the Judiciary, Subcommittee on Constitutional Amendment, 91st Cong., 2nd Sess., 1970, pp. 335–337.

3. The Women's Action Alliance Agenda, 1975
   Women's Action Alliance, leaflet, 1975, in Gerda Lerner, *The Female Experience: An American Documentary* (Indianapolis: Bobbs-Merrill, 1977), pp. 458–462.

4. Phyllis Schlafly Attacks the ERA, 1982
   Phyllis Schlafly, "The Case Against the ERA," *Radcliffe Quarterly* (Cambridge, Mass.: Radcliffe College, 1982).

5. NOW Proposes an Expanded Bill of Rights, 1989
   National Organization of Women, "Expanded Bill of Rights for the 21st Century," 1989, in Toni Carabillo *et al., Feminist Chronicles, 1953–1993* (Los Angeles: Women's Graphics, 1993), p. 247.

Chapter 32:
Document Set 1 Credits

CHAPTER 32

Confronting the Evil Empire by Proxy: Central America as a Battleground

Although the main target of Reagan administration foreign policy was the Soviet Union, one of the key battlegrounds for the ideological struggle against the "Evil Empire" was Central America. Your textbook stresses the president's overt and covert attempts to unhorse the Sandinista government in Nicaragua through support of the contra resistance, itself a product of CIA activities in the unstable area. As the documents suggest, the overall thrust of the Reagan policy was reminiscent of the Eisenhower-Dulles era. When you review these materials, think about continuity in American hemispheric policy, with particular emphasis on the exercise of executive authority.

Start with the brief excerpt from President Reagan's 1985 State of the Union message as an indicator of the goals and assumptions that underlay American policy toward Nicaragua and the contras. Compare the Reagan approach to the Dulles initiative in Guatemala, discussed in Chapter 29. Watch for themes in the history of American response to revolution in the western hemisphere, and think about the relationship between the president's broad objectives, his management style, and the eventual result of an extensive program of covert activity.

It was ultimately the CIA-NSC program of freelance adventurism that created problems for militant anticommunists on the Reagan team. The consequence of concern for American hostages in the Middle East and determination to aid the contras was a scan-

dal of major proportions that severely damaged the administration for much of the president's second term. As you examine the Tower Commission Report and the majority and minority reports of the congressional Iran-contra panels, be conscious of similarities and differences between this crisis and the Watergate affair of the Nixon years (see Chapter 31). Also, compare the president's lack of candor with President Clinton's evasiveness in 1998 and 1999. Assess the constitutional principles at stake in the activities of Lieutenant Colonel Oliver North and National Security Adviser John Poindexter, as described in your textbook.

One reason the national security managers decided to circumvent legislative prohibitions of contra aid was that they shared President Reagan's anti-Sandinista zeal, despite the fact that the administration never succeeded in generating substantial public support for his policy. Review the article by former Assistant Secretary of State for Inter-American Affairs Elliot Abrams and the newsletter of the Inter-Religious Task Force on Central America to identify the shortcomings of U.S. Central American policy and the reasons for public reservations in the United States. Consider the authors' personal agendas as you evaluate their criticisms.

These documents place the Reagan policy in its historical context. Your task is to identify continuities with the past and to analyze the central constitutional and policy issues raised by American interventionism.

Questions for Analysis

1. What was the rationale for the administration's policy of support for the contra insurgency in Nicaragua? What relationship existed between President Reagan's assumptions and those of Oliver North and John Poindexter, as revealed in the documents? To what extent did their objectives justify the means employed to achieve them?

2. Compare the Watergate affair with the Iran-contra scandal, with emphasis on the legitimate uses of power and the constitutional issues involved. Does justice appear to have been served in the handling of the North and Poindexter cases? Why or why not? What evidence bearing on constitutional interpretation may be extracted from the Tower Report and the Senate-House panel reports?

3. Using your textbook as a resource, evaluate Reagan's management/administrative style. What were the implications of the president's approach to his office?

4. Why was President Reagan unable to mobilize public support for his policy toward the contras? What does the evidence suggest about the reasons for public skepticism of the Reagan program in Central America? In what way do the documents reflect the use or misuse of history? What was the result?

5. Using the documents as your major resource, develop a hypothesis with regard to responsibility for the Iran-contra scandal. What conclusions can be drawn from the evidence concerning the question of who knew what when? Why are these important questions?

6. Examining the evidence from a long-term historical perspective, what do you regard as the strengths and weaknesses in American policy toward Latin America? How do the documents demonstrate the problems and opportunities presented by revolutionary movements in the Third World? What is your evaluation of American policies? Defend your position with evidence drawn from the documents.

1. President Ronald Reagan Sets a Tone for Central American Policy, 1985

We must stand by all our democratic allies. And we must not break faith with those who are risking their lives—on every continent, from Afghanistan to Nicaragua—to defy Soviet-supported aggression and secure rights which have been ours from birth.

The Sandinista dictatorship of Nicaragua, with full Cuban-Soviet bloc support, not only persecutes its people, the church, and denies a free press but arms and provides bases for communist terrorists attacking neighboring states. Support for freedom fighters is self-defense and totally consistent with the OAS and UN Charters. It is essential that the Congress continue all facets of our assistance to Central America. I want to work with you to support the democratic forces whose struggle is tied to our own security.

2. The Inter-Religious Task Force Attacks the Administration Program in Nicaragua, 1985, 1986

The level of U.S. intervention in Nicaragua reached new heights in 1985.

On Feb. 21 the facade of "interdiction" fell when Pres. Reagan admitted that the U.S. goal in Nicaragua was to change the "present structure" there and make the Sandinistas cry "uncle."

Last June, after several weeks of intensive lobbying, the Reagan Administration succeeded in persuading the House of Representatives to reverse itself and resume direct aid to the contras. Although the aid was characterized as "humanitarian," Congressional debate revealed that the envisioned support went far beyond any recognized sense of the term and contravened existing international legal standards. . . .

Over the past year the contras do not appear to have gained any significant ground. They cannot capture or hold any towns or territory and are dependent on their ability to seek safe haven from Honduras and (increasingly) Costa Rica. However, even the resumption of lethal military aid (which recent events suggest the Administration is laying the groundwork for) is not likely to alter the military balance. . . .

Meanwhile, the war continued to take tolls on the lives and economy of Nicaragua. A military offensive in the north was fairly successful, causing thousands of contras to flee into Honduras or to scatter in small bands within Nicaragua. . . .

Allegations of atrocities by the U.S.-backed contras continued to be documented with the issuance of two reports last March. A report by former New York State assistant attorney general Reed Brody documented a "distinct pattern" of murders, kidnappings, assaults and torture by the contras. Similar findings were reported by Americas Watch in a report which at the same time found that serious human rights violations on the part of the Nicaraguan government had declined since 1982.

In addition, a Congressional report to the Arms Control and Foreign Policy Caucus confirmed that almost the entire command structure of the FDN was made up of former Somoza National Guard. The report listed the main contributors of private funds going to the contras. The list includes the Unification Church (owner of the Washington Times); the Christian Broadcasting Network; the Veterans of Foreign Wars; the Knights of Malta; CAUSA International (also the Unification Church); Soldier of Fortune Magazine; and several southern-based mercenary groups.

Direct U.S. involvement was also revealed this past year. In March, the *Wall Street Journal* reported the involvement of U.S. personnel in attacks on Nicaragua and violations of its airspace.

Later in the year it was reported that the National Security Council (NSC), a White House agency, helped raise money for the rebels from private sources. Moreover, the NSC, with full knowledge and acquiescence of the White House, helped plan anti-Sandinista military operations despite Congressional prohibitions on such aid. All the while Pres. Reagan continued to deny that the U.S. was violating international law.

Yet the violation of international law was precisely the issue when Nicaragua's presentation before the World Court at the Hague opened on Sept. 12. Nicaragua charged that U.S. support for the contras attempting to overthrow its government was "state terrorism" and in violation of international law.

While the U.S. refused to participate in the case, former CIA analyst David MacMichael testified that CIA strategy was aimed at provoking a violent military response and domestic repression by Nicaragua. While a decision is still pending, observers agreed that by legal standards Nicaragua has a strong case. . . .

By a vote of 222 to 210 the U.S. House of Representatives rejected on March 20 [1986] President Reagan's plan to extend $100 million military and "humanitarian aid" to the contras. . . .

Explanations for the President's defeat varied; ranging from the level of "anti-communist" rhetoric emanating from the White House, the lack of a coherent policy evoking memories of Vietnam, to the opposition of U.S. allies in Latin America to the request. . . .

But the reaction of the public also played a significant role in the defeat. President Reagan went on national television the Sunday night before the vote in an effort to appeal to the American public. But in most Congressional offices phone calls opposing the President outnumbered those who supported him.

Only two weeks earlier, on March 3, nearly 200 religious leaders formed human crosses on the steps of the Capitol, commemorating people killed by the contras in Nicaragua, and accused President Reagan of preferring "terrorism to the pursuit of peace." . . .

The likely passage of any military aid to the contras, even if it is "fenced," takes the United States one step further down the road to the logical conclusion of a failed policy—the ultimate commitment of U.S. military personnel. This point was underscored by recent revelations that the contras, in need of major training, would have to be trained by U.S. advisers were military aid passed.

3. The Tower Commission Assesses Oliver North's Contra Aid Scheme, 1987

As a general matter, LtCol North kept VADM Poindexter exhaustively informed about his activities with respect to the Iran initiative. Although the Board did not find a specific communication from LtCol North to VADM Poindexter on the diversion question, VADM Poindexter said that he knew that a diversion had occurred. Mr. Regan told the Board that he asked VADM Poindexter on November 24, 1986, if he knew of LtCol North's role in a diversion of funds to support the Contras. VADM Poindexter replied that, "I had a feeling that something bad was going on, but I didn't investigate it and I didn't do a thing about it. . . . I really didn't want to know. I was so damned mad at Tip O'Neill for the way he was dragging the Contras around I didn't want to know what, if anything, was going on. I should have, but I didn't." Attorney General Meese told the Board that after talking to LtCol North, he asked VADM Poindexter what he knew about the diversion. "He said that he did know about it. . . . Ollie North had given him enough hints that he knew what was going on, but he didn't want to look further into it. But that he in fact did generally know that money had gone to the Contras as a result of the Iran shipment."

The President said he had no knowledge of the diversion prior to his conversation with Attorney General Meese on November 25, 1986. No evidence has come to light to suggest otherwise. Contemporaneous Justice Department staff notes of LtCol North's interview with Attorney General Meese on November 23, 1986, show North telling the Attorney General that only he, Mr. McFarlane, and VADM Poindexter were aware of the diversion. . . .

On December 21, 1982, Congress passed the first "Boland amendment" prohibiting the Department of Defense and the Central Intelligence Agency from spending funds to overthrow Nicaragua or provoke conflict between Nicaragua and Honduras. The following year, $24 million was authorized for the Contras. On October 3, 1984, Congress cut off all funding for the Contras and prohibited DoD, CIA, and any other agency or entity "involved in intelligence activities" from directly or indirectly supporting military operations in Nicaragua. . . .

The Bid for Private Funding. Because of Congressional restrictions, the Executive Branch turned to private sources to sustain the Contras militarily. In 1985 and 1986, Mr. McFarlane and the NSC staff repeatedly denied any direct involvement in efforts to obtain funds from these sources. Yet evidence before the Board suggests that LtCol North was well aware of these efforts and played a role in coordinating them. The extent of that role remains unclear.

In a memorandum to Mr. McFarlane dated April 11, 1985, LtCol North expressed concern that remaining Contra funds would soon be insufficient. He advised that efforts be made to seek $15 to $20 million in additional funds from the current donors which will "allow the force to grow to 30–35,000." The exact purpose to which these private funds were to be put was unambiguous. A number of memoranda from LtCol North make clear that the funds were for munitions and lethal aid. . . .

Who Knew What?

The Director of the CIA CATF recalls that by 1985, the CIA knew the Contras were receiving significant arms deliveries, some running in value in excess of $6 million, and were spending at a rate in excess of $1 million a month. CIA officials sought to locate the source of the funding. The Director of the CIA CATF told us:

[W]hat we found out was really only one or two people. It was tremendously compartmented inside the resistance organization and no one knew the ultimate source of the money, and very, very few people even know how much there was coming in and out.

Mr. Abrams recalls:

[W]e did not engage in nor did we really know anything about this private network. We knew that it existed. We knew it in part because somebody was giving the Contras guns. . . . [T]hey were instructed to kind of stay away, as the Agency people were, on the grounds that if you got too close, you would end up being accused of facilitating and so forth.

Richard Armitage, Assistant Secretary of Defense, recalls, "[S]everal of us in those groups said, Ollie . . . you're not involved in all this, are you? And he said . . . I have broken no laws."

LtCol North and VADM Poindexter do not seem to have sought the President's approval. In his response to a May 16, 1986, message from Poindexter on the status of the Contra project, LtCol North went on to discuss White House knowledge of his activities. LtCol North speculated that the President must know, indirectly, of his Contra activities.

I have no idea what Don Regan does or does not know re my private U.S. operation but the President obviously knows why he has been meeting with several select people to thank them for their 'support for Democracy' in CentAm.

Later that day VADM Poindexter replied to LtCol North: "Don Regan knows very little of your operation and that is just as well."

4. The Congressional Panel's Conclusions on the Iran-Contra Affair: The Majority View, 1987

Dishonesty and Secrecy

The Iran-Contra Affair was characterized by pervasive dishonesty and inordinate secrecy.

North admitted that he and other officials lied repeatedly to Congress and to the American people about the Contra covert action and Iran arms sales, and that he altered and destroyed official documents. North's testimony demonstrates that he also lied to members of the Executive branch, including the Attorney General, and officials of the State Department, CIA and NSC. . . .

Poindexter and North cited fear of leaks as a justification for these practices. But the need to prevent public disclosure cannot justify the deception practiced upon Members of Congress and the Executive branch officials by those who knew of the arms sale to Iran and the Contra support network. The State and Defense Departments deal each day with the most sensitive matters affecting millions of lives here and abroad. The Congressional Intelligence Committees receive only the most highly classified information, including information of covert activities. Yet, according to North and Poindexter, even the senior officials of these bodies could not be entrusted with the NSC staff's secret because they might leak. . . .

The Administration never sought to hide its desire to assist the Contras so long as such aid was authorized by statute. On the contrary, it wanted the Sandinistas to know that the United States supported the Contras. After enactment of the Boland Amendment, the Administration repeatedly and publicly called upon Congress to resume U.S. assistance. Only the NSC staff's Contra support activities were kept under wraps. The Committees believe these actions were concealed in order to prevent Congress from learning that the Boland Amendment was being circumvented. . . .

Initially, Congress was told that our purpose was simply to interdict the flow of weapons from Nicaragua into El Salvador. Then Congress was told that our purpose was to harass the Sandinistas to prevent them from consolidating their power and exporting their revolution. Eventually, Congress was told that our purpose was to eliminate all foreign forces from Nicaragua, to reduce the size of the Sandinista armed forces, and to restore the democratic reforms pledged by the Sandinistas during the overthrow of the Somoza regime. . . .

Disdain for Law

In the Iran-Contra Affair, officials viewed the law not as setting boundaries for their actions, but raising impediments to their goals. When the goals and the law collided, the law gave way:

The covert program of support for the Contras evaded the Constitution's most significant check on Executive power: The President can spend funds on a program only if he can convince Congress to appropriate the money.

When Congress enacted the Boland Amendment, cutting off funds for the war in Nicaragua, Administration officials raised funds for the Contras from other sources—foreign Governments, the Iran arms sales, and private individuals; and the NSC staff controlled the expenditures of these funds through power over the Enterprise. Conducting the covert program in Nicaragua with funding from the sale of U.S. Government property and contributions raised by Government officials was a flagrant violation of the Appropriations Clause of the Constitution.

In addition, the covert program of support for the Contras was an evasion of the letter and spirit of the Boland Amendment. The President made it clear that while he opposed restrictions on military or paramilitary assistance to the Contras, he recognized that compliance with the law was not optional. "[W]hat I might personally wish or what our Government might wish still would not justify us violating the law of the land," he said in 1983. . . .

Who Was Responsible?

Who was responsible for the Iran-Contra Affair? Part of our mandate was to answer that question, not in a legal sense (which is the responsibility of the Independent Counsel), but in order to reaffirm that those who serve the Government are accountable for their actions. Based on our investigation, we reach the following conclusions:

At the operational level, the central figure in the Iran-Contra Affair was Lt. Col. North, who coordinated all of the activities and was involved in all aspects of the secret operations. North, however, did not act alone.

North's conduct had the express approval of Adm. John Poindexter, first as Deputy National Security Adviser and then as National Security Adviser.

North also had at least the tacit support of Robert McFarlane, who served as National Security Adviser until December 1985.

In addition, for reasons cited earlier, we believe that the late Director of Central Intelligence, William Casey, encouraged North, gave him direction and promoted the concept of an extra-legal covert organization. Casey, for the most part, insulated CIA career employees from knowledge of what he and the NSC staff were doing. Casey's passion for covert operations—dating back to his World War II intelligence days—was well known.

5. A Minority Opinion of the Scandal, 1987

President Reagan and his staff made mistakes in the Iran-Contra Affair. It is important at the outset, however, to note that the President himself has already taken the hard step of acknowledging his mistakes and reacting precisely to correct what went wrong. . . .

The bottom line, however, is that the mistakes of the Iran-Contra Affair were just that—mistakes in judgment, and nothing more. There was no constitutional crisis, no systematic disrespect for "the rule of law," no grand conspiracy, and no Administration-wide dishonesty or coverup. . . .

Nicaragua

By the late spring of 1984, it became clear that the [Nicaraguan] Resistance would need some source of money if it were to continue to survive while the Administration tried to change public and Congressional opinion. To help bridge the gap, some Administration officials began encouraging foreign governments and U.S. private citizens to support the Contras. NSC staff members played a major role in these efforts, but were specifically ordered to avoid direct solicitations. The President clearly approved of private benefactor and third-country funding, and neither he *nor his designated agents* could constitutionally be prohibited from encouraging it. To avoid political retribution, however, the Administration did not inform Congress of its actions. . . .

Because the Boland Amendment is an appropriations rider, it is worth noting that there is no evidence that any substantial amounts of appropriated taxpayer funds were used in support of these efforts. In addition, the NSC staff believed—as we do—that the prohibition did not cover the NSC. At no time, in other words, did members of the President's staff think their activities were illegal. Nevertheless, the NSC staff did make a concerted effort to conceal its actions from Congress. There is no evidence, however, to suggest that the President or other senior Administration officials knew about this concealment. . . .

The Boland Amendment

We do believe . . . that virtually all of the NSC staff's activities were legal, with the possible exception of the diversion of Iran arms sale proceeds to the Resistance. We concede that reasonable people may take a contrary view of what Congress intended the Boland Amendment to mean. . . .

Summary: Nicaragua

. . . (1) The Constitution protects the power of the President, either acting himself or through agents of his choice, to engage in whatever diplomatic communications with other countries he may wish. It also protects the ability of the President and his agents to persuade U.S. citizens to engage voluntarily in otherwise legal activity to serve what they consider to be the national interest. That includes trying to persuade other countries to contribute their own funds for causes both countries support. To whatever extent the Boland Amendment tried to prohibit such activity, they were clearly unconstitutional.

(2) If the Constitution prohibits Congress from restricting a particular Presidential action directly, it cannot use the appropriation power to achieve the same unconstitutional effect. Congress does have the power under the Constitution, however, to use appropriations riders to prohibit the entire U.S. Government from spending any money, including salaries, to provide covert or overt military support to the Contras. Thus, the Clark Amendment prohibiting all U.S. support for the Angolan Resistance in 1976 was constitutional. Some members of Congress who supported the Boland Amendment may have thought they were enacting a prohibition as broad as the Clark Amendment.

The specific language of the Boland Amendment was considerably more restricted, however. . . .

Summary: Diversion

We consider the ownership of the funds that Iranians paid to the Secord-Hakim "Enterprise" to be in legal doubt. There are respectable legal arguments to be made both for the point of view that the funds belong to the U.S. Treasury and for the contention that they do not. If the funds do not belong to the United States, then the diversion amounted to third-country or private funds being shipped to the Contras. If they did belong to the United States, there would be legal questions (although not, technically, Boland Amendment questions) about using U.S.-owned funds for purposes not specifically approved by law. The answer does not seem to us to be so obvious, however, as to warrant treating the matter as if it were criminal.

6. Elliot Abrams Assesses the Impact of the Iran-Contra Scandal on Central American Policy, 1989

Reagan made the establishment of democratic institutions the centerpiece of his Central American policy. In El Salvador, in Guatemala, and in relatively peaceful Honduras, it became U.S. policy to push for transitions, via free elections to democratic governments; and furthermore to encourage those countries to improve their judicial systems, reduce military violence, expand freedom of the press—in short, to build not only democratic governments but democratic societies as well.

This was the tacit agreement: the U.S. would protect Central America from Communism by bottling up and ultimately toppling the Sandinista regime if the Right—civilian and military—would throw its support to a process of democratization, which we for our part would help in every possible way. . . .

By mid-1987, there were 15,000 well-equipped *contras* in the field in Nicaragua, giving the Sandinistas real trouble and moving freely throughout the countryside. In particular, the *contras'* American Redeye missiles rendered the Sandinistas' Soviet-made helicopter gunships marginal to the struggle. Contrary to the claims of congressional liberals, the Sandinistas were very well aware of the wide support for the *contras* among the populace, and of the threat they constituted to the survival of the Communist regime.

It was at this promising point—when Communism was under effective assault in Nicaragua, and democracy was being built in the neighboring countries—that the Iran-*contra* affair erupted.

Thanks to the ensuing scandal, the liberal opponents of Reagan's strategy of backing guerrilla wars against Communism were given a new, unexpected chance to teach once again their version of the "lessons of Vietnam:" that a policy of anti-Communism leads to crises, scandals, adventurism, and even threatens the very integrity of our political system. But instead of combining the admission of serious mistakes with a tough defense of itself and with a frank explanation to the American people of the aims of its Central American strategy, the Reagan administration spun into a panic. High officials were thrown overboard. Two separate investigations into official misconduct (one by the Tower Commission and one by Congress) were launched, and just as quickly overshadowed, as the President, appointing an "independent counsel" before either of these investigations has been concluded, permitted the issue to become one of criminality.

Until now, congressional votes on *contra* aid had always been won or lost by very slim margins. Even Reagan's most important victory, the $100 million in military aid that had been authorized in the fall of 1986, had been wrung out of the Congress by a handful of votes. Now, as a result of the scandal, the tenuous majority that had backed *contra* aid was gone. Nevertheless Central America was still there, and the administration felt duty-bound to try to maintain its policy somehow.

In this weakened condition, the White House entered into negotiations in July 1987 with its former ally Jim Wright, now the Speaker of the House, a Texas Democrat with a pro-*contra* constituency. The product of these negotiations was the Wright-Reagan plan, under which Ronald Reagan agreed for the first time to link *contra* aid to Sandinista promises of reform, rather than to the *contras'* real battlefield needs.

It is hard to blame Central American leaders too much for the panic which characterized their initial reaction to this plan. They represented small, weak nations whose internal peace and stability could be upset in a weekend by Castro or Ortega. And if they sat and faced the future much surer about Castro's intentions and Ortega's than about our own, then their panic was not unfounded.

But the particular form of panic to which they succumbed was a disastrous one. For in a single day, the four Central American democratic leaders swept away the foundations of the policy which had been sustaining them, and presented to Daniel Ortega a very great gift. This they did at a summit meeting in Esquipulas, Guatemala, when they adopted the "peace plan" set forth by President Oscar Arias of Costa Rica, under which the *contras* would be disarmed and disbanded in exchange for Ortega's paper pledges of Jeffersonian democracy.

Now the road to democracy no longer required *contras* to eliminate Communists, but instead required agreements with Communists to eliminate the *contras*. Not even Iran-*contra* was so serious a blow to the Reagan administration's Central America policy as this.

7. Berke Breathed on the Rule of Law in America, 1989

BLOOM COUNTY by Berke Breathed

© 1989, Washington Post Writers Group. Reprinted with permission.

Chapter 32:
Document Set 2 References

1. President Ronald Reagan Sets a Tone for Central American Policy, 1985
   Ronald Reagan, "State of the Union Address," February 6, 1985.
2. An Inter-Religious Task Force Attacks the Administration Program in Nicaragua, 1985, 1986
   Inter-Religious Task Force on Central America, *Update Central America,* December 1985, March 1986.
3. The Tower Commission Assesses Oliver North's Contra Aid Scheme, 1987
   Excerpted from *The Tower Commission Report: The Full Text of the President's Special Review Board,* (New York: Bantam Books, 1987), pp. 54–57, 475–476.
4. The Congressional Panel's Conclusions on the Iran-Contra Affair: The Majority View, 1987

   Congressional Quarterly Almanac, 100th Cong., 1st Sess., 1987 (Washington, D.C.: Congressional Quarterly, Inc., 1987), pp. 101, 103.
5. A Minority Opinion of the Scandal, 1987
   Congressional Quarterly Almanac, 100th Cong., 1st Sess., pp. 107, 109, 111.
6. Elliot Abrams Assesses the Impact of the Iran-Contra Scandal on Central American Policy, 1989
   Elliot Abrams, "The Deal in Central America," *Commentary,* Vol. 87 (May 1989).
7. Berke Breathed on the Rule of Law in America, 1989
   Berke Breathed, "Bloom County," *Washington Post,* January 7, 1989.

Chapter 32:
Document Set 2 Credits

CHAPTER 32

DOCUMENT SET 3
Decision for War: An End to the "Vietnam Syndrome"?

As the international community moved cautiously beyond the Cold War, new challenges tested President George Bush's vaguely defined "new world order." Even before world leaders absorbed the impact of the momentous events in the expiring Soviet Union, a new threat to world stability arose when Saddam Hussein's Iraqi troops occupied Kuwait in August 1990. As your textbook notes, President Bush deftly crafted a United Nations coalition that reversed the invasion. For the president, the greatest challenge lay in persuading the American public and a reluctant Congress that U.S. military intervention in the Middle East was justified. This document set examines the issues that brought about the conflict, focusing on the historic Senate debate that ended in a congressional authorization of force.

Your analysis of the documents should seek to understand the influence of recent U.S. history on the discourse over the wisdom of military action. Be especially aware of the Vietnam War's impact on the thinking of the American political leaders who bore responsibility for authorizing the president to use force. Ask yourself how the Vietnam experience shaped the arguments advanced by participants in the Senate debate. Compare the Bush administration's approach to that of the Johnson administration in 1965 (see Chapter 30, Document Set 1).

To understand the complexities of the political disagreement that divided the Congress, you will need to assess the state of U.S. public opinion in January 1991. One expression of popular uncertainty may be found in the statement issued in November 1990 by the National Council of Churches of Christ. Evaluate the council's criticism of the Bush policies and its recommended alternatives. Its preference for a nonmilitary solution to the Kuwait crisis mirrored the widespread doubts that plagued Americans on the eve of the Senate debate.

As you analyze the conflicting arguments over the question of war, try to identify the issues at stake. Think about the separation of powers in the American constitutional system, placing emphasis on the war powers debate that had become so divisive in the 1960s. Consider also the post–World War II tradition of bipartisanship in foreign policy and the issues it has created in recent years. Finally, make a judgment about the potential utility of economic sanctions as a means of influencing Iraqi policy and behavior. Evaluate and account for the positions taken by both Republicans and Democrats.

The political drama of January 1991 reflected deep divisions within American society over the use of war as an instrument of foreign policy. Whatever the positions taken, contemporary observers asserted that the congressional debates constituted an extraordinary exercise in democracy.

But was it? James Bennet's searing critique of the U.S. media raises disturbing questions about the objectivity and reliability of the press coverage that preceded the decision for war. As you review Bennet's arguments, think about the relationships among media analysis, public information, and the ability to legislate responsibility. Is informed decision making possible in a modern, centralized state?

Questions for Analysis

1. The Gulf War proved very popular with the American public. How do you account for this positive response? How was it possible for a deeply divided public to react with such emotional enthusiasm to a war that so many Americans had opposed in early January?

2. What do the documents reveal about the influence of the Vietnam War on American public attitudes concerning the role of the United States in world affairs? To what extent do the backgrounds of the participants in the Senate debate shed light on the impact of the "Vietnam syndrome" on U.S. foreign policy? Have American concerns about foreign military interventions lessened since the Gulf War?

3. What were the basic arguments for and against U.S. military action in January 1991? Evaluate the positions taken. Explain why their proponents advanced these arguments. In view of Hussein's continued provocations, judge the war's results.

4. What evidence do the documents contain pertaining to the significance of executive leadership in the modern state? In what ways did the president influence the development of the national debate over the Gulf crisis? What were the results?

5. Evaluate the media's role in creating an informed public during the early debate over the issues at stake in the Gulf crisis. What do the documents reveal about the influence of the press in modern American society and politics? Do you believe that the press fulfilled its responsibility to the public between August 1990 and January 1991? What were the implications of the media's handling of the issues?

1. President Bush Frames the Debate, 1990

On August 6, in response to the unprovoked Iraqi invasion of Kuwait, I ordered the deployment of U.S. military forces to Saudi Arabia and the Persian Gulf to deter further Iraqi aggression and to protect our interests in the region. What we've done is right, and I'm happy to say that most members of Congress and the majority of Americans agree.

From the very beginning, we and our coalition partners have shared common political goals—the immediate, complete and unconditional withdrawal of Iraqi forces from Kuwait, restoration of Kuwait's legitimate government, protection of the lives of citizens held hostage by Iraq, both in Kuwait and Iraq, and restoration of security and stability in the Persian Gulf region. To achieve these goals, we and our allies have forged a strong diplomatic, economic and military strategy to force Iraq to comply with these objectives. The framework of this strategy is laid out in ten United Nations resolutions overwhelmingly supported by the United Nations Security Council. . . .

After consultation with King Fahd and our other allies, I have today directed the secretary of defense to increase the size of U.S. forces committed to

Desert Shield to insure that the coalition has an adequate offensive military option should that be necessary to achieve our common goals. Toward this end, we will continue to discuss the possibility of both additional allied force contributions and appropriate United Nations actions. . . .

Questions and Answers

Q. Mr. President, it sounds like you're going to war. You have moved from a defensive position to an offensive position and you have not said how many more troops you are sending or really why.

A. Well, I said why right now, and I hope that it's been very clear to the American people.

Q. Well is there—are there new reasons that have moved this posture?

A. No, I'm just continuing to do what we feel is necessary to complete our objectives, to fulfill our objectives that have been clearly stated.

Q. Well, are you going to war?

A. I'm not—we—I would love to see a peaceful resolution to this question. And that's what I want.

2. The Churches of Christ Call for Alternative Solutions, 1990

Two months ago, on September 14, 1990, the Executive Coordinating Committee of the National Council of the Churches of Christ in the USA addressed a message to its member communions on the Gulf crisis. That message condemned Iraq's invasion and occupation of Kuwait, raised serious questions about the decision of the U.S. government to send

troops to the Gulf region and about the growing magnitude of U.S. presence, noting that the extent of the commitment of U.S. forces and weaponry was the largest since the Vietnam war. Since then, the U.S. has more than doubled the number of troops sent to the region to a number approaching a half million persons.

The message also questioned the apparent open-ended nature of the U.S. military involvement in the Middle East and the failure on the part of the administration clearly to state its goals. President Bush and administration officials have done little to clarify either of these points. Indeed the rationales offered for the steady expansion of U.S. presence have often been misleading and sometimes even contradictory. Early statements that U.S. forces had been deployed for the defense of Saudi Arabia or the enforcement of U.N. sanctions have been supplanted by suggestions of broader goals, including expulsion of Iraqi forces from Kuwait by military means, or even offensive action against Iraq itself. The nation still has not been told in clear and certain terms what would be required for the withdrawal of U.S. troops. . . .

Resolution on the Gulf and Middle East Crisis: The General Board of the National Council of Churches, meeting in Portland, Oregon, November 14–15, 1990, recognizing its solidarity with the Christians of the Middle East and with the Middle East Council of Churches:

Urges the government of Iraq to release immediately all those citizens of other nations being held against their will in Kuwait or Iraq and to withdraw immediately its troops and occupation forces from Kuwait.

Calls for the continued rigorous application of the sanctions against Iraq authorized by the United Nations Security Council until such time as it withdraws its forces from Kuwait.

Reiterates its opposition to the withholding of food and medicine as a weapon against civilian populations.

Encourages the secretary-general of the United Nations to exercise fully his own good offices in pursuit of a rapid negotiated resolution of the present conflict in the Gulf.

Calls upon the president and U.S. Congress to pursue every means for a negotiated political solution to the crisis in the Gulf, including direct negotiations with Iraq.

Reiterates support for the convening under U.N. auspices of an international conference for a comprehensive peace in the Middle East, as a means of implementing United Nations Security Council resolutions on Israel and Palestine, Lebanon and Cyprus, recognizing that the present crisis cannot be isolated from the unresolved issues of the region as a whole.

Calls for an immediate halt to the buildup and withdrawal of U.S. troops from the Gulf region except those which might be required and explicitly recommended by the Security Council of the United Nations in accordance with the relevant provisions of the United Nations charter.

Calls upon the U.S. government to give leadership to the institution of an immediate and complete embargo under U.N. auspices on arms transfers to the Middle East.

3. Senator John Kerry Questions the President's Leadership, 1991

MR. KERRY: Mr. President, I wish, like everyone else here, that we were not at this moment talking about sending people to another war. . . .

The question of being ready and certain is important to many of us of the Vietnam generation. We come to this debate with a measure of distrust, with some skepticism, with a searing commitment to ask honest questions and with a resolve to get satisfactory answers so that we are not misled again.

I might add that I also come to this debate determined that whatever happens we will not confuse a war with the warriors. I am determined that our

troops will receive complete and total support. And, that if we do go to war, I am committed that we do everything in our power to accomplish our mission with minimum casualties and bring the troops home to the gratitude and respect they deserve.

But until the first shot is fired I remain troubled by the unanswered questions and by the human considerations. . . .

There is a rush to war here. I do not know why, but there is a rush to war. There is a rush to have this thing over with. Somehow I can not help but feel that if we were squared off against a stronger nation there would not be such a rush. Our history with the Soviet Union makes that clear. But with Iraq—we know we can win or think we know we can win. We know they are surrounded. We know our high-technology weapons and targeting capabilities can overwhelm the Iraqi military. And so we think we can get it over with an "acceptable level of casualties." . . .

Are we supposed to go to war simply because one man—the President—makes a series of unilateral decisions that put us in a box—a box that makes that war, to a greater degree, inevitable? Are we supposed to go to war because once the President has announced something publicly, to reverse or question him is somehow detrimental to the Nation despite the fact we are a coequal partner in government?

Obviously, such an argument and such an approach to the governing process of this country makes Congress nothing more than a rubber stamp and literally renders inoperative our coequal decisionmaking responsibility in a matter of war and peace. It might be wise to remind ourselves that we still are a nation of laws and not of men; that we still elect our Presidents: We do not crown them. We had a revolution more than 200 years ago to settle that question and the Constitution put the war-making power in Congress's hands precisely to avoid the very individual decisionmaking—that places us in the box we are told we are in today. . . .

We are in this position today because the President of the United States made a series of decisions that have put us in this position, not because we made them or because we fail to make them. The memory of Vietnam says to all of us that it is far, far better that we risk curbing in or reining in this rush to war now, rather than trying to get the American people [to] support it at some time down the road after the shooting has started. Nothing, nothing could faster bring us a repetition of the divisions and

the torment this Nation faced during the 1960's and 1970's.

Mr. President, in my heart and in my gut and in my mind I do not believe in sending people to war unless it is imperative. And it is not, in my view, imperative that in the next few days we send soldiers to fight a war. We are at this grave moment deciding whether or not we do so for two fundamental reasons: Because President Bush unilaterally decided to increase the troops to 430,000 and because he set a deadline.

We are not here because oil is not reaching the shores of the United States or our economy is crippled.

We are not here because there has been an attack or there is the imminent threat of one.

We are not here because the world has decided that we have to go to war.

We are not here because the vital interests of the United States are somehow more at stake today than they will be in 3 weeks or 3 months or a year.

We are here because the policy of one man suggests that we do not have the patience to wait this out and see if we can settle it differently. . . .

This obvious truth is contrary to the testimony of our own intelligence estimates. As CIA Director William Webster testified before the Congress just 1 month ago—on December 5, 1990—the CIA estimated that sanctions would need another 9 months to be effective—only then could we determine the extent to which they were working.

That means that according to the Director of the CIA, we cannot conclude that sanctions are ineffective until next September. . . .

I end my comments coming back to where I began: Are we ready for what this country and our countrymen will witness and bear? Have we come to the moment, each of us, with the values and interests at stake to call on each of us to send our own children to die?

4. Senator John McCain Urges Resistance to Aggression, 1991

MR. McCAIN: Mr. President, I rise in opposition to the resolution which is before us, and in support of a resolution which would, if necessary—and I emphasize only if necessary—give the President the support of this body for the use of force. It is only by supporting our President that we can achieve the goals of our national policy and meet our urgent national security requirements in the Middle East. . . .

Mr. President, during this debate we hear references time and time again to the Vietnam war and how people want no more Vietnams. We hear that from the President. No one wants another Vietnam. The President does not, and neither does anyone in this body who has addressed this issue. Clearly, neither we, nor the American people seek a replay of that tragic chapter in our Nation's history.

Yet, this resolution could force a "Vietnam" upon us. If we drag out this crisis and do not act decisively and bring it to a successful resolution, we face the prospect of a much longer and bitter war.

If we must use force, we must use it quickly and decisively. We must never again drift into a major conflict in slow stages, denying its seriousness, and setting political rules and constraints that make victory impossible. . . .

. . . Mr. President, this is a critical point in history. We determine at this moment whether we, in the first crisis of the post-cold war era, can act together with the United Nations and every other civilized nation in the word, to prevent naked international aggression of the most heinous and disgraceful kind. It is clear to me that if we fail to act, our New World order will be inevitably a succession of dictators, or more Saddam Husseins. There is an abundance around this globe of real or would-be dictators who will see a green light. They will see a green light for aggression, and a green light for annexation of its weaker neighbors. We will have created a threat to the stability of this entire globe.

5. Senator George Mitchell Chooses Economic Sanctions Over War, 1991

MR. MITCHELL: Mr. President, first I want to say that every Member of the Senate firmly shares the convictions expressed by the Senator from Georgia with respect to the support of American military personnel, our men and women, in the event that hostilities break out. That support is firm and unshakable. . . .

The President has submitted to the Congress a written request for authorization to use military force. That is the title of the resolution. In the current circumstances, clearly, it would be of such a scope and intensity that can only be described as war. So the second resolution is, plainly, by its own words, and by the circumstances which exist in the Persian Gulf, an authorization for war. Of that there can be no doubt or dispute. That is what we will be voting for or against today.

I urge my colleagues to vote against authorizing an immediate war.

I have discussed two things we have heard a lot about. Let me close by discussing something we have heard little about. It is this question: In the event of war, why should it be an American war, made up largely of American troops, American casualties, American deaths? The first resolution, the Nunn resolution, directly addresses this concern by supporting "efforts to increase the military and financial contributions made by allied nations." The second resolution does not mention the subject.

Certainly, the United States has a high responsibility to lead the international community in opposing aggression. . . .

It may become necessary to use force to expel Iraq from Kuwait. But because war is such a grave undertaking, with such serious consequences, we should make certain that war is employed only as a last resort. War carries with it great costs and high risk.

The possibilities of spending billions of dollars; a greatly disrupted oil supply and oil price increases; a war widened to include Israel, Turkey, or other allies; the long-term American occupation of Iraq; increased instability in the Persian Gulf region;

long-standing Arab enmity against the United States; a return to isolationism at home. All of these risks are there.

But the largest risk, the greatest risk, the most profound risk is that of the loss of human life. How many people will die? How many young Americans will die? And for the families of those young Americans who die, for every one of us, the truly haunting question will be: Did they die unnecessarily? No one will ever be able to answer that question, for if we go to war now, no one will ever know if sanctions would have worked, if given a full and fair chance.

I urge my colleagues to vote for the first resolution, the Nunn resolution to vote for continuing economic sanctions and diplomatic pressure. I urge my colleagues to vote against the second resolution, to vote against an authorization for immediate war.

6. A Critique of the Media's Role in the Debate Over War, 1990

It's hard to recall now that in the first days after Iraq invaded Kuwait, sending any American troops—much less 430,000 of them—to the Middle East never seemed inevitable. In fact, it didn't even seem probable, since many lawmakers didn't like the idea. . . .

You don't have to oppose the American troop deployment in the Middle East to worry about the singular absence of public debate—in the House and Senate, in the major papers, on TV—during those first few weeks. You just have to believe that good debate makes good policy. The initial deployment and its subsequent spectacular growth came as surprises: We progressed almost magically from a projected ceiling of 50,000 troops to nine times that number. Likewise, we faded from "The mission of our troops is wholly defensive" (George Bush's words) into trying "to ensure that the coalition has an adequate offensive military option" (George Bush's words). Meanwhile, the national dailies and *Nightline* provided blow-by-blow accounts and occasionally ran some tougher stories analyzing U.S. interest in the Persian Gulf and the president's goals—whether we were preparing to fight only for oil, whether it was feasible to push for Saddam Hussein's ouster. On the op-ed pages, there was some grumbling back and forth as to whether those goals were worth chasing. But there was almost no discussion in any of these influential, supposedly adversarial sources of news about the *means* the president had chosen and what human cost they'd entail. . . .

On November 8, after the elections and while Congress was in recess, the consensus-building, slow and cautious Bush made the announcement that he was adding another 200,000 troops to beef up our offensive capability in the Middle East. That evening, Ted Koppel expressed some confusion: "I have a sense that we have taken sort of a major step forward from being. . . in a defensive posture to avoid an invasion of Saudi Arabia, to moving into a totally different kind of posture."

This shouldn't have come as such a shock, since for more than two months the nation's top dailies and *Nightline* had been running news that suggested American forces were preparing to attack, not only defend. Just as *Nightline* and the three papers never pointed out that the official size of the deployment was steadily racheting upward, none of them firmly came to grips with the fact that the initial line that the U.S. had deployed its forces for "wholly defensive" purposes had been crumbling from the getgo. . . .

On August 29, on *Nightline*, Dick Cheney told Sam Donaldson, "Well, again we'll come back to the proposition that our dispositions in the region are defensive. We're there to deter and to defend. . . . [B]ut we're not there in an offensive capacity, we're not there threatening Iraq." Those M-1 tanks slipped Donaldson's mind, evidently, since he didn't pursue the issue. Koppel's astonishment on November 8 was no doubt feigned, but he was making an important point: No one (including Koppel) had been telling the average American that it was part of U.S. policy to prepare to launch an attack. That was a strategy, by the way, that a majority of Americans opposed. . . .

On *Nightline* on November 8, Koppel discussed with his old mentor, Henry Kissinger, Bush's decision to double the size of the American forces in Saudi Arabia. After fielding several questions about the wisdom of the government's action, Kissinger grumpily observed, "America seems to specialize in putting 300,000 or more troops somewhere and afterwards starting to debate how important that is."

Koppel shot back: "Well, that's because there was never any opportunity to have a debate beforehand."

Later, Kissinger backpedaled a bit: "I'm not saying that shouldn't be—no, I'm not saying we shouldn't have a debate, but I'm saying that the debate must take into account what has already happened."

Koppel: "But what has already happened has happened without the benefit of the debate, that's precisely the point."

And whose fault, Ted, is that?

Chapter 32:
Document Set 3 References

1. President Bush Frames the Debate, 1990
   News Conference, November 8, 1990, in Micah L. Sifry and Christopher Cerf, eds., *The Gulf War Reader* (New York: Random House, 1991), pp. 228–229.

2. The Churches of Christ Call for Alternative Solutions, 1990
   National Council of Churches of Christ, Message, November 14–15, 1990, in Sifry and Cerf, pp. 230–231, 233.

3. Senator John Kerry Questions the President's Leadership, 1991
   John Kerry, Speech, January 11, 1991, *Congressional Record,* 102nd Cong., 1st Sess., 1991, pp. S249–252, 254.

4. Senator John McCain Urges Resistance to Aggression, 1991
   John McCain, Speech, January 11, 1991, *Congressional Record,* 102nd Cong., 1st Sess., 1991, pp. S230, 232.

5. Senator George Mitchell Chooses Economic Sanctions over War, 1991
   George Mitchell, Speech, January 12, 1991, *Congressional Record,* 102nd Cong., 1st Sess., 1991, pp. S368–369.

6. A Critique of the Media's Role in the Debate over War, 1990
   James Bennet, "How They Missed That Story," *Washington Monthly* (December 1990).

Chapter 32:
Document Set 3 Credits

CHAPTER 33

Health Security for All Americans: Great Expectations

The textbook indicates that the Clinton administration's failure to enact health care reform in 1994 damaged the president's political credibility as he attempted to advance his agenda before midterm elections. With Hillary Rodham Clinton in charge of the effort, an unwieldy health care reform task force developed a reform measure that promised universal coverage with complex cost controls exercised through regional health care purchasing cooperatives. As noted in the text, administration reformers misjudged American opinion and produced a sweeping proposal for more extensive changes than the public was prepared to accept.

The following documents reflect the diversity of opinion surrounding the health care controversy that came to symbolize the ineffectiveness of Clinton's early years in office. As you review the evidence, try to determine why the proposed reforms were not enacted. Be alert to the economic and social forces that worked against alterations in the nation's health care delivery system. As you examine editorial reaction to the health care crisis, consider the reasons behind the opinions expressed.

A second issue raised by the health care debate involved the institutional mechanisms employed by the Clinton administration to achieve its objectives. Central to the president's approach was his decision to entrust the task to the first lady. Analyze President Clinton's reasons for making this choice and explore the response to his action. Probe the sources for clues to the sharp reaction to the leadership role assumed by Hillary Rodham Clinton.

Finally, the documents reveal serious problems in the American health care system in the early 1990s. As you relate the arguments presented by the proponents of reform to the textbook description of the struggle, account for the emergence of this problem as a critical issue in 1993. Connect the divisive discussion of new delivery systems to the campaign of 1992 and the Clinton program. Ask yourself why Americans were willing to examine this public policy question at this time.

As you consider the timeliness of the administration's decision to embrace health care reform, be aware of the successes and failures of the modern American medical care delivery system. Note the problems cited by critics and defenders of the existing structure and consider the implications of their findings for the preservation of the modern "social safety net." Think also about the task force's proposal to establish a system of "managed competition" rather than a "single payer" program. Evaluate the Clinton reform proposal as a remedy for the ills of the American health care system.

While assessing the Clinton administration's health care reform, think about the issue in its historical context. Link the Clinton proposal with the earlier development of the American social welfare state, ranging from Franklin D. Roosevelt's Social Security Act of 1935 to the proposals and achievements of the Truman and Johnson administrations. Close examination of the ill-fated American Health Security Act and the controversy it generated will enable you to observe continuity in the history of social reform in the twentieth-century United States.

Questions for Analysis

1. How do the documents shed light on the reasons for the failure of the Clinton health care reform proposal?

2. What was Hillary Rodham Clinton's role in the fight for health care reform? What do the primary sources reveal about the Clintons' perceptions of the first lady's responsibilities? How did observers react to the high profile she assumed? How did her activities and procedures influence the discussion of the issue and the outcome of the debate?

3. Compare and contrast the ideas advanced by the Clinton administration with the ideas and accomplishments of earlier generations of social reformers. How does the evidence clarify the pressures and handicaps confronting proponents of national health care coverage in the United States?

4. Use the documents to analyze the positive and negative aspects of the existing health care delivery system in the United States. Why is such an enormously productive economic system unable to meet the medical needs of all citizens at the end of the twentieth century?

1. Hillary Rodham Clinton Justifies Health Care Reform, 1993

Every month, two million Americans lose their insurance for some period of time. Every day, thousands of Americans discover that despite years of working hard and paying for health insurance, they are no longer covered. . . . And business owners, large and small, struggle to stay afloat while providing coverage for their families and employees.

Each time someone loses health coverage or is denied insurance, their experience becomes another chapter in a growing national tragedy. Anxiety and fear about the cost of health care affect tens of millions of Americans—those with health insurance and those without. Even those with the very best benefits worry that their insurance might not be there tomorrow or may no longer be affordable.

Over the past months, I have had the extraordinary opportunity of listening to thousands of Americans talk about health care. . . .

The concerns that were expressed again and again—from those who need care and those who give care—convinced me of one point: although America can still proudly boast the world's finest health professionals and astounding medical advances, our health care system is broken. If we go on

without change, the consequences will be devastating for millions of Americans and disastrous for the nation in human and economic terms.

As a mother, I can understand the feeling of helplessness that must come when a parent cannot afford a vaccination or well-child exam. As a wife, I can imagine the fear that grips a couple whose health insurance vanishes because of a lost job, a layoff or an unexpected illness. As a sister, I can see the inequities and inconsistencies of a health care system that offers widely varying coverage, depending on where a family member lives or works. As a daughter, I can appreciate the suffering that comes when a parent's treatment is determined as much by bureaucratic rules and regulations as by doctors' expertise. And as a woman who has spent many years in the workforce, I can empathize with those who labor for a lifetime and still cannot be assured they will always have health coverage.

As an American citizen concerned about the health of our system, I stand with you as we confront this challenge that touches all of us. We can and will achieve lasting, meaningful change.

2. President William Jefferson Clinton Challenges Congress to Enact Reform, 1993

. . . If Americans are to have the courage to change in a difficult time, we must first be secure in our most basic needs. Tonight I want to talk to you about the most critical thing we can do to build that security.

This health care system of ours is badly broken and it is time to fix it. . . .

In spite of all the work we've done together and all the progress we've made, there's still a lot of people who say it would be an outright miracle if we passed health care reform. But my fellow Americans, in a time of change, you have to have miracles. . . .

And now, it is our turn to strike a blow for freedom in this country. The freedom of Americans to live without fear that their own nation's health care system won't be there for them when they need it.

It's hard to believe that there was once a time in this century when that kind of fear gripped old age. When retirement was nearly synonymous with poverty, and older Americans died in the street. That's unthinkable today, because over a half a century ago Americans had the courage to change—to create a Social Security system that ensures that no Americans will be forgotten in their later years.

Forty years from now, our grandchildren will also find it unthinkable that there was a time in this country when hardworking families lost their homes, their savings, their businesses, lost everything simply because their children got sick or because they had to change jobs. Our grandchildren will find such things unthinkable tomorrow if we have the courage to change today.

This is our chance. This is our journey. And when our work is done, we will know that we have answered the call of history and met the challenge of our time. . . .

3. The President's Health Security Plan, 1993

The Problem

All Americans, those who have health insurance and those who do not, understand that serious problems exist in the health care system:

- **Americans lack security.** One out of four people—or 63 million people—will lose health insurance coverage for some period during the next two years. Thirty-seven million Americans have no insurance and another 22 million lack adequate coverage.

  Losing or changing a job often means losing insurance. Becoming ill or living with a chronic medical condition can mean losing insurance coverage or not being able to obtain it.

- **Health care costs are rising faster than other sectors of the economy.** Precipitous growth in health care costs robs workers of wages, fuels the growth of the federal budget deficit and puts affordable care out of reach for millions of Americans.

  Left unchecked, rising health care costs will consume almost two-thirds of the increase in Gross Domestic Product for each American for the rest of the decade. . . .

Overview

The American Health Security Act guarantees comprehensive health coverage for all Americans regardless of health or employment status. Health coverage continues without interruption if Americans lose or change jobs, move from one area to another, become ill or confront a family crisis.

Through a system of regional and corporate health alliances that organize the buying power of consumers and employers, the American Health Security Act stimulates market forces so that health plans and providers compete on the basis of quality, service and price.

Under the Act health plans must meet national standards on benefits, quality and access to care but each state may tailor the new system to local needs and conditions. Thus the program encourages local innovation within a national framework.

It frees the health care system of much of the accumulated burden of unnecessary regulation and paperwork, allowing doctors, nurses, hospitals and other health providers to focus on providing high-quality care.

Creating Security

The American Health Security Act enhances the security of the American people by extending universal coverage in [an] environment that improves quality and controls rising costs:

- All employers contribute to health coverage for their employees, creating a level playing field among companies.

- Everyone shares the responsibility to pay for coverage.
- Limits on out-of-pocket payments protect American families from catastrophic costs, while subsidies ease the burden on low-income individuals and small employers.
- A comprehensive benefit package with no lifetime limits on medical coverage guarantees access to a full range of medically necessary or appropriate services.
- Elderly and disabled Americans receive coverage for outpatient prescription drugs under Medicare for the first time.
- Guaranteed choice of health plans and providers enhances choice for many Americans.
- No health plan may deny enrollment to any applicant because of health, employment or financial status nor may they charge some patients more than others because of age, medical condition or other factors related to risk.
- All health plans meet national quality standards and provide useful information that allows consumers to make valid comparisons among plans and providers.

- Separate programs increase federal support for long-term care and improve the quality and reliability of private long-term care insurance. . . .

Expanding Access to Care

The American Health Security Act invests in the development of an adequate health care system in areas with inadequate service. Those investments hold the promise of improving the availability and quality of health care in rural communities and urban neighborhoods.

- Health alliances assume responsibility for building health networks in rural and urban areas with inadequate access.
- National loan programs support the efforts of local health providers to develop community-based plans.
- Investments in new health programs such as school-based clinics and community clinics expand access to care for underserved populations.
- Financial incentives attract health professionals to areas with inadequate care. . . .

4. The Press Helps Shape the Debate, 1993

A. Questions on Hillary Rodham Clinton's Role in the Deliberative Process, 1993

Who elected Hillary Rodham Clinton? The answer, of course, is that no one did. But, then, no one elected any other member of Bill Clinton's senior staff or Cabinet. . . .

Mrs. Clinton indeed may become the most powerful First Lady in American history. . . .

Hillary's considerable talents are not in dispute. In Arkansas, she skillfully managed a committee that pushed through a string of education reforms. And she has had a much smoother first week in the White House than the president. That said, assigning the First Lady such a high-visibility role entails enormous political risks.

One obvious danger is that many Americans may resent her top-level involvement in the extraordinarily difficult issue of health care reform. A recent poll shows voters are split right down the middle on whether the president's wife should have a say in major policy decisions, with 47 percent supporting the idea and 45 percent opposed. If Mrs. Clinton's participation becomes a controversial matter itself, it will only complicate the president's efforts to straighten out the health care problem.

And what will happen if the recommendation from Mrs. Clinton's task force is one the president does not want to embrace? Will it be difficult for him to reject publicly his own wife's proposal?

If, in the end, Mrs. Clinton fails to deliver on the high expectations imposed by her new position, the responsibility will rest not with her but with the occupant of the Oval Office. As always, the buck stops on the president's desk.

B. *The Washington Post* Frames the Debate, 1993

The two great issues in health care reform point in opposite directions: One is extending protection to the one-seventh of the population that is without insurance at any one time; the other is controlling costs. As a society, we tend to be better at the first of these tasks—providing benefits—than at the second one of imposing discipline. It's always more pleasant to say yes to a lot of people than it is to say no, and we've provided health care insurance on a mass basis before, as in Medicare and Medicaid. We more or less know how to do it. There are plenty of problems associated with broadening coverage or making it universal—what mechanisms to use, the array of benefits to provide, how to pay the cost—but those are well within the bounds of normal political experience and expertise. . . .

. . . The likelihood is that the planners, for good substantive as well as political reasons, will start trying to achieve cost control with as little direct government involvement as possible. At some point in this business, the dividing line between a private and public system begins to blur, but we would guess they are likely to try a system of "managed care" first (which the government would structure even though it would be privately run), and turn to a more direct government role in the form of fee schedules, more or less binding budgets and the rest, only if that failed.

That might be the right way to proceed, but it ought to be explicitly done. The first step should leave open the possibility of the second if the first fails. Our own sense is that managed care is too frail a reed and won't stem the costs, but perhaps that's wrong. Here again, Medicare is precedent if not quite model. In deference to the medical profession, it was set up with minimal controls over practice and cost. Now, in an effort to control costs, the government dictates not just price but, through the device of price, many aspects of practice as well. Even in health care, he who pays the piper ultimately calls the tune; it just takes longer. And that's the lengthy process in which, on behalf of us all, the administration and Congress are now engaged.

C. Auto Industry Concerns, 1993

The Big Three want some relief from their rising health care costs, but UAW President Owen Bieber promised Monday that the union would strike if the companies tried to touch retiree health benefits. So the domestic automakers appear to be turning to government for a bailout. The idea is that Uncle Sam would put the muscle on auto buyers to subsidize the benefits of the Big Three's workers and retirees. . . .

So the Big Three are lobbying President Clinton and his health care task force for the formation of an auto sector health care "cooperative" that would socialize health costs. The government would impose a 1-percent to 1.5-percent tax on each car, including those from the Japanese and emerging German transplants. The tax revenue would be redistributed mostly back to the Big Three, however, to eliminate their cost disadvantage. . . .

It seems unlikely that the American public is going to want to help the Big Three out of their bargaining difficulties, especially if there are no concessions by the UAW this summer. The union doesn't like to admit that it is part of the problem and doesn't improve matters by advocating its own disastrous bailout plan, a single-payer national health care system. . . .

Detroit and the UAW should press Washington to cut the costs of doing business, including relief from nutty environmental, safety and other regulations, as a way to level the playing field. And if health care benefits are making the Big Three uncompetitive, then they should solve that problem the same way it was created: at the bargaining table.

D. An Endorsement of State Initiative from Connecticut, 1993

Several state governments are not waiting for the Clinton administration to develop a national healthcare policy. They are working on their own plans, as well they should.

Letting states set some of the details of health-insurance coverage would allow various approaches to be tested in the marketplace, among them networks of purchasing cooperatives and so-called single-payer systems that would place everyone in one insurance program. . . .

The Clinton administration is busily working on a national plan, of course. To be meaningful, that plan would have to establish the goals of universal access and cost controls for every state. But experimentation at the state level is a wise approach toward national reform. . . .

The states should exercise their freedom to experiment with cost controls and insurance coverage. The United States is not likely to find a single solution for several years—if ever.

5. The Reform Consensus, 1993

FIRST OF ALL, WE'RE AGAINST CAPS ON PREMIUMS...

INSURANCE COMPANIES

PRIMARILY, WE'RE AGAINST PRICE CONTROLS...

DOCTORS   HOSPITALS

AUTH

FIRST, WE'RE AGAINST EMPLOYERS PAYING FOR WORKERS' HEALTH INSURANCE...

SMALL BUSINESS

WE'RE ALL FOR HEALTH REFORM... ...BUT FIRST THINGS FIRST!

6. Religious Conservatives Define Health Care Reform, 1994

. . . Religious conservatives favor reforming the health care system to provide the highest quality care for American families at an affordable price. The health care plan that President Clinton proposed in 1993 to great fanfare was a bureaucratic, Byzantine, European-style syndicalist nightmare with no precursor in the American experience. Its price controls and high taxes would have led to the rationing of basic medical services, millions of lost jobs, and taxpayer-funded abortion on demand. Religious conservatives favor a free market, pro-family alternative. There are serious problems with the current health care system that can and should be fixed. Some needed reforms include portability of policies, allowing workers to take their insurance with them when they change jobs. American workers do not lose their life or automobile insurance when they change jobs; they should not lose health care coverage either. In addition, we should eliminate previous condition restrictions, enact real malpractice reform, create voluntary purchasing pools to lower premiums, enact medical savings accounts for catastrophic care, and provide tax credits to enable low-income families to purchase health insurance. These common sense reforms can be enacted without interfering with the sacrosanct doctor-patient relationship and without adversely affecting the quality of care. . . .

7. Bob Woodward Analyzes the Decision-Making Process, 1994

. . . Clinton's key economic advisers and others also had their doubts and challenged the health care plan being devised by Hillary and Magaziner. Bentsen was disturbed that health had not been subjected to the collegial deliberative process of the economic plan, but was handled back channel with Magaziner trying to keep all the information to himself. He argued that the resulting plan was not politically attainable in Congress. Clinton could have a great victory with a smaller, less ambitious plan, and afterwards win more reforms incrementally. Altman said privately that the emerging plan was "too big, too expensive and too fast." Rubin invoked the law of unintended consequences, arguing that such rapid change for so much of the economy was impossible and that to attempt it could prompt unanticipated and harmful results. Tyson wrote memos to Hillary recommending moderation.

Gergen was mystified by the decision making. At one meeting, five possible options were to be discussed by the advisers but the more free-market options were summarily dropped. Then at the next meeting, Hillary unilaterally announced the decision for an option that called for a bigger government role than Gergen thought wise or possible. Where did this come from? he wondered.

Clinton had worked it out with Hillary and Magaziner. . . .

Chapter 33:
Document Set 1 References

1. Hillary Rodham Clinton Justifies Health Care Reform, 1993
   Hillary Rodham Clinton, "Foreward," *Health Security: The President's Report to the American People* (Washington, D.C.: White House Domestic Policy Council, 1993), pp. ix–xi.

2. President William Jefferson Clinton Challenges Congress to Enact Reform, 1993
   William Jefferson Clinton, "Address of the President to the Joint Session of Congress," September 22, 1993, in *Health Security: The President's Report to the American People,* pp. 89, 106.

3. The President's Health Security Plan, 1993
   "The American Health Security Act," in *The President's Health Security Plan: The Clinton Blueprint* (Washington, D.C.: White House Domestic Policy Council, 1993), pp. 3, 4–6, 8–9.

4. The Press Helps Shape the Debate, 1993
   A. Questions on Hillary Rodham Clinton's Role in the Deliberative Process, 1993
      San Diego Union-Tribune, January 30, 1993.

   B. *The Washington Post* Frames the Debate, 1993
      The Washington Post, January 27, 1993.
   C. Auto Industry Concerns, 1993
      The Detroit News, April 28, 1993.
   D. An Endorsement of State Initiative from Connecticut, 1993
      The Hartford Courant, April 24, 1993.

5. The Reform Consensus, 1993
   Philadelphia Inquirer, March 31, 1993, Universal Press Syndicate, in Oliver Trager, ed., *America's Health Care Crisis* (New York: Facts on File, 1993), p. 50.

6. Religious Conservatives Define Health Care Reform, 1994
   Ralph Reed, *Politically Incorrect: The Emerging Faith Factor in American Politics* (Dallas: Word Publishing, 1994), p. 262.

7. Bob Woodward Analyzes the Decision-Making Process, 1994
   Bob Woodward, *The Agenda: Inside the Clinton White House* (New York: Simon & Schuster, 1994), p. 316.

Chapter 33:
Document Set 1 Credits

CHAPTER 33

The "Revolution" of 1994: Realignment or Readjustment?

After two years under Clinton's leadership, voter disenchantment with Washington politics and ineffective government resulted in what seemed at the time a sea change in American politics. The New Deal–Fair Deal coalition had been crumbling since the 1960s, and in 1994, Republican conservatives succeeded in wresting control of Congress from a Democratic party that, despite President Clinton's efforts to cast it in a new, moderate light, remained committed to the policies and constituencies that had sustained it as the guarantor of the welfare state. The following documents explore the issues and concerns that led to a "sharp right turn." Your task is to determine why these political changes occurred and assess the long-term implications of the new and volatile voter preferences of the mid-1990s.

As noted in your textbook, the key figure in the Republican electoral success in 1994 was conservative Congressman Newt Gingrich of Georgia, who organized and directed the attack on welfare state liberalism. Examine the documents to determine which of Gingrich's ideas resonated with voters and why the electorate responded to them as they did. As you review the widely publicized Contract with America, try to account for the apparent popular acceptance of its fundamental principles. Relate these ideas to the changing socioeconomic base of the modern Republican party.

Your analysis of the new Republican coalition should reveal the extent to which the "culture wars" of the 1990s came to influence political preferences and outcomes. Explore the relationship between the Republican victories and the rise of religious conservatives as a potent force in American politics. What was the socioeconomic basis for the growth of the Christian Coalition and how were its ideas reflected in the Republican program? Connect the concerns of the religious right with the moral vision espoused by the new conservatives brought to Washington by the "revolution" of 1994.

Your analysis of the Republican vision for America's future will lead to an assessment of character issues in national political life. As the 1990s wore on, the relentless conservative attack on President Clinton gained impetus while taking on an increasingly personal tone. The Clinton scandals focused on the president's moral lapses, which came to light as a result of the Paula Jones case and the revelations of his sexual relationship with Monica Lewinsky. By late 1999, President Clinton stood impeached as a result of alleged perjury and obstruction of justice. As you review the assault on Clinton, ask yourself why conservatives harbored such an extreme dislike for the president and relate their animosity to the moral perspective of the new Republican majority.

Despite his character flaws and often unclear vision for America's future, the president remained popular at century's end. In an ironic turn of events, Democrats defied historical electoral patterns by registering gains in the congressional elections of 1998, thereby raising doubts about the permanence of the "revolution" of 1994. Use the documents to guide your assessment of the new conservatism and the shifting party preferences of the 1990s. Take note of the interests and ideas represented in the sources and use your knowledge of this background to assess the final outcome of the political upheaval of the Clinton era.

Questions for Analysis

1. Use the documents to identify the socioeconomic and ideological roots of the Republican party's new voter base in the 1990s. How had cultural, social, and demographic changes influenced the new party preferences of the Clinton era?

2. How did character issues become important factors in American politics as the 1990s came to an end? How did moral questions influence the growth of the new Republican majority?

3. What do the documents reveal about the permanence of political party loyalties in the 1990s? How may the election results from 1994 to 1998 be used to predict the future direction of American political choices?

4. What do the programs, platforms, and actions of the competing political forces of the 1990s reveal about American attitudes toward government as the

twentieth century ended? How have popular expectations of government changed? In what areas do you find continuity with the past? What are the implications of the "revolution" of 1994 for the future of the welfare state in the United States?

5. What evidence may be found in the documents to support or refute the contention that progressive political ideas could enjoy a resurgence in the wake of the Clinton impeachment crisis?

1. The Republican Contract with America, 1994

. . . As Republican Members of the House of Representatives and as citizens seeking to join that body we propose not just to change its policies, but even more important, to restore the bonds of trust between the people and their elected representatives. That is why, in this era of official evasion and posturing, we offer instead a detailed agenda for national renewal, a written commitment with no fine print.

This year's election offers the chance, after four decades of one-party control, to bring to the House a new majority that will transform the way Congress works. That historic change would be the end of government that is too big, too intrusive, and too easy with the public's money. It can be the beginning of a Congress that respects the values and shares the faith of the American family. . . .

Opening-Day Checklist

The very first day of a Republican House will bring marked change to the business as usual seen in the House of Representatives since 1954. As part of an opening-day checklist, the new Republican leadership will:

- Apply all laws to Congress.
- Cut the number of committees and subcommittees, and cut committee staffs by a third.
- Limit the terms of committee chairs and ranking members.
- Ban "proxy" (ghost) voting in committee.
- Implement an "honest numbers" budget with a zero baseline.
- Require committee meetings to be open to the public.
- Require a three-fifths majority to pass a tax increase.
- Audit the House's books with an independent firm.

After changing the way the House does business, Republicans will change the business the House does. Instead of passing bills that pile taxes, spending, and regulations ever higher, we'll scale back government to make it more efficient and ease the burden on taxpayers and small business people.

Ten Bills: Signed Promises, Specific Goals

1. *Balanced budget amendment/line-item veto.*

2. *Stop violent criminals:*
   —effective death penalty provisions;
   —greater emphasis on prison funding and law enforcement.

3. *Welfare reform:*
   —discourages illegitimacy and teen pregnancy by prohibiting welfare to minor mothers and denying increased AFDC for additional children while on welfare;
   —cuts spending for welfare programs;
   —ends welfare for families collecting AFDC for five years and for noncitizens;
   —requires welfare recipients to work.

4. *Protect our kids:*
   —child support enforcement;
   —tax incentives for adoption;
   —strengthening rights of parents in their children's education;
   —stronger child pornography laws;
   —an elderly dependent care tax credit.

5. *Tax cuts for families:*
   —a $500-per-child family tax credit;
   —reforming the anti-marriage bias in the tax code;
   —. . . "American Dream Savings Accounts" in the form of individual retirement accounts (IRAs) for first-time home buyers, education expenses, and retirement.

6. *Strong national defense:*
   —no U.S. troops under UN command;
   —building budget firewalls between defense and nondefense spending to prevent raids on the defense budget;
   —creating a missile defense system against rogue dictatorships like North Korea.

7. *Raise the senior citizens' earning limit:*
   —increases the earnings limit to at least $30,000;
   —repeals the Clinton tax hikes on Social Security benefits;
   —provides tax incentives for private long-term care insurance.

8. *Economic growth and regulatory reform:*
   —capital gains cut and indexation;
   —neutral cost recovery;
   —risk assessment/cost-benefit analysis;
   —strengthening the Regulatory Flexibility Act;
   —unfunded mandates reforms.

9. *Common sense legal reforms:*
   —"loser pays" to stop frivolous lawsuits;
   —limits on punitive damages;
   —honesty in evidence to exclude "junk science."

10. *Congressional term limits:*
    —a first-ever vote on term limits for members of Congress to replace career politicians with citizen legislators, ...

2. Conservative Christians Influence the Electoral Outcome, 1994

. . . [O]n Election Day 1994, religious conservative voters turned out in the largest numbers ever recorded in the modern political era. An exit poll conducted by the Luntz Research Corporation found that 33 percent of all voters were religious conservatives and that they voted 70 percent Republican and only 24 percent Democrat. An incredible 40 percent of all the votes Republican candidates received came from evangelicals and their pro-family Catholic allies. On the night of the election, I [Ralph Reed] sat in a hotel room in Washington watching the returns roll in from across the nation. It was past three o'clock in the morning when the final results from California came in and I realized the full breadth of the victory. The Republicans had gained control of Congress for the first time in forty years, and conservative Christians had played a central part in the drama. . . .

. . . With abortion, our concern is a matter of caring for a mother facing the trauma of an unplanned pregnancy and caring for a child who has no voice of its own. In the reform of a broken educational system, our concern means giving the poor and minorities the opportunity to send their children to safer, better schools. In the area of welfare, our concern seeks to end the disaster of federal programs from Washington that have ended up hurting the very people they were supposed to help. In trying to pass tax relief for middle-class families, we are seeking to relieve the crushing financial pressure that can lead to family breakup. In each case, our goal is not to legislate our theology. It is to strengthen the family, protect the children, and defend the rights of the poor and marginalized. . . .

In practice, this effort will be rather different from the government-centered campaigns that came to define the Social Gospel and the Great Society. Our efforts will not commence with massive government programs or with grand promises of sure-fire solutions hatched in Washington, D.C. The failure of this approach is undeniable: rather than rolling up their sleeves to actually care for people, the liberals preferred instead to legislate measures from Washington that would somehow make it all go away. But those honorable intentions spawned a hierarchical, uncaring bureaucracy driven by powerful interest groups, and a downward spiral of hopelessness and despair that has led many to conclude that things today are actually worse than when Lyndon Johnson declared war on poverty a generation ago. . . .

Yet our vision for a compassionate society does not exclude a role for government. Under our guidelines, local and state government assistance for orphans, widows, the disabled, and those unable to work would continue, but churches, synagogues, and the faith community would be called upon to help more, and the tax code would be rewritten to provide greater incentives for charitable giving. . . .

3. A Skeptical View of the Contract, 1995

. . . Americans say they want less government, especially less government from Washington. The Contract with America and the drive for devolution are responses to this popular outcry. . . .

It is perfectly clear how negatively Americans now feel toward government in general and the federal government in particular. What remains entirely unclear, however, is whether the mass public, national lawmakers, and state and local government leaders are prepared to do what would be necessary to shrink substantially the size and scope of the national government, devolve major chunks of federal responsibilities, and live with the huge changes in American life that must result from any serious and sustained effort to reverse a half-century of "big government." Some evidence suggests that the antigovernment, anti-Washington consensus is 3,000 miles wide but only a few miles deep.

Exhibit A is the Contract with America itself. The Contract preserves the national government's role in making, administering, and funding the vast and varied array of post–New Deal and post–Great Society domestic policies and programs. That the Contract is considered so "revolutionary" by so many testifies only to the rhetorical resurgence of pre–Hoover era ideas about politics and governance in America. For without the Contract, each year into the next century America will have several trillion dollars worth of national government. And if every jot and tittle of the Contract were approved America would have several trillion dollars worth of national

government for as many years to come. Viewed historically, the Contract represents the final consolidation of the bedrock domestic policies and programs of the New Deal, the Great Society, the post–Second World War defense establishment, and, most importantly, the deeply rooted national political culture that has grown up around them.

Exhibit B is the federal budget. One does not need to be steeped in the esoterica of the budgeting process to recognize that devolving or even zeroing out a $17-billion-a-year "mandatory spending" program like Aid to Families with Dependent Children (AFDC, the welfare program that offers benefits to about 14 million people each month) would make only a trivial difference in the size and scope of a national government which presently spends over ten times as much each year on medicare (the health care program that offers insurance to 37 million senior citizens), fifteen times as much on the military and national defense, and almost twenty times as much on Social Security (which provides benefits to about 94 percent of all elderly households). . . .

Unless we are totally mistaken, a generation from now America is still going to have lots and lots of government, much of it from Washington. Whatever else happens, therefore, we hope that the debate over the Contract with America, devolution, and the administrative realities of American federalism causes many Americans, and not just public management specialists, to begin to rediscover government.

4. The "Revolution" That Wasn't, 1998

They were the self-described revolutionaries, the peasants with pitchforks who were not outside but inside the castle walls. They came to Washington to shake things up. They disdained compromise and prided themselves on their purity. They were going to slice and dice the federal budget no matter how much it hurt. In the beginning they ran around like kids who had taken over the classroom.

Largely because of their number and the historic nature of the 1994 election, the freshmen roared into town believing only they knew the truth of what was

best for the country. They dismissed anyone who had the temerity to disagree with them, and they believed they had a mandate from the voters for their agenda. . . .

Americans didn't want the federal government dismantled. They just wanted it to work better, to do what it is supposed to do. Government can't do everything, but it must do some things, and in many cases it can do them better than it's doing them now. That's what people elect politicians to do: to make government work better and to find solutions to national problems. . . .

The Republicans held onto control of the House in 1996, but only by the slimmest of margins. Their narrow majority coupled with their failure to recapture the White House had a dramatic impact on the agenda they were able to pursue in the 105th Congress. Another factor was Newt Gingrich's problems. . . .

And the new GOP members elected in 1996 were a pale imitation of the previous freshman class. They were older and more moderate and had more traditional political experience than the class of '94. "They don't have the fervor we had. . . . I see the reform aspect of our agenda getting blunted pretty bad," Hilleary told me. There was also a lot less lockstep unity among the Republicans; party leaders were having trouble holding their troops together. Since their margin was so small, the defection of just a handful of Republicans could doom a piece of legislation. Not that the 105th Congress actually seemed to be doing that much.

They had managed to win reelection and to hold the majority, but they were acting like losers instead of winners. Feeling that they had been beaten over the head on Medicare and some other issues by the Democrats and the labor unions, the Republicans seemed unwilling to attempt anything too difficult or ambitious in the 105th Congress. The 1996 election had "scared the bejesus" out of the GOP moderates, according to one member. Their ranks had been thinned,

especially in the Northeast. In Massachusetts two moderates had been defeated, leaving the state's 12-member congressional delegation without a single Republican. . . .

The most substantive legislative action of the first year of the 105th Congress was the budget deal between the congressional Republicans and Clinton. The deal was a departure from the budget-balancing struggle of the previous Congress. The agreement included significant increases in domestic spending for education and children's health benefits, which Clinton wanted. And there was a package of tax cuts that Republicans sought. It was the kind of incremental, something-for-everyone deal that the Republicans would never have considered at the beginning of the 104th Congress. In many ways it also signaled a return to business as usual. . . .

The freshmen of 1994 knew that their legacy was tenuous. It would depend not only on the congressional election of 1998 but the presidential contest of 2000. What happened in the first year of the 105th Congress made it clear that the achievements of the 104th Congress could easily be reversed, especially if the Republicans lost control of the House and failed to recapture the presidency. As Graham told me, "We could be a footnote, or we could be fundamental change. That's not decided yet."

5. *The Nation* Detects the Demise of the Conservative Revolution, 1998

A. Good News for Democrats

Let's start with the good news. The 1998 elections are proof that the Republican Party is in disarray and that the "conservative revolution" does indeed seem to be ending. . . .

Mainstream support for choice, education, the environment and racial toleration was evident in the rejection of many Republican candidates. So, too, as evidenced by successful state initiatives in Washington, Arizona and Massachusetts . . . , was voter support for raising the minimum wage and cleaning up campaign finance—two natural planks in a national progressive program. The defeat of two ballot measures criminalizing "partial birth" abortion, in Washington and Colorado, [was] also heartening, as were victories ranging from the Congressional win of Tammy Baldwin, a Wisconsin advocate of

"healthcare for all," to Florida's approval of a tougher gun control law. And this time around there can be no question that minorities and union members were decisive in the Democrats' success. At a time when the GOP's hard base was listless, these groups mobilized to save their party—a fact that may someday be noted by party leaders. Last, and a source of great happiness to those of us in New York, Senator Alfonse D'Amato is history. After eighteen years in office, he was turned out by Democratic Congressman Charles Schumer.

Democrats won a number of key races, among them the governorship of California, which will put them in a strong position going into the 2000 presidential election. Senator Barbara Boxer even managed to fend off a strong challenge by depicting her foe, Matt Fong, as "too conservative" for California, the state of Ronald Reagan. The Democrats also won several big races in the South, including governorships in South Carolina and Alabama and a Senate seat in North Carolina, suggesting that the Republicans' hopes of putting a lock on that region are premature.

On Capitol Hill, the Democrats managed to pick up four (or possibly five) seats in the House (where the progressive bloc grew by about a dozen including Baldwin, an openly lesbian nonincumbent). Wisconsin Senator Russ Feingold, the Democratic campaign finance reform advocate, survived a massive GOP money blitzkrieg after he pledged to abide unilaterally by strict soft-money limits. . . .

The elections also provided an implicit rebuke to the forces of impeachment—and to the media pundits who have spent the past few months reviewing Clinton's sins and predicting his demise. Although four out of ten voters cited impeachment as their main motivation, they were divided about evenly pro and con. It is hardly likely anymore that House Republicans will have the stomach and votes to drag out an impeachment process that has proven such a millstone around the party's neck. Meanwhile, a majority of voters cited bread-and-butter issues, particularly education, which according to a recent New York Times/CBS News poll, Americans view Democrats as better able to tackle.

But—reality check—the GOP's steady advance in the nineties still leaves the party in a solid position. It controls thirty-one governor's offices (including those in seven of the eight largest states), both houses of Congress (with a commanding majority in the Senate) and seventeen state legislatures (whereas in 1990 it reigned in only six). The GOP seems to have struck its high-water mark, but it's not such a bad one for the party. . . .

B. Farewell to the Architect of the Revolution

Newt Gingrich's hasty departure after the elections was a fitting finale to a career that was both meteoric and plodding. After he won election to the House in 1978—having opportunistically switched from a Rockefellerish Republican to a New Right conservative—Gingrich carefully planned the unthinkable: a Republican takeover of the House that would catapult a mediocre history professor and his grab bag of Big Ideas into the Speaker's chair. He patiently worked the back bench; he relentlessly pursued Democrats on ethics charges (hah!), and he instilled a can-do attitude into the stodgy House Republican

caucus. Then, in what seemed a flash, it was showtime, and, talking revolution all the while, Gingrich led Republicans on a predictable course: tax cuts for the well heeled, favors for corporate special interests like the tobacco and gun lobbies, vicious assaults on social programs, pandering to the Christian right and attacks on health and safety standards for the workplace and the environment.

Now his colleagues have decided that the Era of Newt lasted one election too long. There appear to have been two sets of objections: PR and fervor. Most Republicans could see that it didn't win votes to be associated with a loudmouth whom 58 percent of the public found distasteful. And House conservatives—who believe that were their party *more* conservative it would pull in more votes—had relegated Gingrich to the sell-out category because he blinked in the government-shutdown showdown with the President and was not sufficiently confrontational. The party's poor election performance and Gingrich's miscalculation about the usefulness of Monica-related ads provided justification for the boot-Newt movement. . . .

C. Hopes for a Progressive Revival

Democratic success in the midterm elections, and deep divisions in Republican ranks, signal the end of the 1994 conservative "revolution." Newt Gingrich's stunning announcement that he would leave Congress (we shall miss him as a very useful *bête noire* and locus of Democratic campaign strategy) only confirms this view. The ultimate pork-barrel "revolutionary" has finally met the end of history: his own.

But while progressives should welcome Democratic gains and Republican disarray, neither should be accepted as the limits of what is possible, much less as occasion for much self-congratulation. To be sure, progressive forces did a lot of very hard and good work. They can and should claim credit for revving up the union and minority base that was key throughout. And they can claim as their own the spectacular minimum-wage victory in Washington State, the campaign finance reform victories in Massachusetts and Arizona, and too many specific targeted races to count. But the end result still leaves Republicans dominating state legislatures, holding both houses of Congress and with a better-than-even shot at taking the presidency in 2000. And while the results were, in partisan terms, certainly better than expected, they amounted to very little by way of a mandate for new public action. The Democrats, after all, are not exactly the progressive party we would like them to be. Nevertheless, this election again confirmed what the polls and other election results have been telling us for years: Even as conservatives continue to win money-driven legislative battles, and progressive values continue to lose out in public policy, there is a huge potential out there for a new progressive electoral politics. . . .

Chapter 33:
Document Set 2 References

1. The Republican Contract with America, 1994
   Contract with America (New York: Times Books, 1994), pp. 7, 15–18.

2. Conservative Christians Influence the Electoral Outcome, 1994
   Ralph Reed, *Active Faith: How Christians Are Changing the Soul of American Politics* (New York: The Free Press, 1996), pp. 186–187.

3. A Skeptical View of the Contract, 1995
   John J. DiIulio, Jr., and Donald F. Kettl, *Fine Print: The Contract with America, Devolution, and the Administrative Realities of American Federalism* (Washington, D.C.: Brookings Institution, 1995), pp. 59–60, 66.

4. The "Revolution" That Wasn't, 1998
   Linda Killian, *The Freshmen: What Happened to the Republican Revolution?* (Boulder, Colo.: Westview Press, 1998), pp. 414, 417, 421, 425, 433–434.

5. *The Nation* Detects the Demise of the Conservative Revolution, 1998
   A. Good News for Democrats
      The Nation, November 23, 1998, pp. 3–4.
   B. Farewell to the Architect of the Revolution
      The Nation, November 30, 1998, p. 3.
   C. Hopes for a Progressive Revival
      Katrina vanden Heuvel, "Come Together: Building a Progressive Majority," *The Nation*, December 7, 1998, p. 11.